Dedication

This book is dedicated to my wife Claudia and my children Kristen and Ryan.
  Scott Jarol

To my wife Roberta; I could not have done this without you. And to my children, Angela and Tony, may they never stop reaching for their dreams.
  Anthony Potts

About the Authors

Scott Jarol, a noted author and contributing editor for *PC TECHNIQUES* Magazine, has spent the last 18 years as a consultant and programmer. A multimedia producer with his Phoenix-based company, Media Terra Inc., Scott specializes in natural history, science, and adventure travel titles. His company's latest commercial multimedia product is *Explore the Grand Canyon*. He lives in Phoenix with his wife, Claudia, and two children, Kristen and Ryan.

Anthony Potts is an Associate Editor and author for *PC TECHNIQUES* Magazine. He has been working for the past 5 years on multimedia development, Internet applications, and computer animation. He lives in Phoenix, Arizona with his wife, Roberta, and two children, Angela and Anthony.

Visual Basic 4 Multimedia
Adventure Set

Scott Jarol

Anthony Potts

CORIOLIS GROUP BOOKS

Publisher	*Keith Weiskamp*
Editor	*Michelle Stroup*
Layout Production	*Rob Mauhar*
Indexer	*Lenity Mauhar*

Trademarks: Microsoft is a trademark and Windows is a registered trademark of Microsoft Corporation. All other brand names and product names included in this book are trademarks, registered trademarks, or trade names of their respective holders.

Distributed to the book trade by IDG Books Worldwide, Inc.

Library of Congress Cataloging-in-Publication Data

Jarol, Scott
    Visual Basic 4 multimedia adventure set / Scott Jarol, Anthony Potts
        p. cm.
    Includes Index
    ISBN 1-883577-45-4 : $39.99

Printed in the United States of America

10 9 8 7 6 5 4 3 2 1

Contents

Chapter 6   Exploring Imaging— From Pixels to Palettes   143

Chapter 7   Palette Animation and ROPs   179

Chapter 13   The Magic of Animation   433

Chapter 14   Better Animation   465

Chapter 15   Exploring Waveform Audio   489

Chapter 16   Using the Musical Instrument Digital Interface   531

Chapter 18   Exploring OCXs and OLE Automation   607

Chapter 19   Developing with PC Video   645

Introduction

I t's been barely a year since we published the first edition of this book—but what a year! Back then, CD-ROM multimedia was just beginning to achieve some commercial success. Titles were appearing at a slow but steady rate, and computer manufacturers had begun to sell multimedia-capable systems, which meant little more than the addition of a CD-ROM drive and a sound card. Today it's hard to find any vendor selling a personal computer without multimedia capabilities.

Multimedia is everywhere—and not just on CD-ROM. The fastest growing segment of the Internet is the World Wide Web, a global hyper-linked multimedia system. The Web, which is based on a standard document format known as Hypertext Markup Language, or HTML, enables anyone with access to the Internet to publish their own online multimedia documents, with links to any number of other Web "pages" or to a variety of other Internet resources.

Besides witnessing the revolution occurring in the world of multimedia, we've seen significant changes in our tools. With the introduction of Windows 95, followed immediately by Visual Basic 4.0, Microsoft has rushed us all into the brave new world of 32-bit applications. The promises of the 32-bit world include speed, reliability, and enriched resources, which should lead, in turn, to the development of even more sophisticated applications.

It was time, we realized, to create a whole new edition of this book.

What's New

First of all, to help with the transition to Windows 95, you'll find that the code in this book now includes API declarations for both 16- and 32-bit Windows, organized with VB's new conditional compilation, so the same program can be compiled for either environment with minimal changes to the code.

In this new version, we've also made some big changes to the hypermedia engine to make it compatible with HTML, which, thanks to the World Wide Web, has become the *de facto* standard for hypertext.

And best of all, we've gone an extra step and built a real Web browser, complete with support for inline images. The code in this book gives you the tools for building your own *hybrid* multimedia projects—presentations that combine disk-based media with up-to-the-minute information pulled live from the Internet.

Also new to this edition is coverage of several useful custom controls, including handy TCP/IP interface OCXs, which will enable you to write your own Internet applications in VB.

Why Use Visual Basic for Multimedia?

In the introduction to the previous book, I claimed that Visual Basic was an excellent development system for interactive multimedia. After completing a commercial product titled *Explore the Grand Canyon*, a product based on many of the techniques presented in the first edition, I believe more than ever on that assertion. Windows programming can be a bear with conventional programming languages, so most multimedia developers turn tail and opt for more generic, but less flexible *authoring systems*.

Authoring systems are the multimedia equivalent of page layout software. They make it easy to assemble photographs, illustrations, music, sound bites, animation, and video clips into lively onscreen presentations. Many offer a variety of built-in special effects and interactive controls that make it possible to produce engaging presentations with just a few mouse clicks. But most lock you into their own way of doing things. They're not *extendible*, which means that the only effects and controls you get are the ones built into the product.

Visual Basic (VB), on the other hand, is a completely extendible development system. Almost any feature not supported directly by VB itself is available in the form of either a Windows *dynamic link library* (DLL), or a *custom control*. And with the new Windows *object linking and embedding* (OLE) system, entire programs—even other multimedia authoring systems—can become custom controls, embedded in and controlled by our own VB programs.

VB gives you the power and flexibility of a true programming language, along with the simplicity and rapid development time of an authoring system. In this book, we are going to show you how far VB can take you. We'll use just a few custom controls and one amazing DLL, but VB is so powerful in its own right that we'll have time to discuss only a few of the hundreds of other add-on products presently available that can energize your multimedia productions.

Who Is This Book For?

If you want to learn how to get the most out of VB, then this book is for you. Although we'll be focusing "like a laser beam" on multimedia programming, the programming principles will apply to any kind of VB project. We'll be calling dozens of functions from both the 16- and 32-bit Windows Application Programming Interfaces (APIs), along with some functions not found in the core Windows libraries. We'll also cover a variety of other VB programming topics, including database programming, code organization, custom controls, and subclassing, which is a technique for adding new capabilities to an existing control.

If you're new to Windows multimedia programming, VB 4, or to both, don't worry. We'll try to make learning the Windows Multimedia System as easy as possible. We will, however, assume that you have at least a basic working knowledge of Windows and VB programming and using custom controls. Since several existing books—not to mention the fine manuals packaged with the program—introduce and thoroughly explain the concepts of programming in VB, we won't rehash them here. We will, however, discuss why we've chosen VB as a multimedia development system, and review concepts that pertain directly to the projects in this book. After all, the best way to learn how to use something is to use it. In this book, we'll work our way up from basic principles to working systems, so even if you're beginning with only minimal knowledge of VB, you'll pick up quite a bit along the way.

Programmers who work in the lower-level languages—C, C++, and Pascal—will also benefit. The concepts that we study in this book will apply to all multimedia programming projects in Windows. In fact, many programmers use Visual Basic as a prototyping tool for projects they intend to implement in other languages, and almost all PC programmers, regardless of their language preferences, understand code written in Basic. With Visual Basic, we can concentrate on concepts peculiar to multimedia without getting lost in all the Windows overhead.

What We Will Do

Unlike most Basic language programming compendia, which offer tips, tricks, and techniques on a variety of unrelated projects, this book focuses on one unifying concept. The programs we'll create in the course of the text will all add functionality to either the presentation engine or to the authoring tools. Every bit of this book will introduce or clarify multimedia concepts, and each programming project will build upon the last.

In most of the projects, we will call functions from the Windows API. Many VB programmers never crack open the API, which is a shame because they don't know what they're missing. The API is a programmer's treasure trove. Many of the capabilities that seem to be missing from VB were omitted intentionally because they are so easily accessible from the API. Most of the 1,500 or so Windows API functions belong to families. For example, the graphic device interface (GDI) includes dozens of drawing and typesetting functions. We won't be able to use all the functions in every group, but we'll cover enough of them to kindle your understanding of those we miss.

The API functions reside in a set of DLLs. Functions in DLLs can be called at runtime from any language that supports dynamic linking, which today includes languages as diverse as C++, Word Basic, WordPerfect Macros, and VB. The Windows operating system itself is a set of DLLs. So is the multimedia system. And third-party software developers are publishing new DLLs all the time, offering everything from advanced statistical functions to spelling checkers to 3D graphics engines. VB provides an easy interface to most functions located in DLLs, which you'll discover in Chapter 2.

What You Will Need

To complete most of the projects in this book, all you need is Visual Basic 4 and a multimedia-capable PC, which consists primarily of a Windows system and a sound card. To produce commercial multimedia titles, however, you'll need to invest in all kinds of stuff: a scanner, one or more image editing and drawing programs, an animation program, a WAV audio editing program, and a video digitizer and a video source, such as a VCR or camcorder or both.

If you decide to delve more deeply into multimedia development, or even just use some of the many commercial titles, you'll need a multimedia-compatible computer, which includes the following hardware and software:

- A 486DX2 or higher processor.
- At least 8 MB of memory (16 MB or more is ideal).
- A Super VGA display system (256 colors or more). You will need a VGA display system set to at least 800×600 resolution with 65,000 colors to run the *Explore the Grand Canyon* multimedia sampler.
- A Windows-compatible sound board, which must support PCM playback for WAV files, MIDI playback through a synthesizer, and an internal audio mixer.
- A CD-ROM drive with a minimum average seek time of .5 second (remarkably slow) and a sustained transfer rate of 150 kilobytes per second (you'll want a drive with an average seek time no greater than 250 milliseconds; several manufacturers now offer seek times under 150 milliseconds).
- Windows 3.1 or later (Windows 95 preferred, and required by some of the projects).

If your system isn't already equipped for multimedia, we recommend that you buy one of the many upgrade kits, now available through almost all PC vendors. We've done it both from individual components and from kits, and we believe that upgrade kits can save you from a configuration nightmare.

Even with Windows 95's Plug & Play capabilities, installing new hardware can be a headache. These kits usually include a sound board, a CD-ROM drive, software drivers, and a bundle of multimedia titles. Or better yet, buy a new computer, pre-configured with a high-quality sound card and a quad-speed CD-ROM drive. It's the quickest way to get going and sample the state-of-the-art multimedia technology.

As a general rule, we'll try to avoid extensions to VB. We'll write all the projects in VB and use Windows API functions. In a couple of cases, we'll use some functions from DLLs written in other languages. And in a few projects, we'll use custom controls (included on the companion CD-ROM) to add capabilities otherwise unavailable to VB programmers. We wish all the code could be written in pure VB, but when you're dealing with real-time events, sometimes you have to program "to the metal."

Take the Test Drive

For a sample of what you can do with VB, take a look at the demonstration version of *Explore the Grand Canyon*, a new product by Media Terra, published by the Coriolis Group. The demo version is included on the companion CD-ROM, and you'll find complete installation instructions in Appendix C. To run this program, you'll need a VGA display system set to at least 800×600

Using the Explore the Grand Canyon *program.*

resolution with 65,000 colors (a 1 MB video card supporting high color). You will also need at least 8 MB of RAM and 8 MB of available hard disk space. With the exception of the 3D graphics system (which was written in Borland's Object Pascal, the language in the new Delphi programming system) and a handful of custom controls, the multimedia engine for *Explore the Grand Canyon* was written entirely in VB. Run the file GCSETUP.EXE from the root directory on the CD-ROM to begin the installation program, then just follow the instructions. More information is included in Appendix C.

Our Adventure Itinerary

The most logical way to organize this book would be in sections—sound, images, video, and so on. But that would be too dull. Instead, we've mixed up the material a little, working through all the topics, and gradually adding features to the multimedia engine along the way.

We'll begin, in Chapter 1, with a couple of simple experiments to demonstrate a few of the multimedia capabilities built into Windows and VB. We'll also review a few VB programming concepts.

In Chapter 2, we'll discuss VB's multimedia qualities, and share some of the trials and tribulations of developing a commercial multimedia title.

In Chapter 3, we'll break ground for the Magic Multimedia Engine by building the first version of the HTML-based hypertext system.

Chapters 4 and 5 will take us into the Windows Multimedia API. First, we'll add some multimedia capabilities to the hypertext system. Then, we'll explore the various high-level and low-level functions of the MMSYSTEM.DLL by playing WAV files—six different ways.

We'll seek out the Windows Palette Manager in Chapters 6 and 7 and learn to display and manipulate bitmaps using exclusively API functions. We'll use that knowledge in Chapter 8 to create awesome visual effects.

Chapters 9 and 10 bring us back to hyperlinking. But instead of text, you'll learn how to place hotspots on images. We'll start out with simple rectangles, but by the time we finish, we'll have a powerful hotspot editor that will let us draw and test a hotspot over any irregularly shaped object.

Chapter 11 returns to our hypertext system. For the first time, our hypertext and image hotspot systems will come together to form the Hypermedia Engine. We'll also expand both subsystems by adding scrolling capabilities.

Once we have a working hypermedia engine, the next step, presented in Chapter 12, will be to modify it into a powerful HTML viewer, the foundation for our full-blown Web browser.

In Chapters 13 and 14, we'll explore the world of graphic animation. The emphasis here is on sprites, the interactive form of animation that powers most video games and other graphic simulations.

In Chapter 15, we return to waveaudio. We'll use the knowledge of the low-level functions we studied in Chapter 5 to manipulate WAV data at the byte-level. Then, we'll explore the remarkable WaveMix DLL, an experimental library distributed by Microsoft that lets us do real-time mixing of up to eight WAV files for simultaneous playback—in stereo! We'll also show you an easy way to record WAV files from your VB programs.

In Chapter 16, we'll tackle the Musical Instrument Digital Interface, known as MIDI, a real-time networking system originally designed to control synthesizers. Although MIDI's intended domain was music, the power of MIDI has barely been tapped by multimedia developers. You may be surprised to learn just what your sound card can do.

One of the major components of the Windows Multimedia System is the Media Control Interface (MCI). By the time we get to Chapter 17, we'll have used a few simple MCI commands to play multimedia files, including WAV audio, MIDI music, and AVI video. In this chapter, we'll look at some of the MCI's other capabilities by building two very different audio CD players.

In Chapter 18, we'll explore some powerful custom controls, including one that we'll help us tap directly into the Internet, enabling us to complete our VB Web browser.

Our last adventure takes us into the dazzling world of digital video. Microsoft has generously provided us with the complete VfW runtime libraries, production utilities, and Development Kit. We'll use the custom controls in the VfW DK to develop our own video capture utility (which requires a video capture card) and to perform controlled video playback (no special hardware required). At the end, we'll have come full circle, adding video playback controls to the Magic Hypermedia Engine, which we'll use to produce the Grand Canyon mini-multimedia presentation.

Let's hit the trail!

Acknowledgments

So many people have contributed to this project that it's hard to remember everyone, but a few names stand out. We offer our deepest gratitude to Keith Weiskamp and Jeff Duntemann, who sheparded this project from earliest conception to completion. We also wish to thank Darrin Chandler, not only for his invaluable technical insights, but for his encouragement and support. Our other technical alter-ego was Dan Haygood, programmer extraordinaire.

Several artists have contributed to this book, including Susan Haygood, who drew the moth (or, if you prefer, butterfly) sprites for the animation programs; Kane Clevenger of Tier 3 Productions, who drew the dictionary pages for the FLIPBOOK program; and James Cowlin, whose gorgeous landscape photographs appear in several program examples, including the *Explore the Grand Canyon* sample program.

We also wish to thank Nels Johnson of The San Francisco Canyon Company, who contributed his knowledge and insight into the profoundly technical world of digital video; MIDI programming wizard Arthur Edstrom of Artic Software, Inc., for sharing the program (VB MIDI Piano) described in Chapter 16, and helped solve several MIDI mysteries; James Tyminski, who contributed the VB Messenger custom control that made MIDI input possible; Angel Diaz of Microsoft Corporation for creating the WaveMix DLL and for his generous support of this "unsupported" product; and Rick Segal, the Multimedia Evangelist of Microsoft Corporation, for contributing the entire Video for Windows system.

We would also like to send a big thank you to Edward Toupin and Tanny Bear. Mr. Toupin graciously allowed us to put his Internet protocol OCX controls onto the CD-ROM. Tanny is the man responsible for creating the Webster custom control that is also on the companion CD-ROM. Both of these guys deserve a lot of credit for creating some impressive controls.

Many thanks to The Coriolis Group Books production team, including eagle-eyed copy editor Michelle Stroup, designer and layout artist Brad Grannis and Rob Mauhar. We would also like to thank Karen Watterson and Phil Kunz.

We are all indebted to the companies that contributed clip art for the companion CD-ROM. These include Adobe Systems; AJS Publishing, Inc.; Andover Advanced Technologies; Cambium Development Corp.; Crisp Technology Inc.; Data Techniques, Inc.; First Byte; Interactive Publishing Corporation; Media-Pedia Video Clips, Inc.; Media Architects; Microsoft Corporation; Rainbow Imaging; Software Interphase; and Ulead Systems, Inc.

Finally, we would like to thank our families for putting up with us as we created this book. We thank them for their patience with our zombie-like behavior. We promise, no more books—for now.

Find out how the new
Visual Basic 4 and
Windows 95—with their 32-bit
support—provide the right
platforms for developing
multimedia applications.

The Visual Basic 4 and Windows 95 Connection

Everyone is talking about Visual Basic 4 and Windows 95—and has been for quite some time now. And it's no wonder. Microsoft spent more money and resources promoting and launching Windows 95 than most software companies acquire in their lifetime. Of course, critics have been complaining about Windows 95's shortcomings ever since it was introduced to the world—it is not a true 32-bit operating system, it still needs DOS, it won't run all of your old software as well as Windows 3.1 could, and it was released two years late. But most developers, especially those of us who are creating cutting-edge applications like multimedia products, are increasingly won over to Windows 95's enhanced features. Let's face it, Windows 95's true multitasking and multithreading capabilities will certainly make our software run better than ever and its new built-in multimedia capabilities will give it more power and flexibility than any other operating system.

1

The challenge now is to find a way to take advantage of the 32-bit power of Windows 95. Fortunately, that's where Visual Basic 4 comes in. Visual Basic started the visual development revolution when version 1 was released four years ago. Since that time, each new version has introduced new features, capabilities, and power, such as VBX custom controls, Access database engine, and Windows API support, to help developers create more and more unique applications—including multimedia products. VB's latest release can bring you into the core of Windows 95 development where you can really take advantage of 32-bit and multimedia programming.

In this chapter, we'll look at both Windows 95 and VB 4 to see what new features are in store to help us create powerful multimedia applications. If you haven't done much Windows 95 (32-bit) programming with VB 4, this introduction will help you see what you've been missing. Although VB 4 has garnered much attention because of Windows 95, you'll see that it offers quite a number of new features in its own right, including OCX support, conditional compilation, better memory management, and enhanced database support.

Windows 95—32 Bits at Last!

When you start up Windows 95, the first thing you'll notice is that its user interface, as shown in Figure 1.1, makes Windows 3.1 look like something out of the stone age. The new interface controls, Task Bar and Explorer file manager, provide the types of desktop tools that users have been demanding for years. If you are lucky enough to have a multimedia application developed for Windows 95, you'll soon discover that the built-in multimedia capabilities are the best they've ever been. Windows 3.1 offered a good platform for multimedia development, but Windows 95's speed increase and unique features, including Plug & Play, AutoRun, and better sound and video drivers, make it tough to beat. Many multimedia developers who felt Windows would never be as good as the Mac for creating and running multimedia are starting to take a serious second look.

But the real power of Windows 95 isn't found by just exploring its new interface. When you get under the hood, you'll encounter its biggest change—support for 32-bit applications. What exactly does this do for you? Well, that depends on the actual application you're developing. If you are creating a database-driven multimedia program like the ones we'll be developing in this book, you could possibly double the bandwidth at which information can be moved around in memory. Does this mean that all of your VB programs can

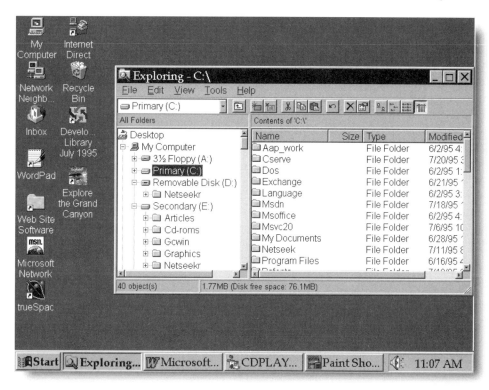

Figure 1.1   *The Windows 95 interface with the new Explorer.*

be recompiled under VB 4 as 32-bit apps, so that they will instantly run twice as fast under Windows 95? Not quite. First, due to compatibility reasons, not all Windows API calls truly take advantage of the full potential of the new 32-bit environment. For example, VB's built-in database engine still must handle 16-bit applications as well, so it has to use a little bit of it's processing bandwidth to watch for those exceptions. The more you work with Windows 95, the more you'll find that many API functions that you might have thought were implemented as 32-bit operations are still running as 16-bit tasks. Second, even if you could truly double the data transfer rate of an application, the application won't spend all of its time transferring information to and from memory—it still must perform other operations such as I/O, sending and receiving messages to and from Windows, and performing general house-keeping chores. Unfortunately, because many of these tasks are performed by making Windows API calls that are still written to support both 16- and 32-bit programs, there will be some communication overhead required.

The Power of Multitasking and Multithreading

Where can you get the biggest performance boost with Windows 95? The answer lies in Windows 95's ability to perform preemptive multitasking and multithreading. But isn't Windows 3.1 a multitasking environment? Well yes, but it's a *non-preemptive* multitasking system. This means that an application running under Windows 3.1 must manually tell the operating system when it is ready to hand control over to another program, as shown in Figure 1.2. In other words, a Windows 3.1 application retains control of the system until it decides to give it up—and if it decides not to give up control for one reason or another, the other programs are out of luck. Think of this like trying to catch a shuttle bus at a New York airport. Imagine that a shuttle pulls up and someone in front of you jumps in but stands in the doorway, and the shuttle just sits there idle (with the door open). You can't climb aboard because the person in front of you has taken control over the bus. To get a ride, you'd wait until the person decides to step off the shuttle. Although the shuttle has room for more passengers, you can't use it because it is *non-preemptive*.

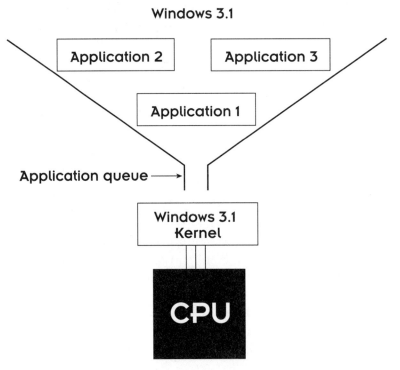

Figure 1.2 *The process of multitasking under Windows 3.1.*

Windows 95, on the other hand, uses preemptive, time-slice-based multitasking that schedules tasks to be completed and hands them off to the CPU when it is ready, as shown in Figure 1.3. When a new application is launched, Windows 95 schedules it to run even though there may be other applications already running. This system is much more efficient, because it allows the operating system to have complete control over how applications are scheduled, rather than the other way around. This approach prevents any single task from dominating the system.

But Windows 95 scheduling system doesn't stop here. It takes the multitasking idea one step further by letting a single application run multiple *threads*. (Windows 3.1 deals only with processes—Windows 95 deals with threads.) A thread can be a single program running somewhere in memory, or it can be just a single operation of the program. So, every application can run on at least one thread at any time, but it can also spawn multiple threads at any time, and therefore may perform multiple tasks simultaneously, as shown in Figure 1.4. Where Windows 3.1 lets you run more than one application at once, Windows 95 lets multiple applications run multiple threads, all at the same time. The key here is figuring out how to take advantage of threads. Once you start thinking about it, you'll realize just how powerful threads can be when used effectively. For example, we are using a pre-release version of

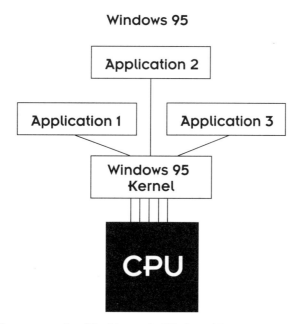

Figure 1.3 *The process of multitasking under Windows 95.*

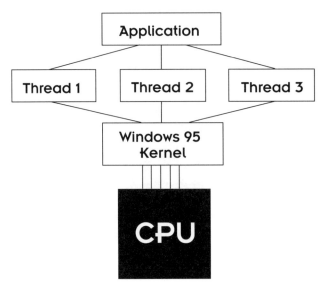

Figure 1.4 *Processing applications using multiple threads.*

Word 7.0 for Windows 95 to write this book. Word 7.0 uses threads in many ways in order to increase its own efficiency, as well as yours. One of the most useful ways it uses threads is to perform spell-checking while you type. While we are typing, Word is simultaneously running a thread that is checking the words we just typed. If you don't think that sounds powerful, just wait until you use it and see how helpful and fast this feature is.

In a multimedia context, threads can be used in any number of ways. In this area, you'll see previously undreamed of uses for threads, because developers of mass-market products have not had access to an operating system that could handle threads and true multitasking. One possible use for threads is to make interactive video clips. With Windows 3.1, playback of videos was a very processor-intensive undertaking. Now, with Windows 95, the use of 32-bit addressing increases the throughput and speeds up playback. This gives us a little bit of our processor time back. What do we do with it? How about using the extra processor cycles to run a thread that checks for mouse movement and clicks within a video window? Later in this book we'll show you how to create hotspots in images. You could take this technology one step further and create animated hotspots for videos. Using threads, you could track a region as it moved around in a video and respond to mouse movements and clicks within that region. Under Windows 3.1 this would be a mighty tough task, but with Windows 95 it just takes some initial time and effort to create the hotspot information and develop the code to deal with the mouse.

Multiple Input Queues

Another improvement that Windows 95 has introduced is the addition of multiple input queues. Windows 3.1 provides a single input queue that keeps track of input messages such as key presses and mouse clicks while an open application is busy. Windows 95 gives each open thread its own input queue, which has the advantage that no one process can slow things down if it is responding slowly to its messages.

This is a feature that you may not be aware of because it already does what you would have expected Windows 3.1 to do. When a task has been taken over by the processor, the mouse pointer still functions. When the processor frees up, all the mouse movements and clicks that occurred when the processor was busy are executed. Under Windows 3.1, all the mouse activity that occurs is assigned to a single process. Because Windows 3.1 keeps track only of where a mouse event occurs, such as a mouse click, events can't be assigned to different tasks. For example, assume you are running an application and another window becomes active before you click the mouse. The new windows will get the click, instead of the old window that you thought you had originally clicked on. This problem is fixed under Windows 95. A separate queue is created for each open thread. When a click is registered for a thread, Windows 95 keeps track of not only where the click took place, but what window was clicked, even when the processor is busy.

Text-Based Application Support

Windows 95 gives you more power and flexibility with text-based applications as well. With previous versions of Windows, text-based applications were inconvenient. They either required the full screen, or slowed down the system too much. Now, with Windows 95, a special type of window is available, called a *console*. A console window provides a standard text-based, command-prompt environment. The big advantage that Windows 95 offers is that these programs now run in windows that act just like all the other windows. So, you can resize DOS boxes or use the mouse within any text-based application, just like you can for regular Windows programs.

32-Bit Addressing

Another important feature introduced by Windows 95 is *flat addressing*. Windows 95 applications can use memory from a pool of 4 gigabytes of virtual memory! Not only is this amount significantly higher than the memory pool available with Windows 3.1, but this memory resides in a flat address space. Unlike DOS and Windows 3.1, which use *segmented memory*, Windows 95 treats memory as though it were linear, which means that access speed is improved and memory management is much simpler from a programmer's point of view. Due to the use of virtual memory, each application has as much memory as it could possibly need (as long as you have the RAM and disk space).

The shift to 32-bit addressing has changed the way some messages are passed to a Windows 95 program versus a Windows 3.1 program. Most of the change is in the way the messages are organized, and also in the format of the values being passed. The most common change you will see is the switch from two-byte integers to four-byte *Long* integers. But, be warned, not every message and function has changed, so you can't just expect that all values will come in as Longs if they were regular integers before.

These are not all the changes that have been made to the Windows operating system, just some of the big ones that you will have to pay attention to when programming for the 32-bit environment.

What's New with Visual Basic 4?

The single biggest change in Visual Basic 4 is its upgrade to 32-bit Windows. As we said, this does not mean that every program you convert to VB 4 will run twice as fast. What it does mean is that a good programmer, backed with some useful tips, can create applications that run faster and more robustly under Windows.

Actually, many of VB 4's most predominant changes have occurred in areas we won't even deal with—client/server features. Microsoft has now added a third level to the VB hierarchy. With the release of VB 3, two product options were available: the Standard Edition, which provided the basic Visual Basic environment, and the Professional Edition, which added more controls and more powerful database support features. The new level introduced with VB 4, the Enterprise Edition, adds features like remote automation and a component manager. This edition has little benefit to us as multimedia developers, but if you find yourself hanging out in the IS department of your company, you're likely to hear many programmers discussing these features.

32-Bit Programming

So, why should you be using VB 4 to create your multimedia applications? 32-bit access is the obvious answer. Not only do we get faster access to memory, but we get more flexibility with variables. For example, the **String** variable under 32-bit VB 4 can hold more than two billion characters of information, compared to only 64,000 under 16-bit VB. This makes it much easier to process large multimedia files directly in VB without having to worry about complex Windows API calls.

32-Bit Custom Controls

VB 4 also allows us to use the newer OCX custom controls that have been custom-built for the 32-bit environment. All VB custom controls are written in other languages, especially C and C++. These controls are written using lower-level calls that can make good use of the newer 32-bit environment. Because of this, a multimedia control that performs 32-bit image manipulation will work faster, and therefore, *your* application will run faster. We'll explore some of the advantages and disadvantages to using the OCX controls a little later in this chapter. We've also devoted an entire chapter in this book to showing you how to use off-the-shelf controls to create your own multimedia applications.

Resource Files Support

Resource files have been used for many years by programmers in the C environment, to store all kinds of information. As a VB developer, you can now use Windows resource files. This offers you a way to isolate strings, bitmaps, icons, graphics, and even custom data such as AVI files, into a single file. You can also use resource files to store different versions of the same data, so that a single set of source code could be used to create applications with multilingual capabilities. To localize an application in a foreign language, you could simply switch the resource file from the English version to another language such as Spanish, Dutch, and so on. Any localized strings or graphics can then be extracted from the new resource file at run time.

New Database Features

Another considerable change in the new version of VB is the increased database functionality. The new Enterprise edition of VB 4 provides many tools for developing distributed applications based on VB's powerful database engine. (Microsoft doesn't plan on getting rich by just selling copies of VB to multimedia developers. The big money is in corporate database development areas—client/server systems. So, that's where many of the upgrades have been focused.)

The Enterprise edition adds the ability to easily and quickly access components, OLE objects, and resources over a network. No longer do individual programmers need to work on separate projects. With the new network capabilities, they can use a central set of tools and resources. This ensures that each programmer is using the same tools as everyone else.

The features offered by the Enterprise edition will come in handy for anyone developing applications in teams. For the individual programmer, the Professional edition is perfect, but in a team environment, the Enterprise edition is the way to go. It gives you tools to keep track of what is being developed by who, and keeps track of changes to individual projects and components so that every member of your team is up to date on what others are doing. You'll also know if the components being used by one person are identical to those being used by another. This feature circumvents some major pitfalls; for example, if two team developers were using different versions of a component, they might discover that when their parts of the overall application are brought together, they don't work with one another.

We don't have to worry about these issues in the context of this book, but if you are working for a corporation, or plan to, then you need to become familiar with these tools and ideas. According to Microsoft, professional developers account for more than 85 percent of VB sales.

Windows 95 versus Windows NT

Ever since the announcement of Windows 95 more than two years ago, developers have been debating whether Windows NT is a better 32-bit operating system than Windows 95. Originally, it seemed that Microsoft planned Windows 95 to be a user's stepping stone to Windows NT. Microsoft knew they couldn't force everyone to go out and buy a monster machine with 32 MB of RAM to run Windows NT, so why not create an operating system that provided the basic 32-bit features, but wouldn't be as demanding on the hardware budget?

As Windows 95 evolved over the course of its extended beta testing period, many of the features in Windows NT migrated into Windows 95. Of course, Windows NT is a more powerful 32-bit operating system than Windows 95. But you can bet that Windows 95 will remain a popular operating system to run your multimedia applications for quite a few years. Personally, we'd like to see more users running Windows NT in the near future because it is an extremely stable and robust environment. Many of the problems and delays that impacted the release of Windows 95 are associated with compatibility issues. Microsoft needed to ensure that Windows 95 would run all of the major 16-bit Windows applications, otherwise they'd be hearing from a lot of angry customers. So, they sacrificed some speed to gain compatibility.

But don't think that having to support the thousands of 16-bit apps has turned Windows 95 into a crippled operating system. It simply means that Microsoft has had to do some incredible work, just to create what they did.

With Windows NT, Microsoft did not need to create a system that was compatible with every Windows program ever created. Their goal was to build a no-compromises, 32-bit environment that would lead them into the next century. Unfortunately, to achieve this goal, Windows NT has become one of the most resource-intensive environments for desktop computers. When NT was released in 1993, those resource demands really hurt its acceptance into the PC marketplace. But as hardware prices have fallen, systems capable of effectively running NT can be purchased for a modest sum. We think that when NT is released next year with the Windows 95 user interface (Cairo), many users will migrate toward this system.

But what about today? Well, in terms of personal users, the scales clearly tip towards Windows 95. Its new user interface is much more efficient to use and more aesthetically pleasing. The release of Windows 95 should be one of the biggest boons to the computer hardware market ever seen. Why? Because everyone will want the latest and greatest hardware to keep up with Windows 95. Plug and Play, built-in multimedia features, and higher system demands will push users into acquiring new hardware, especially more memory and larger hard drives. If you plan on doing any serious multimedia work or connecting to a network, you'll want to load your PC with at least 8 megabytes of RAM, and 16 megabytes is even a better idea. At least a gigabyte of hard drive space is probably a safe start. The release of Windows 95, even with the delay, is likely to be the most revolutionary event in the modern era of computing.

OCXs versus VBXs

The switch to OCXs in VB 4 was really a necessity. The problem with VBXs is that they are limited to running under 16-bit environments. The use of VBXs in previous versions of VB created one of the largest contingents of third party developers ever seen. There are thousands of VBX custom controls available that can easily add instant functionality to your applications—everything from 3D graphics to voice recognition is available in a VBX. Microsoft could have just introduced a 32-bit version of the VBX, but they decided to take this technology one step further and add support for the powerful OLE architecture within custom controls. These controls can now be used in all types of situations.

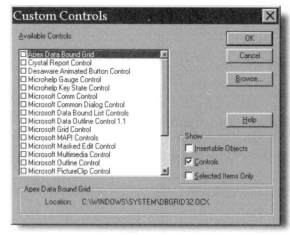

Figure 1.5   *The Custom Control Upgrade dialog box.*

Unfortunately, the 32-bit version of VB 4 does not support VBXs at all. This can be a real drawback for programmers who have VBX controls that they have relied on to program with in VB 3. Now, they will either have to wait for the OCX versions to come out or they can find a way to hard-code the functions of the obsolete VBX themselves. If you really need to use VBXs, the 16-bit version of VB 4 can use both VBXs and 16-bit OCXs. Are you getting confused yet? We have not been able to find out from Microsoft why they did not support VBXs in the 32-bit version of VB 4. We can only assume that the support for the VBXs was too complicted and was not compatible with the 32-bit upgrades to the language. When you do load in your old code, it will be checked to see if it uses VBXs. If one is found that has a corresponding OCX, VB will ask you if your code should be upgraded to use the OCX version. Figure 1.5 shows the Custom Control Upgrade dialog box that you will see when you load code that uses VBXs that can be updated to OCXs.

Plug and Play with Multimedia

The Plug and Play abilities of Windows 95 provide some interesting possibilities for VB 4 programmers. If a multimedia app is running on a laptop and the user hot-swaps a new video capture card into the PC Card slot, your application needs to be able to respond. Windows 95 will handle the setup and installation of the card, then your app needs to figure out that it has been added. This is done with the **SystemInfo** control. This control gives VB programs the ability to react gracefully to new hardware, even in the middle of the program's execution. The documentation on this control was minimal with the Beta version of VB 4, so check out the documentation you received with the full release version, to get more details.

If you plan on selling your application, and you want to say that it is "Windows 95 Ready," you need to make sure that your program can handle these situations. Microsoft has placed some pretty stiff requirements onto developers who want to say their apps are compatible with Windows 95. One of the requirements is that your app can handle Plug and Play events. Your app also has to run under Windows 95 or Windows NT, and be fully OLE-2-compliant. If you can handle all that, then you *might* be able to say your app is "Windows 95 Ready."

AutoPlay

Another new feature of Windows 95 is AutoPlay. AutoPlay is a simple device that checks CD-ROMs when they are first placed into the computer. If there is a file called AUTORUN.INF, Windows 95 performs the actions specified in the file. It acts a lot like a batch file did under DOS. Here is an example of an AUTORUN.INF:

```
[autorun]
OPEN=AUTORUN\AUTORUN.EXE
ICON=AUTORUN\WIN95CD.ICO
```

This code simply tells Windows to open the AUTORUN\AUTORUN.EXE file, and since it is an executable, Windows will run it.

Your first thought may be; what good is it? Well, once you see it in action, you will understand. Most readers of this book are probably pretty computer savvy, but the people who will be using your software may not be. So you need to write your applications to meet the user's skill level, and not yours. AutoPlay simplifies the process of setting up and installing your software, and makes program execution automatic. The real time-saver is that users of your software will no longer have to go hunting for the icon or the SETUP.EXE file. Every time a CD is loaded into the computer, you can instruct Windows 95 to either begin the setup process or execute the main program file. From a user's standpoint, it doesn't get much easier than that.

Programming 16-Bit Applications

What do you do if you want to create an application that will run under multiple platforms? For instance, assume you are creating a consumer-oriented multimedia program that you want to be a big hit and sell millions of copies. You could design it to run only under Windows 95 or Windows NT, but that could really limit your market. (You'd miss out on all of the buyers who are not ready to move to 32-bit Windows.) You could create separate VB programs, one to run under 16-bit Windows and the other to run under 32-bit Windows. Unfortunately, this approach would be difficult to manage. You'd need two teams of programmers as well as an efficient way to create both versions at the same time. As an alternative, you could just create a 16-bit program and sacrifice performance under 32-bit environments to gain compatibility. All are options, but none sound very good.

Using Conditional Compilation

Fortunately, VB 4 gives us an out. To create native applications that may be used under Windows 3.1 as well as Windows 95, you must be able to build separate executables for each environment. To accomplish this, VB 4 supports the technology of *conditional compilation*. This technique involves using the same source code to create separate 16- and 32-bit executables. A special type of **If..Then** statement is provided so that VB 4 can determine the type of environment an application is being compiled under, and then it can easily go about its business and create the appropriate code. One situation in which this technique is extremely useful is when declaring API function calls. If your app is running under Windows 3.1 and a call is made to a 32-bit function in a DLL, you'll get an error. Conversely, if your app is running under Windows 95 and you make a call to a 16-bit function, the operating system *thunks* down to 16-bit code, which slows things down tremendously. Thunking is the term used to describe what happens when Windows 95 needs to execute older and slower 16-bit code. If you are trying to write fast, 32-bit multimedia applications, thunking is something you want to avoid like the plague.

Let's look at sample section of code that uses conditional compilation statements with VB 4:

```
#If Win32 Then          ' Windows 95 Code
    Declare Function mciSendString Lib "winmm.dll" Alias "mciSendStringA" _
      (ByVal lpstrCommand As String, ByVal lpstrReturnString As String, _
      ByVal uReturnLength As Long, ByVal hwndCallback As Long) As Long
#Else                          ' Windows 3.1 Code
    Declare Function mciSendString Lib "MMSystem" (ByVal lpstrCommand As String, _
      ByVal lpstrReturnString As String, ByVal uReturnLength As Integer, _
      ByVal hwndCallback As Integer) As Long
#End If
```

As you can see, conditional compilation is really rather simple. The compiler encounters the #**If** statement and realizes that it needs to determine the environment for which it is compiling. The argument **Win32** is a special constant that tells VB4 that the code following should be compiled as 32-bit Windows code. If a statement like this is encountered, on the other hand, VB 4 will compile the code for 16-bit Windows:

```
#If Win16 Then          ' Windows 16 Code
    Declare Function mciSendString Lib "MMSystem" (ByVal lpstrCommand As String, _
        ByVal lpstrReturnString As String, ByVal uReturnLength As Integer, _
        ByVal hwndCallback As Integer) As Long
#End If
```

When an **#IF** conditional compilation statement is used, typically you'll want to provide an **#ELSE** statement to provide optional statements that will be used if the first part of the statement fails. As shown in our first example, if the code is being compiled for a 32-bit environment, the first API function is declared; otherwise, the second one is used for the 16-bit environment.

Continuing Long Lines

In our conditional compilation examples, note that an underscore character (_) is placed at the end of some of the lines. This is the symbol that you now use in VB 4 to break a long line of code and continue it on the next line. You can break a line of code at any point as long as you enter the underscore character preceded by a space. Throughout this book, you'll see this symbol used quite a bit so that we can make our longer lines of code fit on the page.

For most simple VB programs, you can just do a compile, and VB will create the correct version. But if you use 32-bit-specific API calls and VB functions, then conditional compilation is a life-saver. This method allows you to simultaneously create both versions, without having to worry about keeping track of two sets of source code. If you are using the 16-bit versions of VB 4, it automatically compiles 16-bit executables. If you are using the 32-bit version, on the other hand, you need to tell it which type of executable you want. VB 4 defaults to 32-bit, so you actually only need to tell it when you want to compile for 16-bit. This is accomplished by using the Options dialog box. Let's take a look.

Open the Options dialog box by clicking on the Tools menu item. Then, choose Options to bring up the Options dialog box as shown in Figure 1.6. Notice the tab options for Environment, Project, Editor, and Advanced. Click the Advanced tab. This displays options for automatically updating VBXs, conditional compilation, error trapping, and other advanced features. The

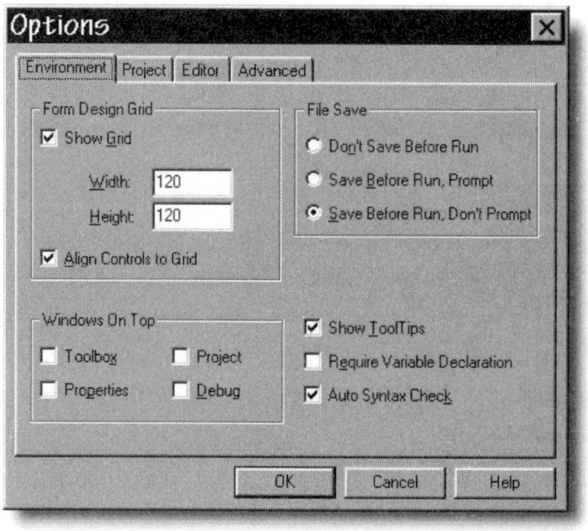

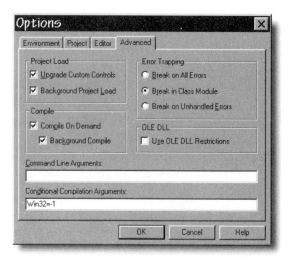

Figure 1.6   *Using the Options dialog.*

item we are interested in is the Conditional Compilation Arguments text box, where you can enter arguments, and VB will check to see what type of compile it should perform. If the box is empty, 32-bit VB 4 defaults to a 32-bit compile. If you want it to perform a 16-bit compile, you need to enter the argument "Win32=-1" into the text box, as shown in Figure 1.7, and when you compile your program the next time, VB will create a 16-bit executable.

You need to be extremely careful when working with conditional compilation—it is very easy to crash 16-bit Windows with poorly coded apps. Calling

Figure 1.7   *Using the Advanced options to specify a conditional compilation setting.*

the correct API functions is only the beginning. You also need to make sure that the arguments passed to all the API calls match up. By using the wrong type of variable with your API calls, you might quickly become a GPF expert! For instance, many of the 32-bit API functions now take arguments as Long Integers, where their 16-bit counterparts used standard Integers. In this situation, several things can happen. Most likely, you will get calling convention errors because the function is expecting a different type of variable. The next possibility is that the function will accept the variable, but because it is of the wrong type, the function will not do what is expected, and might return a value that is wrong. There are also instances in which the function will still work, but these cases are rare, and you should always code your applications to use the correct variable types.

The answer to all our conditional compilation issues is to use the **If..Then** statements in conjunction with the conditional compilation identifier (#). Just be careful where you use them. For many of the projects in this book, we decided not to go through the entire process of creating completely cross-platform-ready code. We have included all the correct API function calls for 16- and 32-bit, but we felt that using all the conditional compilation statements in the code would just confuse things. This is especially true of the lower-level projects that get into memory management and byte-by-byte string manipulation. These projects get so involved with the API function calls that conditional compilation increases the size of the application by 50 percent. Many of the programs will function in 16-bit Windows without any changes, aside from recompiling. However, other projects will need some modification so that the variable types will work correctly. None of the projects are 32-bit specific, so you should have very little trouble using them under Windows 3.1 with minimal changes.

For those of you still interested in 16-bit multimedia, we have included all the code from the original version of this book that was written for 16-bit VB 3. The projects are located in the \VBMAGIC\16BIT subdirectory on the companion CD-ROM. You may also want to check out the hypermedia system we created there. It is completely different than the one in this book, and not as powerful, but it might give you some insights when customizing the projects in this book for use in your own applications.

Wrapping It Up

Well, we've given you an introduction into the world of Visual Basic 4 and Windows 95. Next, we are going to take our first tentative steps into the Windows multimedia system. We'll slowly traverse our way down into the depths of the Windows 95 operating system. By the time we're done, you will have a basic understanding of almost all aspects of multimedia under Windows 95. So hang on tight, and get ready for some challenging multimedia development!

Chapter 2

Visual Basic 4 and
Windows 95 make
perfect partners for
developing many
types of multimedia
applications.

Visual Basic 4 Meets Multimedia

Ah, multimedia! Sit back, throw your feet up on your desk, fire up your computer, and get lost in a world of adventure and fun—a world where you can explore historical events and fascinating places by watching videos and participating in interactive stories. Or journey into the Grand Canyon and raft down the awesome rapids of the Colorado river. That's multimedia as it should be. But when you try to create apps like this, you'll discover multimedia development is practically a black art, and you'll need all the help you can get.

Gone are the days when a program required only a few algorithms, a database, and some interface code in order to come to life. As multimedia takes PCs into the twenty-first century, traditional programming languages and development tools alone simply won't cut it anymore. With sound, music, video, 3D animation, scrolling images, hypertext, and online services to support, you'll need a visual development environment that provides the right multimedia connections.

And that's where Visual Basic (VB) comes in. Instead of drowning in minute technical details in a complex language like C++ or using a dedicated multimedia authoring system that locks you into its own way of doing things (and there are certainly many of them competing for the spotlight), you can have the best of both worlds by using VB and letting your creativity soar.

Go Interactive

The multimedia we'll be exploring in this book isn't the boring "slide show" stuff that first emerged when the multimedia world arrived at the PC's doorstep. The demand for multimedia products has been high and so has the temptation for just throwing "shovel ware" software together on a CD-ROM. Our interest is in creating adventurous, interactive multimedia that brings new worlds to the user, not just slide shows with sound.

Imagine being able to watch any part of a basketball game from any player's position. You could put yourself in Hakeem Alajuwon's shoes as he spins around Shaq for a graceful dunk, or you could follow around the official as he breaks up a fight. If you want to replay a shot, you could click your mouse and step back in time for a moment. That's interactive. You get to be part of the experience rather than just a spectator watching from a distance.

Creating quality interactive multimedia takes a lot of knowledge and the right tools. You must know how to present your information and how to manipulate it in real time. Of course, you won't become an instant content expert from reading this book, but you will learn how to create the tools to process your multimedia images, sound files, music, animation, video, and hypertext. We'll start by exploring some of the tools that Windows 95 provides for manipulating these components, and then we'll create our own. You'll be amazed by the multimedia power and flexibility that VB brings to the table.

Exploring the Windows 95 Multimedia System

The Windows Multimedia System, which is built into Windows 95, provides a set of services that you can use in your programs to manipulate sound, graphics, and video. Windows 95 (or Windows 3.1, or Windows 3.0 with Multimedia Extensions) also includes some multimedia utilities that give you instant access to these capabilities. However, Windows 95 offers some major advantages over the previous versions. The Sound Recorder, for instance, will let you add digitized sounds, such as oral annotations, to Word documents, Excel spreadsheets, or other apps that support Windows Object Linking and Embedding (OLE). The Media Player utility will play back *WAV* files, *MIDI* sequencer files, or *AVI* video files (that's video as in television video, not PC display video) right from your hard disk or CD-ROM drive. Media Player can also play standard audio CDs on your CD-ROM drive, and if you load the right drivers, it can operate video laser disks, video tape decks, and other external devices equipped with serial or *SCSI* interfaces.

Windows 95 uses the same programs as previous versions, but the big difference is that they have been upgraded to 32 bits. That means twice the bandwidth, and therefore, twice the resolution. In audio terms, you may not notice a big change, but with video clips, you will see a tremendous improvement. This is because video takes so much more processing power than audio does. Look at it this way—a thirty-second compact disc quality WAV file takes up almost five megabytes. If you think that's a lot, a thirty-second full-screen AVI file compressed with a 32-bit CODEC (compression/decompression algorithm) can take up a whopping 30 megabytes of disk space!

So you can see how it would be helpful to be able to pass that information through as fast as possible. Now, just because you are still using 16-bit Windows, doesn't mean you should forget video, just be careful how and where you use it. If you have to have full screen animation, than forget AVI files altogether; look to MPEG. As this book was being written, software-based MPEG was difficult at best, so we did not cover it. However, by the time this book gets on the shelves, there should be a new set of standards for software-based MPEG compression and decompression that will make it much easier for the average programmer to use, mostly because you do not have to worry about any proprietary hardware standards. Now, back to what we will teach you.

No Programming Necessary

Not everyone aspires to multimedia fame. Some of us just want to use sound and pictures to make a point or to assist with day to day tasks, or just to play music. Fortunately, you can use Windows 95 Multimedia features without ever touching a programming language or an authoring system. Let's explore a simple example.

Start up any Windows app that supports Object Linking and Embedding, such as Microsoft Word or Excel. Create or load any file. Then, locate the option that enables you to insert a Windows object into a document. In Word, choose Insert, Object. Word will display the dialog box shown in Figure 2.1.

Choose Sound from the Object Type list box to open the Sound Recorder utility. You can record from a microphone plugged into your sound card or you can record from a CD playing in your CD-ROM drive, press the record button (the little red button) on the Sound Recorder, and say something. Try to be as profound as Alexander Graham Bell when he tested his first telephone ("Watson, come here I need you!"). But keep it brief; digital audio recordings gobble disk space if you are recording at a high-quality level!

Figure 2.1 *The Microsoft Word Insert Object dialog box allows you to insert Windows objects into a document.*

When you're done, close the Recorder. Word will display a microphone icon in your document as shown in Figure 2.2.

You may insert text as you please before or after this *embedded object*. To replay your recording, just double click on the microphone icon. If you transmit your document by email to other people who use Word for Windows, they too will see the Recorder icon and can replay your message.

By the way, you can embed existing recordings just as easily as new ones by selecting Media Clip from the Object Type list box. When the Media Player appears, choose Device, Sound from the menu. Then, open and play any WAV file. When you're done, close Media Player. In this case, Word will display the Media Player icon rather than the Sound Recorder's microphone. Double click on the icon to replay the sound.

If you want a little more flexibility but are truly wary of programming, you can use an authoring system to build presentations. Without programming, you can get to all the same *kinds* of services (sound, graphics, animation, and video) as you can with programming; you just won't have as much flexibility in how you present them.

These handy utilities perform some amazing operations behind the scenes. And Microsoft has given us most of the functions we need to build our own programs to manipulate the devices and data that comprise the Multimedia System. They're contained in a Windows *Dynamic Link Library* (*DLL*) called WINMM.DLL. Just like any other Windows *Application Programming Interface* (*API*) functions, we can call these functions from our own apps.

Figure 2.2   *Microsoft Word document with an embedded Recorder object.*

Windows Programming—A Black Art?

Windows programming resembles no other type of programming that most of us have ever encountered. The Windows graphical user interface (GUI) is designed to make programs look similar. Obviously, you can only go so far in this direction, or all programs would look exactly the same. But many apps, especially productivity programs like word processors and spreadsheets, share dozens of common operations. For example, all word processors offer cursor movement, printing, rulers, cut and paste operations, and a variety of other features. And all programs need navigation tools so you can get from one option or data field to another.

Windows provides functions that perform many of these common operations. In fact, the Windows 95 Application Programming Interface (API) offers almost 2,000 functions! Some do spectacular things, like playing back a video file with a single call; others perform small, specialized operations like reporting the position of the cursor. To program a Windows app, all you have to do is stack up a series of calls to the appropriate Windows functions.

Right!

A Windows app carries on an intimate relationship with the operating system. Like young lovers, they exchange messages at a frantic rate. Almost any time something happens in Windows, whether it's in your app or another one running at the same time, Windows sends your app a message, offering it an opportunity to respond. Often the response triggers a flurry of exchanges. You may already be familiar with the infamous *WinProc*, the often gargantuan procedure familiar to C/C++ Windows programmers that consists primarily of a lengthy case statement piled high with procedures that respond to messages. This is where the work of a Windows app happens.

To write a Windows app—at least one that works reliably—you have to anticipate all the messages your app might receive and need to act upon.

Unless you write your application in VB.

Visual Basic as a Windows Development System

Prepare yourself for a suspicious claim:

You can accomplish a lot more in a lot less time with VB than you can with one of the traditional languages like C, C++, or Pascal. (I mean regular old Pascal, not the new Object Pascal of Borland's Delphi, but that is another book altogether!)

Languages like C/C++ are necessary for writing tight, fast code for projects like device drivers or communication programs. These languages have more direct access to the lower-level capabilities of the hardware and operating system. But most of us want to write applications and utilities that solve higher-level day-to-day problems like amortizing loans or storing information about clients and patients. To create the low-level services of the Windows Multimedia System, you would need a language like C or Pascal. To reach in and grab hold of those services and bring them to life without a ton of code, VB provides the ticket.

VB Takes Care of Windows Housekeeping Chores for You

Huge sections of the Windows API perform routine functions like opening and closing windows, managing memory, formatting text, and displaying scroll bars. Since most Windows apps use these features, they tend to call the same functions and respond to the same messages over and over. With VB, the details for many of the basic Windows housekeeping chores like these are taken care of for you. VB calls hundreds of API functions and responds to all the appropriate messages behind the scenes. You only need to fill in the blanks.

It's Event Driven

To program in Windows, you have to think in Windows, and Windows is a world of events. Almost anything an app does in Windows is a response to an event. Windows notifies your program of each event by sending it a message.

VB is designed around this event-driven model. If you click on a command button in a typical Windows program, some program code would need to be called to perform an operation. VB provides you with built-in event handlers for standard events, such as mouse clicks, so that you can easily create truly event-driven programs. VB even goes one step further and incorporates the event-driven nature of Windows into the VB development environment. For example, you can click on a command button to open a window and display your code as you are designing your programs.

Interactive Development Puts the User First

VB offers the most interactive way to develop interactive programs. The ease with which you can add controls helps you to design and modify your programs so that they work and feel just right for your users.

When you create a program with a traditional language, the initial focus is on the task you want to automate. Once you think you know how to solve the tough problems, you begin to grind out the code. Along the way, you build the user interface: menus, windows, interactive controls, data entry fields, and so on.

But with VB, you begin with the most important component—the user.

Visual Programming Power

Visual design is a handy feature for creating many types of Windows apps. For interactive multimedia, it's essential. Interactive multimedia is a new medium—a visual medium. The success of a project depends on how the user can interact with it. A movie director would never hand over a script to his crew and wait in his office for the final film footage. Much of what ends up on the screen is discovered on the set. When you design your multimedia title, you need feedback every step of the way. Are the buttons too big? Too small? Too many? Does the picture get lost among the controls? Can you read the text without covering the images?

With VB, you can fine-tune your apps as you work. And, if you still need low-level horsepower, this book will give you the map to guide you as you machete your trail through the API jungle.

Easy-to-Use Support of the API

Although some of the Windows API functions deliver their goods to us through the VB back door, many do not. Some of them must be called directly, which, thankfully, is easy. (Actually, it isn't so much that the API functions are difficult to understand individually. The tricky part is finding the right combinations to successfully complete the task at hand.) To prove just how easy it is, let's try one.

Playing Multimedia with a Few Lines of Code

Our first VB multimedia project shows you how to use the **mciExecute()** multimedia API call to play a WAV file.

Start up VB and create a new form called MCIPlay. Place one control on it: a Command Button named ExecuteMCICommand. Set the **Caption** Property of this button to "Execute MCI Command."

Next, click on the ExecuteMCICommand button. VB should display the framework for the **Click** event shown in Figure 2.3. We're going to call upon the services of the simplest function in the multimedia API—**mciExecute()**. This function executes MCI commands.

The function **mciExecute()** takes a single argument, a string, which contains a plain English command as shown in Listing 2.1. In this simple example, all we want to do is play a WAV file. The MCI "play" command will automatically open and close the WAV device for us.

Listing 2.1 ExecuteMCICommand_Click() Event Procedure

```
Sub ExecuteMCICommand_Click ()
    Dummy% = mciExecute("play c:\windows\tada.wav")
    End Sub
```

Make sure you add the following declarations:

```
#If Win32 Then
    Private Declare Function mciExecute Lib "winmm" _
      (ByVal lpstrCommand As String) As Long
#Else
    Private Declare Function mciExecute Lib "MMSystem" _
      (ByVal CommandString As String) As Integer
#End If
```

mciExecute() is a true *function*, not a *procedure*, or subprocedure as procedures are called in VB; it returns a long integer value that indicates success or failure. Since we don't plan to act upon that result, we're just catching the result in a dummy integer variable.

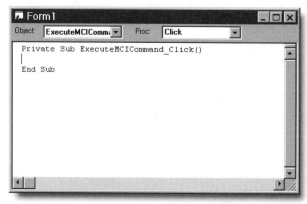

Figure 2.3 *The VB Code window with the ExecuteMCICommand_Click() event procedure displayed.*

If Windows 95 is installed on a drive other than C:, make the appropriate change to the command string argument. Then, run the program and click on the Command Button. You can insert the name of any WAV file into this command. Try it out and give it a listen!

Actually, you can insert the name of any MCI-supported data file into the play command. Windows 95 comes with a sample MIDI sequencer file called CANYON.MID. Replace the WAV filename with the name of this MIDI file and run the program again.

```
Dummy% = mciExecute("play c:\windows\canyon.mid")
```

Unlike the brief WAV files, CANYON.MID will play for a couple of minutes.

I would be misleading you if I told you that all the Windows multimedia API calls were this easy to use. Many functions take several arguments. Often you have to follow arcane rules to pass arguments from VB to Windows functions. Some functions work only in combination with other functions. Other functions that were present in Windows 3.1 have been taken out of Windows 95 and, of course, all the new 32-bit functions are new to Windows programming. And other functions don't work from VB at all! In Chapter 4, we'll begin to look at the Windows API in general and at the multimedia functions in particular. By the time we've finished with our presentation system, you'll know how to use many of the key functions that will propel our programs into the multimedia age.

The Essential VB Ingredients

Before we begin programming in earnest, let's rummage around in the VB closet and figure out what we can use. We'll start by sorting the components we'll be needing into their proper compartments.

A VB program usually consists of a least one *form* on which we find one or more objects, in the form of *controls*. Controls have *properties*, which define their appearance and general behavior, and *event procedures,* which determine what will happen when the control is activated by one or several operator actions, or *events*.

Forms Present

Forms are actually objects themselves, and like control objects, they offer some event procedures. For most purposes, we generally think of a form as a frame within which to place controls. In general, we'll abide by that convention, although we'll also see that plain unpopulated forms can perform some useful functions in screen presentation, as well.

Objects Behave

Most of the real action takes place within controls. Much of the activity on the screen requires the services of more than one control. A Command Button, for example, might load a bitmap image into a Picture Box. Each type of control offers its own selection of event procedures. Some overlap; but many do not.

Properties Define

Properties determine states, such as background color or the name by which we'll reference the control elsewhere within our program.

Events Happen

Events usually trigger everything that happens in VB programs. In fact, if you write a program that loops away on its own, without regard to events—which you *can* do—you'll effectively disable Windows, and may be forced to reboot the computer. An infinite loop in a Windows program will hang your system just as well as an infinite loop in a DOS program. But thanks to multitasking, there's more to crash.

The concept of multimedia events extends beyond Windows programming, as you'll see when we discuss the Musical Instrument Digital Interface, or MIDI, in Chapter 16.

Functions, Procedures, and Methods Work

Functions and *procedures* contain program statements that manipulate data. When we want something done, we call a procedure; when we want something back, we call a function. Event procedures are special procedures that Windows and VB call when something happens in Windows that might affect a particular form or control. VB also includes dozens of other functions that perform common operations like trimming strings of their leading or trailing spaces, or calculating the cosine of an angle.

Forms and controls offer a special type of procedure that performs work under program control rather than in response to user events. These procedures are defined as integral components of their host objects. In objected-oriented programming, such procedures are called *methods*. VB, by the way, though object-oriented in its design, doesn't permit us to define our own objects and methods, at least not from within the language itself. It is therefore, object-oriented, but not *internally extensible*. How's that for colliding jargon?

The difference between a method and any other procedure that is built into the language is that a method belongs to its host object and usually modifies a property of that object, whereas a general purpose procedure accepts and modifies conventional data elements, such as variables, constants, and arrays—most of the time. You can write procedures that modify an object's properties. The difference between these two components will just continue to get fuzzier, and I promised a brief review, so we'll move on.

Modules Organize

Considering the way we scatter code around in a VB program, you have to wonder whether we're still entitled to call it "structured." The VB programming system—and it is a system, not just a language—dictates not only syntax, but architecture. In fact, the apparently chaotic organization of a VB program reflects a purer form of the structured ideal than the linear listings required by traditional programming languages. Like protein molecules, procedures perform distinct operations. They offer a single entry point and a single exit. The order in which we create them matters only to the extent that one procedure cannot call another unless the one being called already exists.

Yet, within any given program, procedures tend to cluster. So-called low-level procedures perform minute repetitive tasks and tend to call built-in language or operating system features. Higher-level procedures call on low-level procedures, so much so that the low-level procedures sometimes obscure the identity of the host language. Several procedures may perform related tasks, like disk and file management.

As we write event procedures for our VB programs, we find that we want to write procedures we can call upon over and over again without duplicating their code. We may even want to bag some of these tools to tote them from one program to another. So we place them in *modules.*

You can add general procedures and functions to a form, but if you create a separate module to store those items, they can be called by procedures in other forms, as well. And if you add that module file to another project, the same code can be called from modules or forms in both projects. Throughout this book we'll bundle code into modules that you can incorporate into your own projects.

Code Style Clarifies

The most overlooked component of any language is overlooked because it isn't a component, but a philosophy. *Code style* illuminates a program's rails and switches. A digital computer runs a program in a particular order. That order is determined by a set of critical statements that divert the processor into loops and branches. You can weave as many loops and branches into your program as you wish, and as long as you obey the language's rules of syntax, the interpreter or compiler doesn't care how your code looks. But *you* should care, because if *you* can't follow it, it probably doesn't work the way you think.

The most obvious element of code style is *indentation*. This apparently trivial technique has fanned some hot debates. Everyone has personal views on indentation, and since none of the mainstream languages impose indentation style, we all stick to our own guidelines. This discussion won't shed any light on multimedia, so we'll just say that we'll try to indent our code in order to clarify its structure. We never write code without indentation—not even tiny programs—but we are not purists and our style may not satisfy your needs. We recommend two things: Develop or adopt a style, and *apply it consistently*. Inconsistent indentation can hang you as surely as no indentation, maybe worse—we don't expect any help from unformatted code, but randomly formatted code plays pranks on us.

The second key element of code style is *scoping*. The VB manuals explain scoping pretty well, as do some of the many introductory texts on the language. We won't waste your time by repeating the same technical discussion. Think of scoping as containment, like a nest of Chinese boxes. When you're done with a program, nothing should show outside those boxes, except what you need to run that program. And at each layer within, the same rule pertains: nothing more or less than you need should appear outside that level of scope. Each time you declare a variable, consider where you'll use it, then put it in the smallest box you can. By eliminating global variables, passing information around as arguments instead, you'll write more reusable code. Remember, structured programming is the artful hiding of details. This rule too, we will try to follow as closely as possible.

Intrinsic Multimedia Features

You'll find yourself using a large assortment of VB's features to write any serious application. Thus, any VB feature could be considered useful for multimedia projects. But some of VB's features turn out to be particularly useful. Let's take a closer look.

Forms, Image Boxes, and Picture Boxes, for example, are essential multimedia tools, both in obvious and—as we'll learn in Chapter 3—surprising ways. These three *objects* share several useful capabilities, like the **Picture** property and **Graphics** methods.

Forms are the platforms on which we'll stage our productions. To make effective presentations, we need to think carefully about forms, how many to display, how to size them, and how to move them.

Graphics *methods* provide essential graphic capabilities to our programs at runtime, whereas **Graphics** *controls* take the form of lines, boxes, and circles with which we can decorate our forms at design-time.

VB also lets us add pictures to our applications either at design-time or at runtime. We can move them, resize them, and remove them. With a simple technique based on control arrays, we can even animate them. We'll use Picture Boxes, Images, Text Boxes, and forms themselves extensively in our applications. And we'll end up using most of their properties and methods. By layering these elements and manipulating their properties at runtime, we can really get the show moving. Let's try a simple example.

Moving Pictures

This project shows you how to use a few VB programming tricks to move a picture around in a window.

First, we need a form. We won't need to reference the **Name** property, so you can name the form anything you wish. On the form, place a Frame control and stretch it to proportions similar to those shown in Figure 2.4. The Frame control is represented in the toolbox by a rectangle with the letters "Frame1" in the top border.

Next, click on the Picture Box control icon in the toolbox. The Picture Box is represented by a picture of a desert vista. Place the Picture Box inside the Frame control. We need to align the upper-left corners of the Picture Box and Frame controls so that the Frame disappears, but before we do that, let's assign an image to the Picture Box so we can keep track of it.

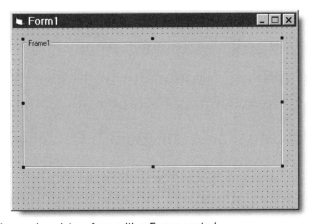

Figure 2.4 *The moving picture form with a Frame control.*

The accompanying CD-ROM contains a subdirectory called \VBMAGIC\ IMAGES. In it you will find a file called YAKIDAWN.BMP. We want to assign this file to the **Picture** property of the Picture Box.

Now you can slide the Picture Box up into position. This requires a little practice; you may tend to accidentally switch contexts and find yourself dragging the Frame instead of the Picture Box, but it can be done. The easiest way to clean up the edges is to set the **Top** and **Left** properties of the Picture Box to 0 in the VB Properties Window. **Top** and **Left** determine the position of the Picture Box relative to its container, in this case, the Frame.

We need to change one other property of the Picture Box, **AutoSize**. Set this property to True.

> **Note:** *You can switch a* Boolean *property (a property with either of two values: True or False) by double clicking anywhere on its line in the Properties list.*

The **AutoSize** property causes the Picture Box to match its size to the height and width of the currently active Picture—the image assigned to the **Picture** property. The picture is much larger than what we can see on the screen. To see the entire picture as shown in Figure 2.5, open the file in Windows 95 Paint (Paintbrush in Windows 3.1) application.

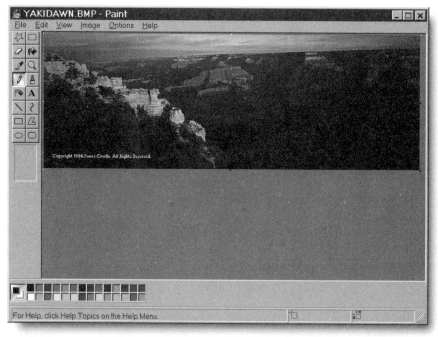

Figure 2.5   *The entire YAKIDAWN.BMP image.*

The Frame masks the Picture Box so we can only see the portion of the picture that is visible through the Frame.

Place a Timer control anywhere on the form. The Timer will disappear at runtime so it doesn't matter where it goes. If you put more than one Timer on a form, you may want to locate them on or near the other controls to which they're most closely related. Timers service only one event, the **Timer** event, and have only seven properties.

The only Timer properties that affect us are **Enabled**, which must be True, and **Interval**. The **Interval**, measured in milliseconds, determines how often the **Timer** event occurs. Actually, the Timer control can't tick any more often than the system timer, which ticks 18 times per second, so the shortest meaningful interval is one eighteenth of a second, or about 56 milliseconds. We are going to use the Timer to animate our image, and we want the smoothest motion we can coax from it, so set the **Interval** to 56.

We're going to use the **Timer** event to slide the Picture Box from right to left behind the Frame, creating the illusion that we're panning the landscape. Listing 2.2 shows the code needed for the **Timer1_Timer()** event procedure.

Listing 2.2   Timer1_Timer() Event Procedure

```
Sub Timer1_Timer ()
   Picture1.Left = Picture1.Left - 15
End Sub
```

The **Left** property indicates the position of the Picture Box control relative to the left edge of its container. We measure this value in *twips*, VB's default *Scale Mode*. Twips provide a device-independent scale for measuring screen objects. One twip equals 1/1440th of a logical inch, or 1/567th of a logical centimeter. The benefit of using the twips scale measurement is that the size of an object remains reasonably constant, regardless of screen resolution (not always the case with pixels). As we subtract twips from **Picture1.Left**, increasing its negative magnitude, the whole Picture control slides further and further left of the left edge of the Frame. The negative value indicates how many twips the control's left edge rests from position zero, the Frame's left edge. Run the program to see what happens.

Don't forget to stop the program after the image disappears. To prevent the Picture Box from sliding right on past us, let's add a terminating condition. The new version of our event procedure is shown in Listing 2.3.

Listing 2.3   The New Timer1_Timer() Event Procedure

```
Sub Timer1_Timer ()
   Picture1.Left = Picture1.Left - 15
```

```
   If Picture1.Left = -(Picture1.Width - Frame1.Width) Then
     Timer1.Enabled = False
   End If
End Sub
```

With the **Width** property, we can stop the motion of the image either by diverting around the subtraction statement, or, as we've done here, by disabling the Timer. By disabling the Timer, we free some system resources. We want the motion to cease when the right edges of the image and the Frame meet. The difference between the Picture Box width and the Frame width tells us how much of the image will be hanging out to the left of the Frame when that happens. **Picture1.Left** will contain a negative value, so we negate the difference of the object widths before comparing the two values.

That's animation with five lines of code—seven if you're particular—no function calls, and one bitmap. Now *that's* intristic multimedia.

We'll look at some more animation techniques in Chapters 8, 13, and 14.

The Professional Edition MCI Control

The Professional Edition of VB 4 comes with a custom control called the *MCI OLE custom control.* You can operate all kinds of devices with this control, including the system's sound card, Microsoft's AVI (Audio-Video Interleave) files, CD-Audio, and external VCRs and video disk players. But you don't *need* the MCI control to operate many of these devices. In fact, the MCI control can be cumbersome when all you want to do is play back a WAV file or a MIDI sequence. Yet, as an interface to external devices, the MCI control can come in handy.

Missing Links

As good as VB is at displaying screens with text, still images, and controls, plus its ability in responding to user activity, it provides no intrinsic support for the most exciting multimedia elements: sound, animation, and video. If you plan to use Windows' multimedia features, unless you own the Professional Edition, you have no choice but to venture outside the secure confines of VB. And even if you do own the Professional Edition, you'll find it easier to accomplish some things without the MCI control.

In many cases, VB will serve us well as an application framework, tending to the menial tasks of Windows management. For much of what we'll do, we'll rely on VB's numerous features, especially when it comes to the user interface. With its assortment of Scroll Bars, List Boxes, Image controls, and various buttons, we can assemble some attractive, functional forms.

Where VB leaves off, we'll look to the Windows API. Sometimes we'll have to sneak past VB, intentionally avoiding its zealous attempts to protect us from the fearsome machinery below.

The Making of *Explore the Grand Canyon*

Throughout this book we'll feature some multimedia development projects created by different developers to give you some insight into the way other developers work. For our first example, we'll look at a unique multimedia product titled *Explore the Grand Canyon* that was developed with both Visual Basic and Borland's Delphi. This product, shown in Figure 2.6, is based on a highly-interactive explorer model and provides both a 2D and 3D adventure of the awesome Grand Canyon. Three years in the making, it represents the largest-ever assembled collection of media on the Grand Canyon. Here you'll find the work of some of the Canyon's finest photographers, writers, artists, geologists, and explorers all woven together in an interactive worldwide multimedia adventure. Using a custom multimedia engine, this unique CD-ROM links to the Internet with Coriolis' NetSeeker™ to allow users to dynamically link in new content with the click of a button.

Figure 2.6 *The interface to Explore the Grand Canyon.*

Here are some interesting design notes from Scott Jarol, the developer of *Explore the Grand Canyon*:

In 1992, when we first started working on *Explore the Grand Canyon*, our first task was to choose our tools. Even back then, multimedia developers had enough options that selecting development tools had already become one of the major production tasks. As programmers, my partner and I suffered from a severe case of "not invented here" syndrome, an affliction that often causes technical people to shrug off other people's work as cute prototypes. To us, authoring systems were just impediments to our grand visions. We believed that to do innovative work, we had to code it all ourselves. And to a certain extent, we still believe that's true. After all, you don't see too many hit computer games built with authoring systems. Authoring systems bundle complicated technology into neatly wrapped, easy-to-use packages, where it can be shared by all. But game developers don't want to share technology. In the world of computer games, technical innovation is the force that drives products into the marketplace. Witness the cyclone of oneupsmanship spawned by *Castle Wolfenstein* and its even nastier cousin *Doom*.

Okay, that's fine for multimedia products intended to entertain us, but what about those that are supposed to—what, bore us? If interactive multimedia has had any philosophical impact so far, it has been the institutionalization of the once-closeted belief that successful information delivery is a form of entertainment. That's why so many of us have succumbed to verbal atrocities like "edutainment." Game or encyclopedia, interactive multimedia is entertainment.

And that's why, even in the face of ever-receding deadlines, we thumbed our noses at authoring systems—sort of. The fact is, the boundaries between programming tools and authoring systems are beginning to blur, a phenomenon that we exploited in *Explore the Grand Canyon*. In the end we found that we could combine tools to achieve the results we were after.

Creating a Multimedia Engine

The Grand Canyon is a big subject. As we began to study the Canyon, we found that most of the information we were gathering fell into one of six categories: geology, geography, archaeology, history, fauna, and flora. But the last thing we wanted to do with the Canyon was chop and box it. The best way to understand the Canyon is by studying its resources in context. We decided that to do justice to the Grand Canyon, we needed to bring it to our users. So, in the impractical fashion typical of many programmers, we began by assigning ourselves a monumental technical challenge.

Early on, the design for the project revolved around a 3D re-creation of the Canyon, dotted with hotspots, each of which would trigger some kind of multimedia event or events. We also wanted to display hyperlinked text and images, which could, in turn, interact with the 3D model and a 2D topographic map. The goal was to place as much of the content into the canyon as we could. Users could learn about John Wesley Powell's historic expeditions down the Colorado River by listening to Powell and his companions describe the enormous rapids they faced, while looking at pictures of those rapids, listening to their roar, and better yet, while "standing" at the actual locations in the canyon where the events took place. Just as in real life, elusive bighorn sheep would appear occasionally along the river and trails. By clicking on a picture of an animal, you could learn more about its survival tactics. As in an adventure game, we wanted users to explore a Canyon haunted with its natural and human history.

Unfortunately, real-time 3D graphics programming is a complex task. It's math intensive, and often requires a mind-meld with the underlying computer hardware to squeeze every last drop of performance from it. Not the stuff Macromind Director was meant to handle. So, our own graphics wizard Dan Haygood took the plunge into Borland's new Delphi programming system. Although easier to use than most other high-level computer languages, Delphi's Object Pascal still requires a programmer's skills. Dan worked feverishly away on the 3D model for more than four months. Eventually, he managed to mold fifteen million elevation values into an attractive interactive model of the Canyon, complete with shading, coloring, and a blue gradient sky.

In the meantime, we had already abandoned Delphi's older brother, Borland Pascal 7.0 for Windows, to construct our multimedia engine, the part of the program that would display hyperlinked text, maps, photographs, and video clips. The development process was just too slow. Our completion deadline had come and gone—twice—and we still had no multimedia engine. We began to reconsider the idea of using an authoring system, but our technical requirements just overwhelmed them. We had three thousand true-color images (over a gigabyte), two hundred megabytes of sound, hundreds of pages of text, and a huge topographical map and 3D model that shared over a thousand hotspots, all of which needed to communicate with each other. To display all that visual material, handle the live mixing of sound effects, narration and music, and to pack it all on a CD-ROM, we needed heavy-duty data compression, and some powerful multimedia management techniques. And we no longer had time to write the code to do it all ourselves. That was when we began to seriously think about moving the multimedia engine into either Borland's Delphi or Microsoft's Visual Basic.

We had extolled the virtues of VB in the first edition of this book as a multimedia development system, but had never used VB for more than the prototype of the Grand Canyon project. Visual Basic was one of the first Windows development system to embrace the so-called software component model. Software components, often called "custom controls," enable programmers to cobble together complete programs from one or more pre-existing components. Each custom control is a separate little program that performs a unique task, or set of related tasks. With any luck, a component is written by someone who has thought really hard about those tasks, and has added enough features to support just about any contingency. Components for VB and other programming systems now come in hundreds of varieties, from heart-shaped buttons to video playback windows, to complete spreadsheets. We knew from experience that by combining the relatively straightforward programming language in VB with the right set of custom controls we could get a hypermedia engine up and running in a matter of weeks, rather than the months that would have been required to program and debug it in a more complex language like C++.

Delphi also offers a component-based programming system, but Borland's product was so new that third-party support had not yet generated the variety of components now available to VB programmers. The user-interface is often the most difficult part of any programming project, especially when it comes to interactive multimedia, and custom controls make interface programming almost effortless. Delphi's programming language provided the raw speed and power needed for the 3D model, but for now, Visual Basic would offer the most flexible platform for the program's multimedia engine. We knew the time had come to practice what we had preached.

Unfortunately, by this time, we were also so mired in the editorial work that we couldn't spare any time to code—which is good, because it's not our strongest suit anyway—and Dan had his hands full with the 3D model. Instead of delaying the project by several more months, we hired a local multimedia consulting firm, Soft Reel Graphics, to take on the VB implementation.

Our hunch panned out when SRG's Chris Coppola and Shane Edmonds whipped together the first version of the system in a few days. Selecting two particularly handy custom controls had eliminated many crucial technical issues.

The FXCmp Custom Control by ImageFX (Rochester, NY) supported the extremely efficient LEAD Technologies, Inc. CMP compression scheme, which squeezed our 3000 photographs and illustrations into just 110 megabytes. FXCmp could not only expand the images in fractions of a second, with no noticeable loss of quality, it could also perform transitions, such as wipes, dissolves, and side-to-side pushes. The only preparation step was to open LEAD Technologies's LEADView image editor and batch compress all the images from Windows BMP files to LEAD CMP files. To load a picture into FXCmp, you just set its Picture property to the file name of the image; everything else is automatic. Incidentally, image compression has a double benefit. Obviously, efficient compression enables you to pack more images on to the disk, but smaller files also load more quickly—even when you factor in decompression time—which improves your program's overall performance.

To handle hypertext we worked a little harder. Although we had implemented a simple hypertext system for the projects in my book, we wanted something that could handle formatted text, including indentations, color changes, and text attributes, such as bold and italics. The ALLTEXT HT/Pro custom control by Bennet-Tec Information Systems, Inc. provided many of the features we needed—and quite a few that we didn't. This powerful control is actually a complete text editor-in-a-box. We didn't intend to offer any editing capabilities to our users, so we ended up disabling many of the control's features. We also wanted to feed our text to the control in Rich Text Format (RTF), which is easily exported from most Windows word processors, including Microsoft Word. The ALLTEXT HT/Pro control handles RTF nicely; the problem is that each topic, no matter how brief, needed to be an independent RTF document, complete with all the standard RTF header information. Instead of spending days or weeks implementing a proprietary hypertext system, SRG spent hours writing a program that would slice up our RTF files into individual topics that the custom control could digest. You should also be aware that the Bennet-Tec control does not handle hyperlinking automatically. All it does is detect clicks on designated words or phrases, and notify your VB program by calling a VB *event procedure.* Event procedures are the heart and soul of VB programming. Events occur whenever something happens in your program that requires a response. One of the simplest event procedures is called the Click event, which happens when the user clicks a button. When you first load a custom control into a new program, its event procedures show up as empty boxes, which you must fill with your own program code to perform the appropriate response. In our multimedia engine, the ALLTEXT's ATXChange event triggers multimedia activity. Custom controls do not replace programmers, they just make their jobs easier, which accelerates development and helps to minimize bugs.

Over the following weeks, Chris and Shane patiently listened to our change requests and bug reports, and gradually molded our general design into a powerful multimedia engine, complete with hypertext, image transition effects, irregularly-shaped image hotspots, floating video windows, popup glossaries, and hotspotted maps.

The moment of truth came when Dan and Chris implanted the 3D model into the hypermedia system. In one long day of surgery, they stitched together the two programs, written in two distinct languages, into a seemlessly integrated system. Clicking a hotspot in the Delphi-based 3D model now caused pictures to appear in the VB-based Browser window, along with sound effects, narration, and music.

About the same time we were bringing our hypermedia engine to life, our publisher, The Coriolis Group, showed us a new technology they had just developed. As computer book publishers, they were becoming frustrated with the fact that software distributed on their book's companion disks was becoming outdated before the books hit the shelves. To solve that problem they invented NetSeeker, a client/server Internet utility that enables their readers to instantly download and update their software over the Internet with a single mouse click. Coriolis Group's publisher, Keith Weiskamp asked me whether the same technology could be adapted to offer ongoing updates to users of *Explore the Grand Canyon*. At first we resisted the idea—we really just wanted to finish what we had started—but it didn't take long to realize the value that NetSeeker could add to our product. But how were we going to perform piecemeal updates to such a complex hypermedia system?

Once again, VB, or—more precisely—VB's Data Access features came to the rescue. SRG's Chris and Shane had decided to store all the links and media catalog information in an Access database, which in turn would be installed on the user's local hard drive. Even 3D and map hotspots were stored in the database as records, which meant that to add a new hotspot, all we needed to do was add a record to the appropriate data table. Chris worked with Coriolis's Tony Potts to devise an interface that would enable NetSeeker to download additional media elements (pictures, audio clips, etc.) to the user's hard drive, along with a database supplement, which *Explore the Grand Canyon* would automatically absorb the next time it was run. If we had used a multimedia authoring system, this enhancement might not have been practical. And because we control our own code, we can continue to refine this feature, as bandwidth increases, to support the integration of online media without downloading. So, just like a game developer, we've turned proprietary technology into a competitive advantage.

Of course, not everything has been rosy. Component software development demands compromise. For example, the image display control we've used, ImagesFX's FXCmp Custom Control, offers plenty of nice transition effects, but like any other custom control, it doesn't allow for orchestrated effects. So the behavior of the controls on the screen is somewhat limited. Each time we rearrange our images, we have to hide them, shuffle them around, then reactivate them once in their new positions—the electronic equivalent of theatrical blackouts for fast stage-set changes. Limitations like this make it difficult to do polished presentations, something that users of Macromind Director take for granted. On the other hand, screen layouts in our system automatically adapt themselves to whatever group of pictures happen to be on the screen at any given time. We had to make some sacrifices, but we also enjoyed some hefty windfall benefits.

Our approach is not for everyone. And I don't mean that in a condescending way. The creative talent behind any multimedia project matters far more than the tools. A good product is a good product, and many outstanding products have been implemented with authoring systems. But for each project, consider all your options. The time it takes to master a tool is actually a small portion of the time it takes to complete an entire production. New tools mean new options. Don't let comfort define your boundaries.

What's Next?

We'll start our multimedia presentation kit in Chapter 3 by building a hypertext system based on the Hypertext Markup Language (HTML), which we'll create entirely with plain vanilla VB. HTML is the language used to create Web pages for the World Wide Web. By using HTML we'll be able to create an especially powerful and flexible engine that can be used to present multimedia from your own PC or it can be extended to build multimedia applications that work across the World Wide Web. As the multimedia industry is quickly moving from delivery engines that work on a single platform to integrated systems that can work transparently across client/server networks, you'll be ahead of the pack by learning how to build your own powerful development tools.

To create powerful
multimedia applications
with VB 4, you'll want your
own custom multimedia engine.
In this chapter we'll create a
flexible engine that uses HTML
as the hypermedia language.

Building a
Multimedia Engine

I f you've been watching the computer industry explode over the past few
years, you've probably witnessed the growth of CD-ROM and online information networks that support multimedia, like the World Wide Web. From
3D games to dinosaur adventures to interactive encyclopedias, CD-ROM has
ushered in a new age of desktop computing. And it's no wonder. A CD-ROM
holding thousands of images and millions of words can bring the magical
world of multimedia to your PC. But to really make use of all the interesting
data forms that can be stored on a CD-ROM, you'll need a way to organize
process and link together your crowd-generating images, intriguing sounds,
dazzling video, and important text.

And that's where *hypermedia* comes in. Hypermedia isn't a new miracle
cure, though. It's simply a way of organizing information—text, graphics,
pictures, video, and so on—so that you can create powerful, interactive interfaces. If you've used multimedia products on the World Wide Web, you're
already aware of the benefits of hypermedia. For example, when you click on
the name of a street in an electronically displayed street atlas and a document

43

window pops up to give you directions, you're experiencing the power of hypermedia at work. Or when you surf the Web with a browser like Netscape and click on a hyperlink, it is through the magic of hypermedia that you can quickly be transported to a new online location to experience new sights and sounds.

Because hypermedia is the foundation of interactive multimedia, this is the best place to start. We'll introduce you to some of the hypermedia key concepts, such as hyperlinks and hypertext. Then, we'll show you how to write the VB code to support hypertext. And because hypermedia systems tend to resemble each other in many ways, you'll be able to create a hypermedia system that you can adapt to a variety of multimedia projects.

For our major project in this chapter we'll create a very useful multimedia engine that uses HTML or Hypertext Markup Language—the hypertext language for the World Wide Web. HTML is a great foundation for building a multimedia engine because it provides everything needed to link documents with text, images, video, sound, and animation. Instead of creating our own specialized language, we can benefit by using a language like HTML that has really been tested in the field, and has become a global standard. As a bonus, the multimedia engine that we develop can be adapted for use as an interactive Web browser. How's that for power?

The Explosion of Hypermedia

Just a few years ago, hypermedia-based systems were regarded as lab experiments. Apple Computer brought hypermedia into the mainstream when they released the innovative HyperCard for the Mac. Since that time, a number of unique applications have emerged that incorporate hypermedia capabilities. Even the help systems of most major software products now use hypermedia techniques that are inherent in the Windows Help system (WinHelp). Over the past year, the Internet and especially the World Wide Web have brought the power of hypermedia to the masses. With a simple Web browser, a user can access a dazzling multimedia world of everything from music samples of popular rock bands to interactive encyclopedias. As the Web continues to grow, more and more people are experiencing the power of hypermedia, while software developers are scrambling to develop tools and applications to help users take advantage of a world that is dynamically connected.

In a hypermedia presentation, you can navigate by jumping from topic to topic, or topic to media element—picture, sound, video, and so on. You can also locate information by clicking on keywords and icons in specially-prepared documents. Such a document could consist of text or graphics, or a combination of both. For example, you could click on a particular spot in a world map and voilà!—you'd have an article about the history of Portugal on your screen. Then, as you're getting your history lesson, you could click on the word "currency," and guess what? Up comes an article about Portuguese currency, along with pictures of various bank notes and coins.

Some visionaries like Ted Nelson claim that soon all information—magazine articles, books, newspapers, scientific papers, stock quotes, network news stories, movies, music, everything—will be available as hypermedia. This information could be available online and accessible by satellite from your personal computer. Of course, someone will need to convert all of this stuff into an electronic form. The raw data will undergo information renewal, transforming into entirely new works at the hands of skilled multimedia producers.

Organized Chaos—The Magic of Hyperlinking

Hypermedia systems are designed so that you can explore information in a variety of formats by activating *hyperlinks*. A hyperlink operates like an underground tunnel to connect points of data together. These pieces of data may appear in an application as "highlighted" text, a picture with a "hot" spot, a graphic embellishment, or an icon. (Since the field of hypermedia is so new, many creative techniques for representing hyperlinks are just starting to emerge.)

In more traditional- or document-based systems, the term *hypertext* is used to refer to text-based information that is connected with hyperlinks. Some hypertext documents mix two or more kinds of markers, each one performing a different function. Figure 3.1 shows how VB 4 uses hyperlinks with its hypertext-based help system.

Hyperlinking can serve many purposes. Sometimes you may want to look up a term and then return to what you were doing. Other times you may discover a subtopic that you want to explore more thoroughly, so you jump to another topic, and leave your previous work completely. And occasionally, you may want to refresh your knowledge on a subject, or acquire some background information, then return to your point of departure. Good hypermedia browsers like Netscape provide a history feature so that you can keep track of the links you've previously explored and easily return to them later. If you get lost as you are exploring, you can also backtrack.

The manner in which hyperlinks are placed in a multimedia application can determine how useful the application will be. If too few links are used, the user might feel too constrained. (After all, a multimedia application is suppose to be more fun and interesting than flipping pages in a book.) On the other hand, if too many links are used, the user might feel like he or she

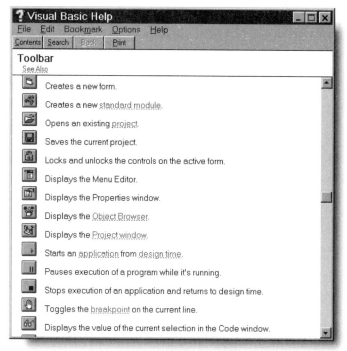

Figure 3.1 *A typical hypertext screen from the VB help system.*

is trapped in a maze. Figure 3.2 shows how an organized hypermedia system stacks up against a disorganized one.

If you add links (hotspots) to images, it's important to make sure that your users can locate them. Otherwise, a user might not even realize that hotspots are provided and they'll end up skipping over something important. If you've spent much time surfing the Web, you've probably already experienced this type of situation. Many Web pages use graphics images with "mappable" links, however, the links are often so hard to detect that typically a user will not even realize that they can click on the image to access additional information.

The network of linked pathways provides the first and most-used layer of interactivity. And this is where the relationship between content and interface begins. In the publishing world, authors and editors have to choose and stick to a single structure for each publication they create. Sometimes the material will dictate the structure. But sometimes the structure that at first seems most natural ends up being the least effective—and the most boring!

Fortunately, most topics become fascinating—almost magical—when they are examined from a variety of angles. On paper, one word follows another, paragraph after paragraph, chapter after chapter. With hyperlinks, on the

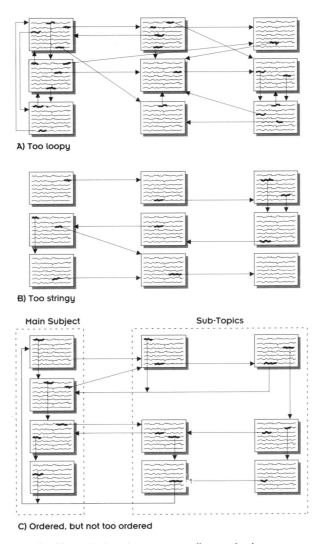

Figure 3.2 *An organized hypertext system versus a disorganized one.*

other hand, you can connect thoughts and ideas in much more creative ways, which is the main benefit of the hyperlinking approach.

Before we started this book, we created a working outline. We used Microsoft Word's Outline View feature so we could move freely through our material, expanding and collapsing headings, jumping from section to section, adding and removing topics as new ideas emerged. As you can guess, the finished outline—a portion of which is shown in Figure 3.3—defined a book organized by subject categories—a section for images, one for sound, another for text, and so on.

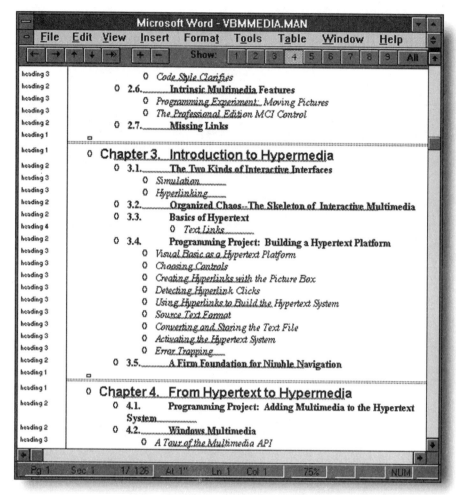

Figure 3.3 *Part of an early outline for this book as it appears in Microsoft Word.*

When the outline was finished, we realized that the book really needed a different, more creative approach. So we reorganized the material into chapters that began with basic concepts, then built upon those concepts, intertwining ideas, techniques, and fun projects to complete the multimedia adventure set. We actually needed to maintain two outlines, one that organized the book by subject, and another that split subjects into smaller chunks spread across multiple chapters. At one point, we even began to contemplate creating a third structure that would be organized by technical issues, so we could sort through the programming projects more easily! If we had created this book as a hypermedia document, we could have offered the different views of the outline as interfaces. Hypermedia gives the option of using any number of different interfaces, and can even display them all at the same time!

Many of the hyperlinks you incorporate into your productions will be utilitarian—digressions on subtopics or simple glossary lookups. But hyperlinking is also an editorial lantern that enables you to illuminate the secret passages through your ideas and concepts.

Using Hyperlinks with *Explore the Grand Canyon*

When we created the *Explore the Grand Canyon* multimedia adventure, we wanted to give the user the experience of playing an adventure game. To accomplish this, we included thousands of links that access all types of content—video, text, photos, music, voice narration, sound effects, and so on. The "surprise" element comes from the fact that a user doesn't always know what he or she will get when a hotspot is selected. As shown in Figure 3.4, hotspots are arranged in an explorer-type map. When a hotspot is selected, a pop-up window presents a list of topics. Selecting one of the topics will present the user with some type of multimedia content. The goal is to encourage the user to explore to find interesting material. When the user finds something of interest, he or she can interact with the material presented by clicking on additional links.

Figure 3.4 *Implementing links with* Explore the Grand Canyon.

Figure 3.5   *Using different types of hotspots in an image.*

Another technique used to enhance the "explorer" nature of the multimedia experience involves adding different types of hotspots to pictures. When a picture is displayed in the multimedia viewer, the user can move the mouse pointer around within the image and the pointer will change. For example, one type of pointer looks like a plant icon as shown in Figure 3.5. When the user clicks on a hotspot referenced by this icon, information about plant life in the Grand Canyon is displayed. Overall, we found this to be a very effective way to link different types of contextual information into a picture.

Hyperlinking on the Information Superhighway

Hypertext and hyperlinking have recently been getting a tremendous amount of press due to their use in the Hypertext Markup Language (HTML) that the World Wide Web is based on. This standardized protocol is a simple way to create hypertext documents and be able to share them with the world, regardless of what type of hardware you own. With HTML, a Windows user with a Web browser can get on to the Internet and travel to Web sites created by people all over the world who use different kinds of hardware and operating systems. A person working within Windows 95, for example, can download pages from people who have created documents using Unix, DOS,

Windows 3.1, NextStep, or other operating systems. The point here is that HTML provides a standardized style for writing documents. This standardization is directly responsible for the popularity of the Web. That, as well as its graphical nature, which allows Web page creators to easily add images, sounds, video, or any type of multimedia format they wish. The only problem right now with the Web is that its multimedia features demand phenomenal bandwidth. A typical Windows user working with a modem can receive about 28,000 bits per second at best. Downloading an average video file of two or three megabytes can take half an hour! Needless to say, not too many people will sit at their computers that long each time they click on a video link, waiting for files to download.

If we could ignore physics for a while, we could say the answer would be to simply speed up our connection. Unfortunately, phone companies have to follow physical laws, and the current phone technology will not allow data transfer much over the current best of 28.8 Kbps without special connections and dedicated lines. Thus, from a PC user's point of view, the answer is to use multimedia wisely and sparingly within an online document. This can be said of all multimedia documents, not just HTML. If you create a program that tries to display too many videos, or plays too many simultaneous sounds, things tend to get bogged down. Besides, not everybody using your software will have a 300 MHz Pentium and 128 MB of RAM, so you need to decide what the lowest common denominator will be for your software, and design for that. (Or, if you can't entirely give up the slick effects, you could have separate versions for different systems.)

Regardless of technical bottlenecks, however, HTML has rapidly emerged as the standard for online interactive publishing. And for that reason we decided to completely rewrite the hypermedia engine from the first edition of this book, and turn it into an HTML-driven engine that can also eventually serve not only as an interactive multimedia engine, but also as the heart of a Web browser.

Getting to Hypertext

So far, we've been singing the praises of hypermedia and, in particular, hyperlinks. Throughout the rest of this chapter, we'll focus on techniques for creating a hypertext system with VB 4. In the next chapter, we'll expand the code presented here to create more powerful hypermedia support tools. We'll also take a look at the Windows 95 multimedia API.

Creating Text Links

To set up a hypertext system, you'll need to link up text-based information using *anchors* and *destinations*. An *anchor* is simply a designated word or phrase in your text that links up to other information. When a user selects the anchor by clicking the mouse or pressing a key on the keyboard, the *destination* gets triggered. In a hypertext-only system, selecting an anchor will only display new text. A more sophisticated system can display a graphic image, run a video clip, play a sound, or even execute another program.

The actual form a hypertext link takes will depend on the format of the source documents you adapt or create for your hypertext system. A hyperlink may advance the user to the beginning of a topic or to a particular line within a lengthy passage. (For documents composed of many brief topics, short enough to fit entirely on the screen, either type of link would produce the same result.) In lengthy documents that remain essentially linear, you could link from word to word or from phrase to phrase. In a presentation that incorporates two or more separate but whole documents, a hyperlink might take the user directly to the top of a document, or to any point within another document. Figure 3.6 shows some examples of hyperlinks in a hypertext system.

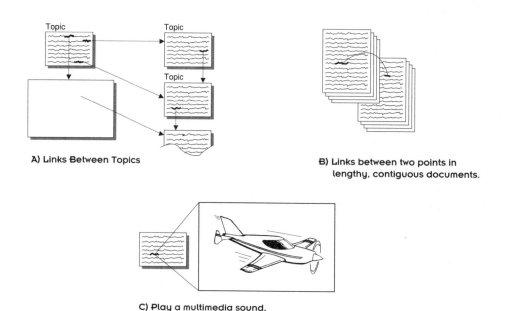

A) Links Between Topics

B) Links between two points in lengthy, contiguous documents.

C) Play a multimedia sound, animation, or video, and return.

Figure 3.6 *Types of hyperlinks used in a hypertext system.*

Creating a Hypertext System

Now that we've explored the basics of hyperlinking and hypertext, let's build our own hypertext system. We'll start by creating a simple hypertext project that uses VB's event-driven interface. Then, we'll build on this project to add additional features, such as pop-up message windows, support for hypertext source files, and a hypertext compiler. In Chapter 11, we'll use Windows API calls to attach multimedia events to our hypertext screens, linking them directly to the "hot" words embedded in the text.

Visual Basic as a Hypertext Platform

VB practically jumps up and screams to become a multimedia development platform. With its powerful controls (and more appearing every day), direct support for bitmapped graphics, and a remarkable event-driven interface, VB gives you more flexibility than you'll find with other multimedia development environments. VB also provides a relatively straightforward interface to the Windows API, as you'll see in the next chapter.

Unfortunately, VB doesn't provide a control for hypertext linking, so we must roll our own. We'll need to display text that contains highlighted "hotlinks," which, when clicked on, cause the system to display the text page (known as a topic or subject) that elaborates on or defines the highlighted word. If all this seems like too much work for you, take heart; there are controls available to perform these operations, but custom controls require extra resources, and by creating our own system we can customize it without any limitations or restraints placed on us by someone else's code. Besides, we are going to hold your hand as we walk you through the process of building this system, so you will not be alone.

Searching for the Right Control

Of all the controls included with VB, there are three possible options for our hypertext system:

- Text Box
- Combination of Labels and Command Buttons
- Picture Box

Let's examine each of these approaches with a critical eye.

- **Text Box** This control is designed to display and edit text. It even supports the standard Windows mouse techniques for selecting text and performing clipboard operations. Unfortunately, it doesn't provide many mouse events for external programmed responses because it offers its own internal mouse-dependent editing functions. The second problem is that the Text Box control doesn't support internal variable formatting. Text is always displayed with the same attributes, so we can't highlight hotlinks. It looks like we'll have to scrap the Text Box control for now.

- **Labels and Command Buttons** A combination of labels and command buttons can be used to implement our hypertext system (see Figure 3.7). All *plain* text (text that isn't hotlinked) could appear on the form as Labels. To display a hotlink, we could place a Command Button between Labels and set the button's caption to the word or phrase to which we wanted to link. Then, all we'd need to do is respond to the Mouse Click event for the command buttons.

  Displaying text this way would require some fancy footwork. If our hypertext system had multiple screens, we would need to place controls at runtime and neatly align them into well formatted text. Although this approach might work, we'd find ourselves buried in the mechanics of formatting text. Let's forget it; this is too much work and not very attractive!

- **Picture Box** This control provides several features to facilitate text formatting. Within a single Picture Box, we can mix *typefaces, type size, character attributes,* and even *color.* Now we're talking. We can easily highlight the hotlinks by boldfacing, underlining, or using color contrast.

  But there is a catch; words displayed in the Picture Box are stored as bitmapped images—no longer words, but just pictures of words. While the Text Box can hand us its contents whole or as bits and pieces of strings, the Picture Box can't tell us anything about its contents except the coordinates of the *insertion point,* and the locations of mouse events.

  Fortunately, we don't really need to know the actual word on which the user has clicked. To achieve a "hyper jump," only three things are needed:

  - *When* the user clicks on a hotlink

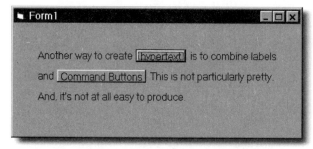

Figure 3.7   *A patchwork of Label and Command Button controls.*

- *Which* link the user clicks on
- The *destination subject*

The Picture Box's **MouseDown** event can tell us when and where a click has occurred, and we can keep a table that correlates screen coordinates (actually Picture Box coordinates) with destination subjects. Figure 3.8 shows an example of how the Picture Box control can be used to implement our hypertext system.

Creating Hyperlinks with the Picture Box

For our first hyperlink programming project, we'll use VB's Picture Box control and set up a simple form so that we can create our basic hypertext system. Here are the steps to follow:

1. Create a form called HTEXT1.FRM using the instructions provided in the next section, *Creating the Form.*
2. Add the code for HTEXT1.FRM. This form requires the procedures **ParseText()** (Listing 3.1), **ParseHTML()** (Listing 3.2), and **PrintLine()** (Listing 3.3).
3. Add the support code to handle the **OpenButton_Click** event (Listing 3.4) and the code for the **NewLine()** procedure (Listing 3.5).

 This project is stored in the subdirectory \VBMAGIC\HYPRTXT1 in the files HTEXT1.VBP, HTEXT1.FRM, and GLOBCONS.BAS.

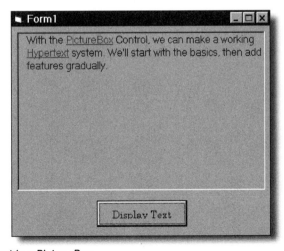

Figure 3.8   *Hypertext in a Picture Box.*

Running the Simple Pre-Hypertext Program

If you run the program and click the Display Text Command Button, you should see a text string in the Picture Box with the tagged words highlighted in blue and underlined, as shown in Figure 3.9.

Although this program displays the hotlink word underlined and in color, it doesn't yet respond to mouse clicks. We'll add this feature later.

Creating the Form

Our new form actually requires two controls: a Picture Box that occupies most of the form area, and a Command Button. On the Picture Box, set the **Picture** property to (none), and set **AutoRedraw** to True. On the Command Button, set the **Caption** property to "Display Text." We'll use the default control name of Picture1, but we'll change Command1's **Name** property to "OpenButton." Check out Figure 3.10 to see how the form should be set up. In the form itself, we'll retain the default **Name** property of Form1. (You can use the file HTEXT1.FRM on the companion CD-ROM.)

Getting the Text Ready

Before we can display hypertext with highlighted hotlinks, we need to define a format for our *source text*. As we discussed earlier, we want to eventually add Web browsing functions to this application, so we should start using HTML right from the beginning. (See Appendix A for a review of the HTML format.) To get started, all you need to know is the basic structure of HTML,

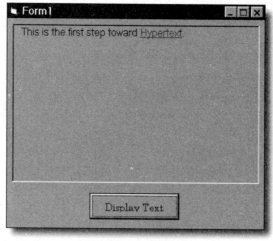

Figure 3.9 *The text with a highlighted hotlink.*

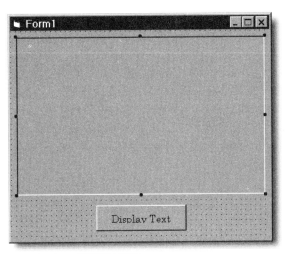

Figure 3.10 *Setting up the form HTEXT1.FRM.*

which revolves around text and tags. Tags are used to describe what is going on with the displayed text.

Here's an example of a sentence with a hotlink:

```
This sentence uses the word <A HREF="L1">hotlink</A> as the link.
```

In this case, the word "hotlink" serves as the hyperlink or hotspot. The word "L1" serves as the target link or label. Whenever the hotspot is selected, a jump is made to the location of the document where the label "L1" is placed. The initial letter tag **<A>** is one of the most important tags used in writing HTML documents. It is used to denote the beginning of a link. The link can be to another document, to a point within the same document, to an image, or any file the author wants. This is a very versatile and much used tag. The 'A' tells us that whatever follows should be a link. The 'HREF' part of the tag tells us that the quoted text that follows contains the link information. The second 'A' proceeded by a forward slash, **</A>**, indicates that we should stop treating the text as a link, and return to the previous formatting.

The formatting for other tags is very similar. An initial tag tells the browser to begin formatting in the specified way, and then another tag tells the browser when to stop. This type of formatting is used throughout the HTML specification to indicate formats like bolding, underlining, font size, and destination links.

Here's an example of a sentence with an italicized phrase:

```
This sentence is not very <I>interesting</I>.
```

The first **<I>** tag tells an HTML interpreter to start formatting text in italics and the second tag, **</I>** tells the interpreter to stop formatting the text. If the terminating tag is omitted, any remaining text will continue to be formatted with italics. Although we could write a whole book about writing documents in HTML, we just want to give you a good start here. Make sure you read Appendix A for more information on writing HTML documents. As we use HTML tags in this book we'll point out some of the basics of this useful formatting language.

> **Note:** *The hypertext test string used with this project will be placed in the* **OpenButton_Click()** *event procedure. (For more information, see the section* Adding the Support Code.*)*

Adding the Code to the Form Module

To perform the text processing tasks, we'll need the procedure **ParseText()**. This procedure is designed to process the string until it runs into a tag character (<). The "<" symbol always indicates the beginning of an HTML tag. If your HTML string was made up of all text, with no tags, **ParseText()** would only have to send a single string to the **PrintLine()** procedure. That probably won't happen too often, but if it does, we will be ready. The other operation that **ParseText()** performs is stripping out the HTML tags when they are encountered and sending them to the **ParseHTML()** procedure.

Listing 3.1　ParseText() Procedure from HTEXT1.FRM

```
Private Sub ParseText(Text)
   ' Set base text attributes
   Picture1.ForeColor = BLACK
   Picture1.FontBold = False
   Picture1.FontUnderline = False
   Picture1.FontItalic = False
   Picture1.FontStrikethru = False
   Picture1.FontSize = 12
   ' Indent a little from the left border if at edge
   If Picture1.CurrentX < 200 Then
      Picture1.CurrentX = 200
   End If
   ' Check to see if there is any HTML tags in the string
   If InStr(Text, "<") Then
      While InStr(Text, "<") ' Don't stop parsing until all tags are gone
         ' Print line up to tag
         PrintLine Left(Text, InStr(Text, "<") - 1)
         ' Pull HTML info from tag and parse
         ParseHTML Mid(Text, InStr(Text, "<") + 1, InStr(Text, ">") - 1 - _
            InStr(Text, "<"))
         ' Strip away text up to the end of the HTML tag
```

```
        Text = Right(Text, Len(Text) - InStr(Text, ">"))
    Wend
  End If
  ' Print remaining string
  PrintLine Text
End Sub
```

This procedure begins by setting up the base attributes of our Picture Box control. Then, it indents the control slightly to make the layout a little more aesthetically pleasing. The next few lines are the important ones. The **InStr()** function tells us if there are any HTML tags in the string. It does this by searching for the less-than symbol (<). If it finds one, it enters a while loop that cycles through the string until all of the tags have been removed. Whenever a tag is encountered, the **ParseHTML()** procedure is called, which does the dirty work of parsing the tag. In a sense, it serves as the heart of our hypermedia engine. As we later add more features to our engine, we'll be updating this procedure. For now, let's look at how it is called so that we can see how HTML tags are parsed:

```
ParseHTML Mid(Text, InStr(Text,"<") + 1, InStr(Text,">") - 1 - InStr(Text,"<"))
```

Now, that's a handful! This line of code must find the beginning and the end of the tag and pull the text out from between the tag symbols ("<" and ">"). The text extracted is then sent to the **ParseHTML()** procedure. To accomplish this, we use the **Mid()** function, which allows us to copy any part of a string. This function requires three parameters: the string to be copied from, the first character to copy, and the string's length. The string to be copied from is just the text string itself. The beginning character is found by using the **InStr()** function to search for the initial "<" symbol. Of course, we have to add one position to the starting point because we want to skip over the "<" symbol. Finally, we calculate the length of the string by counting the number of characters between the terminating tag symbol ">" and the position of the "<" symbol for the starting tag. Notice that we need to subtract a value of 1 from the position of the closing symbol ">" to calculate the correct length.

Let's look at an example to see how this parsing system works. Assume that we have a string of text that contains an HTML tag pair as shown here:

```
This is a <B>test string</B> for parsing.
```

Figure 3.11 indicates how this text would be parsed. The starting point is the character "B" placed inside the tag symbols. The length of the string for parsing turns out to be just one character. Subtract one to miss the symbol,

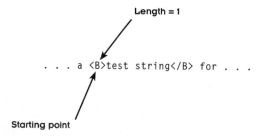

Figure 3.11   *Parsing a sample text string.*

then subtract the length to the less-than symbol. What we end up with is the actual text between the first tag **<B>**, which is just "B".

After we have copied the HTML information, we need to truncate the main text string using the **Right()** function. When all the tags have been parsed, we exit the **While** loop and call the **PrintLine()** procedure once more to make sure that no text is left in the buffer.

Processing HTML Commands

Once an HTML tag has been encountered and the tag symbols are stripped off, the **ParseHTML()** procedure shown in Listing 3.2 performs its magic. Even though we are only supporting two HTML tags at this point—A and /A—a **Case** statement is used. This will keep us from ending up with a complicated list of nested **If-Then** statements later, when we add the code for other tags.

Listing 3.2   ParseHTML() General Procedure from HTEXT1.FRM

```
Private Sub ParseHTML(HTML)
Dim TempColor As Long
Dim TempUnderline As Boolean

    ' Remove any leading or trailing spaces
    ' and switch to all uppercase
    Select Case (UCase(HTML))
       Case "A "        'Begin Link
          TempColor = Picture1.ForeColor
          TempUnderline = Picture1.Font.Underline
          Picture1.ForeColor = vbBlue
          Picture1.Font.Underline = True
       Case "/A"        'End link
          Picture1.ForeColor = TempColor
          Picture1.Font.Underline = TempUnderline
    End Select
End Sub
```

The **Case** statement first converts the HTML input keyword to all uppercase.

The first option processes input that consists of only the letter 'A.' This signifies the beginning of a link. At this stage we need to change the font style. We've decided to take the approach used by other popular Web browsers like Netscape and highlight the text link by underlining it and displaying it in blue. We also need to store our Picture Box's font color and underline status in a temporary variable so that we can switch them back when the link is switched off.

Keep in mind that the code for processing the HTML **<A>** tag is not complete at this stage. Our sample program is only designed to process a link by highlighting it. Later we'll add code to make the link active so that it can reference other material when the link is selected.

The second option in the **Case** statement is responsible for switching off the link for us. All we have to do here is reset the color and underline properties back to their original setting. That's it for HTML tags for our program at this point, but don't worry—we'll be adding plenty more next.

The last major procedure in this project is the **PrintLine()** procedure (Listing 3.3), which takes the parsed text strings and outputs them to the Picture Box.

Listing 3.3   PrintLine() Procedure from HTEXT1.FRM

```
Private Sub PrintLine(Text)
Dim NextWord As String

    While InStr(Text, Chr$(32)) 'While there is a space
       NextWord = Left(Text, InStr(Text, Chr$(32))) 'Copy first word from
                                                     'text string
       Text = Right(Text, (Len(Text) - InStr(Text, Chr$(32)))) 'Clip first word
       If (Picture1.CurrentX + Picture1.TextWidth(NextWord)) > _
             Picture1.ScaleWidth Then
          NewLine
          Picture1.Print NextWord;
       Else
          Picture1.Print NextWord;
       End If
    Wend
    'Clean-up and print remaining text
    If (Picture1.CurrentX + Picture1.TextWidth(NextWord)) > _
          Picture1.ScaleWidth Then
       NewLine
       Picture1.Print Text;
    Else
       Picture1.Print Text;
    End If
End Sub
```

This procedure pulls one word at a time off the text string. Each word is checked to see if it will fit when placed on the Picture Box. If it does, the

Print method is used to output the string. If the text does not fit, the **NewLine()** procedure is called to advance to the next line. This avoids text being clipped from the screen.

Adding the Support Code

Now that we have the key procedure **ParseText()** in place, we can fill in the supporting code to process the **OpenButton_Click()** event procedure. This event calls **ParseText()** with a test string, as the code in Listing 3.4 shows.

Listing 3.4   OpenButton_Click() Event Procedure from HTEXT1.FRM

```
Private Sub OpenButton_Click()
   Const TestString$ = "With the PictureBox Control, we can make a working _
      <A >Hypertext</A> system. We'll start with the basics, then add _
      features gradually. "
   ParseText TestString$
End Sub
```

Finally, Listing 3.5 shows the simple **NewLine()** procedure.

Listing 3.5   NewLine() Procedure from HTEXT1.FRM

```
Private Sub NewLine()
   Picture1.Print
   Picture1.CurrentX = 200
End Sub
```

This procedure looks pretty simple, but is called so often that the one line of code we can save every time we want a new line really adds up.

Detecting Hyperlink Clicks

Let's expand our first hypertext project and add a detection feature for processing hyperlinks. Now, when the user selects a hotlink, a message box will pop up. Here are the steps to follow:

1. Create a form with filename HTEXT2.FRM.
2. Create the array data structure called **HyperLinkElement** to process hyperlinks. This array is defined in the new code module HTEXT2.BAS (Listing 3.6).
3. Create the code module for the HTEXT2.FRM form. This form requires modified versions of the procedures **PrintLine()** (Listing 3.7) and **ParseHTML()** (Listing 3.8). We also need to reuse

the **ParseText()** procedure (Listing 3.1) from the first project, but that does not need to be changed.

4. Add new declarations to HTEXT2.FRM (Listing 3.9).

5. Add the support code for the **MouseDown()** event procedure (Listing 3.10).

 This project is stored in the subdirectory \VBMAGIC\HYPRTXT2 in the files HTEXT2.VBP, HTEXT2.FRM, HTEXT2.BAS, and GLOBCONS.BAS.

Using the Program

With this project we've added a simple user interface to our hypertext system. To test it out, select Run, Start from the VB menu bar (or press F5, or click on the Run button on the Toolbar). Click on the boldface hotlink word in the program to display the message box.

Building the Form

For this project, we'll need a form module identical to the one in the previous project. If you wish, you can remove the default form from the new project and use the File, Add File option on the VB menu bar to add the form HTEXT1.FRM. Then, select File, Save File As from the menu and save the form with the filename HTEXT2.FRM. Again, you may retain the form's **Name** property of Form1, or change it as you please.

Building the Data Structure

Highlighted hotlinks won't do us any good until we can detect and interpret mouse clicks on them. To keep track of the hotlinks, we must record their screen locations. Then, when the user clicks the mouse button, we can check the mouse coordinates against our list of hotlinks to determine whether a link has been selected, and, if so, return the name of the destination subject.

To code this feature, we must define a data structure that describes the *hot zone* and the link target. Since words occupy rectangular regions, we can keep track of their locations by recording the positions of their four sides, as shown in Figure 3.12.

Since each screen may contain one or several hotlinks, we'll use an array called **HyperLinkElement** to keep track of all the links on a given screen (see Listing 3.6). An element of this array consists of a record, or in VB, a **Type** containing five fields: **Left**, **Top**, **Right**, **Bottom**, and **DestinationSubject**.

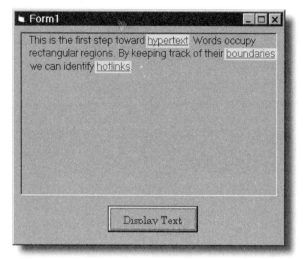

Figure 3.12   *Words occupy rectangular regions.*

Listing 3.6   Declarations Section from HTEXT2.BAS

```
Type HyperLinkElement
    Left As Integer
    Top As Integer
    Right As Integer
    Bottom As Integer
    DestinationSubject As String
End Type
```

Structures defined with the **Type** statement must be declared in the declarations section of a code module, not in the form module. To create the new code module, select File, New Module from the VB menu bar. The next time you save the project, VB will ask you to name the module. Call it HTEXT2.BAS.

To use the array, we must declare an array of **HyperLinkElement** in the declarations section of Form1 (stored in the file HTEXT2.FRM):

```
Dim HyperLinkArray(100) As HyperLinkElement
```

Notice here that we've assigned an arbitrary size to this array. The array needs only enough elements to hold the largest number of hotlinks that would ever appear on a single subject screen. (If your topics contain 100 elements per screen, you need to seriously rethink your structure.)

Creating the New Code

We'll modify the **PrintLine()** procedure in HTEXT2.FRM (Form1) so it will build the **HyperLinkElement** array whenever it is sent text to be printed as a link (see Listing 3.7). We already know when we've stumbled across a hotlink, so all we have to do is store its coordinates when we begin printing it, and again when printing is complete. We also need to determine a procedure in case a hyperlink is cut into two pieces when it goes off the edge of the Picture Box.

You will notice that the **PrintLine()** procedure does some intersecting things when it encounters a link that flows off the edge of the Picture Box. It almost looks like it is setting the **Bottom** and **Top** variables of the **HyperLinkArray** element before we have set the **Left** and **Top**. Actually, this section of code will never be called until a link has been started, and that can only happen in the **ParseHTML()** subroutine (Listing 3.8), so you should look over both routines to understand what is happening.

We can determine our current position in the Picture Box at any time by checking the **CurrentX** and **CurrentY** properties. When we place a hotlink on the screen, we can set its **Left** boundary by recording **CurrentX** before printing, and its **Right** boundary by recording **CurrentX** after printing. The **CurrentY** property gives us the **Top** boundary; to find the **Bottom** boundary, simply add the value of the **TextHeight** property to the **CurrentY** property. To split a hyperlink between two lines, record the **Right** and **Bottom** boundaries, then start a new **HyperLinkElement** after a **NewLine** call.

Listing 3.7   PrintLine() Procedure from HTEXT2.FRM

```
Private Sub PrintLine(Text)
Dim NextWord As String

   While InStr(Text, Chr$(32)) 'While there is a space
      NextWord = Left(Text, InStr(Text, Chr$(32))) 'Copy first word from
                                                   'text string
      Text = Right(Text, (Len(Text) - InStr(Text, Chr$(32)))) 'Clip first word
                                                              'from text string
      If (Picture1.CurrentX + Picture1.TextWidth(NextWord)) > _
            Picture1.ScaleWidth Then
         If IsLink Then 'Truncated Link
            HyperLinkArray(LinkArrayPos).Bottom = Picture1.CurrentY + _
               Picture1.TextHeight("A")
            HyperLinkArray(LinkArrayPos).Right = Picture1.CurrentX
            LinkArrayPos = LinkArrayPos + 1
         End If
         NewLine
         HyperLinkArray(LinkArrayPos).Top = Picture1.CurrentY
         HyperLinkArray(LinkArrayPos).Left = Picture1.CurrentX
         HyperLinkArray(LinkArrayPos).DestinationSubject = _
            HyperLinkArray(LinkArrayPos - 1).DestinationSubject
```

```
        Picture1.Print NextWord;
    Else
        Picture1.Print NextWord;
    End If
Wend
'Clean-up and print remaining text
If (Picture1.CurrentX + Picture1.TextWidth(NextWord)) > _
        Picture1.ScaleWidth Then
    If IsLink Then 'Truncated Link
        HyperLinkArray(LinkArrayPos).Bottom = Picture1.CurrentY + _
            Picture1.TextHeight("A")
        HyperLinkArray(LinkArrayPos).Right = Picture1.CurrentX
        LinkArrayPos = LinkArrayPos + 1
    End If
    NewLine
    HyperLinkArray(LinkArrayPos).Top = Picture1.CurrentY
    HyperLinkArray(LinkArrayPos).Left = Picture1.CurrentX
    HyperLinkArray(LinkArrayPos).DestinationSubject = _
        HyperLinkArray(LinkArrayPos - 1).DestinationSubject
    Picture1.Print Text;
Else
    Picture1.Print Text;
End If
End Sub
```

The major change in this procedure from the previous version is the addition of the assignment statements that are used to record the graphical boundaries of the link word when the procedure realizes that a link is in progress. In this case, a **NewLine** call needs to be made:

```
If IsLink Then 'Truncated Link
    HyperLinkArray(LinkArrayPos).Bottom = Picture1.CurrentY + _
        Picture1.TextHeight("A")
    HyperLinkArray(LinkArrayPos).Right = Picture1.CurrentX
    LinkArrayPos = LinkArrayPos + 1
End If
NewLine
HyperLinkArray(LinkArrayPos).Top = Picture1.CurrentY
HyperLinkArray(LinkArrayPos).Left = Picture1.CurrentX
HyperLinkArray(LinkArrayPos).DestinationSubject = _
    HyperLinkArray(LinkArrayPos - 1).DestinationSubject
Picture1.Print Text;
```

Expanding the New HTML Parser

The procedure presented in Listing 3.8 is where the bulk of the work is done whenever a link is found. Because of the highly modular nature of the **Case** statement used in the previous version of our **ParseHTML()** procedure, new code is easy to add to process hyperlinks. Our basic goal here is to take the HTML **<A>** anchor tag one step further and add support for clickable text links. This is easily accomplished by simply adding more code to the two **Case** options.

Listing 3.8 ParseHTML() Procedure from HTEXT2.FRM

```
Private Sub ParseHTML(HTML)
Dim TempColor As Long
Dim TempUnderline As Boolean
Dim LinkSubject As String

   ' Switch to all uppercase before the Case statement
   Select Case (UCase(HTML))
     Case "A"       'Begin Link
        TempColor = Picture1.ForeColor
        TempUnderline = Picture1.Font.Underline
        Picture1.ForeColor = vbBlue
        Picture1.Font.Underline = True
        LinkSubject = Right(HTML, ((Len(HTML) - InStr(HTML, Chr$(34)))))
        LinkSubject = Left(LinkSubject, InStr(LinkSubject, Chr$(34)) - 1)
        HyperLinkArray(LinkArrayPos).DestinationSubject = LinkSubject
        HyperLinkArray(LinkArrayPos).Top = Picture1.CurrentY
        HyperLinkArray(LinkArrayPos).Left = Picture1.CurrentX
        IsLink = True
     Case "/A"      'End link
        HyperLinkArray(LinkArrayPos).Bottom = Picture1.CurrentY + _
           Picture1.TextHeight("A")
        HyperLinkArray(LinkArrayPos).Right = Picture1.CurrentX
        LinkArrayPos = LinkArrayPos + 1
        Picture1.ForeColor = TempColor
        Picture1.Font.Underline = TempUnderline
        IsLink = False
   End Select
End Sub
```

When we supported the **<A>** tag in the previous project, we simply added code to implement the most basic format of the tag:

```
This is the simplest <A>form</A> of the anchor tag.
```

In this case, only the word "form" would be highlighted. No action or hyperlink would be assigned. To assign an action (or trigger) to a hotspot, we need to implement what is called an anchor definition, using a variation of the basic **<A>** tag:

```
<A HREF="Link">
```

Here *Link* specifies a file, image, sound, or whatever else the link is meant to trigger. The term "HREF" is an HTML keyword that indicates a hyperlink reference is being defined. In practice, a tag like this would be used as follows:

```
Click <A HREF="BIRDS.WAV">here</A> to hear a sound.
```

The word "here" would be defined as the link and it would be highlighted when the sentence is displayed. If the user clicks on this word, the sound file BIRDS.WAV would be played.

The new code we'll add to support this feature is all pretty straightforward. We'll parse the tag and assign trigger (action) to the variable **LinkSubject**. Once it has been properly parsed, it will be assigned to **DestinationSubject**. The **DestinationSubject** is very important because it tells the program what to do after a mouse click. But for now, we only need to display textual information in a message box.

For this project, our trigger ("Link") will be a descriptive phrase or word. To support this, we simply need to parse the string out from between the quotation marks. This task is accomplished with these two lines of code:

```
LinkSubject = Right(HTML, ((Len(HTML) - InStr(HTML, Chr$(34)))))
LinkSubject = Left(LinkSubject, InStr(LinkSubject, Chr$(34)) - 1)
```

Here is another case where all of the built-in VB string formatting and manipulating functions come in handy. First, we use the **Right()** function to get everything to the right of the first quotation mark. (The **InStr()** function searches for the quotation mark represented by using **Chr$(34)**.) Then, we use the **Left()** function to wipe out the final quotation and everything to the right of it. Next, we set the **DestinationSubject** equal to the resulting string. We will use pretty much the same code in the rest of the hypertext and hypermedia projects, but we will also take the parsed link and figure out what to do with it.

Adding New Declarations

As we mentioned earlier, we need to add a declaration for the support array. We'll also need to add a few other declarations to support our new linking features. Listing 3.9 shows the four new declarations you should add to Form1.

Listing 3.9   Declarations Section from HTEXT2.FRM

```
Option Explicit

Dim HyperLinkArray(100) As HyperLinkElement
Dim LinkArrayPos As Integer
Dim IsLink as Boolean
```

Adding the Support Code

We're just about ready to wrap up our second project. The only task remaining is to add the **MouseDown()** event.

We'll test the hotlinks by popping up a message box each time the user clicks on a hotlink, as shown in Figure 3.13. This will tell us whether our hypertext control actually works. You might expect this code to appear in the Picture Box's **Click** event, but the **Click** event does not receive position coordinates. Instead, we'll add our code to the **Picture1_MouseDown()** event procedure (Listing 3.10), which provides us with the mouse position as the single-precision, floating-point values **X** and **Y**.

Listing 3.10   Picture1_MouseDown() Event Procedure from HTEXT2.FRM

```
Private Sub Picture1_MouseDown(Button As Integer, Shift As Integer,
  _X As Single, Y As Single)
Dim Index As Integer

    For Index = 0 To LinkArrayPos
       If (X > HyperLinkArray(Index).Left) And _
          (X < HyperLinkArray(Index).Right) And _
          (Y > HyperLinkArray(Index).Top) And _
          (Y < HyperLinkArray(Index).Bottom) Then
          MsgBox "This is a link to " + _
             HyperLinkArray(Index).DestinationSubject,  64, "Link Destination"
          Exit For
       End If
    Next Index
End Sub
```

Figure 3.13   *A message box triggered by a hotlink.*

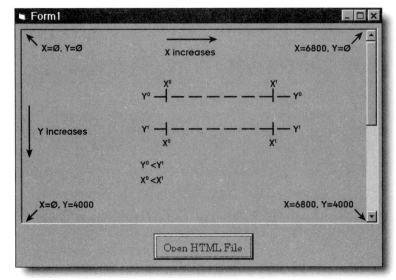

Figure 3.14   *Coordinate system within the Picture Box*

Note: *The comparisons may look confusing because here the Y axis runs top-to-bottom. The upper-left corner of the Picture Box is position X=0, Y=0, so the **Bottom** boundary has a greater value than the **Top** boundary, as shown in Figure 3.14.*

Extending the Hypertext System

We added a useful pop-up message feature to test hypertext links in the previous project. But pop-up messages hardly constitute real hypertext. What we need is a system that can actually change the contents of the screen when hotlinks are selected. In addition, we'll want to be able to store and process longer text that has multiple hypertext links and anchors. We have several other small additions to make to our hypertext system, including a scrolling window and file loading capabilities. We also need to add support for more of the HTML tags so that we can give our hypertext documents a little style.

To create such a system, we'll need to store hypertext data in a source file and then find a way to read the information into our system for parsing. What we'll end up with is a core "HTML" engine that you can use as is or easily extend to create your own multimedia applications. Because of the popularity of HTML and the Web, new tags and features are being added constantly. Therefore, the design of the procedure that parses HTML tags is easily extendible to support additional tags.

Extending the Hypertext System with HTML Files

Let's extend our hypertext system one more time by adding more useful hotlink processing features and a hypertext storage system. Here are the steps to follow:

1. Create a form using the filename HYPRTXT3.FRM. We'll start by using the form from the last project. But we need to add two very important controls. First, we'll create another Picture Box that contains the first Picture Box. This new control will allow us to scroll the other Picture Box inside of it. Of course, scrolling capabilities wouldn't be very useful without a scroll bar, so we'll add one of those too.

2. Add the required definitions to the **Declarations** section of the main form (Listing 3.11).

3. Add the code to the form module HYPRTXT3.FRM. This form requires the **ParseText()** procedure from the first project in this chapter (Listing 3.1) and the **PrintLine()** procedure from the second project (Listing 3.7). We will also need a modified version of the **ParseHTML()** procedure (Listing 3.12) that will be able to handle more of the HTML tags.

4. Update the **Picture1_MouseDown()** event procedure (Listing 3.13) and the **OpenButton_Click()** event procedure (Listing 3.14).

5. Add the code for a **LoadHTMFile()** function (Listing 3.15) to read in the HTML files, and add the code for the **ScrollBar_Change()** property procedure (Listing 3.16).

 This project is stored in the subdirectory \VBMAGIC\HYPRTXT3 in the files HYPRTXT3.VBP, HYPRTXT3.FRM, HYPRTXT3.BAS, and GLOBCONS.BAS. You'll also need the files HYPRTXT3.HTM, and HPRTXT3B.HTM.

Setting Up the New Form

Let's start with the new form by increasing its size a little. The basic form is shown in Figure 3.15. The smaller size used for the previous two projects was fine for testing and demonstrating basic hypertext principles, but now we want to be able to display *real* content, so we should probably give ourselves more room to work with.

Figure 3.15 *Creating the basic form for the multimedia engine.*

Next, we need to add a second Picture Box to act as a container for our initial Picture Box. Start by placing the new Picture Box anywhere on the main form. Rename it to **PictureFrame** to make sure we can keep track of the two Picture Boxes. Next, we need to change the parent control of the **Picture1** Picture Box from the main form to the new Picture Box. The easiest way to do this is to cut it from the form and paste it into the new Picture Box. To accomplish this, first highlight the initial Picture Box and perform a cut operation, which will place the control into the Windows clipboard.

There are several ways to cut a control in VB. The fastest way is to use the keyboard command Ctrl+X. Or, you can select Edit I Cut from the menu bar or right-button click on the desired control to display a pop-up menu that lists the cut command. After you "cut" the control it will disappear—but don't worry, it won't be removed permanently. The control is still there—it is just in memory, waiting to be reused. However, don't wait too long to use it; the Picture Box could be overwritten if you are using other Windows applications, which also have access to the clipboard. Next, highlight the **PictureFrame** Picture Box, and perform a paste operation. This will copy the Picture Box we stored in memory to the **PictureFrame** control, and thereby change the parent of **Picture1** from the main form to the **PictureFrame** control. This allows us to add scrolling because we can move the **Picture1** control or resize it to see whatever is within the **PictureFrame** control.

The controls won't look quite right just yet, so let's change a few of their properties. First, and most importantly, change the **AutoRedraw** property of

PictureFrame to **True**. This property saves us a lot of time by automatically redrawing the screen when necessary. Otherwise, we would have to respond to **Paint** events every time a new word is printed or whenever the window is resized or another window is placed over it. There really isn't any reason you would want to go through the labor of controlling that stuff yourself, unless you receive pleasure from performing tedious, time-consuming procedures. Now we need to make the **Picture1** control look transparent so that the hypertext appears on the **PictureFrame** control. We accomplish this by setting the **Appearance** property to **FLAT**, and the **BorderStyle** property to **NONE**. This will make the control look as if it's a part of the **PictureFrame** control, instead of dropped on top of it. Another important property to check is the **FontTransparent** property. Set to **True** by default, if changed, the property will produce results less than desirable for this project.

Finally, we need to properly size the **Picture1** control. The width is a personal choice. You can make the control as wide as its parent control, but this would cause the displayed text to flow right into the sides. Let's move them in a little on both sides for the margin used in the previous chapters. Fortunately, this time we don't need to write any code to calculate margin settings. For a different look, just move the sides in or out. The top of the **Picture1** control should be aligned with the top of the **PictureFrame** control. The easiest way to do that is to set the **Top** property of **Picture1** to zero. Since the parent control of **Picture1** is **PictureFrame** and not the form itself, **Picture1** will move right up to the top of the **PictureFrame** and not to the top of the form.

The only size we haven't set is the **Height** property. We decided to make the control tall to accommodate a huge HTML file. After the hypertext is displayed we can resize the **Picture1** control to the size of the text. When we first tried this technique, we were worried about using too much memory. But, since the extra space of the control does not contain any data, this technique does not use extra resources—stored is only a number representing the size of the control.

Another option for sizing the control is to start with a small Picture Box and resize it every time a new line of text is added. This method has several problems. First, resizing a control each time is extremely slow. (In our tests, the drawing time for an average HTML file went from under a second to about three seconds.) The second problem is figuring out how much to increase the size of the control for each new line. If we were displaying just text, this calculation would be easy. But we want to add images later on and there is no easy way to pre-determine the size of each image. If an image's size isn't correctly calculated, the image will be clipped. So, we decided to go with the big control and resize it once when the layout is complete.

The other control we need to add is the scroll bar, which we decided to right-align within the PictureFrame control. However, there is no reason you couldn't put the control anywhere on the form. It's up to you. Change the name property of the scroll bar to **ScrollBar** for ease of coding.

Adding the Required Declarations

Before continuing, we need to add the declarations shown in Listing 3.11 to Form1 (filename HYPRTXT3.FRM) so that all of our new hypertext processing features will be supported.

Listing 3.11   Declarations Section from HYPRTXT3.FRM

```
Option Explicit

Type HyperLinkElement
    Left As Integer
    Top As Integer
    Right As Integer
    Bottom As Integer
    DestinationSubject As String
End Type

Type AnchorElement
    Name As String
    VPosition As Integer
End Type

Dim HyperLinkArray(100) As HyperLinkElement
Dim AnchorArray(100) As AnchorElement
Dim LinkArrayPos As Integer
Dim AnchorArrayPos As Integer
Dim IsLink As Boolean
Dim Text As String
```

Defining the HTML Format

Now we need to define the HTML authoring conventions to create our hypertext in a text editor. To perform hyperlinks, our program has to know the *destination subject.* Therefore, each subject in the hypertext file needs a name we can link to, and each hotlink embedded in the text must indicate the destination subject, or target, to which it is linked. That's how subjects bind, or "relate," to links.

When we used the HTML **<A>** tag in the previous two projects, we just implemented a basic link. Now we'll go one step further and add the capability to link to a destination subject.

Destination *subjects* in HTML are tagged much the same way source links are tagged—with one major difference. Instead of using the *HREF* variable we used for hypertext links, destination subjects use the *NAME* variable. So, we'll need to add the ability to parse that information out of the string that is sent to the **ParseHTML()** procedure.

To refresh your memory, we previously set up an HTML **<A>** tag that defines a link using a format like this:

```
<A HREF="IMAGE.GIF">Hypertext systems</A>
```

In this case, the file IMAGE.GIF would be displayed when the link is selected. To implement links that can take us to other HTML files or to other locations within a file, we'll need to support an extended version of the **<A>** tag. Let's take a look at the two forms of the **<A>** tag and then we'll explore a few examples:

```
<A HREF=URL
    NAME=Anchor-text>text</A>
```

The first thing you might be wondering is, "what the heck is a URL?" The term URL stands for universal resource locator. In the realm of the Internet and the World Wide Web, a URL serves as an all-in-one type address. It can reference a Web site, another file, or another location within the same document. To define a source and destination point within the same document, two **<A>** tags would be used. One would include the *HREF* variable and the other would use the *NAME* variable. For example, this first tag would set up a link named "Link1" at the middle of a sentence:

```
Set up a target link at the <A NAME="Link1">middle</A> of this sentence.
```

Later in the document, a source link could be defined so that when a highlighted word is selected the user will be taken to the middle of the above sentence:

```
Click <A HREF="#Link1">here</A> to jump.
```

The **<A>** tag that uses the *NAME* variable defines the target destination of the link, and the **<A>** tag with the *HREF* variable defines the source link. Notice that the "#" symbol is required to indicate that the link being defined references an anchor point—in this case, Link1. If this symbol is omitted, an HTML interpreter will assume that you want to open a file named Link1.

In addition to defining a source link that can jump to a target in the same document, you can link to a target in another file. Here's an example of how this type of link is defined:

```
Click <A HREF="DOC2.HTM#Link1">here</A> to jump.
```

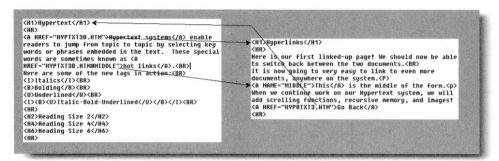

```
<H1>Hypertext</H1>
<HR>
<A HREF="HYPTXT3B.HTM">Hypertext systems</A> enable
readers to jump from topic to topic by selecting key
words or phrases embedded in the text.  These special
words are sometimes known as <A
HREF="HYPTXT3B.HTM#MIDDLE">hot links</A>.<BR>
Here are some of the new tags in action:<BR>
<I>Italics</I><BR>
<B>Bolding</B><BR>
<U>Underlined</U><BR>
<I><B><U>Italic-Bold-Underlined</U></B></I><BR>
<HR>
<H2>Heading Size 2</H2>
<H4>Heading Size 4</H4>
<H6>Heading Size 6</H6>
<HR>
```

```
<H1>Hyperlinks</H1>
<HR>
Here is our first linked-up page! We should now be able
to switch back between the two documents.<BR>
It is now going to very easy to link to even more
documents, anywhere on the system.<P>
<A NAME="MIDDLE">This</A> is the middle of the form.<p>
When we continue work on our Hypertext system, we will
add scrolling functions, recursive memory, and images!
<A HREF="HYPRTXT3.HTM">Go Back</A>
<HR>
```

Figure 3.16   *Two of the HTML files used with the multimedia engine.*

When the user clicks on the word "here" they will be taken to the location in DOC2.HTM where the anchor "Link1" is defined.

Figure 3.16 shows two of the HTML files used with this project. Notice the arrows showing where the links and their anchors are. You might want to take a few minutes to look over these files to get a better idea how HTML tags are written.

The HTML files are provided on the companion CD-ROM as HYPRTXT3.HTM, HPRTXT3B.HTM, and HPRTXT3C.HTM. If you point to other files in a destination subject, make sure that the file is in the same directory, or that you use full path names. (We will make this process a little cleaner later in the book.) Also, if you break a line in mid-sentence, add an extra space on the end to separate the words when the program later concatenates the lines into paragraph strings.

Adding the New HTML Features

The next step is to make the required changes to the **ParseHTML()** procedure. This is one of the more drastic additions, so we'll go slow. First, we need to change the responses for the tags used previously, and we need to add responses in the **Case** statement that can handle all of the other HTML tags. (Well, not *all* of them, but we will cover the basics.) Table 3.1 shows the HTML tags that are supported for now. Notice that most of the HTML tags supported come in pairs. The heading tags **<H1>**, **<H2>**, down to **<H6>** are all implemented.

The updated version of **ParseHTML()** is presented in Listing 3.12. As you can see, the **Case** statements have grown considerably. If you want to add support for additional tags, this is the first place that you should turn to. Many of the formatting tags such as **<B>** and **<U>** are very easy to implement. On the other hand, the more extended version of the **<A>** tag requires a bit more code.

Table 3.1 *The HTML Tags Implemented in the Multimedia Engine*

Tag	Description
<H1> </H1>	Displays text as a top level heading
...	
<H6> </H6>	Displays text as the lowest level heading
<B> </B>	Displays text in bold
<U> </U>	Displays text as underlined text
<I> </I>	Displays text in italics
<TT> </TT>	Displays text in a typewriter style
<STRONG> </STRONG>	Displays text using the strong format
<EM> </EM>	Displays text using an emphasized format
<CITE> </CITE>	Displays text as a citation
<PRE> </PRE>	Displays text exactly as it's formatted in a file
 	Breaks a line
<P>	Starts a new paragraph
<HR SIZE=>	Displays a horizontal rule
<A> </A>	Defines an anchor

Listing 3.12   The ParseHTML() Procedure from HYPRTXT3.FRM

```
Private Sub ParseHTML(HTML)
Dim TempColor As Long
Dim TempFontSize As Integer
Dim TempUnderline As Boolean
Dim LinkSubject As String
Dim LinkSubjectFile As String
Dim LinkSubjectLink As String
Dim LinkType As String
Dim TagType As String
Dim HRSize As Long

    ' Switch to all uppercase and pull off characters up to
    ' first space. If no spaces, then return whole string
    If InStr(HTML, Chr$(32)) Then
      TagType = Left(HTML, InStr(HTML, Chr$(32)) - 1)
    Else
      TagType = HTML
    End If
    Select Case UCase(TagType)
       Case "BR"             'Line Break
          NewLine
```

```
    Case "P", "/P"        'End Paragraph
       If Picture1.CurrentX > 0 Then NewLine
       NewLine
    Case "HR"             'Horizontal Rule
       ' Check for 'SIZE' tag within HTML
       If InStr(UCase(HTML), "SIZE=") Then
          HRSize = Val(Right(HTML, Len(HTML) - InStr(HTML, "SIZE=") - 4))
       Else
          HRSize = 1
       End If
       If Picture1.CurrentX > 0 Then NewLine
       TempColor = Picture1.ForeColor ' Store previous foreground(font) color
       Picture1.ForeColor = vbBlack
       ' Draw horizontal and vertical portions of black section of rectangle
       Picture1.Line (0, (Picture1.CurrentY + (Picture1.TextHeight("A") _
          / 2)))- (Picture1.ScaleWidth - 1, (Picture1.CurrentY + _
          (Picture1.TextHeight("A") / 2)))
       Picture1.Line (0, Picture1.CurrentY)-(0, Picture1.CurrentY + 1 + HRSize)
       Picture1.ForeColor = vbWhite
       ' Draw horizontal and vertical portions of white section of rectangle
       Picture1.Line (1, (Picture1.CurrentY))-(Picture1.ScaleWidth, _
          (Picture1.CurrentY))
       Picture1.Line (Picture1.ScaleWidth - 1, Picture1.CurrentY - HRSize)- _
          (Picture1.ScaleWidth - 1, Picture1.CurrentY)
       Picture1.ForeColor = TempColor ' Reset to old color
       Picture1.CurrentY = Picture1.CurrentY + Picture1.TextHeight("A") / 2
       Picture1.CurrentX = 0
    Case "A"              'Begin Link or Anchor
       ' If there are quotation marks present, then we know
       ' that the link subject is the string between the quotation marks.
       ' Else take everything from the right of the equal sign
       ' up to, but not including, the next space encountered.
       If InStr(HTML, Chr$(34)) Then
          LinkSubject = Right(HTML, ((Len(HTML) - InStr(HTML, Chr$(34)))))
          LinkSubject = Left(LinkSubject, InStr(LinkSubject, Chr$(34)) - 1)
       Else
          LinkSubject = Right(HTML, ((Len(HTML) - InStr(HTML, Chr$(61)))))
          If InStr(LinkSubject, Chr$(32)) Then
             LinkSubject = Left(LinkSubject, InStr(LinkSubject, Chr$(32)) - 1)
          End If
       End If
       ' The link type is the variable before the subject.
       ' So, lets grab the characters up to the equal
       ' sign first, then strip off everything up
       ' to the final space.
       LinkType = Left(HTML, InStr(HTML, Chr$(61)) - 1)
       While InStr(LinkType, Chr$(32))
         LinkType = Right(LinkType, ((Len(LinkType) - InStr(LinkType, _
           Chr$(32)))))
       Wend
       Select Case LinkType
          Case "HREF"    ' Link
             If Not IsLink Then
                TempColor = Picture1.ForeColor
```

```
                    TempUnderline = Picture1.Font.Underline
                    Picture1.ForeColor = vbBlue
                    Picture1.Font.Underline = True
                    HyperLinkArray(LinkArrayPos).DestinationSubject = LinkSubject
                    HyperLinkArray(LinkArrayPos).Top = Picture1.CurrentY
                    HyperLinkArray(LinkArrayPos).Left = Picture1.CurrentX
                    IsLink = True
                 End If
            Case "NAME"     ' Anchor
                 AnchorArray(AnchorArrayPos).Name = UCase(LinkSubject)
                 AnchorArray(AnchorArrayPos).VPosition = Picture1.CurrentY
                 AnchorArrayPos = AnchorArrayPos + 1
         End Select
   Case "/A"               'End link or Anchor
      If IsLink Then
         HyperLinkArray(LinkArrayPos).Bottom = Picture1.CurrentY + _
            Picture1.TextHeight("A")
         HyperLinkArray(LinkArrayPos).Right = Picture1.CurrentX
         LinkArrayPos = LinkArrayPos + 1
         Picture1.ForeColor = TempColor
         Picture1.Font.Underline = TempUnderline
         IsLink = False
      End If
   Case "/H1", "/H2", "/H3", _
      "/H4", "/H5", "/H6" 'Headings Off
      If Picture1.CurrentX > 0 Then NewLine
      Picture1.Font.Size = 12
   Case "H1"               'Heading 1
      If Picture1.CurrentX > 0 Then NewLine
      Picture1.Font.Size = 30
   Case "H2"               'Heading 2
      If Picture1.CurrentX > 0 Then NewLine
      Picture1.Font.Size = 24
   Case "H3"               'Heading 3
      If Picture1.CurrentX > 0 Then NewLine
      Picture1.Font.Size = 20
   Case "H4"               'Heading 4
      If Picture1.CurrentX > 0 Then NewLine
      Picture1.Font.Size = 16
   Case "H5"               'Heading 5
      If Picture1.CurrentX > 0 Then NewLine
      Picture1.Font.Size = 10
   Case "H6"               'Heading 6
      If Picture1.CurrentX > 0 Then NewLine
      Picture1.Font.Size = 8
   Case "EM"               'Bold On
      Picture1.Font.Bold = True
      Picture1.Font.Italic = True
   Case "/EM"              'Bold Off
      Picture1.Font.Bold = False
      Picture1.Font.Italic = False
   Case "B", "STRONG"      'Bold On
      Picture1.Font.Bold = True
```

```
        Case "/B", "/STRONG"  'Bold Off
           Picture1.Font.Bold = False
        Case "U"              'Underline On
           Picture1.Font.Underline = True
        Case "/U"             'Underline Off
           Picture1.Font.Underline = False
        Case "I", "CITE"      'Italic On
           Picture1.Font.Italic = True
        Case "/I", "/CITE"    'Italic Off
           Picture1.Font.Italic = False
        Case "PRE"            'Exact Text On
           Picture1.Font = "Courier New"
            PreFormat = True
        Case "/PRE"           'Exact Text Off
           Picture1.Font = "Times New Roman"
           PreFormat = False
        Case "TT"             'Typewriter Text On
           Picture1.Font = "Courier New"
        Case "/TT"            'Typewriter Text Off
           Picture1.Font = "Times New Roman"
     End Select
End Sub
```

Many of the new tags are pretty straightforward. The text formatting routines all follow the same format:

```
Case "X"
   Do Something
Case "/X"
   Undo that Something
```

Things start to get a little complicated in the routine that handles the 'A' tag. This tag denotes the beginning of a new link or anchor, so we have a lot to figure out here. The code for handling a standard link has not changed, but we now need to check to see if it is a link or an anchor. They both have identical formats, except for the bit of text that specifies a link (HREF) or anchor (NAME). To figure this information, we use the **Left()** function to copy the information to the left of the equal sign. Then we use the **Right()** function to copy any information between the equal sign and any spaces to the left. After that is done, we end up with the type of link or anchor within the **LinkType** variable, then we can do a simple check to see if it is a link or anchor. If it is a link, then we use the code from the last project. If it is an anchor, we need to add that information to the **AnchorArray()** array of information, which is used by the **Picture1_MouseDown()** event procedure to move the document to the correct position for viewing the anchor destination.

Picture1_MouseDown() now needs to respond differently to a click on a hotlink. Instead of displaying a pop-up message, we want it to load and display the appropriate subject, as the code shown in Listing 3.13 indicates.

Listing 3.13   The Picture1_MouseDown() Event Procedure from HYPRTXT3.FRM

```
Private Sub Picture1_MouseDown(Button As Integer, Shift As Integer, _
    X As Single, Y As Single)
Dim Index As Integer
Dim Index2 As Integer
Dim LinkSubject As String
Dim LinkSubjectFile As String
Dim LinkSubjectLink As String

    ' Check for loaded text
    If Picture1.CurrentY = 0 Then Exit Sub
    ' Step through Hypertext links
    For Index = 0 To LinkArrayPos
        If (X > HyperLinkArray(Index).Left) And _
           (X < HyperLinkArray(Index).Right) And _
           (Y > HyperLinkArray(Index).Top) And _
           (Y < HyperLinkArray(Index).Bottom) Then
           LinkSubject = HyperLinkArray(Index).DestinationSubject
           ' Check for '#' symbol to see if there is a specific destination
           If InStr(LinkSubject, Chr$(35)) Then
              ' Parse file and link information
              LinkSubjectFile = Left(LinkSubject, InStr(LinkSubject, Chr$(35)) - 1)
              LinkSubjectLink = Right(LinkSubject, (Len(LinkSubject) - _
                 InStr(LinkSubject, Chr$(35))))
              ' Check for non-null file name
              If Not LinkSubjectFile = "" Then
                 Text = LoadHTMLFile(LinkSubjectFile)
                 ParseText Text
              End If
              ' Search for Anchor and move to correct position
              For Index2 = 0 To AnchorArrayPos - 1
                 If AnchorArray(Index2).Name = LinkSubjectLink Then
                    Picture1.Top = -AnchorArray(Index2).VPosition
                    Exit For
                 End If
              Next Index2
           Else ' No specific destination subject, just load file
              Text = LoadHTMLFile(LinkSubject)
              ParseText Text
           End If
           Exit For
        End If
    Next Index
    ' Change value of scroll bar to reflect size of document
    ScrollBar.Value = -Picture1.Top
End Sub
```

Let's break this procedure down for a better understanding of how it works. It starts off as before, cycling through the array of links until it finds one that matches all the coordinates. When it finds a match, it copies the **HyperLinkArray().DestinationSubject** variable into the string **LinkSubject**. Next, it checks to see if the separator symbol '#' is in the string. If it is, then we know that we at least have to find an anchor point, and if there is a file name also, we need to load the file first. If they exist, these lines of code parse out the file name and link name:

```
LinkSubjectFile = Left(LinkSubject, InStr(LinkSubject, Chr$(35)) - 1)
LinkSubjectLink = Right(LinkSubject, (Len(LinkSubject) - InStr(LinkSubject, _
   Chr$(35))))
```

Basically, they search for the '#' (ASCII code 35) symbol and pull off the characters to the right or left of it. Then they check to see if there is a value within the **LinkSubjectFile** variable. If there is, we know that we have to load a new file before we search for the anchor point. To search for the anchor point, start another cycling loop that searches through the **AnchorArray().Name** variable for a match. When it finds one, it will change the **Top** property of the **Picture1** component so that the destination anchor is lined up with the top of the screen. If it can't find the anchor, it does nothing, and moves on. The final line of code changes the value of the scroll bar so that it matches up with the position of the picture box. If the picture box is at the top, so is the scroll bar. If it is halfway up the page, then the scroll bar moves to halfway down.

Next, we need to change the **OpenButton_Click()** (see Listing 3.14) to call **LoadHTMLFile()** and load the initial file:

Listing 3.14　OpenButton_Click() Event Procedure from HYPRTXT3.FRM

```
Private Sub OpenButton_Click()
   Text = LoadHTMLFile(App.Path & "/HYPRTXT3.HTM")
   ParseText Text
End Sub
```

Loading and Scrolling

All that's left to do is add the code for the **LoadHTMLFile()** function (Listing 3.15) and the **ScrollBar_Change()** event procedure (Listing 3.16).

The **LoadHTMLFile()** function uses a very simple technique to load a text file (or HTML) into a string. Let me stop here to say something about strings. It may seem a little odd to load an entire file into a single string, but let's look at the trade-offs. Using a single string is definitely easy; no arrays or databases to deal with. We do lose some of the searching functionality that we might have with an array of strings, but creative programming can overcome that. The only other valid concern is size. Under Windows 3.1, a string variable can hold 2^16 (about 64K) characters of information. Most documents used in HTML will easily fit in 64K, but the few that won't can become a real problem. There are two solutions to this problem. You can create a simple array of strings to hold the entire file (which is not too tough), or use a 32-bit operating environment (such as Windows 95 or Windows NT). A 32-bit OS will allow 2^31 characters of information to be placed in a single string variable—that's about 2 billion characters! This should be more than enough to handle any book ever written, let alone our little HTML files.

Listing 3.15 shows the complete code for the **LoadHTMLFile()** function.

Listing 3.15 LoadHTMLFile() Function from HYPRTXT3.FRM

```
Private Function LoadHTMLFile(FileName As String) As String
Dim TempText As String
Dim Fnum As Integer

    LoadHTMLFile = ""
    ' Acquire number for free file
    Fnum = FreeFile
    ' Load HTML contents into string
    Open FileName For Input As #Fnum
    ' Loop until end of file
    Do While Not EOF(Fnum)
        ' Read line into temporary string
        Line Input #Fnum, TempText
        ' Add line to document string
        LoadHTMLFile = LoadHTMLFile & TempText
    Loop
End Function
```

This function starts by initializing the return buffer. We then call the **FreeFile()** function to get the number of an available file location. For a simple program like ours, you could get away with giving it a hard-coded number, but to be able to open many files simultaneously (trust us—eventually, you'll want to), you'll need to use the **FreeFile()** function. After finding a viable file number, call the **Open** statement to open the desired file and set it up for reading. The **Open** statement takes the filename access type and free file number as variables. When it's done, the file stored in the **Fnum** location can be directly accessed for reading by the **Line Input** statement. This simple statement grabs successive lines of text from a file and places it into the specified variable. By looping until we reach the end of the file, the statement quickly places the contents of the file into our string variable, which is passed back when the function terminates.

The final bit of programming involves the scroll bar. The goal is to move the **Picture1** control up or down depending on the location of the scroll bar. Listing 3.16 shows you the code involved.

Listing 3.16   ScrollBar_Change() Event Procedure from HYPRTXT3.FRM

```
Private Sub ScrollBar_Change()
   ' Check for active document
   If Picture1.CurrentY = 0 Then
      ScrollBar.Value = 0
      Exit Sub
   End If
   ' Move top of Picture1 with inverse relation to the scroll bar
   Picture1.Top = -ScrollBar.Value
End Sub
```

This code first checks to make sure that a file is loaded; after all, there is no reason to do any work if there's nothing to show. If it passes that check, it sets the **Top** property of the **Picture1** control equal to the inverse of the scroll bar's value.

Running the Complete Hypertext Program

We're finally ready to take our new program for a test drive. To do this, click on the **OpenButton** button to open the hypertext file. The first subject from the source text file should appear on the screen as shown in Figure 3.17. If you have provided sufficient hotlinks, you can move freely among the subject screens. If you haven't, you might find yourself trapped in a dead end, in which case your only choice is to terminate execution using any of the three handy controls designed for this purpose: the form's own Control menu, VB's End option on the Run menu, or the End button on the Toolbar.

Adding Error Trapping Support

If we were to add error trapping to our previous project, we'd have a much larger and more complex program on our hands. To avoid obscuring the subject at hand, throughout this book we'll neglect most error trapping. Don't follow this bad example in your own projects.

The runtime errors that you need to look out for fall into three categories:

- I/O errors that occur as a result of missing files, invalid drive specifications, or malfunctioning hardware

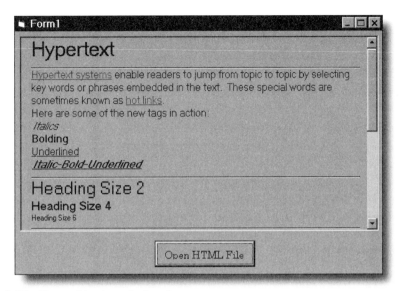

Figure 3.17 *The working hypertext system.*

- Errors in the source text that trip up the parser and prevent it from parsing the source text
- Poorly designed hyperlinks that lead the user into inescapable circular traps

VB provides some valuable features for runtime error trapping. The *VB Programmer's Guide* provides detailed examples of error trapping functions for some of the file I/O operations. You should study these functions and incorporate similar error traps into your programs. The goal of runtime error trapping is to prevent the user from ever encountering an error that terminates the execution of the program. If you plan to distribute your multimedia projects, whether as a commercial release, or as a corporate information system, or for any other purpose in which other people will need to use it without your personal guidance, then you must scrutinize your programs, and plug every chink with some sort of fail-safe mechanism.

As for errors in the source text, you'll get no help from VB. In our code, we've assumed that all hyperlinks will be properly terminated and delimited, and that once compiled, the hyperlinked text will provide open passage. Neither of these assumptions is prudent. See if you can devise methods for validating your source text, and for reporting compilation errors. Once your multimedia projects grow beyond a handful of topics, you'll find that time invested in error trapping is time well spent.

A Firm Foundation for Nimble Navigation

We've now constructed the most essential mechanisms for a hypertext—or a hypermedia—platform that is based on the flexible HTML. We discovered that the Picture Box control offered us the most flexibility with the fewest obstacles for creating our hypertext system. We then developed data structures and algorithms that we used to place hyperlinks on the screen, to detect clicks on those links, and to retrieve and display the text to which those links point.

Hypertext is only one of several navigational tools we can provide to the readers of our electronic documents. We'll present some of the others in later chapters. But first, let's add some multimedia features and get to the heart of the Windows Multimedia API.

To develop great multi-media apps with Visual Basic, you'll want to learn everything you can about the Windows 95 Multimedia API.

Introducing the Windows 95 Multimedia System

Thanks to Windows 95 and Visual Basic, the step from hypertext to full hypermedia is shorter than you might suspect. The Windows Multimedia API offers several interfaces to help you get there. In Chapter 2, you learned about ways to call the simple **mciExecute()** function to plug in multimedia features. Now, we are going to explain the Windows 95 multimedia system in much more detail.

This system provides both low-level and high-level sets of functions. The low-level set, which includes numerous functions for WAV, MIDI (musical instrument digital interface), and movie player operations, is the largest of the two. The high-level set, which consists primarily of six functions, provides an easy-to-use, high-level interface. As you might guess, the low-level functions call device drivers and require more programming. The high-level functions, on the other hand, hide the details as they pass messages to the

Media Control Interface (*MCI*), which interprets the messages and calls the low-level functions to access the appropriate device drivers.

To perform important low-level tasks, such as writing utilities for mixing and editing WAV files or synchronizing sounds with other multimedia activities such as animation, we'll need the flexibility and precision timing of the low-level interface. For now, since we only want to play existing multimedia files, the high-level interface will work just fine.

Let's continue where we left off in Chapter 3 and expand on our HTML-driven hypermedia engine. After we explore the high-level multimedia interface, we'll add a multimedia connection to our engine. Then, we'll work our way through the levels of the multimedia interface by exploring a couple of ways to play WAV files. In Chapter 5, we'll move down a few levels and show you how to get closer to the MCI and work with low-level audio functions.

A Look at the High-Level MCI

Although the high-level MCI imposes a few limitations, it's still packed with useful features. It exists mainly to isolate us from the actual device drivers by providing a common interface for all multimedia devices. Using this interface, many of the same instructions will work whether we want to play CD audio, WAV files, MIDI sequences, or video discs.

The MCI comes in two flavors: the Command-Message Interface and the Command-String Interface. The difference between the two interfaces is simple. When you call the Command-Message function **mciSendCommand()**, you pass it a numeric constant and a data structure filled with constants, strings, or pointers to other structures that indicate what operation you want the MCI to perform. When you call the Command-String function **mciSendString()**, you pass it a text string. The two functions execute the same commands—they just expect the commands in different formats.

In their *Multimedia Programmer's Workbook*, Microsoft states that the Command-Message Interface is "more versatile if your application controls an MCI device directly." They also say that the Command-String Interface is slower. (After all, it's really just a translator that converts string commands into data structures for the Command-Message interface.) Both statements may well be true, but the Command-String Interface offers a couple of advantages. First, you don't need a long list of data structures and constant declarations to establish names for all the command messages. Second—and this Microsoft *does* mention—the Command-String Interface can execute scripts provided by the end user without intermediate interpretation. (You can pass operator text directly to the **mciSendString()** function, that is, if the operator knows the MCI command syntax.)

Adding Multimedia to the HTML Hypertext Engine

Our goal now is to extend the HTML-based hypertext engine we constructed in the previous chapter by adding sound. We can easily do this by using **mciExecute()**—the function that strips the Command-String Interface down to its bare bones. This function accepts a plain English text string as a single parameter. Unlike other MCI command functions, **mciExecute()** doesn't return an error code. Instead, when we call **mciExecute()**, the MCI performs its own error trapping and displays message boxes whenever an error occurs. Because these errors are non-fatal, your programs can go about their business, even when one or more multimedia devices aren't working. Although this function won't support a complex application that requires a dialog between the user and various multimedia devices, it does offer the easiest way to play back WAV (digitized sound), MIDI (synthesized music and sound effects), MMM (movie/animation), AVI (audio/video interleave), and other standard multimedia files.

Plugging into the High-Level MCI

This project allows you to play a multimedia file when a hyperlink is selected. To incorporate the MCI interface, follow these steps:

1. Create a new form called HYPRTXT4.FRM. Begin with the form created in the last project in Chapter 3, HYPRTXT3.FRM, or make a copy of that file and add it to the new project.
2. Add a declaration for **mciExecute()** to the project's global code module, HYPRTXT4.BAS (Listing 4.1).
3. Modify the **Picture1_MouseDown()** event procedure used in the last hypertext project in Chapter 3 (Listing 4.2).
4. Create a new hypertext file to test out the multimedia interface (Listing 4.3).

 You'll find this project in the subdirectory \VBMAGIC\HYPRTXT4, in the files HYPRTXT4.MAK, HYPRTXT4.FRM, HYPRTXT4.BAS, GLOBCONS.BAS, HYPRTXT4.HTM, HYPTXT4B.HTM, and HYPTXT4C.HTM.

Setting Up the Multimedia Interface

Once the new form has been created, we need to add the API function declaration shown in Listing 4.1 to the global code module. This is the first project we have created that uses the conditional compilation feature of VB 4, so make sure you understand it well. If you have to, go back to Chapter 1 and study it more.

Listing 4.1   Revised Declarations Section of HYPRTXT4.BAS

```
#If Win32 Then
    Declare Function mciExecute Lib "winmm" _
      (ByVal lpstrCommand As String) As Long
#Else
    Declare Function mciExecute Lib "MMSystem" _
      (ByVal lpstrCommand As String) As Integer
#End If
```

Next, we need to modify the **Picture1_MouseDown()** event procedure. (Recall that this is the event procedure we used in Chapter 3 to test our HTML-driven hyperlinks.) In **Picture1_MouseDown()**, we'll perform a little extra parsing on the destination subject. We can play any multimedia file by passing the command string **"Play <filename.ext>"** to **mciExecute()**. Since we already have the ability to determine if a destination subject is a link or a filename, all we need to do is determine what kind of file is specified. The easiest way to do this it to use the **Right** function to pull the file extension from the filename, which we find by grabbing everything to the right of the period in the **LinkSubject** string variable. Then, we simply use a **Select Case** statement to pick out which file type we are dealing with. If the extension is equal to "HTM" then we use our previous code, and open a new HTML file. If the extension is equal to "WAV", "MID", or "AVI", we know we are dealing with a multimedia filename. If we find such a string, we'll feed it to **mciExecute()** as the object of a **"Play"** command sentence. Listing 4.2 provides the new version of **Picture1_MouseDown()**.

Listing 4.2   Picture1_MouseDown() Event Procedure from HYPRTXT4.FRM

```
Private Sub Picture1_MouseDown(Button As Integer, Shift As Integer, X As Single,
Y As Single)
Dim Index As Integer
Dim Index2 As Integer
Dim LinkSubject As String
Dim LinkSubjectFile As String
Dim LinkSubjectLink As String

    ' Check for loaded form
    If Picture1.CurrentY = 0 Then Exit Sub
    ' Step through Hypertext links
    For Index = 0 To LinkArrayPos
        If (X > HyperLinkArray(Index).Left) And _
```

```
                (X < HyperLinkArray(Index).Right) And _
                (Y > HyperLinkArray(Index).Top) And _
                (Y < HyperLinkArray(Index).Bottom) Then
                LinkSubject = HyperLinkArray(Index).DestinationSubject
                ' Check for '#' symbol to see if there is a specific destination
                If InStr(LinkSubject, Chr$(35)) Then
                    ' Parse file and link information
                    LinkSubjectFile = Left(LinkSubject, InStr(LinkSubject, Chr$(35)) - 1)
                    LinkSubjectLink = Right(LinkSubject, (Len(LinkSubject) - _
                        InStr(LinkSubject, Chr$(35))))
                    ' Check for non-null file name
                    If Not LinkSubjectFile = "" Then
                        Text = LoadHTMLFile(LinkSubjectFile)
                        ParseText Text
                    End If
                    ' Search for Anchor and move to correct position
                    For Index2 = 0 To AnchorArrayPos - 1
                        If AnchorArray(Index2).Name = LinkSubjectLink Then
                            Picture1.Top = -AnchorArray(Index2).VPosition
                            Exit For
                        End If
                    Next Index2
                Else ' No specific destination subject, just load file
                    Select Case UCase(Right(LinkSubject, Len(LinkSubject) - _
                        InStr(LinkSubject, Chr$(46))))
                        Case "HTM"
                            Text = LoadHTMLFile(LinkSubject)
                            ParseText Text
                        Case "WAV", "MID", "AVI"
                            Dummy = mciExecute("Play " + LinkSubject)
                    End Select
                End If
                Exit For
            End If
        Next Index
        ' Change value of scroll bar to reflect size of document
        ScrollBar.Value = -Picture1.Top
End Sub
```

The function **mciExecute()** returns a Long value to indicate if it succeeds or fails. We're ignoring it by assigning it to **Dummy**. Later on, we'll learn what to do with the return values, but for now it's okay to just ignore it.

That's it! You can add a hotlink to the HTML source file that specifies a multimedia filename, including the path if necessary, and try it out. Listing 4.3 provides a couple of sample HTML files. If you still aren't up to speed with writing HTML tags, you should review Chapter 3 and Appendix A. To help you navigate, we'll give you a quick guided tour of the structures of the two HTML files presented in Listing 4.3.

Listing 4.3   HYPRTXT4.HTM and HYPTXT4C.HTM Sample Source Text Files

HYPRTXT4.HTM:

```
<H1>Hypertext</H1>
<HR>
Want to try some <A HREF="HYPTXT4C.HTM">sound?</A>
<HR>
<A HREF="HYPTXT4B.HTM">Hypertext systems</A> enable readers to jump from topic
to topic by selecting key words or phrases embedded in the text.
These special words are sometimes known as <A HREF="HYPTXT4B.HTM#MIDDLE">hot
links</A>.<BR> Here are some of the new tags in action:<BR>
<I>Italics</I><BR>
<B>Bolding</B><BR>
<U>Underlined</U><BR>
<I><B><U>Italic-Bold-Underlined</U></B></I><BR>
<HR>
<H2>Heading Size 2</H2>
<H4>Heading Size 4</H4>
<H6>Heading Size 6</H6>
<HR>
```

HYPTXT4C.HTM:

```
<H1>How about some sound...</H1>
<HR>
Here are a couple of neat sounds to try out:<P>
1. <A HREF="ERROR.WAV">Wave file one</A><P>
2. <A HREF="HASTA.WAV">Wave file two</A><P>
3. <A HREF="TEST.MID">MIDI file</A><P>
<HR>
```

The HYPERTXT4.HTM file starts with a main heading enclosed in a pair of
<H1> tags. This is the top-level heading that can be created with HTML. Any
text included between these tags will be displayed in bold face. If the terminating tag **</H1>** is omitted, everything in the document will be formatted as
a top-level heading. The next tag used is **
,** which forces a line break.
Everything contained within an HTML file is displayed as one continuous
stream unless manual breaks are specified by using the **
** or **<P>** tags.

The first link defined in the file is found in this sentence:

```
Want to try some <A HREF="HYPTXT4C.HTM">sound?</A>
```

Here, when the user clicks on the word "sound," the HTML file
HYPTXT4C.HTM will be automatically loaded and displayed. Recall that the
HREF variable is assigned the name of a file to load when used with the **<A>**
(anchor) tag. The first part of the tag, **<A HREF=**"HYPTXT4C.HTM"**>**, specifies the action that should occur when a link is selected, the second part,

"sound," specifies the highlighted link, and the final part, **</A>**, terminates the anchor definition. Again, if you left out the terminating tag, all the text in the document until the next **</A>** would be displayed as the link.

After the first anchor is defined, you'll find more text and a few more anchors. One worth noting is the one found as part of this line of text:

```
known as <A HREF="HYPTXT4B.HTM#MIDDLE">hot links</A>.<BR>
```

This is actually similar in format to the other anchor definition we looked at. But look closely and you'll see the "#" character used with the *HREF* variable assignment. In this case, we are defining a link to an actual *location* in another file. The file that will be opened is named HYPTXT4B.HTM and the location in the file that we'll jump to is referenced by the label MIDDLE. If you looked at the file HTPTXT4B.HTM, you'd find an anchor definition in the middle of the file that looks like this:

```
<A NAME="MIDDLE"> ... /A>
```

This is the actual spot the user would be taken to when the link "hot links" is selected.

The remainder of the HTML tags in HYPRTXT4.HTM perform some formatting magic. Here we are showing how text can be displayed in italics, bold, underline, and different heading sizes. Notice that we can also group formatting tags together to put text in more than one format. For example, this line displays text in three formats at the same time:

```
<I><B><U>Italic-Bold-Underlined</U></B></I><BR>
```

The HYPTXT4C.HTM file contains the required tags to play sound files. Here we are showing how both WAV and MID files can be played. When one of the corresponding links are selected, the appropriate sound file will be loaded and played. If you have sound files of your own that you'd like to play, simply edit one of the **<A>** tag definitions. That's all there is to it.

The best part about our system is that you can add other multimedia features. For example, you might want to display a bitmap or activate a CD player. For true hypermedia, you may even want to create hotspot regions on bitmapped images. We'll do all of these things in later chapters using a combination of VB and a few Windows 95 API functions. But first, let's look at the Windows Multimedia System in more detail.

Exploring the Windows Multimedia System

The Windows multimedia system functions are located in several dynamic link libraries, or DLLs. In fact, all Windows operating system functions reside in DLLs. The Windows 95 operating system, *sans* multimedia, comes in three libraries: Kernel32, GDI32 (graphic device interface), and User32. These files contain all of the more than 1,000 or so functions that define Windows 95 services.

Almost all graphics functions reside in the GDI32. When you create a multimedia project, you will inevitably call numerous GDI32 functions, which include functions for drawing shapes, writing text, defining and changing colors, and many other graphics operations. Because the three main Windows libraries are more fundamental to Windows programming than to the multimedia system, we'll skip them for now and return to them in later chapters.

A Tour of the Multimedia API

The multimedia system provides an interface to several services:

- WAV audio playback and recording
- Synthesizer audio and MIDI
- Animation playback
- Video playback
- Joystick services
- High-resolution timing
- Operation of external media devices

Except for the lower-level animation functions, which you'll find in MMP.DLL, the functions that control these services reside in WINMM.DLL (MMSYSTEM.DLL in Windows 3.1). These functions can be further divided into two classes: the low-level and high-level multimedia interfaces. The function **mciExecute()**, which we used earlier to add multimedia playback capabilities to our hypertext system, belongs to the high-level interface. In fact, you might say that **mciExecute()** represents the *highest* level of the high-level interface because it parses MCI commands and performs its own error trapping.

Let's descend into the multimedia interface one level at a time. We'll do this by calling upon several of the functions that we can use to play WAV files.

Using High-Level Multimedia Functions: MessageBeep() and sndPlaySound()

As we mentioned earlier, the high-level interface includes the MCI—a kind of universal control language for media devices—and two sound functions: **MessageBeep()** and **sndPlaySound()**. You could say that **MessageBeep()** and **sndPlaySound()** sit atop the summit of the multimedia interface. Why? Because they perform a single high-level function—playing WAV files. In addition, you don't need to know anything about the underlying data structures—such as the WAV audio data itself—to use them.

Of theses two functions, **MessageBeep()** is the most specialized. It takes a single parameter, a flag that indicates a system alert level. If you've explored VB's **MsgBox** statement (or function), you may know that among the many *message types* it will accept are four special types that indicate system alerts: **MB_ICONSTOP**, **MB_ICONQUESTION**, **MB_ICONEXCLAMATION**, and **MB_ICONINFORMATION**. These four message box flags cause the message box to display icons: a stop sign, a question mark, an exclamation point, and the letter "i", respectively. These four VB message flags correspond to four Windows flags: **MB_ICONHAND**, **MB_ICONQUESTION**, **MB_ICONEXCLAMATION**, and **MB_ICONASTERISK**. Their names may differ, but their values match.

Now if you use the registry editing program RegEdit, you can look through the default system sounds, or peek at some of the sound schemes. Look in HKEY_USERS/.DEFAULT/APPEVENTS/SCHEMES/APPS/.DEFAULT to find all current sound possibilities and their associated WAV files (or in the **[sounds]** section of your WIN.INI file for Windows 3.1). You'll find a list that looks something like Figure 4.1.

These entries assign sounds, in the form of WAV files, to system events. Notice that four of the events in this list correspond to the four Windows message flags. By calling **MessageBeep()** with one of these four flags, you will cause Windows to look up the appropriate sound in the Registry or WIN.INI, and play it.

Actually, **MessageBeep()** is not a function at all; it's a procedure because it doesn't return anything—no error code, no handles, no success flag—nothing. If you hand it a flag value that it doesn't recognize, it simply plays the **SystemDefault** sound.

You can also use **sndPlaySound()** to play message beeps. This function is actually more useful than **MessageBeep()** because it can play other WAV files in your system and not just the sounds that have been assigned to system

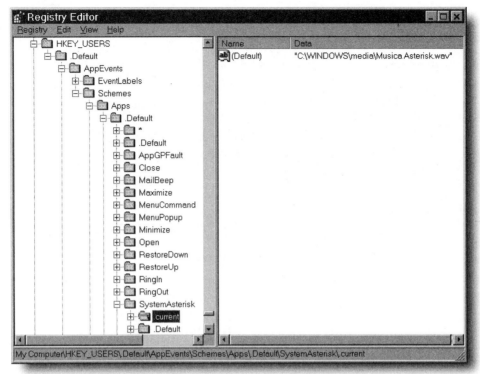

Figure 4.1   *System sounds registry entries.*

events in the Registry. The **sndPlaySound()** function takes two arguments and returns a Long value that represents a Boolean result.

Integer versus Boolean Values

A nice feature that has been added to VB in this release is the addition of Boolean type values. In previous versions of VB, you had to assign Boolean values to integers, in the form of ones and zeros. Now, you can directly use actual Boolean values, which helps when using Boolean functions like **AND**, **OR**, **NOT**, and so on.

Playing WAV Files with MessageBeep()

Let's begin a new project that demonstrates **MessageBeep()**. We'll call it **MCIPlay1**. As we descend into the multimedia interface, we'll add to this project, adding in new functions that demonstrate the various ways to play WAV and other types of multimedia files.

> To test out **MessageBeep()**, follow these steps:
>
> 1. Create a new form called MCIPLAY1.FRM.
> 2. Add the required declarations to MCIPLAY1.FRM (Listing 4.4).
> 3. Create a code module called MCIPLAY1.BAS, and add the required declarations (Listing 4.5).
> 4. Add a Command Button to MCIPLAY1.FRM to play a WAV file.
> 5. Add code for the **MessageBeepButton_Click()** event procedure (Listing 4.6).
>
> *This project is located in the subdirectory \VBMAGIC\MCIPLAY1, in the files MCIPLAY1.VBP, MCIPLAY1.FRM, and MCIPLAY1.BAS. These files will also be used for the second project in this chapter.*

Creating the MCIPlay Project: Version 1

To start, add the declaration shown in Listing 4.4 to the declarations section of MCIPLAY1.FRM. (Remember, this is a new form that you should create.)

Listing 4.4 From the Declarations Section of MCIPLAY1.FRM

```
Option Explicit

#If Win32 Then
    Private Declare Sub MessageBeep Lib "user32" (ByVal wType As Long)
#Else
    Private Declare Sub MessageBeep Lib "User" (ByVal wAlert As Integer)
#End If
```

As this declaration indicates, **MessageBeep()** actually resides in the "User32" DLL in Windows 95 and in the "User" DLL in 16-bit Windows.

To call **MessageBeep()**, you'll need at least one of the four values assigned to the six constants shown in Listing 4.5.

Listing 4.5 From the Declarations Section of MCIPLAY1.BAS

```
Global Const MB_ICONHAND = &H10
Global Const MB_ICONSTOP = MB_ICONHAND
Global Const MB_ICONQUESTION = &H20
Global Const MB_ICONEXCLAMATION = &H30
Global Const MB_ICONASTERISK = &H40
Global Const MB_ICONINFORMATION = MB_ICONASTERISK
```

These constants could be declared at the form level, without the **Global** keyword of course, but since we're going to need a *code module* eventually, we might as well start one now. Notice that we've named the code module **MCIPLAY1.BAS**.

Next, we'll add a Command Button to the form and set its caption to "Message Beep," as shown in Figure 4.2. It also wouldn't hurt to change its **Name** property to something more descriptive than Command1. I recommend "MessageBeepButton."

Finally, we'll need to add one statement in the **MessageBeepButton_Click()** event procedure as shown in Listing 4.6.

Listing 4.6　MessageBeepButton_Click Event Procedure from MCIPLAY1.FRM

```
Sub MessageBeepButton_Click ()
   MessageBeep MB_ICONEXCLAMATION
End Sub
```

> **Note:** *If you wish, you can use the Sound applet in the Windows Control Panel to change the system sounds. Windows 95 even allows you to create entire schemes of sounds, so you can fully customize your interface.*

MessageBeep() allows us to abandon old-fashioned beeps in favor of digitized sounds for system signals. Because of its limited capabilities, you wouldn't want to use it as a multimedia presentation function. However, when you build your multimedia apps, you could use message beeps for system signals, just as you would with other types of applications. The system sounds variables are there to ensure that all Windows apps produce the

Figure 4.2　*The first step of our Windows sound system.*

same message beeps, whether those are the default sounds, or sounds installed by the user.

Playing WAV Files with sndPlaySound()

This second sound project allows you to play any WAV file using the **sndPlaySound()** function. Here are the steps to follow:

1. Add a new declaration to MCIPLAY1.FRM (Listing 4.7).
2. Add the required declarations to the MCIPLAY1.BAS code module (Listing 4.8).
4. Add the necessary controls to MCIPLAY1.FRM.
5. Update the **PlaySoundButton_Click()** event (Listing 4.9).

Running the New MCIPlay Project

To test **sndPlaySound()**, run the program MCIPlay and type the name of a WAV file, including its path, into the Command String Text Box that appears at the top of the form. Then, click on the Command Button labeled "sndPlaySound." Figure 4.3 shows an example of the program as it is running.

You can also enter the name of a system sound, such as "SystemAsterisk" or "SystemExit." **sndPlaySound()** first searches the sounds section of the Registry and WIN.INI for a matching string. If it doesn't find one, it looks in the disk directory. If it still doesn't find a match, it plays the "SystemDefault" sound. You might expect an empty string to produce either an error or the "SystemDefault" sound. Don't count on it. When you call the function with an empty (or null) string, it simply plays nothing.

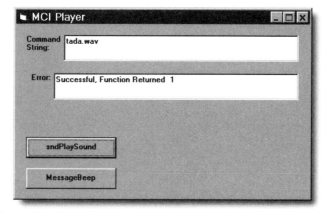

Figure 4.3   The **sndPlaySound()** function in action.

The only way we have found to produce a return value of **False** is to disable the device driver for the sound card. **sndPlaySound()** is remarkably robust, which makes it handy for simple sound playback applications.

By the way, all of the high-level MCI functions will play system sounds. We won't bother to explore that option further, but it's there if you need it.

Expanding the MCIPlay Project: Version 1

Instead of creating a whole new project, we'll add to MCIPLAY1.FRM from the previous project. This time, revise the declaration section of MCIPLAY1.FRM as shown in Listing 4.7.

Listing 4.7   From the Declarations Section of MCIPLAY1.FRM

```
Option Explicit

#If Win32 Then
    Private Declare Sub MessageBeep Lib "user32" (ByVal wType As Long)
    Private Declare Function sndPlaySound Lib "winmm" Alias "sndPlaySoundA" _
      (ByVal lpSound As String, ByVal Flags As Long) As Long
#Else
    Private Declare Sub MessageBeep Lib "User" (ByVal wAlert As Integer)
    Private Declare Function sndPlaySound Lib "MMSystem" (ByVal lpSound As _
      String, ByVal flag As Integer) As Integer
#End If
```

For the first parameter, **lpSound**, we pass a *long pointer* to a string that contains either a filename or the name of a system sound. For the second parameter, **flag**, we pass an long integer value that comprises one or more *Flags*.

Many of the Windows API functions take **flag** parameters. These parameters are also an integral component of *windows messages*. In decimal terms, the value of each flag is a factor of two. The first flag has a decimal value of 1 (2 raised to the power of 0), the second flag has a decimal value of 2, the third has a value of 4, and so on. So each flag value represents one bit in the two byte integer. An integer flag block can therefore hold up to 16 flags simultaneously (sometimes **flag** parameters are represented by 4 bytes, or in VB, *long integers*, which can hold 32 flags). To set multiple flags, just add their values together, or better yet, combine them with a logical **Or** operation.

The six flags that **sndPlaySound()** supports need to be added to the declarations section of MCIPLAY1.BAS (Listing 4.8).

Listing 4.8   From the Declarations Section of MCIPLAY1.BAS

```
Global Const SND_SYNC = &H0      ' decimal 0, play synchronously (the default)
Global Const SND_ASYNC = &H1     ' decimal 1, play asynchronously
```

```
Global Const SND_NODEFAULT = &H2    ' decimal 2, don't use default sound
Global Const SND_MEMORY = &H4       ' decimal 4, lpSound points to a memory file
Global Const SND_LOOP = &H8         ' decimal 8, loop the sound
Global Const SND_NOSTOP = &H10      ' decimal 16, don't stop any playing sound
```

For now, we'll only use the first two **SND** flags. **SND_SYNC** causes the system to play a WAV file *synchronously*. This means that a program will stand at attention until **sndPlaySound()** has finished playing the sound. Since **SND_SYNC** has a 0 value, it actually represents the absence of a flag. It also represents the default behavior of the function. **SND_ASYNC** causes **sndPlaySound()** to return control to a program immediately after starting playback, even as the WAV file continues to play *asynchronously* in the background. If **sndPlaySound()** succeeds, it returns **True**; otherwise, it returns **False**.

To demonstrate this function, we'll add three more controls to MCIPlay: a Command Button named **PlaySoundButton**, and two Text Boxes named **CommandStringText** and **ErrorText**, which are shown in Figure 4.4. Let's also label the Text Boxes and clear their initial **Text** properties.

In the **PlaySoundButton_Click()** event procedure, we'll accept a **SoundName** as user input through the **CommandStringText** Text Box. We'll then interpret the result of the play operation and display a message in **ErrorText** to indicate success or failure. The new version of this event is shown in Listing 4.9.

Listing 4.9   PlaySoundButton_Click() Event Procedure from MCIPLAY1.FRM

```
Private Sub PlaySoundButton_Click()
Dim Successful As Integer
Dim SoundName As String
```

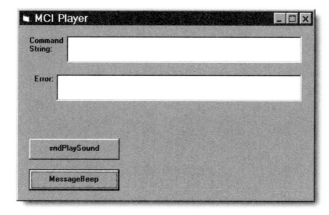

Figure 4.4   *Form layout for simple sounds project.*

```
    SoundName = CommandStringText.Text
    Successful = sndPlaySound(SoundName, SND_ASYNC)
    If Successful Then
        ErrorText.Text = "Successful, Function Returned " + Str$(Successful)
    Else
        ErrorText.Text = "Unsuccessful, Function Returned " + Str$(Successful)
    End If
End Sub
```

In the next chapter, we'll add four more buttons to this program to demon-strate some of the other ways to play sound.

It's time for us to get under the hood and take an in-depth look at the Windows 95 Media Control Interface.

Inside the Windows Multimedia System

The Windows Media Control Interface, or MCI, provides a common interface to a variety of multimedia devices, including *Audio Video Interleave* (AVI) playback, animation players, VCRs, video disk players, CD players, and the wave audio and synthesizer systems on our sound cards. Continuing where we left off in Chapter 4, we'll show you how to play WAV files using MCI functions. Then we'll move down a level to show you how to use low-level audio functions.

Using the MCI

With the MCI functions, we can send commands—such as start, stop, and pause—to any of these devices, as if we were pushing a button on the front panel of a VCR or CD player. The particular commands available for each device depend on the capabilities of the device itself. For example, a wave audio device can record, but a CD player can only play. To send MCI commands to multimedia devices, we pass them as arguments to any of three

MCI command functions. Along with the command functions, the MCI includes two support functions.

All MCI function names begin with the prefix *mci* and are arranged in three short groups:

- Command-Message Interface
  mciSendCommand()
  mciGetDeviceID()
- Command-String Interface
  mciSendString()
  mciExecute()
- Command-String *and* Command-Message Interfaces
  mciGetErrorString()
  mciSetYieldProc()

The extra function, **mciSetYieldProc()**, enables the MCI to carry on a dialog with your application when you issue an MCI command with the **WAIT** flag. The **WAIT** flag instructs the MCI not to return control to the program until the current operation is complete. For example, if you instruct the MCI to play a several-minute-long MIDI music sequencer file and issue the command with the **WAIT** flag, the MCI will freeze your program until the entire sequence has played. However, if you do not include the **WAIT** flag in your command, the MCI will immediately return control to your program and play the MIDI file in the background. Both methods have their uses. **mciSetYieldProc()** enables a program to track the progress of a command executed with the **WAIT** flag. However, VB does not support this kind of interaction with the API, so we can't use this function (unless we want to write a custom control in a lower-level language, like C). That's fine; we don't need it.

The two high-level command interfaces, Command-Message and Command-String, both perform the same functions. They send commands to the multimedia system, instructing it to play WAV files or MIDI files, to execute operations similar to those you would perform with the remote control on your home entertainment system. Recall that the difference between these two interfaces is mainly the difference between words and numbers. You've already seen one of the easiest ways to play a wave audio file—**mciExecute()**. For the sake of completeness, we've added a demonstration function for **mciExecute()**. We won't bother to make this a separate project, but you can easily test it out with the Command Button we added to the MCIPLAY2.FRM. Figure 5.1 shows the modified dialog box for MCIPLAY2.VBP and Listing 5.1 shows the code.

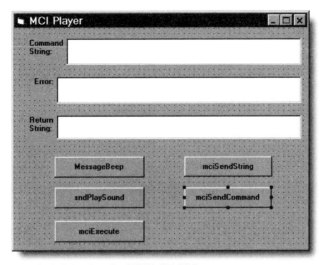

Figure 5.1   *The modified dialog box for MCIPLAY2.VBP*

Listing 5.1   ExecuteButton_Click Event Procedure from MCIPLAY2.FRM

```
Sub ExecuteButton_Click ()
Dim Successful As Integer
Dim CommandString As String
    CommandString = CommandStringText.Text
    Successful = mciExecute(CommandString)
    If Successful Then
        ErrorText.Text = "Successful " + Str$(Successful)
      Else
        ErrorText.Text = "Unsuccessful " + Str$(Successful)
      End If
End Sub
```

Making WAVes with mciSendString() and mciSendCommand()

Let's scoot down the ladder another rung and explore **mciSendString()** and **mciSendCommand()**. These functions are useful for playing WAV files. Since **mciSendString()** is the simplest, we'll start with it first.

The formal declaration (known in Windows SDK circles as its *prototype*) for **mciSendString()** looks like this:

```
DWORD FAR PASCAL mciSendString(lpstrCommand, lpstrRtnString, wRtnLength, hCallback)
```

And here it is translated into VB:

```
Declare Function mciSendString Lib "winmm" (ByVal lpstrCommand As String, _
    ByVal lpstrReturnString As String, ByVal uReturnLength As Long, ByVal _
    hwndCallback As Long) As Long
```

We can also play WAV files with **mciSendCommand()**. Let's take a look at its standard prototype:

```
DWORD mciSendCommand(wDeviceID, wMessage, dwParam1, dwParam2)
```

Here again, is the translation into VB:

```
Declare Function mciSendCommand Lib "winmm" (ByVal wDeviceID As Long, ByVal _
    uMessage As Long, ByVal dwParam1 As Long, ByVal dwParam2 As Long) As Long
```

We can refine this definition one step further by naming the third and fourth parameters more descriptively than they are in the Multimedia Development Kit (MDK) documentation:

```
Declare Function mciSendCommand Lib "winmm" (ByVal wDeviceID As Long, ByVal _
    uMessage As Long, ByVal dwFlags As Long, ByVal dwCommandParameters As Long) _
    As Long
```

Here, an MCI message requires a group of parameters, which we deliver by wrapping them in a *user-defined* **Type** and passing that structure by reference. That's how the folks at Microsoft managed to consolidate all the myriad MCI operations into a single interface function. Otherwise, you would need a separate function for each operation, each with its own parameter list. Instead of all those functions with separate parameter lists, we call a single function and tell it where to find its parameters.

Playing WAV Files with mciSendString()

In this second version of the MCIPlay project, we'll add Command Buttons that call both **mciSendString()** and **mciSendCommand()**. Playing a WAV file with the MCI command strings requires these steps:

1. Add a declaration for **mciSendString()** to MCIPLAY2.FRM (Listing 5.2).
2. Add a Command Button and Text Box to MCIPLAY2.FRM.
3. Add code for the **SendStringButton_Click()** event procedure (Listing 5.3).

This project is found in the subdirectory \VBMAGIC\MCIPLAY2, in the files MCIPLAY2.VBP, MCIPLAY2.FRM, and MCIPLAY2.BAS.

Creating the MCIPlay Project: Version 2

In the sample project MCIPLAY2.VBP, we begin where we left off with MCIPLAY1.VBP in Chapter 4. If you are creating this project yourself, you'll find it helpful to copy the files from the previous project before you begin. Add the declaration shown in Listing 5.2 to the declarations section of MCIPLAY2.FRM.

Listing 5.2 The Declarations Section of MCIPLAY2.FRM

```
Option Explicit

#If Win32 Then
    Private Declare Function mciExecute Lib "winmm" (ByVal lpstrCommand _
        As String) As Long
    Private Declare Sub MessageBeep Lib "user32" (ByVal wType As Long)
    Private Declare Function sndPlaySound Lib "winmm" Alias "sndPlaySoundA" _
        (ByVal lpszSoundName As String, ByVal uFlags As Long) As Long
    Private Declare Function mciGetErrorString Lib "winmm" Alias _
        "mciGetErrorStringA" (ByVal dwError As Long, ByVal lpstrBuffer As String, _
        ByVal uLength As Long) As Long
    Private Declare Function mciSendCommand Lib "winmm" Alias "mciSendCommandA" _
        (ByVal wDeviceID As Long, ByVal uMessage As Long, _
        ByVal dwParam1 As Long, ByVal dwParam2 As Long) As Long
    Private Declare Function mciSendString Lib "winmm" Alias "mciSendStringA" _
        (ByVal lpstrCommand As String, ByVal lpstrReturnString As String, _
        ByVal uReturnLength As Long, ByVal hwndCallback As Long) As Long
    Private Declare Function lstrcpy Lib "kernel32" Alias "lstrcpyA" _
        (ByVal lpString1 As Any, ByVal lpString2 As Any) As Long
#Else
    Private Declare Function mciExecute Lib "MMSystem" (ByVal CommandString _
        As String) As Integer
    Private Declare Sub MessageBeep Lib "User" (ByVal wAlert As Integer)
    Private Declare Function sndPlaySound Lib "MMSystem" _
        (ByVal lpSound As String, ByVal flag As Integer) As Integer
    Private Declare Function mciSendString Lib "MMSystem" _
        (ByVal lpstrCommand As String, ByVal lpstrRtnString As Any, _
        ByVal wRtnLength As Integer, ByVal hCallback As Integer) As Long
    Private Declare Function mciSendCommand Lib "MMSystem" (ByVal wDeviceID _
        As Integer, ByVal wMessage As Integer, ByVal dwParam1 As Long, _
        dwParam2 As Any) As Long
    Private Declare Function lstrcpy Lib "Kernel" (lp1 As Any, lp2 As Any) As Long
    Private Declare Function mciGetErrorString Lib "MMSystem" (ByVal dwError _
        As Long, ByVal lpstrBuffer As String, ByVal wLength As Integer) As Integer
#End If
```

Next, drop in another Command Button, set its **Name** property to **SendStringButton**, and set its **Caption** property to **mciSendString**. Finally, add a Text Box, and set its **Name** property to **ReturnStringText**. You might find it helpful to add a label to the new Text Box. The new version of MCIPlay is shown in Figure 5.2.

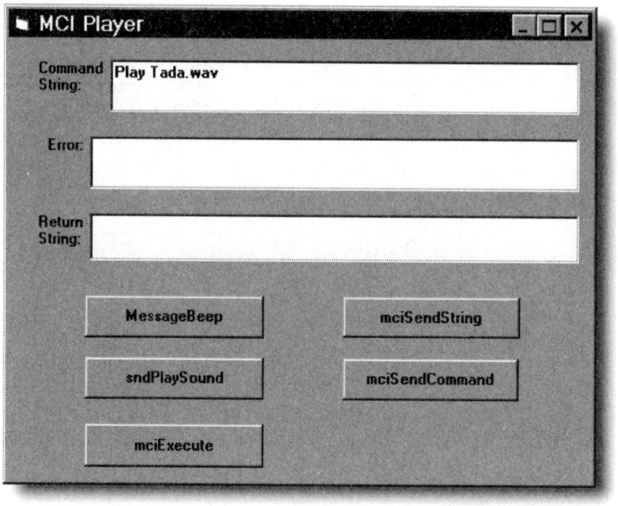

Figure 5.2   *MCIPLAY2 loaded and cocked with a command string.*

You could play sounds by simply inserting the following trial version of the **SendStringButton_Click()** event:

```
Sub SendStringButton_Click ()
Dim Dummy As Long
    Dummy = mciSendString("play c:\windows\tada.wav", ByVal 0&, 0, 0)
End Sub
```

This minimalistic procedure illustrates how little you need to exercise the Command-String Interface, but it also ignores some useful and, frankly, essential features. Unlike **mciExecute()**, **mciSendString()** doesn't benefit from the built-in error trapping dialog boxes. When a command fails, the user will receive no feedback unless you collect the error code returned by the function and act upon it.

In addition to error codes, the Command-String Interface can also return information about an MCI device, which it does by setting **lpstrRtnString**. This opens all kinds of new capabilities not available with **mciExecute()**. To add error checking support, we'll use the version of **SendStringButton_Click()** shown in Listing 5.3.

Listing 5.3   SendStringButton_Click() Event Procedure from MCIPLAY2.FRM

```
Private Sub SendStringButton_Click()
Dim mciError As Long
Dim ReturnString As String * 512
Dim Dummy As Long
```

```
Dim mciErrorString As String * 256
Dim CommandString As String

    ErrorText.Text = ""
    CommandString = CommandStringText.Text
    mciError = mciSendString(CommandString, ByVal ReturnString, _
        Len(ReturnString) - 1, 0&)
    Dummy = mciGetErrorString(mciError, mciErrorString, 255)
    ErrorText.Text = mciErrorString
    ReturnStringText.Text = ReturnString
End Sub
```

Notice that neither the **"Play"** command, nor the target filename appear in this procedure because we have not hard coded them, so that the the filename and action can be easily entered and changed while running the program.

To play a WAV file, type the entire command into the Text Box labeled "Command String," then click on the mciSendString button, as shown in Figure 5.3.

A Closer Look at mciSendString() and mciGetErrorString()

A closer inspection of Listing 5.2 shows that **mciSendString()** takes four parameters. This first parameter is a string that tells the MCI what to do. The second parameter supplies the memory address of a buffer through which the MCI can return a message. The third parameter specifies the length of the return buffer. (The MCI uses this information to determine the length of the message that it can return.) Finally, the fourth parameter is used to set up a *callback* function. (We'll explain this a little later.)

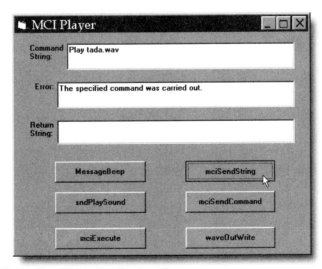

Figure 5.3   *The mciSendString function in action.*

If you look at the names of the first and second parameters, **lpstrCommand** and **lpstrRtnString**, you'll notice that their prefixes identify them as long pointers (lp) to strings (str). When we pass strings from VB to API functions, we normally declare them with the **ByVal** keyword. For most data types, **ByVal** indicates that the contents of the variable, rather than its memory address, is being passed. But, in combination with a string variable, **ByVal** performs a special function.

Normally, when we pass parameters by value, they remain unchanged. The target procedure receives a copy of the variable rather than the variable itself. Thus, if the procedure changes the variable, those changes affect only its local copy, not the original value. Once the program returns from that function, the modified value vanishes. A variable passed by reference, VB's default behavior, enjoys no such protection. If the target function changes its value, then the value has changed outside that function as well. But when we use the **ByVal** keyword to pass strings, its meaning changes. We cannot pass VB strings to API functions by value. The **ByVal** keyword instead causes VB to convert the string to a C-style (or *zero-terminated*) string. If the API function changes the string, then when we return from the function, we will find the new value in our string variable—just as we would with a variable of any other data type passed by reference. Upon returning from the called function, VB converts the zero-terminated string back into a VB string. To pass a string to a DLL other than to one written specifically for VB, we must pass the string with **ByVal**. Why, then, have we declared the second parameter, **lpstrRtnString**, without the **ByVal** keyword?

Many MCI commands produce return strings containing such information as track lengths, numbers of tracks, and device mode. The **"Play"** command, however, does not produce a return string. So, rather than provide a useless buffer, we instead want to tell the API function that no buffer exists. We can do this by sending it a zero, or ***NULL*** value in place of a memory address. But we can't pass a **NULL** value if we declare the parameter as a string. VB would report a data type mismatch. If we sent a null string, as indicated by an empty pair of quotation marks (""), VB would just pass along the address of an empty string. But we want to pass a **NULL** *address*, indicating the complete absence of a string. To gain a little flexibility, we declare this parameter **As Any**. We may then pass either a string or a numeric value to **mciSendString()**. When we call **mciSendString()**, we must always precede the value of **lpstrRtnString** with **ByVal** to force VB to pass it either as a zero-terminated string, or as a long integer zero. That's why, for the second parameter, **ByVal** appears in the call to **mciSendString()** rather than in its declaration. You must still always use **ByVal** when you call **mciSendString()**, whether you pass it a **NULL** address or a string buffer. The VB documentation does not explain why you cannot just declare

```
ByVal <string variable> As Any
```

but since Microsoft knows more about the internal workings of VB than we do, we're inclined to follow their instructions!

When we do need **lpstrRtnString**, we pass either a fixed-length string, or a variable-length string that's been pre-filled with spaces, specifying its length because the Windows API cannot extend variable-length strings. When **mciSendString()** fills in a return string, it starts with the first byte pointed to by the string reference, then continues filling as many subsequent bytes as it needs to hold the entire string. If we were to supply a variable-length string that was too short to hold the return string, **mciSendString()** would write into memory not allocated to that string, quite possibly overwriting some other crucial data. By declaring and passing a fixed-length string, we reserve a large enough block of memory to hold any value returned by the API function.

In Chapter 16, you'll see how we can use the **lpstrRtnString** parameter to retrieve status and position information from MCI devices.

We're now ready to get back to the last parameter of **mciSendString()**. It performs a function, known as a *callback*, which is not available to us from within VB; however, many API functions perform callbacks. A callback is a means by which an API function can notify a program that it has completed an operation. Callbacks work in one of two ways: They either call an independent function written by the programmer to service the callback, or, like **mciSendString()**, they send a message to a window, which must contain the code to service the callback. In the latter case, the callback works just like any other Windows event, except that instead of responding to an action performed by the user—like a mouse click or a resize event—the program responds to an action requested by an API function. Unfortunately, VB provides no intrinsic support for programmer-defined events. The only way we could respond to the **MM_MCINOTIFY** message generated by **mciSendString()** would be to write a custom control in an HTL (Holy-Trinity Language). (When we write our own controls, we also get to define which events to support.) For now, we'll just tell **mciSendString()** not to send a notification message by passing a zero value as the callback handle. Actually, it wouldn't even send the **MM_MCINOTIFY** message unless we changed the command string to:

```
"play c:\windows\tada.wav notify"
```

Along with **mciSendString()**, we've slipped in another new function, **mciGetErrorString()**. Take a look at its declaration:

```
Win32:
Declare Function mciGetErrorString Lib "winmm" (ByVal dwError As Long, _
   ByVal lpstrBuffer As String, ByVal uLength As Long) As Long

Win16:
Declare Function mciGetErrorString Lib "MMSystem" (ByVal dwError As Long, _
   ByVal lpstrBuffer As String, ByVal wLength As Integer) As Integer
```

In the first parameter, we pass the error code returned by **mciSendString()** (or by **mciSendCommand()**, as you'll soon see). The second and third parameters once again define a buffer for a return string and its length, respectively. The return value of **mciGetErrorString()** is—believe it or not—an error code. After all, we could feed it an invalid error code to begin with, which would be an error (error trapping can become very convoluted).

Playing WAV Files with mciSendCommand()

This next addition to the MCIPlay project requires these simple steps:

1. Add the declarations shown in Listing 5.4 to MCIPLAY2.FRM.
2. Add code for the **SendCommandButton_Click()** event procedure to MCIPLAY2.FRM (Listing 5.5).
3. Add the global constants (Listing 5.6).

This project, which is a continuation of the previous project, can be found in the directory \VBMAGIC\MCIPLAY2, in the files MCIPLAY2.VBP, MCIPLAY2.FRM, and MCIPLAY2.BAS.

Expanding the MCIPlay Project: Version 2

To play a WAV file using the **mciSendCommand()** as presented in Listing 5.4.

Listing 5.4   Data Structures Needed to Play a WAV File with the MCI Command-Message Interface, Declared in MCIPLAY2.BAS

```
Option Explicit

Type MCI_WAVE_OPEN_PARMS
    dwCallback As Long
    wDeviceID As Integer
    wReserved0 As Integer
    lpstrDeviceType As String
```

```
            lpstrElementName As String
            lpstrAlias As String
            dwBufferSeconds As Long
End Type

Type MCI_PLAY_PARMS
        dwCallback As Long
        dwFrom As Long
        dwTo As Long
End Type
```

The **"Play"** message in the Command-Message Interface does not perform implied open and close operations. So, to play a WAV file, we will need to issue three command messages: open, play, and close. Two of these, open and play, take parameter blocks.

MCI_WAVE_OPEN_PARMS is just a slightly extended version of the more generic structure **MCI_OPEN_PARMS**, which lacks the field **dwBufferSeconds**. If you do not wish to specify a buffer length, you can use **MCI_OPEN_PARMS**. **MCI_PLAY_PARMS** holds the parameters for the play command, although we won't use any of them in this example.

The next step involves adding the **SendCommandButton_Click()** event procedure code in Listing 5.5.

Listing 5.5   The SendCommandButton_Click() Event Procedure from MCIPLAY2.FRM

```
Private Sub SendCommandButton_Click()
Dim Dummy As Long
Dim mciError As Long
Dim mciOpenParms As MCI_WAVE_OPEN_PARMS
Dim mciPlayParms As MCI_PLAY_PARMS
Dim mciFlags As Long
Dim wDeviceID As Long
Dim mciErrorString As String * 256

    ErrorText.Text = ""
    mciOpenParms.dwCallback = 0&
    mciOpenParms.wDeviceID = 0
    mciOpenParms.wReserved0 = 0
    mciOpenParms.lpstrDeviceType = "waveaudio"
    mciOpenParms.lpstrElementName = "c:\windows\media\tada.wav"
    mciOpenParms.lpstrAlias = 0&
    mciOpenParms.dwBufferSeconds = 0&
    mciFlags = MCI_OPEN_TYPE Or MCI_OPEN_ELEMENT
    mciError = mciSendCommand(0, MCI_OPEN, mciFlags, mciOpenParms)
    If mciError = 0 Then
        wDeviceID = mciOpenParms.wDeviceID
        mciError = mciSendCommand(wDeviceID, MCI_PLAY, MCI_WAIT, mciPlayParms)
```

```
    If mciError = 0 Then
        mciError = mciSendCommand(wDeviceID, MCI_CLOSE, 0, ByVal 0&)
    End If
End If
Dummy = mciGetErrorString(mciError, mciErrorString, 255)
ErrorText.Text = mciErrorString
```

This procedure, actually a complete program except for declarations, uses several constants. Remember when we said that the difference between the Command-String Interface and the Command-Message Interface was largely the difference between words and numbers? This is what we meant. You'll find definitions of them all in the Microsoft *Multimedia Programmer's Reference*, but not their values. For their numeric values, you'll have to look in the file WIN32API.TXT (WINMMSYS.TXT for 16-bit Windows) that comes with VB (normally copied by VB Setup to the subdirectory \VB\WINAPI). For this example, we need the six standard constants shown in Listing 5.6.

Listing 5.6   The Global MCI Constants Needed to Play a WAV File

```
Global Const MCI_OPEN = &H803            ' Command Message
Global Const MCI_PLAY = &H806            ' Command Message
Global Const MCI_CLOSE = &H804           ' Command Message
Global Const MCI_OPEN_TYPE& = &H2000&    ' Command Flag
Global Const MCI_OPEN_ELEMENT& = &H200&  ' Command Flag
Global Const MCI_WAIT& = &H2&            ' Command Flag
```

The first several lines of the **SendCommandButton_Click()** event procedure set the parameter values required by the **Open** command message. The first three are easy.

```
mciOpenParms.dwCallback = 0&
mciOpenParms.wDeviceID = 0
mciOpenParms.wReserved0 = 0
```

VB doesn't support callbacks, so we set the first field to 0. We don't know the **DeviceID** yet; the MCI will assign one and return its value in the **wDeviceID** field when we execute the **Open** command. The third field contains a 0. According to the Microsoft documentation, this field is reserved—and that's that.

We don't want to assign an alias to the device, and we don't need to specify a buffer length, so we set both of these parameters to 0.

```
mciOpenParms.lpstrAlias = 0&
mciOpenParms.dwBufferSeconds = 0&
```

Next, we need to set the flags that tell the Command-Message Interface how to interpret the information we've passed in the **mciOpenParms** structure.

```
mciFlags = MCI_OPEN_TYPE Or MCI_OPEN_ELEMENT
```

Boolean operations like *Or* can look misleading. Unlike a Boolean decision, such as those found in **If** statements and **While** loops, the **Or** operator in this assignment statement performs a *bitwise* operation that actually combines the two flags. Let's look first at a trivial case.

Bits can carry one of two values, 0 or 1. Let's say we have two bits, A and B. If both A and B start out with 0 values, then the expression "A Or B" returns 0. If either A or B, or both A and B are set to 1, then the expression "A Or B" returns 1. Now let's expand that one step to two whole bytes full of bits.

```
A = 00000001
B = 00000010
```

When we **Or** A and B, VB performs the **Or** operation on each bit, comparing the first bit (or more correctly, the lowest-order bit, counting from right to left) of A with the first bit of B, then the second bit of A with the second bit of B, and so on. The result of "A Or B" in this case will produce a byte with two bits set to 1:

```
A Or B = 00000011
```

The **flag** parameter is a four-byte value. Each bit in the four bytes represents one flag, for a total of 32 possible flags. Several flags are defined in Table 5.1.

By the way, these flags notify the MCI that we're supplying both the device type and the name of the file, or *element*, that we want it to play. We could actually omit the device type. The MCI can determine the device type by

Table 5.1 *Flags Defined for the MCI_OPEN Command*

Flag	Hexadecimal	Binary Value
MCI_OPEN_TYPE&	&H2000&	00000000 00000000 00100000 00000000
MCI_OPEN_ELEMENT&	&H200&	00000000 00000000 00000010 00000000
MCI_OPEN_TYPE& Or MCI_OPEN_ELEMENT&	&H2200&	00000000 00000000 00100010 00000000

looking up the file extension in the system registry, or the **[mci extensions]** section of the WIN.INI file for Windows 3.1.

Once we've set all our flags, pointers to strings, and other parameters, we can send the messages:

```
mciError = mciSendCommand(0, MCI_OPEN, mciFlags, mciOpenParms)
If mciError = 0 Then
   wDeviceID = mciOpenParms.wDeviceID
   mciError = mciSendCommand(wDeviceID, MCI_PLAY, MCI_WAIT, mciPlayParms)
   If mciError = 0 Then
      mciError = mciSendCommand(wDeviceID, MCI_CLOSE, 0, ByVal 0&)
   End If
End If
Dummy = mciGetErrorString(mciError, mciErrorString, 255)
ErrorText.Text = mciErrorString
```

The **MCI_WAIT** flag that accompanies the **MCI_PLAY** message instructs the MCI not to return control to our program until the play operation is complete. Without this flag we can go on about our business while the WAV file plays in the background. However, when we send the **MCI_CLOSE** message, the MCI aborts the play operation. To play the WAV file *asynchronously,* we would need to find some other way to close the device upon completion. For HTL (Holy Trinity Language) programmers this is easy; they can write a call-back function and pass the **NOTIFY** flag. For VB programmers, it can be a nuisance, so for now we won't bother.

In one way, we've taken a step backward here by hard-coding the commands to play a WAV file. Unfortunately, because of the data structures it requires for its parameters, the Command-Message Interface doesn't easily adapt to a little exerciser function like the one we created for the Command-String Interface.

For most multimedia applications that we're likely to write with VB, the Command-Message Interface dwells in purgatory between the simple, friendly Command-String Interface and the complex but truly powerful low-level functions that speak directly to the multimedia device drivers. Now you know how to use it. Relax. We won't need **mciSendCommand()** for any of the other projects or exercises in *this* book.

Combing the Depths of the Low-Level Audio Functions

Clearly, the MCI functions that we've investigated do a lot of work behind the scenes. Wave audio data resides in files, which contain not only the *digital sample* values, but also descriptive information that identifies the particular format of that audio data. To replay a WAV file, the multimedia system has to open the file, read and interpret its header information, load the audio data into memory, open the wave audio device, prepare the header, play the sound, unprepare the header, and close both the device and the file. Whew! That's a lot of work!

To accomplish all this, the MCI functions call upon the services of several low-level functions. To perform low-level replay of WAV files, we need to call about a dozen functions. These fall into two groups: functions that read *Resource Interchange File Format (RIFF)* files, and functions that manage wave audio playback.

Before you can even open the wave audio device, you have to know some things about the data you intend to send it. WAV data comes in several formats, various combinations of sampling rate, multiple channels (mono or stereo), and different resolutions (number of bits per sample). We'll talk about WAV formats in greater detail in Chapter 14. For now, all you need to know is that this information appears in a format block—known in RIFF terminology as a *chunk*—near the beginning of each WAV file.

The Mysteries of RIFF Files

As Figure 5.4 indicates, RIFF files are hierarchical structures—chunks contain chunks, which may again contain chunks.

The highest-level chunk is the RIFF chunk itself. Chunks carry labels, known officially as *chunk IDs*. If you peek at a WAV file with a file viewer, you'll see that the first four bytes literally contain the characters *R*, *I*, *F*, and *F*.

To read and write RIFF files, you use a standard data structure called **MMCKINFO**, for "multimedia chunk information." In VB, the structure looks like this:

```
' RIFF chunk information data structure
Type MMCKINFO
    ckid As FOURCC          ' chunk ID
    cksize As Long          ' chunk size
    fccType As FOURCC       ' form type or list type
    dwDataOffset As Long    ' offset of data portion of chunk
    dwFlags As Long         ' flags used by MMIO functions
End Type
```

The first and third fields actually contain simple four-character, fixed-length strings:

```
Type FOURCC
    Chars As String * 4
End Type
```

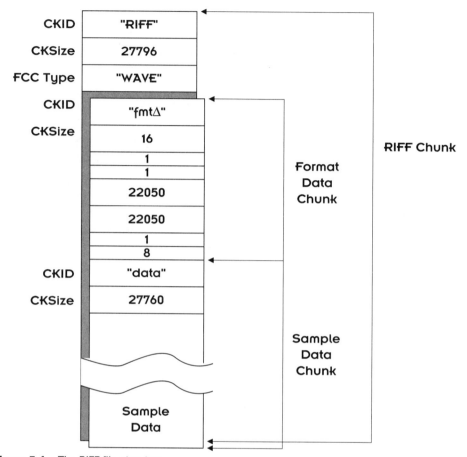

Figure 5.4 *The RIFF file structure.*

This **FOURCC** substructure is just a convention created for C programmers who don't have such straightforward string operations.

To keep you from getting as confused as we did, let us state now that **MMCKINFO** *does not define a data file record!* We use **MMCKINFO** only to exchange information with the *multimedia file I/O functions*. Although chunks do adhere to a couple of well-defined structures, they vary in size, which means we can't just read them into, or write them from, simple, fixed-length record buffers.

All chunks start with at least two common fields: the chunk ID and the chunk size, which, coincidentally, correspond to the first two fields of **MMCKINFO**. When we use the low-level multimedia function **mmioDescend()** to read a chunk, we will pass it the address of a structure of type **MMCKINFO**, which it will then fill with the appropriate values. This is an important distinction.

When we read records from a file with VB, we often use the **Get** statement. **Get** takes three arguments: the file number, a record number, and the variable name into which we want the data copied. To read a record that contains multiple fields, we can define a record with the **Type** statement, declare a variable of that type, then **Get** a record of the same structure from the disk file. If **MMCKINFO** were a file record type—which it is not—we could do something like this:

```
Dim TheChunk As MMCKINFO          ' Don't even think about doing this!
Get #WaveFile, 1, TheChunk
```

Don't do it! It won't work.

A RIFF file doesn't contain a series of records of uniform structure. Chunks vary in size. The only efficient way to read a RIFF file is to walk through it in the prescribed manner, using the **mmio** (multimedia I/O) functions.

To navigate a RIFF file, you use the functions **mmioDescend()** and **mmioAscend()**. These functions are used to position the file pointer in a chunk. Depending on what type of chunk you want to find, you set either the chunk ID (**ckID**) or the form type (**fccType**), set a search flag, then call **mmioDescend()**. This function will locate the next chunk in the file with the **ckID** or **fccType** you have specified. If you want the next chunk in line, you can descend without specifying the **ckID** or the **fccType**, and the descent function will fill in those fields with the four-character codes it finds in the next chunk.

The WAV File Structure

To better understand how WAV files are accessed, let's look at a sample file. Table 5.2 shows a breakdown of the WAV file TADA.WAV from 16-bit Windows.

At minimum, a WAV file comprises three chunks. The RIFF chunk is the largest container. The whole WAV file is actually a RIFF chunk. The **ckSize,** which appears immediately after the "RIFF" **ckID**, contains a value equal to the file size minus eight bytes—the eight bytes is required to store the RIFF chunk's own **ckID** and **ckSize**. The second and third chunks, known as *subchunks*, are contained within the RIFF chunk. The first of these, the "fmt" chunk, contains the information necessary to fill in a **PCMWAVEFORMAT** structure. The second subchunk, the "data" chunk—by far the largest portion of the file—immediately follows the "fmt" subchunk, and contains all the digital waveform data. The end of the "data" subchunk corresponds to the end of the RIFF chunk. The **ckSize** of the RIFF chunk equals the total number of bytes occupied by the "fmt" and "data" subchunks.

Table 5.2　*The Structure of a Sample WAV File*

Position		Size in Bytes	Contents	Comments
Hex	Dec			
0000	0	4	"RIFF"	Each byte contains one character, ckId
0004	4	4	27796	Equals the file size minus eight bytes, ckSize
0008	8	4	"WAVE"	fccType
000C	12	4	"fmt "	Next ckID; notice the blank, must be four characters
0010	16	4	16	The WAV format chunk is 16 bytes, ckSize
0014	20	2	1	1 indicates a PCM WAV format, wFormatTag
0016	22	2	1	Number of channels, nChannels
0018	24	4	22050	Sampling rate, nSamplesPerSec
001C	28	4	22050	nAvgBytesPerSec
0020	32	2	1	Effectively bytes per sample, nBlockAlign
0022	34	2	8	wBitsPerSample
0024	36	4	"data"	Next ckID; this chunk contains the wave data itself
0028	40	4	27760	Next ckID; size of wave data
002C	44	Depends on Data		The digitized audio data

To make matters worse, RIFF files may contain another type of chunk called a *LIST* chunk. LIST chunks hold additional information, such as copyright notices and other data that describes the content of the main "data" chunk or chunks. At this point, it won't help us to discuss LIST chunks; very few WAV files have any information embedded in them. However, the WAV files that come with Windows 95 *do* contain information about copyrights and subject matter. Most of these files are the ones used for the different sound schemes available in Windows 95. For those of you who are not using Windows 95 yet, Microsoft has added a feature like the one provided for setting color schemes in Windows 3.1. Instead of just selecting colors, you can also choose sounds to play when different events in Windows 95 occur. For example, you could play a sound when a window is minimized or maximized, or when the Recycle Bin is emptied. We only mention them because their presence—or at least their potential presence—will highlight the value of the multimedia file I/O functions, which Microsoft custom-designed for RIFF data files. You'll see what we mean shortly.

A Peek at the Multimedia I/O Functions

You *could* read RIFF files with conventional file I/O functions by calculating offsets and reading blocks of the appropriate sizes. But the multimedia file I/O functions provide intrinsic support for the RIFF format. The best way to understand these functions is to use them.

All of the multimedia file I/O functions begin with the prefix *mmio*. Here is the complete set:

```
mmioOpen()
mmioClose()
mmioSeek()
mmioRead()
mmioWrite()
mmioDescend()
mmioAscend()
mmioCreateChunk()
mmioFOURCC()
mmioStringToFOURCC()
mmioAdvance()
mmioGetInfo()
mmioSetInfo()
mmioInstallIOProc()
mmioSendMessage()
```

Of these fifteen functions, we'll need just five to read and play a WAV file: **mmioOpen()**, **mmioClose()**, **mmioRead()**, **mmioDescend()**, and **mmioAscend()**.

All of these functions can return errors, so to use them properly we have to check the result of each function call to make sure that the operation is performed correctly. Since we need to make several calls to read the WAV file, this error-checking procedure can become a little lengthy. To minimize confusion and make the code more manageable, we could create two separate VB routines, one to open and read a WAV file, and one to play it. And that's what we'll do in the next project.

Playing WAV Files Using Low-Level Functions

This project shows you how to read and play WAV files using the low-level multimedia I/O functions. Just as MCIPLAY2.VBP began where MCIPLAY1.VBP left off, this new project, MCIPLAY3.VBP, will begin with the files from MCIPLAY2.VBP. By the time we're done, the final project will have six Command Buttons, each offering a different way to play WAV files. Here are the steps:

1. Create the code module WAVEPLAY.BAS and add the necessary declarations.
2. Create the function named **OpenWaveFile()** (Listing 5.7) for opening and processing a WAV file.
3. Create the function named **WaveOut()** (Listing 5.8) for playing the WAV file.
4. Add a new Command Button to MCIPLAY3.FRM and use its Click event procedure to open and play the WAV file.

 This version of the MCIPlay project is located in the directory \VBMAGIC\MCIPLAY3, in the files MCIPLAY3.VBP, MCIPLAY3.FRM, MCIPLAY3.BAS, and WAVEPLAY.BAS.

Reading and Processing a WAV File

To read and play a WAV file, we'll need to create a separate code module. We'll call this module WAVEPLAY.BAS and include two new procedures: **OpenWaveFile()** to open and read the file and **WaveOut()** to play it. We'll call both procedures from a Command Button Click event. Let's begin with **OpenWaveFile()**.

The first thing we want to do is open the file, so let's declare the low-level multimedia function, **mmioOpen()**.

```
Win32:
Declare Function mmioOpen Lib "winmm" (ByVal szFileName As String, _
   lpMMIOInfo As Any, ByVal dwOpenFlags As Long) As Long

Win16:
Declare Function mmioOpen Lib "MMSystem" (ByVal szFilename As String,  _
   lpMMIOINFO As Any, ByVal dwOpenFlags As Long) As Integer
```

The first parameter, **szFilename**, specifies the filename. We have enough experience passing strings to the API, so this is easy. Just remember to use **ByVal** in the declaration.

For the second parameter, **lpMMIOINFO**, we could pass a pointer to a **MMIOINFO** data structure, but we don't need this structure. We'll declare this parameter as type **Any** so we can pass it a **NULL** (literal value 0&) pointer.

mmioOpen() performs several operations, and each is selectable by passing flags with the third parameter, **dwOpenFlags**. For this example, we'll need only one flag, **MMIO_READ**.

Add the declaration for **mmioOpen()** to the declarations section of WAVEPLAY.BAS. Then, select New Procedure from the View menu, and declare a new function called **OpenWaveFile()**. When the framework for this function is displayed, simply add a single parameter for passing the filename of the WAV file we intend to open and play. Also, declare the *return type* of the function **As Boolean**:

```
Public Function OpenWaveFile (FileNameAndPath As String) As Boolean
End Function
```

Now we can plug in the **mmioOpen()** function, along with the declaration for the file handle, **hMMIO**.

```
Public Function OpenWaveFile (FileNameAndPath As String) As Boolean
Dim hMMIO As Long

    hMMIO = mmioOpen(FileNameAndPath, ByVal 0&, MMIO_READ)
```

After we've opened the file, we have to locate the *parent chunk* of the RIFF chunk. RIFF files can't contain more than a single parent chunk in the current version of the multimedia I/O system. Thus, this process may seem nonsensical, but future releases probably will support *compound* files (RIFF files that could, for example, contain more than one WAV sound). Besides, the search operation automatically positions the file pointer at the beginning of the data section of the chunk (in this case, the 13th byte in the file), so it isn't a completely wasted effort.

To search for chunks, we'll call upon **mmioDescend()**, which we also declare in WAVEPLAY.BAS:

```
Win32:
Declare Function mmioDescend Lib "winmm" (ByVal hMMIO As Long, _
   lpCk As Any, lpCkParent As Any, ByVal uFlags As Long) As Long

Win16:
Declare Function mmioDescend Lib "MMSystem" (ByVal hMMIO As Integer, _
   lpCk As  Any, lpCkParent As Any, ByVal wFlags As Integer) As Integer
```

To search for a particular type of RIFF chunk—in this case, a RIFF chunk that contains WAV data—we have to specify the *form type*. The form type, which is the third field at the head of a RIFF chunk, identifies the type of data stored in the RIFF chunk. It's also the third field in **MMCKINFO**. We'll declare a variable of type **MMCKINFO** called **MMCkInfoParent**. To search for a RIFF chunk with a form type of WAV, we set the **fccType** field in this record to "WAVE" and call **mmioDescend()**.

```
Public Function OpenWaveFile (FileNameAndPath As String) As Integer
Dim MMCkInfoParent As MMCKINFO
Dim hMMIO As Long
Dim ErrorCode As Long

    hMMIO = mmioOpen(FileNameAndPath, ByVal 0&, MMIO_READ)
    If hMMIO <> 0 Then
      ' Find WAV Parent Chunk
      MMCKInfoParent.fccType.Chars = "WAVE"
      ErrorCode = mmioDescend(hMMIO, MMCKInfoParent, ByVal 0&, MMIO_FINDRIFF)
```

Descending is kind of like reading. The difference is that **mmioDescend()** reads only the fields that describe the chunk. That is, it reads the rind—not the fruit, the data inside the chunk. As we mentioned earlier, all chunks begin with two data fields, the chunk ID (**CkID**) and the chunk size (**CkSize**). Instead of defining two different structures for chunks, Microsoft muddies the definition of a chunk with a kludge: a chunk may also contain a third data field, the form type or list type (**fccType**), which is contained in the first four bytes of the data section of the chunk. Only RIFF and LIST chunks include this "extra" field (form type for RIFF chunks, and list type for LIST chunks, both known as **fccType**).

When you descend into a chunk, **mmioDescend()** fills in the field **dwDataOffset** in the **MMCKINFO** record, which in this case is **MMCkInfoParent**. If you're descending into a RIFF or LIST chunk, **mmioDescend()** will also automatically fill in the **CkID** with either "RIFF" or "LIST."

In the call to **mmioDescend()**, we set the form type to "WAVE" and pass the flag **MMIO_FINDRIFF**. **mmioDescend()** will quickly search the file for its first (and currently, its only) RIFF chunk. When it has finished, we will have a complete description of the RIFF chunk contained in a record called **MMCkInfoParent**.

The RIFF chunk with the form type "WAVE" is the mother of all chunks— at least mother of all other chunks in a WAV file. To search for any other type of chunk, we need to specify the **CkID** and pass (by reference) a record of type **MMCHKINFO** for the parent chunk as the third parameter:

```
Public Function OpenWaveFile (FileNameAndPath As String) As Integer
Dim MMCKInfoParent As MMCKINFO
Dim MMCkInfoChild As MMCKINFO
Dim hMMIO As Long
Dim ErrorCode As Long

    hMMIO = mmioOpen(FileNameAndPath, ByVal 0&, MMIO_READ)
    If hMMIO <> 0 Then
      ' Find WAVE Parent Chunk
```

```
MMCKInfoParent.fccType.Chars = "WAVE"
ErrorCode = mmioDescend(hMMIO, MMCKInfoParent, ByVal 0&, MMIO_FINDRIFF)
If ErrorCode = 0 Then
   ' Find fmt Chunk
   MMCkInfoChild.CkId.Chars = "fmt "
   ErrorCode = mmioDescend(hMMIO, MMCkInfoChild, _
MMCKInfoParent, MMIO_FINDCHUNK)
```

Notice that **MMCkInfoChild.CkID.Chars** is blank-padded to four characters. In this statement, **mmioDescend()** searches the parent chunk for a *format chunk*. This takes little effort because the format chunk begins right after the form type field, at the 13th byte in the file. You can't assume, however, that this will always be the case. Someday you may encounter a WAV file that includes LIST chunks, which appear ahead of the format chunk. If you were to read the file in a conventional fashion, either with standard file I/O, or with the function **mmioRead()**, you would have to identify and skip the LIST chunks. But when we call **mmioDescend()** with the flag **MMIO_FINDCHUNK**, and a **CkId** of "fmt," it will automatically hop directly to the format chunk.

Now we get to read some data:

```
Public Function OpenWaveFile (FileNameAndPath As String) As Integer
Dim MMCKInfoParent As MMCKINFO
Dim MMCkInfoChild As MMCKINFO
Dim hMMIO As Long
Dim ErrorCode As Long
Dim BytesRead As Long

   hMMIO = mmioOpen(FileNameAndPath, ByVal 0&, MMIO_READ)
   If hMMIO <> 0 Then
      ' Find WAV Parent Chunk
      MMCKInfoParent.fccType.Chars = "WAVE"
      ErrorCode = mmioDescend(hMMIO, MMCKInfoParent, ByVal 0&, MMIO_FINDRIFF)
      If ErrorCode = 0 Then
         ' Find fmt Chunk
         MMCkInfoChild.CkId.Chars = "fmt "
         ErrorCode = mmioDescend(hMMIO, MMCkInfoChild, _
            MMCKInfoParent, MMIO_FINDCHUNK)
         If ErrorCode = 0 Then
            ' Read PCM Wave Format Record
            BytesRead = mmioRead(hMMIO, PCMWaveFmtRecord, MMCkInfoChild.CkSize)
```

mmioRead() does what you would expect. It reads from the file specified by **hMMIO** the number of bytes specified by the third parameter. It then places the data in memory, beginning at the address specified by the second parameter. Because we're passing a record of type **PCMWAVEFORMAT** by reference in the second parameter, when we return from **mmioRead()** we should find that it has filled in the wave format record.

Declaring the Wave Format Record

We declare the wave format record in the general declarations section of WAVEPLAY.BAS:

```
Type WAVEFORMAT
   wFormatTag As Integer
   nChannels As Integer
   nSamplesPerSec As Long
   nAvgBytesPerSec As Long
   nBlockAlign As Integer
End Type

Type PCMWAVEFORMAT
   wf As WAVEFORMAT
   wBitsPerSample As Integer
End Type-
-
-
Dim PCMWaveFmtRecord As PCMWAVEFORMAT
```

We also need to declare **mmioRead()**:

```
Win32:
Declare Function mmioRead Lib "winmm" (ByVal hMMIO As Long, _
   pch As Any, ByVal cch As Long) As Long
Win16:
Declare Function mmioRead Lib "MMSystem" (ByVal hMMIO As Integer, _
   pCh As Any, ByVal cCh As Long) As Long
```

After we read the format chunk, we can check to see whether the WAV file at hand contains data that's compatible with our digital waveform output device. If not, we can skip the rest of the procedure. To do this, we'll use a special case of **waveOutOpen()**. Ordinarily, this function is used to open the wave audio output device. In fact, we will use it for just that purpose in our function **WaveOut()**. But we can also call it with a flag named **WAVE_FORMAT_QUERY**, which will compare the contents of the wave format record with the device capabilities as defined in the wave audio device driver. If the file is compatible with the device, **waveOutOpen()** returns zero. We'll look at **waveOutOpen()** in more detail when we write the function **WaveOut()**:

```
Public Function OpenWaveFile(ByVal FileNameAndPath As String) As Boolean
Dim MMCKInfoParent As MMCKINFO
Dim MMCkInfoChild As MMCKINFO
Dim hMMIO As Long
Dim ErrorCode As Long
```

```
Dim BytesRead As Long
Dim Index As Long

   OpenWaveFile = False

   hMMIO = mmioOpen(FileNameAndPath, ByVal 0&, MMIO_READ)
   If hMMIO <> 0 Then
      ' Find WAV Parent Chunk
      MMCKInfoParent.fccType.Chars = "WAVE"
      ErrorCode = mmioDescend(hMMIO, MMCKInfoParent, ByVal 0&, MMIO_FINDRIFF)
      If ErrorCode = 0 Then
         ' Find fmt Chunk
         MMCkInfoChild.ckid.Chars = "fmt "
         ErrorCode = mmioDescend(hMMIO, MMCkInfoChild, _
            MMCKInfoParent, MMIO_FINDCHUNK)
         If ErrorCode = 0 Then
            ' Read PCM Wave Format Record
            BytesRead = mmioRead(hMMIO, PCMWaveFmtRecord, MMCkInfoChild.cksize)
            If BytesRead > 0 Then
               ErrorCode = waveOutOpen(hWaveout, WAVE_MAPPER, _
                  PCMWaveFmtRecord, 0&, 0&, WAVE_FORMAT_QUERY)
```

Somewhere after the format chunk we should find the data chunk. To find the data chunk without making any assumptions about its location, we'll again want to use **mmioDescend()** to search the parent chunk for it. But before we can do that, we first have to *ascend* out of the format chunk:

```
Public Function OpenWaveFile(ByVal FileNameAndPath As String) As Boolean
Dim MMCKInfoParent As MMCKINFO
Dim MMCkInfoChild As MMCKINFO
Dim hMMIO As Long
Dim ErrorCode As Long
Dim BytesRead As Long
Dim Index As Long

   OpenWaveFile = False

   hMMIO = mmioOpen(FileNameAndPath, ByVal 0&, MMIO_READ)
   If hMMIO <> 0 Then
      ' Find WAVE Parent Chunk
      MMCKInfoParent.fccType.Chars = "WAVE"
      ErrorCode = mmioDescend(hMMIO, MMCKInfoParent, ByVal 0&, MMIO_FINDRIFF)
      If ErrorCode = 0 Then
         ' Find fmt Chunk
         MMCkInfoChild.ckid.Chars = "fmt "
         ErrorCode = mmioDescend(hMMIO, MMCkInfoChild, MMCKInfoParent, _
            MMIO_FINDCHUNK)
         If ErrorCode = 0 Then
            ' Read PCM Wave Format Record
            BytesRead = mmioRead(hMMIO, PCMWaveFmtRecord, MMCkInfoChild.cksize)
            If BytesRead > 0 Then
```

```
ErrorCode = waveOutOpen(hWaveout, WAVE_MAPPER, PCMWaveFmtRecord, _
   0&, 0&, WAVE_FORMAT_QUERY)
If ErrorCode = 0 Then
   ' Ascend back one level in the RIFF file
   ErrorCode = mmioAscend(hMMIO, MMCkInfoChild, 0)
```

The first parameter of **mmioAscend()** once again identifies the file, and the second parameter identifies the chunk from which to ascend. The third parameter may someday accept flags, but none have been defined yet by Microsoft, so we'll always set it to 0. Declare **mmioAscend()** like this:

```
Win32:
Declare Function mmioAscend Lib "winmm" (ByVal hMMIO As Long, _
   lpck As Any, ByVal uFlags As Long) As Long

Win16:
Declare Function mmioAscend Lib "MMSystem" (ByVal hMMIO As Integer, _
   lpCk As Any, ByVal wFlags As Integer) As Integer
```

At the end of our ascent, the file pointer will stand at the threshold of the next chunk, which, coincidentally, is the next chunk into which we'll descend.

```
Public Function OpenWaveFile(ByVal FileNameAndPath As String) As Boolean
Dim MMCKInfoParent As MMCKINFO
Dim MMCkInfoChild As MMCKINFO
Dim hMMIO As Long
Dim ErrorCode As Long
Dim BytesRead As Long
Dim Index As Long

   OpenWaveFile = False

   hMMIO = mmioOpen(FileNameAndPath, ByVal 0&, MMIO_READ)
   If hMMIO <> 0 Then
      ' Find WAV Parent Chunk
      MMCKInfoParent.fccType.Chars = "WAVE"
      ErrorCode = mmioDescend(hMMIO, MMCKInfoParent, ByVal 0&, MMIO_FINDRIFF)
      If ErrorCode = 0 Then
         ' Find fmt Chunk
         MMCkInfoChild.ckid.Chars = "fmt "
         ErrorCode = mmioDescend(hMMIO, MMCkInfoChild, _
            MMCKInfoParent, MMIO_FINDCHUNK)
         If ErrorCode = 0 Then
            ' Read PCM Wave Format Record
            BytesRead = mmioRead(hMMIO, PCMWaveFmtRecord, MMCkInfoChild.cksize)
            If BytesRead > 0 Then
               ErrorCode = waveOutOpen(hWaveout, WAVE_MAPPER, _
                  PCMWaveFmtRecord, 0&, 0&, WAVE_FORMAT_QUERY)
               If ErrorCode = 0 Then
                  ' Ascend back one level in the RIFF file
                  ErrorCode = mmioAscend(hMMIO, MMCkInfoChild, 0)
```

```
If ErrorCode = 0 Then
  ' Read data chunk
  MMCkInfoChild.ckid.Chars = "data"
  ErrorCode = mmioDescend(hMMIO, MMCkInfoChild, _
    MMCKInfoParent, MMIO_FINDCHUNK)
```

Throughout this odyssey, our parent chunk has remained, steadfastly, the RIFF chunk. To locate the data chunk, we set the **CkID** in **MMCkInfoChild** to "data" and call **mmioDescend()** again with the flag **MMIO_FINDCHUNK**. If we strike paydirt, it's time to dig out the prize—waveform audio data.

To read in the waveform data we need to supply a buffer. In VB we have limited resources when it comes to manipulating *binary large objects* (BLOBs). WAV files tend to be large—very large. The lowest fidelity WAV format requires 11,025 bytes per second of audio. The WAV files that contain the Windows 95 message beep sounds were recorded at the next highest sampling rate of 22.05 KHz, which means that they occupy 22,050 bytes for each second of playback time.

We now need to create a structure to hold the WAV data. The easiest way to store this information is to use a dynamic array of **Bytes**. The advantage with this approach is that we can reset the size for each individual WAV file without having to use any more memory than we need to. If you are programming for 16-bit Windows, this method cannot be used if you need an array larger than 64,000 bytes—a frustrating limitation of the 16-bit Windows environment. To set the size of the array, we will use the **ReDim Preserve** command to set the size to one less than the size of the WAV chunk. The size needs to be one less than the WAV chunk because we are using a zero-based array. It just so happens that this value is already available to us in the **ckSize** variable of the **MMCkInfoChild**.

Here is the declaration of the **Byte** array that needs to be put into the declaration section of WAVEPLAY.BAS:

```
Dim WaveBuffer() as Byte
```

Now, we need to add the code that redimensions the array:

```
ReDim WaveBuffer(MMCkInfoChild.ckSize - 1)
```

Finally, now that we know how much information to pull in where we are going to put it, we can add the code that actually reads in the WAV information:

```
Dim WaveBuffer(1 To 64000) As byte
```

```
-
-
-
' Read data chunk.
MMCkInfoChild.ckid.Chars = "data"
ErrorCode = mmioDescend(hmmio, MMCkInfoChild, MMCKInfoParent, MMIO_FINDCHUNK)
If ErrorCode = 0 Then
   ReDim WaveBuffer(MMCkInfoChild.ckSize - 1)
   BytesRead = mmioRead(hmmio, WaveBuffer(0), MMCkInfoChild.ckSize)
   If BytesRead > 0 Then
      ' Get a pointer to the Wave data and fill in Wave Header.
      WaveHeader.lpData = lparraycpy(WaveBuffer(0), WaveBuffer(0))
      WaveHeader.dwBufferLength = BytesRead
      WaveHeader.dwFlags = 0&
      WaveHeader.dwLoops = 0&
      OpenWaveFile = True
   Else
   MsgBox "Couldn't read wave data.", MB_ICONSTOP, "RIFF File Error"
End If
```

Next, we call **mmioRead()**, passing the first element of the array **WaveBuffer** as the target buffer in the second parameter, and **MMCkInfoChild.ckSize** as the number of bytes to read in the third parameter.

Finally, if **mmioRead()** returns successfully, we have all the information we need to construct a **WAVEHDR** record. Wave headers are the structures that describe individual WAV buffers. For a variety of reasons, we might wish to play wave audio data by passing it to the driver in segments. We treat each segment as a separate buffer with its own header. The format record, a structure of type **PCMWAVEFORMAT**, describes the format of a single wave audio recording. Each segment of that recording will have its own header, a structure of type **WAVEHDR**. One reason to segment a WAV file into multiple buffers might be to overcome limitations on the size and number of elements of 16-bit Window's strings and arrays. That's not the reason we'll do it, but it's undeniably a valid reason.

```
Type WAVEHDR
   lpData As String
   dwBufferLength As Long
   dwBytesRecorded As Long
   dwUser As Long
   dwFlags As Long
   dwLoops As Long
   lpNext As Variant
   reserved As Long
End Type

Dim WaveHeader As WAVEHDR
```

We'll need **WaveHeader** in both **WaveOut()** and **OpenWaveFile()**, so make sure to include it in the declarations section of WAVEPLAY.BAS to give it a scope that will make it usable by any function within the WAVEPLAY.BAS module.

While the format record describes the sampling rate, number of channels, and bit resolution of a wave audio file, the main purpose of a wave header is to hold the length and location of the wave audio data. In **WaveOut()** we'll use the format record to open the device, and the header to play the data.

When we're done reading the file and preparing the header, we can close the file. Listing 5.7 provides the complete **OpenWaveFile()** function with all its error messages.

Listing 5.7   OpenWaveFile() from WAVEPLAY.BAS

```
Public Function OpenWaveFile(ByVal FileNameAndPath As String) As Boolean
Dim MMCKInfoParent As MMCKINFO
Dim MMCkInfoChild As MMCKINFO
Dim hmmio As Long
Dim ErrorCode As Long
Dim BytesRead As Long

   OpenWaveFile = False

   hmmio = mmioOpen(FileNameAndPath, ByVal 0&, MMIO_READ)
   If hmmio <> 0 Then
     ' Find WAVE Parent Chunk
     MMCKInfoParent.fccType.Chars = "WAVE"
     ErrorCode = mmioDescend(hmmio, MMCKInfoParent, ByVal 0&, MMIO_FINDRIFF)
     If ErrorCode = 0 Then
        ' Find fmt Chunk
        MMCkInfoChild.ckid.Chars = "fmt "
        ErrorCode = mmioDescend(hmmio, MMCkInfoChild, MMCKInfoParent, _
          MMIO_FINDCHUNK)
        If ErrorCode = 0 Then
           ' Read PCM Wave Format Record
           BytesRead = mmioRead(hmmio, PCMWaveFmtRecord, MMCkInfoChild.ckSize)
           If BytesRead > 0 Then
              ErrorCode = waveOutOpen(hWaveOut, WAVE_MAPPER, PCMWaveFmtRecord, _
                0&, 0&, WAVE_FORMAT_QUERY)
              If ErrorCode = 0 Then
                 ' Ascend back one level in the RIFF file.
                 ErrorCode = mmioAscend(hmmio, MMCkInfoChild, 0)
                 If ErrorCode = 0 Then
                    ' Read data chunk.
                    MMCkInfoChild.ckid.Chars = "data"
                    ErrorCode = mmioDescend(hmmio, MMCkInfoChild, _
                      MMCKInfoParent, MMIO_FINDCHUNK)
                    If ErrorCode = 0 Then
                       ReDim WaveBuffer(MMCkInfoChild.ckSize - 1)
```

```
                    BytesRead = mmioRead(hmmio, WaveBuffer(0), _
                       MMCkInfoChild.ckSize)
                    If BytesRead > 0 Then
                       ' Get a pointer to the Wave data and fill in
                       ' Wave Header.
                       WaveHeader.lpData = lparraycpy(WaveBuffer(0), _
                          WaveBuffer(0))
                       WaveHeader.dwBufferLength = BytesRead
                       WaveHeader.dwFlags = 0&
                       WaveHeader.dwLoops = 0&
                       OpenWaveFile = True
                    Else
                    MsgBox "Couldn't read wave data.", MB_ICONSTOP, _
                       "RIFF File Error"
                    End If
                 Else
                    MsgBox "Couldn't find data chunk.", MB_ICONSTOP, _
                       "RIFF File Error"
                 End If
              Else
                 MsgBox "Couldn't ascend from fmt chunk.", MB_ICONSTOP, _
                    "RIFF File Error"
              End If
           Else
              MsgBox "Format not supported by Wave device.", MB_ICONSTOP, _
                 "Wave Data Error"
           End If
        Else
           MsgBox "Couldn't read wave format record.", MB_ICONSTOP, _
              "RIFF File Error"
        End If
     Else
        MsgBox "Couldn't find fmt chunk.", MB_ICONSTOP, "RIFF File Error"
     End If
  Else
     MsgBox "Couldn't find WAVE parent chunk.", MB_ICONSTOP, _
        "RIFF File Error"
  End If
  ' Close WAVE file.
  ErrorCode = mmioClose(hmmio, 0)
Else
  MsgBox "Couldn't open file.", MB_ICONSTOP, "RIFF File Error"
End If
End Function
```

Last, but not least, make sure you update the WAVEPLAY.BAS file with the declaration for **mmioClose()**:

```
Win32:
Declare Function mmioClose Lib "winmm" (ByVal hMMIO As Long, _
   ByVal uFlags As Long) As Long
```

```
Win16:
Declare Function mmioClose Lib "MMSystem" (ByVal hMMIO As Integer, _
   ByVal wFlags As Integer) As Integer
```

We don't have to ascend back out to the RIFF chunk before we close the file. Even if we did, we would still be in the same position—at the end of the file. If some day multimedia file I/O supports compound files—RIFF files that contain multiple RIFF chunks—we may wish to ascend out of one RIFF chunk before descending into, or searching for, the next one.

Playing the WAV File

Once we've extracted the data from the RIFF file and created the three essential data structures (the format record, the wave audio data, and the wave data header), we can use the wave audio device to play the sound. Five steps are required to play the wave audio from the structures stored in memory:

1. Open the wave audio device.
2. Prepare the wave header.
3. Write the data to the device.
4. Unprepare the wave header.
5. Close the device.

As you might assume from the discussion so far, we cannot just call the five functions that perform these steps in rapid-fire succession. Like **OpenWaveFile()**, our next subroutine, **WaveOut()**, will include conditions for verification and failure. Listing 5.8 shows the complete code for **WaveOut()**.

Listing 5.8 WaveOut() from WAVEPLAY.BAS

```
Public Sub WaveOut()
Dim ReturnCode As Long

' Open the wave audio device
   ReturnCode = waveOutOpen(hWaveout, WAVE_MAPPER, PCMWaveFmtRecord, 0&, 0&, 0&)
   If ReturnCode = 0 Then
      ' Prepare the wave output header
      ReturnCode = waveOutPrepareHeader(hWaveout, WaveHeader, Len(WaveHeader))
      If ReturnCode = 0 Then
         ' Write the wave data to the output device
         ReturnCode = waveOutWrite(hWaveout, WaveHeader, Len(WaveHeader))
         ' Wait until finished playing
         If ReturnCode = 0 Then
            Do Until (WaveHeader.dwFlags And WHDR_DONE)
               DoEvents
            Loop
```

```
        End If
        ' Unprepare the wave output header
        ReturnCode = waveOutUnprepareHeader(hWaveout, WaveHeader, _
           Len(WaveHeader))
        If ReturnCode <> 0 Then
           MsgBox "Unable to Unprepare Wave Header", MB_ICONSTOP, "Wave Error"
        End If
        WaveHeader.dwFlags = 0
        ' Close the wave device
        ReturnCode = waveOutClose(hWaveout)
        If ReturnCode <> 0 Then
           MsgBox "Unable to Close Wave Device", MB_ICONSTOP, "Wave Error"
        End If
     Else
        ' Couldn't prepare the header, so close the device
        MsgBox "Unable to Prepare Wave Header", 0, "Wave Error"
        ReturnCode = waveOutClose(hWaveout)
        If ReturnCode <> 0 Then
            MsgBox "Unable to Close Wave Device", MB_ICONSTOP, "Wave Error"
        End If
     End If
  Else
     ' Couldn't open the device so do nothing.
     MsgBox "Unable to Open Wave Device", MB_ICONSTOP, "Wave Error"
  End If
End Sub
```

We begin by opening the device. Although we called **waveOutOpen()** from our function **OpenWaveFile()**, we didn't actually open the wave audio device. We called the function with a special flag called **WAVE_FORMAT_QUERY**, which, instead of opening the device, just verified that the format of the wave file we read was compatible with the wave audio device. This time we'll call **waveOutOpen()** with no flags at all, which really will open the device.

waveOutOpen() expects six parameters. The first parameter is the address of an empty device handle, which the function will fill-in if it successfully opens a wave audio device. This handle is used to perform all subsequent operations with the device. For the second parameter, we specify which wave audio device to open. A Windows system may contain several wave audio devices (the MPC specification requires only one). They will be numbered sequentially, beginning with device 0, if your system contains more than one compatible device. If you want the multimedia system to select the first available driver, you can specify the constant **WAVE_MAPPER**, which has an integer value of -1.

For the third parameter, we pass the address of the wave format structure. The fourth and fifth parameters specify a callback function and information to be used by the callback function. Holy Trinity programmers could use the callback function to carry on a dialog with the wave playback function. Unfortunately, unless we write a custom control, we VB programmers will have to use a more primitive technique to monitor playback. We'll pass **NULL**s in these arguments.

For the last parameter of **waveOutOpen()**, we could pass a flag, as we did in our function **OpenWaveFile()**. However, the only other flags available specify the callback method, and because we won't be using callbacks, we can pass a **NULL** set of flags.

The activities of **waveOutPrepareHeader()** and **waveOutUnprepareHeader()** remain mysterious to us. We can tell you that you must prepare the header before you send wave audio data to the device driver, and that you must unprepare the header before you release the memory occupied by the header and wave audio data. But we have to confess, we can't find any explanation—not even a poor one—of what this preparation actually does. We would guess that whatever these functions do, they have been separated from the function **waveOutWrite()** to facilitate performance. Digital audio output devours processor cycles. When you consider that the Windows multimedia system can play 16-bit stereo wave data at 44.1 KHz, you realize that the output functions can't be bothered with any tasks other than those that must occur in real time. Because they are external to the output function, **waveOutPrepareHeader()** and **waveOutUnprepareHeader()** enable **waveOutWrite()** to offload some overhead. With these functions we can prepare the buffers and headers in advance and feed them to the output function in quick succession. As the device driver finishes with each buffer, it can spit it out and leave the cleanup for us to perform later. Of course, when we call the prepare and unprepare functions, we're still using the processor, but not during the critical handoff between buffer segments.

After we prepare **WaveHeader**, we send it to the wave audio device with **waveOutWrite()**. This function takes three arguments: the handle we received when we opened the device, the memory location of the wave header, and the size of the wave header. Notice that the built-in VB function **Len()** will return the size of a data structure just as easily as it will return the length of a string. We could have supplied the size as a constant value, but it's generally better practice to avoid hard-coded references to structures that may change in the future, especially when functions like **Len()** exist.

After we write out the audio data, we need to unprepare the header and close the device. But we can't do that until the device completes playback, so we loop until **waveOutWrite()** sets the flag **WHDR_DONE** in **WaveHeader**. This is the poor man's alternative to a callback function. If we *could* supply a callback, either in the form of a function or a window handle, we could then instruct **waveOutWrite()** to notify us when it's done. Instead, we just watch for the signal. Notice that this "wait" loop repeatedly executes **DoEvents**.

Under 16-bit Windows, the **DoEvents()** function is very useful because it allows us to process other messages while an application is waiting for something to happen. Without the **DoEvents()** call, it is easy to hang 16-bit Windows if the requirements of a loop are never met. (This condition is known as *non-preemptive multihanging* in 16-bit Windows.) Fortunately, the preemptive multitasking operation of the 32-bit Windows environment provides much more flexibility for dealing with problems like this.

If we don't include the **DoEvents()** call in our loop and the requirements to exit the loop are never met, only our application will hang. Windows 95 will continue to run. With 32-Windows, the scope of the **DoEvents()** function has been reduced from a global function to one that only effects the program that calls the function. Even so, we still do not want our program hanging so badly that we can not exit out of it, so we will leave the **DoEvents()** call in.

When we spot the **WHDR_DONE** flag, we unprepare the header. Then, as always, we must close the wave audio device before we terminate our program or we'll be unable to reopen the device until we restart Windows.

Adding Low-Level Playback to MCIPlay

Now we can add the low-level playback functions to our test program, MCIPLAY3.VBP. We're going to revisit the functions **OpenWaveFile()** and **WaveOut()** in Chapter 14, which is why we placed them in a new code module called WAVEPLAY.BAS. Add a new button to MCIPLAY3.FRM, and set its **Name** property to WaveOutButton, and its **Caption** property to "waveOutWrite," as shown in Figure 5.5. Then, insert the code that appears in Listing 5.9.

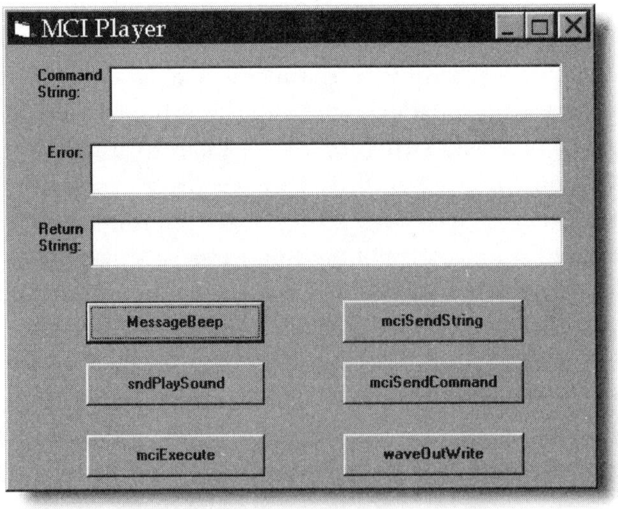

Figure 5.5   *MCIPLAY3.FRM as it appears with all six play buttons.*

Listing 5.9   WaveOutButton_Click Event Procedure from MCIPLAY3.FRM

```
Private Sub WaveOutButton_Click()

    WaveOutButton.Enabled = False
    If OpenWaveFile(App.Path & "\" & CommandStringText.TEXT) Then
        WaveOut
    End If
    WaveOutButton.Enabled = True
    WaveOutButton.SetFocus
End Sub
```

Don't forget to add the declarations to WAVEPLAY.BAS as they appear in Listing 5.10.

Listing 5.10   From the Declarations Section of WAVEPLAY.BAS

```
Option Explicit

Type FOURCC
        Chars As String * 4
End Type

Type WAVEFORMAT
        wFormatTag As Integer
        nChannels As Integer
        nSamplesPerSec As Long
        nAvgBytesPerSec As Long
        nBlockAlign As Integer
End Type

Type WAVEOUTCAPS
        wMid As Integer
        wPid As Integer
        vDriverVersion As Long
        szPname As String * 32
        dwFormats As Long
        wChannels As Integer
        dwSupport As Long
End Type

Type WAVEHDR
        lpData As Long
        dwBufferLength As Long
        dwBytesRecorded As Long
        dwUser As Long
        dwFlags As Long
        dwLoops As Long
        lpNext As Long
        Reserved As Long
End Type
```

```
Type PCMWAVEFORMAT
        wf As WAVEFORMAT
        wBitsPerSample As Integer
End Type

Type MMIOINFO
        dwFlags As Long
        fccIOProc As Long
        pIOProc As Long
        wErrorRet As Long
        htask As Long
        cchBuffer As Long
        pchBuffer As String
        pchNext As String
        pchEndRead As String
        pchEndWrite As String
        lBufOffset As Long
        lDiskOffset As Long
        adwInfo(4) As Long
        dwReserved1 As Long
        dwReserved2 As Long
        hmmio As Long
End Type

Type MMCKINFO
        ckid As FOURCC          ' chunk ID
        ckSize As Long          ' chunk size
        fccType As FOURCC       ' form type or list type
        dwDataOffset As Long    ' offset of data portion of chunk
        dwFlags As Long         ' flags used by MMIO functions
End Type

#If Win32 Then
    Private Declare Function lparraycpy Lib "kernel32" Alias "lstrcpy" _
        (lpString1 As Any, lpString2 As Any) As Long
    Private Declare Function mmioAscend Lib "winmm.dll" (ByVal hmmio As Long, _
        lpck As Any, ByVal uFlags As Long) As Long
    Private Declare Function mmioClose Lib "winmm.dll" (ByVal hmmio As Long, _
        ByVal uFlags As Long) As Long
    Private Declare Function mmioDescend Lib "winmm.dll" (ByVal hmmio As Long, _
        lpck As Any, lpckParent As Any, ByVal uFlags As Long) As Long
    Private Declare Function mmioOpen Lib "winmm.dll" Alias "mmioOpenA" (ByVal _
        szFileName As String, lpmmioinfo As Any, ByVal dwOpenFlags As Long) _
        As Long
    Private Declare Function mmioRead Lib "winmm.dll" (ByVal hmmio As Long, _
        pch As Any, ByVal cch As Long) As Long
    Private Declare Function waveOutClose Lib "winmm.dll" (ByVal hWaveOut _
        As Long) As Long
    Private Declare Function waveOutGetDevCaps Lib "winmm.dll" Alias _
        "waveOutGetDevCapsA" (ByVal uDeviceID As Long, lpCaps As WAVEOUTCAPS, _
        ByVal uSize As Long) As Long
    Private Declare Function waveOutOpen Lib "winmm.dll" (lphWaveOut As Long, _
        ByVal uDeviceID As Long, lpFormat As PCMWAVEFORMAT, ByVal dwCallback _
        As Long, ByVal dwInstance As Long, ByVal dwFlags As Long) As Long
```

```
    Private Declare Function waveOutPrepareHeader Lib "winmm.dll" (ByVal _
        hWaveOut As Long, lpWaveOutHdr As Any, ByVal uSize As Long) As Long
    Private Declare Function waveOutUnprepareHeader Lib "winmm.dll" (ByVal _
        hWaveOut As Long, lpWaveOutHdr As Any, ByVal uSize As Long) As Long
    Private Declare Function waveOutWrite Lib "winmm.dll" (ByVal hWaveOut _
        As Long, lpWaveOutHdr As Any, ByVal uSize As Long) As Long
#Else
    Private Declare Function waveOutGetDevCaps Lib "MMSYSTEM" (ByVal wDeviceID _
        As Integer, lpCaps As WAVEOUTCAPS, ByVal wSize As Integer) As Integer
    Private Declare Function waveOutOpen Lib "MMSYSTEM" (lphWaveOut As Integer, _
        ByVal wDeviceID As Integer, lpFormat As Any, ByVal dwCallback As Long, _
        ByVal dwCallback As Long, ByVal dwFlags As Long) As Integer
    Private Declare Function waveOutClose Lib "MMSYSTEM" (ByVal hWaveOut _
        As Integer) As Integer
    Private Declare Function waveOutPrepareHeader Lib "MMSYSTEM" (ByVal _
        hWaveOut As Integer, lpWaveOutHdr As Any, ByVal wSize As Integer) _
        As Integer
    Private Declare Function waveOutUnprepareHeader Lib "MMSYSTEM" (ByVal _
        hWaveOut As Integer, lpWaveOutHdr As Any, ByVal wSize As Integer) _
        As Integer
    Private Declare Function waveOutWrite Lib "MMSYSTEM" (ByVal hWaveOut _
        As Integer, lpWaveOutHdr As Any, ByVal wSize As Integer) As Integer
    Private Declare Function mmioOpen Lib "MMSYSTEM" (ByVal szFileName _
        As String, lpmmioinfo As Any, ByVal dwOpenFlags As Long) As Integer
    Private Declare Function mmioClose Lib "MMSYSTEM" (ByVal hmmio As Integer, _
        ByVal wFlags As Integer) As Integer
    Private Declare Function mmioDescend Lib "MMSYSTEM" (ByVal hmmio As Integer, _
        lpck As Any, lpckParent As Any, ByVal wFlags As Integer) As Integer
    Private Declare Function mmioAscend Lib "MMSYSTEM" (ByVal hmmio As Integer, _
        lpck As Any, ByVal wFlags As Integer) As Integer
    Private Declare Function mmioRead Lib "MMSYSTEM" (ByVal hmmio As Integer, _
        pch As Any, ByVal cch As Long) As Long
    Private Declare Function lstrcpy Lib "Kernel" (lpString1 As Any, lpString2 _
        As Any) As Long
#End If

Global Const WAVE_MAPPER = -1          ' Device ID for Wave Mapper
Global Const MMIO_READ = &H0&
Global Const MMIO_WRITE = &H1&
Global Const MMIO_READWRITE = &H2&

Global Const MMIO_FINDCHUNK = &H10     ' mmioDescend: find a chunk by ID
Global Const MMIO_FINDRIFF = &H20      ' mmioDescend: find a LIST chunk

Global Const WHDR_DONE = &H1           ' done bit

' flags for dwFlags parameter in waveOutOpen() and waveInOpen()
Global Const WAVE_FORMAT_QUERY = &H1

Dim WaveBuffer() As Byte
Dim hWaveOut As Long
Dim PCMWaveFmtRecord As PCMWAVEFORMAT
Dim WaveHeader As WAVEHDR
```

This may seem like too much trouble just to play WAV files, especially when there are at least five other much simpler methods. It is. But in the most intimate form of interactivity, we will often want to manipulate not only the playback process, but the form and content of the data itself. Wave audio data consists of lengthy streams of binary amplitude values. Those values, when used to drive an analog amplifier and speaker, translate back into sound. Once we have our hands on the binary data itself, we can chop it, filter it, loop it, splice it, mix it, and otherwise modify it—perhaps in real time—to suit our own purposes, and more importantly, to reflect the actions of our users.

You may also notice that the low-level functions we just implemented do not work with all WAV files—in particular, the new compressed WAV files. These files can be read into our buffer without any problems, but when we try and actually open the WAV device, the does not know how to handle the compressed data. We need to find a way to decompress the data that is in our buffer before we try and open the device. For the moment, don't worry this, we will discuss compressed wave audio in more detail in Chapter 15.

The View from the Cellar

We've taken such a direct route down into the multimedia API that we've neglected to pause at each level and survey the territory. The MCI, for example, offers a whole bunch of commands that enable you to manipulate multimedia files as if they were physical media, like audio cassettes or video tapes. You can change your position, ask for the number of tracks, select tracks, set the volume, alter the playback speed, record, pause, and resume. Each device supports a few standard commands, along with a selection of commands unique to its medium.

And although we've focused on wave audio playback, the multimedia system supports several kinds of media, including MIDI for synthesizer control, the Audio Video Interleave format (AVI), graphic animation through the multimedia movie player (MMM), and also external devices such as video tape recorders, video disk players, CD audio players, and Digital Audio Tape (DAT) decks.

At the low level, the Windows multimedia system includes functions to perform all kinds of operations, including buffered file I/O and MIDI sequencing and mapping. In fact, we haven't yet really reached the bottom level; we're standing on the catwalk in the deepest sub-basement, still a few feet above the floor. To perform such time-critical operations as wave audio or MIDI output, the device control functions depend on even lower-level functions, in particular, the multimedia timer, which offers much higher resolution timing than the standard Windows timer. The multimedia system even provides a standard interface for joystick input.

What we have discovered is that the Windows multimedia system offers a variety of approaches to multimedia operation, and that each technique offers unique advantages and disadvantages. For any given multimedia project, or for that matter, for any element of any project, you may choose the approach that provides the most appropriate mixture of accessibility, performance, and control over the data, from simple asynchronous message beeps to byte-by-byte manipulation of digitized sound.

In upcoming chapters, we'll apply many of these techniques, not only to wave audio, but to the other multimedia services as well. So stay tuned.

Once you unlock the mysteries of colors and palettes, you'll be on your way to adding dazzling visual effects to your multimedia applications.

Exploring Imaging— From Pixels to Palettes

T he world of graphics and imaging is a big black hole. The further you go into it, the more you realize there's so much more to discover. But it's worth the journey to see your program come alive with eye-catching screen effects.

In this chapter, we'll explore how Visual Basic and Windows work together to display images. Along the way, you'll learn about bitmaps, color display systems, and color palettes. In the next chapter, we'll cover palette animation and raster operations (ROPs), and a host of other low-level graphics topics. Windows and Visual Basic provide the tools you need to step out of the projection booth and onto the big screen. By mastering the basic imaging techniques, you'll be able to stitch together visual information to make your graphics as captivating and expressive as movies.

Many Windows programmers find the topics of bitmaps and color palettes to be quite mysterious. Once you understand the basics, you'll see how simple it is to use the Windows API to access colors and control palettes.

The Windows Connection—The Graphics Device Interface

Every screen in Windows is a graphic image. (Even a DOS window, which simulates a character-based screen, is drawn with a special font.) The ingenious authors of Windows, faced with a monumental graphics programming task, built a library of functions for drawing colorful borders, buttons, icons, and fonts. Fortunately, they made all those functions available to us by means of the Windows API.

VB handles many of the basic graphics tasks for us by drawing our forms and controls. VB also provides a variety of tools for drawing Picture Boxes, Image Controls, and directly on a form's client area, and even displays *bitmapped images* on these image-ready surfaces. But when images need to be manipulated for special effects such as animation, VB tosses us back into the API.

Most Windows graphics functions reside in a Windows DLL, known as the *Graphics Device Interface* (GDI). We've already used some of them indirectly. When you create and run just about any VB program, many GDI functions are used behind the scenes. This frees you from needing to know about *pixels, palettes,* or *raster operations.* But to write programs that manipulate graphic images, you'll need to know about those things and how to use GDI functions directly. The easiest way to understand GDI functions is to first understand the data structures they manipulate—in particular, bitmaps and color palettes.

Introducing WinG and CreateDIBSection()

Before we jump in and start exploring bitmaps and color palettes, we should introduce you to the new kids on the block for creating lightning-fast Windows graphics: *WinG* and *CreateDIBSection().* The GDI functions just mentioned are great for drawing graphics on the screen, however, they don't provide any means for directly accessing display memory or bitmaps. If you've ever tried to write games or fast-action graphics programs in DOS, you probably know that you can access your video display hardware directly. That's why the graphics in DOS games look so smooth. Windows, on the other hand, limits you to using functions that have more overhead—at least until WinG was released.

So what exactly is WinG? It is a custom DLL created by Microsoft that provides low-level support so that you can work with graphics at the bitmap level. WinG is actually an API that defines a new type of device context called *WinGDC,* and a new type of bitmap called *WinGBitmap.* Included with the WinG API is a set of eight specialized functions for working with this device context and bitmap. For example, you can call a function such as **WinGCreateBitmap()** to create a special type of device independent bitmap (DIB). Then, you can use a WinG device context to access the bits of the bitmap directly, or use standard GDI functions to draw graphics on top of the bitmap. After your bitmaps are set up the way you want them to be, you can copy them directly to the screen. In this respect, you get the best of both worlds: fast low-level bitmap support and the high-level flexibility of GDI functions.

WinG was developed to add fast bitmap display support to Windows 3.1. With Windows 95, Microsoft has added a powerful function named **CreateDIBSection()**, which supports low-level bitmap access.

Understanding Bitmaps

The PC's video system displays a matrix of pixels—little dots of light arranged in a grid. In a *character-based* environment, the video system contains a "hard-coded" set of shapes that represents the standard character set, along with various drawing characters (lines, corners, solid blocks, and so on) and a few symbols (smiling faces, diamonds, spades, and the like). A character is displayed by sending the system an ASCII or ANSI character code. In a *graphic* display system like Windows, the computer and its software define the shapes that appear on the screen, which are represented as bitmapped images. The main benefit with this approach is that pictures and text can be displayed in a variety of sizes, fonts, and styles. Take a look at Figure 6.1 for a better idea of how this works.

What exactly are bitmapped images? They are a collection of data elements that determine which color to display at each screen position. In a *monochrome* (black-and-white) graphic image, each bit represents one screen pixel, zero for black (the absence of color), and one for white (the presence of color). As you'll see soon, bitmaps can describe multi-colored images. The number of bits per pixel determines the number of different colors that can appear in a single bitmap. Besides the single-bit-per-pixel monochrome version, there are three others. Four bits per pixel produces 16 colors, eight bits will support 256 colors, and 24 bits can describe 16,777,216 colors. The bits

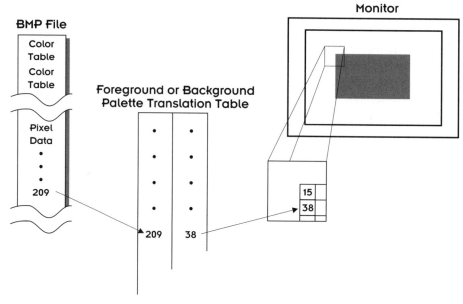

Figure 6.1 *How Windows displays bitmapped images.*

that make up a bitmap are arranged sequentially in the bitmap structure. Keep in mind, however, that the rows are stored in reverse order. That is, the first row in the pixel data section of the bitmap file is actually the bottom row of the image, as illustrated in Figure 6.2.

We'll present the actual structure of a bitmap file in this chapter. In Chapter 7 we'll show you how to work with them in much more detail. For now, remember that each pixel represents the absence or presence of color. And that's where our exploration of the GDI begins—with color and color palettes.

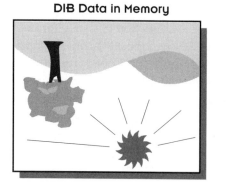
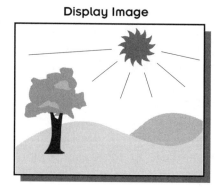

Figure 6.2 *How bitmaps are stored and processed.*

Color and the PC Display System

You can ignore how color works and let Windows and VB do their own thing if you don't need to create interesting visual effects. But what good is a multimedia application if it's not visually interesting? To create the animation and other imaging effects that help users enjoy what they're learning, you'll need to understand how both Windows and your own computer manage color.

What Windows can do with color images is dependent on the capabilities of your display system. The systems supported today come in three classes: VGA, super VGA (SVGA), and true color. (Since the MPC standard specifies VGA as the minimum display capability, we'll ignore the older CGA and EGA systems.) The standard VGA system can display 16 colors simultaneously with a resolution of 640×480. As you'll see, the waters start to get a little muddy when we look at SVGA and true color systems.

Most SVGA systems can theoretically display a dazzling array of 16,777,216 colors. However, only 256 colors out of that vast selection can appear on the screen simultaneously. Some so-called SVGA systems display only 64 simultaneous colors, though these are usually found in color notebook computers. SVGA resolutions start at 640×480 and go up from there—some even exceed 1600×1200 pixels.

Systems that display the full 16 million color range are often called *true color* displays. What does "true color" mean? It is derived from the idea that if a color display shows an extensive range of colors, the images will look natural or "true." True color displays use 24 bits to determine the color of each pixel. The 24 bits are divided into three 8-bit color components that indicate the intensity of the red, green, and blue color components. For this reason, 24-bit colors are referred to as *RGB* colors. Each primary color may vary in intensity according to an integer scale of 0 through 255. When all three RGB components are set to 0, the pixel appears black; when all are set to 255, the pixel is white. The total number of RGB combinations equals 256 cubed, or 16,777,216 colors.

Since older technology like photographs and analog television can display a virtually infinite variety of colors, it may seem presumptuous to call this digital version "true color." But right now, this is the state-of-the-art in desktop computer color technology. In fact, most hardware capable of digitizing color images provides a maximum color resolution of 24 bits, which means that a true color display displays the maximum color resolution found in current image data.

Unfortunately, SVGA systems can't display all of their colors at once because of memory limitations. These systems display at least 307,200 pixels

(640×480) and to produce full 24-bit color requires three bytes for each pixel, a total of 921,600 bytes. Until a couple years ago, having this much dedicated display memory was considered an extravagance. Today, the average SVGA card comes configured with 1024 kilobytes (1 MB) of memory, enough to support 24 bits per pixel at resolutions of 640×480, or 8 bits per pixel at resolutions of 1024×768. Some of the latest display interfaces support resolutions up to 1600×1200, which, at 24 bits of color resolution, would require over 6 MB of display RAM! As memory prices continue to fall, more systems will include 24-bit color displays that can handle high resolutions. But right now, most of the PCs being sold as Windows systems come equipped with 24-bit color displays with only 1 MB of memory, and there are many systems out there that still can only handle 8-bit color information. So this is the standard we should try to accommodate in our programs.

The Magic of Color Palettes

The pictures you'll display in your presentations will likely come in a multitude of different colors. Think about it; a photograph of the emerald Irish rolling hills requires an entirely different set of colors than a picture of Mars. If you wanted to display both images at once, you'd have a real problem on your hands. You would never have enough shades to render both images with any fidelity, even with 256 colors to divide between them. Fortunately, by displaying only one picture at a time, you can ask Windows to swap colors so that each image can activate its own selection of 256 colors—its own *color palette.*

A pixel's color on an 8-bit color display is determined by looking up its 8-bit pixel value in a color table, or *palette,* as shown in Figure 6.3. A palette contains a set of 24-bit RGB color values. The maximum number of color entries in a palette is 256, numbered from 0 through 255. A palette need not contain all 256 entries. Each pixel entry in the display memory contains a value from 0 through 255. This pixel value indicates which palette entry to use to color the pixel. To change the color of a pixel, you have two options: You can either change the index value of the pixel to another palette entry, or change the RGB value of the palette entry itself, which will change the color of all pixels on the screen that reference that palette entry.

Palettized color certainly imposes limitations—the 256 color limitation applies to the entire screen, not just to each window or application—but it also offers two important advantages. First, it makes your uncompressed image files two-thirds smaller than true color images. Second, you can use the built-in Windows palette manipulation functions to perform two popular (and

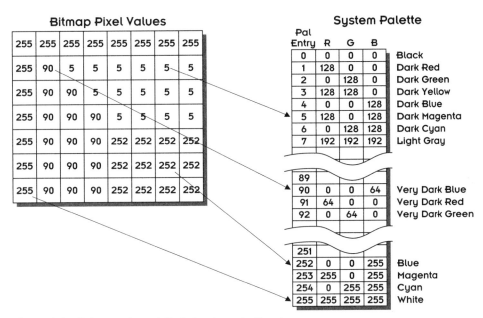

Figure 6.3 *Using a color palette to locate a pixel's color.*

economical) forms of animation: *palette animation* and *color cycling*. We'll explore these techniques later.

Inside the Palette Manager

As we mentioned previously, each displayed image carries its own color palette. In addition, each active window can manipulate the current palette for its own purposes. Remember that the 256 color limitation applies to the entire screen, not just to each window or application. With such limited seating, someone has to play the role of the bouncer. That's where the Windows *Palette Manager* comes in.

Windows uses the Palette Manager to determine which window has control of the palette at any given time. The active window, the one in the foreground, always has priority. If that window doesn't use the palette, the priority goes to the next window in the *z-order* (the order in which windows are stacked on the desktop). Once the window with the highest priority "realizes" its palette as the *foreground palette*, the other windows are signaled in order by the Palette Manager to "realize" their palettes as *background palettes*.

But what does it mean to *realize* a palette? Each image you display has its own color palette (several palettes can be kept in memory simultaneously). A palette stored in memory is called a *logical palette*. The palette in your display system that determines which colors actually appear on the screen is called the *hardware*, or *system palette*. There is only one hardware palette and the Palette Manager maintains a copy of it. When an application wants to activate its own colors, it must select its logical palette into a *device context* and *realize* it, which means that it must ask the Palette Manager to load its logical palette into the system (hardware) palette. This process of realizing a palette is shown in Figure 6.4.

Because palettes vary in size, the Palette Manager doesn't blindly copy a block of 256 color elements from the logical palette to the hardware palette, but loads only as many colors as it finds in each logical palette. The system palette can accommodate multiple logical palettes, as long as the total number of colors does not exceed 256. Furthermore, Windows reserves 20 of the

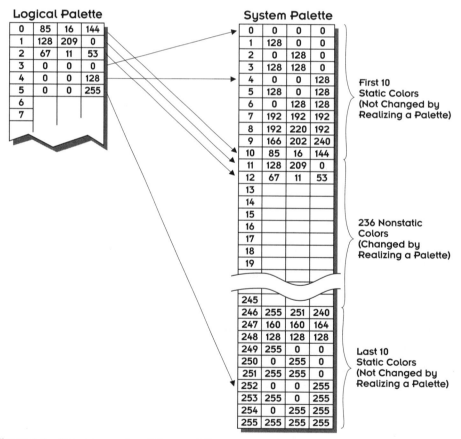

Figure 6.4   *The process of realizing a palette.*

palette entries for its *static colors*—the colors it uses to draw buttons, borders, text, icons, and so on. So we're left with only 236 changeable color slots. But this doesn't mean a palette should include only the 236 colors it needs to support its bitmap. It's wise to convert the palette of any 8-bit image into a Windows *identity palette*, which is a palette that includes the 20 reserved colors, especially if you plan to draw with the palette. Otherwise, you won't be able to use the reserved colors. If you wish, you *can* tamper with the system static colors to extend the range of definable colors all the way up to 256; the GDI provides special functions just for that purpose. But that would violate the Windows prime directive of not interfering with other active applications, since it could dramatically alter their appearance.

The colors in a logical palette often do not occupy the same positions in the system palette that they do in the logical palette. Therefore the Palette Manager must build a cross-reference table, called a *palette mapping*, to load a logical palette into the system palette. This table is used by GDI drawing functions to translate pixel values from logical palette indexes into system palette indexes. As we explained earlier, a pixel's color is determined by looking up its value in a color table. In a *device independent bitmap,* or DIB, the most common form of 256-color bitmap file, the bytes that make up the bitmap pixel data contain values that reference the entries in the color table contained within the file. As the GDI transfers the image from the file to the screen, that is, from a device *independent* bitmap into a device *dependent* bitmap (or DDB), it uses the palette mapping to change the pixel values to reference the correct colors in the system palette. The palette mapping that's created for a logical palette is called the *foreground mapping.*

If the active window does not hog all the palette entries, the remaining slots will be filled with colors from the inactive windows until either all the slots are occupied or until no other windows ask to realize their own palettes. If the foreground window requires all 236 free color slots, all the inactive windows must conform to the active foreground palette. The Palette Manager can also perform this service automatically by mapping colors in the inactive windows to the closest matching colors in the currently realized palette, which occasionally produces amusing (or ugly) results. This is called *background mapping.* Each time the focus changes from one palette-based application to another, the entire realization process starts over.

The difference between device independent and device dependent bitmaps is worth repeating: The pixels in a DIB contain the indexes of the colors in the logical palette that accompany the bitmap, usually a color table stored in the DIB file; the pixels in a DDB contain the indexes of the colors in the system palette. Figure 6.5 illustrates the difference between the two structures. A DIB

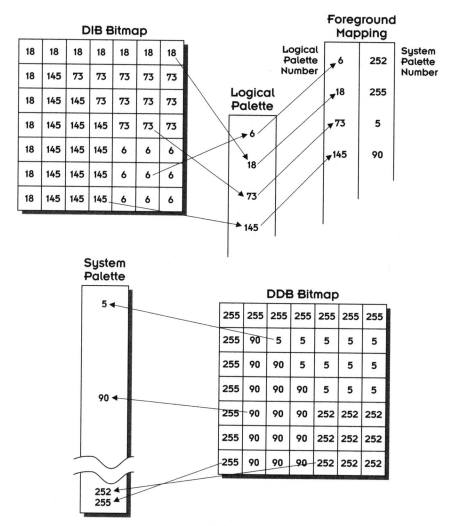

Figure 6.5 *Comparing a DIB with a DDB.*

does not exist in a device context. It must be translated into a DDB either before it's selected into a device context or as it is painted into the device context. The foreground and background palette mappings are the tables used to translate DIBs into DDBs.

Exploring Colors with Visual Basic

VB does a great job of hiding the details of color palette operations. If you just want to display bitmaps in Picture Boxes, you can let VB and the Windows

Palette Manager handle the palette. When VB loads a bitmap that contains its own palette, it loads and realizes that palette automatically. If you load another bitmap, the palette changes again, all behind the scenes. VB can't perform miracles, however, so you'll need to keep in mind the limitations imposed by palettes and the Palette Manager as you prepare your image data. Do not, for example, expect VB to simultaneously and accurately display two or more images with dissimilar palettes.

To program image processing applications, or to perform animation or special effects, you can go over VB's head and talk directly to the Palette Manager. In this section, we'll show you how to work with colors by using both VB and Windows API functions.

Selecting Colors the Easy Way

Before abandoning VB's built-in color capabilities, let's see how far they can take us. VB provides a function named **RGB()** for creating or selecting background, text, and foreground colors. **RGB()** is like a chameleon because its behavior changes under different circumstances. For example, **RGB()** displays colors as dithered colors by default; however, other palettes can be loaded to access more "pure" colors.

Using the RGB() Function

This project shows you how to use **RGB()** to display different colors. Here are the steps to follow:

1. Create a new form named TestRGB and place a Picture Box and Scroll Bars on the form, as shown in Figure 6.6.
2. Insert code for the **ColorBar_Change()** event procedure and the Picture Box's **Paint** event.

 This project is located in the directory \VBMAGIC\TESTRGB, in the files TESTRGB.VBP and TESTRGB.FRM.

Creating the RGB() Program

To start, create the form named TestRGB and place a Picture Box anywhere on the form. Set the Picture Box's **AutoRedraw** property to False. For now, you can ignore the other properties of the Picture Box. Next, place three Scroll Bar controls side by side on the form (see Figure 6.6). You may choose

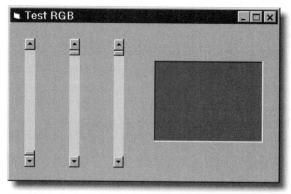

Figure 6.6 *The Test RGB form.*

either variety, horizontal, or vertical. We'll organize the scroll bars into a control array. To do this, simply name them all ColorBar. After you name the second one, VB will ask you to verify that you really want a control array.

You also need to set two properties on all three Scroll Bars: Set the **Max** property to 255, and set the **LargeChange** property to a value of about 5 or 10.

Double click on any of the three bars to display the framework for the **ColorBar_Change()** event procedure. Then, insert the following statement:

```
Picture1.Refresh
```

Because we declared a control array, all three Scroll Bars share the same event procedures. If you hadn't created a control array, you could have placed this same statement in each of the three separate Scroll Bar **Change** events.

Double click on the Picture Box, choose the **Paint** event from the Procedure list box, and insert this line:

```
Picture1.BackColor = RGB(ColorBar(0).Value, ColorBar(1).Value, ColorBar(2).Value)
```

Now run the program. As you move the thumb on the Scroll Bars, the Picture Box will change colors.

Remember that the VB **RGB()** function produces *dithered* colors. This means that it alternates pixels of 20 pure static colors to approximate the color value specified with the red, green, and blue color value arguments. Unless you stand at some distance from the display, dithered colors often resemble psychedelic plaids and checkerboards—not particularly attractive for high impact graphics!

Using More Colors—Loading a Palette

We can do better than dithered colors. The way to go is to use a more extensive palette of "pure colors," which are mixed at the hardware level. This can be done by loading a palette into a specific object such as a Picture Box, form, or Image Box. But none of these objects possesses a Palette property, so how do we load them?

The easiest way is to load a bitmap that contains a color table. In fact, VB comes with three special DIB files that contain a color table and a single pixel—just enough image data for them to qualify as bitmaps. If you load any of the files RAINBOW.DIB, PASTEL.DIB, or BRIGHT.DIB—either at runtime or by assigning them to the **Picture** property of a Picture Box control or a form at design time—the host object acquires access to the color palette contained in that file.

Once you load a color palette into a VB object, you need a way to select individual colors. And that is where VB's color handling begins to falter.

To see how this works, click on the Picture Box to select it and locate its **Picture** property in the Properties window. When you double click on the **Picture** property, VB displays the Load Picture dialog box. Select the VB directory and then select one of the DIB files. We recommend using PASTEL.DIB because its colors differ substantially from the system colors, which makes them easier to recognize as you experiment.

The **Picture** property doesn't show the name of the file. Instead, it simply says "(Bitmap)." Run the program again.

> **Note:** *If you want to remove a bitmap from the **Picture** property later, delete "(Bitmap)" from the property by selecting and deleting it from the edit control near the top of the Properties window. You do not have to delete one bitmap selecting another.*

As you change the Scroll Bar this time, the color of the Picture Box will jump from one palette color to another. Each time you change any of the three color values, **RGB()** locates the color palette entry that most closely matches the color specified. The three Scroll Bars can produce almost seven million combinations of red, green, and blue, but the palette holds no more than 256 colors, so as you change the RGB value, the displayed color will snap to one of those palette entries.

Using the API to Access Colors

Unless you have acutely sensitive color vision and an intuitive grasp of the relationship between numerical and actual color values, VB offers no way to select specific colors from the palette. You would think that with a table of

256 entries you could just choose colors by number. You can, but you need the Windows API.

Windows provides thirteen functions—and for C programmers, six macros—that control and retrieve information from the color palette. Among these you will find the macros used by the VB **RGB()** function to locate the closest matching color.

When referencing a color from an API drawing function, you use not just the three bytes that hold the red, green, and blue color values, but also a fourth byte that contains a flag value. The lowest-order byte contains the value of the red component. The highest-order byte contains a flag that indicates whether the reference is to a dithered color, a palette matched color, or an explicit palette index. The value of the high byte determines how the three lower-order bytes will be used to select a color. When you want to specify the color of a pen or brush in one of the API functions that create those objects, you can set the high byte to one of three values listed in Table 6.1.

This double word (four bytes) value is called a *COLORREF*, or color reference, which means that the proper place to use it is as a parameter in API drawing functions that require a color specifier. Later we'll look at some other structures that also hold color information.

Technically, the four fields in **COLORREF** are byte values, but in the Windows API, **COLORREF** is not a record-style data structure—it is just a long integer. To construct a color reference in VB, you need to pack the three RGB values and the flag byte into a long integer value:

```
Dim ColorReference As Long
ColorReference = RedValue + (GreenValue  * 256) + (BlueValue * 65536) + _
    (FlagValue * 16777216)
```

Table 6.1 *The possible high-order byte values in a GDI color reference.*

High-Byte Value	Result
&H00	Windows dithers the 20 reserved colors as the object is drawn. This is called an RGB color reference.
&H01	Instead of the value of the red color component, the lowest-order byte specifies the number, or index value, of a palette entry, so Windows uses the color it finds in that palette entry. The middle two bytes (bytes 1 and 2) should always contain value &H00. This is called a Palette Index reference.
&H02	Windows locates the palette entry that most closely matches the color determined by the red, green, and blue components specified in the three lower-order bytes. This is called a Palette RGB reference.

Selecting Colors by Numbers

This project uses a handful of API functions to display a palette in a 16×16 unit grid, as shown in Figure 6.7. Here are the steps to follow:

1. Create a new form named PaletExp.
2. Add the declarations (Listing 6.1) and the **Form_Paint()** event procedure (Listing 6.2) to the form.

 This project is located on the companion CD-ROM in the directory \VBMAGIC\PALETEX1, in the files PALETEX1.VBP and PALETEX1.FRM.

Creating the Palette Program

This simple project requires a single, empty form—no controls. Select the form and set its **Name** property to PaletExp and load PASTEL.DIB into its **Picture** property. With the exception of a single constant and its API function declarations, our program will reside entirely in the form's **Paint()** event procedure. The program won't run until we declare the API functions and specify a value for the constant **BLACK_BRUSH**. Insert the declarations shown in Listing 6.1 to the declarations section of the form.

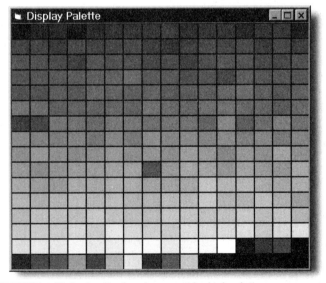

Figure 6.7 *PALETEX1 will display the form's current logical palette.*

Listing 6.1　The Declarations Section from PALETEX1.FRM

```
Option Explicit

#If Win32 Then
    Private Declare Function CreateSolidBrush Lib "gdi32" (ByVal crColor As _
        Long) As Long
    Private Declare Function DeleteObject Lib "gdi32" (ByVal hObject As Long) _
        As Long
    Private Declare Function GetStockObject Lib "gdi32" (ByVal nIndex As Long) _
        As Long
    Private Declare Function Rectangle Lib "gdi32" (ByVal hDC As Long, ByVal X1 _
        As Long, ByVal Y1 As Long, ByVal X2 As Long, ByVal Y2 As Long) As Long
    Private Declare Function SelectObject Lib "gdi32" (ByVal hDC As Long, ByVal _
        hObject As Long) As Long
#Else
    Private Declare Function CreateSolidBrush Lib "GDI" (ByVal crColor As Long) _
        As Integer
    Private Declare Function SelectObject Lib "GDI" (ByVal hDC As Integer, ByVal _
        hObject As Integer) As Integer
    Private Declare Function Rectangle Lib "GDI" (ByVal hDC As Integer, ByVal X1 _
        As Integer,  ByVal Y1 As Integer, ByVal X2 As Integer, ByVal Y2 As _
        Integer) As Integer
    Private Declare Function DeleteObject Lib "GDI" (ByVal hObject As Integer) _
        As Integer
    Private Declare Function GetStockObject Lib "GDI" (ByVal nIndex As Integer) _
        As Integer
#End If

Const BLACK_BRUSH = 4
```

Next, open that code window and enter the code shown in Listing 6.2.

Listing 6.2　The Form_Paint() Event Procedure from PALETEX1.FRM

```
Private Sub Form_Paint()
Dim Row As Integer
Dim Column As Integer
Dim BoxHeight As Integer
Dim BoxWidth As Integer
Dim ColorIndex As Long
Dim hBrush As Integer
Dim Dummy As Integer

    BoxWidth = ScaleWidth \ 16
    BoxHeight = ScaleHeight \ 16
    For ColorIndex = 0 To 255
        Row = ColorIndex \ 16 + 1
        Column = ColorIndex Mod 16 + 1
        hBrush = CreateSolidBrush(&H1000000 Or ColorIndex)
        Dummy = SelectObject(hDC, hBrush)
        Dummy = Rectangle(hDC, (Column - 1) * BoxWidth, (Row - 1) * _
            BoxHeight, Column * BoxWidth, Row * BoxHeight)
```

```
        Dummy = SelectObject(hDC, GetStockObject(BLACK_BRUSH))
        Dummy = DeleteObject(hBrush)
    Next ColorIndex
End Sub
```

Let's explore this procedure from the inside out. First we'll look inside the loop at the series of five function calls that draw the 256 colored rectangles.

The function **CreateSolidBrush()** performs the work of selecting colors. Its sole argument is a long integer—four bytes—which normally defines a color. But here, the logical operator **Or** sets the most significant byte to 1, which, as you may recall, redefines the color reference as an index into the palette. If we omitted the logical operation, leaving the high byte set to 0, the program would display only 256 shades of red, all dithered. With the high byte set to 1, color number 1 means the color defined in palette entry 1; color number 2 means the color defined in palette entry 2, and so on.

Under normal circumstances, we could use the **Line()** method to draw filled rectangles:

```
Line ((Column - 1) * BoxWidth, (Row - 1) * BoxHeight)-(Column * BoxWidth, _
    Row * BoxHeight), (&H1000000 Or ColorIndex), BF
```

But we want to delve a little deeper into the world of Windows colors and use the API calls. Also, in the previous releases of VB, this line would report an illegal function call, because previous versions intentionally prevented us from referencing the color palette by color index. Since we want to go beyond the simple **Line()** method, we instead call directly upon the Windows API function **Rectangle()**. (Isn't it odd that VB offers only its **Line()** method for drawing rectangles, yet Windows provides an explicit rectangle function?)

VB's graphic methods neatly package the steps of creating and selecting brushes, selecting colors, drawing objects, and releasing brushes. But because we're circumventing VB, we have to perform these tasks ourselves.

Creating a Brush

Before we can draw rectangles in the color of our choice, we have to create a brush of that color. Windows supports two kinds of drawing objects: brushes and pens. Brushes are used for filling areas, and pens are used for writing text and for drawing lines and borders. For this program, we will use the default **BLACK_PEN** to draw the outlines of the color rectangles, and we'll create brushes to fill them with the colors from the current palette.

Here are the steps required to create and use a brush:

1. Create a solid colored brush.
2. Select the new brush into the device context.
3. Draw a rectangle.
4. Select the system default brush back into the device context.
5. Destroy the colored brush created in step 1.

Once we create and select a brush, all the subsequent graphic drawing functions we call within that device context will use the brush. To stop drawing or to change colors, destroy the brush and create a new one. You cannot destroy a brush that is active in the device context, so we select the system's default **BLACK_BRUSH** before destroying the brush we've created.

Notice that in the statement that calls **CreateSolidBrush()**, you set the value of the high-order byte not by adding (which seems logical), but with this logical **Or** operation:

```
hBrush = CreateSolidBrush(&H1000000 Or ColorIndex)
```

It's a good idea to use logical operations when setting flags, because it prevents us from adding them more than once, which would produce an entirely incorrect result. Think about it: In this case we are setting the 25th bit, which appears to be equivalent to adding &H01000000 (decimal 16,777,216) to the existing flag block. If we perform a logical **Or** between values &H00000001 and &H01000000, we get &H01000001 (decimal 16,777,217). If we repeat the **Or**, this time combining the result, &H01000001, with the flag value &H01000000, we once again get &H01000001. If we perform these steps again, but add instead of **Or**ing, we start off in the right direction, because &H00000001 + &H01000000 is equal to &H01000001 (decimal 16,777,217). But the second time we add &H01000000, we get &H02000001 (decimal 33,554,433), an outcome which is not at all the same.

Occasionally, you may display a palette on the screen and find that it lacks some or all of the system default colors. When you request a color by its index value, you're asking for the color according to its position in the logical palette, not its position in the system palette. Windows maintains a map between the logical palette and the system palette. If the realized logical palette doesn't include the 20 system default colors, we lose access to them. This doesn't mean they go away—Windows needs those colors to properly display other objects on the desktop, including the desktop itself—we just can't access them because we can only directly reference colors in our logical palette. If you need the system colors, add them to your logical palette. (The palette editor, PalEdit, which Microsoft includes in the Multimedia Development Kit and in Video for Windows, provides a menu option called "Make Identity Palette," which performs this function automatically.)

Now that you know how to display the logical palette, you're ready to change it, or more specifically, to set and change specific colors.

Changing Colors in the Logical Color Palette

In this project we'll use Scroll Bars again to modify colors. But this time, instead of dithering the 20 Windows reserved colors, we'll select individual colors in the logical palette and use the API's palette functions to change their actual RGB values.

1. Create a form named PaletEx2. The completed form is shown in Figure 6.8.
2. Add the **Picture1_Paint()** event procedure (Listing 6.3).
3. Add the **Picture1_MouseDown()** event procedure (Listing 6.4) to select a color for editing.
4. Add the **BigColorBox_Paint()** event procedure (Listing 6.5) to display a larger swatch of the color as it's modified.
5. Add the **ColorScrollBar_Change()** event procedure (Listing 6.6) to update the colors on the screen.
6. Define the **PALETTEENTRY** structure.
7. Add a new code module called PALETEX2.BAS and fill in its declarations section (Listing 6.7).
8. Add declarations to the form (Listing 6.8).
9. Add a **Form_Load()** event procedure to initialize the **ColorSelected** variable (Listing 6.9).

 This project is located in the directory \VBMAGIC\PALETEX2 and includes the files PALETEX2.VBP, PALETEX2.FRM, and PALETEX2.BAS.

Creating the Logical Color Palette Program

For this project we need to confine the palette display to a Picture Box and reintroduce the Scroll Bar control array we used earlier in this chapter to experiment with VB's internal color control (see Figure 6.8).

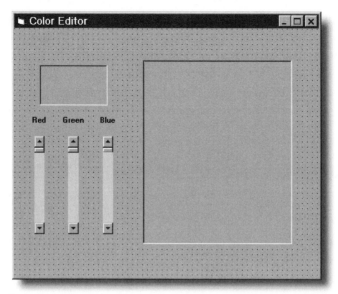

Figure 6.8   *The color editor form, PALETEX2.FRM, at design time.*

We'll display the palette matrix in a Picture Box. When the user clicks in the Picture Box, we'll use the X and Y coordinates provided by the **Picture1_MouseDown()** event procedure to calculate the identity of the color cell selected. We'll then retrieve the color settings from the logical palette, highlight the selection by displaying an oversized rectangle of that color centered on the same position, and set the Scroll Bars to the present RGB values. Each time the user changes a Scroll Bar setting, we'll update the color entry in the logical palette and re-realize that palette into the system palette so that the updated color will appear on the screen.

Let's begin with the **Picture1_Paint()** event procedure that draws the color matrix in **Picture1**. The complete procedure is shown in Listing 6.3.

Listing 6.3   The Picture1_Paint() Event Procedure from PALETEX2.FRM

```
Private Sub Picture1_Paint()
Dim Row As Integer
Dim Column As Integer
Dim BoxHeight As Integer
Dim BoxWidth As Integer
Dim Color As Long
Dim ColorIndex As Long
Dim hBrush As Integer
Dim Dummy As Integer

    hSystemPalette = GetStockObject(DEFAULT_PALETTE)
```

```
    hCurrentPalette = SelectPalette(Picture1.hDC, hSystemPalette, False)
    hSystemPalette = SelectPalette(Picture1.hDC, hCurrentPalette, False)

    BoxWidth = Picture1.ScaleWidth / 16
    BoxHeight = Picture1.ScaleHeight / 16
    For ColorIndex = 0 To 255
        Row = ColorIndex \ 16 + 1
        Column = ColorIndex Mod 16 + 1
        hBrush = CreateSolidBrush(&H1000000 Or ColorIndex)
        Dummy = SelectObject(Picture1.hDC, hBrush)
        Dummy = Rectangle(Picture1.hDC, (Column - 1) * BoxWidth, (Row - 1) * _
            BoxHeight, Column * BoxWidth, Row * BoxHeight)
        Dummy = SelectObject(Picture1.hDC, GetStockObject(BLACK_BRUSH))
        Dummy = DeleteObject(hBrush)
    Next ColorIndex
    If ColorSelected >= 0 Then
        Row = ColorSelected / 16 + 1
        Column = ColorSelected Mod 16 + 1
        hBrush = CreateSolidBrush(&H1000000 Or ColorSelected)
        Dummy = SelectObject(Picture1.hDC, hBrush)
        Dummy = Rectangle(Picture1.hDC, MaxVal((Column - 1.5) * BoxWidth, 0), _
            MaxVal((Row - 1.5) * BoxHeight, 0), (Column + 0.5) * BoxWidth, (Row + _
            0.5) * BoxHeight)
        Dummy = SelectObject(Picture1.hDC, GetStockObject(BLACK_BRUSH))
        Dummy = DeleteObject(hBrush)
    End If
End Sub
```

Much of this procedure comes from **Form_Paint()**, which was used in the previous project. Since we now have several objects in hand, we will explicitly de-reference **Picture1**'s properties. We could leave them alone—since they appear in **Picture1**'s **Paint** event, they default to **Picture1**'s properties—but for the sake of clarity, we have used the verbose form.

The **Paint** event performs two additional operations. To understand the first block of code we've added to **Picture1_Paint()**, we have to look ahead a little.

To *paint* with colors from the logical palette, we need just a color reference with a high byte value of 1 and a handle to the Picture Box's device context, which VB's designers have thoughtfully provided. But to *set* colors in the logical palette, we will also need a handle to the palette itself, which we'll have to fish out ourselves. The intuitive way to accomplish this would be to call an API function that would return a handle. Too bad no such function exists. Instead we'll have to play a little now-you-see-it-now-you-don't shell game with the palette handles.

The API function **GetStockObject()** returns the handle to the default system palette. Actually, this useful function returns a handle to any number of system objects, depending on the constant we supply as its one and only parameter. The constant used is called **DEFAULT_PALETTE**, which is de-fined in the Windows API Declaration Reference as:

```
Global Const DEFAULT_PALETTE = 15
```

You'll need to add this declaration to the declarations section of the code module.

Before we can capture the palette handle, we'll need a place to store it. For the shell game, we're also going to need a place to hold a second handle.

```
Dim hCurrentPalette As Integer
Dim hSystemPalette As Integer
```

Here's the problem. We can't just ask VB for the handle to the palette referenced by **Picture1**. We can, however, select a palette into **Picture1**, or rather into **Picture1**'s device context. Select a palette by passing a handle to a device context and a handle to a palette into a function called **SelectPalette()**. It just so happens that **SelectPalette()** returns the handle of the previously selected palette, so we can con Windows into giving us the handle to the PASTEL palette, by using **SelectPalette()** to switch **Picture1** over to the system palette. Then, once we have the handle to the PASTEL palette, we switch it back into the device context by calling **SelectPalette()** again.

```
hSystemPalette = GetStockObject(DEFAULT_PALETTE)
hCurrentPalette = SelectPalette(Picture1.hDC, hSystemPalette, False)
hSystemPalette = SelectPalette(Picture1.hDC, hCurrentPalette, False)
```

In the first statement, **hSystemPalette** receives the handle to the system default palette, the standard VGA colors. VB has already secretly selected PASTEL's palette into **Picture1**'s device context upon loading the file PASTEL.DIB, so in the second statement we throw in **hSystemPalette** to trick it into tossing us the handle to PASTEL's palette, which we capture into **hCurrentPalette**. Finally, we reselect PASTEL's palette back into the device context from which we snatched it, which harmlessly and without effect reassigns to **hSystemPalette** the handle to the system default palette.

Later we'll use **SelectPalette()** again to select the same logical palette into the device context of the other Picture Box, which we'll call **BigColorBox**. **BigColorBox** will display an even larger sample of the selected color.

The second operation we'll add to **Picture1_Paint()** will display the en-larged version of the selected color rectangle. The **Picture1_MouseDown()** event procedure (coming up next) will identify the color and set a form level variable named **ColorSelected** to the color's index value. In **Picture1_Paint()**, we'll use **ColorSelected** to position and draw the expanded rectangle:

```
If ColorSelected >= 0 Then
    Row = ColorSelected / 16 + 1
    Column = ColorSelected Mod 16 + 1
    hBrush = CreateSolidBrush(&H1000000 Or ColorSelected)
    Dummy = SelectObject(Picture1.hDC, hBrush)
    Dummy = Rectangle(Picture1.hDC, MaxVal((Column - 1.5) * BoxWidth, 0), _
      MaxVal((Row - 1.5) * BoxHeight, 0), (Column + 0.5) * BoxWidth, (Row + _
      0.5) * BoxHeight)
    Dummy = SelectObject(Picture1.hDC, GetStockObject(BLACK_BRUSH))
    Dummy = DeleteObject(hBrush)
End If
```

Now that we've finished with **Picture1_Paint()**, let's examine **Picture1_MouseDown()**. This event procedure (Listing 6.4) identifies the color index and sets the three Scroll Bar **Value** properties.

Listing 6.4 The Picture1_MouseDown() Event Procedure from PALETEX2.FRM

```
Private Sub Picture1_MouseDown(Button As Integer, Shift As Integer, _
    X As Single, Y As Single)
Dim CurrentPaletteEntry As PALETTEENTRY
Dim Row As Integer
Dim Column As Integer
Dim BoxHeight As Integer
Dim BoxWidth As Integer
Dim Dummy As Long

    BoxWidth = Picture1.ScaleWidth / 16
    BoxHeight = Picture1.ScaleHeight / 16
    Row = (Y \ BoxHeight)
    Column = X \ BoxWidth
    ColorSelected = Row * 16 + Column
    Dummy = GetPaletteEntries(hCurrentPalette, ColorSelected, 1, _
            CurrentPaletteEntry)
    SelectingAColor = True
    ColorScrollBar(0).Value = 255 - CurrentPaletteEntry.peRed
    ColorScrollBar(1).Value = 255 - CurrentPaletteEntry.peGreen
    ColorScrollBar(2).Value = 255 - CurrentPaletteEntry.peBlue
    SelectingAColor = False
    Picture1_Paint
    BigColorBox_Paint
End Sub
```

Adding the PALETTEENTRY Data Structure

To retrieve the RGB values for an entry in the logical palette, we have to construct a **PALETTEENTRY**, a four-byte data structure that comprises three color bytes and a flag byte.

```
Type PALETTEENTRY
    peRed As Byte
    peGreen As Byte
    peBlue As Byte
    peFlags As Byte
End Type
```

Notice the similarity between a **PALETTEENTRY** and a **COLORREF**—but there's a catch. They're not the same. First of all, the flag values of a **PALETTEENTRY** are not the same as the flag values of a color reference (more on those later). Second, the bytes are in the wrong order. If we were to declare a **COLORREF** structure (which is entirely theoretical, because there isn't one) it would look like this:

```
Type COLORREF (WARNING! THIS IS NOT AN OFFICIAL DATA STRUCTURE)
    crReferenceType As Byte
    crBlue As Byte
    crGreen As Byte
    crRed As Byte
End Type
```

Remember, a color reference is just a four-byte long integer. The lowest-order byte contains the value of the red component. The highest-order byte contains a flag that indicates whether the reference is to a dithered color, a palette matched color, or an explicit palette index. In the **PALETTEENTRY** structure, however, the whole thing is inverted. If we were to view the four bytes of a **PALETTEENTRY** as a long integer, the lowest-order byte would contain a flag value, and the highest-order byte would contain the value of the red component.

Since **type** declarations are always global, they must be made in the declarations section of a code module, not within a form. Once you define the new data type, you may declare a variable of the defined type anywhere, either locally or globally. The declaration of **PALETTEENTRY** will go into the file PALETEX2.BAS.

We can obtain the RGB color settings for any palette element, or for multiple elements, with the API function **GetPaletteEntries()**, as shown in Listing 6.4. The **PALETTEENTRY** structure is the component from which a logical palette is built. We use it either to set the palette entries in a logical palette, or, as in this example, to retrieve them. This procedure retrieves a single palette entry each time it is called. To get two or more contiguous entries, change the third argument to the appropriate number, and pass an array element as the fourth parameter. Of course, the array must extend far enough beyond the given element to accommodate the number of entries we request. In

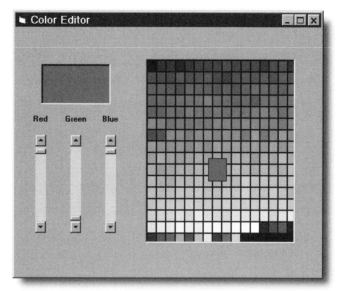

Figure 6.9 *PALETEX2 in action.*

other words, if you ask for 50 palette entries, and you pass in an array element called PaletteEntries(100), then the array **PaletteEntries()** had better be dimensioned to at least 149 elements.

Sometimes the Best Event Is No Event

The global Boolean variable, **SelectingAColor**, is used in the **MouseDown()** event procedure to eliminate unnecessary updates to the palette. Each time the user changes a Scroll Bar, we'll want to update the palette as shown in Figure 6.9. We'll do that in the **ColorScrollBar_Change()** event procedure. But when the user first selects a color for editing, we need to set the **Value** property of all three Scroll Bars to represent the RGB values for that color. When we set the **Value** property, VB also automatically generates an unwanted Scroll Bar **Change** event. We'll use **SelectingAColor** to communicate with the **ColorScrollBar_Change()** event procedure so that it doesn't waste time updating the palette three times as we set the Scroll Bar **Values** here in **Picture1_MouseDown()**. This is one of the pitfalls of event-driven programming; sometimes we trigger events that we would rather not.

Finally, we'll call the **Paint** events for **Picture1** and **BigColorBox** so that **BigColorBox** fills itself with the correct color, and **Picture1** displays its enlarged color cell. Notice that all the actual screen updates take place in the **Paint** events. By confining graphic operations to the **Paint** events, we enable

Windows to redraw our application window correctly whenever it is moved or uncovered.

In the Picture Box named **BigColorBox**, we'll place the **Paint** event shown in Listing 6.5.

Listing 6.5   The BigColorBox_Paint() Event Procedure from PALETEX2.FRM

```
Private Sub BigColorBox_Paint()
Dim hBrush As Long
Dim Dummy As Long

    hSystemPalette = SelectPalette(BigColorBox.hDC, hCurrentPalette, False)
    Dummy = RealizePalette(BigColorBox.hDC)
    hBrush = CreateSolidBrush(&H1000000 Or ColorSelected)
    Dummy = SelectObject(BigColorBox.hDC, hBrush)
    Dummy = Rectangle(BigColorBox.hDC, 0, 0, BigColorBox.ScaleWidth, _
            BigColorBox.ScaleHeight)
    Dummy = SelectObject(BigColorBox.hDC, GetStockObject(BLACK_BRUSH))
    Dummy = DeleteObject(hBrush)
End Sub
```

This procedure paints the entire Picture Box with the solid color selected in the **Picture1_MouseDown** event.

Handling the Scroll Bars

Now we're ready for the scroll bars. All three scroll bars perform the same operations in their **Change** events, so we declare them as a control array, as shown in Listing 6.6.

Listing 6.6   The ColorScrollBar_Change() Event Procedure from PALETEX2.FRM

```
Private Sub ColorScrollBar_Change(Index As Integer)
Dim Dummy As Long
Dim NewPaletteEntry As PALETTEENTRY

    If (Not SelectingAColor) And (ColorSelected > -1) Then
        NewPaletteEntry.peRed = 255 - ColorScrollBar(0).Value
        NewPaletteEntry.peGreen = 255 - ColorScrollBar(1).Value
        NewPaletteEntry.peBlue = 255 - ColorScrollBar(2).Value
        NewPaletteEntry.peFlags = 0

        hSystemPalette = GetStockObject(DEFAULT_PALETTE)
        hCurrentPalette = SelectPalette(Picture1.hDC, hSystemPalette, False)
        Dummy = SetPaletteEntries(hCurrentPalette, ColorSelected, 1, _
                NewPaletteEntry)
        hSystemPalette = SelectPalette(Picture1.hDC, hCurrentPalette, False)
        Dummy = RealizePalette(Picture1.hDC)
```

```
        'Picture1.Refresh
    End If
End Sub
```

To invert the Scroll Bars so that the colors reach their maximum intensity when the thumb is at the top of each bar, we subtract the Scroll Bar values from 255.

As we explained earlier, the Scroll Bars can change in response to two distinct events: when the user moves the thumb or when the user clicks the mouse in **Picture1** to select a palette color. By setting **SelectingAColor** in **Picture1**'s **MouseDown** event, we can prevent the Scroll Bar **Change** event from performing unnecessary updates to the palette. If **SelectingAColor** is **False**, then we can update the color.

The functions **SetPaletteEntries()** and **RealizePalette()** perform the real work. **SetPaletteEntries()**, like its sibling **GetPaletteEntries()**, takes four parameters. The first is a handle to the logical palette. The second and third parameters contain the number of the first palette entry we wish to change and the number of entries to change respectively. Just as we can retrieve several palette entries with a single call to **GetPaletteEntries()**, we can also set several palette entries with a single call to **SetPaletteEntries()**. The fourth parameter is a variable of type **PALETTEENTRY**, which contains the new color settings for the first palette entry we want to change. To change two or more palette entries in the same call, we would declare an array of **PALETTEENTRY** and pass the first element of the array as the fourth parameter of **SetPaletteEntries()**.

Once we've set the new color value, we have to instruct Windows to activate the new logical palette by mapping it into the system palette, which is the purpose of **RealizePalette()**. The new color will not appear on the screen until Windows realizes the logical palette. Technically, we should call the **RealizePalette()** function from within **Picture1**'s **Paint** event. At any time, our program could lose the input focus to another application that realizes a different palette. When our program regains the input focus, Windows will instruct it to repaint itself, and it will first reactivate its own colors by realizing its logical palette. In this case, however, VB does this for us, so we don't need to worry about it.

On to the Final Details

Finally, let's take care of the details. We need to add a code module named PALETEX2.BAS and insert the code from Listing 6.7 into its declarations section.

Listing 6.7   The Declarations Section of PALETEX2.BAS

```
Type PALETTEENTRY
   peRed As Byte
   peGreen As Byte
   peBlue As Byte
   peFlags As Byte
End Type

Global Const BLACK_BRUSH = 4
Global Const DEFAULT_PALETTE = 15
```

In the form's declaration section you'll need to declare all the API functions we've used, along with a few form level variables shown in Listing 6.8.

Listing 6.8   The Declarations Section of PALETEX2.FRM

```
Option Explicit

#If Win32 Then
   Private Declare Function SelectPalette Lib "gdi32" (ByVal hDC As Long, _
      ByVal hPalette As Long, ByVal bForceBackground As Long) As Long
   Private Declare Function CreateSolidBrush Lib "gdi32" (ByVal crColor _
      As Long) As Long
   Private Declare Function DeleteObject Lib "gdi32" (ByVal hObject As Long) _
      As Long
   Private Declare Function GetStockObject Lib "gdi32" (ByVal nIndex As Long) _
      As Long
   Private Declare Function Rectangle Lib "gdi32" (ByVal hDC As Long, ByVal X1 _
      As Long, ByVal Y1 As Long, ByVal X2 As Long, ByVal Y2 As Long) As Long
   Private Declare Function SelectObject Lib "gdi32" (ByVal hDC As Long, _
      ByVal hObject As Long) As Long
   Private Declare Function SetPaletteEntries Lib "gdi32" (ByVal hPalette As _
      Long,  ByVal wStartIndex As Long, ByVal wNumEntries As Long, _
      lpPaletteEntries As PALETTEENTRY) As Long
   Private Declare Function SendMessage Lib "user32" Alias "SendMessageA" _
      (ByVal hWnd As Long, ByVal wMsg As Long, ByVal wParam As Long, _
      lParam As Any) As Long
   Private Declare Function GetPaletteEntries Lib "gdi32" (ByVal hPalette As _
      Long, ByVal wStartIndex As Long, ByVal wNumEntries As Long, _
      lpPaletteEntries As PALETTEENTRY) As Long
   Private Declare Function RealizePalette Lib "gdi32" (ByVal hDC As Long) _
      As Long
#Else
   Private Declare Function SelectPalette Lib "user" (ByVal hDC As Integer, _
      ByVal hPalette As Integer, ByVal bForceBackground As Integer) As Integer
   Private Declare Function RealizePalette Lib "user" (ByVal hDC As Integer) _
      As Integer
   Private Declare Function CreateSolidBrush Lib "GDI" (ByVal crColor As Long) _
      As Integer
   Private Declare Function SelectObject Lib "GDI" (ByVal hDC As Integer, _
      ByVal hObject As Integer) As Integer
```

```
    Private Declare Function Rectangle Lib "GDI" (ByVal hDC As Integer, ByVal X1 _
        As Integer, ByVal Y1 As Integer, ByVal X2 As Integer, ByVal Y2 As _
        Integer) As Integer
    Private Declare Function DeleteObject Lib "GDI" (ByVal hObject As Integer) _
        As Integer
    Private Declare Function GetStockObject Lib "GDI" (ByVal nIndex As Integer) _
        As Integer
    Private Declare Function GetPaletteEntries Lib "GDI" (ByVal hPalette As _
        Integer, ByVal wStartIndex As Integer, ByVal wNumEntries As Integer, _
        lpPaletteEntries As PALETTEENTRY) As Integer
    Private Declare Function SetPaletteEntries Lib "GDI" (ByVal hPalette As _
        Integer, ByVal wStartIndex As Integer, ByVal wNumEntries As Integer, _
        lpPaletteEntries As PALETTEENTRY) As Integer
    Private Declare Function SendMessageByNum Lib "user" Alias "SendMessage" _
        (ByVal hWnd As Integer, ByVal wMsg As Integer, ByVal wParam As Integer, _
        ByVal lParam As Long) As Long
#End If

Dim ColorSelected As Long
Dim hSystemPalette As Long
Dim hCurrentPalette As Long
Dim SelectingAColor As Boolean
```

And just for good measure, we should initialize **ColorSelected** by setting it to -1 in the **Form_Load()** event procedure shown in Listing 6.9.

Listing 6.9   The Form_Load() Event Procedure from PALETEX2.FRM

```
Sub Form_Load ()
    ColorSelected = -1
End Sub
```

Although our program won't permanently update a color table (for that we would have to create or update a device independent bitmap file), it does demonstrate how to manipulate a logical palette and how the logical palette interacts with the system palette. From this kernel you could construct a complete palette editor, an essential component of any image manipulation system.

If it were not for VB repainting the Picture Box every time we change and realize the palette, we could perform some interesting real-time operations on a bitmap by dynamically altering its colors. Fortunately, once again Windows comes to the rescue with a function that will enable us to do this.

Using AnimatePalette() to Edit the Palette

This project shows you how to instantly change colors in the system palette by using the **AnimatePalette()** API function.

1. Copy the files from PALETEX2.MAK and remove the PASTEL.DIB bitmap from the **Picture** property of the Picture Box controls.

2. Add the **Form_Load()** event procedure (Listing 6.10) to create a logical palette from scratch.

3. Modify the **Picture1_Paint()** event procedure (Listing 6.11) to select in our custom palette.

4. Add calls at the end of **Picture1_MouseDown()** (Listing 6.12) to repaint the Picture Boxes.

5. Modify **ColorScrollBar_Change()** (Listing 6.13) to call **AnimatePalette()**.

6. Add the **Form_Unload()** event procedure (Listing 6.14) to dispose of the logical palette.

This project is located in the directory \VBMAGIC\PALETEX3, in the files PALETEX3.VBP, PALETEX3.FRM, and PALETEX3.BAS.

Creating the AnimatePalette() Project

For this project, we'll modify the program from the previous project so that instead of loading a bitmap and mangling its palette, it will create a new logical palette from scratch. We'll then modify the Scroll Bar **Change** event so it calls the API function **AnimatePalette()** instead of **SetPaletteEntries()**. These changes will affect several of the event procedures.

If you wish, copy the files PALETEX2.FRM and PALETEX2.BAS to PALETEX3.FRM and PALETEX3.BAS, respectively. Then start a new project called PALETEX3.VBP and use the VB menu option File | Add File to add the new copies of the form and code modules.

Next, remove the PASTEL.DIB file from the **Picture** property of **Picture1** and, if necessary, from **BigColorBox**. To remove a file from the **Picture** property, select the **Picture** property from the list box, select **(Bitmap)** in the edit box at the top of the property window, then press the Delete key.

We'll begin with the new **Form_Load()** event procedure (see Listing 6.10), where we'll build and activate our custom palette.

Building the Palette

To create a new logical palette, we have to build a Windows data structure called **LOGPALETTE**, then call **CreatePalette()** with that structure. **LOGPALETTE** includes three elements:

```
Type LOGPALETTE
    palVersion As Integer
    palNumEntries As Integer
    palPalEntry(255) As PALETTEENTRY
End Type
```

The first field in **LOGPALETTE** contains a constant, the hexadecimal value 300 (entered as &H300), which originally was meant to indicate the Windows version number. However, the value 300 works for either Windows 95 or Windows 3.1. The second field specifies the number of palette entries in the new palette. The third field in **LOGPALETTE** is not really a field at all, but an array of **PALLETTEENTRY** structures.

Listing 6.10   The Form_Load() Event Procedure from PALETEX3.FRM

```
Private Sub Form_Load()
Dim LogicalPalette As LOGPALETTE
Dim ColorIndex As Integer
Dim R As Integer, G As Integer, B As Integer

    LogicalPalette.palVersion = &H300
    LogicalPalette.palNumEntries = 216
    For R = 1 To 6
        For G = 1 To 6
            For B = 1 To 6
                ColorIndex = ((R - 1) * 36) + ((G - 1) * 6) + (B - 1)
                LogicalPalette.palPalEntry(ColorIndex).peRed = R * (255 \ 6)
                LogicalPalette.palPalEntry(ColorIndex).peGreen = G * (255 \ 6)
                LogicalPalette.palPalEntry(ColorIndex).peBlue = B * (255 \ 6)
                LogicalPalette.palPalEntry(ColorIndex).peFlags = PC_RESERVED
            Next B
        Next G
    Next R
    hCurrentPalette = CreatePalette(LogicalPalette)
    ColorSelected = -1
End Sub
```

For simplicity's sake, the loop in the middle of the **Form_Load()** event procedure creates only 216 colors, the maximum cubed integer under 256. You may substitute any method you wish as a color generator. Remember though, that Windows reserves 20 entries in the system palette for default system colors, so unless you modify the system palette (which requires a special set of API functions, and is *not* recommended), Windows will never realize more than 236 of your colors.

CreatePalette() takes the information stored in the **LOGPALETTE** structure, makes a living logical palette out of it, and returns the palette handle. The colors in our new palette, however, will not become available for screen painting until we realize the palette, which we'll do in the **Picture1_Paint()** event procedure.

Using the Custom Palette

In **Picture1_Paint()** (Listing 6.11), we can dispense with the shell game we used before to grab the palette handle—our call to **CreatePalette()** in **Form_Load** has returned a palette handle, which we've captured in the form level variable **hCurrentPalette**.

Listing 6.11 The Picture1_Paint() Event Procedure from PALETEX3.FRM

```
Private Sub Picture1_Paint()
Dim Row As Integer
Dim Column As Integer
Dim BoxHeight As Integer
Dim BoxWidth As Integer
Dim ColorIndex As Long
Dim hBrush As Integer
Dim dummy As Integer

    hSystemPalette = SelectPalette(Picture1.hDC, hCurrentPalette, False)
    dummy = RealizePalette(Picture1.hDC)
    BoxWidth = Picture1.ScaleWidth / 16
    BoxHeight = Picture1.ScaleHeight / 16
    For ColorIndex = 0 To 255
        Row = ColorIndex \ 16 + 1
        Column = ColorIndex Mod 16 + 1
        hBrush = CreateSolidBrush(&H1000000 Or ColorIndex)
        dummy = SelectObject(Picture1.hDC, hBrush)
        dummy = Rectangle(Picture1.hDC, (Column - 1) * BoxWidth, (Row - 1) * _
                BoxHeight, Column * BoxWidth, Row * BoxHeight)
        dummy = SelectObject(Picture1.hDC, GetStockObject(BLACK_BRUSH))
        dummy = DeleteObject(hBrush)
    Next ColorIndex
    If ColorSelected >= 0 Then
        Row = ColorSelected \ 16 + 1
        Column = ColorSelected Mod 16 + 1
        hBrush = CreateSolidBrush(&H1000000 Or ColorSelected)
        dummy = SelectObject(Picture1.hDC, hBrush)
        dummy = Rectangle(Picture1.hDC, MaxVal((Column - 1.5) * BoxWidth, 0), _
                MaxVal((Row - 1.5) * BoxHeight, 0), (Column + 0.5) * BoxWidth, _
                (Row + 0.5) * BoxHeight)
        dummy = SelectObject(Picture1.hDC, GetStockObject(BLACK_BRUSH))
        dummy = DeleteObject(hBrush)
    End If
End Sub
```

The rest of this procedure remains unchanged from the example shown in Listing 6.3.

You'll also want to slightly modify **Picture1_MouseDown()** (Listing 6.12) by adding calls at the end to the Picture **Paint** event procedures.

Listing 6.12   The Picture1_MouseDown() Event Procedure from PALETEX3.FRM

```
Private Sub Picture1_MouseDown(Button As Integer, Shift As Integer, X _
    As Single, Y As Single)
Dim CurrentPaletteEntry As PALETTEENTRY
Dim Row As Integer
Dim Column As Integer
Dim BoxHeight As Integer
Dim BoxWidth As Integer
Dim dummy As Long

    BoxWidth = Picture1.ScaleWidth / 16
    BoxHeight = Picture1.ScaleHeight / 16
    Row = (Y \ BoxHeight)
    Column = X \ BoxWidth
    ColorSelected = Row * 16 + Column
    dummy = GetPaletteEntries(hCurrentPalette, ColorSelected, 1, _
            CurrentPaletteEntry)
    SelectingAColor = True
    ColorScrollBar(0).Value = 255 - CurrentPaletteEntry.peRed
    ColorScrollBar(1).Value = 255 - CurrentPaletteEntry.peGreen
    ColorScrollBar(2).Value = 255 - CurrentPaletteEntry.peBlue
    SelectingAColor = False
    Picture1_Paint
    BigColorBox_Paint
End Sub
```

In the previous project, where we used **SetPaletteEntries()** to change colors, each time we changed the color and realized the palette the Windows Palette Manager issued a **WM_PALETTECHANGED** message to all the active windows, including VB. This caused **Picture1** to refresh repeatedly as we moved the color change Scroll Bars. **AnimatePalette()**, however, will not only change colors in the logical palette, but also directly in the system palette, which means we don't have to call **RealizePalette()** every time we change the selected color. Without the call to **RealizePalette()**, the Picture Boxes never receive Paint messages from the Palette Manager. So unless we call the **Paint** events explicitly after we set the Scroll Bar values, **Picture1** and **BigColorBox** won't always refresh, which means that the enlarged color cell won't appear, and **BigColorBox** won't display the selected color.

Plugging In the AnimatePalette() API Function

Next, let's modify the **ColorScrollBar_Change()** event procedure so it calls **AnimatePalette()** instead of **SetPaletteEntries()**.

Listing 6.13 The ColorScrollBar_Change() Event Procedure from PALETEX3.FRM

```
Private Sub ColorScrollBar_Change(Index As Integer)
Dim NewPaletteEntry As PALETTEENTRY

    NewPaletteEntry.peRed = 255 - ColorScrollBar(0).Value
    NewPaletteEntry.peGreen = 255 - ColorScrollBar(1).Value
    NewPaletteEntry.peBlue = 255 - ColorScrollBar(2).Value
    NewPaletteEntry.peFlags = PC_RESERVED
    If Not SelectingAColor Then
        AnimatePalette hCurrentPalette, ColorSelected, 1, NewPaletteEntry
    End If
End Sub
```

Only palette entries flagged as **PC_RESERVED** can be altered by **AnimatePalette()**. That's why we have to set the palette entry's flag byte to this value (hex 01) here and when we create the logical palette. This flag also prevents other windows from mapping their logical palettes to the reserved color entries, which confines the effects of color changes to the active window. Consequently, if you set all or most of the palette entries to **PC_RESERVED**, as we've done here, other windows will have to make do with the remaining colors. Sometimes that means that other bitmaps have no colors available to them except the 20 Windows reserved colors.

> **Note:** Do not confuse colors defined with **PC_RESERVED** with the Windows reserved colors. The sole purpose of **PC_RESERVED** is to enable palette animation and to confine its effects to the active window. Colors marked as **PC_RESERVED** are reserved not by Windows, but by the application.

To round out this program, shown in Figure 6.10, we need to dispose of the palette we created in the **Form_Load()** procedure. This is accomplished by using the **Form_QueryUnload()** event procedure shown in Listing 6.14. We'll call again upon the **DeleteObject()** API function, but first we have to "unselect" our palette from the device contexts of the two Picture Boxes.

Listing 6.14 The Form_QueryUnload() Event Procedure from PALETEX3.FRM

```
Private Sub Form_QueryUnload(Cancel As Integer, UnloadMode As Integer)
Dim dummy As Integer
Dim hSystemPalette As Integer
Dim hDummyPalette As Integer

    hSystemPalette = GetStockObject(DEFAULT_PALETTE)
    hDummyPalette = SelectPalette(Picture1.hDC, hSystemPalette, False)
    hDummyPalette = SelectPalette(BigColorBox.hDC, hSystemPalette, False)
    dummy = DeleteObject(hCurrentPalette)
End Sub
```

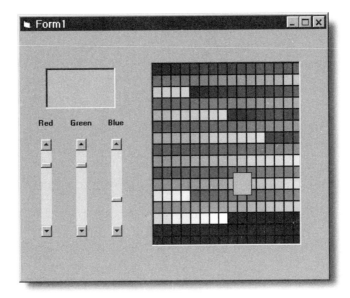

Figure 6.10   Using **AnimatePalette()** in the PALETEX3 project.

If we were to call **DeleteObject()** without first deselecting the palette from the device contexts, we would likely crash Windows. We know—we've done it, several times.

By the way, you may be wondering why we didn't just put the clean-up code straight into the **Form_Unload().** Well, VB won't run the **Form_Unload()** event procedure unless you use the Control menu button or the Control menu Close option to end your program. If you click on the End button on the Toolbar, your program will stop running, but you may leave behind unfinished business. Each time you run this particular program, it will eat enough memory to hold the newly created palette. If you repeatedly run and end the program with the Toolbar controls, you'll gnaw away at memory by about a kilobyte at a time. If you click on the Control menu button to stop the program properly, **Form_Unload()** will release the memory occupied by the palette. But, by placing the code into the **Form_QueryUnload()** procedure, we avoid that problem.

The projects we've completed in this chapter have used about half of the 14 API palette functions. In the next two chapters, we'll use these functions, along with many other GDI functions to perform some fancy graphical effects.

Explore the worlds of color palettes and raster operations and how they help you to produce some truly amazing images.

Chapter 7

Palette Animation and ROPs

Would you like to be able to get down to the hardware level and create some animated visual effects? With the help of a few powerful Windows API calls and some unique pixel and raster operations, you can bring your Visual Basic apps to life.

We're now ready to embark on the second phase of our amazing journey into imaging techniques. This time, we'll go a little deeper into the graphics black hole and see what new mysteries we can uncover. Along the way, we'll add to our imaging construction set. In particular, we'll show you how to use color palettes to perform a useful type of animation. Then, we'll look at some clever techniques for performing animation by manipulating pixels using raster operations. In the last part of the chapter, we'll explore the powerful Windows API **BitBlt()** function for performing magic with bitmap images. We'll show you how this special API call can be used to quickly copy bitmaps.

The Magic of Color Palette Animations

With direct access to the system palette, we can perform certain kinds of animation—animation that requires no actual changes to the displayed bitmap. With this technique, sometimes known as color cycling, we can simulate running water, atmospheric effects, lighting changes, and even moving objects without resorting to more resource-intensive, multi-frame animation methods. But don't let the terminology mislead you. Remember, **AnimatePalette()** doesn't activate a process; it just sets the palette entries indicated by its second and third parameters to the new colors you specify in its fourth parameter. These changes appear immediately on the screen, without the usual intermediate step of realization, which, when called repeatedly, creates the illusion of movement. Think of **AnimatePalette()** as a way to change displayed colors in real time—a tool with which to animate, not an engine.

Marquee Lights with Palette Animation

We'll now draw a series of colored dots to represent light bulbs around the perimeter of an otherwise blank form, then use palette animation to set them in motion, like the traveling lights on a theater marquee. Here's what we'll do:

1. Create a form with filename MARQUEE.FRM with no visible controls.
2. Insert the global and form level declarations (Listings 7.1 and 7.2).
3. Add these four form event procedures: **Form_Load()**, **Form_Paint()**, **Form_Resize()**, and **Form_Unload()** (Listings 7.3 through 7.5).
4. Add the Timer control and write its **Timer()** event procedure (Listing 7.6).

This project is located in the directory \VBMAGIC\MARQUEE, in the files MARQUEE.VBP, MARQUEE.FRM, and MARQUEE.BAS.

Creating the Marquee Project

Start a new project and set the form's **Scale Mode** property to type 3 - Pixel. We'll borrow most of the global declarations used in Chapter 4's final project. Listing 7.1 shows the complete set of global variables that should be assigned to MARQUEE.BAS.

Listing 7.1 The Global Declarations from MARQUEE.BAS

```
Option Explicit

Type PALETTEENTRY
    peRed As Byte
    peGreen As Byte
    peBlue As Byte
    peFlags As Byte
End Type

Type LOGPALETTE
    palVersion As Integer
    palNumEntries As Integer
    palPalEntry(4) As PALETTEENTRY
End Type

Global Const BLACK_BRUSH = 4
Global Const PC_RESERVED = &H1  '  palette index used for animation
```

You won't need the constant **DEFAULT_PALETTE** for this program, so we've removed it from the global declarations.

We can also pare down the form level declarations as shown in Listing 7.2.

Listing 7.2 The Declarations Section of MARQUEE.FRM, Based on the Declarations in PALETEX3.FRM

```
Option Explicit

#If Win32 Then
    Private Declare Sub AnimatePalette Lib "gdi32" (ByVal hPalette As Long, _
        ByVal wStartIndex As Long, ByVal wNumEntries As Long, _
        lpPaletteColors As PALETTEENTRY)
    Private Declare Function CreatePalette Lib "gdi32" _
        (lpLogPalette As LOGPALETTE) As Long
    Private Declare Function CreateSolidBrush Lib "gdi32" _
        (ByVal crColor As Long) As Long
    Private Declare Function DeleteObject Lib "gdi32" (ByVal hObject As Long) _
        As Long
    Private Declare Function Ellipse Lib "gdi32" (ByVal hDC As Long, ByVal X1 _
        As Long, ByVal Y1 As Long, ByVal X2 As Long, ByVal Y2 As Long) As Long
    Private Declare Function GetStockObject Lib "gdi32" (ByVal nIndex As Long) _
        As Long
    Private Declare Function RealizePalette Lib "gdi32" (ByVal hDC As Long) _
        As Long
    Private Declare Function SelectObject Lib "gdi32" (ByVal hDC As Long, _
        ByVal hObject As Long) As Long
    Private Declare Function SelectPalette Lib "gdi32" (ByVal hDC As Long, _
        ByVal hPalette As Long, ByVal bForceBackground As Long) As Long
#Else
    Private Declare Function CreatePalette Lib "GDI" (lpLogPalette As LOGPALETTE) _
        As Integer
```

```
    Private Declare Function SelectPalette Lib "User" (ByVal hDC As Integer, _
        ByVal hPalette As Integer, ByVal bForceBackground As Integer) As Integer
    Private Declare Function RealizePalette Lib "User" (ByVal hDC As Integer) _
        As Integer
    Private Declare Function CreateSolidBrush Lib "GDI" (ByVal crColor As Long) _
        As Integer
    Private Declare Function SelectObject Lib "GDI" (ByVal hDC As Integer, _
        ByVal hObject As Integer) As Integer
    Private Declare Function DeleteObject Lib "GDI" (ByVal hObject As Integer) _
        As Integer
    Private Declare Function GetStockObject Lib "GDI" (ByVal nIndex As Integer) _
        As Integer
    Private Declare Function Ellipse Lib "GDI" (ByVal hDC As Integer, ByVal X1 _
        As Integer, ByVal Y1 As Integer, ByVal X2 As Integer, ByVal Y2 _
        As Integer) As Integer
    Private Declare Sub AnimatePalette Lib "GDI" (ByVal hPalette As Integer, _
        ByVal wStartIndex As Integer, ByVal wNumEntries As Integer, _
        lpPaletteColors As PALETTEENTRY)
#End If

Dim hSystemPalette As Long
Dim hCurrentPalette As Long
Dim PaletteEntries(4) As PALETTEENTRY
Dim hPaintBrush(3) As Long
Dim LogicalPalette As LOGPALETTE
```

We've eliminated a few of the API function declarations we used in PALETEX3.BAS, and added a new one, **Ellipse()**. We also don't need all the variables we used for palette editing, and we can trim the **PaletteEntries** array down to five elements (0 through 4). We've added the array **hPaintBrush** to hold the handles of four individually colored brushes. With this approach, we don't have to create and destroy the brushes repeatedly as we draw the four separate shades of yellow, which we use to indicate varying degrees of brightness along the series of light bulbs. We've also moved the declaration of **LogicalPalette** to the form level, because we'll need it in two event procedures.

Adding the Event Procedures

We'll support four form events: **Load**, **Paint**, **Unload**, and **Resize**. The **Form_Load()** event procedure will again create the palette (see Listing 7.3).

Listing 7.3   The Form_Load() Event Procedure from MARQUEE.FRM

```
Private Sub Form_Load()
Dim ColorIndex As Integer

    LogicalPalette.palVersion = &H300
    LogicalPalette.palNumEntries = 4
    For ColorIndex = 0 To 3
```

```
        LogicalPalette.palPalEntry(ColorIndex).peRed = 127 + ColorIndex * 128 / 3
        LogicalPalette.palPalEntry(ColorIndex).peGreen = 127 + ColorIndex * 128 / 3
        LogicalPalette.palPalEntry(ColorIndex).peBlue = 0
        LogicalPalette.palPalEntry(ColorIndex).peFlags = PC_RESERVED
    Next ColorIndex
    hCurrentPalette = CreatePalette(LogicalPalette)
    'Form_Paint
End Sub
```

In this program, we declare the structure **LOGPALETTE** (in MARQUEE.BAS) with an array of only five elements:

```
Type LOGPALETTE
    palVersion As Integer
    palNumEntries As Integer
    palPalEntry(4) As PALETTEENTRY
End Type
```

You'll also notice that in the field **LogicalPalette.palNumEntries** we've specified only four elements. For this program we only need to create four live palette entries, but we'll use the fifth entry as a temporary buffer when we begin the palette cycling. You'll see what we mean when we get to the **Timer** event. It doesn't hurt to declare a **palPalEntry** array that's larger than the size specified in **palNumEntries**; the extra entries will be ignored by **CreatePalette()**.

The other big event procedure is **Form_Paint()**, which is shown in Listing 7.4. Once we finish writing this procedure, the rest is easy.

Listing 7.4   The Form_Paint() Event Procedure from MARQUEE.FRM

```
Private Sub Form_Paint()
Dim TopPos As Integer
Dim LeftPos As Integer
Dim BoxHeight As Integer
Dim BoxWidth As Integer
Dim DotWidth As Integer
Dim ColorIndex As Long
Dim Dummy As Integer

    hSystemPalette = SelectPalette(MarqueeForm.hDC, hCurrentPalette, False)
    Dummy = RealizePalette(MarqueeForm.hDC)
    For ColorIndex = 0 To 3
        hPaintBrush(ColorIndex) = CreateSolidBrush(&H1000000 Or ColorIndex)
    Next ColorIndex
    MarqueeForm.Cls
    DotWidth = MarqueeForm.ScaleWidth / 24
    ColorIndex = 0
    TopPos = DotWidth / 2
```

```
      MarqueeForm.CurrentX = DotWidth * 1.5
      Do While CurrentX < (ScaleWidth - DotWidth * 2)
         Dummy = SelectObject(MarqueeForm.hDC, hPaintBrush(ColorIndex))
         Dummy = Ellipse(MarqueeForm.hDC, CurrentX, TopPos, CurrentX + DotWidth, _
            TopPos + DotWidth)
         CurrentX = CurrentX + DotWidth * 1.5
         ColorIndex = ColorIndex + 1
         ColorIndex = ColorIndex Mod 4
      Loop
      LeftPos = MarqueeForm.ScaleWidth - DotWidth * 1.5
      CurrentY = DotWidth * 1.5
      Do While CurrentY < (ScaleHeight - DotWidth * 1.5)
         Dummy = SelectObject(MarqueeForm.hDC, hPaintBrush(ColorIndex))
         Dummy = Ellipse(MarqueeForm.hDC, LeftPos, CurrentY, LeftPos + DotWidth, _
            CurrentY + DotWidth)
         CurrentY = CurrentY + DotWidth * 1.5
         ColorIndex = ColorIndex + 1
         ColorIndex = ColorIndex Mod 4
      Loop
      TopPos = MarqueeForm.ScaleHeight - DotWidth * 1.5
      CurrentX = MarqueeForm.ScaleWidth - DotWidth * 2.5
      Do While CurrentX > DotWidth * 1.5
         Dummy = SelectObject(MarqueeForm.hDC, hPaintBrush(ColorIndex))
         Dummy = Ellipse(MarqueeForm.hDC, CurrentX, TopPos, CurrentX + DotWidth, _
            TopPos + DotWidth)
         CurrentX = CurrentX - DotWidth * 1.5
         ColorIndex = ColorIndex + 1
         ColorIndex = ColorIndex Mod 4
      Loop
      LeftPos = DotWidth / 2
      CurrentY = MarqueeForm.ScaleHeight - 2 * DotWidth
      Do While CurrentY > DotWidth * 1.5
         Dummy = SelectObject(MarqueeForm.hDC, hPaintBrush(ColorIndex))
         Dummy = Ellipse(MarqueeForm.hDC, LeftPos, CurrentY, LeftPos + DotWidth, _
            CurrentY + DotWidth)
         CurrentY = CurrentY - DotWidth * 1.5
         ColorIndex = ColorIndex + 1
         ColorIndex = ColorIndex Mod 4
      Loop
      Dummy = SelectObject(MarqueeForm.hDC, GetStockObject(BLACK_BRUSH))
      For ColorIndex = 0 To 3
         Dummy = DeleteObject(hPaintBrush(ColorIndex))
      Next ColorIndex
End Sub
```

As you can see, this procedure is pretty complex. Let's break it down into manageable pieces. First, we'll do some initialization.

```
      hSystemPalette = SelectPalette(MarqueeForm.hDC, hCurrentPalette, False)
      Dummy = RealizePalette(MarqueeForm.hDC)
```

Remember, when you work with logical palettes you should always select and realize your palette in the **Paint** event. This effectively returns control of the system palette to your program whenever it regains the focus.

This next segment, the **For** loop, creates one GDI brush for each of the four colors created in **Form_Load()**:

```
For ColorIndex = 0 To 3
    hPaintBrush(ColorIndex) = CreateSolidBrush(&H1000000 Or ColorIndex)
Next ColorIndex
```

Next, we'll clear the form, set a variable to the diameter we want to use for the colored dots, and initialize a counter called **ColorIndex** to the first color, zero.

```
MarqueeForm.Cls
DotWidth = MarqueeForm.ScaleWidth / 24
ColorIndex = 0
```

The bulk of the **Paint** event consists of four loops, each of which draws a series of dots along one edge of the form's client area. Except in the details of positioning and vertical versus horizontal orientation, all these loops are similar. The first one draws the dots along the top edge of the form:

```
ColorIndex = 0
' Get a starting Y position
TopPos = DotWidth / 2
' Get a starting X position
MarqueeForm.CurrentX = DotWidth * 1.5
Do While CurrentX < (ScaleWidth - DotWidth * 2)
    Dummy = SelectObject(MarqueeForm.hDC, hPaintBrush(ColorIndex))
    Dummy = Ellipse(MarqueeForm.hDC, CurrentX, TopPos, CurrentX + DotWidth, _
        TopPos + DotWidth)
    CurrentX = CurrentX + DotWidth * 1.5
    ColorIndex = ColorIndex + 1
    ColorIndex = ColorIndex Mod 4
Loop
```

The **Ellipse()** API function takes a handle to the device context and two pair of coordinates, the upper-left and lower-right corners of the rectangle that bound the ellipse.

```
Win32:
Declare Function Ellipse Lib "gdi32" (ByVal hDC As Long, ByVal X1 As Long, _
        ByVal Y1 As Long, ByVal X2 As Long, ByVal Y2 As Long) As Long
```

```
Win16:
Declare Function Ellipse Lib "GDI" (ByVal hDC As Integer, ByVal X1 As Integer, _
    ByVal Y1 As Integer, ByVal X2 As Integer, ByVal Y2 As Integer) As Integer
```

To draw a circle, make sure the two corners define a square instead of a rectangle.

We bet you're wondering why we just don't consolidate these four loops into two: one for the top and bottom rows, and one for the left and right columns. Here's the reason: The separation of the loops allows us to easily keep track of which color we're on (or more precisely, which palette entry we're on) as we start to draw each row or column. Since the dot diameter depends on the width of the form and not its height, we won't know how many dots will fit in each column until we draw them. Okay, we could pre-calculate that, but then we would have to deal with still more numbers to determine the correct starting color for each of the four sides. In any case, you may wish to refine the arithmetic to produce more consistent alignment of the dots within the form's boundaries.

When we finish painting the dots, we select the default **BLACK_BRUSH** back into the device context, and destroy our four colored brushes.

```
    Dummy = SelectObject(MarqueeForm.hDC, GetStockObject(BLACK_BRUSH))
    For ColorIndex = 0 To 3
        Dummy = DeleteObject(hPaintBrush(ColorIndex))
    Next ColorIndex
End Sub
```

The other two form event procedures, shown in Listing 7.5, perform the required housekeeping chores.

Listing 7.5 The Form_QueryUnload() and Form_Resize() Event Procedures from MARQUEE.FRM

```
Sub Form_QueryUnload (Cancel As Integer)
Dim Dummy As Long

    Timer1.Enabled = False
    Dummy = DeleteObject(hCurrentPalette)
    hSystemPalette = GetStockObject(DEFAULT_PALETTE)
    hDummyPalette = SelectPalette(MarqueeForm.hDC, hSystemPalette, False)
    Dummy = DeleteObject(hCurrentPalette)
End Sub

Sub Form_Resize ()
    Form_Paint
End Sub
```

Supporting the Timer Event

Finally, we reach the climax of this story, the **Timer** event. Before you can add this event, you'll need a Timer control. You can place it anywhere on the form. We left ours in the center. The Timer comes in handy for animation, because after all, it can be made to fire—if somewhat irregularly—several times per second. Listing 7.6 shows the complete **Timer1_Timer()** event procedure.

Listing 7.6   The Timer1_Timer() Event Procedure from MARQUEE.FRM

```
Private Sub Timer1_Timer()
Dim ColorIndex As Integer

   For ColorIndex = 4 To 1 Step -1
      LogicalPalette.palPalEntry(ColorIndex) = _
         LogicalPalette.palPalEntry(ColorIndex - 1)
   Next ColorIndex
   LogicalPalette.palPalEntry(0) = LogicalPalette.palPalEntry(4)
   AnimatePalette hCurrentPalette, 0, 4, LogicalPalette.palPalEntry(0)
End Sub
```

The **For** loop and the following assignment statement shift the colors one position to the right in the four-element palette array, and rotate the last element (array element 3) back to the beginning (array element Ø). Array element 4 serves only as a temporary storage position.

We call **AnimatePalette()** with four arguments. The first specifies the handle of the currently realized palette. The second specifies the index of the first entry in the currently realized logical palette, in this case entry 0. The third argument indicates the number of entries we want to change (four). And for the last argument we pass a pointer (which we do by leaving off the **ByVal** keyword) to the first element in the palette entry array, which contains the new color values for the entries in the logical palette. Each time the Timer ticks, the colors rotate their positions in the logical palette, and **AnimatePalette()** updates the system palette directly so the changes appear on the screen almost instantaneously.

That's it. Take the program out for a test drive, and you'll see the marquee lights shown in Figure 7.1.

Remember to stop your program from the Control-menu button on the form rather than with the VB End button or the Run|End menu option. Otherwise, you'll leave an orphan palette in memory. We cannot stress enough how diligent we must be in releasing resources, and how carefully this must be done. At best, a failure to release resources will gradually eat away available memory. At worst, a release performed without unselecting the object from all device contexts will cause an instant General Protection Failure.

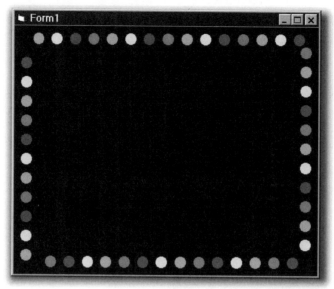

Figure 7.1   *Marquee lights simulated with the* **AnimatePalette()** *API Function.*

Pixels and Raster Operations

When you get right down to it, drawing on a graphics display amounts to nothing more than setting color values for individual pixels. That is, as long as we begin with a neutral background.

But what is a "neutral" background? White, the most common background color, is represented by 24 bits set to 1 (or true), which literally means the maximum presence of color. The opposite of white is, of course, black, which is represented by 24 bits set to 0—the total absence of color. To display a bitmapped image, we could disregard the existing colors of the drawing context, and replace every bit of every pixel with the bits from our new image. That's what happens when we invoke the **LoadPicture()** function to display a bitmap in a form, Picture Box, or Image control.

But sometimes, instead of replacing an existing image altogether, we only need to draw on top of it, or combine images. How do you do this? It's relatively easy with the addition of *raster operations*, or *ROPs*. Raster operations determine what happens when we try to place one pixel on top of another. (Impossible? Yes and no, but more on this in a moment.) Windows provides two sets of raster operation codes in Windows, the *ROP* codes and the *ROP2* codes. But just what is a raster operation? Let's begin another project to see.

When Is a Pen a "Not Pen"?

In this simple project, we'll take our first look at ROPs. Follow these steps to see how a raster operation affects a simple box drawing:

1. Open a new VB project. Go to the **Form_MouseDown** event procedure and insert the following line:

```
Line (X, Y)-Step(1000, 1000), , B
```

This command draws a square measuring 1001 twips on a side, beginning at the present cursor location, each time you click the left mouse button.

2. In the Properties window, set the **DrawMode** to 6, which VB calls *Invert*. Figure 7.2 shows you the effect Invert has in a drawing. It will be easier to see what's happening with thicker lines, so set the **DrawWidth** property to at least 5 (Figure 7.3).

 You'll find this project in the subdirectory \VBMAGIC\NOTPEN, in the files NOTPEN.VBP and NOTPEN.FRM.

That's it. Run the program. When you click the mouse anywhere on the form's client area, VB will draw a square. You may be surprised to learn that the color of the square's borders will depend entirely on the color of the background. To see this, stop the program and change the **BackColor** property of the form (double click on the **BackColor** property in the Properties window to display the VB Color Palette, then click on any color cell to select

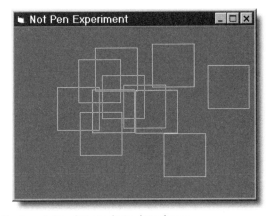

Figure 7.2 *Using the Invert drawing mode to draw boxes.*

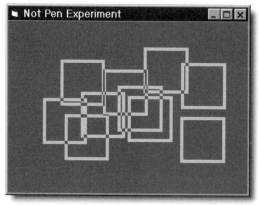

Figure 7.3   *The same program using a thicker brush.*

it). Now, when you run the program again and click the mouse, the squares will be drawn in a different color. Ordinarily, you would expect the **ForeColor** property to determine the current drawing color, but when the **DrawMode** is set to Invert, the foreground color is irrelevant. Try it. Change the **ForeColor** property and run the program again. You'll get the same result. The color of the square will always depend exclusively on the background color.

As we mentioned previously, there are two sets of raster operation codes in Windows, the *ROP* codes and the *ROP2* codes. The raster operations available in the **DrawMode** property of a form or Picture Box control are the simpler *binary raster operation*, or ROP2 codes, so called because they define the effects of combining only two pixels, a pen pixel and a destination pixel. As you can see in the **DrawMode** property, there are 16 ROP2 codes. (Later we'll talk about the ternary raster operators, or ROP codes, which combine as many as three pixels.)

Mixing Pixels

As was pointed out earlier, it is these raster operations that determine what happens when we try to place one pixel on top of another. This is, of course, impossible. Our display systems can display only one pixel at a time in each pixel position. But by combining the values of pixels in various ways, we can produce electronic effects that imitate physical effects such as color blending and transparency. And as an added bonus, we can do things that would be impossible with that goop we call paint.

Let's dissect the ROP2 code used in the previous project. A raster operation is a Boolean operation performed on two or more pixel values. That's all. Take the simplest case, a black pen on a white background. In the Windows default palette, black is stored in palette location 0, or binary 00000000, and white is stored in position 255, or binary 11111111. In the language of the Windows API, the raster operation that VB calls **Invert** is actually called **R2_NOT**. The logical **Not** operator performs the simplest of all Boolean operations—it flips the bits, so zeros become ones and ones become zeros. In fact, in the strictest sense, the **Invert** drawing mode doesn't perform a *binary* raster operation at all, because it doesn't combine the values of two pixels. It just flips the bits of the pixel that's already displayed in the device context. If the background is white, then drawing with the **Not** pen changes pixels to black; drawing over the pixels that have changed to black will change them back to white.

This works for other colors, too. If you set the background to the color stored in logical palette position 5, for example, the **Not** pen will change the color to the one stored in position 250.

```
Not   0000 0101  5
=     1111 1010  250
```

In all, Windows offers 16 binary raster operations. For the complete list, see Table 7.1.

> **Note:** *We don't know who created the term binary raster operation, but as terminology goes, this one is a real dog. Technically, all raster operations are binary, because they perform bitwise logical operations on pixel values. But in API terms, a binary raster operation is a ROP performed on two pixels. So, although all raster operations are performed on binary values, some raster operations are* binary *binary raster operations. Just remember that the binary raster operations are the 16 ROP2 codes.*

ROPs and the Split System Palette

In a true color display system, raster operations are performed on the whole RGB values of the pixels. This approach makes the results predictable. If you invert red, which is RGB value &H0000FF, you'll get cyan, RGB value &HFFFF00. If you invert blue (&HFF0000), you'll get yellow (&H00FFFF). But on a palette-based display, the ROPs operate on the pixels' palette references, not on their actual RGB values.

The division of the Windows system colors into two groups of ten, positioned at opposite ends of the palette, is meant to provide some semblance of meaningful behavior when colors are inverted. White inverts to black, dark blue inverts to bright yellow, light blue inverts to dark yellow, and so

Table 7.1   *The 16 Binary Raster Operations*

Windows Name	Visual Basic Name	Boolean Operation
R2_BLACK	1 - Blackness	&H00
R2_NOTMERGEPEN	2 - Not Merge Pen	Not (Pen Or Destination)
R2_MASKNOTPEN	3 - Mask Not Pen	(Not Pen) And Destination
R2_NOTCOPYPEN	4 - Not Copy Pen	Not Pen
R2_MASKPENNOT	5 - Mask Pen Not	Pen And (Not Destination)
R2_NOT	6 - Invert	Not Destination
R2_XORPEN	7 - Xor Pen	Pen XOr Destination
R2_NOTMASKPEN	8 - Not Mask Pen	Not (Pen And Destination)
R2_MASKPEN	9 - Mask Pen	Pen And Destination
R2_NOTXORPEN	10 - Not Xor Pen	Not (Pen XOr Destination)
R2_NOP	11 - Nop	Destination (Do nothing)
R2_MERGENOTPEN	12 - Merge Not Pen	(Not Pen) Or Destination
R2_COPYPEN	13 - Copy Pen	Pen
R2_MERGEPENNOT	14 - Merge Pen Not	Pen Or (Not Destination)
R2_MERGEPEN	15 - Merge Pen	Pen Or Destination
R2_WHITE	16 - Whiteness	&HFF

on. When raster operations apply to system palette references 10 through 245, however, the results can become meaningless. If, for example, palette entries 15 and 240 (which are binary complements) contained similar colors, the inversion could become so subtle that it may not even be visible. On a display system that works internally on an 18-bit model, the two colors may even look identical.

Unfortunately, we have to learn to live with this problem. It isn't practical to reorganize the palettes of most 256 color images to pair up the complementary colors. For one thing, the logical palettes of most photographic images tend to contain many similar colors in subtle shades—some images may contain no complementary colors at all. For most purposes, it hardly matters that inverted colors don't produce their complements. The **Inverted** pen and its close cousin, the **XOr** pen, are used primarily to draw contrasting lines across background bitmaps. In most cases, lines and filled shapes drawn with these pens will contrast enough with the background to stand out.

We've only scratched the surface of the binary raster operations, and they only hint at the power of the ternary raster operations. In later chapters we'll use some of the ROP2 codes. But right now, let's move on to the even more powerful ternary ROP codes, and the API functions that bring them to life.

Processing Bitmaps—Using BitBlt Functions

Although VB does support the Windows drawing modes, and provides reasonably flexible methods and controls for drawing bitmaps, it lacks an interface to one of Windows most powerful graphical features, the ***BitBlt*** (pronounced "bit blit") functions. In a nutshell, **BitBlt()** and its cousins **PatBlt()**, **StretchBlt()**, **SetDIBitsToDevice()**, and **StretchDIBits()**, copy bitmaps or pieces of bitmaps from one device context to another.

The blt functions not only copy images from place to place, some of them can combine as many as three bitmaps, using any of 256 distinct raster operations. The granddaddy of all blt functions is **BitBlt()**:

```
Win32:
    Private Declare Function BitBlt Lib "gdi32" (ByVal hDestDC As Long, ByVal X
    As Long, ByVal Y As Long, ByVal nWidth As Long, ByVal nHeight As Long, ByVal
    hSrcDC As Long, ByVal XSrc As Long, ByVal YSrc As Long, ByVal dwRop As Long)
    As Long

Win16:
    Private Declare Function BitBlt Lib "gdi" (ByVal hDestDC As Integer, ByVal X
    As Integer, ByVal Y As Integer, ByVal nWidth As Integer, ByVal nHeight As
    Integer, ByVal hSrcDC As Integer, ByVal XSrc As Integer, ByVal YSrc As
    Integer, ByVal dwRop As Long) As Integer
```

With nine arguments, the declaration for this function can look pretty intimidating. But it's not at all difficult to use. Let's review the parameters in order (using 32-bit conventions).

hDestDC   This is the handle to the *destination* device context. For example, if you were using **BitBlt()** to copy an image from Picture1 to Picture2, you would pass Picture2.hDC as the first argument.

X   A four-byte integer representing the X coordinate, usually in pixels, of the upper-left corner of the destination rectangle. This need not be zero; you may blt the source image to any location within the destination device context.

Y   A four-byte integer representing the Y coordinate of the upper-left corner of the destination rectangle.

nWidth   A four-byte integer representing the width of the destination rectangle. These measurements are given in *logical units*. For most of our purposes that means pixels, but Windows does support other measurement systems, most notably inches and millimeters. Watch out, though; Windows API functions do not support VB twips!

nHeight A four-byte integer representing the height of the destination rectangle.

hSrcDC The handle to the *source* device context. In our example, from the description of the first argument, you would pass Picture1.hDC as this parameter.

XSrc A long integer representing the X coordinate of the upper-left corner of the source rectangle. Keep in mind that the *origin* (coordinates 0,0) is in the upper-left corner of any client area. X values increase from left to right; Y values increase from top to bottom. (Although you can change this, we'll stick to the default.)

YSrc A long integer representing the Y coordinate of the upper-left corner of the source rectangle.

dwROP A long integer representing one of the 256 raster operation codes. For a simple copy, this would be set to **SRCCOPY**, which is a Windows constant with a value of &HCC0020.

BitBlting—The Quick and Easy Recipe

The easiest way to understand **BitBlt()** is to see it in action. Let's do a simple experiment in which we'll copy part of an image in one Picture Box to a second Picture Box on the same form as shown in Figure 7.4. Follow these steps to try out the **BitBlt()** function:

1. Start a new VB program with a single form, and place two Picture Box controls side by side on the form.

2. Set the **ScaleMode** properties of both Picture Boxes to type 3 - Pixel. Set the **Picture** property of Picture1 to any bitmap you have handy. Then add a Command Button, setting its **Name** property to CopyButton and its caption to Copy Picture.

3. Fill in the **CopyButton_Click()** event procedure and the declarations section of the form as they appear in Listings 7.7 and 7.8.

This project is located in the subdirectory \VBMAGIC\BITBLTEX, in the files BITBLTEX.VBP and BITBLTEX.FRM.

Listing 7.7   The CopyButton_Click() Event Procedure from BITBLTEX.FRM

```
Private Sub CopyButton_Click()
Dim Dummy As Long

    Dummy = BitBlt(Picture2.hDC, 0, 0, Picture2.ScaleWidth, _
           Picture2.ScaleHeight, Picture1.hDC, 0, 0, SRCCOPY)
End Sub
```

Listing 7.8   The Declarations Section from BITBLTEX.FRM

```
Option Explicit

#If Win32 Then
    Private Declare Function BitBlt Lib "gdi32" (ByVal hDestDC As Long, ByVal X _
        As Long, ByVal Y As Long, ByVal nWidth As Long, ByVal nHeight As Long, _
        ByVal hSrcDC As Long, ByVal XSrc As Long, ByVal YSrc As Long, _
        ByVal dwRop As Long) As Long
#Else
    Private Declare Function BitBlt Lib "gdi" (ByVal hDestDC As Integer, ByVal X _
        As Integer, ByVal Y As Integer, ByVal nWidth As Integer, ByVal nHeight _
        As Integer, ByVal hSrcDC As Integer, ByVal XSrc As Integer, ByVal YSrc _
        As Integer, ByVal dwRop As Long) As Integer
#End If

Const SRCCOPY = &HCC0020
```

We've oversimplified this experiment for the sake of clarity. For one thing, we've assumed that Picture2 won't be larger than Picture1. **BitBlt()** doesn't

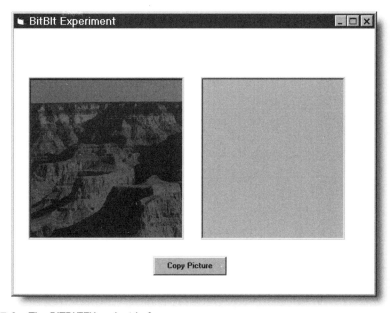

Figure 7.4   *The BITBLTEX project before a copy.*

automatically *clip* to the dimensions of the source device context when the source is smaller than the destination, which means it would copy portions of the screen outside the Picture Box to fill the client area of Picture2. We also have failed to grab the palette from Picture1 and select it into Picture2. The colors display properly, however, because the image has already been mapped in Picture1 to the system palette by VB. **BitBlt()** makes no attempt to re-map the pixel values; it just copies them as they are to the new device context. As long as the appropriate logical palette remains selected and realized into the system palette, both the original image and the copy will display correctly.

We'll show you how to use the blt functions to do a bunch of exciting things in later chapters. But before you can do much more than blast pieces of pictures from window to window, you have to understand the effects of raster operations. In the our next project we're going to combine ROPs and **BitBlt()** to demonstrate what happens when you run bitmaps through the Boolean wringer.

The Standard Windows Raster Operations

In this project, we'll try out the 15 standard raster operations. Because they're so useful, the creators of Windows have given these ROP codes their own names, in the form of Windows constants. Here's what we'll do:

1. Build the TestROPS form stored in the file ROPEXP1.FRM.
2. Add the **Form_Load()** event procedure to the form (Listing 7.9).
3. Add the **ResultPic_Paint()** event procedure (Listing 7.10) and the **ROPList_Click()** event procedure (Listing 7.11) to the form.
4. Add the necessary declarations to the form (Listing 7.12).

This project is located in the subdirectoy \VBMAGIC\ROPEXP1, in the files ROPEXP1.VBP and ROPEXP1.FRM.

Creating the Form

For this program, we'll need a single form, with three small Picture Box controls and a List Box. Set the **Name** property of the form to TestROPS. The first Picture Box, which we'll call SourcePic, will contain a bitmap in the form of a monochrome icon called WHITEDOT.ICO. The second Picture Box, called DestPic, will contain another monochrome icon called CORNERS.ICO. We're using black-and-white images here because their trivial mappings to palette entries &H00 and &HFF make it much easier to discern the effects of raster operations; remember, black represents a binary value of all zeros, white represents all ones. Any logical operation we perform on black and white pixels will produce black or white pixels as a result—no funny colors to worry about here.

You might try to size the Picture Box controls so they just fit the icon images, which are always 32×32 pixels. Set the **ScaleMode** to 3 - Pixel for all three Picture Boxes, which allows you to specify the **ScaleWidth** and **ScaleHeight** properties in pixels. By specifying this **ScaleMode** for the form, you will also be able specify the external control dimensions, determined by the **Height** and **Width** properties, in pixels. Otherwise, you must use VB's own peculiar scale mode, *twips* (1/1440 of an inch—based on average screen size). You may have to play with the dimensions to get them neatly framed, but don't worry too much about it because the program will work even if the Picture Boxes are oddly sized. Name the third Picture Box ResultPic, leave its **Picture** property unassigned, and set its **AutoRedraw** property to False.

Loading the List Box with the ROP Codes

In the List Box we'll build a list of the fifteen ROP codes that are blessed with names. With 256 possible raster operations, many look pretty esoteric; some have probably never been used. But fifteen of them turn up often enough that they earned their place among the named Windows constants. These widely used ROPs are listed in Table 7.2, along with the logical operations they perform. The code that loads the List Box resides in the **Form_Load()** event procedure as shown in Listing 7.9.

Listing 7.9   The Form_Load() Event Procedure from ROPEXP1.FRM

```
Private Sub Form_Load()
   ROPSList.AddItem "SRCCOPY = &HCC0020"
   ROPSList.AddItem "SRCPAINT = &HEE0086"
   ROPSList.AddItem "SRCAND = &H8800C6"
   ROPSList.AddItem "SRCINVERT = &H660046"
   ROPSList.AddItem "SRCERASE = &H440328"
   ROPSList.AddItem "NOTSRCCOPY = &H330008"
   ROPSList.AddItem "NOTSRCERASE = &H1100A6"
   ROPSList.AddItem "MERGECOPY = &HC000CA"
   ROPSList.AddItem "MERGEPAINT = &HBB0226"
   ROPSList.AddItem "PATCOPY = &HF00021"
   ROPSList.AddItem "PATPAINT = &HFB0A09"
   ROPSList.AddItem "PATINVERT = &H5A0049"
   ROPSList.AddItem "DSTINVERT = &H550009"
   ROPSList.AddItem "BLACKNESS = &H000042&"
   ROPSList.AddItem "WHITENESS = &HFF0062"
End Sub
```

Table 7.2   *The 15 Named Ternary ROP Codes*

Name	Logical Operation	Value
SRCCOPY	Source	&HCC0020&
SRCPAINT	Source Or Destination	&HEE0086&
SRCAND	Source And Destination	&H8800C6&
SRCINVERT	Source XOr Destination	&H660046&
SRCERASE	Source And (Not Destination)	&H440328&
NOTSRCCOPY	Not Source	&H330008&
NOTSRCERASE	Not (Source Or Destination)	&H1100A6&
MERGECOPY	Source And Pattern	&HC000CA&
MERGEPAINT	(Not Source) Or Destination	&HBB0226&
PATCOPY	Pattern	&HF00021&
PATPAINT	((Not Source) Or Pattern) Or Destination	&HFB0A09&
PATINVERT	Pattern XOr Destination	&H5A0049&
DSTINVERT	Not Destination	&H550009&
BLACKNESS	0	&H000042&
WHITENESS	1	&HFF0062&

The Paint Event

The **ResultPic_Paint()** event procedure (Listing 7.10) will do the work of "blting" the two images to ResultPic, with the ROP code chosen from the List Box. Things are a little turned around here. We refer to the two bitmaps as the source and destination images. The purpose of the ROP is to control what happens when we lay the source bitmap over the destination. If you look at the **Paint** event, you'll see that although it looks like we're picking up both images and combining them into **ResultPic**, we're really copying the bitmap contained in **DestPic** to **ResultPic** before each ROP-based transfer. We do use a ROP code to do this, **SRCCOPY**, but as its name implies, **SRCCOPY** performs no transformation on the image. It just copies an image from one device context to another, overwriting any image that may have been there before. We then use the selected ROP code with **BitBlt()** to blt the **SourcePic** into the copy of the destination bitmap that sits in **ResultPic**.

Listing 7.10   The ResultPic_Paint() Event Procedure from ROPEXP1.FRM

```
Private Sub ResultPic_Paint()
Dim ROPType As Long
```

```
Dim Param As String
Dim Dummy As Integer

   DestPic.Cls
   Param = ROPSList.Text
   ROPType = Val(Mid$(Param, InStr(Param, "=") + 1))

   Dummy = BitBlt(ResultPic.hDC, 0, 0, 31, 31, DestPic.hDC, 0, 0, SRCCOPY)
   Dummy = BitBlt(ResultPic.hDC, 0, 0, 31, 31, SourcePic.hDC, 0, 0, ROPType)
End Sub
```

The second **BitBlt()** in the **Paint** event performs the raster operation selected from the List Box by combining the image in SourcePic with the image in ResultPic. Figure 7.5 shows ROPEXP1 performing a SCRPAINT operation.

Finishing the Program

The **ROPSList_Click()** event procedure will do nothing but call **ResultPic_Paint()**.

Listing 7.11   The ROPSList_Click() Event Procedure from ROPEXP1.FRM

```
Sub ROPSList_Click ()
   ResultPic_Paint
End Sub
```

Before you can run this program, you'll need to declare the **BitBlt()** function and **SRCCOPY** (Listing 7.12).

Listing 7.12   The Declarations Section of ROPEXP1.FRM

```
Option Explicit

#If Win32 Then
   Private Declare Function BitBlt Lib "gdi32" (ByVal hDestDC As Long, ByVal X _
      As Long, ByVal Y As Long, ByVal nWidth As Long, ByVal nHeight As Long, _
      ByVal hSrcDC As Long, ByVal XSrc As Long, ByVal YSrc As Long, _
      ByVal dwRop As Long) As Long
#Else
   Private Declare Function BitBlt Lib "gdi" (ByVal hDestDC As Integer, ByVal X _
      As Integer, ByVal Y As Integer, ByVal nWidth As Integer, ByVal nHeight _
      As Integer, ByVal hSrcDC As Integer, ByVal XSrc As Integer, ByVal YSrc _
      As Integer, ByVal dwRop As Long) As Integer
#End If

Const SRCCOPY = &HCC0020
```

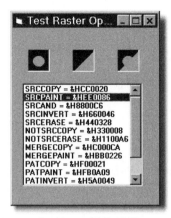

Figure 7.5 *The ROPEXP1 project performing a SRCPAINT operation.*

The SRCINVERT ROP Code—Up Close and Personal

The **SRCINVERT** ROP code demonstrates a logical operation that finds its way into all kinds of situations. When you run ROPEXP1 and select **SRCINVERT** from the List Box, you'll notice that the resulting image more closely resembles a combination of the source and destination images than that produced by any of the other ROPs. The image retains the entire dot shape, as well as the opposed corners. **SRCINVERT** performs an exclusive-or operation, annotated as **XOr**, between the source and destination image pixel values. An **XOr** sets to 1 only those bits set in either the destination or source pixel, but not those that are set in both. The color inversion of half of the dot in the lower-right corner is caused by this property of the **XOr** operator. This area in both the source and destination images is colored white, all bits set to 1 (only because logical palette entry 255 happens to reference RGB color &HFFFFFF, which also represents all bits set). When **XOr** finds a bit set to 1 in both pixels, it changes the result to 0, resulting in a negative image wherever the dot overlaps the white areas of the other image.

The other interesting property of **SRCINVERT** is that it can reverse itself. If you could reapply the source image to the resulting image, again with the **XOr** operation, the dot would disappear. (Try modifying the program to test this out.) The semi-circle in the upper-left corner in both the source image and the resulting image is white. When you apply **XOr** to two white pixels, you get black, which would remove the semi-circle from that corner. The semi-circle in the lower-right corner is white in the source image and black in the resulting image. **XOr** would change those pixels to white, removing the black semi-circle from the lower corner. Poof—no more dot! See Table 7.3 for

Table 7.3 *Repeating an XOr Operation Results in the Same Value as the Original Destination Bit*

Source Bit	Destination Bit	Result A	Source Bit	Result B
0	XOr 0	= 0	XOr 0	= 0
1	XOr 0	= 1	XOr 1	= 0
0	XOr 1	= 1	XOr 0	= 1
1	XOr 1	= 0	XOr 1	= 1

a better understanding of this unique occurrence. You might find it difficult to imagine this effect in multi-colored images, but it works just the same. Just think of the pixels as binary numbers. Bits is bits. And for any given destination bit, two **XOr** operations with the same source bit cancel out. In fact, the same operation works on full 24-bit color bitmaps.

The **XOr** operation turns up in many other useful ROP codes, and we'll be using it in the next chapter to do some cool things to pictures.

Some of the ROP codes we've tested with the program ROPEXP1.VBP appear to produce identical results. **MERGECOPY**, **PATPAINT**, **PATCOPY**, and **PATINVERT** all appear to do nothing to the destination image. There's a perfectly good explanation for this. They don't. The ternary ROP codes (as opposed to the binary ROP2 codes) combine the pixels of not just two, but three bitmaps, and until we plug in the third bitmap, some of these ROPs appear to work the same. In Chapter 8, you'll not only meet this mysterious stranger, but in the process you'll learn how to build a bitmap from the inside out. Then you'll learn how to combine all this knowledge of pixels, palettes, and raster operations to perform knockout visual effects.

Learn how to take our basic techniques of raster operations one step further to create dazzling visual effects.

Advanced Imaging— Special Visual Effects

In the previous two chapters, we explored how Windows displays pictures. You learned how the Palette Manager works in 8-bit color mode, and how to modify and transfer images, or portions of images, with some simple blts and raster operations. Now it's time to pull this information together and expand on it for performing visual trickery, like dissolving one picture into another. The techniques presented in this chapter can easily be incorporated into your own custom multimedia applications. We'll start by exploring a simple dissolve you can easily use to add an animated effect to images as they are displayed. In order to create the dissolve effect, we'll need to revisit ROPs and the flexible pattern brush. As we work our way into more bitmap trickery, we'll also show you how to combine bitmaps to create interesting visual effects.

Introducing the Dissolve

For decades, filmmakers have used dissolves to produce the visual effect of fading from one image into another. To produce this effect on movie film, all you have to do is expose each frame of the film to both pictures (the original and the end result), gradually decreasing the intensity of one while increasing the intensity of the other, frame by frame, until the original image has vanished.

Creating a dissolve with your computer, however, is another story. You could simulate the photographic process on a true color display by shifting the value of each pixel from its color in the first image to its color in the second image. Unfortunately, this process would take a long time for bitmaps of any significant size—even on a lightning-fast PC. Of course, you could perform the dissolve steps, capture them, then play the whole thing back as an animation. That would be fine if you knew the order of all the transitions you wanted in your presentation, but it could prohibit spontaneous dissolves, especially if you have a large number of images.

Another approach is to replace one image with the other, pixel by pixel. But this process *looks* digital. Also, when you try to use this technique on an 8-bit display, you once again bump into the palette problem. If each image is composed from a palette of 256 colors, then the combined images that appear during the dissolve could require as many as 512 colors, which the display system can't provide. It's easy to dissolve from one image to another if the images share a common palette, or if each of the images uses only a few colors so that their combined palettes don't require more than 256 palette entries. But the general-purpose solution to this problem needs to anticipate the worst case.

There is a compromise. By combining the pixel-by-pixel replacement technique with a color translation, you can generate a pretty attractive dissolve. Raster operations will work on either a true color or palettized display, but for 8-bit images, the color translation becomes practical only with the assistance of the Palette Manager.

Let's begin by digging deeper into raster operations and bitmaps.

ROPs Revisited

At the end of Chapter 7, we pointed out that some of the raster operations we tested in the ROPEXP1 project produced identical results, because some of the fifteen named ROP codes manipulate three bitmaps, instead of just two.

The third bitmap, the one conspicuously absent from our last project, is the *Pattern Brush*. Brushes are special square bitmaps, eight pixels on a side, that fill an area with a repeating pattern. You most often see them used with GDI functions that draw shapes. But you can also use them with **BitBlt()** to add repeating patterns to entire bitmaps, or to combinations of bitmaps.

In our next project, ROPEXP2, we'll add the brush bitmap to **BitBlt()**. To do that, we have to create the brush, which we can do either by drawing it or by generating it from within our program. Because brushes are such small bitmaps, this is a good time to show you how a bitmap is built, from the ground up. Although a slight digression here, building bitmaps is a skill you need to master before we get to the dissolve project later in this chapter.

Building a Bitmap

This project shows you how to create a brush and use it in the **BitBlt()** function. Here are the steps to follow:

1. Create a new form with filename ROPEXP2.FRM.
2. Add the function **CreateTheBrush()** (Listing 8.1) to the form.
3. Add the event procedures, **BrushPic_Paint()**, **ResultPic_Paint()**, and **Form_Load()** (Listings 8.2 through 8.4).
4. Place the ROP names and their hex codes in a text file named ROPSLIST.TXT.
5. Create a code module named ROPEXP2.BAS and add the required declarations (Listing 8.5).

You'll find this project in the subdirectory \VBMAGIC\ROPEXP2, in the files ROPEXP2.VBP, ROPEXP2.FRM, ROPEXP2.BAS, and ROPSLIST.TXT.

Inside the Bitmap Data Structures

The entire bitmap creation process for this project resides in the **CreateTheBrush()** function. The **Type** declarations for the structures used by this function are located in ROPEXP2.BAS. Let's start by looking at the device-independent bitmap (DIB) data structures needed, and then we'll write the **CreateTheBrush()** function.

The DIB data structure consists of either four or five major elements, depending on whether the structure is in memory or on a disk file. In this project, we'll be using the four-headed variety (we'll get to the fifth element later). The first of these components, the **BITMAPINFOHEADER**, indicates the dimensions of the bitmap, the total number of bytes in the image, and the number of color bits per pixel:

```
Type BITMAPINFOHEADER '40 bytes
    biSize As Long
    biWidth As Long
    biHeight As Long
    biPlanes As Integer
    biBitCount As Integer
    biCompression As Long
    biSizeImage As Long
    biXPelsPerMeter As Long
    biYPelsPerMeter As Long
    biClrUsed As Long
    biClrImportant As Long
End Type
```

The second DIB element is the color table, which consists of a series of four-byte structures of type **RGBQUAD**, similar, but not identical to **PALETTEENTRY** and the long integer color reference. This is the third type of four-byte color structure, and once again, its fields have been shuffled:

```
Type RGBQUAD
    rgbBlue        As Byte
    rgbGreen       As Byte
    rgbRed         As Byte
    rgbReserved    As Byte
End Type
```

The **BITMAPINFOHEADER** and its related **RGBQUAD**s are gathered together under one roof in the third type of DIB element, a structure called **BITMAPINFO**:

```
Type BITMAPINFO
    bmiHeader As BITMAPINFOHEADER
    bmiColors(1) As RGBQUAD
End Type
```

The number of elements in the array **bmiColors()** depends on the number of colors specified in the field **biClrUsed** in the **BITMAPINFOHEADER**. If you set **biClrUsed** to 0, then the **bmiColors()** must contain the exact number of colors defined by **biBitCount**. In other words, if **biBitCount** equals 8, then **bmiColors()** must include 256 elements, which requires an upper bound of 255. For a bit count of 4, dimension the array to 15, for a total of 16 elements. You may enter a number other than zero in **biClrUsed** to specify a number of colors fewer than the maximum allowed by the bit count. In a true color bitmap, **biBitCount** equals 24, **biClrUsed** equals 0, and **BITMAPINFO** includes no **RGBQUAD**s.

The first field in our **BITMAPINFOHEADER**, named **biSize**, must equal 40, the number of bytes in the structure itself. In the second and third fields, **biWidth** and **biHeight**, specify the bitmap dimensions in pixels. A brush is always 8×8, so enter 8 for both dimensions.

The field **biPlanes** reflects a method of organizing pixel data normally not used in Windows bitmaps. Instead of lining up the three-byte RGB values of a 24-bit image sequentially, you could create three separate 8-bit bitmaps—one for the red, green, and blue color components—each with one byte per pixel. This would be a three plane bitmap. Since Windows bitmaps are not organized in planes, we always set **biPlanes** to 1.

biCompression may be set to one of three values. The constant names for those values are **BI_RGB**, **BI_RLE4**, and **BI_RLE8**, whose values are &H0, &H2, and &H1, respectively. **BI_RGB** indicates that the bitmap is not compressed. The other two values indicate which of the two *run length encoding* (RLE) methods have been used to compress the bitmap. The advantage of RLE bitmaps is that they occupy less memory and disk space. Their disadvantage is that they have to be decompressed as they are displayed, so they slow things down, sometimes considerably. We won't discuss RLE bitmaps any further in this book, but you should note that compressed bitmaps do exist.

By pretending that RLE (and other compressed) bitmaps don't exist, we also get to skip the field **biSizeImage**. For non-compressed bitmaps, the GDI can figure out the number of bytes in the pixel buffer from the dimensions and the color depth. But when you specify a compression method of **BI_RLE4** or **BI_RLE8**, the GDI wants to know the number of bytes in the compressed image data.

biXPelsPerMeter and **biYPelsPerMeter** can be used to specify the resolution of the bitmap on the absolute scale of pixels per meter. You may never encounter a bitmap in which these fields contain any value other than zero, meaning that they are ignored.

The last field in **BITMAPINFOHEADER**, **biClrImportant**, is also rarely used. It specifies how many of the colors in the color table are needed to reasonably display the image. Almost all bitmap files assume that all colors are critical, so this field is set to 0. The display of 256 color images is at the whim of the Palette Manager anyway!

The fourth DIB element is the series of bytes that contain the pixel data itself, not a structure declared with the **Type** command, but a contiguous data buffer large enough to hold the entire bitmap. For the little bitmap in this project, we use a fixed-length string as the pixel buffer. You might expect the entire monochrome brush bitmap to fit into 8 bytes (8 pixels by 8 pixels, 1 bit per pixel). But the number of bytes in each row of bitmap pixels must be evenly divisible by 4, meaning that each row uses a minimum of four bytes. (No such restriction exists on the *number* of rows.) So, we have to build our brush in a 32 byte buffer, in which each row will contain one byte of pixel data and three bytes of padding.

Adding CreateTheBrush()

We're now ready to add the main bitmap function, which is shown in Listing 8.1.

Listing 8.1   The CreateTheBrush() Function from ROPEXP2.FRM

```
Private Function CreateTheBrush() As Integer
Dim hCompBitmap As Long
Dim BrushBitmapInfo As BITMAPINFO
Dim Counter As Integer
Dim PixelData As String * 32
Dim Dummy As Long
Dim Row As Integer
Dim Column As Integer

    ' Fill in BITMAPINFOHEADER
    With BrushBitmapInfo.bmiHeader
     .biSize = 40
     .biWidth = 8
     .biHeight = 8
     .biPlanes = 1
     .biBitCount = 1
     .biCompression = BI_RGB
     .biSizeImage = 0
     .biXPelsPerMeter = 0
     .biYPelsPerMeter = 0
     .biClrUsed = 0
     .biClrImportant = 0
    End With

    ' Set the color table values for the brush to
    ' black and white.
    With BrushBitmapInfo.bmiColors(0)
        .rgbBlue = 0
        .rgbGreen = 0
        .rgbRed = 0
        .rgbReserved = 0
    End With
    With BrushBitmapInfo.bmiColors(1)
        .rgbBlue = 255
        .rgbGreen = 255
        .rgbRed = 255
        .rgbReserved = 0
    End With
```

```
' Initialize brush bitmap pixel data to all white.
For Counter = 0 To 7
    Mid$(PixelData, Counter * 4 + 1, 1) = Chr$(&HFF)
Next Counter
' Create checkerboard monochrome bitmap, i.e. 50% gray dither
For Counter = 0 To 63
    Row = Counter \ 8
    Column = Counter Mod 8
    If (Row Mod 2 = 0) Xor (Column Mod 2 = 0) Then
        Mid$(PixelData, Row * 4 + 1, 1) = Chr$(Asc(Mid$(PixelData, _
            Row * 4 + 1, 1)) And (Not (2 ^ Column)))
    End If
Next Counter

hCompBitmap = CreateDIBitmap(BrushPic.hDC, BrushBitmapInfo.bmiHeader, _
    CBM_INIT, PixelData, BrushBitmapInfo, DIB_RGB_COLORS)
'hCompBitmap = CreateBitmap(8, 8, 1, 1, PixelData)
CreateTheBrush = CreatePatternBrush(hCompBitmap)
Dummy = DeleteObject(hCompBitmap)
End Function
```

Let's take this function apart. The first part fills in the data needed for the **BITMAPINFOHEADER** structure. Then, we move on to the color table. Notice here that we need two entries in our color table, one for black and one for white. We use single-byte variables in **RGBQUAD** to hold the color values (as in the previous chapter when we used the structure **PALETTEENTRY**). For black, set all the color fields to 0, and for white, set them all to their maximum value of 255.

Next, we initialize the bitmap so all its pixel bits reference the white color table entry:

```
For Counter = 0 To 7
    Mid$(PixelData, Counter * 4 + 1, 1) = Chr$(&HFF)
Next Counter
```

You could easily set all the byte values to &HFF, including the pad bytes. We just want to make it clear that *only* the first byte of each four affects the outcome. Did you notice anything unusual about the **Mid$()** function? Instead of counting characters in strings beginning with 0, we begin with 1. That's why the expression in the position parameter in **Mid$()** adds 1 to **Counter * 4**.

After we've initialized the brush, we can set every other pixel bit to reference the black color table entry. And that's exactly what happens in the second **For** loop:

```
For Counter = 0 To 63
    Row = Counter \ 8
```

```
   Column = Counter Mod 8
   If (Row Mod 2 = 0) Xor (Column Mod 2 = 0) Then
      Mid$(PixelData, Row * 4 + 1, 1) = _
         Chr$(Asc(Mid$(PixelData, Row * 4 + 1, 1)) And (Not (2 ^ Column)))
   End If
Next Counter
```

Bitwise Boolean Trickery

We have to use a little bitwise Boolean trickery to change individual bits from a value of 1, which represents white, to a value of 0, which represents black. We use the VB functions **Mid$()** and **Asc()** to pull out an individual byte. Then, to set one bit in that byte, we create a pattern of bits, called a *bit mask*, in which the bit we want to change equals 0, and all the other bits equal 1. To get the pattern, we first create a complementary value in which the bit we want to change equals 1 and all other bits equal 0. The decimal equivalent of a binary number with one bit set always equals a power of 2. So, we set one bit by raising 2 to the power of the column number (0 through 7). We then **Not** that result to get the complement, which leaves us with a binary mask in which one bit equals 0 and the other seven bits equal 1. When we **And** that mask with the existing byte, all the bits remain unchanged except the single bit we have selected, which will switch from 1 to 0. This technique is illustrated in Figure 8.1.

A checkerboard bitmap in which pixels alternate between black and white will produced a 50 percent gray dither.

Working with Brushes

It takes two steps to convert our DIB into a GDI brush. First, we have to convert it into a device-dependent bitmap (DDB). Believe it or not, that's the job of the API function **CreateDIBitmap()**. Despite its name, this function does not create a DIB; instead it converts a DIB into a DDB. You see, before you can display a device *independent* bitmap, you must convert it into a

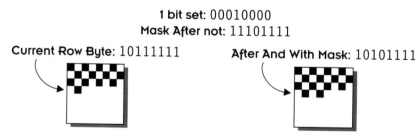

1 bit set: 00010000
Mask After not: 11101111

Current Row Byte: 10111111   **After And With Mask:** 10101111

Figure 8.1 *Using a bit mask to change monochrome pixel values.*

device *dependent* bitmap. The conversion process transforms a bitmap from its native color mode into the color mode supported by the active display system. When your display system is set to 256 color mode, each pixel represents one byte in video memory. Our monochrome brush bitmap contains one bit per pixel. **CreateDIBitmap()** converts each bit of the monochrome DIB into one byte in the corresponding DDB by first looking up the color reference in the DIB's color table. Next, the function compares that color to the colors in the logical palette currently selected into the device context specified in the first argument. Since we have not explicitly selected a palette into the device context of **BrushPic**, Windows will use the **DEFAULT_PALETTE**, which contains the 20 reserved colors, including black and white. The first and last entries in the system palette contain black and white respectively, so each byte of the DDB will reference either palette entry &H00 or palette entry &HFF. The monochrome DIB becomes a 256 color DDB that uses only two of the 256 available colors. The GDI stores this DDB in memory and returns a handle to it through **CreateDIBitmap()**.

CreateDIBitmap() takes six arguments:

```
Win32:
Declare Function CreateDIBitmap Lib "gdi32" (ByVal hDC As Long, _
    lpInfoHeader As BITMAPINFOHEADER, ByVal dwUsage As Long, _
    ByVal lpInitBits As String, lpInitInfo As BITMAPINFO, ByVal wUsage As Long) _
    As Long
```

```
Win16:
Declare Function CreateDIBitmap Lib "GDI" (ByVal hDC As Integer, _
    lpInfoHeader As BITMAPINFOHEADER, ByVal dwUsage As Long, _
    ByVal lpInitBits As String, lpInitInfo As BITMAPINFO, ByVal wUsage _
    As Integer) As Integer
```

The first argument specifies the device context. The function will convert the DIB to a DDB based on the capabilities of this device context. In other words, if the device context belongs to an 8-bit color display buffer, **CreateDIBitmap()** will return a handle to an 8-bit bitmap.

A long pointer to a **BITMAPINFOHEADER** is passed as the second argument. As we've done many times in previous experiments, we pass a pointer to a structure by declaring this argument *without* the **ByVal** keyword.

The third argument determines whether **CreateDIBitmap()** creates an initialized bitmap. If you pass the function a value of 0 in this argument, it will create a raw bitmap. You may then use other GDI functions to draw on that bitmap. The pixels of the uninitialized bitmap will contain whatever values happen to lie in memory. If you choose to create a new bitmap this way, be sure to initialize it with one of the drawing functions. Also, to create an uninitialized bitmap, pass the next three arguments to the function as NULL (zero). To create a bitmap based on the values in the **BITMAPINFOHEADER** and the pixel data, however, set this third argument to the constant **CBM_INIT**, which has a long integer value of &H4&.

For the fourth argument we pass the 32-byte, fixed-length string that we're using as a pixel buffer. By declaring this argument **ByVal**, we instruct VB to convert it to a null-terminated string. Since this is a fixed-length string, VB will make sure Windows allocates enough space for all 32 bytes, plus the null terminator.

The fifth argument takes a pointer to the **BITMAPINFO** structure, which contains not only a second copy of the **BITMAPINFOHEADER**, but more importantly, the color table.

Finally, for the last argument, we specify whether the color table values inside the **BITMAPINFO** structure, passed in parameter five, contain references to the currently realized palette, or to explicit RGB colors. In this case, we'll ask for RGB colors. We'll use the other method in a later project.

To make a brush from the bitmap, we call another API function, **CreatePatternBrush()**, which takes as its sole argument a handle to a bitmap, and returns a handle to a brush. A pattern brush is just a special class of bitmap, one that GDI painting functions can repeat like a rubber stamp to fill an area. In ROPEXP2, the drawing areas measure 32 pixels on a side, so **BitBlt()** will automatically repeat the 8×8 brush pattern 16 times as it draws the **ResultPic**.

Other Ways to Build a Brush

In Windows programming, you often find more than one trail through the API wilderness. As an alternative to **CreateDIBitmap()**, take a look at **CreateBitmap()** and **CreateBitmapIndirect()**. With **CreateBitmap()**, you can create a monochrome bitmap using nothing more than the pixel data itself—no **BITMAPINFOHEADER**, no color table—just bits. Watch out for the structure of the pixel data however, because this function does not expect the bitmap lines to end on 32 bit boundaries, so an 8×8 monochrome bitmap would fit neatly into 8 bytes. To create a color bitmap with this function, you must know which colors are in the system palette, and where they are located, because the function does not convert a DIB into a DDB. The pixel data must already represent a DDB when you hand it over. The other function, **CreateBitmapIndirect()**, also expects DDB pixel data, which is indirectly referenced (hence its name) by its single argument, a pointer to a structure called **BITMAP**.

> For the most direct method of creating a pattern brush, use the function **CreateDIBPatternBrush()**, which consolidates the two functions **CreateDIBitmap()** and **CreatePatternBrush()** into one. To use this function, you'll need to construct a *packed DIB*, which consists of a complete DIB stored contiguously in memory, containing the **BITMAPINFO** structure followed immediately by the pixel data. The word *packed* simply means that the elements are contiguous—not that they are compressed in any way. Later in this chapter, we'll study some handy memory management functions that you could use to pack the DIB.
>
> For more information on these functions and structures, see the Windows SDK or any good API reference.

Brushes 'n' Bits

It doesn't pay to go any further until we know that the pattern brush we've created has come out as intended. We'll fill a Picture Box control with the brush pattern, which will give us a chance to use another blt function called **PatBlt()**. This function is called from the **BrushPic_Paint()** event procedure, as shown in Listing 8.2.

Listing 8.2 The BrushPic_Paint() Event Procedure from ROPEXP2.FRM

```
Private Sub BrushPic_Paint()
Dim hBrush As Long
Dim hOldBrush As Long
Dim Dummy As Long

    hBrush = CreateTheBrush()
    hOldBrush = SelectObject(BrushPic.hDC, hBrush)
    Dummy = PatBlt(BrushPic.hDC, 0, 0, BrushPic.ScaleWidth, _
        BrushPic.ScaleHeight, PATCOPY)
    ' You could also use BitBlt() to paint the
    ' pattern into the BrushPic DC:
    ' Dummy = BitBlt(BrushPic.hDC, 0, 0, BrushPic.ScaleWidth,
    '     BrushPic.ScaleHeight, 0, 0, 0, PATCOPY)
    Dummy = SelectObject(BrushPic.hDC, hOldBrush)
    Dummy = DeleteObject(hBrush)
End Sub
```

Notice that **PatBlt()** takes only six arguments:

```
Win32:
Declare Function PatBlt Lib "gdi32" (ByVal hDC As Long, _
    ByVal X As Long, ByVal Y As Long, ByVal nWidth As Long, _
    ByVal nHeight As Long, ByVal dwRop As Long) As Long
```

```
Win16:
Declare Function PatBlt Lib "GDI" (ByVal hDestDC As Integer, _
    ByVal X As Integer, ByVal Y As Integer, ByVal nWidth As Integer, _
    ByVal nHeight As Integer, ByVal dwROP As Long) As Integer
```

Just like **BitBlt()**, the first argument takes the destination device context. The second and third arguments determine the starting position of the pattern fill operation, while the fourth and fifth arguments specify the width and height of the area to be painted with the brush. The last argument takes a ROP code. The ROP code determines how **PatBlt()** will combine the pattern with the existing bitmap, as shown in Figure 8.2. You could pass any of the 256 ternary ROP codes to **PatBlt()**, but only those that include the brush or the destination will do anything (**BLACKNESS** or **WHITENESS** will also work, in their usual ways).

Note: *For a complete list of the ternary ROP codes, see the Microsoft Windows Programmers's Reference: Vol. 5, Messages, Structures, and Macros.*

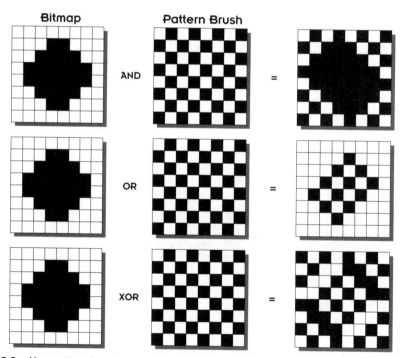

Figure 8.2 *How pattern brushes combine with monochrome or colored bitmaps in Boolean raster operations.*

To use the brush, we first select it into the device context of **BrushPic**. The function **SelectObject()** returns the handle of the previously selected object of the same type, which we save in **hOldBrush**. In this case, that happens to be the handle to the default **BLACK_BRUSH**. We then call **PatBlt()** with the **PATCOPY** ROP code, which replaces the current contents of the device context with the repeating brush pattern. Finally, we restore the old brush and delete our pattern brush.

We have to perform a similar set of steps in **ResultPic_Paint()** (see Listing 8.3), except that we'll use **BitBlt()** instead of **PatBlt()**, and send everything to the device context of ResultPic.

Listing 8.3   The ResultPic_Paint() Event Procedure from ROPEXP2.FRM

```
Private Sub ResultPic_Paint()
Dim hBrush As Long
Dim hOldBrush As Long
Dim ROPType As Long
Dim Param As String
Dim Dummy As Long

    DestPic.Cls
    Param = ROPSList.TEXT
    ROPType = Val(Mid$(Param, InStr(Param, " &") + 1, 11))

    hBrush = CreateTheBrush()
    hOldBrush = SelectObject(ResultPic.hDC, hBrush)
    Dummy = BitBlt(ResultPic.hDC, 0, 0, 33, 33, DestPic.hDC, 0, 0, SRCCOPY)
    Dummy = BitBlt(ResultPic.hDC, 0, 0, 33, 33, SourcePic.hDC, 0, 0, ROPType)
    Dummy = SelectObject(ResultPic.hDC, hOldBrush)
    Dummy = DeleteObject(hBrush)
End Sub
```

We've made another change in ROPEXP2. In the ROP project presented in Chapter 7, we hard-coded the initialization of the **ROPSList** List Box. This time we moved the ROP names and their hex codes into a text file named ROPSLIST.TXT. Some day, when you have nothing better to do, you may add the 241 remaining ROP codes to that file. The **Form_Load()** event procedure shown in Listing 8.4 picks up whatever it finds there.

Listing 8.4   The Form_Load() Event Procedure from ROPEXP2.FRM

```
Private Sub Form_Load()
Dim TempString As String
Const ROPSListFile = 1

    Open App.Path + "\ROPSList.Txt" For Input As ROPSListFile
    Do While Not EOF(ROPSListFile)
```

```
      Input #ROPSListFile, TempString
      If InStr(TempString, "&") > 0 Then
          ROPSList.AddItem TempString
      End If
   Loop
   Close #ROPSListFile
End Sub
```

Adding the Data Structures

To wrap up the project, we need to create the code module and add the
declarations in Listing 8.5. Because we had to create a separate code module
to accommodate the **Type** declarations, for clarity, we moved the external
function declarations and constants there as well.

Listing 8.5 The Declarations Section from ROPEXP2.BAS

```
Option Explicit

Type BITMAPINFOHEADER '40 bytes
    biSize          As Long
    biWidth         As Long
    biHeight        As Long
    biPlanes        As Integer
    biBitCount      As Integer
    biCompression   As Long
    biSizeImage     As Long
    biXPelsPerMeter As Long
    biYPelsPerMeter As Long
    biClrUsed       As Long
    biClrImportant  As Long
End Type


Type RGBQUAD
    rgbBlue      As Byte
    rgbGreen     As Byte
    rgbRed       As Byte
    rgbReserved  As Byte
End Type


Type BITMAPINFO
    bmiHeader As BITMAPINFOHEADER
    bmiColors(1) As RGBQUAD
End Type

#If Win32 Then
    Declare Function BitBlt Lib "gdi32" (ByVal hDestDC As Long, ByVal X As Long, _
        ByVal Y As Long, ByVal nWidth As Long, ByVal nHeight As Long, _
        ByVal hSrcDC As Long, ByVal XSrc As Long, ByVal YSrc As Long, _
        ByVal dwRop As Long) As Long
    Declare Function CreateDIBitmap Lib "gdi32" (ByVal hDC As Long, _
        lpInfoHeader As BITMAPINFOHEADER, ByVal dwUsage As Long, _
```

```
            ByVal lpInitBits As String, lpInitInfo As BITMAPINFO, B_
            yVal wUsage As Long) As Long
        Declare Function CreatePatternBrush Lib "gdi32" (ByVal hBitmap As Long) _
            As Long
        Declare Function DeleteObject Lib "gdi32" (ByVal hObject As Long) As Long
        Declare Function SelectObject Lib "gdi32" (ByVal hDC As Long, _
            ByVal hObject As Long) As Long
        Declare Function PatBlt Lib "gdi32" (ByVal hDC As Long, ByVal X As Long, _
            ByVal Y As Long, ByVal nWidth As Long, ByVal nHeight As Long, _
            ByVal dwRop As Long) As Long
#Else
        Declare Function CreateDIBitmap Lib "GDI" (ByVal hDC As Integer, _
            lpInfoHeader As BITMAPINFOHEADER, ByVal dwUsage As Long, _
            ByVal lpInitBits As String, lpInitInfo As BITMAPINFO, _
            ByVal wUsage As Integer) As Integer
        Declare Function CreatePatternBrush Lib "GDI" (ByVal hBitmap As Integer) _
            As Integer
        Declare Function DeleteObject Lib "GDI" (ByVal hObject As Integer) As Integer
        Declare Function SelectObject Lib "GDI" (ByVal hDC As Integer, _
            ByVal hObject As Integer) As Integer
        Declare Function BitBlt Lib "GDI" (ByVal hDestDC As Integer, ByVal X _
            As Integer, ByVal Y As Integer, ByVal nWidth As Integer, ByVal nHeight _
            As Integer, ByVal hSrcDC As Integer, ByVal XSrc As Integer, ByVal YSrc _
            As Integer, ByVal dwRop As Long) As Integer
        Declare Function PatBlt Lib "GDI" (ByVal hDestDC As Integer, ByVal X _
            As Integer, ByVal Y As Integer, ByVal nWidth As Integer, ByVal nHeight _
            As Integer, ByVal dwRop As Long) As Integer
#End If

'  Pre-defined Raster Operation Constants

Global Const SRCCOPY = &HCC0020
Global Const SRCPAINT = &HEE0086
Global Const SRCAND = &H8800C6
Global Const SRCINVERT = &H660046
Global Const SRCERASE = &H440328
Global Const NOTSRCCOPY = &H330008
Global Const NOTSRCERASE = &H1100A6
Global Const MERGECOPY = &HC000CA
Global Const MERGEPAINT = &HBB0226
Global Const PATCOPY = &HF00021
Global Const PATPAINT = &HFB0A09
Global Const PATINVERT = &H5A0049
Global Const DSTINVERT = &H550009
Global Const BLACKNESS = &H42&
Global Const WHITENESS = &HFF0062
Global Const MergeMask = &HAC0744

Global Const BI_RGB = 0&
Global Const CBM_INIT = &H4&
Global Const DIB_RGB_COLORS = 0
'Global Const DIB_PAL_COLORS = 1
```

Now you can try out the ROPs that use pattern brushes. As an exercise, work out the results you would expect from **PATPAINT**. The funny-looking code that appears beside each ROP hex code in the list box represents the Boolean raster operation in *reverse polish notation* (RPN). We've included these for reference only; you can't pass them to any API function, but most reference guides to the Windows API present ROPs in this form. The RPN expression for **PATPAINT** is DPSnoo (*not* pronounced "Dee Pee Snoo"). For the VB translation of this expression, see Table 7.2.

Combining Bitmaps

We now have many tools under our belts for working with palettes, blts, and raster operations. We're well on our way to the image dissolve effect. Next, let's figure out which ROP code will enable us to combine two images.

Imagine that you're holding two photographs in your hand, one on top of the other. You can't see the bottom photo because photographic prints are opaque. You can simulate the digital dissolve process by poking hundreds of tiny holes in the top image, evenly spaced across the entire picture. Through the holes you could then see little bits of the bottom photo. You could go over the entire image again with your needle, this time adding more holes between the first set. As the holes increase in number, first by hundreds, then by thousands, the bottom image becomes clearer and clearer. After several rounds of hole poking, the top picture disintegrates, leaving the bottom image unobscured.

To speed things up a little, you could make a little hole puncher by sticking several pins through a piece of cork or rubber. Then you could punch dozens of holes with each pop. And that's exactly what we're going to do with a pattern brush.

The brush created in the ROPEXP2 project consists of alternating white and black pixels—a checkerboard pattern. If we think of that pattern not as a checkerboard, however, but as a fine mesh, we can easily imagine that we could see a bitmap through the holes represented by the black pixels. Stepping through the dissolve, we'll create brushes with ever increasing numbers of black pixels.

Now all we need to do is deduce which ROP code will combine the brush and the two images to generate the proper effect.

Hunting through Raster Operations

Windows raster operations have an undeserved reputation as a black art. Choosing a raster operation is one of the hardest things to do in Windows graphics programming. But like any programming problem, all you need to do is break the process into manageable steps. To mix the pixels of two images, we need to do two things:

1. Use the pattern brush to make black holes in the destination bitmap.
2. Fill the holes with the corresponding pixels from the source bitmap.

For the first step, only one logical operator is needed. If you **And** a pixel with a binary value of 00000000—representing the black palette entry—with any other pixel value, you will get only one result: 00000000. 10101010 **And** 00000000 equals 00000000; 11110000 **And** 00000000 equals 00000000, and so on. In Boolean logic, only 1 **And** 1 equals 1. But what happens to the pixels in the destination when we **And** them with the white pixels in the pattern brush? Nothing. Because once again, only the pixel bits that equal 1 in the destination will yield 1 when we **And** them with pattern pixel bits that equal 1. 10101010 **And** 11111111 equals 10101010; 11110000 **And** 11111111 equals 11110000. Pixels that are black in the pattern brush become black in the destination bitmap, while pixels that are white in the pattern brush remain unchanged in the destination bitmap. So, step one looks like this:

(Pattern **And** Destination)

Next, we have to combine the source bitmap with the result of step 1 so that only the pixels that lie under the black holes show through. This step is trickier. Because any of the three logical operators will blend the bits of the colored pixels from both images, we have to perform another masking operation to eliminate the pixels we don't want from the source image. Step 2 splits into two tasks. First we change all the unwanted pixels to black, then we press the two pictures together.

To mask all but the pixels we want added to the awaiting destination bitmap, we invert the mask with a **Not** operator. In Boolean logic, **Not** changes all 1s to 0s, and all 0s to 1s. Then, in the third step, we use the **And** operator again, this time between the inverted pattern and the source image:

((**Not** Pattern) **And** Source)

Whoops—still one step to go. In this last step, we want to combine the results of steps 1 through 3. We know that **And** won't work, because each pair of pixels includes one colored pixel from either of the images, facing one black pixel from the opposite image. Thus, an **And** would blacken the whole picture. An **Or**, however, will retain the bits from each colored pixel exactly as they appear in their native bitmaps. In fact, since one member of each pixel pair is black, an **Xor** would work just as well. The complete raster operation expression looks like this:

(Pattern **And** Destination) **Or** ((**Not** Pattern) **And** Source)

In reverse polish notation it looks like this:

PDaSPnao

Don't bother looking in the table of the fifteen named ROP codes for that one—you won't find it. With a little Boolean algebra, we could derive an equivalent expression, one that does appear in the table. But there's an easier way. The Windows API defines a set of pre-defined binary constants, one representing each of the three types of bitmaps, which we can grind through our equation to directly calculate the hexadecimal identification number of the correct ROP code.

Let's work through the steps:

1. Combine the pattern brush and the destination to make black holes in the destination.

    The pattern brush and the destination bitmap are represented by the binary constants 11110000 and 10101010, respectively. 11110000 **And** 10101010 equals 10100000.

2. Invert the pattern brush.

    Not 11110000 equals 00001111.

3. Combine the result of step 2 with the source bitmap, which is represented by the binary constant 11001100.

    00001111 **And** 11001100 equals 00001100.

4. **Or** the results of steps 1 and 3.

    10100000 **Or** 00001100 equals 10101100.

The ROP code we want is 10101100, which is hexadecimal value &HAC. ROP codes are actually long integers. The highest-order byte always equals &H00. The second highest-order byte represents the ROP identification number. The two lower-order bytes contain codes that help the ROP engine construct the correct sequence of machine instructions to perform the raster operation. ROPs are like tiny programs, or macros. For the sake of speed, the

GDI assembles a temporary program in memory, enabling the blt function to perform the raster operation without calling subfunctions. The lower-order bytes don't help us identify the ROP code, but we must include them when we reference the ROP code in a blt operation.

If we look up raster operation &HAC in the ROP table, we find that its logical expression looks a little different from ours:

SPDSxax

But regardless of appearance, the two expressions are logically equivalent, which we could prove by again grinding the bitmap binary constants. Go right ahead.

> **Note:** *The expression given in the ROP table may seem less intuitive than the one we derived by our step-by-step method, but you can still make sense of it if you remember that an **Xor** operation is reversible (just do it over again). In the expression SPDSxax, you see two **Xor** operations. The first combines the source and destination bitmaps. The second de-combines all the pixels untouched by the pattern brush. The middle step combines the effects of the **Not** and both **And** operations from our version of the expression. Instead of performing one **And**, then inverting the pattern to perform the second **And**, you can perform the **And** on the combined bitmaps. When you perform the final **Xor**, the blackened pixels are filled with the pixels from the source bitmap, while simultaneously the source pixels are reversed out of the unblackened destination pixels.*

According to the standard table of Windows ternary ROP codes, the complete hex value of the &HAC ROP code is &H00AC0744. To test this raster operation, add it to ROPSLIST.TXT and run ROPEXP2, as shown in Figure 8.3.

That takes care of the ROP code. Now we can start the dissolve project.

Creating the Basic Digital Dissolve

In the program BITBLTEX, which we created in Chapter 7, we used **BitBlt()** and the simple **SRCCOPY** raster operation to copy an image from one Picture Box to another. Let's make that program more interesting by creating a series of black and white pattern brushes, tossing in our newly discovered ROP code, and dissolve the image from one Picture Box to the other.

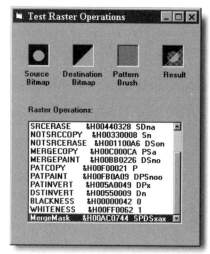

Figure 8.3 *You can use the program ROPEXP2 to test any raster operation.*

The First Dissolve

This project shows you how to dissolve two bitmap images.

1. Create the new form DSLVEXP.FRM.
2. Add the **CreateDissolveBrush()** function (Listing 8.6) and the **CreatePixelSetSequence()** procedure (Listing 8.7) to the form.
3. Add the supporting event procedures, **Picture2_Paint()**, **DissolveButton_Click()**, **Timer1_Timer()**, **Picture2_Click()**, and **Form_Load()** (Listings 8.8 through Listings 8.12).
4. Add the necessary declarations to DSLVEXP.FRM (Listing 8.13) and DSLVEXP.BAS (Listing 8.14).

This project is located in the directory \VBMAGIC\DSLVEXP in the files DSLVEXP.VBP, DSLVEXP.FRM, DSLVEXP.FRX, DSLVEXP.BAS, and PIXELLST.TXT.

Setting Up the Dissolve

In the ROPEXP2 project presented earlier, we created a function named **CreateTheBrush()**, which built a DIB from the ground up, then converted it to a DDB, from which it made a pattern brush. For this new project, we need to modify that function to produce one of a series of pattern brushes. Each successive version of the brush will contain a greater percentage of black pixels than its predecessor. We'll call the new function **CreateDissolveBrush()**, and we'll tell it which version of the brush we want by passing it an integer argument by the name of **DissolveStep** (see Listing 8.6).

Listing 8.6 The CreateDissolveBrush() Function from DSLVEXP.FRM

```
Private Function CreateDissolveBrush(DissolveStep As Integer) As Integer
Dim hCompBitmap As Long
Dim BrushBitmapInfo As BITMAPINFO
Dim Counter As Integer
Dim PixelData As String * 32
Dim Dummy As Long
Dim Row As Integer
Dim Column As Integer

    With BrushBitmapInfo.bmiHeader
        .biSize = 40
        .biWidth = 8
        .biHeight = 8
        .biPlanes = 1
        .biBitCount = 1
        .biCompression = 0
        .biSizeImage = 0
        .biXPelsPerMeter = 0
        .biYPelsPerMeter = 0
        .biClrUsed = 0
        .biClrImportant = 0
    End With

    ' Set the color table values for
    ' the brush to black and white.
    With BrushBitmapInfo.bmiColors(0)
        .rgbBlue = 0
        .rgbGreen = 0
        .rgbRed = 0
        .rgbReserved = 0
    End With
    With BrushBitmapInfo.bmiColors(1)
        .rgbBlue = 255
        .rgbGreen = 255
        .rgbRed = 255
        .rgbReserved = 0
    End With

    ' Initialize brush bitmap pixel data to all white.
    For Counter = 0 To 7
        Mid$(PixelData, Counter * 4 + 1, 1) = Chr$(&HFF)
    Next Counter

    ' Set the bits representing the black pixels to 0.
    For Counter = 1 To DissolveStep * (64 / NumberOfSteps)
        Row = (PixelSetSequence(Counter) - 1) \ 8
        Column = (PixelSetSequence(Counter) - 1) Mod 8
```

```
        Mid$(PixelData, Row * 4 + 1, 1) = Chr$(Asc(Mid$(PixelData, Row * 4 + 1, _
            1)) And (Not (2 ^ Column)))
    Next Counter

    ' Convert the DIB into a DDB and create the pattern brush.
    hCompBitmap = CreateDIBitmap(Disolve1.hDC, BrushBitmapInfo.bmiHeader, _
        CBM_INIT, PixelData, BrushBitmapInfo, DIB_RGB_COLORS)
    CreateDissolveBrush = CreatePatternBrush(hCompBitmap)
    Dummy = DeleteObject(hCompBitmap)
End Function
```

The code that distinguishes **CreateDissolveBrush()** from **CreateThe-Brush()** is the **For** loop that sets the black pixels:

```
For Counter = 1 To DissolveStep * (64 / NumberOfSteps)
    Row = (PixelSetSequence(Counter) - 1) \ 8
    Column = (PixelSetSequence(Counter) - 1) Mod 8
    Mid$(PixelData, Row * 4 + 1, 1) = Chr$(Asc(Mid$(PixelData, Row * 4 + 1, 1)) _
        And (Not (2 ^ Column)))
Next Counter
```

Instead of simply flipping every other bit, this code uses a series of pixel numbers, stored in an array called **PixelSetSequence()**, to identify the pixels that should be changed to black for any given step in the dissolve. We tried several approaches to generate this sequence algorithmically, and failed. Every series we created caused the resulting brush to produce visible patterns in the combined bitmaps. Some made nice plaids, others drew stripes. But we wanted brushes that would produce gray-scale dithers, so that when the blt repeated the brush, you would see one uniform pattern of points instead of wallpaper patterns. So we gave up and hand-dithered it. The results of our intensive research efforts (we drew them with pencil on graph paper) are contained in a text file called PIXELLST.TXT, and the procedure that reads the contents of that file into the array **PixelSetSequence()** is called **CreatePixelSetSequence()** (see Listing 8.7).

Listing 8.7   The CreatePixelSetSequence() Procedure from DSLVEXP.FRM

```
Private Sub CreatePixelSetSequence()
Dim Counter As Integer
Dim PixelNumberString As String * 5
Const PixelListFile = 1

    Open App.Path & "\PixelLst.TXT" For Input As #PixelListFile
    For Counter = 1 To 64
        Input #PixelListFile, PixelNumberString
        PixelSetSequence(Counter) = Val(PixelNumberString)
    Next Counter
End Sub
```

We've numbered the pixels from 1 to 64. We'll leave it to you to find the magic pattern to do away with this kluge.

The constant **NumberOfSteps** determines the number of pixels that are set to black at each step. We have set it to 8, so each successive brush adds 8 black pixels. If you set **NumberOfSteps** to 16, each brush will add 4 black pixels. The value of **NumberOfSteps** must divide evenly into 64. We believe our hand-picked pixel list works best for a value of 8 or 16.

> **Note:** *Don't forget that DIB data begins with the last row, so row 0 in the* **CreateDissolveBrush()** *is actually row 7 on the screen. The whole pattern is upside down.*

Adding the Event Procedures

It's now time to add the five event procedures that we'll need. Once again, the brush meets blt and ROP in the event procedure **Picture2_Paint()** (see Listing 8.8).

Listing 8.8   The Picture2_Paint() Event Procedure from DSLVEXP.FRM

```
Private Sub Picture2_Paint()
Dim hRgn As Long
Dim Dummy As Long
Dim hOldBrush As Long

    hBrush = CreateDissolveBrush(DissolveStep)
    hOldBrush = SelectObject(Picture2.hDC, hBrush)
    Dummy = BitBlt(Picture2.hDC, 0, 0, Picture2.ScaleWidth, _
        Picture2.ScaleHeight, Picture1.hDC, 0, 0, &HAC0744)
    Dummy = SelectObject(Picture2.hDC, hOldBrush)
    Dummy = DeleteObject(hBrush)
End Sub
```

With the form level variable **DissolveStep**, we create the appropriate brush. We then select it into the device context of Picture2, and **BitBlt()** the image over from Picture1, using ROP code &HAC0744. Finally, we replace the default **BLACK_BRUSH**, and delete the brush we created, which, like all the brushes, live only briefly.

The rest of this program is easy. We'll need a trigger to get things going, and some way to fire off and keep track of the dissolve steps. For these tasks, we'll add a Command Button named DissolveButton and a Timer control. The **DissolveButton_Click()** event procedure starts the timer, as Listing 8.9 indicates.

Listing 8.9   The DissolveButton_Click() Event Procedure from DSLVEXP.FRM

```
Sub DissolveButton_Click ()
   DissolveButton.Enabled = False
   Timer1.Enabled = True
End Sub
```

The **Timer1_Timer()** event procedure advances the **DissolveStep** timer, as shown in Listing 8.10.

Listing 8.10   The Timer1_Timer() Event Procedure from DSLVEXP.FRM

```
Sub Timer1_Timer ()
   If DissolveStep < NumberOfSteps Then
      DissolveStep = DissolveStep + 1
      Picture2_Paint
   Else
      Timer1.Enabled = False
   End If
End Sub
```

We've also added similar code to **Picture2_Click()** (see Listing 8.11) so you can single-step through the dissolve. Just click on the Picture2 Command Button instead of the DissolveButton Command Button.

Listing 8.11   The Picture2_Click() Event Procedure from DSLVEXP.FRM

```
Sub Picture2_Click ()
   If DissolveStep < NumberOfSteps Then
      DissolveStep = DissolveStep + 1
      Picture2_Paint
   End If
End Sub
```

To complete the set of event procedures, add **Form_Load()** from Listing 8.12.

Listing 8.12   The Form_Load() Event Procedure from DSLVEXP.FRM

```
Sub Form_Load ()
   CreatePixelSetSequence
   DissolveStep = 0
End Sub
```

Adding the Declarations

The dissolve project requires two sets of declarations. One set is placed in the DSLVEXP.FRM form (Listing 8.13) and the other set should be placed in the declarations section of DSLVEXP.BAS (Listing 8.14).

Listing 8.13 The Declarations Section from DSLVEXP.FRM

```
Option Explicit

Dim hBrush As Variant
Dim PixelSetSequence(64) As Integer
Dim DissolveStep As Integer
Const NumberOfSteps = 8
```

Listing 8.14 The Declarations Section from DSLVEXP.BAS

```
Option Explicit

Type BITMAPINFOHEADER
    biSize As Long
    biWidth As Long
    biHeight As Long
    biPlanes As Integer
    biBitCount As Integer
    biCompression As Long
    biSizeImage As Long
    biXPelsPerMeter As Long
    biYPelsPerMeter As Long
    biClrUsed As Long
    biClrImportant As Long
End Type

Type RGBQUAD
    rgbBlue As Byte
    rgbGreen As Byte
    rgbRed As Byte
    rgbReserved As Byte
End Type

Type BITMAPINFO
    bmiHeader As BITMAPINFOHEADER
    bmiColors(1) As RGBQUAD
End Type

Declare Function CreateDIBitmap Lib "gdi32" (ByVal hDC As Long, lpInfoHeader _
    As BITMAPINFOHEADER, ByVal dwUsage As Long, ByVal lpInitBits As String, _
    lpInitInfo As BITMAPINFO, ByVal wUsage As Long) As Long
Declare Function DeleteObject Lib "gdi32" (ByVal hObject As Long) As Long
Declare Function SelectObject Lib "gdi32" (ByVal hDC As Long, ByVal hObject _
    As Long) As Long
Declare Function BitBlt Lib "gdi32" (ByVal hDestDC As Long, ByVal X As Long, _
    ByVal Y As Long, ByVal nWidth As Long, ByVal nHeight As Long, ByVal hSrcDC _
    As Long, ByVal XSrc As Long, ByVal YSrc As Long, ByVal dwRop As Long) _
    As Long
Declare Function StretchBlt% Lib "gdi32" Alias "StretchBlt%" (ByVal hDC%, _
    ByVal X%, ByVal Y%, ByVal nWidth%, ByVal nHeight%, ByVal hSrcDC%, ByVal _
    XSrc%, ByVal YSrc%, ByVal nSrcWidth%, ByVal nSrcHeight%, ByVal dwRop&)
Declare Function CreatePatternBrush Lib "gdi32" (ByVal hBitmap As Long) As Long
```

```
Global Const SRCCOPY = &HCC0020
Global Const SRCPAINT = &HEE0086
Global Const SRCAND = &H8800C6
Global Const SRCINVERT = &H660046
Global Const SRCERASE = &H440328
Global Const NOTSRCCOPY = &H330008
Global Const NOTSRCERASE = &H1100A6
Global Const MERGECOPY = &HC000CA
Global Const MERGEPAINT = &HBB0226
Global Const PATCOPY = &HF00021
Global Const PATPAINT = &HFB0A09
Global Const PATINVERT = &H5A0049
Global Const DSTINVERT = &H550009
Global Const BLACKNESS = &H42&
Global Const WHITENESS = &HFF0062
Global Const BLACKONWHITE = 1
Global Const WHITEONBLACK = 2
Global Const COLORONCOLOR = 3
Global Const BI_RGB = 0&
Global Const BI_RLE8 = 1&
Global Const BI_RLE4 = 2&
Global Const TRANSPARENT = 1
Global Const OPAQUE = 2

Global Const CBM_INIT = &H4&

Global Const DIB_RGB_COLORS = 0
Global Const DIB_PAL_COLORS = 1
```

To run this program, you'll need a couple of images. For Picture1, select any 8-bit color bitmap. Because we haven't dealt with the color palette yet at all, for Picture2 start with a bitmap that uses only the Windows reserved colors—try a Windows wallpaper bitmap, such as WINLOGO.BMP. Once you've installed the pictures, run the program.

Ghost of a Window

We started with a simple **BitBlt()** test program. Although not especially useful, it did illustrate how to use the blt functions. Then, we added the ability to dissolve from one Picture Box to another. Still not particularly useful—why would you want to dissolve to an image that already appears in the Picture Box next door? You wouldn't. But there is a way to make the source Picture Box invisible, and it doesn't require any changes to the program code.

DSLVEXP.FRM has two Picture Box controls, Picture1 and Picture2. Just change the **Visible** property of Picture1 to False, and change its **AutoRedraw** property to True, then run the program again. Picture1 will disappear from the form, but when you click the Do Dissolve Command Button, the image assigned to the **Picture** property of Picture1 will still materialize in Picture2.

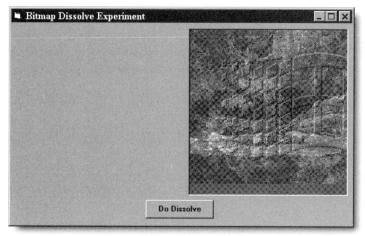

Figure 8.4   *DSLVEXP.FRM with an invisible Picture1 and halfway through the dissolve.*

Figure 8.4 shows this new approach—it looks as if we've pulled a rabbit out of our hat.

By activating its **AutoRedraw** property and making it invisible, we turned a simple Picture Box control into a special kind of GDI phantom, known as a *memory device context*. Just like a screen device context, we can draw on a memory device context, and we can transfer pixel data to or from its bitmap with blt functions. We just can't see it. We'll take a closer look at memory device contexts in the next project.

Dueling Palettes Revisited

The dissolve project we just created looked pretty good. Unfortunately, it's easy to break. To see what we mean, set the **Picture** property of Picture2 to any 256 color image, then run the program again. If both Picture controls are visible, you'll see that the colors of only one or the other are active in the system palette, so one image will look as if it's been retouched by Andy Warhol. The dissolve doesn't improve the situation. Although the final image contains only the pixels of the source, their colors all come from the logical palette that VB selected into the device context of Picture2 when it loaded the original bitmap. The pixels in both images belong to DDBs. By definition, all bitmaps become device dependent by the time they reach the display. The pixel values in those bitmaps reference system palette entries, not logical palette entries. So, the color of any given pixel will depend on the color that occupies the entry in the system palette referenced by the pixel value, even if that color happens to belong to another bitmap.

As we explained in the previous chapter, a palette-aware window should respond to certain messages sent by the Palette Manager by attempting to temporarily remap its logical palette to the current system palette. VB Picture controls do not always do this. Instead, whenever a Picture Box control loses the focus to another window that uses the palette, its colors may go haywire.

Copying the bitmap to a new device context won't fix the problem. The **BitBlt()** function simply copies pixel values from the source device context to the destination device context, which means that if they reference nonsensical colors to begin with, they will point to the same nonsensical colors when they arrive in their new locations. To solve this problem, we have to grab the DIBs before VB gets hold of them and turns them into DDBs. We can then remap the pixels by comparing the color tables in the two DIBs. That may sound like a time-consuming job, but the API includes a blt function that can convert the images to DDBs, combine their pixels with raster operations, and map their colors to a common palette all at the same time. In the next project, we'll show you how to suck a DIB right out of its file and blast it on the screen with the hardest-working blt function of all. By the time we finish, we'll be doing complete 256-color digital dissolves.

Dissolve-in-a-Box

1. Create the form DSLVEXP.FRM and add its code (Listing 8.15).
2. Add the code for the DIB2.BAS code module (Listing 8.16 and 8.17).
3. Add the code for the PALETTE.BAS code module (Listing 8.18).
4. Add the code for the DISSOLVE.BAS code module (Listings 8.19 through 8.23).

Creating the Amazing Dissolve

To demonstrate the code modules that perform the dissolve, we'll create a simple form with three controls: a Picture Box, a Command Button, and a Timer. When the form first loads, it will dissolve the Picture Box from its pure background color to the first image. When you click on the Command Button, the first image will dissolve to a second image, as shown in Figure 8.5.

By taking a look at Listing 8.15, you'll see that DISSOLVE.FRM contains little code; it simply calls functions and subprocedures in the other code modules.

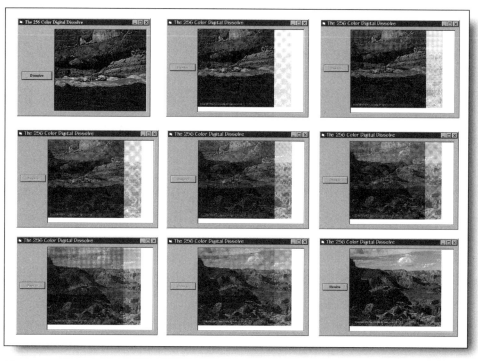

Figure 8.5 *A dissolve in progress in the form DISSOLVE.FRM from the program DISSOLVE.VBP.*

Listing 8.15   The DISSOLVE.FRM Program Code

```
VERSION 4.00
Begin VB.Form DslvF1
    AutoRedraw      =    -1  'True
    Caption         =    "The 256 Color Digital Dissolve"
    ClientHeight    =    4650
    ClientLeft      =    2220
    ClientTop       =    2790
    ClientWidth     =    6990
    BeginProperty Font
        name            =    "MS Sans Serif"
        charset         =    0
        weight          =    700
        size            =    8.25
        underline       =    0    'False
        italic          =    0    'False
        strikethrough   =    0    'False
    EndProperty
    Height          =    5100
    Left            =    2160
    LinkTopic       =    "Form1"
    ScaleHeight     =    4650
```

```
    ScaleWidth        =    6990
    Top               =    2400
    Width             =    7110
    Begin VB.Timer DissolveTimer
        Enabled       =    0    'False
        Interval      =    56
        Left          =    600
        Top           =    3900
    End
    Begin VB.CommandButton DissolveButton
        Caption       =    "Dissolve"
        Default       =    -1   'True
        Height        =    435
        Left          =    180
        TabIndex      =    1
        Top           =    2400
        Width         =    1635
    End
    Begin VB.PictureBox Picture1
        Height        =    4272
        Left          =    1920
        ScaleHeight   =    281
        ScaleMode     =    3    'Pixel
        ScaleWidth    =    325
        TabIndex      =    0
        Top           =    180
        Width         =    4932
    End
End
Attribute VB_Name = "DslvF1"
Attribute VB_Creatable = False
Attribute VB_Exposed = False

Option Explicit

Private Sub DissolveButton_Click()
    'DissolveToImage app.path & "\housrock.bmp", DissolveTimer, DissolveButton
    DissolveToImage App.Path & "\kaibab.bmp", DissolveTimer, DissolveButton
End Sub

Private Sub DissolveTimer_Timer()
    DoDissolveStep Picture1, DissolveTimer, DissolveButton
End Sub

Private Sub Form_Load()
    InitializeDissolve
    DissolveToImage App.Path & "\housrock.bmp", DissolveTimer, DissolveButton
End Sub

Private Sub Form_QueryUnload(Cancel As Integer, UnloadMode As Integer)
    DissolveTimer.Enabled = False
    Picture1.Enabled = False
    DissolveUnload Picture1
End Sub
```

```
Private Sub Picture1_Click()
   DoDissolveStep Picture1, DissolveTimer, DissolveButton
End Sub

Private Sub Picture1_Paint()
   DissolvePaint Picture1
End Sub
```

The code that does the real work resides in three modules: DIB2.BAS, DISSOLVE.BAS, and PALETTE.BAS. The majority of the code is found in the ten functions assigned to DISSOLVE.BAS. You should already be familiar with two of the functions in DISSOLVE.BAS—**CreatePixelSetSequence()** and **CreateDissolveBrush()**, which we used in the previous project. The code modules—DSLVEXP.FRM, DIB2.BAS, and PALETTE.BAS—contain only a few functions and some declarations. Let's put this project together by writing each of the three code modules.

Reading Bitmaps—DIB2.BAS

Now we need to add a set of functions for reading and manipulating bitmaps and their palettes. To resolve the palette debacle, we're going to relieve VB of its artistic responsibilities by extracting images from their disk files, loading them into memory, then blting them to their device contexts. The procedure that reads DIB files is called **ReadBitmapFile()**, and you'll find it in DIB2.BAS (see Listing 8.16).

Listing 8.16   The ReadBitmapFile() Procedure from DIB2.BAS

```
Sub ReadBitmapFile(ByVal FileName As String, bmFileHeader As BITMAPFILEHEADER, _
   bmInfo As BITMAPINFO, PixelData As ByteArray)

   Open FileName For Binary As #1
   ' Read the header structures.
   Get #1, 1, bmFileHeader
   Get #1, , bmInfo
   ' Read the pixel data
   ReDim PixelData.TheBytes(bmInfo.bmiHeader.biSizeImage - 1)
   Get #1, , PixelData.TheBytes
   Close #1
   PixelData.Initialized = True
End Sub
```

Only three commands are needed to open the file and read the header information:

```
Open FileName For Binary As #1
' Read the header structures.
```

```
Get #1, 1, bmFileHeader
Get #1, , bmInfo
```

The rest of the code actually pulls the image information out of the file and places it into our array of bytes in **PixelData.TheBytes**. This code will not work very well in a 16-bit environment because 16-bit VB puts a 32K limit on arrays. So, this code, in a 16-bit environment, would only hold 32K worth of image—not very much. Luckily, 32-bit VB and the flat memory model of Windows 95 clears these problems up by giving us almost unlimited array sizes.

Since we have already read in the header information from the bitmap, we know many things about the file. Most important at this stage is the image size in bytes, which is stored in the **bmInfo.bmiHeaderSizeImage** variable. Because we need to resize our image array to hold that number of bytes, we use the **ReDim** command to change the end field of the array to one less then **bmInfo.bmiHeaderSizeImage**. We use one less because the array is zero-based.

```
' Read the pixel data
  ReDim PixelData.TheBytes(bmInfo.bmiHeader.biSizeImage - 1)
  Get #1, , PixelData.TheBytes
  Close #1
  PixelData.Initialized = True
```

If you are forced to use a 16-bit environment, then check out the project by the same name in the /OLDBOOK subdirectory on the companion CD where you will find all the 16-bit projects from the VB3 version of this book. Without the unlimited array size, you are forced to start playing with binary large objects (BLOBs) and memory management. And, let us tell you, the segmented memory model of Windows 3.1 is no joy to work with. VB code compiled under a 16-bit environment will still work in Widows 95, but reverse compatibility is much harder.

Wrapping Up DIB2.BAS

DIB2.BAS also contains a "Min" function, which will return the lesser of two long integers passed as arguments, along with the DIB-related declarations (Listing 8.17).

Listing 8.17   The Function MinLong() and the Declarations Section from DIB2.BAS

```
Function MinLong(ByVal A As Long, ByVal B As Long)
  If A < B Then
    MinLong = A
```

```
         Else
             MinLong = B
         End If
    End Function


Option Explicit

Type ByteArray
    TheBytes()      As Byte
    Initialized     As Boolean
End Type

Type BITMAPINFOHEADER
    biSize          As Long
    biWidth         As Long
    biHeight        As Long
    biPlanes        As Integer
    biBitCount      As Integer
    biCompression   As Long
    biSizeImage     As Long
    biXPelsPerMeter As Long
    biYPelsPerMeter As Long
    biClrUsed       As Long
    biClrImportant  As Long
End Type


Type RGBQUAD
    rgbBlue         As Byte
    rgbGreen        As Byte
    rgbRed          As Byte
    rgbReserved     As Byte
End Type

Type BITMAPINFO
    bmiHeader As BITMAPINFOHEADER
    bmiColors(0 To 255) As RGBQUAD
End Type

Type INDEXBITMAPINFO
    bmiHeader As BITMAPINFOHEADER
    bmiColorIndexes(0 To 255) As Integer
End Type

Type BITMAPFILEHEADER
    bfType As Integer
    bfSize As Long
    bfReserved1 As Integer
    bfReserved2 As Integer
    bfOffBits As Long
End Type

Global Const SRCCOPY = &HCC0020
Global Const SRCPAINT = &HEE0086
Global Const SRCAND = &H8800C6
```

```
Global Const SRCINVERT = &H660046
Global Const SRCERASE = &H440328
Global Const NOTSRCCOPY = &H330008
Global Const NOTSRCERASE = &H1100A6
Global Const MERGECOPY = &HC000CA
Global Const MERGEPAINT = &HBB0226
Global Const PATCOPY = &HF00021
Global Const PATPAINT = &HFB0A09
Global Const PATINVERT = &H5A0049
Global Const DSTINVERT = &H550009
Global Const BLACKNESS = &H42&
Global Const WHITENESS = &HFF0062
Global Const BLACKONWHITE = 1
Global Const WHITEONBLACK = 2
Global Const COLORONCOLOR = 3
Global Const BI_RGB = 0&
Global Const BI_RLE8 = 1&
Global Const BI_RLE4 = 2&
Global Const TRANSPARENT = 1
Global Const OPAQUE = 2

Global Const CBM_INIT = &H4&

#If Win32 Then
    Public Declare Function CreateCompatibleDC Lib "gdi32" (ByVal hdc As Long) _
        As Long
    Public Declare Function DeleteDC Lib "gdi32" (ByVal hdc As Long) As Long
    Public Declare Function CreateCompatibleBitmap Lib "gdi32" (ByVal hdc _
        As Long, ByVal nWidth As Long, ByVal nHeight As Long) As Long
    Public Declare Function CreateDIBitmap Lib "gdi32" (ByVal hdc As Long, _
        lpInfoHeader As BITMAPINFOHEADER, ByVal dwUsage As Long, _
        ByVal lpInitBits As String, lpInitInfo As INDEXBITMAPINFO, ByVal wUsage _
        As Long) As Long
    Public Declare Function CreateDIBitmapByPal Lib "gdi32" Alias _
        "CreateDIBitmap" (ByVal hdc As Long, lpInfoHeader As BITMAPINFOHEADER, _
        ByVal dwUsage As Long, ByVal lpInitBits As String, lpInitInfo _
        As INDEXBITMAPINFO, ByVal wUsage As Long) As Long
    Public Declare Function DeleteObject Lib "gdi32" (ByVal hObject As Long) _
        As Long
    Public Declare Function SelectObject Lib "gdi32" (ByVal hdc As Long, ByVal _
        hObject As Long) As Long
    Public Declare Function BitBlt Lib "gdi32" (ByVal hDestDC As Long, ByVal x _
        As Long, ByVal y As Long, ByVal nWidth As Long, ByVal nHeight As Long, _
        ByVal hSrcDC As Long, ByVal XSrc As Long, ByVal YSrc As Long, ByVal _
        dwRop As Long) As Long
    Public Declare Function SetDIBitsToDevice% Lib "gdi32" Alias _
        "SetDIBitsToDevice%" (ByVal hdc#, ByVal x#, ByVal y#, ByVal dx#, ByVal _
        dy#, ByVal SrcX#, ByVal SrcY#, ByVal Scan#, ByVal NumScans#, ByVal Bits _
        As String, BitsInfo As BITMAPINFO, ByVal wUsage#)
    Public Declare Function StretchDIBits Lib "gdi32" (ByVal hdc As Long, _
        ByVal x As Integer, ByVal y As Integer, ByVal dx As Integer, ByVal dy _
        As Integer, ByVal SrcX As Integer, ByVal SrcY As Integer, ByVal _
        wSrcWidth As Integer, ByVal wSrcHeight As Integer, lpBits As Any, _
        lpBitsInfo As BITMAPINFO, ByVal wUsage As Long, ByVal dwRop As Long) _
        As Long
```

```
'   Public Declare Function StretchDIBits Lib "gdi32" (ByVal hdc As Long, _
        ByVal x As Integer, ByVal y As Integer, ByVal dx As Integer, ByVal dy _
        As Integer, ByVal SrcX As Integer, ByVal SrcY As Integer, ByVal _
        wSrcWidth As Integer, ByVal wSrcHeight As Integer, lpBits As Any, _
        lpBitsInfo As BITMAPINFO, ByVal wUsage As Integer, ByVal dwRop As Long) _
        As Long
#Else
    Public Declare Function CreateCompatibleDC Lib "GDI" (ByVal hdc As Integer) _
        As Integer
    Public Declare Function DeleteDC Lib "GDI" (ByVal hdc As Integer) As Integer
    Public Declare Function CreateCompatibleBitmap Lib "GDI" (ByVal hdc _
        As Integer, ByVal nWidth As Integer, ByVal nHeight As Integer) As Integer
    Public Declare Function CreateDIBitmap Lib "GDI" (ByVal hdc As Integer, _
        lpInfoHeader As BITMAPINFOHEADER, ByVal dwUsage As Long, ByVal _
        lpInitBits As String, lpInitInfo As BITMAPINFO, ByVal wUsage As Integer) _
        As Integer
    Public Declare Function CreateDIBitmapByPal Lib "GDI" Alias "CreateDIBitmap" _
        (ByVal hdc As Integer, lpInfoHeader As BITMAPINFOHEADER, ByVal dwUsage _
        As Long, ByVal lpInitBits As String, lpInitInfo As INDEXBITMAPINFO, _
        ByVal wUsage As Integer) As Integer
    Public Declare Function DeleteObject Lib "GDI" (ByVal hObject As Integer) _
        As Integer
    Public Declare Function SelectObject Lib "GDI" (ByVal hdc As Integer, _
        ByVal hObject As Integer) As Integer
    Public Declare Function BitBlt Lib "GDI" (ByVal hDestDC As Integer, _
        ByVal x As Integer, ByVal y As Integer, ByVal nWidth As Integer, _
        ByVal nHeight As Integer, ByVal hSrcDC As Integer, ByVal XSrc As Integer, _
        ByVal YSrc As Integer, ByVal dwRop As Long) As Integer
    Public Declare Function SetDIBitsToDevice Lib "GDI" (ByVal hdc As Integer, _
        ByVal DestX As Integer, ByVal DestY As Integer, ByVal nWidth As Integer, _
        ByVal nHeight As Integer, ByVal SrcX As Integer, ByVal SrcY As Integer, _
        ByVal nStartScan As Integer, ByVal nNumScans As Integer, ByVal lpBits _
        As Long, lpBitsInfo As BITMAPINFO, ByVal wUsage As Integer) As Integer
    Public Declare Function StretchDIBits Lib "GDI" (ByVal hdc As c, ByVal _
        DestX As Integer, ByVal DestY As Integer, ByVal nDestWidth As Integer, _
        ByVal nDestHeight As Integer, ByVal SrcX As Integer, ByVal SrcY _
        As Integer, ByVal nSrcWidth As Integer, ByVal nSrcHeight As Integer, _
        ByVal lpBits As Long, lpBitsInfo As BITMAPINFO, ByVal wUsage As Integer, _
        ByVal dwRop As Long) As Integer
#End If
```

Inside PALETTE.BAS

PALETTE.BAS requires one procedure—**ConstructPaletteFromColorTable()**.
Of course, we'll also need to include some declarations in this module. Listing 8.18 shows the complete code for PALETTE.BAS.

Listing 8.18   The Declarations Section and the ConstructPaletteFromColorTable() Procedure from PALETTE.BAS

```
Option Explicit

Type PALETTEENTRY
    peRed As Byte
    peGreen As Byte
    peBlue As Byte
    peFlags As Byte
End Type

Type LOGPALETTE
    palVersion As Integer
    palNumEntries As Integer
    palPalEntry(255) As PALETTEENTRY
End Type

Type ColorSteps
    iRed As Long
    iGreen As Long
    iBlue As Long
End Type


Global Const BLACK_BRUSH = 4
Global Const DEFAULT_PALETTE = 15
Global Const PC_RESERVED = &H1   ' palette index used for animation
Global Const CF_PALETTE = 9
Global Const DIB_RGB_COLORS = 0 ' color table in RGBTriples
Global Const DIB_PAL_COLORS = 1


#If Win32 Then
    Public Declare Function CreateSolidBrush Lib "gdi32" (ByVal crColor As Long) _
        As Long
    Public Declare Function DeleteObject Lib "gdi32" (ByVal hObject As Long) _
        As Long
    Public Declare Function GetStockObject Lib "gdi32" (ByVal nIndex As Long) _
        As Long
    Public Declare Function ReleaseDC Lib "user32" (ByVal hWnd As Long, ByVal _
        hdc As Long) As Long
    Public Declare Function Rectangle Lib "gdi32" (ByVal hdc As Long, ByVal X1 _
        As Long, ByVal Y1 As Long, ByVal X2 As Long, ByVal Y2 As Long) As Long
    Public Declare Function SelectObject Lib "gdi32" (ByVal hdc As Long, _
        ByVal hObject As Long) As Long
    Public Declare Function SelectPalette Lib "gdi32" (ByVal hdc As Long, _
        ByVal hPalette As Long, ByVal bForceBackground As Long) As Long
    Public Declare Function SetPaletteEntries Lib "gdi32" (ByVal hPalette _
        As Long, ByVal wStartIndex As Long, ByVal wNumEntries As Long, _
        lpPaletteEntries As PALETTEENTRY) As Long
    Public Declare Function GetPaletteEntries Lib "gdi32" (ByVal hPalette _
        As Long, ByVal wStartIndex As Long, ByVal wNumEntries As Long, _
        lpPaletteEntries As PALETTEENTRY) As Long
    Public Declare Function RealizePalette Lib "gdi32" (ByVal hdc As Long) _
        As Long
```

```
    Public Declare Function GetDC Lib "user32" (ByVal hWnd As Long) As Long
    Public Declare Function CreatePalette Lib "gdi32" (lpLogPalette _
        As LOGPALETTE) As Long
    ' This function isn't used in this program, but it's a member of the family:
    ' Public Declare Sub AnimatePalette Lib "gdi32" (ByVal hPalette As Long,
    '    ByVal wStartIndex As Long, ByVal wNumEntries As Long, lpPaletteColors _
    '    As PALETTEENTRY)
#Else
    Public Declare Function SelectPalette Lib "User" (ByVal hdc As Integer, _
        ByVal hPalette As Integer, ByVal bForceBackground As Integer) As Integer
    Public Declare Function RealizePalette Lib "User" (ByVal hdc As Integer) _
        As Integer
    Public Declare Function GetDC Lib "User" (ByVal hWnd As Integer) As Integer
    Public Declare Function ReleaseDC Lib "User" (ByVal hWnd As Integer, _
        ByVal hdc As Integer) As Integer
    Public Declare Function CreateSolidBrush Lib "GDI" (ByVal crColor As Long) _
        As Integer
    Public Declare Function SelectObject Lib "GDI" (ByVal hdc As Integer, _
        ByVal hObject As Integer) As Integer
    Public Declare Function Rectangle Lib "GDI" (ByVal hdc As Integer, ByVal X1 _
        As Integer, ByVal Y1 As Integer, ByVal X2 As Integer, ByVal Y2 _
        As Integer) As Integer
    Public Declare Function DeleteObject Lib "GDI" (ByVal hObject As Integer) _
        As Integer
    Public Declare Function GetStockObject Lib "GDI" (ByVal nIndex As Integer) _
        As Integer
    Public Declare Function GetPaletteEntries Lib "GDI" (ByVal hPalette As _
        Integer, ByVal wStartIndex As Integer, ByVal wNumEntries As Integer, _
        lpPaletteEntries As PALETTEENTRY) As Integer
    Public Declare Function SetPaletteEntries Lib "GDI" (ByVal hPalette As _
        Integer, ByVal wStartIndex As Integer, ByVal wNumEntries As Integer, _
        lpPaletteEntries As PALETTEENTRY) As Integer
    Public Declare Function CreatePalette Lib "GDI" (lpLogPalette As LOGPALETTE) _
        As Integer
    ' This function isn't used in this program, but it's a member of the family:
    ' Public Declare Sub AnimatePalette Lib "GDI" (ByVal hPalette As Integer, _
    '    ByVal wStartIndex As Integer, ByVal wNumEntries As Integer, _
    '    lpPaletteColors As PALETTEENTRY)
#End If

Global ColorSelected As Long
Global hSystemPalette As Long
Global hCurrentPalette As Long
Global CurrentPaletteEntry As PALETTEENTRY
Global NewPaletteEntry As PALETTEENTRY
Global PaletteEntries(256) As PALETTEENTRY

Sub ConstructPaletteFromColorTable(ColorTable() As RGBQUAD, LogicalPalette _
    As LOGPALETTE)
Dim Counter As Integer

    For Counter = 0 To 255
        With LogicalPalette.palPalEntry(Counter)
            .peRed = ColorTable(Counter).rgbRed
```

```
            .peGreen = ColorTable(Counter).rgbGreen
            .peBlue = ColorTable(Counter).rgbBlue
            If (Counter > 9) And (Counter < 246) Then
                .peFlags = PC_RESERVED
            Else
                .peFlags = 0
            End If
        End With
    Next Counter
    LogicalPalette.palVersion = &H300
    LogicalPalette.palNumEntries = 256
End Sub
```

By declaring the first parameter of this function with a pair of empty paren-
theses, we enable VB to pass it an entire array, which, in this case, is the color
table from our freshly read DIB.

ConstructPaletteFromColorTable() translates color table entries into
logical palette entries. The logical palette is also an array, but because it belongs
to the **Type**-declared structure **LOGPALETTE**, instead of passing in the array,
we pass the entire structure just by reference. That way we can also set
palVersion and **palNumEntries**, rounding out a complete logical palette.

We'll be calling **ConstructPaletteFromColorTable()** from the general
procedure **DissolveToImage()**, which we'll cover in the next section.

Inside DISSOLVE.BAS

We're now ready for the workhorse module. Here we have a lot of ground to
cover, so let's break the module into its different functions. We'll start by
making a subtle, but essential, change to the function **CreateDissolveBrush()**,
as shown in Listing 8.19

Listing 8.19   The function CreateDissolveBrush() from DISSOLVE.BAS

```
Function CreateDissolveBrush(DissolveStep As Integer, ByVal hdc As Integer) _
    As Integer
Dim hCompBitmap As Long
Dim BrushBitmapInfo As INDEXBITMAPINFO
Dim Counter As Integer
Dim PixelDataChunk As String * 32
Dim Dummy As Long
Dim Row As Integer
Dim Column As Integer

    With BrushBitmapInfo.bmiHeader
        .biSize = 40
        .biWidth = 8
        .biHeight = 8
        .biPlanes = 1
```

```
        .biBitCount = 1
        .biCompression = 0
        .biSizeImage = 0
        .biXPelsPerMeter = 0
        .biYPelsPerMeter = 0
        .biClrUsed = 0
        .biClrImportant = 0
    End With

    BrushBitmapInfo.bmiColorIndexes(0) = 0
    BrushBitmapInfo.bmiColorIndexes(1) = 255

    For Counter = 0 To 7
        Mid$(PixelDataChunk, Counter * 4 + 1, 1) = Chr$(&HFF)
    Next Counter
    For Counter = 1 To DissolveStep * (64 / NumberOfSteps)
        Row = (PixelSetSequence(Counter) - 1) \ 8
        Column = (PixelSetSequence(Counter) - 1) Mod 8
        Mid$(PixelDataChunk, Row * 4 + 1, 1) = Chr$(Asc(Mid$(PixelDataChunk, _
            Row * 4 + 1, 1)) And ((Not (2 ^ (7 - Column))) - &HFF00))
    Next Counter

    hCompBitmap = CreateDIBitmapByPal(hdc, BrushBitmapInfo.bmiHeader, _
        CBM_INIT, PixelDataChunk, BrushBitmapInfo, DIB_PAL_COLORS)
    CreateDissolveBrush = CreatePatternBrush(hCompBitmap)
    Dummy = DeleteObject&(hCompBitmap)
End Function
```

As we discussed in the previous project, we normally create a bitmap by preparing a structure of type **BITMAPINFO**, which contains a **BITMAPINFOHEADER** followed by a color table in the form of an array of **RGBQUAD**s. When the GDI converts this bitmap to a DDB, it maps the colors by matching the RGB values in the table to the RGB values in the currently realized logical palette. Here's the problem we discovered: Colors are matched in order, starting at the beginning of the palette. If the currently realized logical palette contains a pure white color entry in its non-reserved color list—the colors in entries 10 through 245—then when the color matching takes place, the white pixels in the monochrome bitmap will be set to reference that earlier entry instead of entry 255. When that happens, the ROPs will no longer be manipulating white pixels with values of 255, and the monochrome bitmap no longer functions as a mask.

Fortunately, there is an alternate way to specify the color information. Instead of building a table of RGB values, we can create an array of 16-bit integers that specify color indexes into the currently realized logical palette. Oddly enough, although the Windows Programmer's Reference clearly discusses this approach, there is no pre-defined structure, like **BITMAPINFO**, to handle a color palette index array. So, we made one up:

```
Type INDEXBITMAPINFO
   bmiHeader As BITMAPINFOHEADER
   bmiColorIndexes(0 To 255) As Integer
End Type
```

We declare the **BrushBitmapInfo** structure with this type:

```
Dim BrushBitmapInfo As INDEXBITMAPINFO
```

Then we set the color values to the palette entries for black and white:

```
BrushBitmapInfo.bmiColorIndexes(0) = 0
BrushBitmapInfo.bmiColorIndexes(1) = 255
```

And finally, we call **CreateDIBitmapByPal()**, an *alias* of the API function **CreateDIBitmap()**:

```
hCompBitmap = CreateDIBitmapByPal(hDC, BrushBitmapInfo.bmiHeader, _
       CBM_INIT, PixelData, BrushBitmapInfo, DIB_PAL_COLORS)
```

Here's the declaration for the aliased form of the **CreateDIBitmap()** API function:

```
Win32:
Declare Function CreateDIBitmapByPal Lib "gdi32" Alias "CreateDIBitmap" _
   (ByVal hdc As Long, lpInfoHeader As BITMAPINFOHEADER, _
   ByVal dwUsage As Long, ByVal lpInitBits As String, _
   lpInitInfo As INDEXBITMAPINFO, ByVal wUsage As Long) As Long

Win16:
Declare Function CreateDIBitmapByPal Lib "GDI" Alias "CreateDIBitmap" _
   (ByVal hDC As Integer, lpInfoHeader As BITMAPINFOHEADER, _
   ByVal dwUsage As Long, ByVal lpInitBits As String, _
   lpInitInfo As INDEXBITMAPINFO, ByVal wUsage As Integer) As Integer
```

In the **lpInitInfo** argument, we pass the **INDEXBITMAPINFO** structure instead of **BITMAPINFO**, and we set the **wUsage** parameter to **DIB_PAL_COLORS** to indicate that the color table contains integer palette indices.

Next, we'll write **CreatePaletteSequenceArray()** (see Listing 8.20), which will create the series of palettes needed to handle the dissolve.

Listing 8.20 The CreatePaletteSequenceArray() Procedure from DISSOLVE.BAS

```
Sub CreatePaletteSequenceArray(CurrentPalette As LOGPALETTE, NewPalette _
   As LOGPALETTE)
```

```
'  This procedure will take the palette belonging to
'  the currently displayed image, and the palette
'  belonging to the new image, and will construct a
'  series of six intermediate palettes.  The eight
'  palettes will then be used to soften the transition
'  between images.
'
'  The palette array is declared globally.

Dim PalCounter As Integer
Dim PalEntryCounter As Integer

    If CurrentPalette.palNumEntries <> 256 Then
        LSet palettes(1) = NewPalette
    Else
        LSet palettes(1) = CurrentPalette
    End If
    LSet palettes(8) = NewPalette
    For PalEntryCounter = 0 To 255
        PalStepArray(PalEntryCounter).Red = _
            (CInt(NewPalette.palPalEntry(PalEntryCounter).peRed) - _
            palettes(1).palPalEntry(PalEntryCounter).peRed) \ 7
        PalStepArray(PalEntryCounter).Green = _
            (CInt(NewPalette.palPalEntry(PalEntryCounter).peGreen) - _
            palettes(1).palPalEntry(PalEntryCounter).peGreen) \ 7
        PalStepArray(PalEntryCounter).Blue = _
            (CInt(NewPalette.palPalEntry(PalEntryCounter).peBlue) - _
            palettes(1).palPalEntry(PalEntryCounter).peBlue) \ 7
    Next PalEntryCounter
    For PalCounter = 2 To 7
        For PalEntryCounter = 0 To 255
            palettes(PalCounter).palPalEntry(PalEntryCounter).peRed = _
                MaxInt(MinInt(((palettes(PalCounter - _
                    1).palPalEntry(PalEntryCounter).peRed) + _
                    PalStepArray(PalEntryCounter).Red), 255), 0)
            palettes(PalCounter).palPalEntry(PalEntryCounter).peGreen = _
                MaxInt(MinInt(((palettes(PalCounter - _
                1).palPalEntry(PalEntryCounter).peGreen) + _
                PalStepArray(PalEntryCounter).Green), 255), 0)
            palettes(PalCounter).palPalEntry(PalEntryCounter).peBlue = _
                MaxInt(MinInt(((palettes(PalCounter - _
                1).palPalEntry(PalEntryCounter).peBlue) + _
                PalStepArray(PalEntryCounter).Blue), 255), 0)
            If (PalEntryCounter > 9) And (PalEntryCounter < 246) Then
                palettes(PalCounter).palPalEntry(PalEntryCounter).peFlags = _
                    PC_RESERVED
            Else
                palettes(PalCounter).palPalEntry(PalEntryCounter).peFlags = 0
            End If
        Next PalEntryCounter
        palettes(PalCounter).palVersion = &H300
        palettes(PalCounter).palNumEntries = 256
    Next PalCounter
End Sub
```

To understand what this procedure does, imagine that a particular palette entry—say entry 217—contains a color consisting of pure red in the palette of the current image and pure blue in the palette of the new image. (This is unlikely, not to mention unnecessary, in the real world, because the reserved colors include pure red and pure blue at palette entries 249 and 252.) In seven steps, we want to gradually change the color &H00 &H00 &HFF into the color &HFF &H00 &H00. If you take the difference of the red component in the two colors, you get &HFF, or the decimal 255. 255 divided by 7 equals approximately 36. So, with each step we need to add decimal value -36 to the red component. For the blue component, we do just the reverse. The blue component of palette entry 217 begins with a value of 0, and must end at decimal 255, so we need to add +36 at each step. The eight versions of palette entry 217 would contain the values that appear in Table 8.1.

In the final step of the dissolve, we jump directly to the correct palette for the new image, instead of adding the palette step values.

The first loop in **CreatePaletteSequenceArray()** builds an array of these step values, one for each red, green, and blue component of each palette entry, for a total of 768 values. The second loop uses these values to build the six intermediate logical palettes.

Notice that we've set the flags of the 236 modifiable colors to **PC_RESERVED**. Although this program doesn't use **AnimatePalette()** to shift colors, the **PC_RESERVED** flags prevent colors from mapping too wildly. (When we've finished, try setting the flag both ways to compare the results.)

At this point, we have a DIB waiting in the wings, a set of palettes to ease the transition from one image to the other, and a function to generate the brushes as we step through the dissolve. We'll pull everything together in a procedure called **DissolvePaint()**, as shown in Listing 8.21.

Table 8.1 *A Seven-Step Transition from Pure Red to Pure Blue*

Palette Number	Blue Component	Green Component	Red Component
1	0	0	255
2	36	0	219
3	72	0	183
4	144	0	111
6	180	0	75
7	216	0	39
8	255	0	0

Listing 8.21 The DissolvePaint() Procedure from DISSOLVE.BAS

```
Sub DissolvePaint(DissolvePicture As PictureBox)
Dim hMemDC As Long
Dim hMemBitmap As Long
Dim hOldMemBitmap As Long
Dim ErrCode As Long
Dim hOldPalette As Long
Dim hDisolveBrush As Long
Dim hOldBrush As Long
Dim OldImage As Long
Dim OldImageWidth As Integer
Dim OldImageHeight As Integer
Dim NewImageWidth As Integer
Dim NewImageHeight As Integer

    If DissolveStepForPainting < 1 Then Exit Sub
    ' Builds a memory device context where the dissolve
    ' will be performed.
    hMemDC = CreateCompatibleDC(DissolvePicture.hdc)
    hMemBitmap = CreateCompatibleBitmap(DissolvePicture.hdc, _
        DissolvePicture.ScaleWidth, DissolvePicture.ScaleHeight)
    hOldMemBitmap = SelectObject(hMemDC, hMemBitmap)
    ErrCode = Rectangle(hMemDC, 0, 0, DissolvePicture.ScaleWidth, _
        DissolvePicture.ScaleHeight)

    ' Switch the context index.
    OldImage = (NewImage + 1) Mod 2

    ' Assign image dimension info to shorthand reference variables.
    OldImageWidth = bmInfo(OldImage).bmiHeader.biWidth
    OldImageHeight = bmInfo(OldImage).bmiHeader.biHeight
    NewImageWidth = bmInfo(NewImage).bmiHeader.biWidth
    NewImageHeight = bmInfo(NewImage).bmiHeader.biHeight

    ' Select the palette activated by DoDissolveStep() into
    ' the memory and display DCs.
    ErrCode = SelectPalette(hMemDC, hPalette, False)
    hOldPalette = SelectPalette(DissolvePicture.hdc, hPalette, False)
    ErrCode = RealizePalette(DissolvePicture.hdc)
    ' Throw away the palette belonging to the previous step or image,
    ' unless this is the first image (you can't delete the
    ' default palette).
    If (hOldPalette <> DEFAULT_PALETTE) And (hOldPalette <> hPalette) Then
        ErrCode = DeleteObject(hOldPalette)
    End If

    If PixelData(NewImage).Initialized Then
        ' Create the appropriate dissolve brush for the current step,
        ' and select it into the MemDC.
        hDisolveBrush = CreateDissolveBrush(DissolveStepForPainting, _
            DissolvePicture.hdc)
        hOldBrush = SelectObject(hMemDC, hDisolveBrush)
```

```
        ' Paint the old image into the MemDC with an inverted brush.
        If PixelData(OldImage).Initialized Then
            ErrCode = StretchDIBits(hMemDC, 0, 0, OldImageWidth, OldImageHeight, _
                0, 0, OldImageWidth, OldImageHeight, _
                PixelData(OldImage).TheBytes(0), bmInfo(OldImage), _
                DIB_RGB_COLORS, &HCF0224) ' Performs ROP SPno
        End If
        ' Paint the new image into the MemDC with the dissolve ROP.
        ErrCode = StretchDIBits(hMemDC, 0, 0, NewImageWidth, NewImageHeight, _
            0, 0, NewImageWidth, NewImageHeight, PixelData(NewImage).TheBytes(0), _
            bmInfo(NewImage), DIB_RGB_COLORS, &HAC0744) ' Performs ROP SPDSxax
        ' Rapidly transfer the contents of the MemDC to the screen.
        ErrCode = BitBlt(DissolvePicture.hdc, 0, 0, DissolvePicture.ScaleWidth, _
            DissolvePicture.ScaleHeight, hMemDC, 0, 0, SRCCOPY)

        ' Replace the default brush in the MemDC and
        ' delete the dissolve brush.
        ErrCode = SelectObject(hMemDC, hOldBrush)
        ErrCode = DeleteObject(hDisolveBrush)
    End If

    ' Delete the MemDC, then delete the MemBitmap.
    ErrCode = SelectObject(hMemDC, hOldMemBitmap)
    ErrCode = SelectPalette(hMemDC, DEFAULT_PALETTE, False)
    ErrCode = DeleteDC(hMemDC)
    ErrCode = DeleteObject(hMemBitmap)
End Sub
```

The first part of **DissolvePaint()** creates a memory device context.

```
hMemDC = CreateCompatibleDC(DissolvePicture.hDC)
hMemBitmap = CreateCompatibleBitmap(DissolvePicture.hDC,
        DissolvePicture.ScaleWidth, DissolvePicture.ScaleHeight)
hOldMemBitmap = SelectObject(hMemDC, hMemBitmap)
ErrCode = Rectangle(hMemDC, 0, 0, DissolvePicture.ScaleWidth,
        DissolvePicture.ScaleHeight)
```

A memory device context is like a shadow of a screen device context. You can perform all the same operations on a memory device context that you can perform on the screen, but they're invisible. The only way to see the bitmap created or changed in a memory device context is to transfer the image to a visible device context, usually the screen. We've chosen to use a memory device context as a scratch pad for the dissolve, because it helps disguise some of the slower painting that occurs with complex raster operations. It still takes longer than straight **SRCCOPY** blting, but the messy mechanics remain hidden backstage. When we've completed each dissolve step, we can use **SRCCOPY** and **BitBlt()** to rapidly transfer the resulting image to the screen.

There is another, perhaps more important, reason for using a memory device context. Windows is a multitasking environment; when one window covers another, the covered bitmap is lost. When its parent window rises back to the top of the z order, it needs some way to redraw the rectangular area, or areas, that have just been uncovered. In some cases, it's just as easy to redraw each element whenever necessary, for example, when the only things drawn in the device context are text or controls or simple graphic elements. But for complex bitmap patterns such as photographs, you can use a memory device context as a buffer to manipulate and store the image behind the scenes. Then, whenever you need to display or restore the screen image, you can just blt it from the memory device context. That's exactly what happens when you enable the **AutoRedraw** property of a Picture Box or form in VB.

To build a memory device context, call the function **CreateCompatibleDC()**, passing it a single argument, the handle to the screen device context you want to shadow. Then use **CreateCompatibleBitmap()** to make a bitmap with the same dimensions and color resolution as the screen device context. Before you can draw on the bitmap, you have to select it into the memory device context with **SelectObject()**. The GDI doesn't automatically initialize the bitmap, so it will contain a random pattern of pixels determined by whatever happens to lie in memory. To clean things up, we've used the **Rectangle()** function to draw a filled rectangle that covers the entire bitmap. **Rectangle()** will use whatever brush it finds selected into the device context. The default brush is pure white, so **Rectangle()** will whitewash the bitmap to a nice clean drawing surface. See the declaration sections in DISSOLVE.BAS and DIB2.BAS for the declarations of these GDI functions.

The next line of code in **DissolvePaint()** identifies which image is which.

```
OldImage = (NewImage + 1) Mod 2
```

During a dissolve, we have two DIBs in memory: the **OldImage** and the **NewImage**. To keep track of them, we've declared three arrays of two elements each:

```
Global bmFileHeader(1) As BITMAPFILEHEADER
Global bmInfo(1) As BITMAPINFO
Global PixelData(1) As ByteArray
Dim NewImage As Integer
```

Each time we dissolve to a new image, we load the bitmap header information, and the handle to the pixel data into whichever of the two elements is free at the time. When the program first loads, we set **NewImage** to 0, so the first DIB goes into the first array element. When we load the second image, we change the value of **NewImage** to 1 and load the DIB data into the second array element. During the dissolve, we know that the elements that do not hold the new image must hold the old image, so in **DissolvePaint()**, **OldImage** equals **(NewImage + 1) Mod 2**. When we get to the higher-level procedures a little later, we'll show you how we ping-pong the images between the two sets of array elements.

The next four statements do nothing but provide a shorthand for the lengthy references to the image dimensions:

```
OldImageWidth = bmInfo(OldImage).bmiHeader.biWidth
OldImageHeight = bmInfo(OldImage).bmiHeader.biHeight
NewImageWidth = bmInfo(NewImage).bmiHeader.biWidth
NewImageHeight = bmInfo(NewImage).bmiHeader.biHeight
```

Next, we select the appropriate palette into both the memory device context and the screen device context:

```
' Select the palette activated by DoDissolveStep() into
' the memory and display DCs.
 ErrCode = SelectPalette(hMemDC, hPalette, False)
hOldPalette = SelectPalette(DissolvePicture.hdc, hPalette, False)
 ErrCode = RealizePalette(DissolvePicture.hdc)
' Throw away the palette belonging to the previous step or image,
' unless this is the first image (you can't delete the
' default palette).
 If (hOldPalette <> DEFAULT_PALETTE) And (hOldPalette <> hPalette) Then
   ErrCode = DeleteObject(hOldPalette)
 End If
```

We have to realize the palette into the screen device context, **DissolvePicture.hDC**, to get the Palette Manager to load it into the system palette. Under normal circumstances, a memory device context cannot control the system palette.

Since the palettes we create for each step of the dissolve exist only until the next step, we can destroy the previous palette after we select the next palette into the device context, unless it happens to be the system default palette.

The final step before we perform the dissolve is to create the pattern brush:

```
If PixelData(NewImage).Initialized Then
    ' Create the appropriate dissolve brush for the current step,
    ' and select it into the MemDC.
```

```
hDisolveBrush = CreateDissolveBrush(DissolveStepForPainting, _
    DissolvePicture.hdc)
hOldBrush = SelectObject(hMemDC, hDisolveBrush)
```

We don't need the brush in the screen device context, because we're going to perform all our complex raster operations in the memory device context. We'll use **SRCCOPY**, which doesn't use a pattern brush, to blt the image from the memory device context to the screen device context.

Once we've created the memory device context, selected the palette, and created the pattern brush, we can perform the blting operations that combine the DIBs into the memory device context.

```
' Paint the old image into the MemDC with an inverted brush.
If PixelData(OldImage).Initialized Then
    ErrCode = StretchDIBits(hMemDC, 0, 0, OldImageWidth, OldImageHeight, _
    0, 0, OldImageWidth, OldImageHeight, PixelData(OldImage).TheBytes(0), _
    bmInfo(OldImage), DIB_RGB_COLORS, &HCF0224) ' Performs ROP SPno
End If
' Paint the new image into the MemDC with the dissolve ROP.
ErrCode = StretchDIBits(hMemDC, 0, 0, NewImageWidth, NewImageHeight, 0, _
    0, NewImageWidth, NewImageHeight, PixelData(NewImage).TheBytes(0), _
    bmInfo(NewImage), DIB_RGB_COLORS, &HAC0744) ' Performs ROP SPDSxax
' Rapidly transfer the contents of the MemDC to the screen.
ErrCode = BitBlt(DissolvePicture.hdc, 0, 0, DissolvePicture.ScaleWidth, _
    DissolvePicture.ScaleHeight, hMemDC, 0, 0, SRCCOPY)
```

This section of code performs three separate blt operations. In the first two, we use a new function, **StretchDIBits()**, to combine the two images with the pattern brush. **StretchDIBits()** looks a lot like **StretchBlt()**, and performs a similar function. However, unlike **StretchBlt()**, which copies a DDB from one device context into another, **StretchDIBits()** copies a DIB from memory directly into a device context, converting it into a DDB as it goes. Compare the 32-bit declarations for these two blt functions:

```
Declare Function StretchBlt Lib "gdi32" (ByVal hdc As Long, ByVal x As Long, _
    ByVal y As Long, ByVal nWidth As Long, ByVal nHeight As Long, _
    ByVal hSrcDC As Long, ByVal xSrc As Long, ByVal ySrc As Long, _
    ByVal nSrcWidth As Long, ByVal nSrcHeight As Long, ByVal dwRop As Long) _
    As Long

Declare Function StretchDIBits Lib "gdi32" (ByVal hdc As Long, ByVal x As Long, _
    ByVal y As Long, ByVal dx As Long, ByVal dy As Long, ByVal SrcX As Long, _
    ByVal SrcY As Long, ByVal wSrcWidth As Long, ByVal wSrcHeight As Long, _
    lpBits As Any, lpBitsInfo As BITMAPINFO, ByVal wUsage As Long, ByVal dwRop _
    As Long) As Long
```

In the declaration of **StretchBlt()**, you find two parameters that specify device contexts: one for the destination, the first argument; and one for the source, the sixth argument. In the **StretchDIBits()**, you find a place for only the destination device context. In place of the source device context, this function requires a pointer to the pixel data, a pointer to the **BITMAPINFO** structure that describes that pixel data, and an argument called **wUsage**, which specifies whether the color table data in **BITMAPINFO** contains palette indexes or RGB colors (just like the **dwUsage** argument in the **CreateDIBitmap()** function, which we used to make the pattern brush).

We have to use **StretchDIBits()** instead of **BitBlt()** or **StretchBlt()** because we want to map the colors of both images to the palette currently selected into the memory device context. Remember, **BitBlt()** copies literal pixel values from one location to another. It makes no attempt to match colors from one device context to the other. But because **StretchDIBits()** starts out with the DIB data, it has to map each color in its color table to the system palette as it converts the image to a DDB. That's how we get the two images to share the six intermediate palettes. The first call to **StretchDIBits()** retranslates the existing image to the intermediate palette. The second call to **StretchDIBits()** then translates the pixel values of the new image as it combines its pixels with those of the pattern brush and the existing image. When the dissolve ends, we have two versions of the new image: the DDB that appears on the screen, and the DIB that we hold in memory for the next dissolve.

We've added another raster operation in the first call to **StretchDIBits()**. This is just a refinement. The real work is done by the ROP code we derived earlier in this chapter. But this additional raster operation solves one slight problem. When dissolving from a larger image to a smaller image, you must get rid of the portions of the old image that lie outside the dimensions of the new image. Let me briefly explain how we arrived at this ROP code.

To make the periphery of the larger image fade away as the new image dissolves in, we realized that we could invert the pattern brushes and use them to gradually change the pixels in the image to pure white, the background color. After inverting each brush, we used an **Or** operation between the inverted brush and the image, which made an image full of white holes. To calculate the correct ROP code, we performed these two steps on the binary constants representing a brush and a source image. Then we looked up the code in the ROP table.

For the final blt operation, we use **BitBlt()**, the quickest blt function, to **SRCCOPY** the image to the screen. The rest, shown below, is cleanup:

```
' Replace the default brush in the MemDC and
  ' delete the dissolve brush.
```

```
        ErrCode = SelectObject(hMemDC, hOldBrush)
        ErrCode = DeleteObject(hDisolveBrush)
    End If

    ' Delete the MemDC, then delete the MemBitmap.
    ErrCode = SelectObject(hMemDC, hOldMemBitmap)
    ErrCode = SelectPalette(hMemDC, DEFAULT_PALETTE, False)
    ErrCode = DeleteDC(hMemDC)
    ErrCode = DeleteObject(hMemBitmap)
End Sub
```

When we're done with each **Paint** event, we restore the default brush to
the memory device context, delete the dissolve brush, and delete the memory
device context and its bitmap.

Now that we have the underlying elements of the dissolve in place, we
need a mechanism to trigger a dissolve and tick off the steps. Listing 8.22
shows the procedures that fulfill those roles.

Listing 8.22   The DissolveToImage() and DoDissolveStep() Procedures from DISSOLVE.BAS

```
Sub DissolveToImage(FileName As String, DissolveTimer As Timer, _
    DissolveTrigger As Control)
Dim NewPalette As LOGPALETTE

    DissolveTrigger.Enabled = False
    NewImage = (NewImage + 1) Mod 2
    DissolveStep = 1
    If PixelData(NewImage).Initialized = False Then
        ReadBitmapFile FileName, bmFileHeader(NewImage), bmInfo(NewImage), _
            PixelData(NewImage)
        ConstructPaletteFromColorTable bmInfo(NewImage).bmiColors(), NewPalette
        CreatePaletteSequenceArray palettes(8), NewPalette
        DissolveTimer.Enabled = True
    End If
End Sub

Sub DoDissolveStep(DissolvePicture As PictureBox, DissolveTimer As Timer, _
    DissolveTrigger As Control)

    hPalette = CreatePalette(palettes(DissolveStep))
    DissolveStepForPainting = DissolveStep
    InvalidateRect DissolvePicture.hWnd, ByVal 0, False
    'DissolvePicture.Refresh
    If DissolveStep >= 8 Then
        DissolveTimer.Enabled = False
        DissolveTrigger.Enabled = True
    Else
        DissolveStep = DissolveStep + 1
    End If
End Sub
```

DissolveToImage() disables the control that initiated the dissolve, passed in as the third parameter. It then switches the value of **NewImage** to the free index into the DIB information arrays (either 1 or 0), and sets the **DissolveStep** to 1.

After calling **ReadBitmapFile()** in order to read the DIB into its memory structure, **DissolveToImage()** then calls **ConstructPaletteFromColorTable()**, followed by **CreatePaletteSequenceArray()**, which takes the two logical palettes belonging to the current image on the screen and the newly read image in memory, and interpolates six intermediate palettes.

Finally, after it has read the bitmap and set up the palettes, **DissolveToImage()** enables the Timer control specified in the second parameter.

The next procedure, **DoDissolveStep()** performs one step of the dissolve by building a logical palette and invalidating the client area of the Picture Box control, which triggers a **Paint** event. It then increments **DissolveStep**. When the dissolve is complete, it disables the Timer control passed in as the second parameter, and enables the control that triggers a new dissolve, passed in as the third parameter.

You'll notice that these procedures won't do anything until called by an event procedure somewhere. Instead of embedding this code directly in the event procedures, we've placed it in a code module. Things get turned a little inside out. Instead of code embedded in event procedures, we end up with procedures that expect to receive controls as arguments. In this sample program, **DoDissolveStep()** is called by a **Timer** event. Any timer will do, because the procedure never explicitly references a Timer by its own name. Instead, it expects the event procedure that controls the dissolve to pass the Timer control as a parameter. Since the dissolve will likely be controlled by a Timer control, the event procedure will be the **Timer** event, which means that with each tick, the Timer control will pass itself to **DoDissolveStep()**, along with the control that initiated the dissolve and the Picture Box control on which the image will appear. Similarly, the Picture Box control will pass itself to **DissolvePaint()** whenever it executes its **Paint** event. By placing this code in a separate module, we make it a general-purpose library that we can add to any program that needs to perform dissolves.

In the sample program, we call **DissolveToImage()** from the **Form_Load** event first, and then from a Command Button **Click** event. We could just as easily have used a List Box, or the hypertext system we built in Chapters 3 and 4.

Wrapping Up DISSOLVE.BAS

DISSOLVE.BAS also contains a few support functions and some declarations. You'll find them in Listing 8.23.

Listing 8.23   The Declarations and Remaining Functions from DISSOLVE.BAS

```
Option Explicit

#If Win32 Then
    Private Declare Function CreatePatternBrush Lib "gdi32" (ByVal hBitmap _
        As Long) As Long
    Private Declare Function Rectangle Lib "gdi32" (ByVal hdc As Long, ByVal _
        X1 As Long, ByVal Y1 As Long, ByVal X2 As Long, ByVal Y2 As Long) As Long
    Private Declare Sub InvalidateRect Lib "user32" (ByVal hWnd As Long, _
        lpRect As Any, ByVal bErase As Long)
#Else
    Private Declare Function CreatePatternBrush Lib "GDI" (ByVal hBitmap _
        As Integer) As Integer
    Private Declare Function Rectangle Lib "GDI" (ByVal hdc As Integer, _
        ByVal LeftX As Integer, ByVal TopY As Integer, ByVal RightX As Integer, _
        ByVal BottomY As Integer) As Integer
    Private Declare Sub InvalidateRect Lib "User" (ByVal hWnd As Integer, _
        ByVal lpRect As Long, ByVal bErase As Integer)
#End If

Const NumberOfSteps = 8
Dim PixelSetSequence(64) As Integer
Dim DissolveStep As Integer
Dim DissolveStepForPainting As Integer

Global bmFileHeader(1) As BITMAPFILEHEADER
Global bmInfo(1) As BITMAPINFO
Global PixelData(1) As ByteArray
Dim NewImage As Integer

Dim hPalette As Long
Global palettes(1 To 8) As LOGPALETTE
'Global NewPalette As LOGPALETTE

Type PALSTEP
    Red As     Long
    Green As Long
    Blue As    Long
End Type

Dim PalStepArray(255) As PALSTEP

Sub DissolveUnload(DissolvePicture As PictureBox)
Dim ResultCode As Long

    ResultCode = SelectPalette(DissolvePicture.hdc, DEFAULT_PALETTE, False)
    If hPalette <> 0 Then
        ResultCode = DeleteObject(hPalette)
    End If
End Sub
```

```
Sub InitializeDissolve()

    NewImage = 0
    PixelData(NewImage).Initialized = False
    PixelData((NewImage + 1) Mod 2).Initialized = False
    hPalette = 0
    CreatePixelSetSequence
End Sub

Function MaxInt(A As Integer, B As Integer)
    If A > B Then
        MaxInt = A
    Else
        MaxInt = B
    End If
End Function

Function MinInt(A As Integer, B As Integer) As Integer
    If A < B Then
        MinInt = A
    Else
        MinInt = B
    End If
End Function
```

The primary purpose of **DissolveUnload()** is to reselect the default system palette into Picture1 before destroying the latest logical palette.

Using the Dissolve Program

Our program works best with DIBs that use a Windows *identity palette.* An identity palette is a logical palette that includes the 20 reserved colors in their proper locations, 10 at the beginning and 10 at the end. Identity palettes help to prevent all kinds of odd mapping effects. Since a logical palette can really claim only 236 of the system palette entries, an image with 256 colors will have 20 of its colors mapped to other colors in the palette. Sometimes the Palette Manager does less than an ideal job of performing that palette reduction. Your images will look much better if you preprocess them with a utility, such as Microsoft's BitEdit/PalEdit combination, which comes with Video for Windows and with the Multimedia Development Kit. Some shareware image editing tools also offer this function.

Expanding the Dissolve

The dissolve construction set leaves plenty of room for optimization. We have intentionally sacrificed performance for clarity. But that shouldn't stop you from poking around in the GDI and experimenting with alternative approaches. Here are just a few suggestions:

- Use **CreateDIBSection()** (formerly part of the WinG API) to speed up image transfer.
- Use **AnimatePalette()** instead of creating and realizing new palettes for each step.
- Maintain the memory device context throughout the dissolve.
- Build all the pattern brushes before you begin the dissolve.

Now that you understand bitmaps inside out and backwards, from pixels to palettes to raster operations, you're ready to create your own special effects. Knock someone's socks off.

Learn how to bring your
VB multimedia applications
to life by adding interactive
hotspots to your images.

The Art of
Hyperimaging

I f something in a picture grabs your attention, you should be able to click on it and find out what it is or what it does. In this chapter we'll look at a few ways to create hotspots on pictures that can activate any of the multimedia features we've presented. We'll explore a few hypermedia projects to see how Windows operates as a hypermedia system. We'll show you some basic techniques to use to define rectangular hotspots by creating a useful hotspot editor. With this editor, you'll be able to define hotspots and save them in a format so that they can be used in other multimedia apps. In Chapter 10 we'll create a more powerful hotspot editor for defining irregular-shaped regions. Then, in Chapter 11 we'll build a powerful hypermedia engine that handles hotspots of any shape or size. You'll be able to use this engine for your own multimedia projects.

We have a lot of ground to cover, so let's get started.

Windows Is Hypermedia!

Every time you click on a button, drag a scroll bar, or select a list box item in a Windows app, you're engaging in a kind of hypermedia. When you click your mouse pointer on a button, Windows detects that the click has occurred within a particular region of the display. It then performs the appropriate actions, which usually include redrawing the button to create the illusion that it has been depressed and released. Some controls even open entire dialog boxes. If you click in the right place on one picture, Windows may display another picture with its own hotspot regions in the form of controls.

Using Controls as Pictures

You probably won't want to use controls for every type of visual hyperlinking but they provide a good starting point. Besides, it's a good idea to step back every once in a while and try to imagine new uses for old tools. Figure 9.1 shows a simple experiment in which we have built a bar chart from a control array of six Command Buttons.

You might expect Command Buttons to be short and fat rather than tall and thin. You might also expect them to keep their shapes when you click on them. But in this program, we have turned buttons into bars that shrink and grow.

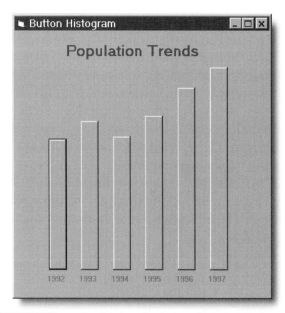

Figure 9.1   *HISTOBTN.FRM creates this bar chart at runtime.*

Rather than stretch them randomly, we set up a simple relationship between them. Any bar (button), when clicked on, will change its size in proportion to the difference in size between itself and its neighbor to the left. The procedure that performs this operation, **BarButton_Click()**, is shown in Listing 9.1.

Listing 9.1   The BarButton_Click() Procedure

```
Private Sub BarButton_Click(Index As Integer)
   If BarButton(Index).Height > 192 Then ' in Twips
      If Index > 0 Then
         BarButton(Index).Top = BarButton(Index).Top - 0.05 * _
            (BarButton(Index).Height - BarButton(Index - 1).Height)
         BarButton(Index).Height = MaxInt(BarButton(Index).Height + 0.05 * _
            (BarButton(Index).Height - BarButton(Index - 1).Height), 192)
      Else
         BarButton(Index).Top = BarButton(Index).Top - 0.05 * _
            BarButton(Index).Height
         BarButton(Index).Height = MaxInt(BarButton(Index).Height * 1.05, 192)
      End If
   End If
End Sub
```

This code actually exaggerates the curve formed by the tops of the bars in a somewhat less than predictable fashion. You could also use the **Click** event to pop up a Message Box that explains the reasons for the rise or fall in population for that particular year.

To jazz up this demonstration, you could easily substitute Labels or some other control for the Command Buttons. But Command Buttons have their own qualities. They expect to be touched. You don't need a label that says "Press the Bars for Further Information."

Using Controls as Hotspot Buttons

Now let's move on to the core of this chapter—how to add hotspots to images. By images, we mean bitmap graphics. You could scan photographs or drawings to create your images, or paint them with a drawing program such as Fractal Painter. You could even use VB to draw them directly into your Picture Box controls. It doesn't matter how you create your images, because pixels are pixels, and as we discovered in Chapter 3, a hotspot is nothing more than a region on the screen. Once you define that region, you can use the **MouseDown()** event procedure to fire off any multimedia event you wish.

As you discovered in the bar chart program, Command Buttons don't make the greatest hotspots. For one thing, they're opaque; you don't want to cover up your attractive images with boring Command Buttons. Fortunately, VB provides us with two other controls that can sit invisibly on top of pictures, and yet remain active. These are the Label and Image controls. Let's see what they can do for us.

Creating Hotspots with Label and Image Controls

This project uses Labels and Image controls to set up hotspots on an image. To create the project, all you'll need to do is make a new form, add a picture, and include the controls.

There is a simple example of this hotspot technique in the directory \VBMAGIC\HOTSPOT1, in the files HOTSPOT1.VBP, HOTSPOT1.FRM, and HOTSPOT1.FRX.

Start a new VB project, select the **Picture** property of the form, and add a bitmap. Anything will do. Next, place a Label control on the picture. It will appear as blank rectangle. Size the Label so it covers some object in the image as closely as possible. Remove the caption from the Label by double clicking on the **Caption** property in the Properties window and pressing the Delete key. Finally, change the **BackStyle** property to 0 - Transparent. The only evidence of the Label will be its frame handles. Once you click elsewhere on the form, all visible traces of it will vanish from the image. But when you click on the area it covers, it reappears. Double clicking on the area instructs VB to display its **Click** event procedure. All you need to do is add the code to kick off the appropriate multimedia event.

You can do the same thing with an Image control. And, as a bonus, the Image control will work with its default property settings. The other advantage the Image control has over a Label is that it will display a border during development time so you won't lose track of it.

To use the control-based method of hyperimaging for a large number of images, you would need a way to create and place controls over the images at runtime. You could keep track of their locations and sizes in a simple database, either using VB's ordinary file I/O, or with its Data Access features. You could then use a control array to generate as many controls as you need to cover all the hotspots of any particular image. When you finished displaying an image, you could delete all but the one Label or Image control that must remain as a placeholder for the control array.

Since you have to keep track of the locations and dimensions of the hotspots anyway, it would be nice if you could create them directly on the client area of the form or Picture Box, without scattering controls all over the place. We're sure you won't be surprised when we tell you that the Windows API once again comes to our aid with a pair of almost unbelievably simple functions that do just what we need. Follow me to the next project in our multimedia adventure.

Using Rectangular Window Regions

The GDI includes a family of functions that create and manipulate *regions*. A region is simply a bounded area of the screen. Just like the other GDI objects we explored in Chapters 5 and 6, regions have handles. One function, named **CreateRectRgn()**, constructs a Windows region from two pair of coordinates that specify the upper-left corner and lower-right corner of a rectangle, and return a handle that we can store in an integer variable:

```
Win32:
Public Declare Function CreateRectRgn Lib "gdi32" (ByVal X1 As Long, ByVal Y1 _
    As Long, ByVal X2 As Long, ByVal Y2 As Long) As Long

Win16:
Declare Function CreateRectRgn Lib "GDI" (ByVal X1 As Integer, ByVal Y1 _
    As Integer, ByVal X2 As Integer, ByVal Y2 As Integer) As Integer
```

Thanks to another GDI function named **PtInRegion()**, regions make handy mouse traps.

```
Win32:
Public Declare Function PtInRegion Lib "gdi32" (ByVal hRgn As Long, ByVal X _
    As Long, ByVal Y As Long) As Long

Win16:
Declare Function PtInRegion Lib "GDI" (ByVal hRgn As Integer, ByVal X _
    As Integer, ByVal Y As Integer) As Integer
```

In Chapter 3, we kept track of hotlink words or phrases in hypertext topic windows by recording their rectangular boundaries. Then, in the **MouseDown()** event procedure, we compared the mouse position coordinates to the rectangular boundaries to determine whether a mouse click occurred within any of those rectangles. With these two new API functions, we can do the same thing with fewer steps.

To intercept mouse clicks in a particular section of the screen, we can mark that area with a region, then pass the handle to that region and the coordinates of the **MouseDown()** event procedure to **PtInRegion()**, which will return either **True** or **False**.

Before calling the **CreateRectRgn()** and **PtInRegion()** functions, we need some way to determine the positions and dimensions of the rectangular regions we want to use as hotspots. Here's our solution: We can write a VB hotspot editor that lets us draw rectangles over bitmaps, test them, and save them in a file for later use in our hypermedia system. The editor will be a great addition to our multimedia construction set.

Creating a Visual Basic Hotspot Editor

This is one of the bigger projects we've created so far—so hold on to your hat. A number of steps are required, but the editor is actually easy to put together.

1. Create the main form HOTSPOT2.FRM and add the **Form_Load()** and **Form_Unload()** event procedures (Listing 9.1).
2. Add the global variables for the project to the module HOTSPOT2.BAS (Listing 9.2).
3. Add the form's **Mouse** events for drawing hotspot regions (Listings 9.3 through 9.5).
4. Add the **TestOption_Click()** event procedure (Listing 9.6) to test out hotspots and the **DefineOption_Click()** event procedure (Listing 9.7) to define hotspots.
5. Add the **DeleteRegion()** procedure (Listing 9.8) to HOTSPOT2.BAS to delete hotspot regions.
6. To support a menu system, add the **LoadOption_Click()** event procedure to HOTSPOT2.FRM (Listing 9.9) and the **InitRecordBuffer()** procedure to HOTSPOT2.BAS (Listing 9.10).
7. To save hotspot records, add the **SaveOption_Click()** event procedure to HOTSPOT2.FRM (Listing 9.11) and the **SaveHotspotRecord()** procedure to HOTSPOT2.BAS (Listing 9.12).
8. Almost there! Create the form HTSPT2F2.FRM and add the necessary support event procedures (Listings 9.13 and 9.16).
9. Add the **EditOption_Click()** event procedure (Listing 9.17), the **NewOption_Click()** event procedure (Listing 9.18), and the **DeleteOption_Click()** event procedure (Listing 9.19).

This project is located in the directory \VBMAGIC\HOTSPOT2 in the files HOTSPOT2.VBP, HOTSPOT2.FRM, HOTSPOT2.BAS, HTSPT2F2.FRM, and GLOBCONS.BAS. You will also need the Common Dialog custom control, located in the file COMDLG32.OCX (CMDIALOG.VBX for Windows 3.1). VB Setup normally installs this file in your \WINDOWS\SYSTEM directory.

How the Hotspot Editor Works

Before you explore this project, take a few minutes to run the editor just to get to know how it works. Figure 9.2 shows the editor with a bitmap image loaded. The editor allows you to load in a bitmap image, draw your hotspots with the mouse, and then save them.

To display an image, choose File|Load Picture, then use the Open file dialog box to locate and select a bitmap image. When the picture appears on the form, you may use the mouse to draw and test hotspot regions.

Each time you press the mouse button, the editor will begin drawing a new rectangle. You won't see the new figure until you stretch it into one or two dimensions by moving the mouse. When you release the mouse button, the rectangle will remain locked at its last position and size until you restart the process by pressing the mouse button again.

After you draw a rectangle, choose Mode|Test. When you click inside the rectangle, you should hear TADA.WAV. When you click outside the rectangle, you should hear DING.WAV.

Designing the Hotspot Editor

Our editor requires two forms: HOTSPOT2.FRM and HTSPTF2.FRM. The first form contains the **Mouse** event procedures for drawing hotspot regions and the menu system for the project. We'll create the HTSPTF2.FRM form to retrieve and edit hotspots that we have already saved in a file. We'll be taking a closer look at this form later. For now, let's create the main form.

Create a new form and set its **Name** property to HotSpot2F1. Next, set the **DrawMode** property to 6 - Invert, and save it in a file named HOTSPOT2.FRM.

Figure 9.2   *The rectangular hotspot editor.*

We'll need a pair of event procedures for loading and unloading the form. These procedures are shown in Listing 9.1.

Listing 9.1   The Form_Load() and Form_Unload() Event Procedures from HOTSPOT2.FRM

```
Private Sub Form_Load()

    NewOption.Enabled = False
    EditOption.Enabled = False
    SaveOption.Enabled = False
    DeleteOption.Enabled = False
    CurrentHotspotRecordNumber = 0
    DrawingRectangle = False
    Open App.Path + "\ImagLink.Dat" For Random As ImageLinkFile Len = _
        Len(HotSpotRecord)
    InitRecordBuffer
End Sub

Private Sub Form_Unload(Cancel As Integer)

    DeleteRegion hRectRgn
    Close ImageLinkFile
End Sub
```

Form_Load() is needed to initialize the variables we'll be using. It also contains the code for opening a data file so that the editor can store the newly created hotspot regions. We'll look at this procedure in a little more detail when we discuss how hotspot regions are saved. The **Form_Unload()** procedure is responsible for removing any stray regions that have been left lying around in memory and closing our link file.

Speaking of variables, where should we declare them? In HOTSPOT2.FRM? No. Remember that our project requires two forms and both of them will need to access the variables and the four API functions that are used. We'll need to put declarations in HOTSPOT2.BAS. Listing 9.2 shows the complete set.

Listing 9.2   The Declarations Section of HOTSPOT2.BAS

```
Option Explicit

Type HotSpotRecords
    Image As String * 128
    Target As String * 128
    TopX As Integer
    TopY As Integer
    BottomX As Integer
    BottomY As Integer
End Type
```

```
Global Const ImageLinkFile = 1
Global HotSpotRecord As HotSpotRecords
Global hRectRgn As Long
Global CurrentImageFilename As String
Global CurrentHotspotRecordNumber As Long
Global AnchorX As Integer
Global AnchorY As Integer
Global EndX As Integer
Global EndY As Integer

#If Win32 Then
    Public Declare Function CreateRectRgn Lib "gdi32" (ByVal X1 As Long, _
        ByVal Y1 As Long, ByVal X2 As Long, ByVal Y2 As Long) As Long
    Public Declare Function DeleteObject Lib "gdi32" (ByVal hObject As Long) _
        As Long
    Public Declare Function PtInRegion Lib "gdi32" (ByVal hRgn As Long, _
        ByVal X As Long, ByVal Y As Long) As Long
    Public Declare Function mciExecute Lib "winmm" (ByVal lpstrCommand As _
        String) As Long
#Else
    Public Declare Function CreateRectRgn Lib "GDI" (ByVal X1 As Integer, _
        ByVal Y1 As Integer, ByVal X2 As Integer, ByVal Y2 As Integer) As Integer
    Public Declare Function PtInRegion Lib "GDI" (ByVal hRgn As Integer, _
        ByVal X As Integer, ByVal Y As Integer) As Integer
    Public Declare Function DeleteObject Lib "GDI" (ByVal hObject As Integer) _
        As Integer
    Public Declare Function mciExecute Lib "MMSystem" _
        (ByVal CommandString As String) As Integer
#End If
```

We start out with the declaration of the data structure **HotSpotRecords**. This structure is used to store and retrieve file records containing hotspot information. Next, you'll find the declarations of the nine global variables needed. Finally, HOTSPOT2.BAS declares the API functions we'll be using to draw and define hotspot regions. Let's take a closer look.

Setting the Bait—Outlining Hot Regions

We need to create the three event procedures to support the mouse. So let's get to it. Double click on the main form and open the **MouseDown()** event procedure. Listing 9.3 provides the code required for **Form_MouseDown()**.

Listing 9.3   The Form_MouseDown() Event Procedure of HOTSPOT2.FRM

```
Private Sub Form_MouseDown(Button As Integer, Shift As Integer, X As Single, _
    Y As Single)
Dim Dummy As Integer

    If DefineOption.CHECKED And (Len(CurrentImageFilename) > 0) Then
        Line (AnchorX, AnchorY)-(EndX, EndY), , B
```

```
        AnchorX = X
        AnchorY = Y
        EndX = X
        EndY = Y
        DrawingRectangle = True
    Else
        ' Test whether click is in region.
        If PtInRegion(hRectRgn, X, Y) Then
            Dummy = mciExecute("play c:\windows\media\tada.wav")
        Else
            Dummy = mciExecute("play c:\windows\media\ding.wav")
        End If
    End If
End Sub
```

This procedure initiates the drawing process. We need a flag to tell the other mouse event procedures that we're in the middle of drawing a rectangle, so we set **DrawingRectangle** to **True**. Next, we call the **Line()** method to erase any rectangle we may have drawn previously. The first time we press the mouse button, both vertices lie at the origin (the upper-left corner) of the client area, so nothing will happen. We then initialize both vertices to the current position of the mouse, as returned by the **x** and **y** arguments of the **Form_MouseDown()** procedure.

Next, we need to add the **Form_MouseMove()** event procedure (Listing 9.4).

Listing 9.4   The Form_MouseMove() Event Procedure from HOTSPOT2.FRM

```
Private Sub Form_MouseMove(Button As Integer, Shift As Integer, X As Single, _
    Y As Single)

    If DrawingRectangle Then
        ' Undraw the previous rectangle.
        Line (AnchorX, AnchorY)-(EndX, EndY), , B
        ' Record the new coordinates of
        ' the new end point.
        EndX = X
        EndY = Y
        ' Draw the new rectangle.
        Line (AnchorX, AnchorY)-(EndX, EndY), , B
    End If
End Sub
```

Each time we move the mouse, we need to erase the previously drawn rectangle and draw a new one from the anchor point to the new mouse location. Because we have set the **DrawMode** to **Invert**, the first call to the **Line()** method erases the old rectangle by drawing right over it. We then grab the new end points and draw the new rectangle.

Finally, to complete the drawing operation, we turn to the **Form_MouseUp()** event procedure shown in Listing 9.5.

Listing 9.5   The Form_MouseUp() Event Procedure from HOTSPOT2.FRM

```
Sub Form_MouseUp (Button As Integer, Shift As Integer, x As Single, y As Single)
    If DrawingRectangle Then
        EndX = x
        EndY = y
        DrawingRectangle = False
    End If
End Sub
```

Nothing complicated here. We just capture the final end point and set **DrawingRectangle** to **False**. Now we need to convert the rectangle we've drawn into a Windows region.

Drawing or Testing?

Our editor must be set up so that we can switch between drawing mode and testing mode. We've added a menu to the form with an option called Mode. This option contains two suboptions labeled Define and Test. We'll use check marks to indicate which option is active. Define will turn on the drawing mode, and Test will create the rectangular Windows region. Listing 9.6 shows the **TestOption_Click()** event procedure.

Listing 9.6   The TestOption_Click() Event Procedure from HOTSPOT2.FRM

```
Sub TestOption_Click ()
    DefineOption.Checked = False
    TestOption.Checked = True
    hRectRgn = CreateRectRgn(AnchorX, AnchorY, EndX, EndY)
End Sub
```

The first two lines of this procedure just switch the check mark on the menu from the Define option to the Test option. The third and last line call the API function **CreateRectRgn()** to register the rectangle with Windows as an official region.

Go back and look closely at the **Form_MouseDown()** event procedure (Listing 9.3). Notice we used the **Checked** property of the **DefineOption** menu item to split the **MouseDown()** event procedure into two clauses, one for each mode. The truth clause of the **If** statement performs this procedure's part in the drawing operation. The **Else** clause, which handles test mode, calls the API function **PtInRegion()**, passing it the handle to the rectangular region, along with the **X** and **Y** coordinates of the mouse pointer. **PtInRegion()** returns **True** or **False**, so we can use another **If** statement to respond to the **MouseDown()** event procedure. We've called upon the services of our old friend **mciExecute()** to announce whether the event occurs inside or outside of the region.

For proper symmetry, we'll need to support the **DefineOption_Click** event. Listing 9.7 provides the required event procedure.

Listing 9.7 The DefineOption_Click() Event Procedure from HOTSPOT2.FRM

```
Sub DefineOption_Click ()
   DefineOption.Checked = True
   TestOption.Checked = False
   DeleteRegion hRectRgn
End Sub
```

First, we switch the check mark. Then we call **DeleteRegion()**, a new general procedure shown in Listing 9.8. We must place this procedure in the code module, HOTSPOT2.BAS, because it will be called from two different forms.

Listing 9.8 The DeleteRegion() General Procedure from HOTSPOT2.BAS

```
Sub DeleteRegion (hRgn As Integer)
   If hRgn <> 0 Then
      If DeleteObject(hRgn) Then
         hRgn = 0
      Else
         MsgBox "Unable to Delete Region", 48, "GDI Error"
      End If
   End If
End
```

This simple procedure checks whether **hRgn** has been set, presumably with a previous call to **CreateRectRgn()**. If it has, it deletes the region referenced by the handle by calling the API function **DeleteObject()**, then sets **hRgn** to zero. If it cannot delete the region, it displays a warning. A failure to delete a region will not prevent the program from continuing, but it will leave an orphan region in memory, which will harmlessly remain there for the rest of the Windows session.

That's all it takes to create and use hotspots with Windows regions. First, you define the boundaries. Then, you create the region. And finally, you test whether a mouse click has occurred within the region.

Table 9.1   *File MENU Suboptions from HOTSPOT1.FRM*

Menu Caption	Menu Name
Load Picture	LoadOption
New Hotspot	NewOption
Edit Saved Hotspot	EditOption
Save Hotspot	SaveOption
Delete Hotspot	DeleteOption
Quit	QuitOption

Adding the Menu System

Most of the work we've done so far on this program helps us just to define our region boundaries. But in order to use these regions, you must associate them with images and save them somewhere.

It's time to add the menu system for loading images and creating and saving hotspots. First, view the form and display the Menu Design window. Second, add a File menu to the menu bar. Then add the options listed in Table 9.1.

If it is not yet visible, add the Common Dialog Control custom control to the project. This custom control allows you to invoke the *Common Dialog* for opening files, saving files, printing, and other common tasks. This **Open** dialog box, shown in Figure 9.3, looks and operates like the file dialog boxes found throughout the VB development environment. When you add CMDIALOG.OCX to the project, VB will add its icon to the Toolbox. (It's a

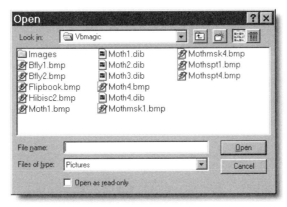

Figure 9.3   *We'll use the Common Dialog for opening files.*

little schematic window with a dark caption bar and a few controls.) Double click on the Toolbox button (or click once and drag) to place one Common Dialog control on the form. It doesn't matter where you place it, because it's invisible at runtime. Change the **Name** property of the Common Dialog control to ImageFileDialog. Set the **DefaultExt** property to *.BMP;*.DIB, and the **Filter** property to Pictures | *.BMP;*.DIB.

To support our menu system, we'll need to add event procedures for each of the menu options shown in Table 9.1. The **LoadOption_Click()** event procedure has three distinct groups of statements, as shown in Listing 9.9.

Listing 9.9　The LoadOption_Click() Menu Event Procedure from HOTSPOT2.FRM

```
Private Sub LoadOption_Click()

    NewOption.Enabled = True
    EditOption.Enabled = True
    SaveOption.Enabled = False
    DeleteOption.Enabled = False
    CurrentHotspotRecordNumber = 0
    DrawingRectangle = False
    InitRecordBuffer
    AnchorX = 0
    AnchorY = 0
    EndX = 0
    EndY = 0
    DeleteRegion hRectRgn
    ImageFileDialog.Action = 1
    If ImageFileDialog.FileName <> "" Then
        CurrentImageFilename = ImageFileDialog.FileName
        HotSpot2F1.Picture = LoadPicture(CurrentImageFilename)
    End If
End Sub
```

The first four lines turn on or off four of the other options in the File menu. Once an image is loaded, you can ask to create a new hotspot or edit an existing hotspot. You can't save or delete a hotspot until you create one or retrieve one from the hotspot file (which we haven't yet created).

The next eight lines initialize the hotspot editor. The variable **CurrentHotspot-RecordNumber** will eventually hold the record number of a hotspot that has already been recorded in the hotspot file. The general procedure **InitRecordBuffer()** will clear all the fields in a global structure called **HotSpotRecord**, which we'll use to store and retrieve hotspot records from the file.

The last five lines of code activate the **ImageFileDialog** in its "Open" file mode. The user may then use the drive, directory, and file list boxes to select an image file. When the program returns from the Open file dialog box, the **FileName** property of **ImageFileDialog** will contain the path and filename of the selected file. Since we'll need that again later, copy it to a variable called **CurrentImageFilename**, then pass it to the VB function **LoadPicture()** to assign the image to the **Picture** property of the form.

Before this procedure will work, we need to add the general procedure **InitRecordBuffer()**, which is shown in Listing 9.10.

Listing 9.10   The General Procedure InitRecordBuffer() from HOTSPOT2.BAS

```
Sub InitRecordBuffer()

    HotSpotRecord.Image = ""
    HotSpotRecord.Target = ""
    HotSpotRecord.TopX = 0
    HotSpotRecord.TopY = 0
    HotSpotRecord.BottomX = 0
    HotSpotRecord.BottomY = 0
End Sub
```

Drawing with Inverted Colors

You'll notice that the lines that form the rectangles are not solid, but look more like negative versions of the pixels they cover. The **DrawMode** we selected for the form, **6 - Invert**, flips the bits of each pixel value, either from one to zero, or zero to one. The pixel values then reference colors in the opposite side of the system palette. The result often looks like a photographic negative. If you are in High Color or True Color mode, it is, but if you are 256 color mode, it isn't, unless each color in the palette happens to be paired with its RGB complement at the position in the palette determined by its 8-bit binary complement. Most of the Windows reserved colors try to look like complementary pairs, but even they are impostors. The only colors in the system palette that always enjoy this symmetry are black and white.

Saving Hotspots—A Simple Filing System

Now that we can draw hotspots over images, we need a way to store and edit them to be able to use them in the hypermedia system. At the beginning of this project, we defined a data structure in HOTSPOT2.BAS called **HotSpotRecords** (Listing 9.2). Let's now explore how it is used to store and retrieve file records:

```
Type HotSpotRecords
    Image As String * 128
```

```
      Target As String * 128
      TopX As Integer
      TopY As Integer
      BottomX As Integer
      BottomY As Integer
   End Type
```

First, we'll need a data file. In the **Form_Load()** event procedure for the main form, we'll open or create a file called IMAGLINK.DAT.

```
Sub Form_Load ()
   NewOption.Enabled = False
   EditOption.Enabled = False
   SaveOption.Enabled = False
   DeleteOption.Enabled = False
   CurrentHotspotRecordNumber = 0
   DrawingRectangle = False
   Open App.Path + "\ImagLink.Dat" For Random As ImageLinkFile Len = _
      Len(HotSpotRecord)
   InitRecordBuffer
End Sub
```

This procedure also disables most of the other File menu options, because they won't mean anything until we load an image file. If the files exists, the **Open** statement will open it; if it doesn't exist, **Open** will create and open it. The application property **App.Path** will force the data file into the same directory from which the program was invoked.

After you open an image file and draw a hotspot, you'll want to save its coordinates, along with the name of the image file and a hotlink target. That will be the job of the File | Save Hotspot menu option and its event procedure **SaveOption_Click()**, shown in Listing 9.11.

Listing 9.11   The SaveOption_Click() Menu Event Procedure from HOTSPOT2.FRM

```
Private Sub SaveOption_Click()
Dim TempString As String

   TempString = RTrim$(HotSpotRecord.Target)
   TempString = InputBox$("Enter a Hyperlink Target string of "& _
      "up to 128 characters:", "Enter Target", TempString)
   If Len(TempString) > 0 Then
      HotSpotRecord.Image = CurrentImageFilename
      HotSpotRecord.Target = TempString
      HotSpotRecord.TopX = AnchorX
      HotSpotRecord.TopY = AnchorY
      HotSpotRecord.BottomX = EndX
      HotSpotRecord.BottomY = EndY
```

```
      SaveHotspotRecord HotSpotRecord, CurrentHotspotRecordNumber
      DeleteOption.Enabled = True
   End If
End Sub
```

We already know the filename and path of the image because we saved it in the string variable **CurrentImageFilename** when we loaded the picture into the form. We also know the hotspot coordinates, which we created with the drawing operation. The only thing we don't know is the target to which we want the hotspot linked, so we have to ask for it.

The VB function **InputBox$()** will display a simple dialog box with a prompt, a title, and a text box into which the user may type a response. (See Figure 9.4 to see what this function accomplishes.) The third parameter of **InputBox$()** enables us to display a default response. For a new hotspot, this default will come from a freshly initialized **HotSpotRecord**, which means it will be blank. Later, when we implement the Edit Hotspot option, the variable **TempString** will pass the existing target string to **InputBox$()**.

After we set the fields of the **HotSpotRecord**, we call the general procedure **SaveHotspotRecord()** (Listing 9.12), passing the record and a file position.

Listing 9.12   The SaveHotspotRecord() General Procedure from HOTSPOT2.BAS

```
Sub SaveHotspotRecord (HotSpotRecord As HotSpotRecords, RecordPos As Long)
    Dim Counter As Long
    Dim FileSize As Long
    Dim TempRecord As HotSpotRecords
    Dim BlankFound As Integer
    If RecordPos = 0 Then
        BlankFound = False
        FileSize = LOF(ImageLinkFile) \ Len(HotSpotRecord)
        Counter = 0
        Do Until (Counter >= FileSize) Or BlankFound
            Counter = Counter + 1
            Get ImageLinkFile, Counter, TempRecord
            BlankFound = (Len(RTrim$(TempRecord.Image)) = 0)
        Loop
```

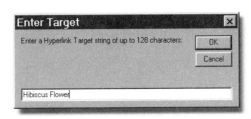

Figure 9.4   *The InputBox$() function will display a dialog box to request the target string for the hotspot.*

```
        If BlankFound Then
            RecordPos = Counter
        Else
            RecordPos = FileSize + 1
        End If
    End If
    Put ImageLinkFile, RecordPos, HotSpotRecord
    End Sub
```

For new records, **SaveHotspotRecord()** looks for the first available record position in the file. A record that contains a blank filename in the **Image** field is considered free. If all the records are occupied, it appends the new record to the end of the file. If **RecordPos** contains a value other than zero, **SaveHotspotRecord()** writes the record back to the specified position.

Retrieving Hotspot Records

Our next requirement is to be able to retrieve and edit hotspots that we have already saved in the file. And that's where the HTSPT2F2.FRM, shown in Figure 9.5, comes in. Create this form and set its **Name** property to HotSpot2F2. Remember to save it in a file named HTSPT2F2.FRM.

The form has three controls: a List Box named **HotSpotList** and two Command Buttons named **CancelButton** and **LoadButton**. The **Form_Load()** event procedure, shown in Listing 9.13, loads **HotSpotList** with the names of all the hotspots in the file that belong to the currently loaded image.

Listing 9.13   The Form_Load() Event Procedure from HTSPT2F2.FRM

```
Private Sub Form_Load()
Dim RecordCounter As Long
Dim FileLength As Integer
Dim TempHotspotRecord As HotSpotRecords

    LoadButton.Enabled = False
    HotSpotList.Clear
    FileLength = LOF(ImageLinkFile) / Len(TempHotspotRecord)
    For RecordCounter = 1 To FileLength
        Get ImageLinkFile, RecordCounter, TempHotspotRecord
        If RTrim$(TempHotspotRecord.Image) = CurrentImageFilename Then
            HotSpotList.AddItem RTrim$(TempHotspotRecord.Image) + " - " + _
                RTrim$(TempHotspotRecord.Target)
            HotSpotList.ItemData(HotSpotList.NewIndex) = RecordCounter
        End If
    Next RecordCounter
End Sub
```

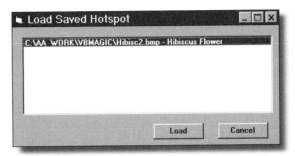

Figure 9.5 *The HTSPT2F2.FRM form will allow us to retrieve and edit existing hotspots.*

We use the **ItemData** property of the List Box to store the record positions of the hotspot records, so we can replace one or more of them later without searching for them.

To select a hotspot for editing and display it on HotSpot2F1, we'll accept either a double click on the **HotSpotList** item, or a single click on the Load Command Button. The procedures that handle this work are shown in Listing 9.14.

Listing 9.14 The HotspotList_DblClick() and LoadButton_Click() Event Procedures from HTSPT2F2.FRM

```
Private Sub HotspotList_DblClick()
    CurrentHotspotRecordNumber = HotSpotList.ItemData(HotSpotList.ListIndex)
    LoadHotSpot CurrentHotspotRecordNumber
End Sub

Private Sub LoadButton_Click()
    CurrentHotspotRecordNumber = HotSpotList.ItemData(HotSpotList.ListIndex)
    LoadHotSpot CurrentHotspotRecordNumber
End Sub
```

These simple event procedures both call a general procedure, **LoadHotSpot()**, shown in Listing 9.15.

Listing 9.15 The LoadHotSpot() General Procedure from HTSPT2F2.FRM

```
Private Sub LoadHotSpot(RecordPos As Long)

    Get ImageLinkFile, RecordPos, HotSpotRecord
    AnchorX = HotSpotRecord.TopX
    AnchorY = HotSpotRecord.TopY
    EndX = HotSpotRecord.BottomX
    EndY = HotSpotRecord.BottomY
    HotSpot2F1.SaveOption.Enabled = True
    HotSpot2F1.DeleteOption.Enabled = True

    Unload HotSpot2F2
End Sub
```

The other Command Button, **CancelButton**, just unloads the form. Its event procedure is provided in Listing 9.16.

Listing 9.16 The CancelButton_Click() Event Procedure from HTSPT2F2.FRM

```
Sub CancelButton_Click ()
    Unload HotSpot2F2
End Sub
```

Defining the Other Menu Options

Back in the main form, HOTSPOT2.FRM, the File | Edit Saved Hotspot option kicks off the process of loading a hotspot record. Listing 9.17 shows the procedure needed for this task.

Listing 9.17 The EditOption_Click() Menu Event Procedure from HOTSPOT2.FRM

```
Private Sub EditOption_Click()

    HotSpot2F1.Line (AnchorX, AnchorY)-(EndX, EndY), , B
    DeleteRegion hRectRgn
    HotSpot2F2.Show MODAL
    If TestOption.CHECKED Then
        hRectRgn = CreateRectRgn(AnchorX, AnchorY, EndX, EndY)
    End If
    HotSpot2F1.Refresh
End Sub
```

EditOption_Click() first uses the **Line()** method to erase any rectangle already visible in the client area. It then deletes any lingering Windows area, and opens HotSpot2F2 as a *modal* form. One difference between a modal and a *modeless* form is that when Windows displays a modal form, no other window in the application can receive input, either from the keyboard or the mouse, until the modal form is unloaded or hidden. The other difference has a more profound impact on the code in this **Click** event. The five lines of code that follow **HotSpot2F2.Show** build the new rectangular region and redraw the screen to display the rectangle on the image. If we showed the second form *modelessly*, these last lines would execute immediately. Then when the user selected a hotspot from the Hotspot List Box and returned to **HotSpot2F1**, the region and the rectangular coordinates might belong to two different region records. When you **Show** a modal form, execution of code in the calling procedure is suspended until the modal form is hidden or unloaded. In effect, the modal form behaves like a subprocedure. (Message Boxes are modal forms.) You should specify the modal option on a form whenever it doesn't make sense to continue program execution until the subform gathers information from the user. The global constant **MODAL**, with a value of 1, is located in the file GLOBCONS.TXT, which we've imported into GLOBCONS.BAS.

Next, we need a way to clear an existing hotspot from the editor window and start a new one. For that, we'll write the **NewOption_Click()** event procedure as shown in Listing 9.18.

Listing 9.18   The NewOption_Click() Menu Event Procedure from HOTSPOT2.FRM

```
Private Sub NewOption_Click()

    SaveOption.Enabled = False
    DeleteOption.Enabled = False
    CurrentHotspotRecordNumber = 0
    InitRecordBuffer
    Line (AnchorX, AnchorY)-(EndX, EndY), , B
    AnchorX = 0
    AnchorY = 0
    EndX = 0
    EndY = 0
    TestOption.CHECKED = False
    DefineOption.CHECKED = True
    DeleteRegion hRectRgn
End Sub
```

Once again, we use the **Line()** method and the **Invert DrawMode** to undraw the current rectangle. We then initialize all the variables, set the Mode menu options to indicate that the program is in Define mode, and if necessary, delete the current region.

Deleting Hotspot Records

We have one more menu option to finish, Delete Hotspot. The procedure that processes this menu option is **DeleteOption_Click()**, shown in Listing 9.19.

Listing 9.19   The DeleteOption_Click() Menu Event Procedure from HOTSPOT2.FRM

```
Private Sub DeleteOption_Click()
Dim Response As Integer

    If CurrentHotspotRecordNumber > 0 Then
        Response = MsgBox("Are you sure you want to delete this Hotspot?", _
            MB_YESNO + MB_ICONQUESTION, "Warning!")
        If Response = IDYES Then
            SaveOption.Enabled = False
            DeleteOption.Enabled = False
            InitRecordBuffer
```

```
        SaveHotspotRecord HotSpotRecord, CurrentHotspotRecordNumber
        CurrentHotspotRecordNumber = 0
        Line (AnchorX, AnchorY)-(EndX, EndY), , B
        AnchorX = 0
        AnchorY = 0
        EndX = 0
        EndY = 0
        TestOption.CHECKED = False
        DefineOption.CHECKED = True
        DeleteRegion hRectRgn
      End If
   Else
      MsgBox "There is no region to delete.", 48, "Delete Error"
   End If
End Sub
```

This procedure performs many of the same operations as **NewOption_Click()**. The only significant differences are the **MsgBox()** prompt that offers an opportunity to cancel the deletion, and the call to **SaveHotspotRecord**. The second **MsgBox()**, the one that warns when users try to delete an undefined region, should never appear if you have properly enabled and disabled menu options throughout the program.

What's Next?

Wow. Creating our rectangular hotspot editor was a big job. In our hyperimaging adventures, we've uncovered some powerful Windows programming techniques to help automate the process of defining hotspot regions.

We're now ready to move on and enter the next dimension of hyperimaging. When we arrive, you'll learn how to create a much more versatile hotspot editor for defining irregularly shaped hotspots.

It's now time to explore real-world objects and create more functional hyperimaging projects.

Chapter

10

Hyperimaging: The Next Dimension

Imagine trying to bring the feel of the Grand Canyon into your home. You could hang up a big photograph in your living room, but that wouldn't be very interactive. You really want to *feel* like you're there—almost as if you could soar over the canyon like an eagle, locate a hidden gorge, dive down into the canyon, and jump on a raft and splash down the Colorado river.

In Chapter 9, we learned to create rectangular hotspot regions. Unfortunately, the real world isn't made up of rectangles. (Think how boring life would be if it were!) To create multimedia adventures like the real-world Grand Canyon project, you'll need a way to jigsaw pictures of the real world into irregularly-shaped hotspots. Once you accomplish this task, you'll be able to click on any part of a picture and set off a multimedia event, like playing a video or zooming in for greater detail.

Mastering Irregular Hotspots

To bring the non-rectangular world of cars, planes, dinosaurs, and nature into our multimedia apps, we need to create irregularly shaped hotspots.

Let's begin by developing another hotspot editor for our multimedia construction set. For now, we'll start with the drawing and testing features. Then, in the next project, we'll adapt the code we wrote in Chapter 9 for the rectangular hotspot editor into an editor for irregularly shaped regions.

Drawing Irregularly Shaped Images

This project shows you how to draw irregularly shaped images using the mouse and then test out the regions you've drawn.

1. Create the form HOTSPOT3.FRM to use as the hotspot drawing area.
2. Add the event procedures that make it possible to quickly draw complex shapes on the form's client area (Listings 10.1 through 10.4).
3. Add the **DeleteRegion()** general procedure to HOTSPOT3.BAS (Listing 10.5).
4. Fill in the **Paint** event to redraw the current polygon (Listing 10.6).
5. Add the menu support procedures (Listing 10.7 and 10.8).
6. Add the necessary declarations (Listing 10.9 and 10.10).

> *This project is located in the directory \VBMAGIC\HOTSPOT3, in the files HOTSPOT3.VBP, HOTSPOT3.FRM, and HOTSPOT3.BAS.*

Running the Program—Testing the Polygon Hotspots

By running the HOTSPOT3 program, you'll see that it starts in Define mode, as shown in Figure 10.1. To begin drawing a polygon, click the mouse button and release it anywhere on the client area of the form. The first line segment will then follow your cursor until you click again to lock in the second point. Then the second line will follow the cursor. Add several sides to the figure. When you feel you've made a complex enough region, like that in Figure 10.1, place the cursor close to the first point and click again. The line that was following you will let go of the cursor and join the first vertex, sealing off the polygon. If you click again anywhere on the client area, the program will display the message box that tells you the polygon is closed. To draw another polygon, you must first select New from the File menu.

To test the hotspot region, select Testing Region from the Mode menu. Then click in and around your polygon to prove that it works. To stop the program, choose Close from the Control menu of the form or select Quit from the File menu. If you stop the program from the VB menu bar, you may

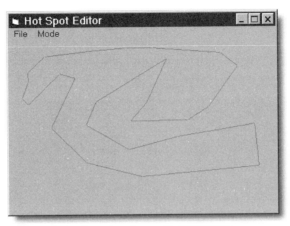

Figure 10.1   *Drawing irregularly shaped regions with HOTSPOT3.*

leave an orphaned region in memory, which will remain there throughout the Windows session.

Creating the Form

We'll begin the project with a new form. Set the Form's **Name** property to **HotSpot3F1** and save it as HOTSPOT3.FRM. Set the **AutoRedraw** and **ClipControls** properties to False, set the **ScaleMode** to 3 - Pixel, and set the **DrawMode** to 6 - Invert.

We won't need to place any controls on the form, but we do need to begin with a few menu options. Open the Menu Design window and add the menus and options shown in Table 10.1. Figure 10.2 shows the completed form.

Drawing Polygons

In this project we'll use the **MouseDown** and **MouseMove** events to draw the outlines of our polygon hotspot regions. But unlike the editor in Chapter 9, this drawing program doesn't use the **MouseUp** event to complete a figure.

Table 10.1   *The HOTSPOT3.FRM Menus*

Menu Caption	Menu Name	Option Caption	Option Name
Property	Property	Property	Property
File	FileMenu	New	NewOption
		Quit	QuitOption
Mode	ModeMenu	Defining Region	DefineOption
		Testing Region	TestOption

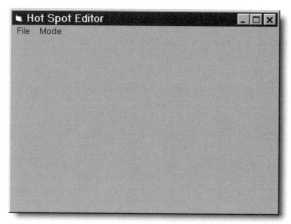

Figure 10.2 *The HotSpot3F1 form, the main form for our polygon hotspot test editor.*

When we were drawing rectangles, we needed to define only two points, opposite corners. The procedure for drawing a rectangle meshed nicely with the **MouseDown-MouseMove-MouseUp** sequence of events. Unfortunately, it takes more than two points to define a non-rectangular polygon. To mark each corner, or *vertex*, we need to click and release the mouse button repeatedly, which means we can't use the **MouseUp** event to wrap things up.

So when is a polygon complete? When it's closed. For each mouse click, we'll add a new vertex to the polygon and check the distance to the starting point. We'll close the loop either when the latest click comes within 10 pixels of the starting point, or when we fill up the array of vertex points—whichever comes first.

The **Form_MouseDown()** event procedure looks similar to the one in HOTSPOT2.FRM, but there's a big difference as shown in Listing 10.1.

Listing 10.1   The Form_MouseDown() Event Procedure from HOTSPOT3.FRM

```
Private Sub Form_MouseDown(Button As Integer, Shift As Integer, X As Single, _
   Y As Single)
Dim Dummy As Integer

   If DefineOption.Checked Then
      If DrawingPolygon Then
         DrawingPolygon = Not VertexFinishesPolygon(X, Y)
         PreviousX = X
         PreviousY = Y
      Else
         Dummy = mciExecute("play c:\windows\media\ding.wav")
         MsgBox "This polygon region is closed", 16, "Drawing Error"
      End If
```

```
      Else
         ' Test whether click is in region.
         If PtInRegion(hPolyRgn, X, Y) Then
            Dummy = mciExecute("play c:\windows\media\tada.wav")
         Else
            Dummy = mciExecute("play c:\windows\media\ding.wav")
         End If
      End If
End Sub
```

In HOTSPOT2.FRM, the **MouseDown** event erased the previously drawn rectangle by drawing over it in **Invert DrawMode**. It then set new anchor and end points. The version of **MouseDown** in this program doesn't draw or erase anything, leaving that task to **MouseMove**. Until the polygon is finished, **MouseDown** calls a general function named **VertexFinishesPolygon()** at each click of the mouse button, as shown in Listing 10.2

Listing 10.2   The VertexFinishesPolygon() General Function from HOTSPOT3.FRM

```
Private Function VertexFinishesPolygon(X As Single, Y As Single) As Integer

   If (CurrentPointIndex > 0) And ((Sqr((X - PolygonVertices(0).X) ^ 2 + _
      (Y - PolygonVertices(0).Y) ^ 2) <= 10) Or (CurrentPointIndex = 99)) Then
      HotSpot3F1.Line (PolygonVertices(CurrentPointIndex).X, _
         PolygonVertices(CurrentPointIndex).Y)-(PreviousX, PreviousY)
      HotSpot3F1.Line (PolygonVertices(CurrentPointIndex).X, _
         PolygonVertices(CurrentPointIndex).Y)-(PolygonVertices(0).X, _
         PolygonVertices(0).Y)
      VertexFinishesPolygon = True
   Else
      CurrentPointIndex = CurrentPointIndex + 1
      PolygonVertices(CurrentPointIndex).X = X
      PolygonVertices(CurrentPointIndex).Y = Y
      VertexFinishesPolygon = False
   End If
End Function
```

First, this function checks whether the polygon has more than one vertex and whether it's time to close it. If so, it erases the last line segment drawn by **MouseMove**, draws the line that closes the polygon, and returns **True**. Otherwise it adds the new vertex to the array and returns **False**. We've split out this function only for clarity; it's called from just one place, **Form_MouseDown**.

Listing 10.3 shows the **Form_MouseMove()** event procedure.

Listing 10.3   The Form_MouseMove() Event Procedure from HOTSPOT3.FRM

```
Private Sub Form_MouseMove(Button As Integer, Shift As Integer, X As Single, _
    Y As Single)

    If DrawingPolygon And (CurrentPointIndex > -1) Then
        Line (PolygonVertices(CurrentPointIndex).X, _
            PolygonVertices(CurrentPointIndex).Y)-(PreviousX, PreviousY)
        PreviousX = X
        PreviousY = Y
        Line (PolygonVertices(CurrentPointIndex).X, _
            PolygonVertices(CurrentPointIndex).Y)-(PreviousX, PreviousY)
    End If
End Sub
```

Like the **Form_MouseMove()** event procedure we used in HOTSPOT2.FRM, this procedure erases and redraws the lines as you move the mouse across the client area. But instead of a rectangle, it stretches a single line from the latest vertex to the mouse pointer. Until you close the polygon by clicking within the 10-pixel radius of ground zero, or by filling up the vertex array, the line will follow you wherever you go.

With all these things to keep track of—the array of vertices and its number of points stored, the current state of completion, the lines on the screen, the region handle—you know we're going to need an initialization procedure. Listing 10.4 shows **InitPolygonEditor()**—the right person for this job.

Listing 10.4   The InitPolygonEditor() General Procedure from HOTSPOT3.FRM

```
Private Sub InitPolygonEditor()
Dim I As Integer

    DeleteRegion hPolyRgn
    If CurrentPointIndex > 1 Then
        For I = 1 To CurrentPointIndex
            Line (PolygonVertices(I - 1).X, PolygonVertices(I - 1).Y)- _
                (PolygonVertices(I).X, PolygonVertices(I).Y)
        Next I
        If Not DrawingPolygon Then
            Line (PolygonVertices(CurrentPointIndex).X, _
                PolygonVertices(CurrentPointIndex).Y)-(PolygonVertices(0).X, _
                PolygonVertices(0).Y)
        End If
    End If
    CurrentPointIndex = -1
    DrawingPolygon = True
End Sub
```

This procedure cleans up any polygon or polygon pieces lying around by disposing of the region handle, drawing over the polygon in the client area with the Invert pen, and resetting **CurrentPointIndex** to **-1**. The general procedure **DeleteRegion()**, shown in Listing 10.5, comes from the previous hotspot projects, and it resides in HOTSPOT3.BAS.

Listing 10.5   The DeleteRegion() General Procedure from HOTSPOT3.BAS

```
Sub DeleteRegion(hRgn As Integer)
   If hRgn <> 0 Then
      If DeleteObject(hRgn) Then
         hRgn = 0
      Else
         MsgBox "Unable to Delete Region", 48, "GDI Error"
      End If
   End If
End Sub
```

Redrawing Polygons

Event-driven programming really begins to test us when we write drawing programs. For predictable results, we have to consider not only how the various mouse events need to behave, but also all the things that can happen to our client area during and after the drawing process. What happens, for example, when you bring the hotspot editor back to the foreground after switching to another application? We expect the program to return the picture to the state it was in before we covered it. And to do that, it's going to need a **Form_Paint()** event procedure. So that's what we'll do. Take a look at Listing 10.6 to see how this is done.

Listing 10.6   The Form_Paint() Event Procedure from HOTSPOT3.FRM

```
Private Sub Form_Paint()
Dim I As Integer

   If CurrentPointIndex > 1 Then
      For I = 1 To CurrentPointIndex
         Line (PolygonVertices(I - 1).X, PolygonVertices(I - 1).Y)- _
            (PolygonVertices(I).X, PolygonVertices(I).Y)
      Next I
      If Not DrawingPolygon Then
         Line (PolygonVertices(CurrentPointIndex).X, _
            PolygonVertices(CurrentPointIndex).Y)-(PolygonVertices(0).X, _
            PolygonVertices(0).Y)
      End If
   End If
End Sub
```

This procedure will redraw the outline of the polygonal hotspot whenever the client area becomes uncovered, moves, or changes size. But it won't work unless you've properly set both the **AutoRedraw** and **ClipControls** properties of the form HotSpot3F1. If you set **AutoRedraw** to True, you don't need the **Paint** event at all, and you don't need to worry about **ClipControls**. However, if you set **AutoRedraw** to **False** then you must also set **ClipControls** to **False**. When **AutoRedraw** is **False** and **ClipControls** is **True**, VB will repaint the entire client area whenever it detects the need to repaint any portion of it. The problem with indiscriminately repainting everything is that the Invert pen will erase areas that were never covered in the first place, causing the lines in the newly exposed area to reappear and, all others to vanish. When you set **ClipControls** to **False**, however, VB repaints only newly exposed areas, restoring the image to its original condition.

Starting a New Polygon

We have one last drawing detail to handle before we fill in the remaining menu options and the declarations. If you decide to select the New menu option before you've closed off a polygon, you'll trail a stray line from the last point you set to the edge of the client area. To clean up the extra line, we have to check whether we're in drawing mode. If so, erase the line by re-drawing it. Listing 10.7 shows the menu procedure that handles this task.

Listing 10.7   The NewOption_Click() Event Procedure from HOTSPOT3.FRM

```
Private Sub NewOption_Click()

    If DrawingPolygon Then
        Line (PolygonVertices(CurrentPointIndex).X, _
            PolygonVertices(CurrentPointIndex).Y)-(PreviousX, PreviousY)
    End If
    InitPolygonEditor
    TestOption.Checked = False
    DefineOption.Checked = True
End Sub
```

The **MouseMove()** event procedure won't draw any lines when **DrawingPolygon** is **False**, so we want to execute the **Line()** method in the **NewOption_Click()** event procedure only when **DrawingPolygon** is **True**.

The last three lines of the **NewOption_Click()** event procedure set things up so we can draw a new polygon. Obviously, if we've cleared the current polygon, make sure the program is in Define mode, not Test mode.

Tidying Up—The Remaining Code for HOTSPOT3

The last three menu option **Click** events and the **Form_Load()** and **Form_Unload()** event procedures perform some simple housekeeping, such as switching the check mark on the Define and Test mode options, and creating and deleting the hotspot region. This code is shown in Listing 10.8.

Listing 10.8   The Remaining Event Procedures in HOTSPOT3.FRM

```
Private Sub DefineOption_Click()

    TestOption.Checked = False
    DefineOption.Checked = True
    DeleteRegion hPolyRgn
End Sub

Private Sub Form_Load()

    InitPolygonEditor
End Sub

Private Sub Form_Unload(Cancel As Integer)

    DeleteRegion hPolyRgn
End Sub

Private Sub TestOption_Click()

    If DrawingPolygon Then
        MsgBox "Cannot Test Incomplete Polygon", 48, "Error"
    Else
        DefineOption.Checked = False
        TestOption.Checked = True
        hPolyRgn = CreatePolygonRgn(PolygonVertices(0), CurrentPointIndex + 1, 0)
    End If
End Sub

Private Sub QuitOption_Click()

    Form_Unload (0)
    End
End Sub
```

Finally, we need to add the declarations to HOTSPOT3.FRM (Listing 10.9) and HOTSPOT3.BAS (Listing 10.10).

Listing 10.9   The Declarations Section from HOTSPOT3.FRM

```
Option Explicit

Dim hPolyRgn As Integer
Dim PolygonVertices(99) As POINTAPI
Dim PreviousX As Integer
Dim PreviousY As Integer
Dim CurrentPointIndex As Integer
Dim DrawingPolygon As Boolean
```

Listing 10.10   The Declarations Section from HOTSPOT3.BAS

```
Option Explicit

Type POINTAPI
    X As Long
    Y As Long
End Type

#If Win32 Then
    Public Declare Function DeleteObject Lib "gdi32" (ByVal hObject As Long) _
        As Long
    Public Declare Function mciExecute Lib "winmm" (ByVal lpstrCommand _
        As String) As Long
    Public Declare Function PtInRegion Lib "gdi32" (ByVal hRgn As Long, ByVal X _
        As Long, ByVal Y As Long) As Long
    Public Declare Function CreatePolygonRgn Lib "gdi32" (lpPoints As POINTAPI, _
        ByVal nCount As Long, ByVal nPolyFillMode As Long) As Long
#Else
    Public Declare Function CreatePolygonRgn Lib "gdi32" (lpPoints As POINTAPI, _
        ByVal nCount As Long, ByVal nPolyFillMode As Long) As Long
    Public Declare Function DeleteObject Lib "gdi32" (ByVal hObject As Long) _
        As Long
    Public Declare Function mciExecute Lib "winmm" (ByVal lpstrCommand _
        As String) As Long
    Public Declare Function PtInRegion Lib "gdi32" (ByVal hRgn As Long, ByVal X _
        As Long, ByVal Y As Long) As Long
#End If
```

Adding Polygon Hotspots to Images

Now we'll combine what we learned in our last two projects, HOTSPOT2.VBP
(Chapter 8) and HOTSPOT3.VBP, to write a polygon editor that lets us draw
irregularly shaped hotspots over bitmap images and save them in a data file.
In the next chapter, we'll pull them back out and put them to work in our
hypermedia system.

Although this program closely resembles HOTSPOT2, it varies considerably in the details. We'll highlight the most significant differences here, but
don't make any assumptions about the housekeeping procedures. One flaky
flag can break the whole thing. Study the code.

Watch for three important differences between this and the two previous
projects. First, we'll add a Picture Box control, where we'll do all our drawing. Second, we'll shift around some code, primarily from the main form to
the code module. Finally, we'll use the data access features of VB to store our
hotspots in a Microsoft Access database. These changes will help us get ready
to add hyperimaging to our hypermedia system.

The Powerful (Irregular) Hotspot Editor

This editor draws and saves irregular (polygon) hotspot regions. Here are the steps we'll follow:

1. Create two forms, HotSpot4F1, saved as the file HOTSPOT4.FRM, and HotSpot4F2, saved as the file HTSPT4F2.FRM.
2. Set up the **Mouse** events to perform the drawing operations (Listings 10.11 through 10.13).
3. Create the database file structure.
4. Save and retrieve hotspots from the database file (Listings 10.14 through 10.17).

 *This project is located in the directory \VBMAGIC\HOTSPOT4, in the files HOTSPOT4.VBP, HOTSPOT4.FRM, HOTSPOT4.BAS, HTSPT4F2.FRM, DATACONS.BAS, and GLOBCONS.BAS. You'll also need the Common Dialog control, which is located in the file CMDIALOG.OCX. VB Setup normally installs this, and its other OCX files in your \WINDOWS\SYSTEM directory. You can either load the files individually, or use the **Tools|Custom Controls** menu option to bring up a dialog box of all the controls that came with VB 4.*

Running the New Hotspot Editor

When you start the HOTSPOT4 program, you'll see the form shown in Figure 10.3. The first time you run this program, it will create an Access database file called IMAGES.MDB. The file should appear in the same directory as HOTSPOT4.VBP. Before you can begin drawing polygons, you must first load a picture into the Picture Box by choosing File|Load Picture. Use the resulting dialog box to select any Windows bitmap image file (*.BMP or *.DIB).

Draw a polygon outline around some portion of the image, and then choose File|Save Hotspot. The program prompts you to enter a hyperlink target string. For now, enter anything; we'll create working target strings in the next chapter. When you click on OK, the program will add a new record to the Image Table in IMAGES.MDB.

Of course, you have to properly terminate the program and dispose of any active region. Simply choose File|Quit, or choose Close from the form's Control menu. That's all there is to it.

Figure 10.3   *Running HOTSPOT4.*

Creating the Forms

Start with a new project and set the **Name** property of the first form to HotSpot4F1. You won't need to worry about the **DrawMode**, **ScaleMode**, **AutoRedraw**, or **ClipControls** properties of the form, because we're going to do all our drawing in a Picture Box.

Open the Menu Design window and create two menus, one labeled &File and one labeled &Mode. Under the File menu, add the options listed in Table 10.2.

Under the Mode menu, add the &Defining Region and &Testing Region options. Name them **DefineOption** and **TestOption**, respectively.

We'll need two controls on this form. First, drop in a Picture Box. We'll only have one Picture Box in the whole project, so we'll just leave its **Name**

Table 10.2   *The File Menu Options from HOTSPOT4.FRM*

Menu Caption	Menu Name
&Load Picture	LoadOption
&New Hotspot	NewOption
&Edit Saved Hotspot	EditOption
&Save Hotspot	SaveOption
&Delete Hotspot	DeleteOption
&Quit	QuitOption

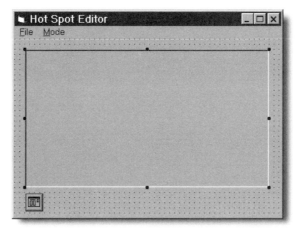

Figure 10.4 *Creating the main form for the image hotspot editor.*

property set to the default, Picture1. This is where we'll be drawing our polygon hotspots, so stretch it out to fill most of the client area of the form, as shown in Figure 10.4. Set the Picture Box's **AutoRedraw** and **ClipControls** properties to False, set its **ScaleMode** to 3 - Pixel, and set its **DrawMode** to 6 - Invert.

The second control we'll add will be a Common Dialog. Make sure the file CMDIALOG.VBX is listed in the Project window. If not, select File | Add File from the VB menu bar, and locate this file in the Windows System directory (usually C:\WINDOWS\SYSTEM). Once you've added the .VBX file to the project, you'll find the Common Dialog control in the VB Toolbox. The icon for the control looks like a miniature window with a few controls drawn on it. You can place the Common Dialog control anywhere on the form's client area; remember, it will become invisible at runtime.

To add the second form, select File | New Form. Set the **Name** property of the form to HotSpot4F2. Also, set its **BorderStyle** to 1 - Fixed Single and its **Caption** to "Open a Hotspot."

On this form we'll need three controls, one List Box and two Command Buttons. Set the **Name** property of the List Box to HotSpotList. Set the **Caption** properties of the two Command Buttons to "Load Hotspot" and "Cancel." Set their **Name** properties to LoadButton and CancelButton, respectively. Figure 10.5 shows what this form looks like.

Programming the Main Form

The **MouseDown()** and **MouseMove()** event procedures have hardly changed at all, except that they now belong to Picture1 rather than the form. The **Line()** methods in **MouseMove()** include explicit de-references to Picture1,

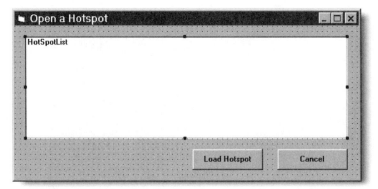

Figure 10.5   *The HotSpot4F2 form.*

although their relationship to the control is implied. Listing 10.11 shows the complete code for **Picture1_MouseMove()**.

Listing 10.11   The Picture1_MouseMove() Event Procedure from HOTSPOT4.FRM

```
Private Sub Picture1_MouseDown(Button As Integer, Shift As Integer, _
    X As Single, Y As Single)
Dim Dummy As Integer

    If DefineOption.CHECKED And (Len(CurrentImageFilename) > 0) Then
        If DrawingPolygon Then
            DrawingPolygon = Not VertexFinishesPolygon(X, Y)
            PreviousX = X
            PreviousY = Y
        Else
            Dummy = mciExecute("play c:\windows\ding.wav")
            MsgBox "This polygon region is closed", 16, "Drawing Error"
        End If
    Else
        ' Test whether click is in region.
        If PtInRegion(hPolyRgn, X, Y) Then
            Dummy = mciExecute("play c:\windows\media\tada.wav")
        Else
            Dummy = mciExecute("play c:\windows\media\ding.wav")
        End If
    End If
End Sub
```

We have to modify the general function **VertexFinishesPolygon()** in the same way, and this time the change is necessary. Here's why. General functions defined in a form module belong to that form, and any method we use without an explicit object reference would belong to the form. To guarantee that the **Line()** methods draw on the Picture Box instead of the form, we have to change their object references to Picture1, as shown in Listing 10.12.

Listing 10.12   The VertexFinishesPolygon() General Function from HOTSPOT4.FRM

```
Private Function VertexFinishesPolygon(X As Single, Y As Single) As Boolean

    If (CurrentPointIndex > 0) And ((Sqr((X - PolygonVertices(0).X) ^ 2 + _
        (Y - PolygonVertices(0).Y) ^ 2) <= 10) Or (CurrentPointIndex = 99)) Then
        Picture1.Line (PolygonVertices(CurrentPointIndex).X, _
            PolygonVertices(CurrentPointIndex).Y)-(PreviousX, PreviousY)
        Picture1.Line (PolygonVertices(CurrentPointIndex).X, _
            PolygonVertices(CurrentPointIndex).Y)-(PolygonVertices(0).X, _
            PolygonVertices(0).Y)
        VertexFinishesPolygon = True
        SaveOption.Enabled = True
    Else
        CurrentPointIndex = CurrentPointIndex + 1
        PolygonVertices(CurrentPointIndex).X = X
        PolygonVertices(CurrentPointIndex).Y = Y
        VertexFinishesPolygon = False
    End If
End Function
```

In HOTSPOT3.FRM, we duplicated the code that draws (or erases) the polygon in **InitPolygonEditor()** and the **Form_Paint()** event procedure. In our new version, we'll place that code in a general procedure called **DrawPolygon()**, which will now reside in HOTSPOT4.BAS, as shown in Listing 10.13.

Listing 10.13   The DrawPolygon() General Procedure from HOTSPOT4.BAS

```
Sub DrawPolygon(VertexArray() As POINTAPI, LastArrayIndex As Integer, ThePicture
As PictureBox, CompletePolygon As Integer)
Dim I As Integer

    If LastArrayIndex > 0 Then
        For I = 1 To LastArrayIndex
            ThePicture.Line (VertexArray(I - 1).X, VertexArray(I - 1).Y)- _
                (VertexArray(I).X, VertexArray(I).Y)
        Next I
        If CompletePolygon Then
            ThePicture.Line (VertexArray(LastArrayIndex).X, _
                VertexArray(LastArrayIndex).Y)-(VertexArray(0).X, VertexArray(0).Y)
        End If
    End If
End Sub
```

This procedure reveals the reason for plugging in Picture1 instead of continuing to use the form as the drawing surface. Later, when we use our hotspots in actual multimedia presentations, we may occasionally want to draw the outlines of the hotspot regions. To produce such a general purpose version of the procedure, we'll need to pass in the display control as an argument, which means that we have to give it an *object type*. We can't use the types **Form** and **PictureBox** interchangeably, so we have to pick one or the other. Since Picture Boxes will give us the most flexibility in later programming projects (not just those in this book), that's what we'll use here.

Storing Polygon Regions

In the project HOTSPOT2.MAK, we used VB's regular file I/O to store records in a binary data file. We defined the record with the **Type** statement:

```
Type HotSpotRecords
   Image As String * 128
   Target As String * 128
   TopX As Integer
   TopY As Integer
   BottomX As Integer
   BottomY As Integer
End Type
```

We then used the **Put** and **Get** statements to store and retrieve records from the data file.

To use the same method for polygon hotspots, we would need to modify the record structure to accommodate a complete set of vertices:

```
Type PolygonHotSpotRecords
   Image As String * 128
   Target As String * 128
   VertexArray(99) As POINTAPI
End Type
```

The record structure looks simpler, but it's much larger. Each record of type **HotSpotRecords** occupies 264 bytes, the sum of its two string fields and four two-byte integers. A record of the hypothetical type **PolygonHotSpotRecords** would fill 656 bytes, no matter whether the polygon it represented consisted of only three or eighty-three vertices.

We could split the record into two structures, and therefore two files, one to hold the image filename and target string, and one to hold each vertex. Then we could store just as many points as we needed to define each polygon. To keep track of the vertex records, we could use a linked list structure. If that sounds like a lot of work—believe us, it is!

Even if we were to get all that working, we would still have to figure out ways to sort and search the primary file, and to manage deleted records in both files. Fortunately, VB offers us an alternative to building our own database manager. With version 3.0 of VB, Microsoft introduced the *Data Access* system, which includes a whole bunch of features that enable us to create and maintain databases using the Microsoft Access database engine. With the Data Access features, we can use simple methods to add, change, or delete records. And to top it all off, records in Access databases can store special binary fields, which may vary in length from record to record.

Building the Hotspot Database

Unlike ordinary binary data files, Access data files are not built from records defined with the **Type** statement. Instead, Access records are collections of *field objects* that belong to a *table definition object*. The table definition object, in turn, belongs to the mother of all Access objects, a *database object*.

Let's take a look at the inner workings of the Access database engine. We build a useable database by first creating all the necessary objects. We then assemble them with the **Append** method. First we declare and define **Field** objects, which we **Append** to the **Fields** collection of the **TableDef** object. Next, we define an **Index** object based on the fields in the **Fields** collection and **Append** it to the **Indexes** collection of the **TableDef** object. And finally, we **Append** the whole **TableDef** object to the **Database** object. A **Recordset** may contain many fields, and a **Database** may contain many **Recordsets**. And these are just some of the object types available to us in the Access database system.

We'll call our database ImageDB and store it in a file called IMAGES.MDB. ImageDB will contain only one table, which we'll call ImageTable. The table definition that corresponds to ImageTable will be called **ImageTableDef**, and will contain four field definitions: **ImageFilename**, a 128-byte *text* field; **HotSpotNum**, a long integer field; **LinkTarget**, another 128-byte text field; and **VertexArray**, a *long binary* field. We'll also create an index for the table called **PrimaryKey**, which will be ordered according to the combination of two fields, the **ImageFilename** plus the **HotSpotNum**.

The general function **OpenImageDatabase()**, in HOTSPOT4.BAS (as shown in Listing 10.14), will open the database for business. If the file doesn't exist, it will create it by assembling all the appropriate objects.

Listing 10.14   The OpenImageDatabase() General Function from HOTSPOT4.BAS

```
Function OpenImageDatabase() As Integer
' Opens the file IMAGES.MDB.  If file does
' not exist, this function will create it.
Dim Fld() As New Field
```

```
Dim Idx() As New Index
Dim ImageTableDef As New TableDef
Dim Counter As Integer

    If Len(Dir$(App.Path + "\Images.MDB")) > 0 Then
        Set ImageDB = OpenDatabase(App.Path + "\Images.MDB")
        Set ImageTable = ImageDB.OpenRecordset("ImageTable")
    Else
        ' Create database Images.MDB
        Set ImageDB = CreateDatabase(App.Path + "\Images.MDB", DB_LANG_GENERAL)
        ' Create Image Table
        ImageTableDef.Name = "ImageTable"
        ' Create Fields.
        ReDim Fld(1 To 4)
        Fld(2).Attributes = DB_AUTOINCRFIELD     ' Counter field.
        For Counter = 1 To 4  ' Set properties for fields.
            Fld(Counter).Name = Choose(Counter, "ImageFileName", "HotSpotNum", _
                "LinkTarget", "VertexArray")
            Fld(Counter).Type = Choose(Counter, DB_TEXT, DB_LONG, DB_TEXT, _
                DB_LONGBINARY)
            Fld(Counter).Size = Choose(Counter, 128, 4, 128, 400)
            ImageTableDef.Fields.Append Fld(Counter)
        Next Counter

        ' Create Table Index.
        ReDim Idx(1)
        Idx(1).Name = "PrimaryKey"
        Idx(1).Fields = "ImageFileName;HotSpotNum"
        Idx(1).Primary = True
        Idx(1).Unique = True
        ImageTableDef.Indexes.Append Idx(1)

        ' Create Table.
        ImageDB.TableDefs.Append ImageTableDef
        ImageDB.Close
        Set ImageDB = OpenDatabase(App.Path + "\Images.MDB")
        Set ImageTable = ImageDB.OpenRecordset("ImageTable")
    End If
End Function
```

Although it looks a little lengthy, this function is simple. The only decision it needs to make is whether to open an existing database file or create a new one. The VB **Dir$()** function will return a null string ("") if it can't locate the filename and path, which means you've passed it. If we find the file, we use the **Set** statement and the **OpenDatabase()** function to open the object variable **ImageDB**. There is no permanent relationship between the object variable and the database file. As long as we declare it as a database object, we could use any legal variable name to reference the database object, such as:

```
Dim AnyDatabase As Database
```

The declaration for **ImageDB** is **Global** and you'll find it in the declarations section of HOTSPOT4.BAS, along with the declaration for **ImageTable**. Inside this function we declare three types of local object variables:

```
Dim Fld() As New Field
Dim Idx() As New Index
Dim ImageTableDef As New TableDef
```

Here we use the reserved word **New** to indicate that these objects don't yet exist. To create a new child object, you must declare it as **New**.

To open an existing database, we use two **Set** statements:

```
If Len(Dir$(App.Path + "\Images.MDB")) > 0 Then
   Set ImageDB = OpenDatabase(App.Path + "\Images.MDB")
   Set ImageTable = ImageDB.OpenRecordset("ImageTable")
```

The **Path** property of the **App** object will return the path of the .MAK file for a program running in the VB development environment, or the path of the .EXE file for a compiled program. This is an arbitrary restriction we've placed in the program to make it easier for you to run the sample program; you may remove it if you wish. To turn the project into a general purpose hotspot editor, you'll probably want to add a file dialog box that will let the user select a specific image database file, or choose the location for a new one.

To create a new database, we begin with VB's **CreateDatabase()** function

```
Set ImageDB = CreateDatabase(App.Path + "\Images.MDB", DB_LANG_GENERAL)
```

This statement sets **ImageDB** to the **Database** object type, referencing an empty database definition. Now all we need to do is fill it out.

We begin by assigning the **Name** "ImageTable" to the new table definition. Then we define its four fields:

```
ReDim Fld(1 To 4)
   Fld(2).Attributes = DB_AUTOINCRFIELD     ' Counter field.
   For Counter = 1 To 4  ' Set properties for fields.
      Fld(Counter).Name = Choose(Counter, "ImageFileName", "HotSpotNum", _
         "LinkTarget", "VertexArray")
      Fld(Counter).Type = Choose(Counter, DB_TEXT, DB_LONG, DB_TEXT, _
         DB_LONGBINARY)
      Fld(Counter).Size = Choose(Counter, 128, 4, 128, 400)
      ImageTableDef.Fields.Append Fld(Counter)
   Next Counter
```

The order in which we set the field properties doesn't matter as long as we set all the properties of any given field *before* we **Append** it to the **Fields** collection of the table definition. Since we're going to set most of the properties and **Append** the fields inside the **For** loop, we need to get the one oddball property out of the way first.

The second field, **HotSpotNum** is an *autoincrement* field. That is, every time we add a new record to the table, the database engine automatically sets this field to the next available long integer value. Unlike ordinary binary files, indexed database files provide no meaningful record numbers. So to make sure that every record has a unique identity, it's often useful to add an autoincrement field to the record definition. Since this type of field increments indefinitely (or up to 2,147,483,647, the maximum long integer value), and never reuses the values assigned to deleted records, it also enables us to build indexes that reflect the order in which the records were added to the table. Set the **Attributes** property of the second field before beginning the loop, because none of the other fields has special attributes.

Inside the **For** loop, we use the VB **Choose()** function to select the values of the field properties based on the loop index, an integer variable named **Counter**. The constants **DB_AUTOINCRFIELD**, **DB_TEXT**, **DB_LONG**, **DB_TEXT**, and **DB_LONGBINARY** are defined in the code module DATACONS.BAS. After we assign the field **Name**, **Type**, and **Size** properties, we use the **Append** method to add the fields to the table definition's **Fields** collection, the Access equivalent of a record definition.

Next, we define an **Index** object for the table:

```
ReDim Idx(1)
Idx(1).Name = "PrimaryKey"
Idx(1).Fields = "ImageFileName;HotSpotNum"
Idx(1).Primary = True
Idx(1).Unique = True
ImageTableDef.Indexes.Append Idx(1)
```

By setting the **Primary** property to **True**, we instruct VB to enforce a couple of rules. First, the values of the fields that make up the index—in this case, the fields called **ImageFileName** and **HotSpotNum**—must never contain null values. Second, these fields, when combined, must always produce a unique value. In this case, we've guaranteed uniqueness by making **HotSpotNum** an autoincrement field. The **Unique** property is redundant when **Primary** is set to **True**. *A table can have only one primary index, and the key values in the primary index must be unique for each entry.*

Finally, we append the entire table definition to the database:

```
ImageDB.TableDefs.Append ImageTableDef
```

However, we must first close, then reopen the database before we can use it:

```
ImageDB.Close
Set ImageDB = OpenDatabase(App.Path + "\Images.MDB")
Set ImageTable = ImageDB.OpenRecordset("ImageTable")
```

Saving Hotspot Records

Now that we have our database, we're going to add records to it. Don't worry, adding records to an Access database is easy. Just call the **AddNew** method, assign values to the fields, and call the **Update** method. To replace an existing record, use the **Edit** method instead of **AddNew**. Unlike conventional file systems in which you explicitly read or write a whole record at once, in the VB Data Access system, you position yourself over a record, then assign values to or from individual fields. The record buffer is like a sliding porthole. To edit an existing record, ask VB to position the porthole over it using one of the various search methods. Then call the **Edit** method, which tells it that you intend to change the contents of the record. You can copy data to one field or several, but this doesn't necessitate updating them all. When you ask to add a new record with the **AddNew** method, VB positions the buffer over an empty record. Other than that, there is no difference between adding and replacing a record. In either case, you commit your changes to the file by calling the **Update** method. Listing 10.15 shows the **SaveHotspotRecord()** general procedure that handles all of this for us.

Listing 10.15 The SaveHotspotRecord() General Procedure from HOTSPOT4.BAS

```
Sub SaveHotspotRecord()
Dim TempTarget As String
Dim ArrayString As String

   ArrayString = StringFromArray(PolygonVertices(), CurrentPointIndex)
   If CurrentHotspotRecordID = 0 Then
     ' Add new record
     TempTarget = ""
     TempTarget = InputBox$("Enter a Hyperlink Target string of "& _
       "up to 128 characters: ", "Enter Target", TempTarget)
     If Len(TempTarget) > 0 Then
       ImageTable.AddNew
       ImageTable!ImageFilename = CurrentImageFilename
       ImageTable!LinkTarget = TempTarget
       ImageTable!VertexArray = ArrayString
       ImageTable.Update
     End If
```

```
    Else
      ' Replace existing record
      ImageTable.Seek "=", CurrentImageFilename, CurrentHotspotRecordID
      If Not ImageTable.NoMatch Then
        TempTarget = ImageTable!LinkTarget
        TempTarget = InputBox$("enter a Hyperlink Target string of "& _
            "up to 128 characters: ", "Enter Target", TempTarget)
        If Len(TempTarget) > 0 Then
          ImageTable.Edit
          ImageTable!ImageFilename = CurrentImageFilename
          ImageTable!LinkTarget = TempTarget
          ImageTable!VertexArray = ArrayString
          ImageTable.Update
        End If
      Else
        MsgBox "Unable to Relocate Record", 48, "Database Error"
      End If
    End If
  End If
End Sub
```

Before we can perform either type of update to our hotspot records, we need to set the values of the variables **CurrentImageFilename**, **TempTarget**, and **ArrayString**. We can get the first of these out of the way easily. When we load the image into Picture1, we set **CurrentImageFilename** to the name of the bitmap file chosen from the file dialog box. That value will remain unchanged until we either select another picture to work on, or exit the program. The next easiest field to capture is **TempTarget**. We'll just display an Input Box and ask the user to enter the target string:

```
TempTarget = ""
TempTarget = InputBox$("Enter a Hyperlink Target string of up to 128 characters: _
    ", "Enter Target", TempTarget)
```

To fill in the third field, **ArrayString**, we'll need to be a little trickier. You set a field of type **DB_LONGBINARY** by assigning it the value of a string. So before we can store our vertex array in the database record, we first need to convert it into a string. That's the job of the general function **StringFromArray()**, which is shown in Listing 10.16.

Listing 10.16   The StringFromArray() General Function from HOTSPOT4.BAS

```
Function StringFromArray(VertexArray() As POINTAPI, LastArrayIndex As Integer)
As String
Dim I As Integer
Dim TempString As String

  TempString = ""
  For I = 0 To LastArrayIndex
```

```
        TempString = TempString + Chr$(VertexArray(I).X \ 256)
        TempString = TempString + Chr$(VertexArray(I).X Mod 256)
        TempString = TempString + Chr$(VertexArray(I).Y \ 256)
        TempString = TempString + Chr$(VertexArray(I).Y Mod 256)
    Next I
    StringFromArray = TempString
End Function
```

We store the **X** and **Y** values by converting them into characters and appending them to the variable-length string **TempString**. A character can have any ANSI value from 0 to 255, which means that any single-byte value can be represented by a character. To break a two-byte integer into two character values, we extract the high and low bytes with the integer divide (\) and **Mod** operators. When we're done, we can return a string just long enough to hold the current vertex array.

There's one precaution to take before replacing a record. Make sure that the current record buffer and position match the record you retrieved for editing. To reposition yourself on the record, use the **Seek** method:

```
ImageTable.Seek "=", CurrentImageFilename, CurrentHotspotRecordID
If Not ImageTable.NoMatch Then
    ...
```

The **NoMatch** property will tell you whether you've managed to relocate the record. In most situations you don't need to worry about this step, but in a multi-user environment, unless you provide adequate protection in the form of record locking, it's possible for another user to delete a record while you're working on it.

Retrieving Hotspot Records

To read a hotspot record from the database table, we first locate the record with the **Seek** method. If VB finds the record we've requested, we can set our variables with simple assignment statements. Once it has been located, reading a record requires no special commands or methods. This is the job of the general function **LoadHotSpot()**, shown in Listing 10.17.

Listing 10.17   TheLoadHotSpot() General Function from HOTSPOT4.BAS

```
Function LoadHotSpot(ImageFilename As String, ByVal RecordID As Long) As Integer
Dim TempString As String

    ImageTable.Index = "PrimaryKey"
    ImageTable.Seek "=", ImageFilename, RecordID
```

```
   If Not ImageTable.NoMatch Then
      CurrentImageFilename = ImageTable!ImageFilename
      TempString = ImageTable!VertexArray
      CurrentPointIndex = ArrayFromString(PolygonVertices(), TempString)
      CurrentHotspotRecordID = ImageTable!HotSpotNum
      LoadHotSpot = True
   Else
      LoadHotSpot = False
   End If
End Function
```

The index we've defined for **ImageTable** consists of two fields, **ImageFileName** and **HotSpotNum**. To retrieve a hotspot record, we pass those two values to **LoadHotSpot()**. Inside the function we set the current **Index** to **PrimaryKey**, which is the name we gave to the one and only index of **ImageTable**. Then we use the **Seek** method to search for a match. If we find the record, we assign the field values into our program variables, convert the long binary field back from a string into an array of **POINTAPI** structures, and return **True**.

The Complete Listing of HOTSPOT4

Listings 10.18, 10.19, and 10.20 show the complete listings of HOTSPOT4.FRM, HTSPT4F2.FRM, and HOTSPOT4.BAS. The code modules GLOBCONS.BAS and DATACONS.BAS contain the text files CONSTANT.TXT and DATACONS.TXT that ship with VB. You will most likely find them in your VB directory.

Listing 10.18　HOTSPOT4.FRM

```
VERSION 4.00
Begin VB.Form HotSpot4F1
   Caption         =   "Hot Spot Editor"
   ClientHeight    =   4170
   ClientLeft      =   1770
   ClientTop       =   2730
   ClientWidth     =   6420
   BeginProperty Font
      name         =   "MS Sans Serif"
      charset      =   1
      weight       =   700
      size         =   8.25
      underline    =   0    'False
      italic       =   0    'False
      strikethrough =  0    'False
   EndProperty
   Height          =   4920
   Left            =   1710
```

```
LinkTopic       =    "Form1"
ScaleHeight     =    4170
ScaleWidth      =    6420
Top             =    2040
Width           =    6540
Begin VB.PictureBox Picture1
   ClipControls    =    0       'False
   DrawMode        =    6       'Mask Pen Not
   Height          =    3255
   Left            =    240
   ScaleHeight     =    211
   ScaleMode       =    3       'Pixel
   ScaleWidth      =    387
   TabIndex        =    0
   Top             =    240
   Width           =    5895
End
Begin MSComDlg.CommonDialog ImageFileDialog
   Left            =    240
   Top             =    3600
   _version        =    65536
   _extentx        =    847
   _extenty        =    847
   _stockprops     =    0
End
Begin VB.Menu FileMenu
   Caption            =    "&File"
   Begin VB.Menu LoadOption
      Caption         =    "&Load Picture"
   End
   Begin VB.Menu NewOption
      Caption         =    "&New"
   End
   Begin VB.Menu EditOption
      Caption         =    "&Edit Saved Hotspot"
   End
   Begin VB.Menu SaveOption
      Caption         =    "&Save Hotspot"
   End
   Begin VB.Menu DeleteOption
      Caption         =    "&Delete Hotspot"
   End
   Begin VB.Menu QuitOption
      Caption         =    "&Quit"
   End
End
Begin VB.Menu ModeMenu
   Caption            =    "&Mode"
   Begin VB.Menu DefineOption
      Caption         =    "&Defining Region"
      Checked         =    -1       'True
   End
   Begin VB.Menu TestOption
```

```
        Caption        =    "&Testing Region"
      End
    End
End
Attribute VB_Name = "HotSpot4F1"
Attribute VB_Creatable = False
Attribute VB_Exposed = False
Option Explicit

Dim DrawingPolygon As Integer

Private Sub DefineOption_Click()

    TestOption.CHECKED = False
    DefineOption.CHECKED = True
    DeleteRegion hPolyRgn
End Sub


Private Sub DeleteOption_Click()
Dim Response As Integer

    If CurrentHotspotRecordID > 0 Then
        Response = MsgBox("Are you sure you want to delete this Hotspot?", _
            MB_YESNO + MB_ICONQUESTION, "Warning!")
        If Response = IDYES Then
            ImageTable.Seek "=", CurrentImageFilename, CurrentHotspotRecordID
            If Not ImageTable.NoMatch Then
                ImageTable.Delete
                SaveOption.Enabled = False
                DeleteOption.Enabled = False
                InitPolygonEditor
                DrawPolygon PolygonVertices(), CurrentPointIndex, Picture1, _
                    Not DrawingPolygon
                PreviousX = 0
                PreviousY = 0
                TestOption.CHECKED = False
                DefineOption.CHECKED = True
                DeleteRegion hPolyRgn
            Else
                MsgBox "Unable to Relocate Hotspot Record.", 48, "Database Error"
            End If
        End If
    Else
        MsgBox "There is no region to delete.", 48, "Delete Error"
    End If
End Sub

Private Sub EditOption_Click()

    DrawPolygon PolygonVertices(), CurrentPointIndex, Picture1, Not DrawingPolygon
    DeleteRegion hPolyRgn
    DrawingPolygon = False
    HotSpot4F2.Show MODAL
```

```vba
        If CurrentHotspotRecordID > 0 Then
            SaveOption.Enabled = True
            DeleteOption.Enabled = True
        End If
        If TestOption.CHECKED Then
            hPolyRgn = CreatePolygonRgn(PolygonVertices(0), CurrentPointIndex + 1, 0)
        End If
        HotSpot4F1.Refresh
End Sub


Private Sub Form_Load()

    NewOption.Enabled = False
    EditOption.Enabled = False
    SaveOption.Enabled = False
    DeleteOption.Enabled = False
    CurrentHotspotRecordID = 0&
    DatabaseOpen = OpenImageDatabase()
    InitPolygonEditor
End Sub

Private Sub Form_Resize()

    Picture1.Width = 0.9 * HotSpot4F1.ScaleWidth
    Picture1.Height = 0.9 * HotSpot4F1.ScaleHeight
    Picture1.Left = HotSpot4F1.ScaleWidth \ 2 - Picture1.Width \ 2
    Picture1.Top = HotSpot4F1.ScaleHeight \ 2 - Picture1.Height \ 2
End Sub

Private Sub Form_Unload(Cancel As Integer)
    DeleteRegion hPolyRgn
    ImageTable.Close
    ImageDB.Close
    End Sub


Private Sub InitPolygonEditor()

    DeleteRegion hPolyRgn
    DrawPolygon PolygonVertices(), CurrentPointIndex, Picture1, Not DrawingPolygon
    CurrentPointIndex = -1
    CurrentHotspotRecordID = 0&
    PreviousX = 0
    PreviousY = 0
    DrawingPolygon = True
End Sub

Private Sub LoadOption_Click()

    NewOption.Enabled = True
    EditOption.Enabled = True
    SaveOption.Enabled = False
    DeleteOption.Enabled = False
```

```
        CurrentHotspotRecordID = 0&
        InitPolygonEditor
        ImageFileDialog.Filter = "Bitmaps *.BMP|*.BMP|Device Independent Bitmaps _
            *.DIB|*.DIB"
        ImageFileDialog.Action = 1
        If ImageFileDialog.FileName <> "" Then
            CurrentImageFilename = Mid$(ImageFileDialog.FileName, 3)
            Picture1.Picture = LoadPicture(CurrentImageFilename)
        End If
End Sub


Private Sub NewOption_Click()

    SaveOption.Enabled = False
    DeleteOption.Enabled = False
    CurrentHotspotRecordID = 0&
    If DrawingPolygon And (CurrentPointIndex > -1) Then
        Picture1.Line (PolygonVertices(CurrentPointIndex).X, _
            PolygonVertices(CurrentPointIndex).Y)-(PreviousX, PreviousY)
    End If
    InitPolygonEditor
    TestOption.CHECKED = False
    DefineOption.CHECKED = True
    DeleteRegion hPolyRgn
End Sub

Private Sub Picture1_MouseDown(Button As Integer, Shift As Integer, _
    X As Single, Y As Single)
Dim Dummy As Integer

    If DefineOption.CHECKED And (Len(CurrentImageFilename) > 0) Then
        If DrawingPolygon Then
            DrawingPolygon = Not VertexFinishesPolygon(X, Y)
            PreviousX = X
            PreviousY = Y
        Else
            Dummy = mciExecute("play c:\windows\ding.wav")
            MsgBox "This polygon region is closed", 16, "Drawing Error"
        End If
    Else
        ' Test whether click is in region.
        If PtInRegion(hPolyRgn, X, Y) Then
            Dummy = mciExecute("play c:\windows\media\tada.wav")
        Else
            Dummy = mciExecute("play c:\windows\media\ding.wav")
        End If
    End If
End Sub

Private Sub Picture1_MouseMove(Button As Integer, Shift As Integer, _
    X As Single, Y As Single)
```

```vba
    If DrawingPolygon And (CurrentPointIndex > -1) Then
        Picture1.Line (PolygonVertices(CurrentPointIndex).X, _
            PolygonVertices(CurrentPointIndex).Y)-(PreviousX, PreviousY)
        PreviousX = X
        PreviousY = Y
        Picture1.Line (PolygonVertices(CurrentPointIndex).X, _
            PolygonVertices(CurrentPointIndex).Y)-(PreviousX, PreviousY)
    End If
End Sub

Private Sub Picture1_Paint()

    DrawPolygon PolygonVertices(), CurrentPointIndex, Picture1, Not DrawingPolygon
End Sub

Private Sub QuitOption_Click()

    Form_Unload (0)
    End
End Sub

Private Sub SaveOption_Click()

    SaveHotspotRecord
End Sub

Private Sub TestOption_Click()

    If DrawingPolygon Then
        MsgBox "Cannot Test Incomplete Polygon", 48, "Error"
    Else
        DefineOption.CHECKED = False
        TestOption.CHECKED = True
        hPolyRgn = CreatePolygonRgn(PolygonVertices(0), CurrentPointIndex + 1, 0)
    End If
End Sub

Private Function VertexFinishesPolygon(X As Single, Y As Single) As Boolean

    If (CurrentPointIndex > 0) And ((Sqr((X - PolygonVertices(0).X) ^ 2 + _
        (Y - PolygonVertices(0).Y) ^ 2) <= 10) Or (CurrentPointIndex = 99)) Then
        Picture1.Line (PolygonVertices(CurrentPointIndex).X, _
            PolygonVertices(CurrentPointIndex).Y)-(PreviousX, PreviousY)
        Picture1.Line (PolygonVertices(CurrentPointIndex).X, _
            PolygonVertices(CurrentPointIndex).Y)-(PolygonVertices(0).X, _
PolygonVertices(0).Y)
        VertexFinishesPolygon = True
        SaveOption.Enabled = True
    Else
        CurrentPointIndex = CurrentPointIndex + 1
        PolygonVertices(CurrentPointIndex).X = X
        PolygonVertices(CurrentPointIndex).Y = Y
        VertexFinishesPolygon = False
    End If
End Function
```

Listing 10.19   HTSPT4F2.FRM

```
VERSION 4.00
Begin VB.Form HotSpot4F2
   BorderStyle      =   1   'Fixed Single
   Caption          =   "Open a Hotspot"
   ClientHeight     =   3585
   ClientLeft       =   870
   ClientTop        =   1530
   ClientWidth      =   8325
   BeginProperty Font
      name             =   "MS Sans Serif"
      charset          =   1
      weight           =   700
      size             =   8.25
      underline        =   0   'False
      italic           =   0   'False
      strikethrough    =   0   'False
   EndProperty
   Height           =   4050
   Left             =   810
   LinkTopic        =   "Form1"
   ScaleHeight      =   3585
   ScaleWidth       =   8325
   Top              =   1125
   Width            =   8445
   Begin VB.CommandButton CancelButton
      Caption          =   "Cancel"
      Height           =   492
      Left             =   6360
      TabIndex         =   2
      Top              =   2880
      Width            =   1692
   End
   Begin VB.CommandButton LoadButton
      Caption          =   "Load Hotspot"
      Enabled          =   0   'False
      Height           =   492
      Left             =   4320
      TabIndex         =   1
      Top              =   2880
      Width            =   1692
   End
   Begin VB.ListBox HotSpotList
      Height           =   2400
      Left             =   240
      TabIndex         =   0
      Top              =   240
      Width            =   7815
   End
End
Attribute VB_Name = "HotSpot4F2"
Attribute VB_Creatable = False
```

```vba
Attribute VB_Exposed = False
Option Explicit

Private Sub CancelButton_Click()

    Unload HotSpot4F2
End Sub

Private Sub Form_Load()
Dim Done As Integer

    LoadButton.Enabled = False
    HotSpotList.Clear
    ImageTable.Index = "PrimaryKey"
    ImageTable.Seek ">=", CurrentImageFilename
    If (Not ImageTable.NoMatch) Then
        If (ImageTable!ImageFilename = CurrentImageFilename) Then
            Done = False
            Do While Not Done
                HotSpotList.AddItem ImageTable!ImageFilename + " - " + _
                    ImageTable!LinkTarget
                HotSpotList.ItemData(HotSpotList.NewIndex) = ImageTable!HotSpotNum
                ImageTable.MoveNext
                Done = ImageTable.EOF
                If Not Done Then
                    Done = (ImageTable!ImageFilename <> CurrentImageFilename)
                End If
            Loop
        End If
    End If
End Sub

Private Sub HotSpotList_Click()

    LoadButton.Enabled = True
End Sub

Private Sub HotSpotList_DblClick()
    Dim LoadedHotspot As Integer
    LoadedHotspot = LoadHotSpot(CurrentImageFilename, _
        HotSpotList.ItemData(HotSpotList.ListIndex))
    Unload HotSpot4F2
    End Sub

Private Sub LoadButton_Click()
Dim LoadedHotspot As Integer

    LoadedHotspot = LoadHotSpot(CurrentImageFilename, _
        HotSpotList.ItemData(HotSpotList.ListIndex))
    Unload HotSpot4F2
End Sub
```

Listing 10.20 HOTSPOT4.BAS

```
Attribute VB_Name = "HOTSPOT41"
Option Explicit

Type POINTAPI
    X As Long
    Y As Long
End Type

#If Win32 Then
    Public Declare Function mciExecute Lib "winmm" (ByVal lpstrCommand _
        As String) As Long
    Public Declare Function PtInRegion Lib "gdi32" (ByVal hRgn As Long, ByVal X _
        As Long, ByVal Y As Long) As Long
    Public Declare Function DeleteObject Lib "gdi32" (ByVal hObject As Long) _
        As Long
    Public Declare Function CreatePolygonRgn Lib "gdi32" (lpPoints As POINTAPI, _
        ByVal nCount As Long, ByVal nPolyFillMode As Long) As Long
#Else
    Public Declare Function CreatePolygonRgn Lib "gdi32" (lpPoints As POINTAPI, _
        ByVal nCount As Long, ByVal nPolyFillMode As Long) As Long
    Public Declare Function PtInRegion Lib "GDI" (ByVal hRgn As Integer, _
        ByVal X As Integer, ByVal Y As Integer) As Integer
    Public Declare Function DeleteObject Lib "GDI" (ByVal hObject As Integer) _
        As Integer
    Public Declare Function mciExecute Lib "MMSystem" (ByVal CommandString _
        As String) As Integer
#End If

Global ImageDB As Database
Global ImageTable As Recordset
Global CurrentHotspotRecordID As Long
Global CurrentImageFilename As String
Global hPolyRgn As Integer
Global PolygonVertices(99) As POINTAPI
Global PreviousX As Integer
Global PreviousY As Integer
Global CurrentPointIndex As Integer
Global DatabaseOpen As Integer

Function ArrayFromString(TheVertexArray() As POINTAPI, ByVal TheString _
    As String) As Integer
Dim I As Integer
Dim LastElement As Integer

    LastElement = Len(TheString) \ 4 - 1
    For I = 0 To LastElement
        TheVertexArray(I).X = Asc(Mid$(TheString, I * 4 + 1, 1)) * 256 + _
            Asc(Mid$(TheString, I * 4 + 2, 1))
        TheVertexArray(I).Y = Asc(Mid$(TheString, I * 4 + 3, 1)) * 256 + _
            Asc(Mid$(TheString, I * 4 + 4, 1))
    Next I
```

```
      ArrayFromString = LastElement
End Function

Sub DeleteRegion(hRgn As Integer)

    If hRgn <> 0 Then
        If DeleteObject(hRgn) Then
            hRgn = 0
        Else
            MsgBox "Unable to Delete Region", 48, "GDI Error"
        End If
    End If
End Sub

Sub DrawPolygon(VertexArray() As POINTAPI, LastArrayIndex As Integer, _
    ThePicture As PictureBox, CompletePolygon As Integer)
Dim I As Integer

    If LastArrayIndex > 0 Then
        For I = 1 To LastArrayIndex
            ThePicture.Line (VertexArray(I - 1).X, VertexArray(I - 1).Y)- _
                (VertexArray(I).X, VertexArray(I).Y)
        Next I
        If CompletePolygon Then
            ThePicture.Line (VertexArray(LastArrayIndex).X, _
                VertexArray(LastArrayIndex).Y)-(VertexArray(0).X, VertexArray(0).Y)
        End If
    End If
End Sub

Function LoadHotSpot(ImageFilename As String, ByVal RecordID As Long) _
    As Integer Dim TempString As String

    ImageTable.Index = "PrimaryKey"
    ImageTable.Seek "=", ImageFilename, RecordID
    If Not ImageTable.NoMatch Then
        CurrentImageFilename = ImageTable!ImageFilename
        TempString = ImageTable!VertexArray
        CurrentPointIndex = ArrayFromString(PolygonVertices(), TempString)
        CurrentHotspotRecordID = ImageTable!HotSpotNum
        LoadHotSpot = True
    Else
        LoadHotSpot = False
    End If
End Function

Function OpenImageDatabase() As Integer
'   Opens the file IMAGES.MDB.  If file does
'   not exist, this function will create it.
Dim Fld() As New Field
Dim Idx() As New Index
Dim ImageTableDef As New TableDef
Dim Counter As Integer
```

```
    If Len(Dir$(App.Path + "\Images.MDB")) > 0 Then
        Set ImageDB = OpenDatabase(App.Path + "\Images.MDB")
        Set ImageTable = ImageDB.OpenRecordset("ImageTable")
    Else
        ' Create database Images.MDB
        Set ImageDB = CreateDatabase(App.Path + "\Images.MDB", DB_LANG_GENERAL)
        ' Create Image Table
        ImageTableDef.Name = "ImageTable"
        ' Create Fields.
        ReDim Fld(1 To 4)
        Fld(2).Attributes = DB_AUTOINCRFIELD      ' Counter field.
        For Counter = 1 To 4  ' Set properties for fields.
            Fld(Counter).Name = Choose(Counter, "ImageFileName", "HotSpotNum", _
                "LinkTarget", "VertexArray")
            Fld(Counter).Type = Choose(Counter, DB_TEXT, DB_LONG, DB_TEXT, _
                DB_LONGBINARY)
            Fld(Counter).Size = Choose(Counter, 128, 4, 128, 400)
            ImageTableDef.Fields.Append Fld(Counter)
        Next Counter

        ' Create Table Index.
        ReDim Idx(1)
        Idx(1).Name = "PrimaryKey"
        Idx(1).Fields = "ImageFileName;HotSpotNum"
        Idx(1).Primary = True
        Idx(1).Unique = True
        ImageTableDef.Indexes.Append Idx(1)

        ' Create Table.
        ImageDB.TableDefs.Append ImageTableDef
        ImageDB.Close
        Set ImageDB = OpenDatabase(App.Path + "\Images.MDB")
        Set ImageTable = ImageDB.OpenRecordset("ImageTable")
    End If
End Function

Sub SaveHotspotRecord()
Dim TempTarget As String
Dim ArrayString As String

    ArrayString = StringFromArray(PolygonVertices(), CurrentPointIndex)
    If CurrentHotspotRecordID = 0 Then
        ' Add new record
        TempTarget = ""
        TempTarget = InputBox$("Enter a Hyperlink Target string of up to 128 "& _
            "characters: ", "Enter Target", TempTarget)
        If Len(TempTarget) > 0 Then
            ImageTable.AddNew
            ImageTable!ImageFilename = CurrentImageFilename
            ImageTable!LinkTarget = TempTarget
            ImageTable!VertexArray = ArrayString
            ImageTable.Update
        End If
```

```
      Else
          ' Replace existing record
          ImageTable.Seek "=", CurrentImageFilename, CurrentHotspotRecordID
          If Not ImageTable.NoMatch Then
             TempTarget = ImageTable!LinkTarget
             TempTarget = InputBox$("enter a Hyperlink Target string of up to 128"& _
                "characters: ", "Enter Target", TempTarget)
             If Len(TempTarget) > 0 Then
                ImageTable.Edit
                ImageTable!ImageFilename = CurrentImageFilename
                ImageTable!LinkTarget = TempTarget
                ImageTable!VertexArray = ArrayString
                ImageTable.Update
             End If
          Else
             MsgBox "Unable to Relocate Record", 48, "Database Error"
          End If
      End If
   End If
End Sub

Function StringFromArray(VertexArray() As POINTAPI, LastArrayIndex As Integer) _
   As String
Dim I As Integer
Dim TempString As String

   TempString = ""
   For I = 0 To LastArrayIndex
      TempString = TempString + Chr$(VertexArray(I).X \ 256)
      TempString = TempString + Chr$(VertexArray(I).X Mod 256)
      TempString = TempString + Chr$(VertexArray(I).Y \ 256)
      TempString = TempString + Chr$(VertexArray(I).Y Mod 256)
   Next I
   StringFromArray = TempString
End Function
```

Hotspots: The Next Generation

The programs we've written in this chapter work just well enough to get some hotspots on to our images. You'll find many other ways to expand their capabilities—you just need to look. For one thing, as we said in an earlier chapter, you should take greater pains to trap errors. You may also want to add an option that displays or tests all the hotspots for an image simultaneously, just as they'll be used in a working presentation. Or, you may want to fix up HOTSPOT4 so you can change a hotspot's vertex array without first deleting the whole record from the database. The more you look, the more you'll find.

As a matter of fact, there's one great way to improve on polygon regions with the API function we've used in HOTSPOT3 and HOTSPOT4, **CreatePolygonRgn()**. This function helps us make regions that consist of either one polygon, or multiple polygons joined at common vertices (just cross some of your own lines when drawing the polygon). But what do you do when you have several separate hotspots on your image that all have the same hyperlink target? You could make separate hotspot regions for each of them. Or you could call upon the services of yet another API function, called **CreatePolyPolygonRgn()**.

```
Win32:
Declare Function CreatePolyPolygonRgn Lib "gdi32" Alias "CreatePolyPolygonRgn" _
    (lpPoints As POINT, lpPolyCounts As Long, ByVal nCount As Long, ByVal _
    nPolyFillMode As Long) As Long

Win16:
Declare Function CreatePolyPolygonRgn Lib "GDI" (lpPoints As POINTAPI, _
    lpPolyCounts As Integer, ByVal nCount As Integer, ByVal nPolyFillMode _
    As Integer) As Integer
```

The difference between this function and **CreatePolygonRgn()** is in the second argument, **lpPolyCounts**. In this parameter, we would pass a pointer to a second array, a simple array of integer values in which each integer specifies how many points in the first array belong to each separate polygon. For example, let's say we had an array of 25 vertices, and a second array of three integers that contained the values 3, 12, and 10. This would describe a Windows region that consisted of three distinct polygons. The first three points in the vertex array would define a triangle, the next 12 points would describe a second polygon, and the last 10 would describe a third.

When we called **PtInRegion()** with the handle to the PolyPolygon region, it would return **True** if the click had occurred anywhere within any of the three polygons. Three regions act like one. Pretty neat, huh?

To implement PolyPolygon regions, both the drawing functions of the program and the storage system would have to be modified, but if you need this much flexibility, you should be able to modify HOTSPOT4 to support it.

Now that you know how to create and activate hotspots in both text and images, let's put all this knowledge to work. Our next adventure takes us into a true hypermedia realm—one of sound, music, images, and video.

With a little more HTML
support, we'll easily be able
to add a number of extensions
to our evolving multimedia
engine.

Expanding the VB
Multimedia Engine

Get ready for a big multimedia project. It's time to pull together some of the things we've learned in the first ten chapters and build a much more powerful multimedia engine that will let us link hotspots with text, sound, music, and video. We will also show you how to use a database to store the textual information instead of HTML files, and then we will incorporate a flexible scripting feature.

In Chapter 2 we showed you how easy it is to use VB to trigger multimedia events. We also looked at the basic techniques involved in parsing HTML files. Then, in Chapter 3, we used VB to build a hypertext engine that let us jump from topic to topic by clicking on hotlinked words in the text itself. In Chapter 4 we added some multimedia features to the hypertext engine so that hotlinked words in the hypertext could play back video, MIDI music, or any other event supported by the Windows Multimedia API. In Chapter 5 we delved deeper into the API, using waveform audio to try a variety of functions. Chapters 6, 7, and 8 covered the elements of image display and special effects. And in the previous two chapters, we built an editor that enabled us to map out hotspots on our images. We've come a long way.

In this chapter, we're going to draw on this knowledge to expand our hypermedia system. First, we're going to briefly revisit hypertext and turn our hypertext system into a code module that we can call from any program. Then, we'll hook in image hotspots so we can hop back and forth between pictures and text. Later in the chapter, we'll flesh out the hypermedia engine with some powerful new navigation and display features, as well as move all the HTML files into a single database. The goal is to make our multimedia engine more "database" driven. This design approach will make it much easier for you to create your own multimedia applications because it reduces the development work down to creating HTML instructions and inserting them into a database.

Repackaging the Hypertext

In Chapters 9 and 10, we wrote a program for creating irregularly shaped hotspots. But instead of adding the functions and procedures that performed the dissolve to the program's main form, we placed them in their own code module called HOTSPOT4.BAS. We put related functions together in these handy packages so that we can move them from one project to another without extensive modifications.

Generally, lower-level functions package more neatly than higher-level, program-specific functions. There are no clear guidelines for writing your program. When we write new VB programs, we often place more code than we should in the form module. After all, when we want to use the **MouseDown** event, why not put the code in the event procedure that belongs to the form or control? Once we get everything working, though, we try to find ways to pull the code out of the form and into its own module. Then, when we want to write another program that uses the same functions, we can just select File I Add File from the VB menu bar and hook the module right into our project.

The first step in turning our hypertext system into a full-fledged *hypermedia* system is to take as much code as possible out of the form module and put it into its own code module. A module named HYPRMED1.BAS will contain nearly all the code that handles hypermedia events. Along with the code from the form module, we'll add the capability to handle images.

The General Purpose Hypermedia Engine

This project presents the steps for creating the new and improved hypertext engine.

1. Copy the form and code modules from HYPRTXT4.VBP. This project was created in Chapter 3 and can be found on the companion CD-ROM under the \VBMAGIC\HYPRTXT4 subdirectory.
2. Open a new VB project file called HYPRMED1.VBP.
3. Move all the key procedures and functions from the form module to the code module.
4. Modify the code to make it reusable for future projects. The listings that we'll be creating include Listings 11.1 through 11.5.

 You'll find this project in the subdirectory \VBMAGIC\HYPRMED1 in the files HYPRMED1.VBP, HYPRMED1.FRM, HYPRMED1.BAS, and GLOBCONS.BAS. You will also see all of the HTML files and the multimedia files.

Preparing the Project

We're going to use most of the code from HYPRTXT4.FRM and HYPRTXT4.BAS with only a few changes here and there, so the best way to start this project is to make copies of those files. Follow these steps:

1. Create a new form with a PictureBox control for text, and an Image control for our images.
2. Use the Windows 95 Explorer to copy HYPRTXT4.FRM to HYPRMED1.FRM.
3. Use the Windows 95 Explorer to copy HYPRTXT4.BAS to HYPRMED1.BAS.
4. Choose File | New Project from the VB menu bar.
5. In the Project window, highlight FORM1.FRM, which is usually the first entry in the list, and choose File | Remove File from the VB menu bar.
6. If you wish, use the File | Remove File option to remove all the extra .OCX and .VBX files from the project. We won't use any of them for this project.
7. To add the form module to the project, select File | Add File from the VB menu bar. Use the controls in the Add File dialog box to locate and select HYPRMED1.FRM.
8. To add the first code module to the project, choose File | Add File from the VB menu bar. Then use the Add File dialog to select HYPRMED1.BAS.

9. To add the second code module to the project, choose File | Add File and use the Add File dialog box to select GLOBCONS.BAS.

10. Choose File | Save Project As and save the project as HYPRMED1.VBP.

You should now have a project consisting of one form module and two code modules. Don't try to run it yet—it won't work!

Modifying the Form Module

When we first wrote HYPRTXT4, we added the code module only to hold the global constants and three **Type** declarations. In this project, we'll remove the global constants and move all the code from HYPRMED1.FRM into the new version of the code module, HYPRMED1.BAS.

HYPRMED1.FRM currently contains seven variable declarations, five general procedures, and four event procedures. Table 11.1 lists all of these declarations and procedures.

Let's begin by moving all the declarations and general procedures to HYPRMED1.BAS. We'll perform the following steps eight times to move all the general procedures and the declarations to the code module.

1. Select the entire function or procedure in HYPRMED1.FRM, then select Edit | Cut from the VB menu bar.

2. Open the code window of HYPRMED1.BAS, and display the declarations section. Place the insertion point on a new line at the end of the declarations section.

3. Select Edit | Paste from the VB menu. VB will move the procedure into its own section and add its name to the procedure list box at the top of the code window.

When we're done, we'll end up with a nearly empty version of HYPRMED1.FRM, as shown in Listing 11.1.

Listing 11.1   The New, Lean Version of HYPRMED1.FRM

```
VERSION 4.00
Begin VB.Form Form1
   BorderStyle     =   1  'Fixed Single
   Caption         =   "Form1"
   ClientHeight    =   6735
   ClientLeft      =   120
   ClientTop       =   495
   ClientWidth     =   9480
   Height          =   7260
```

Table 11.1 *The Current Inventory of HYPRMED1.FRM*

Variable or Routine	Description
Declarations:	
Dim HyperLinkArray(100) As HyperLinkElement	Array that holds information about the location and destination of hypertext links
Dim AnchorArray(100) As AnchorElement	Array that holds information about the location of hypertext anchor keywords
Dim LinkArrayPos As Integer	Counter for present position in the hyperlink array
Dim AnchorArrayPos As Integer	Counter for present position in the anchor array
Dim IsLink As Boolean	Boolean value that keeps track of when a link is being parsed during display
Dim Text As String	Global variable that holds the complete string of HTML text that is read from the HTML file
Dim Dummy As Variant	Handyman variable that is used to accept values when calling API functions that need to return a value we don't need to keep track of
General Procedures:	
Function LoadHTMLFile()	Loads the HTML file from the disk and into a text string
Sub NewLine()	Advances the current line in the output display
Sub ParseHTML()	HTML information is passed to this subroutine, which then parses it and makes the proper changes to the current status of the output display
Sub ParseText()	Accepts a text string and separates the regular text from the HTML tags, then sends them to their respective subroutines to be displayed or parsed
Sub PrintLine()	Does the actual output of text onto the display control
Event Procedures:	
Sub Form_Load()	Initializes variables
Sub Picture1_MouseDown()	Checks to see if a hypertext link has been hit; if so, it loads the file specified by the links destination variable
Sub OpenButton_Click()	Calls the LoadHTMLFile() function and the ParseText() subroutine
Sub ScrollBar_Change()	Adjusts the position of the output display control to match the position of the scroll bar

```
KeyPreview       =    -1   'True
Left             =    60
LinkTopic        =    "Form1"
ScaleHeight      =    6735
ScaleWidth       =    9480
Top              =    30
WhatsThisHelp    =    -1   'True
Width            =    9600
Begin VB.PictureBox PictureFrame
    AutoRedraw        =    -1   'True
    BeginProperty Font
        name          =    "MS Sans Serif"
        charset       =    0
        weight        =    400
        size          =    12
        underline     =    0    'False
        italic        =    0    'False
        strikethrough =    0    'False
    EndProperty
    Height         =    6375
    Left           =    5640
    ScaleHeight    =    6315
    ScaleWidth     =    3675
    TabIndex       =    0
    Top            =    120
    Width          =    3735
    Begin VB.VScrollBar ScrollBar
        Height        =    6300
        LargeChange   =    1500
        Left          =    3420
        Max           =    1000
        SmallChange   =    100
        TabIndex      =    2
        Top           =    0
        Value         =    1
        Width         =    255
    End
    Begin VB.PictureBox TextPicBox
        Appearance    =    0    'Flat
        AutoRedraw    =    -1   'True
        BackColor     =    &H00C0C0C0&
        BorderStyle   =    0    'None
        ClipControls  =    0    'False
        BeginProperty Font
            name          =    "MS Sans Serif"
            charset       =    0
            weight        =    400
            size          =    12
            underline     =    0    'False
            italic        =    0    'False
            strikethrough =    0    'False
        EndProperty
        ForeColor      =    &H80000008&
        Height         =    1e5
```

```
            Left              =    120
            ScaleHeight       =    1.00005e5
            ScaleWidth        =    3225
            TabIndex          =    1
            Top               =    0
            Width             =    3230
         End
      End
      Begin VB.Image ImagePicBox
         BorderStyle      =    1    'Fixed Single
         Height           =    6375
         Left             =    120
         Stretch          =    -1   'True
         Top              =    120
         Width            =    5415
      End
   End
End
Attribute VB_Name = "Form1"
Attribute VB_Creatable = False
Attribute VB_Exposed = False

Private Sub Form_Load()
   LinkArrayPos = 0
   AnchorArrayPos = 0
   IsLink = False

   UpdateHtml App.Path & "/HYPRMED1.HTM", TextPicBox, ImagePicBox, ScrollBar
End Sub

Private Sub ScrollBar_Change()
   ' Check for active document
   If TextPicBox.CurrentY = 0 Then
      ScrollBar.VALUE = 0
      Exit Sub
   End If
   ' Move top of Picture1 with inverse relation to the scroll bar
   TextPicBox.Top = -ScrollBar.VALUE
End Sub

Private Sub TextPicBox_MouseDown(Button As Integer, Shift As Integer, X As
Single, Y As Single)
   MouseClick TextPicBox, X, Y, ImagePicBox, ScrollBar
End Sub
```

Passing Controls as Arguments

Notice that when we call certain procedures, we pass many of the controls
from our form as arguments. When the program was self-contained and all
the code was placed in the form module, the general procedures could directly reference the controls because they were contained within the same
module. But to encapsulate the code in a code module, we need to pass the

controls by reference. That way, when we reuse the code, we can name the controls whatever we wish without having to modify the code module. Take a look at the abbreviated version of **PrintLine()** in Listing 11.2. In HYPRTXT4.FRM, this procedure had only one parameter, **Text**, which contained the next batch of text to be displayed in text PictureBox. In the previous version, all the **Print** method calls in the procedure directly referenced **Picture1** (for instance, **Picture1.Print**). In the new version of this procedure, we pass in the PictureBox as an argument, then reference it by its argument name, **TextPicBox**.

Listing 11.2   A Portion of the PrintLine() General Procedure from HYPRMED1.BAS

```
Private Sub PrintLine(Text, TextPicBox As PictureBox)
Dim NextWord As String

   While InStr(Text, Chr$(32)) 'While there is a space
   ...
        TextPicBox.Print NextWord;
     Else
        TextPicBox.Print NextWord;
     End If
   ...
     NewLine TextPicBox
     HyperLinkArray(LinkArrayPos).Top = TextPicBox.CurrentY
     HyperLinkArray(LinkArrayPos).Left = TextPicBox.CurrentX
     TextPicBox.Print Text;
   Else
     TextPicBox.Print Text;
   End If
End Sub
```

Several other procedures take controls from the main form as arguments: the new version of **NewLine()**, **ParseHTML()**, **ParseText()**, **PrintLine()**, **UpdateHTML()**, and the new procedures **LoadImage()** and **MouseClick()**. We're now ready to present the complete code for HYPRMED1.BAS, which is shown in Listing 11.3.

Listing 11.3   HYPRMED1.BAS

```
Attribute VB_Name = "Module2"
Option Explicit

Type HyperLinkElement
    Left As Integer
    Top As Integer
    Right As Integer
```

```vb
    Bottom As Integer
    DestinationSubject As String
End Type

Type AnchorElement
    Name As String
    VPosition As Integer
End Type

#If Win32 Then
    Declare Function mciSendString Lib "winmm.dll" Alias "mciSendStringA" _
        (ByVal lpstrCommand As String, ByVal lpstrReturnString As String, _
        ByVal uReturnLength As Long, ByVal hwndCallback As Long) As Long
#Else
    Declare Function mciSendString Lib "mmsystem" (ByVal lpstrCommand As String, _
        ByVal lpstrReturnString As String, ByVal uReturnLength As Integer, _
        ByVal hwndCallback As Integer) As Long
#End If

Dim HyperLinkArray(100) As HyperLinkElement
Dim AnchorArray(100) As AnchorElement
Dim LinkArrayPos As Integer
Dim AnchorArrayPos As Integer
Dim IsLink As Boolean
Dim Text As String
Dim Dummy As Variant

Private Function LoadImage(Filename As String, Destination As Image)
Dim ImageRatio As Integer
Dim FrameRatio As Integer

'    Set TempPicture = LoadPicture(Filename)
'    ImageRatio = CInt(TempPicture.Width * 1000 / TempPicture.Height)
'    FrameRatio = CInt(Destination.Width * 1000 / Destination.Height)
'    If ImageRatio > FrameRatio Then
'       Destination.Width = Destination.Width
'       Destination.Height = Destination.Width * ImageRatio / 1000
'    Else
'       Destination.Width = Destination.Height * ImageRatio / 1000
'       Destination.Height = Destination.Height
'    End If
'    Set Destination.picture = TempPicture
    Set Destination.picture = LoadPicture(Filename)
End Function

Public Sub MouseClick(TextPicBox As PictureBox, X As Single, Y As Single, _
    ImagePicBox As Image, ScrollBar As VScrollBar)
Dim Index As Integer
Dim Index2 As Integer
Dim LinkSubject As String
Dim LinkSubjectFile As String
Dim LinkSubjectLink As String
```

```
    ' Check for loaded form
    If TextPicBox.CurrentY = 0 Then Exit Sub
    ' Step through Hypertext links
    For Index = 0 To LinkArrayPos
        If (X > HyperLinkArray(Index).Left) And _
            (X < HyperLinkArray(Index).Right) And _
            (Y > HyperLinkArray(Index).Top) And _
            (Y < HyperLinkArray(Index).Bottom) Then
            LinkSubject = HyperLinkArray(Index).DestinationSubject
            ' Check for '#' symbol to see if there is a specific destination
            If InStr(LinkSubject, Chr$(35)) Then
                ' Parse file and link information
                LinkSubjectFile = Left(LinkSubject, InStr(LinkSubject, Chr$(35)) - 1)
                LinkSubjectLink = Right(LinkSubject, (Len(LinkSubject) - _
                    InStr(LinkSubject, Chr$(35))))
                ' Check for non-null file name
                If Not LinkSubjectFile = "" Then
                    Text = LoadHTMLFile(LinkSubjectFile)
                    ParseText Text, TextPicBox, ImagePicBox, ScrollBar
                End If
                ' Search for Anchor and move to correct position
                For Index2 = 0 To AnchorArrayPos - 1
                    If AnchorArray(Index2).Name = LinkSubjectLink Then
                        TextPicBox.Top = -AnchorArray(Index2).VPosition
                        Exit For
                    End If
                Next Index2
            Else ' No specific destination subject, just load file
                Select Case UCase(Right(LinkSubject, Len(LinkSubject) - _
                    InStr(LinkSubject, Chr$(46))))
                    Case "HTM"
                        Set ImagePicBox.picture = LoadPicture()
                        Text = LoadHTMLFile(LinkSubject)
                        ParseText Text, TextPicBox, ImagePicBox, ScrollBar
                    Case "WAV", "MID", "AVI"
                        Dummy = mciSendString("Play " + App.Path + "\" + LinkSubject, _
                            0, 0, 0)
                    Case "BMP", "RLE", "ICO", "WMF"
                        Set ImagePicBox.picture = LoadPicture()
                        LoadImage LinkSubject, ImagePicBox
                End Select
            End If
            Exit For
        End If
    Next Index
    ' Change value of scroll bar to reflect size of document
    ScrollBar.VALUE = -TextPicBox.Top
End Sub

Public Sub UpdateHtml(FileToLoad As String, TextPicBox As PictureBox, _
    ImagePicBox As Image, ScrollBar As VScrollBar)
Dim Text As String
```

```vb
    Text = LoadHTMLFile(FileToLoad)
    ParseText Text, TextPicBox, ImagePicBox, ScrollBar
End Sub
Private Function LoadHTMLFile(Filename As String) As String
Dim TempText As String
Dim Fnum As Integer

    LoadHTMLFile = ""
    ' Acquire number for free file
    Fnum = FreeFile
    ' Load HTML contents into string
    Open Filename For Input As #Fnum
    ' Loop until end of file
    Do While Not EOF(Fnum)
        ' Read line into temporary string
        Line Input #Fnum, TempText
        ' Add line to document string
        LoadHTMLFile = LoadHTMLFile & TempText
    Loop
End Function


Private Sub NewLine(TextPicBox As PictureBox)
    TextPicBox.Print
End Sub


Private Sub ParseHTML(HTML, TextPicBox As PictureBox, ImagePicBox As Image)
Dim TempColor As Long
Dim TempFontSize As Integer
Dim TempUnderline As Boolean
Dim LinkSubject As String
Dim LinkSubjectFile As String
Dim LinkSubjectLink As String
Dim LinkType As String
Dim HRSize As Integer

    ' Switch to all uppercase and pull off first two characters
    Select Case (Left(UCase(HTML), 2))
        Case "H1"       'Heading 1
            If TextPicBox.CurrentX > 0 Then NewLine TextPicBox
            TextPicBox.Font.Size = 24
        Case "H2"       'Heading 2
            If TextPicBox.CurrentX > 0 Then NewLine TextPicBox
            TextPicBox.Font.Size = 21
        Case "H3"       'Heading 3
            If TextPicBox.CurrentX > 0 Then NewLine TextPicBox
            TextPicBox.Font.Size = 18
        Case "H4"       'Heading 4
            If TextPicBox.CurrentX > 0 Then NewLine TextPicBox
            TextPicBox.Font.Size = 15
        Case "H5"       'Heading 5
            If TextPicBox.CurrentX > 0 Then NewLine TextPicBox
            TextPicBox.Font.Size = 9
        Case "H6"       'Heading 6
            If TextPicBox.CurrentX > 0 Then NewLine TextPicBox
```

```
        TextPicBox.Font.Size = 6
   Case "/H"        'Bold On
      If TextPicBox.CurrentX > 0 Then NewLine TextPicBox
      TextPicBox.Font.Size = 12
   Case "B"         'Bold On
      TextPicBox.Font.Bold = True
   Case "/B"        'Bold Off
      TextPicBox.Font.Bold = False
   Case "U"         'Underline On
      TextPicBox.Font.Underline = True
   Case "/U"        'Underline Off
      TextPicBox.Font.Underline = False
   Case "I"         'Italic On
      TextPicBox.Font.Italic = True
   Case "/I"        'Italic Off
      TextPicBox.Font.Italic = False
   Case "BR"        'Line Break
      NewLine TextPicBox
   Case "P", "/P" 'End Paragraph
      If TextPicBox.CurrentX > 0 Then NewLine TextPicBox
      NewLine TextPicBox
   Case "HR"                'Horizontal Rule
      TextPicBox.ScaleMode = 3
      ' Check for 'SIZE' tag within HTML
      If InStr(UCase(HTML), "SIZE=") Then
         HRSize = Val(Right(HTML, Len(HTML) - InStr(HTML, "SIZE=") - 4))
      Else
         HRSize = 1
      End If
      If TextPicBox.CurrentX > 0 Then NewLine TextPicBox
      TempColor = TextPicBox.ForeColor ' Store previous foreground(font) color
      TextPicBox.ForeColor = vbBlack
      ' Draw horizontal and vertical portions of black section of rectangle
      TextPicBox.Line (0, (TextPicBox.CurrentY + (TextPicBox.TextHeight("A") _
         / 2)))-(TextPicBox.ScaleWidth - 1, (TextPicBox.CurrentY + _
         (TextPicBox.TextHeight("A") / 2)))
      TextPicBox.Line (0, TextPicBox.CurrentY)-(0, TextPicBox.CurrentY + 1 _
         + HRSize)
      TextPicBox.ForeColor = vbWhite
      ' Draw horizontal and vertical portions of white section of rectangle
      TextPicBox.Line (1, (TextPicBox.CurrentY))-(TextPicBox.ScaleWidth, _
         (TextPicBox.CurrentY))
      TextPicBox.Line (TextPicBox.ScaleWidth - 1, TextPicBox.CurrentY - _
         HRSize)-(TextPicBox.ScaleWidth - 1, TextPicBox.CurrentY)
      TextPicBox.ForeColor = TempColor ' Reset to old color
      TextPicBox.CurrentY = TextPicBox.CurrentY + _
         TextPicBox.TextHeight("A") / 2
      TextPicBox.CurrentX = 0
      TextPicBox.ScaleMode = 1
   Case "A "        'Begin Link or Anchor
      ' If there are quotation marks present, then we know
      ' that the link subject is the string between the quotation marks.
      ' Else take everything from the right of the equal sign
      ' up to, but not including, the next space encountered.
```

```
      If InStr(HTML, Chr$(34)) Then
         LinkSubject = Right(HTML, ((Len(HTML) - InStr(HTML, Chr$(34)))))
         If InStr(HTML, Chr$(34)) Then
            LinkSubject = Left(LinkSubject, InStr(LinkSubject, Chr$(34)) - 1)
         End If
      Else
         LinkSubject = Right(HTML, ((Len(HTML) - InStr(HTML, Chr$(61)))))
         If InStr(LinkSubject, Chr$(32)) Then
            LinkSubject = Left(LinkSubject, InStr(LinkSubject, Chr$(32)) - 1)
         End If
      End If
      ' The link type is the variable before the subject.
      ' So, lets grab the characters between up to the
      ' equal sign first, then strip off everything up
      ' to the final space.
      LinkType = Left(HTML, InStr(HTML, Chr$(61)) - 1)
      While InStr(LinkType, Chr$(32))
        LinkType = Right(LinkType, ((Len(LinkType) - InStr(LinkType, _
           Chr$(32)))))
      Wend
      Select Case LinkType
         Case "HREF" ' Hypermedia Jump
            If Not IsLink Then
               TempColor = TextPicBox.ForeColor
               TempUnderline = TextPicBox.Font.Underline
               TextPicBox.ForeColor = vbBlue
               TextPicBox.Font.Underline = True
               HyperLinkArray(LinkArrayPos).DestinationSubject = LinkSubject
               HyperLinkArray(LinkArrayPos).Top = TextPicBox.CurrentY
               HyperLinkArray(LinkArrayPos).Left = TextPicBox.CurrentX
               IsLink = True
            End If
         Case "NAME" ' Anchor
            AnchorArray(AnchorArrayPos).Name = UCase(LinkSubject)
            AnchorArray(AnchorArrayPos).VPosition = TextPicBox.CurrentY
            AnchorArrayPos = AnchorArrayPos + 1
      End Select
   Case "/A"        'End link
      If IsLink Then
         HyperLinkArray(LinkArrayPos).Bottom = TextPicBox.CurrentY + _
            TextPicBox.TextHeight("A")
         HyperLinkArray(LinkArrayPos).Right = TextPicBox.CurrentX
         LinkArrayPos = LinkArrayPos + 1
         TextPicBox.ForeColor = TempColor
         TextPicBox.Font.Underline = TempUnderline
         IsLink = False
      End If
   Case "IM"        'Image
      ' If there are quotation marks present, then we know
      ' that the image name is the string between the quotation marks.
      ' Else take everything from the right of the equal sign
      ' up to, but not including, the next space encountered.
      If InStr(HTML, Chr$(34)) Then
         LinkSubject = Right(HTML, ((Len(HTML) - InStr(HTML, Chr$(34)))))
```

```
                LinkSubject = Left(LinkSubject, InStr(LinkSubject, Chr$(34)) - 1)
            Else
                LinkSubject = Right(HTML, ((Len(HTML) - InStr(HTML, Chr$(61)))))
                If InStr(LinkSubject, Chr$(32)) Then
                    LinkSubject = Left(LinkSubject, InStr(LinkSubject, Chr$(32)) - 1)
                End If
            End If
            LoadImage LinkSubject, ImagePicBox
    End Select
End Sub

Private Sub ParseText(Text As String, TextPicBox As PictureBox, _
    ImagePicBox As Image, ScrollBar As VScrollBar)

    ' Reset PictureBox
    TextPicBox.Cls
    TextPicBox.Top = 0
    TextPicBox.Height = 10000
    ' Initialize Arrays
    Erase HyperLinkArray
    LinkArrayPos = 0
    Erase AnchorArray
    AnchorArrayPos = 0
    ' Set base text attributes
    TextPicBox.ForeColor = BLACK
    TextPicBox.FontBold = False
    TextPicBox.FontUnderline = False
    TextPicBox.FontItalic = False
    TextPicBox.FontStrikethru = False
    TextPicBox.FontSize = 12
    ' Check to see if there is any HTML tags in the string
    If InStr(Text, "<") Then
        While InStr(Text, "<") ' Don't stop parsing until all tags are gone
            ' Print line up to tag
            PrintLine Left(Text, InStr(Text, "<") - 1), TextPicBox
            ' Pull HTML info from tag and parse
            ParseHTML Mid(Text, InStr(Text, "<") + 1, InStr(Text, ">") - 1 - _
                InStr(Text, "<")), _
            TextPicBox, ImagePicBox
            ' Strip away text up to the end of the HTML tag
            Text = Right(Text, Len(Text) - InStr(Text, ">"))
        Wend
    End If
    ' Print remaining string
    PrintLine Text, TextPicBox
    NewLine TextPicBox
    TextPicBox.Height = TextPicBox.CurrentY
    ScrollBar.MAX = TextPicBox.CurrentY
    ScrollBar.LargeChange = TextPicBox.Parent.Height
End Sub

Private Sub PrintLine(Text, TextPicBox As PictureBox)
Dim NextWord As String
```

```
    While InStr(Text, Chr$(32)) 'While there is a space
        NextWord = Left(Text, InStr(Text, Chr$(32))) 'Copy first word from
                                                      'text string
        Text = Right(Text, (Len(Text) - InStr(Text, Chr$(32)))) 'Clip first word
        If (TextPicBox.CurrentX + TextPicBox.TextWidth(NextWord)) > _
            TextPicBox.ScaleWidth Then
            If TextPicBox.ForeColor = vbBlue Then 'Truncated Link
                HyperLinkArray(LinkArrayPos).Bottom = TextPicBox.CurrentY + _
                    TextPicBox.TextHeight("A")
                HyperLinkArray(LinkArrayPos).Right = TextPicBox.CurrentX
                LinkArrayPos = LinkArrayPos + 1
                HyperLinkArray(LinkArrayPos).DestinationSubject = _
                    HyperLinkArray(LinkArrayPos - 1).DestinationSubject
            End If
            NewLine TextPicBox
            HyperLinkArray(LinkArrayPos).Top = TextPicBox.CurrentY
            HyperLinkArray(LinkArrayPos).Left = TextPicBox.CurrentX
            TextPicBox.Print NextWord;
        Else
            TextPicBox.Print NextWord;
        End If
    Wend
    'Clean-up and print remaining text
    If (TextPicBox.CurrentX + TextPicBox.TextWidth(NextWord)) > _
        TextPicBox.ScaleWidth Then
        If TextPicBox.ForeColor = vbBlue Then 'Truncated Link
            HyperLinkArray(LinkArrayPos).Bottom = TextPicBox.CurrentY + _
                TextPicBox.TextHeight("A")
            HyperLinkArray(LinkArrayPos).Right = TextPicBox.CurrentX
            LinkArrayPos = LinkArrayPos + 1
            HyperLinkArray(LinkArrayPos).DestinationSubject = _
                HyperLinkArray(LinkArrayPos - 1).DestinationSubject
        End If
        NewLine TextPicBox
        HyperLinkArray(LinkArrayPos).Top = TextPicBox.CurrentY
        HyperLinkArray(LinkArrayPos).Left = TextPicBox.CurrentX
        TextPicBox.Print Text;
    Else
        TextPicBox.Print Text;
    End If
End Sub
```

Much of the code shown here still performs the same tasks performed in HYPRTXT4.FRM, but now the code is completely separate and reusable. Trust us when we say that this will make things much easier later on, especially if you want to improve the engine and add more features. A single module could get very complicated, very quickly. Figure 11.1 illustrates the difference between using a single module versus separate code modules for code. This method allows you to separate the elements of your project, thereby making it easier to code, easier to understand when there is a problem, and faster because you are not using the same code twice in your application.

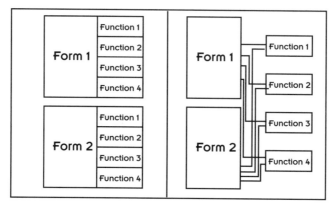

Figure 11.1 *Using a single module versus separate code modules.*

Adding Support for Images

While moving the code into its own module, we slipped in support for images. Let's stop for a second and examine what we did in order to add simple support for images. First of all, we rearranged the form itself to make it more intuitive and attractive. Then, we added an Image control that will receive whatever image is called for in the HTML. Figure 11.2 shows how everything should look, although there is no reason you can't change things to suit your own sensibilities—that's the beauty of using reusable code.

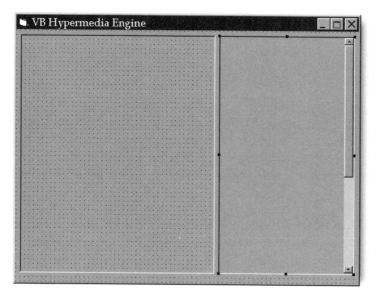

Figure 11.2 *Laying out the main form for our new hypermedia engine.*

Introducing the HTML IMG Tag

In order to support images with our hypermedia engine, we'll need to implement the HTML image (IMG) tag. The IMG tag is perhaps one of the most complicated tags in HTML. It has more variables than most other tags. It is also treated differently in different browsers. Table 11.2 lists the IMG tag variables, their possible values, and their function.

When used in conjunction with each other, you can come up with some really interesting ways to display images. For example, look at the following HTML:

```
<IMG ALIGN=LEFT BORDER=5 HSPACE=10 VSPACE=5 WIDTH=150 HEIGHT=200
SRC="FACE.GIF">
<IMG ALIGN=RIGHT BORDER=5 HSPACE=10 VSPACE=5 WIDTH=150 HEIGHT=200
SRC="FACE.GIF">
<CENTER><H1> The Quick Brown Fox Jumped Over the Lazy Dog!</H1>
</CENTER>
```

Table 11.2 *The IMG Tag Variables*

Variable	Arguments	Description
SRC	Filename	Image to Display
ALT	Any text string	The text if images are turned off
ALIGN	TOP	Aligns the top edge of the image with the top of the tallest text
	MIDDLE	Aligns the center of the image with the bottom of the text
	BOTTOM	Aligns the bottom of the image with the bottom of the text
	ABSMIDDLE	Aligns the center of image with the center of the text
	LEFT	Aligns the image to the left side of the screen and allows text to wrap around the right side of the image
	RIGHT	Aligns the image to the right side of the screen and allows text to wrap around the left side of the image
LOWSRC	Filename	Low res image to display while large image is loading
HSPACE	Integer	Horizontal space between image and text
VSPACE	Integer	Vertical space between image and text
WIDTH	Integer	Image is stretched to this width
HEIGHT	Integer	Image is stretched to this height
BORDER	Integer	Sets the width of the border around an image. Can be used to create borders on normal images, or can get rid of borders on linked images by setting it to 0.

If you are using a newer browser, this entry will display the FACE.GIF image on the left side of the display, and on the right side of the display at the same height. Both images will be stretched to fit into a region that is 150 pixels wide and 200 pixels tall. The images will have borders that are 5 pixels wide, and the text that wraps around them will be offset by 10 pixels horizontally and five pixels vertically. Finally, the text will be wrapped between them and centered. Check out Figure 11.3 to see what they look like.

With a little practice, you can come up with some pretty neat effects by using images in different ways. For more information on the image tag and HTML in general, see Appendix A.

We have coded our new engine so that images will be loaded whenever the parser comes across an **IMG** keyword in the HTML text. Here is the section from **ParseHTML()** that handles this task:

```
Case "IM"       'Image
  ' If there are quotation marks present, then we know
  ' that the image name is the string between the quotation marks.
  ' Else take everything from the right of the equal sign
  ' up to, but not including, the next space encountered.
  If InStr(HTML, Chr$(34)) Then
     LinkSubject = Right(HTML, ((Len(HTML) - InStr(HTML, Chr$(34)))))
```

Figure 11.3   *Using the IMG tag to display images with the Netscape browser.*

```
    LinkSubject = Left(LinkSubject, InStr(LinkSubject, Chr$(34)) - 1)
Else
    LinkSubject = Right(HTML, ((Len(HTML) - InStr(HTML, Chr$(61)))))
    If InStr(LinkSubject, Chr$(32)) Then
      LinkSubject = Left(LinkSubject, InStr(LinkSubject, Chr$(32)) - 1)
    End If
End If
LoadImage LinkSubject, ImagePicBox
```

Notice that we only need to check for the first two letters, "IM." This code works by first recognizing that an **IMG** argument has been parsed. Then, we check to see if the file name for the image is in quotes. If it is in quotes, we strip off the quotes. If not, we simply take all of the text up to either the first space (if there is one), or the entire string. Then, we call our subroutine **LoadImage()**, passing it the file name of the image, and the argument that points by reference to the Image control that will receive the image. For now, we won't support all the IMG tag variables used for image alignment, sizing, or displaying borders. When we extend the multimedia engine later in this book and create our own Web browser, we'll implement more of the IMG tag features.

The other way that images can be displayed is by clicking on a highlighted text that has an image file as a destination subject. For this condition, we use a **Select** statement in our new **MouseClick()** subroutine (Listing 11.4) that checks to see which type of file has been referenced and then loads the appropriate one.

Listing 11.4   The MouseClick() General Procedure from HYPRMED1.BAS

```
Public Sub MouseClick(TextPicBox As PictureBox, X As Single, Y As Single, _
    ImagePicBox As Image, ScrollBar As VScrollBar)
Dim Index As Integer
Dim Index2 As Integer
Dim LinkSubject As String
Dim LinkSubjectFile As String
Dim LinkSubjectLink As String

    ' Check for loaded form
    If TextPicBox.CurrentY = 0 Then Exit Sub
    ' Step through Hypertext links
    For Index = 0 To LinkArrayPos
      If (X > HyperLinkArray(Index).Left) And _
         (X < HyperLinkArray(Index).Right) And _
         (Y > HyperLinkArray(Index).Top) And _
         (Y < HyperLinkArray(Index).Bottom) Then
         LinkSubject = HyperLinkArray(Index).DestinationSubject
         ' Check for '#' symbol to see if there is a specific destination
```

```
        If InStr(LinkSubject, Chr$(35)) Then
           ' Parse file and link information
           LinkSubjectFile = Left(LinkSubject, InStr(LinkSubject, Chr$(35)) - 1)
           LinkSubjectLink = Right(LinkSubject, (Len(LinkSubject) - _
              InStr(LinkSubject, Chr$(35))))
           ' Check for non-null file name
           If Not LinkSubjectFile = "" Then
              Text = LoadHTMLFile(LinkSubjectFile)
              ParseText Text, TextPicBox, ImagePicBox, ScrollBar
           End If
           ' Search for Anchor and move to correct position
           For Index2 = 0 To AnchorArrayPos - 1
              If AnchorArray(Index2).Name = LinkSubjectLink Then
                 TextPicBox.Top = -AnchorArray(Index2).VPosition
                 Exit For
              End If
           Next Index2
        Else ' No specific destination subject, just load file
           Select Case UCase(Right(LinkSubject, Len(LinkSubject) - _
              InStr(LinkSubject, Chr$(46))))
              Case "HTM"
                 Set ImagePicBox.picture = LoadPicture()
                 Text = LoadHTMLFile(LinkSubject)
                 ParseText Text, TextPicBox, ImagePicBox, ScrollBar
              Case "WAV", "MID", "AVI"
                 Dummy = mciSendString("Play " + App.Path + "\" + _
                    LinkSubject, 0, 0, 0)
              Case "BMP", "RLE", "ICO", "WMF"
                 Set ImagePicBox.picture = LoadPicture()
                 LoadImage LinkSubject, ImagePicBox
           End Select
        End If
        Exit For
     End If
  Next Index
  ' Change value of scroll bar to reflect size of document
  ScrollBar.VALUE = -TextPicBox.Top
End Sub
```

As you can see, we can handle other Windows-based graphics files in addition to BMPs because Visual Basic handles all the details behind the scene. To see how **MouseClick()** works, let's stop for a minute and take a look at the argument list:

```
Public Sub MouseClick(TextPicBox As PictureBox, X As Single, Y As Single, _
   ImagePicBox As Image, ScrollBar As VScrollBar)
```

This certainly looks like a handful. Actually, it's not as complicated as it appears. To easily take charge over the output of our parsed HTML, we need to pass a number of controls as arguments. Let's step through the arguments one by one. The **TextPicBox** is our main text display control, it's obvious why we need that. And, of course, we need the **X** and **Y** arguments to pass in the coordinates of the mouse click. We also need the **ImagePicBox** argument because if a hotspot that points to an image has been clicked, we need to know where to display the image. Finally, we need to pass the **ScrollBar** argument, so that if a new HTML file is specified as a hotspot's destination, we can resize our scroll bar when the new file is displayed.

Sometimes we also need to pass controls as arguments—even when the routine we are passing them to does not use them! This happens more than you might think, for instance, we may want to call another routine in the external module that uses the control even though the routine we are passing the control to does not use it. In such a case, the routine acts like a distributor—we pass it all the controls as arguments that it needs, as well as the controls that it will need to pass on to other routines.

One thing you will quickly notice when you play with this version of the multimedia engine is that the images look distorted when they appear. This is because we set the **Stretch** property on the **ImagePicBox** control to **True**. You will see why we did this in the next project.

Refining the Hypermedia Engine

At this stage of development of the hypermedia engine, we are going to fix the distortion image problem and add support for hotspots within the images. It will not be at all difficult to implement these features, especially the hotspots, because we have already completed all required background work. Back in Chapter 10 we created a completely independent code module called HOTSPOT4.BAS that has almost all the code we need, ready to implement hotspots in images. We will now extend the code module from HYPRMED1.BAS so that it can handle image hotspots as well as image scaling and justification.

Refining the Hypermedia Engine

This project adds some new capabilities to our hypermedia engine. Here are the steps to follow:

1. Create a new form with two PictureBox controls, one for text and one for images.
2. Add the code module HYPRMED1.BAS to the project and rename it HYPRMED2.BAS.

3. Copy HOTSPOT4.BAS to HOTSPOT.BAS and fill in the functions we need to use the polygon hotspots we created in Chapter 10 (Listings 11.5 through 11.7).

5. Complete the remaining event procedures in HYPRMED1.FRM (Listings 11.8 through 11.12).

You'll find this program in the subdirectory \VBMAGIC\HYPRMED2 in the files HYPRMED2.VBP, HYPRMED2.FRM, HYPRMED2.BAS, HOTSPOT.BAS, GLOBCONS.BAS, and DATACONS.BAS. Once again, we will need all the HTML files and media files. This time, though, we have placed the multimedia files in the MEDIA directory to keep them separate from our actual code modules.

Running the Magic Hypermedia Engine

By running the program, you'll see the window shown in Figure 11.4. Notice that the subject "HyperMedia" is displayed just as it was in all the previous hypertext projects. But this time, the image of the Grand Canyon is scaled correctly, and clicking on the copyright information causes a WAV file to be

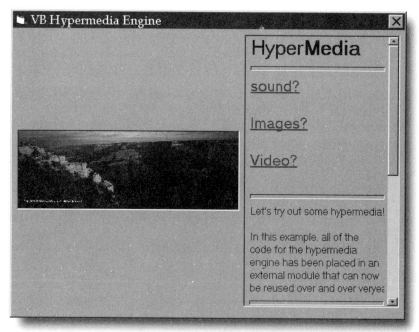

Figure 11.4 *The almost-complete hypermedia engine at work.*

played. This illustrates how a hotspot can be added to an image. You might want to experiment with the program for a while to see where all the hotspots are and how they work.

We have also placed the compiled version of HOTSPOT4 in the application directory so that you can easily create new hotspots, or edit the ones we have created. Keep in mind that the **ImageTable** in IMAGES.MDB won't change by itself. You have to update the field **ImageFilename**, so it contains the correct path for the bitmap file.

Try adding your own images to the system. Use the hotspot editor to define the hotspots, then add hotlinks to the HTML file that point to the pictures. Remember not to create any dead ends—although if you do, you can always stop the program. If you get really ambitious, you can always increase the size of **HyperLinkArray** (in the declarations section of HYPRMED2.BAS) to support more hypertext subjects. Although if you ever have more than 100 subjects within one page of text, you should consider cutting back. The only time you may have a large amount of links is in a list or index, if you happen to include one in your application.

Creating the Form

Now that we've seen what the new engine will do, let's get going on building it. Start a new project called HYPRMED2.VBP, which will have two forms. The first form will be saved as HYPRMED2.FRM. You can leave the **Name** property set to Form1, or switch it to something more descriptive. Set the form's **ScaleMode** property to the default, 1 - Twip. You may also wish to set the caption—we used the title *VB Hypermedia Engine*. The second form allows users to get a better view of the images displayed in the ImagePicBox. They will be able to right-button click on any image and the second form will be displayed with the image at its actual size. We'll explain in a minute how the form works, but for now just create a form with a PictureBox control placed on it, as shown in Figure 11.5. Name the form **FloatingForm** and name the PictureBox **FloatingImage**. Finally, set the **AutoSize** property to **True** to cause the PictureBox to automatically resize to fit whatever image is placed in it.

If you remember from the previous project, the images were displayed with apparent distortion. This was caused by using an Image control that stretched the image to fill the shape of the control. This is convenient if we want to scale an image, but the correct aspect ratio (width to height) must be used in order for the image to be displayed properly. The PictureBox control is good for scaling images, because we can set its **AutoSize** property to **True**

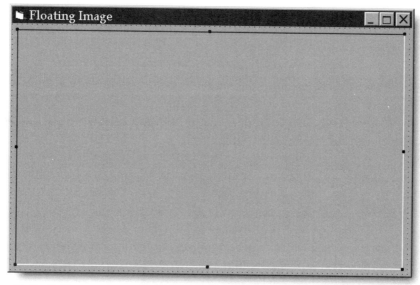

Figure 11.5   *Setting up the form for the floating image.*

and then easily figure out the aspect ratio. Unfortunately, neither control has both of these properties. If they did, we could simply read in the image file, determine the aspect ratio, then resize the control to fit whatever space we have to deal with. Since neither control can do what we need by itself, we can use them both together in order to accomplish our goal.

Here is the process for using both of these controls:

1. Read the image into a PictureBox that has its **AutoSize** property set to **True**.

2. Determine the aspect ratio of the image by dividing the width by the height.

3. Set the size of our Image control so that it takes up as much space as possible, but maintains the aspect ratio of the original image.

4. Copy the **Picture** property from the PictureBox to the Image control.

This may seem a bit complicated, but it works. There are other ways to handle this situation, but this method is fast, simple, and will work under 32-bit and 16-bit environments. If you know that your application will always run in a 32-bit environment, you can use a **Picture** *object* as a buffer instead of a Picture Box. This method is actually faster and less resource-intensive, but it only works in a 32-bit environment. Since we still need to support 16-bit environments, the **Picture** object is out. The other option is to use API calls to gather information about the bitmap, but that's a lot of work, and the benefits are minimal, so we'll just stick with our basic technique and carry on. One other thing: Don't forget to set the **Visible** property of the PictureBox control to **False** so that it does not show up at run time. Check out Figures 11.6 and 11.7 to see our current project at design time and at run time.

Hyperlinking Hotspots

In the project HOTSPOT4.VBP, we wrote a code module called HOTSPOT4.BAS that included the functions and procedures needed to create and test hotspot regions on images. Now we're going to add two new procedures and one function to the new copy of that code module, HOTSPOT.BAS, which we'll use to arm those hotspots.

In our hotspot editor, we could activate and test only one hotspot at a time. But for our hypermedia system, we'll need to simultaneously activate all of the hotspots that belong to an image. For that job, we'll write a procedure called **ActivateHotspots()**, which is shown in Listing 11.5.

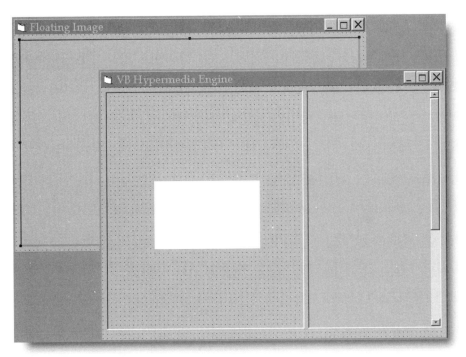

Figure 11.6 *HYPRMED2 at design time with the floating image form in the background.*

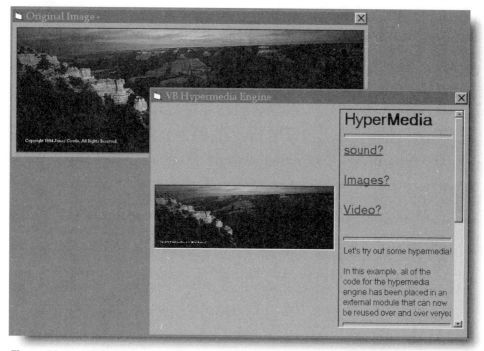

Figure 11.7　*HYPRMED2 at run time with the floating image form in the background.*

Listing 11.5　The ActivateHotspots() General Procedure from HOTSPOT.BAS

```
Public Sub ActivateHotspots(ByVal TheTarget As String)
Dim VertexCount As Integer
Dim TempString As String
Dim StillOnCurrentPicture As Boolean

    DeactivateHotspots
    ImageTable.Index = "PrimaryKey"
    ImageTable.Seek ">=", TheTarget, 1
    If (Not ImageTable.NoMatch) And (Not ImageTable.EOF) Then
        StillOnCurrentPicture = (UCase(ImageTable!ImageFilename) = _
            UCase(TheTarget))
        Do While StillOnCurrentPicture
            ActiveHotspotCount = ActiveHotspotCount + 1
            ActiveHotspots(ActiveHotspotCount).TargetString = ImageTable!LinkTarget
            TempString = ImageTable!VertexArray
            VertexCount = ArrayFromString(PolygonVertices(), TempString)
            ActiveHotspots(ActiveHotspotCount).hPolygonRgn = _
                CreatePolygonRgn(PolygonVertices(0), VertexCount + 1, 0)
            ImageTable.MoveNext
            If ImageTable.EOF Then
                StillOnCurrentPicture = False
            Else
```

```
            StillOnCurrentPicture = (UCase(ImageTable!ImageFilename) = _
                UCase(TheTarget))
        End If
    Loop
    End If
End Sub
```

The first thing this procedure does is call another new procedure, **DeactivateHotspots()**, which we'll cover shortly. For now, suffice to say that **DeactivateHotspots()** simply disposes of all the currently active Windows polygon regions.

To keep track of the currently active hotspots, we'll maintain an array of structures that each hold a region handle and the hotspot's target string:

```
Type ActiveHotspotEntry
    hPolygonRgn As Integer
    TargetString As String * 128
End Type
Dim ActiveHotspots(25) As ActiveHotspotEntry
Dim ActiveHotspotCount As Integer
```

ActivateHotspots() takes a target string as its sole argument, which must always be the path and filename of a bitmap (BMP) or device-independent bitmap (DIB). The procedure then searches the **ImageTable** in the **Images** database to locate all the hotspots for the specified picture. For each entry it finds in the table, **ActivateHotspots()** performs three tasks: it unpacks the vertex array, calls the API function **CreatePolygonRgn()**, and stores the new region handle, along with the hotspot's own target (the one to which the system will jump when the user clicks on the hotspot, *not* the target passed into the procedure) in the next available entry in the **ActiveHotspots** array.

Searching Access Databases

More than half the code in the **ActivateHotspots()** procedure deals with the mechanics of the table search. In particular, you may have noticed that we used a separate variable, **StillOnCurrentPicture**, to control the **Do While** loop. At first, we tried to place the termination test expressions in the **Do While** statement itself:

```
Do While (UCase$(ImageTable!ImageFilename) = UCase$(TheTarget)) And _
    (Not ImageTable.EOF)
    ¬
    ¬
    ¬
    ImageTable.MoveNext
Loop
```

This looks like it should work, but it doesn't. You run into trouble when you run off the end of the file. The **MoveNext** method will shove the file pointer off into limbo when the EOF property returns True, but the record buffer no longer contains a valid record. At that point, instead of returning a null string, any reference to **ImageTable!ImageFilename** causes VB to produce a runtime error. Many computer languages help you out of this conundrum by supporting a feature called short-circuit Boolean evaluation. If this feature detects one Boolean test in the expression that will cause the whole expression to produce a False result, it doesn't bother to evaluate the remaining subexpressions. Sometimes short-circuit evaluation works from right to left, and sometimes from left to right. In VB it doesn't work at all. We can't perform both tests in the same expression. That's why we have used a separate variable to determine when the search has ended. After each turn around the loop, we must check first for the EOF condition:

```
ImageTable.MoveNext
If ImageTable.EOF Then
    StillOnCurrentPicture = False
  Else
    StillOnCurrentPicture = (UCase$(ImageTable!ImageFilename) = _
        UCase$(TheTarget))
  End If
```

If **EOF** is **True**, we set **StillOnCurrentPicture** to **False**—our own short-circuit. If **EOF** is **False**, we can then check whether the new record belongs to the current picture. If not, we set **StillOnCurrentPicture** to **False**, which terminates the loop.

Once we have a bunch of active hotspots, we'll also need some way to get rid of them. For that job, we'll write the **DeactivateHotspots()** general procedure, shown in Listing 11.6.

Listing 11.6　The DeactivateHotspots() General Procedure from HOTSPOT.BAS

```
Public Sub DeactivateHotspots()
Dim HotspotCounter As Integer

  If ActiveHotspotCount > 0 Then
    For HotspotCounter = 1 To ActiveHotspotCount
      DeleteRegion ActiveHotspots(HotspotCounter).hPolygonRgn
    Next HotspotCounter
  ActiveHotspotCount = 0
  End If
End Sub
```

This simple procedure steps through the **ActiveHotspots** array, deleting the polygon hotspot regions, then setting the **ActiveHotspotCount** to zero.

In the HOTSPOT4.MAK project, we tested our new hotspots by passing the mouse coordinates to the API function **PtInRegion()**. Now, in addition to this, we need to check the mouse position against all the active hotspots until we either find a match or run out of hotspots on the image. If the user has clicked on one of the hotspots, we'll need to know the target string so we can perform the appropriate action. To solve this problem, we'll write a function called **TargetFromPointInImage()**, shown in Listing 11.7, that takes the mouse coordinates as arguments, and returns the target string.

Listing 11.7 The TargetFromPointInImage() General Function from HOTSPOT.BAS

```
Public Function TargetFromPointInImage(X As Single, Y As Single, ImageScale _
   As Double) As String
Dim Counter As Integer
Dim Found As Boolean
Dim TempTargetString As String

   TempTargetString = ""
   Found = False
   Counter = 0
   Do While (Counter < ActiveHotspotCount) And (Not Found)
      Counter = Counter + 1
      If PtInRegion(ActiveHotspots(Counter).hPolygonRgn, CInt(X * ImageScale), _
         CInt(Y * ImageScale)) Then
         TempTargetString = RTrim(ActiveHotspots(Counter).TargetString)
         Found = True
      End If
   Loop
   TargetFromPointInImage = TempTargetString
End Function
```

This function steps through the **ActiveHotspots** array, testing the mouse coordinates against each hotspot by passing them to **PtInRegion()** with the handle for the region held in the array element. If it finds a match, it returns the corresponding **TargetString**; otherwise it returns a null string (""). You will also notice the **ImageScale** argument, a value which represents the amount of scaling that has been done to the visible image in order to get it on the screen. We will talk more about that in a minute.

With the additions of **ActivateHotspots()**, **DeactivateHotspots()**, and **TargetFromPointInRegion()**, we've rounded out the HOTSPOT.BAS code module. Now we can hitch together the hotspot and hypertext systems.

Hotspots Meet Hypertext

Let's go back now and simplify a part of the HYPRMED2.BAS module that will make things less complicated and also cut down on our code size. We are going to put all of the code necessary to activate a hypertext jump into a procedure called **DoHyperTextJump()**. This procedure will be able to handle all the possible hypertext jumps and consolidate code that was separated into two procedures before. In HYPERMED1.BAS, the **ImageClick()** and **MouseClick()** subroutines both had code to handle hypermedia links, now they will both contain much less code by utilizing a call to **DoHyperTextJump()**. This procedure takes several arguments in order to handle all the possible links. **DoHyperTextJump()** pulls the extension of the filename off the subject string, then uses a **Select** statement to figure out which type of file it is, and what to do with it. **DoHypermediaJump()** then can do any of several actions:

- If the subject is a media file, it will call the multimedia API function **mciSendString()** to play it.
- If the subject is an image, it will call the **LoadImage()** subroutine in the hypermedia code module, then call the **ActivateHotspots()** in the hotspot code module to initialize the hotspot engine.
- If the right mouse button is pressed, we will load the current image into the **FloatingImage control** and display the **FloatingImage** form.
- If the destination subject is a new subject, load the new HTML text by placing a call to the **LoadHTMLFile()** function, followed by a call to **ParseText()**.

We'll place this procedure, which is shown in Listing 11.8, in the HYPRMED1.BAS code module.

Listing 11.8　The DoHypermediaJump() General Procedure from HYPERMED2.BAS

```
Private Sub DoHyperMediaJump(LinkSubject As String, TextPicBox As PictureBox, _
    ImagePicBox As Image, FloatingImage As PictureBox, ScrollBar As VScrollBar, _
    Button As Integer)
Dim Index As Integer
Dim LinkSubjectFile As String
Dim LinkSubjectLink As String

    ' Check for # symbol. If it is there, then parse out link file and anchor string
    If InStr(LinkSubject, Chr$(35)) Then
        ' Parse file and link information
        LinkSubjectFile = Left(LinkSubject, InStr(LinkSubject, Chr$(35)) - 1)
```

```
        LinkSubjectLink = Right(LinkSubject, (Len(LinkSubject) - _
            InStr(LinkSubject, Chr$(35))))
        ' Check for non-null file name
        If Not LinkSubjectFile = "" Then
            Text = LoadHTMLFile(LinkSubjectFile)
            ParseText Text, TextPicBox, ImagePicBox, ScrollBar
        End If
        ' Search for Anchor and move to correct position
        For Index = 0 To AnchorArrayPos - 1
            If AnchorArray(Index).Name = LinkSubjectLink Then
                TextPicBox.Top = -AnchorArray(Index).VPosition
                Exit For
            End If
        Next Index
    Else ' No specific destination subject, just load file
        Select Case UCase(Right(LinkSubject, Len(LinkSubject) - _
            InStr(LinkSubject, Chr$(46))))
            Case "HTM"
                Text = LoadHTMLFile(LinkSubject)
                ParseText Text, TextPicBox, ImagePicBox, ScrollBar
            Case "WAV", "MID", "AVI"
                Dummy = mciSendString("Play " + App.Path + "\Media\" + _
                    LinkSubject, 0, 0, 0)
            Case "BMP", "RLE", "ICO", "WMF"
                If Button = 2 Then ' If Right Mouse Button is clicked
                    FloatingImage.Parent.Caption = LinkSubject
                    Set FloatingImage.picture = LoadPicture(App.Path + "\Media\" + _
                        LinkSubject)
                    FloatingImage.Parent.Show
                Else ' Left Button
                    LoadImage LinkSubject, ImagePicBox
                    ActivateHotspots UCase(LinkSubject)
                End If
        End Select
    End If

End Sub
```

The two event procedures in HYPRMED2.BAS, **ImageClick()**, shown in Listing 11.9, and **MouseClick()**, shown in Listing 11.10, will now call **DoHypermediaJump()**.

Listing 11.9   The ImageClick() Subroutine from HYPRMED2.BAS

```
Sub ImageClick(Subject As Image, TextPicBox As PictureBox, ImagePicBox As Image, _
    FloatingImage As PictureBox, X As Single, Y As Single, Button As Integer, _
    ScrollBar As VScrollBar, ImageRatio As Double)
Dim LinkSubject As String

    If Button = 2 Then
        FloatingImage.Parent.Caption = "Original Image"
        Set FloatingImage.picture = Subject.picture
```

```
        FloatingImage.Parent.Show
    Else
        LinkSubject = TargetFromPointInImage(X, Y, ImageRatio)
        DoHyperMediaJump LinkSubject, TextPicBox, ImagePicBox, FloatingImage, _
            ScrollBar, 1
    End If
End Sub
```

Listing 11.10   The MouseClick() Subroutine from HYPRMED2.BAS

```
Public Sub MouseClick(TextPicBox As PictureBox, X As Single, Y As Single, _
    ImagePicBox As Image, ScrollBar As VScrollBar, Button As Integer, _
    FloatingImage As PictureBox)
Dim Index As Integer
Dim Index2 As Integer
Dim LinkSubject As String
Dim LinkSubjectFile As String
Dim LinkSubjectLink As String

    ' Check for loaded form
    If TextPicBox.CurrentY = 0 Then Exit Sub
    ' Step through Hypertext links
    For Index = 0 To LinkArrayPos
        If (X > HyperLinkArray(Index).Left) And _
            (X < HyperLinkArray(Index).Right) And _
            (Y > HyperLinkArray(Index).Top) And _
            (Y < HyperLinkArray(Index).Bottom) Then
            LinkSubject = HyperLinkArray(Index).DestinationSubject
            DoHyperMediaJump LinkSubject, TextPicBox, ImagePicBox, FloatingImage, _
                ScrollBar, Button
            Exit For
        End If
    Next Index
    ' Change value of scroll bar to reflect size of document
    ScrollBar.VALUE = -TextPicBox.Top
End Sub
```

More about Our Image Display

The image display in the first incarnation of the hypermedia engine was very simple. Now we need to make it look good and give the user options for viewing images. First, we are going to find the aspect ratio of an image by using a combination of an Image control and a PictureBox control, as shown in Figure 11.8. Next, we need to resize the image so that it fits within whatever space is available, and we might as well center it within that space while we're at it. Most of this work is done in the **LoadImage()** subroutine (Listing 11.11), which is also in HYPRMED2.BAS.

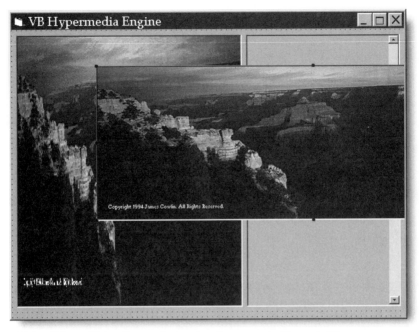

Figure 11.8 *Using a PictureBox control and an Image control to scale bitmaps.*

Listing 11.11 The LoadImage() Subroutine from HYPRMED2.BAS

```
Private Function LoadImage(Filename As String, Destination As Image)
Dim ImageRatio As Double
Dim FrameRatio As Double
Dim MaxWidth As Long
Dim MaxHeight As Long

  MaxWidth = Val(Left(Destination.Tag, InStr(Destination.Tag, Chr(124)) - 1))
  MaxHeight = Val(Right(Destination.Tag, Len(Destination.Tag) - _
    InStr(Destination.Tag, Chr(124))))

  Destination.Visible = False
  Destination.Top = ImageBoxTop
  Destination.Left = ImageBoxleft

  Set Form1.TempPictureBox.picture = LoadPicture(App.Path + "\media\" + _
    Filename)
  ImageRatio = Form1.TempPictureBox.picture.Width / _
    Form1.TempPictureBox.picture.Height
  FrameRatio = MaxWidth / MaxHeight
  If ImageRatio > FrameRatio Then
    Destination.Width = MaxWidth
    Destination.Height = CInt(MaxWidth / ImageRatio)
    Destination.Top = CInt(MaxHeight / 2 - Destination.Height / 2) + _
      ImageBoxTop
```

```
   Else
      Destination.Width = CInt(MaxHeight * ImageRatio)
      Destination.Height = MaxHeight
      Destination.Left = CInt(MaxWidth / 2 - Destination.Width / 2) + _
         ImageBoxleft
   End If

   Set Destination.picture = Form1.TempPictureBox.picture
   Destination.Visible = True

End Function
```

For this subroutine, we need to pass the name of the file to load, and destination of the image. In this case, the destination is the **ImagePicBox** control. We also need to know the maximum space that the control can use, so we can take advantage of the empty **Tag** property that VB gives to all controls. When the program begins, we will place the dimensions of the client space in the **Tag** property of the **ImagePicBox** control. The **Tag** property is a string. We will use the **Str** function to turn the dimensions of the full-size **ImagePicBox** into a string that has a '|' character separating the width and height. We can then parse that information out in the **LoadImage()** subroutine. Once we know the maximum dimensions, we need to figure out if the aspect ratio of the incoming image is greater than the aspect ratio of our client space. If it is, which means that the image's width should be made to fit first, then we can use the aspect ratio of the image to determine the new height. If the aspect ratio of the image is less than the aspect ratio of our client space, we need to first set the height, then determine the width. Once the dimensions are calculated, we'll center the image in the client space and then bring in the picture. While this is going on, it's best to set the **Visible** property of the control that is being manipulated to false, so that the user does not see the control changing sizes repeatedly. Just don't forget to turn the visibility back on!

Now that we have the image on our form, we have a problem. How are we going to handle the image hotspots? The problem stems from the fact that with a scaled image, any coordinate information passed to the hotspot engine will be wrong. To fix this, we need to translate the coordinates of our scaled image back to the original proportions. We also need to translate from twips into pixels by using the **TwipsPerPixelX** and **TwipsPerPixelY** functions in the **ImagePicBox_MouseDown()** event procedure, as shown in Listing 11.12.

Listing 11.12   The ImagePicBox_MouseDown() Event Procedure from HYPRMED2.FRM

```
Private Sub ImagePicBox_MouseDown(Button As Integer, Shift As Integer, _
   X As Single, Y As Single)
Dim TempX As Single
Dim TempY As Single

   TempX = X / Screen.TwipsPerPixelX
   TempY = Y / Screen.TwipsPerPixelY
   ImageClick TextPicBox, ImagePicBox, FloatingForm.FloatingImage, TempX, _
      TempY, Button, ScrollBar, (TempPictureBox.Width / ImagePicBox.Width)
End Sub
```

Now that we have the coordinates in pixels, we need to translate them to the correct scale. To accomplish this, we will send a value to the **ImageClick()** subroutine that represents the compression ratio. To find this ratio, we can take advantage of the fact that we have a full-size version of the image sitting in the background in our temporary PictureBox that we use as a buffer when a new image is loaded. So, all we have to do is divide a dimension from the original image by the respective dimension from the visible **ImagePicBox** control. We chose to use the width, but it doesn't really matter. Next, we pass the actual coordinates of the mouse click, along with the compression ratio, to the **TargetFromPointInImage()** function, which we explained earlier. Here is the key line from **TargetFromPointInImage()** that does the work of rescaling the coordinates of the mouse clicks:

```
If PtInRegion(ActiveHotspots(Counter).hPolygonRgn, CInt(X * ImageScale), _
   CInt(Y * ImageScale)) Then
   TempTargetString = RTrim(ActiveHotspots(Counter).TargetString)
```

As you can see, it's really rather simple now, because we've done most of the figuring beforehand. We simply multiply each coordinate by the **ImageScale** variable.

Filling In the Remaining Event Code

Since we've added support for the image hotspots, we need to update the **Form_Load()** event procedure, as shown in Listing 11.13.

Listing 11.13   The Form_Load() Event Procedure from HYPRMED2.FRM

```
Private Sub Form_Load()
Dim OpenedImageDatabase As Integer
```

```
    LinkArrayPos = 0
    AnchorArrayPos = 0
    IsLink = False
    ImagePicBox.Tag = Str(ImagePicBox.Width) + Chr(124) + Str(ImagePicBox.Height)
    OpenedImageDatabase = OpenImageDatabase()

    UpdateHtml App.Path & "/HYPRMED1.HTM", TextPicBox, ImagePicBox, ScrollBar
End Sub
```

We'll also need to handle the **Unload** event to clean up any active hotspots and close the hotspot database. For that we'll add one procedure call to the **Form_Unload()** event procedure, as shown in Listing 11.14.

Listing 11.14   The Form_Unload() Event Procedure from HYPRMED2.FRM

```
Sub Form_Unload (Cancel As Integer)
    DeactivateHotspots
    ImageTable.Close
    ImageDB.Close
End Sub
```

Using a Database Instead of Text Files

To complete our multimedia engine, let's get rid of all the HTML files. We'll redesign the engine so that it works by obtaining its multimedia data to display and play by accessing a database instead of individual HTML files. Using a database not only gets rid of all the files, but speeds things up, and makes it easier to change things later. The drawback to using a database is that if we decide to distribute our program, which, incidentally, is the point of all this, we will also need to include the runtime version of the database engine, as well as all the support files. With VB 4, those files add up quickly, which you may want to consider before you switch to the database driven multimedia engine.

We are also going to implement a scripting system that will allow multiple hypermedia jumps to take place whenever a link is initiated. This version of the scripting system will accept sound files, video files, and image files.

Before we change any of our code, we need to figure out the layout of our new database. It is important to do your homework on these issues ahead of time, because going back later and changing something can be very difficult. As our needs are pretty simple for this program, we don't even need to consider a relational database, we simply need a standard flat database. We will need only three fields: a **Subject** field to specify the topic of each section, an **HTML** field to hold the actual HTML text, and a **Script** field to hold the script information. Table 11.3 lists the fields and their appropriate data

Table 11.3 *The Layout of Our Hypermedia Database*

Field	Data Type	Size
Subject	Text	50
HTML	Memo	64K
Script	Text	255

types and size. We will use VB's built-in Data Manager to build the database and fill it with information, as shown in Figure 11.9.

To fill the database, you can simply open the HTML files in Notepad or any other text editor, and copy the information into the **HTML** field of the database. Before you do that, though, you need to get rid of the return strings between each line of the HTML file so that the entire string resides on one line. Also, you will need to take all the references to images out of the HTML and copy them into the **Script** field. This version of the hypermedia engine can only show one image at a time, but it would not be very difficult to add support for an array of images. In fact, if you are going to be strictly writing code for Windows 95, there is a new OCX control that you can use called **ImageList** that is well-suited for our multimedia engine.

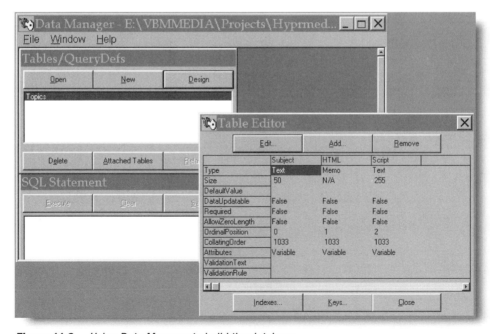

Figure 11.9 *Using Data Manager to build the database.*

The ImagList OCX

The **ImageList** control that comes with VB is a Windows 95-only control that does exactly what you need; it stores arrays of images in a memory buffer that can be easily called up for display or manipulation. You can use this control by activating the Custom Controls dialog box. This menu can be brought up through the menu by picking Tools then Custom Controls, or by simply pressing **Ctrl+T**. Figure 11.10 shows the Custom Control dialog box with the mouse over the check box we want—the Microsoft Windows Custom Controls. This is a single OCX that holds several different Windows 95-specific custom controls.

Completing the Hypermedia Engine

This project adds scripting capability to the multimedia engine, and uses information stored in a database instead of the HTML files. Here are the steps to follow:

1. Create the new database file and copy the information from the HTML files into it, or create new content.
2. Copy all the project files into a new directory, preferably HYPRMED3.
3. Rename HYPRMED2.* files to HYPRMED3.*.
4. Open the new HYPRMED3.VBP project file, and when the error messages signal the file isn't found, continue until the program finishes loading. Then, use the Add File command to add the files that were renamed previously to HYPRMED4.*.
5. Create the subroutines **LoadDatabase(), PlayScript(),** and **EndScript().** We also need one new function—**GetHTMLFromDB().** (See Listings 11.15 To 11.18.)

 You'll find this program in the subdirectory \VBMAGIC\HYPRMED3 in the files HYPRMED3.VBP, HYPRMED3.FRM, HYPRMED3.BAS, HOTSPOT.BAS, GLOBCONS.BAS, and DATACONS.BAS. The HTML files are no longer necessary, but the information must be placed in the database file HYPRMED3.MDB. We will also need all the multimedia files in the MEDIA directory.

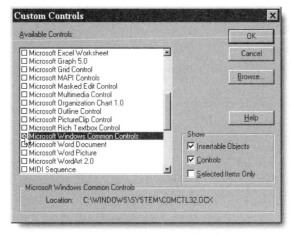

Figure 11.10 *Adding controls in the Custom Controls dialog box.*

Opening the Database

Now that we have created the HTML database, we need to figure out how to use it. The first thing we need to do is load the database. Let's create a new subroutine called **LoadDatabase()** that will activate the database and the table we want to use. Our database processing approach differs slightly from what we used to support the hotspot feature we implemented earlier; we thought it would be helpful to show you a different method. There are actually many ways to interact with databases in VB. For example, we could have used custom controls, or SQL, or any of several third party products. But the Jet database engine that comes with VB is fast, efficient, and VB offers us many options to interact with it, so let's stick with it. If we were using a database that was already made for us and was in another format, we might want to consider using SQL with a custom control. But since we have control over which type of database we are using, the Microsoft Jet database engine is the best choice. Let's take a look at the **LoadDatabase()** subroutine in Listing 11.15, and then we'll explain how it works.

Listing 11.15 The LoadDatabase() Subroutine from HYPRMED3.BAS

```
Public Sub LoadDataBase(DBToLoad As String, TextPicBox As PictureBox, _
   ImagePicBox As Image, ScrollBar As VScrollBar)
Dim Text As String

   Set TopicDB = Workspaces(0).OpenDatabase(DBToLoad)
   Set TopicTable = TopicDB.OpenRecordset("Topics", dbOpenSnapshot)

   Text = GetHTMLFromDB("Subject = 'Main'")
   ParseText Text, TextPicBox, ImagePicBox, ScrollBar
```

```
    PlayScript "Subject = 'Main'", ImagePicBox
End Sub
```

Once again, we need to pass all the controls from the main form as arguments so that they can be passed on to the other routines in our program. The two **Set** statements do all the work of opening the database and the specific table we need. If you have used previous versions of VB to create database apps, the first **Set** statement should look very familiar—but what does the **Workspaces** object represent?

A **Workspace** object defines a session for a user. It operates a lot like an array of databases and their associated information, such as security data and a user base. We'll use the Workspace object to manage the current session or to start an additional session. In a session, you can open multiple databases, manage transactions, and establish security, based on user names and passwords. For example, you can:

- Create a Workspace object using the Name, Password, and UserName properties to establish a named, password-protected session.
- Use the OpenDatabase method to open one or more existing databases on that Workspace.
- Use the BeginTrans, CommitTrans, and Rollback methods to manage nested transaction processing within a Workspace and use several Workspace objects to conduct multiple, simultaneous, and overlapping transactions.
- Use the Close method to terminate a session.

If you want to use the **Workspaces** object collection, you need to let VB know, and tell it how to reference it. VB tries to minimize overhead by not loading information and resources unless you need them. This is critical, because the database engine can use resources fast. To make the database engine available to your application, choose References from the Tools menu and select the appropriate DAO Component Object Library in the References dialog box. For more information, look in VB's help system.

Starting the Jet database engine automatically creates the default workspace, **DBEngine.Workspaces(0)**. The settings of the **Name** and **UserName** properties of the default workspace are "#Default Workspace#" and "Admin", respectively. If security is enabled, the **UserName** property setting is the name of the user who logged on. If you use the **OpenDatabase** method without specifying a **Workspace** object, the default **DBEngine.Workspaces(0)** is used. We will not be using any of the security features of this powerful engine, but it is nice to know they exist, and are relatively simple to use.

Now that we have the database loaded, we need to specify which table we want to use by initiating another **Set** statement. This time, the **Set** statement calls the **OpenRecordset()** function. This function passes the name of the table as a string and the constant **dbOpenSnapshot**. This constant tells the Jet engine that we want to open the table as a snapshot-type Recordset. This means that we simply want to open a static image, or "snapshot" of the table—we don't want to allow any manipulation of the table. This method has two benefits: First, we don't have to worry about our program accidentally changing the database, and second, it speeds up data access. Snapshot-type **Recordset** objects are generally faster to create and access than standard-type **Recordset** objects, because their records are either in memory or stored in temporary disk space, and the Jet database engine doesn't have to deal with page locking or multiuser issues. However, snapshot-type **Recordset** objects consume more local resources than standard-type **Recordset** objects because the entire record is downloaded to local memory. The information stored in our database is relatively small, so the increase in speed is worth using the extra resources.

Now that we have a recordset of our database table stored in memory and accessed by the global variable **TopicTable**, we can call the new **GetHTMLFromDB()** function shown in Listing 11.16.

Listing 11.16   The GetHTMLFromDB() Function from HYPRMED3.BAS

```
Private Function GetHTMLFromDB(Criteria As String) as String

   TopicTable.FindFirst Criteria    ' Find first matching record.
   If Not TopicTable.NoMatch Then   ' Check if record is found.
      GetHTMLFromDB = TopicTable("HTML")
   End If
End Function
```

You can't get much simpler than this. The **FindFirst** method is a very fast and easy way to search a Recordset. You simply pass it a criteria string that specifies the record you are searching for. In this case, the criteria string looks something like this:

```
"Subject = 'Main'"
```

This particular string is telling the **FindFirst** command to search in the field named "Subject" for an entry of "Main." This is a very simple command-message, but with a more elaborate database table, we might call a search with a criteria string like this:

```
"Subject > 'M' and HTML="" and InputDate > #" & Format(mydate, 'm/d/yy' ) & "#"
```

As you can see, this type of searching can get as specific as you need.

Once the search is complete, we check to make sure that a record was found that matched. Next, we return the contents of the HTML field of the found record with this line:

```
GetHTMLFromDB = TopicTable("HTML")
```

This statement tells VB to look in the "HTML" field of the **TopicTable** recordset and return whatever value is there. Now that we have the HTML text loaded into a variable, we can pass it on to our **ParseText** subroutine just the way we did before.

Supporting Scripts

Once text is parsed and displayed, we run into the new call to the **PlayScript()** subroutine. This routine takes two arguments. The first is a database search string expression that will be used to search for the proper script. The second argument is the Image control that will be used if the **PlayScript()** function needs to display any images. Let's take a look at the **PlayScript()** subroutine shown in Listing 11.17.

Listing 11.17   The PlayScript() Subroutine from HYPRMED3.BAS

```
Private Sub PlayScript(SearchParameters As String, ImagePicBox As Image)
Dim ScriptText As String
Dim Command As String
Dim TempTime As Date

    TopicTable.FindFirst SearchParameters    ' Find first matching record.
    If Not TopicTable.NoMatch Then  ' Check if record is found.
       ScriptText = TopicTable("Script")
       If Not ScriptText = "" Then
          Do
             ScriptRunning = True
             If Escape Then
                Escape = False
                Exit Do
             End If
             ' Get first command from script
             If InStr(ScriptText, Chr(124)) Then
                Command = Left(ScriptText, InStr(ScriptText, Chr(124)) - 1)
             Else
                Command = ScriptText
             End If
             ' Do Command
             Select Case UCase(Right(Command, 3))
                Case "WAV", "MID", "AVI"
```

```
            Dummy = mciSendString("Play " + App.Path + "\MEDIA\" + _
                Command, 0, 0, 0)
        Case "BMP", "RLE", "ICO", "WMF"
            LoadImage Command, ImagePicBox
            ActivateHotspots UCase(Command)
        Case Else
            TempTime = DateAdd("s", Val(Command), Now)
            While TempTime > Now
                DoEvents
            Wend
        End Select
        ScriptText = Right(ScriptText, Len(ScriptText) - InStr(ScriptText, _
            Chr(124)))
        Loop While InStr(ScriptText, Chr(124))
    End If
   End If
   ScriptRunning = False
End Sub
```

The routine starts off by searching for the record specified by our search criteria that was passed into the variable **SearchParameters**. If the record is not found, we simply exit the routine. If the record is found, we copy the contents of the "Script" field of the record into the **ScriptText** variable. Next, we make sure that there is actually information in the variable by checking to see if the variable is equal to "" (a Null string). Once we know that we have some useful information, we need to figure out what kind of links they are, and what to do with them.

Then, we start a **Do** loop that will cycle through the script text, picking out the file names and dealing with them accordingly. If we didn't need to play scripts, but just wanted to play single files or display single images, this whole process would be much easier. Scripting, however, is a simple and effective way to add excitement and a feeling of interactivity to your multimedia applications. So, we think it's worth the effort.

First, we need to set the **ScriptRunning** Boolean variable to **True** so that other functions will be able to check and see if a script is presently running. That way, we won't accidentally have multiple scripts running at once.

The next line is important from a user's point of view. We need to check and see if the Escape key has been pressed. This is important if you have long scripts in your database and a user wants to cancel out of the script. He or she can simply press the Escape key and the script will stop playing at the next break. We will get back to how this is done in a minute.

Next, we need to start pulling the individual files out of the script string. Each file name is separated by a "|" character (ASCII code 124). We use the **Left()** function to pull everything off to the left of the delimiting character, then use a **Select** statement to handle the different file extensions. If there is no extension, the **Select** statement defaults to a timer that finds the value of the entry and waits the specified number of seconds before proceeding. For example, in the sample database that comes on the CD-ROM, the "Main" entry in the table has a script string that looks like this:

```
INTRO.BMP|HASTA.WAV|3|YAKIDAWN.BMP|ERROR.WAV|
```

And Table 11.4 shows how this line of the script will be processed when passed to the **PlayScript()** routine.

Here is the code that takes care of the timing:

```
TempTime = DateAdd("s", Val(Command), Now)
While TempTime > Now
    DoEvents
Wend
```

This function finds the current time using the **Now** function. Then it adds the value of the **Command** string to the tim,e using the **DateAdd()** function. This nifty little function can add any amount of time to any date string. For example, assume we wanted to find the date 30 days from now. We could simply call the **DateAdd()** function as shown here:

```
NewTime = DateAdd("d", 30, Now)
```

The first argument is the format of the amount of time we want to add, in this case, "d" stands for days. (In our program we use "s" to specify seconds.) Then, we tell the function the number of days to add—in this case, 30 days. (In our program we tell **DateAdd()** to wait a certain number of seconds.) Finally, we send the time we want it added to. For this example, and in our program, we use the **Now()** function to return the present time, but we could have just as easily sent it any date. The **DateAdd()** function is very useful, so don't forget about it.

Table 11.4 *Processing a Sample Script String*

INTRO.BMP	Display bitmap
HASTA.WAV	Play Sound
3	Wait 3 Seconds
YAKIDAWN.BMP	Display bitmap
ERROR.WAV	Play Sound

Once the current command has been carried out, we extract the remaining text from the script text by using the **Right()** function to pull off everything to the right of the first "|" character. Then, we check to see if there are any more "|" characters left. If there is, we know that we have more commands to carry out in the script. If not, we are done.

Let's go back now to our Escape key processing routine. As we said before, we need a way to stop a script after it has begun. So let's create a subroutine called **EndScript()** , shown in Listing 11.18.

Listing 11.18   The EndScript() Subroutine from HYPRMED3.BAS

```
Public Sub EndScript()
   Escape = True
End Sub
```

Not much to it, but it does play an important role. We now need to add the code that calls this function to the main form's **KeyDown** event procedure, as shown in Listing 11.19.

Listing 11.19   The Form_KeyDown() Event Procedure from HYPRMED3.FRM

```
Private Sub Form_KeyDown(KeyCode As Integer, Shift As Integer)
   If KeyCode = KEY_ESCAPE Then EndScript
End Sub
```

This procedure uses the VB constants to check for the Escape key being pressed. If this key is encountered, the **EndScript()** routine is called, and the script engine is stopped at the next command. Don't forget to set the **KeyPreview** property of the form to **True**. This tells the form that it should pay attention to the keys that are being pressed, even when a control on the form has taken the focus.

Setting Up the Database Connection

We are not quite done with the program. We need to change any routines that previously called the **LoadHTML()** function. Since this function previously loaded the multimedia information from the HTML files, we need to swap them out with a command to point to our **GetHTMLFromDB()** function. Since we already set up the **LoadDatabase()** routine, the only other routine that needs to be changed is the **DoHypermediaJump()** routine, which is shown in Listing 11.20.

Listing 11.20　The New DoHypermediaJump() Subroutine from HYPRMED3

```
Private Sub DoHyperMediaJump(LinkSubject As String, _
   TextPicBox As PictureBox, ImagePicBox As Image, _
   FloatingImage As PictureBox, ScrollBar As VScrollBar, Button As Integer)
Dim Index As Integer
Dim LinkSubjectFile As String
Dim LinkSubjectLink As String

   If LinkSubject = "" Then Exit Sub
   If InStr(LinkSubject, Chr$(35)) Then
      ' Parse file and link information
      LinkSubjectFile = Left(LinkSubject, InStr(LinkSubject, Chr$(35)) - 1)
      LinkSubjectLink = Right(LinkSubject, (Len(LinkSubject) - _
         InStr(LinkSubject, Chr$(35))))
      ' Check for non-null file name
      If Not LinkSubjectFile = "" Then
         Text = GetHTMLFromDB("Subject = '" & LinkSubjectFile & "'")
         ParseText Text, TextPicBox, ImagePicBox, ScrollBar
         PlayScript "Subject = '" & LinkSubjectFile & "'", ImagePicBox
      End If
      ' Search for Anchor and move to correct position
      For Index = 0 To AnchorArrayPos - 1
         If AnchorArray(Index).Name = LinkSubjectLink Then
            TextPicBox.Top = -AnchorArray(Index).VPosition
            Exit For
         End If
      Next Index
   Else ' No specific destination subject, just load file
      Select Case UCase(Right(LinkSubject, Len(LinkSubject) - _
         InStr(LinkSubject, Chr$(46))))
         Case "WAV", "MID", "AVI"
            Dummy = mciSendString("Play " + App.Path + "\Media\" + _
               LinkSubject, 0, 0, 0)
         Case "BMP", "RLE", "ICO", "WMF"
            If Button = 2 Then ' If Right Mouse Button is clicked
               FloatingImage.Parent.Caption = LinkSubject
               Set FloatingImage.picture = LoadPicture(App.Path + "\Media\" + _
                  LinkSubject)
               FloatingImage.Parent.Show
            Else ' Left Button
               LoadImage LinkSubject, ImagePicBox
               ActivateHotspots UCase(LinkSubject)
            End If
         Case Else
            Text = GetHTMLFromDB("Subject = '" & LinkSubject & "'")
            ParseText Text, TextPicBox, ImagePicBox, ScrollBar
            PlayScript "Subject = '" & LinkSubject & "'", ImagePicBox
      End Select
   End If

End Sub
```

The main change here is the switch to the new **GetHTMLFromDB()** function, and the addition of the call to the **PlayScript()** routine. Also, you will notice that we had to get rid of the "HTM" case in the **Select** statement. This is because we no longer are dealing with files, so we just assume that if there is no file extension, it must be a link, and we take it from there. This technique works well, because if for some reason something was not inputted correctly, the **GetHTMLFromDB()** routine will not return anything—which is fine, because the **ParseText()** and **PlayScript()** routines will not produce any errors with a Null string.

Listings 11.21 and 11.22 present the complete code for the fully functional, database-driven, script-enabled Hypermedia engine.

Listing 11.21   The Complete Listing of HYPRMED3.FRM

```
VERSION 4.00
Begin VB.Form Form1
    BorderStyle     =   1   'Fixed Single
    Caption         =   "VB Hypermedia Engine"
    ClientHeight    =   6735
    ClientLeft      =   2220
    ClientTop       =   2085
    ClientWidth     =   9480
    Height          =   7260
    KeyPreview      =   -1  'True
    Left            =   2160
    LinkTopic       =   "Form1"
    MaxButton       =   0   'False
    MinButton       =   0   'False
    ScaleHeight     =   6735
    ScaleWidth      =   9480
    Top             =   1620
    WhatsThisHelp   =   -1  'True
    Width           =   9600
    Begin VB.PictureBox TempPictureBox
        Appearance      =   0   'Flat
        AutoSize        =   -1  'True
        BackColor       =   &H80000005&
        BorderStyle     =   0   'None
        ForeColor       =   &H80000008&
        Height          =   1815
        Left            =   1440
        ScaleHeight     =   1815
        ScaleWidth      =   2895
        TabIndex        =   3
        Top             =   2520
        Visible         =   0   'False
        Width           =   2895
    End
    Begin VB.PictureBox PictureFrame
        AutoRedraw      =   -1  'True
```

```
         BeginProperty Font
            name                =    "MS Sans Serif"
            charset             =    0
            weight              =    400
            size                =    12
            underline           =    0      'False
            italic              =    0      'False
            strikethrough       =    0      'False
         EndProperty
         Height           =    6375
         Left             =    5640
         ScaleHeight      =    6315
         ScaleWidth       =    3675
         TabIndex         =    0
         Top              =    120
         Width            =    3735
         Begin VB.VScrollBar ScrollBar
            Height          =    6300
            LargeChange     =    1500
            Left            =    3420
            Max             =    1000
            SmallChange     =    100
            TabIndex        =    2
            Top             =    0
            Value           =    1
            Width           =    255
         End
         Begin VB.PictureBox TextPicBox
            Appearance      =    0    'Flat
            AutoRedraw      =    -1   'True
            BackColor       =    &H00C0C0C0&
            BorderStyle     =    0    'None
            ClipControls    =    0     'False
            BeginProperty Font
               name                =    "MS Sans Serif"
               charset             =    0
               weight              =    400
               size                =    12
               underline           =    0      'False
               italic              =    0      'False
               strikethrough       =    0      'False
            EndProperty
            ForeColor       =    &H80000008&
            Height          =    1e5
            Left            =    120
            ScaleHeight     =    1.00005e5
            ScaleWidth      =    3225
            TabIndex        =    1
            Top             =    0
            Width           =    3230
         End
      End
   Begin VB.Image ImagePicBox
      BorderStyle     =    1    'Fixed Single
```

```
          Height        =    6375
          Left          =    120
          Stretch       =    -1   'True
          Top           =    120
          Width         =    5415
       End
    End
End
Attribute VB_Name = "Form1"
Attribute VB_Creatable = False
Attribute VB_Exposed = False

Private Sub Form_KeyDown(KeyCode As Integer, Shift As Integer)
   If KeyCode = KEY_ESCAPE Then EndScript
End Sub

Private Sub Form_Load()
Dim OpenedImageDatabase As Integer

   Top = (Screen.Height - Height) / 2
   Left = (Screen.Width - Width) / 2
   Show
   LinkArrayPos = 0
   AnchorArrayPos = 0
   IsLink = False
   ImagePicBox.Tag = Str(ImagePicBox.Width) + Chr(124) + Str(ImagePicBox.Height)
   OpenedImageDatabase = OpenImageDatabase()

   LoadDataBase App.Path & "/HYPRMED3.MDB", TextPicBox, ImagePicBox, ScrollBar
End Sub

Private Sub Form_Unload(Cancel As Integer)
   DeactivateHotspots
   Escape = True
End Sub

Private Sub ImagePicBox_MouseDown(Button As Integer, Shift As Integer, X As
Single, Y As Single)
Dim TempX As Single
Dim TempY As Single

   TempX = X / Screen.TwipsPerPixelX
   TempY = Y / Screen.TwipsPerPixelY
   ImageClick TextPicBox, ImagePicBox, FloatingForm.FloatingImage, TempX, _
      TempY, Button, ScrollBar, (TempPictureBox.Width / ImagePicBox.Width)
End Sub

Private Sub ScrollBar_Change()
   ' Check for active document
   If TextPicBox.CurrentY = 0 Then
      ScrollBar.VALUE = 0
      Exit Sub
   End If
   ' Move top of Picture1 with inverse relation to the scroll bar
   TextPicBox.Top = -ScrollBar.VALUE
End Sub
```

```
Private Sub TextPicBox_MouseDown(Button As Integer, Shift As Integer, _
    X As Single, Y As Single)
    MouseClick TextPicBox, X, Y, ImagePicBox, ScrollBar, Button, _
        FloatingForm.FloatingImage
End Sub
```

Listing 11.22   The Complete Listing of HYPRMED3.BAS

```
Attribute VB_Name = "Module2"
Option Explicit

Type HyperLinkElement
    Left As Integer
    Top As Integer
    Right As Integer
    Bottom As Integer
    DestinationSubject As String
End Type

Type AnchorElement
    Name As String
    VPosition As Integer
End Type

#If Win32 Then
    Declare Function mciSendString Lib "winmm.dll" Alias "mciSendStringA" _
        (ByVal lpstrCommand As String, ByVal lpstrReturnString As String, _
        ByVal uReturnLength As Long, ByVal hwndCallback As Long) As Long
#Else
    Declare Function mciSendString Lib "MMSystem" (ByVal lpstrCommand As String, _
        ByVal lpstrReturnString As String, ByVal uReturnLength As Integer, ByVal _
        hwndCallback As Integer) As Long
#End If

Dim HyperLinkArray(100) As HyperLinkElement
Dim AnchorArray(100) As AnchorElement
Dim LinkArrayPos As Integer
Dim AnchorArrayPos As Integer
Dim IsLink As Boolean
Dim Text As String
Dim Dummy As Variant
Dim Escape As Boolean
Dim ScriptRunning As Boolean

Dim TopicDB As DATABASE
Dim TopicTable As Recordset

Global Const ImageBoxleft = 120
Global Const ImageBoxTop = 120

Public Sub EndScript()
    Escape = True
End Sub
```

```vb
Private Function GetHTMLFromDB(Criteria As String) As String

   TopicTable.FindFirst Criteria    ' Find first matching record.
   If Not TopicTable.NoMatch Then   ' Check if record is found.
      GetHTMLFromDB = TopicTable("HTML")
   End If
End Function


Public Sub LoadDataBase(DBToLoad As String, TextPicBox As PictureBox, _
   ImagePicBox As Image, ScrollBar As VScrollBar)
Dim Text As String

   Set TopicDB = Workspaces(0).OpenDatabase(DBToLoad)
   Set TopicTable = TopicDB.OpenRecordset("Topics", dbOpenSnapshot)

   Text = GetHTMLFromDB("Subject = 'Main'")
   ParseText Text, TextPicBox, ImagePicBox, ScrollBar
   PlayScript "Subject = 'Main'", ImagePicBox
End Sub

Private Sub PlayScript(SearchParameters As String, ImagePicBox As Image)
Dim ScriptText As String
Dim Command As String
Dim TempTime As Date

   TopicTable.FindFirst SearchParameters    ' Find first matching record.
   If Not TopicTable.NoMatch Then   ' Check if record is found.
      ScriptText = TopicTable("Script")
      If Not ScriptText = "" Then
         Do
            ScriptRunning = True
            If Escape Then
               Escape = False
               Exit Do
            End If
            ' Get first command from script
            If InStr(ScriptText, Chr(124)) Then
               Command = Left(ScriptText, InStr(ScriptText, Chr(124)) - 1)
            Else
               Command = ScriptText
            End If
            ' Do Command
            Select Case UCase(Right(Command, 3))
               Case "WAV", "MID", "AVI"
                  Dummy = mciSendString("Play " + App.Path + "\MEDIA\" + _
                     Command, 0, 0, 0)
               Case "BMP", "RLE", "ICO", "WMF"
                  LoadImage Command, ImagePicBox
                  ActivateHotspots UCase(Command)
               Case Else
                  TempTime = DateAdd("s", Val(Command), Now)
                  While TempTime > Now
                     DoEvents
```

```
                     Wend
             End Select
           ScriptText = Right(ScriptText, Len(ScriptText) - InStr(ScriptText, _
               Chr(124)))
        Loop While InStr(ScriptText, Chr(124))
      End If
   End If
   ScriptRunning = False
End Sub


Private Sub DoHyperMediaJump(LinkSubject As String, TextPicBox As PictureBox, _
   ImagePicBox As Image, FloatingImage As PictureBox, ScrollBar As VScrollBar, _
   Button As Integer)
Dim Index As Integer
Dim LinkSubjectFile As String
Dim LinkSubjectLink As String

   If LinkSubject = "" Then Exit Sub
   If InStr(LinkSubject, Chr$(35)) Then
      ' Parse file and link information
      LinkSubjectFile = Left(LinkSubject, InStr(LinkSubject, Chr$(35)) - 1)
      LinkSubjectLink = Right(LinkSubject, (Len(LinkSubject) - _
         InStr(LinkSubject, Chr$(35))))
      ' Check for non-null file name
      If Not LinkSubjectFile = "" Then
         Text = GetHTMLFromDB("Subject = '" & LinkSubjectFile & "'")
         ParseText Text, TextPicBox, ImagePicBox, ScrollBar
         PlayScript "Subject = '" & LinkSubjectFile & "'", ImagePicBox
      End If
      ' Search for Anchor and move to correct position
      For Index = 0 To AnchorArrayPos - 1
         If AnchorArray(Index).Name = LinkSubjectLink Then
            TextPicBox.Top = -AnchorArray(Index).VPosition
            Exit For
         End If
      Next Index
   Else ' No specific destination subject, just load file
      Select Case UCase(Right(LinkSubject, Len(LinkSubject) - _
         InStr(LinkSubject, Chr$(46))))
         Case "WAV", "MID", "AVI"
            Dummy = mciSendString("Play " + App.Path + "\Media\" + _
               LinkSubject, 0, 0, 0)
         Case "BMP", "RLE", "ICO", "WMF"
            If Button = 2 Then ' If Right Mouse Button is clicked
               FloatingImage.Parent.Caption = LinkSubject
               Set FloatingImage.picture = LoadPicture(App.Path + "\Media\" + _
                  LinkSubject)
               FloatingImage.Parent.Show
            Else ' Left Button
               LoadImage LinkSubject, ImagePicBox
               ActivateHotspots UCase(LinkSubject)
            End If
```

```
            Case Else
                Text = GetHTMLFromDB("Subject = '" & LinkSubject & "'")
                ParseText Text, TextPicBox, ImagePicBox, ScrollBar
                PlayScript "Subject = '" & LinkSubject & "'", ImagePicBox
        End Select
    End If
End Sub

Private Function LoadImage(Filename As String, Destination As Image)
Dim ImageRatio As Double
Dim FrameRatio As Double
Dim MaxWidth As Long
Dim MaxHeight As Long

    MaxWidth = Val(Left(Destination.Tag, InStr(Destination.Tag, Chr(124)) - 1))
    MaxHeight = Val(Right(Destination.Tag, Len(Destination.Tag) - _
        InStr(Destination.Tag, Chr(124))))

    Destination.Visible = False
    Destination.Top = ImageBoxTop
    Destination.Left = ImageBoxleft

    Set Form1.TempPictureBox.picture = LoadPicture(App.Path + "\media\" + _
        Filename)
    ImageRatio = Form1.TempPictureBox.picture.Width / _
        Form1.TempPictureBox.picture.Height
    FrameRatio = MaxWidth / MaxHeight
    If ImageRatio > FrameRatio Then
        Destination.Width = MaxWidth
        Destination.Height = CInt(MaxWidth / ImageRatio)
        Destination.Top = CInt(MaxHeight / 2 - Destination.Height / 2) + _
            ImageBoxTop
    Else
        Destination.Width = CInt(MaxHeight * ImageRatio)
        Destination.Height = MaxHeight
        Destination.Left = CInt(MaxWidth / 2 - Destination.Width / 2) + _
            ImageBoxleft
    End If

    Set Destination.picture = Form1.TempPictureBox.picture
    Destination.Visible = True
End Function


Public Sub MouseClick(TextPicBox As PictureBox, X As Single, Y As Single, _
    ImagePicBox As Image, ScrollBar As VScrollBar, Button As Integer, _
    FloatingImage As PictureBox)
Dim Index As Integer
Dim Index2 As Integer
Dim LinkSubject As String
Dim LinkSubjectFile As String
Dim LinkSubjectLink As String
```

```
    ' Check for loaded form
    If TextPicBox.CurrentY = 0 Then Exit Sub
    ' Step through Hypertext links
    For Index = 0 To LinkArrayPos
        If (X > HyperLinkArray(Index).Left) And _
           (X < HyperLinkArray(Index).Right) And _
           (Y > HyperLinkArray(Index).Top) And _
           (Y < HyperLinkArray(Index).Bottom) Then
           LinkSubject = HyperLinkArray(Index).DestinationSubject
           If ScriptRunning Then Escape = True
           DoHyperMediaJump LinkSubject, TextPicBox, ImagePicBox, FloatingImage, _
               ScrollBar, Button
           Exit For
        End If
    Next Index
    ' Change value of scroll bar to reflect size of document
    ScrollBar.VALUE = -TextPicBox.Top
End Sub


Sub ImageClick(TextPicBox As PictureBox, ImagePicBox As Image, FloatingImage _
    As PictureBox, X As Single, Y As Single, Button As Integer, ScrollBar As _
    VScrollBar, ImageRatio As Double)
Dim LinkSubject As String

    If Button = 2 Then
        FloatingImage.Parent.Caption = "Original Image"
        Set FloatingImage.picture = ImagePicBox.picture
        FloatingImage.Parent.Show
    Else
        LinkSubject = TargetFromPointInImage(X, Y, ImageRatio)
        DoHyperMediaJump LinkSubject, TextPicBox, ImagePicBox, FloatingImage, _
            ScrollBar, 1
    End If
End Sub



Private Sub NewLine(TextPicBox As PictureBox)
    TextPicBox.Print
End Sub



Private Sub ParseHTML(HTML, TextPicBox As PictureBox, ImagePicBox As Image)
Dim TempColor As Long
Dim TempFontSize As Integer
Dim TempUnderline As Boolean
Dim LinkSubject As String
Dim LinkSubjectFile As String
Dim LinkSubjectLink As String
Dim LinkType As String
Dim HRSize As Integer

    ' Switch to all uppercase and pull off first two characters
    Select Case (Left(UCase(HTML), 2))
```

```
Case "H1"        'Heading 1
   If TextPicBox.CurrentX > 0 Then NewLine TextPicBox
   TextPicBox.Font.Size = 24
Case "H2"        'Heading 2
   If TextPicBox.CurrentX > 0 Then NewLine TextPicBox
   TextPicBox.Font.Size = 21
Case "H3"        'Heading 3
   If TextPicBox.CurrentX > 0 Then NewLine TextPicBox
   TextPicBox.Font.Size = 18
Case "H4"        'Heading 4
   If TextPicBox.CurrentX > 0 Then NewLine TextPicBox
   TextPicBox.Font.Size = 15
Case "H5"        'Heading 5
   If TextPicBox.CurrentX > 0 Then NewLine TextPicBox
   TextPicBox.Font.Size = 9
Case "H6"        'Heading 6
   If TextPicBox.CurrentX > 0 Then NewLine TextPicBox
   TextPicBox.Font.Size = 6
Case "/H"        'Bold On
   If TextPicBox.CurrentX > 0 Then NewLine TextPicBox
   TextPicBox.Font.Size = 12
Case "B"         'Bold On
   TextPicBox.Font.Bold = True
Case "/B"        'Bold Off
   TextPicBox.Font.Bold = False
Case "U"         'Underline On
   TextPicBox.Font.Underline = True
Case "/U"        'Underline Off
   TextPicBox.Font.Underline = False
Case "I"         'Italic On
   TextPicBox.Font.Italic = True
Case "/I"        'Italic Off
   TextPicBox.Font.Italic = False
Case "BR"        'Line Break
   NewLine TextPicBox
Case "P", "/P" 'End Paragraph
   If TextPicBox.CurrentX > 0 Then NewLine TextPicBox
   NewLine TextPicBox
Case "HR"               'Horizontal Rule
   TextPicBox.ScaleMode = 3
   ' Check for 'SIZE' tag within HTML
   If InStr(UCase(HTML), "SIZE=") Then
      HRSize = Val(Right(HTML, Len(HTML) - InStr(HTML, "SIZE=") - 4))
   Else
      HRSize = 1
   End If
   If TextPicBox.CurrentX > 0 Then NewLine TextPicBox
   TempColor = TextPicBox.ForeColor ' Store previous foreground(font) color
   TextPicBox.ForeColor = vbBlack
   ' Draw horizontal and vertical portions of black section of rectangle
   TextPicBox.Line (0, (TextPicBox.CurrentY + (TextPicBox.TextHeight("A") _
      / 2)))- _
      (TextPicBox.ScaleWidth - 1, (TextPicBox.CurrentY + _
         (TextPicBox.TextHeight("A") / 2)))
```

```
        TextPicBox.Line (0, TextPicBox.CurrentY)-(0, TextPicBox.CurrentY + 1 _
            + HRSize)
        TextPicBox.ForeColor = vbWhite
        ' Draw horizontal and vertical portions of white section of rectangle
        TextPicBox.Line (1, (TextPicBox.CurrentY))-(TextPicBox.ScaleWidth, _
            (TextPicBox.CurrentY))
        TextPicBox.Line (TextPicBox.ScaleWidth - 1, TextPicBox.CurrentY - _
            HRSize)-(TextPicBox.ScaleWidth - 1, TextPicBox.CurrentY)
        TextPicBox.ForeColor = TempColor ' Reset to old color
        TextPicBox.CurrentY = TextPicBox.CurrentY + _
            TextPicBox.TextHeight("A") / 2
        TextPicBox.CurrentX = 0
        TextPicBox.ScaleMode = 1
Case "A "        'Begin Link or Anchor
    ' If there are quotation marks present, then we know
    ' that the link subject is the string between the quotation marks.
    ' Else take everything from the right of the equal sign
    ' up to, but not including, the next space encountered.
    If InStr(HTML, Chr$(34)) Then
        LinkSubject = Right(HTML, ((Len(HTML) - InStr(HTML, Chr$(34)))))
        If InStr(HTML, Chr$(34)) Then
            LinkSubject = Left(LinkSubject, InStr(LinkSubject, Chr$(34)) - 1)
        End If
    Else
        LinkSubject = Right(HTML, ((Len(HTML) - InStr(HTML, Chr$(61)))))
        If InStr(LinkSubject, Chr$(32)) Then
            LinkSubject = Left(LinkSubject, InStr(LinkSubject, Chr$(32)) - 1)
        End If
    End If
    ' The link type is the variable before the subject.
    ' So, lets grab the characters between up to the
    ' equal sign first, then strip off everything up
    ' to the final space.
    LinkType = Left(HTML, InStr(HTML, Chr$(61)) - 1)
    While InStr(LinkType, Chr$(32))
        LinkType = Right(LinkType, ((Len(LinkType) - InStr(LinkType, _
            Chr$(32)))))
    Wend
    Select Case LinkType
        Case "HREF" ' Hypermedia Jump
            If Not IsLink Then
                TempColor = TextPicBox.ForeColor
                TempUnderline = TextPicBox.Font.Underline
                TextPicBox.ForeColor = vbBlue
                TextPicBox.Font.Underline = True
                HyperLinkArray(LinkArrayPos).DestinationSubject = LinkSubject
                HyperLinkArray(LinkArrayPos).Top = TextPicBox.CurrentY
                HyperLinkArray(LinkArrayPos).Left = TextPicBox.CurrentX
                IsLink = True
            End If
        Case "NAME" ' Anchor
            AnchorArray(AnchorArrayPos).Name = UCase(LinkSubject)
            AnchorArray(AnchorArrayPos).VPosition = TextPicBox.CurrentY
            AnchorArrayPos = AnchorArrayPos + 1
```

```
                End Select
            Case "/A"         'End link
                If IsLink Then
                    HyperLinkArray(LinkArrayPos).Bottom = TextPicBox.CurrentY + _
                        TextPicBox.TextHeight("A")
                    HyperLinkArray(LinkArrayPos).Right = TextPicBox.CurrentX
                    LinkArrayPos = LinkArrayPos + 1
                    TextPicBox.ForeColor = TempColor
                    TextPicBox.Font.Underline = TempUnderline
                    IsLink = False
                End If
        End Select
End Sub


Private Sub ParseText(Text As String, TextPicBox As PictureBox, ImagePicBox As
Image, ScrollBar As VScrollBar)
    ' Reset PictureBox
    TextPicBox.Cls
    TextPicBox.Top = 0
    TextPicBox.Height = 10000
    ' Initialize Arrays
    Erase HyperLinkArray
    LinkArrayPos = 0
    Erase AnchorArray
    AnchorArrayPos = 0
    ' Set base text attributes
    TextPicBox.ForeColor = BLACK
    TextPicBox.FontBold = False
    TextPicBox.FontUnderline = False
    TextPicBox.FontItalic = False
    TextPicBox.FontStrikethru = False
    TextPicBox.FontSize = 12
    ' Check to see if there is any HTML tags in the string
    If InStr(Text, "<") Then
        While InStr(Text, "<") ' Don't stop parsing until all tags are gone
            ' Print line up to tag
            PrintLine Left(Text, InStr(Text, "<") - 1), TextPicBox
            ' Pull HTML info from tag and parse
            ParseHTML Mid(Text, InStr(Text, "<") + 1, InStr(Text, ">") - 1 - _
                InStr(Text, "<")), TextPicBox, ImagePicBox
            ' Strip away text up to the end of the HTML tag
            Text = Right(Text, Len(Text) - InStr(Text, ">"))
        Wend
    End If
    ' Print remaining string
    PrintLine Text, TextPicBox
    NewLine TextPicBox
    TextPicBox.Height = TextPicBox.CurrentY
    ScrollBar.MAX = TextPicBox.CurrentY
    ScrollBar.LargeChange = TextPicBox.Parent.Height
End Sub
```

```
Private Sub PrintLine(Text, TextPicBox As PictureBox)
Dim NextWord As String

    While InStr(Text, Chr$(32)) 'While there is a space
        NextWord = Left(Text, InStr(Text, Chr$(32))) 'Copy first word from
                                                     'text string
        Text = Right(Text, (Len(Text) - InStr(Text, Chr$(32)))) 'Clip first word
        If (TextPicBox.CurrentX + TextPicBox.TextWidth(NextWord)) > _
            TextPicBox.ScaleWidth Then
            If TextPicBox.ForeColor = vbBlue Then 'Truncated Link
                HyperLinkArray(LinkArrayPos).Bottom = TextPicBox.CurrentY + _
                    TextPicBox.TextHeight("A")
                HyperLinkArray(LinkArrayPos).Right = TextPicBox.CurrentX
                LinkArrayPos = LinkArrayPos + 1
                HyperLinkArray(LinkArrayPos).DestinationSubject = _
                    HyperLinkArray(LinkArrayPos - 1).DestinationSubject
            End If
            NewLine TextPicBox
            HyperLinkArray(LinkArrayPos).Top = TextPicBox.CurrentY
            HyperLinkArray(LinkArrayPos).Left = TextPicBox.CurrentX
            TextPicBox.Print NextWord;
        Else
            TextPicBox.Print NextWord;
        End If
    Wend
    'Clean-up and print remaining text
    If (TextPicBox.CurrentX + TextPicBox.TextWidth(NextWord)) > _
        TextPicBox.ScaleWidth Then
        If TextPicBox.ForeColor = vbBlue Then 'Truncated Link
            HyperLinkArray(LinkArrayPos).Bottom = TextPicBox.CurrentY + _
                TextPicBox.TextHeight("A")
            HyperLinkArray(LinkArrayPos).Right = TextPicBox.CurrentX
            LinkArrayPos = LinkArrayPos + 1
            HyperLinkArray(LinkArrayPos).DestinationSubject = _
                HyperLinkArray(LinkArrayPos - 1).DestinationSubject
        End If
        NewLine TextPicBox
        HyperLinkArray(LinkArrayPos).Top = TextPicBox.CurrentY
        HyperLinkArray(LinkArrayPos).Left = TextPicBox.CurrentX
        TextPicBox.Print Text;
    Else
        TextPicBox.Print Text;
    End If
End Sub
```

Extending the Multimedia Engine

Well, that's it! You now have a great base for building your ultimate multimedia project. Don't be afraid to experiment with the HTML, database-driven engine. Try to find ways to customize it, and make it run faster and smoother. If we had time, we could probably write an entire book about things you could do to customize the engine. We will say that customizing the look and feel of the interface would be a good place to start. Try using custom graphics, tool bars, and non-standard images. If you were creating a program for an accounting office, it would be all right to use the standard Windows look and feel. But this is hypermedia, and it is important to find your own "custom" design.

Now that we have created the hypermedia project, let's go back to the hypertext engine that we started this chapter with, and turn it into a Web browser!

We're now going to turn our hypermedia application into a powerful HTML document browser.

The Hypermedia Engine at Work— Building an HTML Browser

The hypermedia project we created in the previous chapter pulled together many of the core elements of a multimedia presentation system. From there we could expand the interface to build all kinds of exciting multimedia projects. But there's another aspect of interactive multimedia: the on-line connection. The World Wide Web, a subset of the Internet, serves up multimedia on a global scale. The future of multimedia may very well be on-line. So in this chapter we're going to take the same hypermedia engine and build it into a highly-functional HTML Web browser. To accomplish this, we need to take a step backward before we leap forward. We will start with the first version of the hypermedia engine, HYPRMED1, and slowly build on it. Only this time, we will focus on displaying documents rather than on displaying multimedia elements.

We need to start by developing a plan for building our Web browser. Here are some of the initial design questions we need to consider:

- What should the form look like?
- What type of interface should we use?
- Should we provide a menu for the HTML viewer?
- Should we include a status bar or command buttons?
- What additional HTML features should the browser support?

Building a Web browser is a big undertaking. There are a number of features we can include and topics to cover including page layout, coding style, user interface design, HTML standards, Web page navigation techniques, and so on. We could have easily written an entire book just on how to build a Web browser! Obviously, we had to scale back our discussion somewhat, since we need to cover our browser in a single chapter. Luckily, most of the HTML engine has been developed and explained in previous chapters. So, in this chapter, we can focus on the finer points of developing a user-friendly interface and customizing our HTML engine.

We'll start by using the multimedia engine developed in the previous chapter. We'll modify the code for this project so that we can add user interface features to our browser, then go a little further and extend the capabilities of our browser by adding support for HTML lists and inline images. Our browser will implement many of the basic HTML tags, but the best part is that you'll easily be able to extend the browser and provide support for additional HTML features as the World Wide Web continues to grow.

User Interface Issues

The multimedia application we built in the previous chapter had a fairly standard user-interface. If you were going to update the engine further for inclusion in a distributed product, you would probably update the interface by including fancy buttons, interesting graphics, and a good color scheme. This is the wise approach to take for a consumer-oriented multimedia product, but what about a more utility-oriented product like a Web browser?

When you create your own multimedia product, you can easily use non-standard colors, fancy graphics, and unique icons and buttons to improve the look and feel of your product, because you are in control of the content that is displayed. However, with an application like a Web browser, the program serves merely as a shell or a tool for displaying information created by other people. Thus, you need to design your interface accordingly.

Our first requirement is to determine who is going to be using our HTML browser. If we were planning to create a browser to be used by all types of people, we would want a standard interface that is very intuitive and easy to use. If our browser was going to be used for a specialized application such as an in-house document viewer, we could customize it further, maybe by adding features like a company logo or company colors.

Since we don't know what you will use this technology for, we are going to develop a fairly standard-looking Windows application, using only the custom controls that come with VB 4. We will not use any custom fonts, nonstandard color schemes, or anything else that is unnecessary for this application. Of course, after learning how the browser works, you can easily add your own customization features.

Repackaging the Hypermedia Engine

Let's begin by looking back at the first project presented in the previous chapter. In that project, we created the HYPRMED1 application that included our HTML engine and basic imaging techniques. Because we put the entire HTML engine within a single module, it's a great place to begin.

Let's examine what that project did and determine what features we need to add or subtract. First, we can get rid of the image window and all the code that activates it. In exchange, we'll add code that places the images directly into our text window and in-between text, just as in other Web browsers. Next, we can stretch the text window to fill the entire client area. We will need to add some buttons for traversing HTML documents and opening new ones. We should also add a status bar to give feedback to the user. These are just a few of the features we are going to add, so let's get started.

The First Stage of Our HTML Document Browser

This project presents the initial changes to our hypermedia engine that will serve as the beginnings of an HTML document browser.

1. Copy the form and code modules from HYPRMED1.VBP. This project was created in Chapter 11 and can be found on the companion CD-ROM in the \VBMAGIC\HYPRMED1 subdirectory.

2. Open a new VB project file called BROWSER1.VBP.

3. Add the files copied from the HYPRMED1 project and rename them to match the main file name.

4. Modify the main form (Figure 12.2).

5. Modify the **MouseClick()**, **ParseHTML()**, and **ParseText()** sub-routines (Listings 12.1 to 12.3).

6. Add the **MouseMove()** subroutine (Listing 12.4).

7. Add the code for the **TextPicBox_MouseMove()** and **PictureFrame_MouseMove()** events (Listings 12.5 and 12.6).

 You'll find this project in the subdirectory \VBMAGIC\BROWSER1 in the files BROWSER1.VBP, BROWSER1.FRM, BROWSER1.BAS, and GLOBCONS.BAS. You will also need the new HTML files and related media files.

Preparing the Project

We are going to use most of the code in HYPRMED1.FRM and HYPRMED1.BAS, with only a few changes here and there, so the best way to start the project is to make copies of those files. Follow these steps:

1. Use the Windows 95 Explorer to copy the HYPRMED1.FRM into a new directory, and rename it as BROWSER1.FRM.

2. Use the Windows 95 Explorer to copy the HYPRMED1.BAS into a new directory, and rename it as BROWSER1.BAS.

3. Choose File | New Project from the VB menu bar.

4. In the Project window, highlight FORM1.FRM, usually the first entry in the list, and choose File | Remove File from the VB menu bar.

5. To add the copied form module to the project, select File | Add File from the VB menu bar. Use the controls in the Add File dialog box to locate and select BROWSER1.FRM.

6. To add the copied code module to the project, select File | Add File from the VB menu bar. Use the controls in the Add File dialog box to locate and select BROWSER1.BAS.

7. To add the second code module to the project, select File | Add File from the VB menu bar. Use the controls in the Add File dialog box to locate and select GLOBCONS.BAS.

8. Choose File | Save Project As and save the project as BROWSER1.VBP.

You should now have a project consisting of one form module and two code modules. Don't try to run it yet!

Modifying the Form Module

Next, we need to resize some of the elements on our form. Figures 12.1 and 12.2 show the before and after of this conversion.

Now we need to delete the **ImagePicBox** picture box control. Then, stretch the **PictureFrame** and **TextPicBox** controls to fill the entire area. Finally, pull the bottom of the form down to make room for our StatusBar control.

The StatusBar control is a Windows 95-specific OCX that is very handy for displaying status information such as key states, date and time, or help information. If you will be programming for 16-bit Windows, then you can custom-build a status bar using a 3D frame control. The StatusBar control offers the advantages of automatic positioning when the form is resized, and it can also handle multiple panels. Hand-coding these features with panel controls is not particularly difficult, but making them work together, and resizing them properly can be a burden—so why not let the StatusBar control do the work for us?

We will eventually be using the StatusBar to show several things, but for now, we will just use it to display the destination subject of any hotspots that the mouse passes over. We will show you how to create the code for that in a minute, so for now you'll have to trust us. Click on Tools | Custom Controls to bring up the Custom Controls dialog box. There, you will see all the OCX

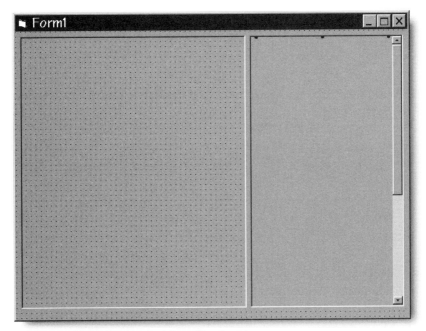

Figure 12.1   *The HYPRMED1 project from Chapter 11.*

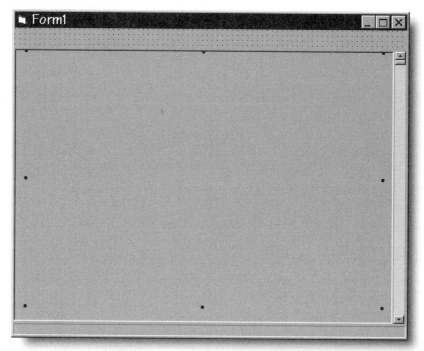

Figure 12.2 *The new BROWSER1 project.*

controls that VB 4 recognizes. Choose the one that says "Microsoft Windows Common Controls." This set of eight powerful controls can be very useful in all types of programming situations. In addition to the StatusBar control, there is also the TabStrip, ToolBar, ProgressBar, TreeView, ImageList, ListView, and Slider controls. Check them out, we think you will find them useful.

To properly configure the StatusBar control, we need to set just a few properties. First let's set the **Name** property to "StatusBar" to make things simple. Next, we need to set the **Style** property. Here we have two options, "1 - Single panel simple text" or "0 - Multiple panels." Since we are only going to be using one panel for now, set it to "1 - Single panel simple text." We also need to set the **Align** property to tell VB where on our form we want **StatusBar** to be positioned. The control can automatically be positioned to take up the full width or height of the control, so all you need to do is set the height or width, respectively. For our needs, let's go with the standard format, and place it on the bottom of the form by setting the **Align** property to "1 - Align Bottom." Then, set the **Height** property to 300. You should also verify that the **Font** property is set so that the font size matches the control.

That's all we have to change, as far as the form goes. Now, let's move on to our code module and see what needs to be changed there. Table 12.1

Table 12.1 *A Current Inventory of BROWSER1.BAS*

Declarations:

Dim HyperLinkArray(100) As HyperLinkElement

Dim AnchorArray(100) As AnchorElement

Dim LinkArrayPos As Integer

Dim AnchorArrayPos As Integer

Dim IsLink As Boolean

Dim Text As String

Dim Dummy As Variant

General Procedures:

LoadHTMLFile()

LoadImage()

MouseClick()

NewLine()

ParseHTML()

ParseText()

PrintLine()

UpdateHTML()

---

shows the functions and subroutines that were copied over when we copied HYPRMED1.BAS to BROWSER1.BAS.

We will be using all of these declarations and procedures except **LoadImage()**, so you can delete it. Now we need to go through several of the procedures and make slight changes so that they work with the new layout. Let's start with the **MouseClick()** subroutine.

Updating MouseClick()

In the hypermedia applications we constructed in previous chapters, the **MouseClick()** subroutine was called when the user clicked on the **TextPicBox** control. **MouseClick()** would then loop through all the elements in the **HyperLinkArray()** array to see if the position of the mouse click fell within any of the boundaries of the displayed hyperlinks. If it found a match, **MouseClick()** would figure out what type of destination it was (image, media, HTML file, and so on) and act upon that finding. For our new program, we only have to change two things. Since we no longer have to place images within a separate control, we can delete the argument in the procedure definition that refers to the "ImagePicBox as Image." You will also need to delete the reference to the **ImagePicBox** control wherever it appears in the code.

The only other necessary change to the **MouseClick()** routine is to delete the **Case** clause that deals with BMP files, since we will no longer be supporting images except those found in the HTML text. Listing 12.1 shows what the code for the **MouseClick()** routine should look like after the changes have been made.

Listing 12.1 The Updated MouseClick() General Subroutine from BROWSER1.BAS

```
Public Sub MouseClick(TextPicBox As PictureBox, X As Single, Y As Single, _
    ScrollBar As VScrollBar)
Dim Index As Integer
Dim Index2 As Integer
Dim LinkSubject As String
Dim LinkSubjectFile As String
Dim LinkSubjectLink As String

    ' Check for loaded form
    If TextPicBox.CurrentY = 0 Then Exit Sub
    ' Step through Hypertext links
    For Index = 0 To LinkArrayPos
        If (X > HyperLinkArray(Index).Left) And _
           (X < HyperLinkArray(Index).Right) And _
           (Y > HyperLinkArray(Index).Top) And _
           (Y < HyperLinkArray(Index).Bottom) Then
            LinkSubject = HyperLinkArray(Index).DestinationSubject
            ' Check for '#' symbol to see if there is a specific destination
            If InStr(LinkSubject, Chr$(35)) Then
                ' Parse file and link information
                LinkSubjectFile = Left(LinkSubject, InStr(LinkSubject, Chr$(35)) - 1)
                LinkSubjectLink = Right(LinkSubject, (Len(LinkSubject) - _
                    InStr(LinkSubject, Chr$(35))))
                ' Check for non-null file name
                If Not LinkSubjectFile = "" Then
                    Text = LoadHTMLFile(LinkSubjectFile)
                    ParseText Text, TextPicBox, ScrollBar
                End If
                ' Search for Anchor and move to correct position
                For Index2 = 0 To AnchorArrayPos - 1
                    If AnchorArray(Index2).Name = LinkSubjectLink Then
                        TextPicBox.Top = -AnchorArray(Index2).VPosition
                        Exit For
                    End If
                Next Index2
            Else ' No specific destination subject, just load file
                Select Case UCase(Right(LinkSubject, Len(LinkSubject) - _
                        InStr(LinkSubject, Chr$(46))))
                    Case "HTM"
                        Text = LoadHTMLFile(LinkSubject)
```

```
                        ParseText Text, TextPicBox, ScrollBar
                    Case "WAV", "MID", "AVI"
                        Dummy = mciSendString("Play " + LinkSubject, 0, 0, 0)
                End Select
            End If
            Exit For
        End If
    Next Index
End Sub
```

Updating ParseHTML()

Now that the mouse clicks will be registered correctly, we need to edit the code that parses the HTML code. Like the **MouseClick()** routine, the **ParseHTML()** (shown in Listing 12.2) routine needs to have the call to the old **LoadImage()** routine deleted. We will not fill in any new code for inline images at this point, but leave the **Case** clause there, so that we can add the code later in the chapter.

Listing 12.2   The Updated ParseHTML() General Subroutine from BROWSER1.BAS

```
Private Sub ParseHTML(HTML, TextPicBox As PictureBox)
Dim TempColor As Long
Dim TempFontSize As Integer
Dim TempUnderline As Boolean
Dim LinkSubject As String
Dim LinkSubjectFile As String
Dim LinkSubjectLink As String
Dim LinkType As String
Dim HRSize As Integer
Dim HRScale As Double

    ' Switch to all uppercase and pull off first two characters
    Select Case (Left(UCase(HTML), 2))
        Case "BR"        'Line Break
            NewLine TextPicBox
        Case "P", "/P"   'End Paragraph
            If TextPicBox.CurrentX > 0 Then NewLine TextPicBox
            NewLine TextPicBox
        Case "HR"                'Horizontal Rule
            If TextPicBox.CurrentX > 0 Then NewLine TextPicBox
            TextPicBox.ScaleMode = 3
            ' Check for 'SIZE' tag within HTML
            If InStr(UCase(HTML), "SIZE=") Then
                HRSize = Val(Right(HTML, Len(HTML) - InStr(HTML, "SIZE=") - 4))
            Else
                HRSize = 1
            End If
            TempColor = TextPicBox.ForeColor ' Store previous foreground(font) color
            TextPicBox.ForeColor = vbBlack
```

```
               ' Draw horizontal and vertical portions of black section of rectangle
               TextPicBox.Line (0, (TextPicBox.CurrentY + _
                  (TextPicBox.TextHeight("A") / 2))- (TextPicBox.ScaleWidth - 1, _
                  (TextPicBox.CurrentY + (TextPicBox.TextHeight("A") / 2)))
               TextPicBox.Line (0, TextPicBox.CurrentY)-(0, TextPicBox.CurrentY + 1 _
                  + HRSize)
               TextPicBox.ForeColor = vbWhite
               ' Draw horizontal and vertical portions of white section of rectangle
               TextPicBox.Line (1, (TextPicBox.CurrentY))-(TextPicBox.ScaleWidth - 1, _
                  (TextPicBox.CurrentY))
               TextPicBox.Line (TextPicBox.ScaleWidth - 1, TextPicBox.CurrentY - _
                  HRSize)- (TextPicBox.ScaleWidth - 1, TextPicBox.CurrentY)
               TextPicBox.ForeColor = TempColor ' Reset to old color
               TextPicBox.CurrentY = TextPicBox.CurrentY + _
                  TextPicBox.TextHeight("A") / 2
               TextPicBox.ScaleMode = 1
               TextPicBox.CurrentX = 0
            Case "A "        'Begin Link or Anchor
               ' If there are quotation marks present, then we know
               ' that the link subject is the string between the quotation marks.
               ' Else take everything from the right of the equal sign
               ' up to, but not including, the next space encountered.
               If InStr(HTML, Chr$(34)) Then
                  LinkSubject = Right(HTML, ((Len(HTML) - InStr(HTML, Chr$(34)))))
                  If InStr(HTML, Chr$(34)) Then
                     LinkSubject = Left(LinkSubject, InStr(LinkSubject, Chr$(34)) - 1)
                  End If
               Else
                  LinkSubject = Right(HTML, ((Len(HTML) - InStr(HTML, Chr$(61)))))
                  If InStr(LinkSubject, Chr$(32)) Then
                     LinkSubject = Left(LinkSubject, InStr(LinkSubject, Chr$(32)) - 1)
                  End If
               End If
               ' The link type is the variable before the subject.
               ' So, lets grab the characters between up to the
               ' equal sign first, then strip off everything up
               ' to the final space.
               LinkType = Left(HTML, InStr(HTML, Chr$(61)) - 1)
               While InStr(LinkType, Chr$(32))
                  LinkType = Right(LinkType, ((Len(LinkType) - InStr(LinkType, _
                     Chr$(32)))))
               Wend
               Select Case LinkType
                  Case "HREF" ' Hypermedia Jump
                     If Not IsLink Then
                        TempColor = TextPicBox.ForeColor
                        TempUnderline = TextPicBox.Font.Underline
                        TextPicBox.ForeColor = vbBlue
                        TextPicBox.Font.Underline = True
                        HyperLinkArray(LinkArrayPos).DestinationSubject = LinkSubject
                        HyperLinkArray(LinkArrayPos).Top = TextPicBox.CurrentY
                        HyperLinkArray(LinkArrayPos).Left = TextPicBox.CurrentX
                        IsLink = True
                     End If
```

```
            Case "NAME" ' Anchor
                AnchorArray(AnchorArrayPos).Name = UCase(LinkSubject)
                AnchorArray(AnchorArrayPos).VPosition = TextPicBox.CurrentY
                AnchorArrayPos = AnchorArrayPos + 1
        End Select
    Case "/A"        'End link
        If IsLink Then
            HyperLinkArray(LinkArrayPos).Bottom = TextPicBox.CurrentY + _
                TextPicBox.TextHeight("A")
            HyperLinkArray(LinkArrayPos).Right = TextPicBox.CurrentX
            LinkArrayPos = LinkArrayPos + 1
            TextPicBox.ForeColor = TempColor
            TextPicBox.Font.Underline = TempUnderline
            IsLink = False
        End If
    Case "IM"         'Image
        ' If there are quotation marks present, then we know
        ' that the image name is the string between the quotation marks.
        ' Else take everything from the right of the equal sign
        ' up to, but not including, the next space encountered.
        If InStr(HTML, Chr$(34)) Then
            LinkSubject = Right(HTML, ((Len(HTML) - InStr(HTML, Chr$(34)))))
            LinkSubject = Left(LinkSubject, InStr(LinkSubject, Chr$(34)) - 1)
        Else
            LinkSubject = Right(HTML, ((Len(HTML) - InStr(HTML, Chr$(61)))))
            If InStr(LinkSubject, Chr$(32)) Then
                LinkSubject = Left(LinkSubject, InStr(LinkSubject, Chr$(32)) - 1)
            End If
        End If
         InLineImage LinkSubject
    Case "H1"        'Heading 1
        If TextPicBox.CurrentX > 0 Then NewLine TextPicBox
        TextPicBox.Font.Size = 24
    Case "H2"        'Heading 2
        If TextPicBox.CurrentX > 0 Then NewLine TextPicBox
        TextPicBox.Font.Size = 21
    Case "H3"        'Heading 3
        If TextPicBox.CurrentX > 0 Then NewLine TextPicBox
        TextPicBox.Font.Size = 18
    Case "H4"        'Heading 4
        If TextPicBox.CurrentX > 0 Then NewLine TextPicBox
        TextPicBox.Font.Size = 15
    Case "H5"        'Heading 5
        If TextPicBox.CurrentX > 0 Then NewLine TextPicBox
        TextPicBox.Font.Size = 9
    Case "H6"        'Heading 6
        If TextPicBox.CurrentX > 0 Then NewLine TextPicBox
        TextPicBox.Font.Size = 6
    Case "/H"        'Bold On
        If TextPicBox.CurrentX > 0 Then NewLine TextPicBox
        TextPicBox.Font.Size = 12
    Case "B"        'Bold On
        TextPicBox.Font.Bold = True
    Case "/B"        'Bold Off
        TextPicBox.Font.Bold = False
```

```
      Case "U"        'Underline On
         TextPicBox.Font.Underline = True
      Case "/U"        'Underline Off
         TextPicBox.Font.Underline = False
      Case "I"         'Italic On
         TextPicBox.Font.Italic = True
      Case "/I"        'Italic Off
         TextPicBox.Font.Italic = False
      End Select
End Sub
```

Updating ParseText()

We will also need to update the **ParseText()** procedure (shown in Listing 12.3) by removing any references to the **ImagePicBox** control. We also need to change the way we size the scroll bar. The scroll bar sizing change is necessary because, by now, we may have documents that are very long. With the old system, you would receive errors when the height of the **TextPicBox** control went beyond 32,767 twips. This happens because many of the numeric properties of controls are still integers. When you try to place a value in an integer-based property that is greater than 32,767 or less than -32,767, an error occurs. To solve this problem, we will preset the **MAX** property of the **ScrollBar** control to 1000, then determine out positions based on the percentages of that value.

Listing 12.3   The Updated ParseText() General Subroutine from BROWSER1.BAS

```
Private Sub ParseText(Text As String, TextPicBox As PictureBox, ScrollBar _
   As VScrollBar)

   ' Reset PictureBox
   TextPicBox.Cls
   TextPicBox.CurrentX = 0
   TextPicBox.Top = 0
   TextPicBox.Height = 50000
   ScrollBar.VALUE = 0
   ' Initialize Arrays
   Erase HyperLinkArray
   LinkArrayPos = 0
   Erase AnchorArray
   AnchorArrayPos = 0
   ' Set base text attributes
   TextPicBox.ForeColor = BLACK
   TextPicBox.FontBold = False
   TextPicBox.FontUnderline = False
   TextPicBox.FontItalic = False
   TextPicBox.FontStrikethru = False
   TextPicBox.FontSize = 12
```

```
' Check to see if there is any HTML tags in the string
Screen.MousePointer = 11
If InStr(Text, "<") Then
    While InStr(Text, "<") ' Don't stop parsing until all tags are gone
        ' Print line up to tag
        PrintLine Left(Text, InStr(Text, "<") - 1), TextPicBox
        ' Pull HTML info from tag and parse
        ParseHTML Mid(Text, InStr(Text, "<") + 1, InStr(Text, ">") - 1 - _
            InStr(Text, "<")), TextPicBox
        ' Strip away text up to the end of the HTML tag
        Text = Right(Text, Len(Text) - InStr(Text, ">"))
        TextPicBox.Refresh
    Wend
End If
' Print remaining string
PrintLine Text, TextPicBox
NewLine TextPicBox
Screen.MousePointer = 0
TextPicBox.Height = TextPicBox.CurrentY
ScrollBar.LargeChange = 1000 * TextPicBox.Parent.Height / TextPicBox.CurrentY
End Sub
```

Wrapping Up the Final Changes

The only other change we need to make is to add support for keeping track of the movement of the mouse pointer. The goal here is to keep the user informed as to what is going on. Eventually, we will provide many types of feedback, but for now, we only want to provide feedback when the user moves the mouse pointer over a hypertext link. The code that accomplishes this looks very much like the code from the **MouseClick()** subroutine. In fact, the first part of the code is identical. Both routines start off by cycling through hyperlink arrays and checking to see if the mouse coordinates fit into the bounding box of the hyperlink. The code changes only in what action is taken when a link is found. Listing 12.4 shows the new **MouseMove()** routine.

Listing 12.4   The Updated MouseMove() General Subroutine from BROWSER1.BAS

```
Public Sub MouseMove(X As Single, Y As Single, StatusBar As StatusBar)
Dim Index As Integer
Dim link As Boolean

    ' Step through Hypertext links
    For Index = 0 To LinkArrayPos
        If (X > HyperLinkArray(Index).Left) And _
            (X < HyperLinkArray(Index).Right) And _
            (Y > HyperLinkArray(Index).Top) And _
            (Y < HyperLinkArray(Index).Bottom) Then
            link = True
            Exit For
```

```
        Else
            link = False
        End If
    Next Index
    If link Then
        If Not StatusBar.SimpleText = HyperLinkArray(Index).DestinationSubject Then
            StatusBar.SimpleText = HyperLinkArray(Index).DestinationSubject
            Screen.MousePointer = 10
        End If
    Else
        If Not StatusBar.SimpleText = "" Then
            StatusBar.SimpleText = ""
            Screen.MousePointer = 0
        End If
    End If
End Sub
```

The code works by searching for a bounding box that our mouse coordinates fall into. When it is found, the Boolean variable **Link** is set to **True**, and we exit the loop by calling the **Exit For** command. Next we perform an **If..Then** statement that checks the **Link** variable. If **Link** is **True**, we perform another **If..Then** that checks to see if the currently displayed text equals the destination subject of the hyperlink that the mouse pointer is over. This is done to keep the status bar from flickering. The flickering would occur without this line, because moving the mouse even a little bit calls the function, each time. And, if we were still over the same hyperlink, the status bar would be updated repeatedly with the same text. You might expect that this would not cause flicker if the text is identical, but VB's refresh is done by resetting the control, which causes a minute, but visible, flicker. If the text is different, we simply set the **SimpleText** property of the **StatusBar** control to equal **HyperLinkArray(Index).DestinationSubject**. While we are at it, let's also change the graphic for our mouse pointer to provide an additional means of giving feedback. This is done by setting the **Screen.MousePointer** property equal to one of the predefined options. We chose option 10, the "Up Arrow," because it gives a nice effect, but does not lose the arrow look.

If **Link** is False, we don't want the status bar to show anything, so we set its **SimpleText** property equal to **Null** by setting it to "". Once again, before we do this, we check to see if the text already is equal to "" so that we don't get any flicker.

Calling the **MouseMove()** routine is simple, you only need to send three variables: the mouse's position on the X axis, the mouse's position on the Y axis, and the name of the status bar control. Listing 12.5 shows the **TextPicBox_MouseMove()** event procedure and the single line that calls **MouseMove()**.

Listing 12.5   The TextPicBox_MouseMove() Event Procedure
from BROWSER1.FRM

```
Private Sub TextPicBox_MouseMove(Button As Integer, Shift As Integer, _
    X As Single, Y As Single)
  MouseMove X, Y, StatusBar
End Sub
```

We also need to place the call into the **PictureFrame_MouseMove()** event
procedure (Listing 12.6) so that if the mouse pointer is moved onto the frame,
the status bar is also blanked. The difference here is that we know that we
want it blanked, so we send the **MouseMove()** routine negative numbers for
the X and Y coordinate. That way, it will never find a link, and will always
blank the status bar.

Listing 12.6   The PictureFrame_MouseMove() Event Procedure
from BROWSER1.FRM

```
Private Sub PictureFrame_MouseMove(Button As Integer, Shift As Integer, _
    X As Single, Y As Single)
  MouseMove -1, -1, StatusBar
End Sub
```

That should do it for our basic HTML document viewer. It is very simple at
this point, but it should display just about any HTML document even if it
leaves out images and a few tags.

Improving the Interface

Now that we have designed and coded the foundation of our HTML document viewer, let's stop for a minute and talk more about our user interface.
The layout we have right now is simple and effective. Since the whole point
of a document viewer is to present the contents of a document without the
interface overshadowing the information that is displayed, we don't need to
worry about spicing up the look of our application.

There are, however, some things we can change or add that will make the
interface more usable. For instance, we offer absolutely no options! Our first
task should be to allow the user the capability of opening any HTML document, not just the ones pointed to in our home page. To accomplish this, let's
take advantage of VB 4's interface to the common control dialogs. These
dialog boxes are the standard dialogs that you will see when you open, save,
or print files. By using these common dialogs, our application will look like
other standard Windows applications. That is exactly what we want for an

application like this, because it provides a familiar interface for all users; they don't have to learn new controls and commands to get around.

Another option we should add is the ability to view previous documents, much like the "Back" command that is used in Netscape and Mosaic. There are two ways to handle this option. First, we could provide a Back button that acts like an "Undo" command, which takes the user back to the previous document. When the user presses this button again, "undoing" the back command, they can be returned to the first document. The second technique is a little more difficult to implement, but provides a much more powerful way to handle recursing. The idea is to let the user press the Back button and recurse through previous documents one by one until they finally get to the document that they began with. If we have a Back function like this, we also need a Forward function to allow users to go forward again, after viewing the document they went "back" to look at. With the Back/Forward system, we need to figure out resolutions for the following questions:

- What should be done if the user backs up a few spots, then picks a link to go somewhere different?
- What should happen to the links that were ahead of a document in the history queue?
- Should links be saved, or should they be erased and a new path started? If they should be saved, how?

Figure 12.3 shows an illustration of how we worked out these issues.

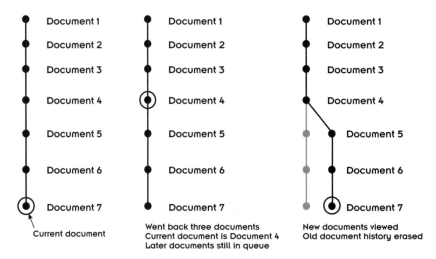

Figure 12.3 The document history chain.

To give you some experience in how the simple and more complex navigational systems operate, we'll implement them both. In the next project, we will use the simple Back button that stores only the last document name. In the third project in this chapter, we will upgrade to the unlimited history system.

Along with providing methods for the user to open files and recurse through the ones they have opened, we need to add simple controls like an exit button. Another feature we are going to add at this point is a text box that the user can use to type in a document name and location, press return, and the document will load. The text box will also be updated whenever a new file is loaded to show the current filename and location.

Finally, we need to be able to let the user resize the main form at any time, and have the controls scale themselves to fit the new size. The Status bar control automatically positions and sizes itself, so we don't have to worry about it. Actually, we only need to resize or move five controls. Figure 12.4 shows you the next iteration of the browser that we will create. Let's get started.

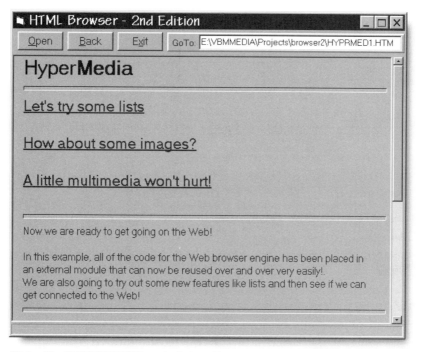

Figure 12.4 *The BROWSER2.VBP project at runtime.*

Extending the Capabilities of Our HTML Document Browser

This project builds on the previous project by implementing some useful user interface controls.

1. Copy the form and code modules from the BROWSER1 project. This project was created earlier in this chapter and can be found on the companion CD-ROM in the \VBMAGIC\BROWSER1 subdirectory.

2. Open a new VB project file called BROWSER2.VBP.

3. Add the files copied from the BROWSER1 project and rename them to match the main file name.

4. Modify the main form (Figure 12.5) and add the new controls and their respective code (Listings 12.7 to 12.9, 12.11, and 12.12).

5. Add the **DoDocJump()** routine (Listing 12.10) to the BROWSER2.BAS code module.

6. Modify the BROWSER2.BAS declaration section, **UpdateHTML()**, **MouseClick()**, **ParseHTML()**, and **ParseText()** subroutines (Listings 12.13 to 12.15).

7. Enter the code for the **Form_Resize()** event procedure (Listing 12.16).

 You'll find this project in the subdirectory \VBMAGIC\BROWSER2 in the files BROWSER2.VBP, BROWSER2.FRM, BROWSER2.BAS, and GLOBCONS.BAS. You will also need the HTML files and related media files.

Updating the HTML Document Browser Project

Once again, we need to transfer the files from the previous project to the current project. By now, you are probably familiar with this process, so we won't elaborate on it any more. If you need a refresher, see the first project in this chapter.

The first step we will take towards updating our browser is to add the new controls to the main form. The changes we make are all centered around the buttons and other controls along the top of the form, as detailed in Figure 12.5. The only other change is one that is mostly hidden from view. That is the Common Dialog control that we will use to let the user open HTML files from the computer's storage systems. This is a 32-bit Windows 95 control, so

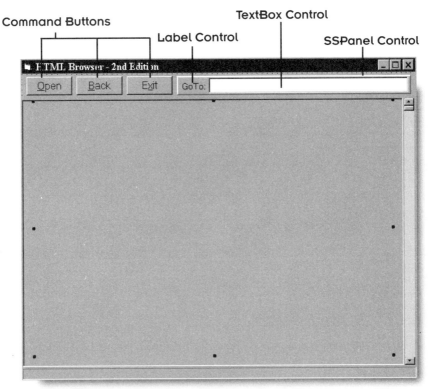

Figure 12.5   *Detail of new controls added to BROWSER2 project.*

it supports long filenames and gives much greater flexibility than the Windows 3.1 version. Place it anywhere on the form and set its **Name** property to "OpenHTMLDialog".

Now we are going to step through each control, and add the code that will make them work.

First, though, let's look at how their properties should be set. Listing 12.7 is the section of BROWSER2.FRM that lists all the controls used on the form and their properties.

Listing 12.7   The Control's Declaration Section from BROWSER2.FRM

```
VERSION 4.00
Begin VB.Form BrowserForm
    Caption         =    "HTML Browser - 2nd Edition"
    ClientHeight    =    7155
    ClientLeft      =    1350
    ClientTop       =    2040
    ClientWidth     =    9480
```

```
Height          =    7665
KeyPreview      =    -1   'True
Left            =    1290
LinkTopic       =    "Form1"
ScaleHeight     =    7155
ScaleWidth      =    9480
Top             =    1590
WhatsThisHelp   =    -1   'True
Width           =    9600
Begin VB.CommandButton ExitBtn
    Caption        =    "E&xit"
    BeginProperty Font
        name         =    "MS Sans Serif"
        charset      =    0
        weight       =    400
        size         =    12
        underline    =    0    'False
        italic       =    0    'False
        strikethrough =   0    'False
    EndProperty
    Height      =    435
    Left        =    2520
    TabIndex    =    6
    Top         =    60
    Width       =    1095
End
Begin VB.CommandButton BackBtn
    Caption        =    "&Back"
    BeginProperty Font
        name         =    "MS Sans Serif"
        charset      =    0
        weight       =    400
        size         =    12
        underline    =    0    'False
        italic       =    0    'False
        strikethrough =   0    'False
    EndProperty
    Height      =    435
    Left        =    1320
    TabIndex    =    5
    Top         =    60
    Width       =    1095
End
Begin VB.CommandButton OpenBtn
    Caption        =    "&Open"
    BeginProperty Font
        name         =    "MS Sans Serif"
        charset      =    0
        weight       =    400
        size         =    12
        underline    =    0    'False
        italic       =    0    'False
        strikethrough =   0    'False
    EndProperty
```

```
      Height          =    435
      Left            =    120
      TabIndex        =    4
      Top             =    60
      Width           =    1095
   End
   Begin VB.PictureBox PictureFrame
      ClipControls    =    0      'False
      Height          =    6255
      Left            =    0
      ScaleHeight     =    6195
      ScaleWidth      =    9105
      TabIndex        =    2
      Top             =    600
      Width           =    9165
      Begin VB.PictureBox TextPicBox
         Appearance      =    0      'Flat
         AutoRedraw      =    -1     'True
         BackColor       =    &H00C0C0C0&
         BorderStyle     =    0      'None
         ClipControls    =    0      'False
         BeginProperty Font
            name            =    "MS Sans Serif"
            charset         =    0
            weight          =    400
            size            =    12
            underline       =    0      'False
            italic          =    0      'False
            strikethrough   =    0      'False
         EndProperty
         ForeColor       =    &H80000008&
         Height          =    6000
         Left            =    240
         ScaleHeight     =    6000
         ScaleWidth      =    8655
         TabIndex        =    3
         Top             =    0
         Width           =    8655
      End
   End
   Begin VB.VScrollBar ScrollBar
      Height          =    6255
      Left            =    9195
      Max             =    1000
      SmallChange     =    10
      TabIndex        =    1
      Top             =    600
      Width           =    255
   End
   Begin MSComDlg.CommonDialog OpenHTMLDialog
      Left            =    9000
      Top             =    0
      _Version        =    65536
```

```
      _ExtentX        =    847
      _ExtentY        =    847
      _StockProps     =    0
      DefaultExt      =    "HTM"
      DialogTitle     =    "Open HTML File"
      Filter          =    "HTML (*.HTM)|*.HTM|Text (*.txt)|*.txt|All Files _
         (*.*)|*.*"
   End
   Begin Threed.SSPanel SSPanel1
      Height          =    450
      Left            =    3720
      TabIndex        =    7
      Top             =    60
      Width           =    5655
      _Version        =    65536
      _ExtentX        =    9975
      _ExtentY        =    794
      _StockProps     =    15
      BackColor       =    12632256
      BevelWidth      =    2
      Begin VB.TextBox FileEntryBox
         BeginProperty Font
            name            =    "MS Sans Serif"
            charset         =    0
            weight          =    400
            size            =    9.75
            underline       =    0    'False
            italic          =    0    'False
            strikethrough   =    0    'False
         EndProperty
         Height          =    355
         Left            =    765
         TabIndex        =    8
         Top             =    40
         Width           =    4815
      End
      Begin VB.Label Label1
         Alignment       =    1    'Right Justify
         AutoSize        =    -1   'True
         Caption         =    "GoTo:"
         BeginProperty Font
            name            =    "MS Sans Serif"
            charset         =    0
            weight          =    400
            size            =    9.75
            underline       =    0    'False
            italic          =    0    'False
            strikethrough   =    0    'False
         EndProperty
         Height          =    240
         Left            =    120
         TabIndex        =    9
         Top             =    120
```

```
        Width           =    570
      End
  End
  Begin ComctlLib.StatusBar StatusBar
    Align              =    2    'Align Bottom
    Height             =    285
    Left               =    0
    TabIndex           =    0
    Top                =    6870
    Width              =    9480
    _Version           =    65536
    _ExtentX           =    16722
    _ExtentY           =    503
    _StockProps        =    68
    BeginProperty Font {FB8F0823-0164-101B-84ED-08002B2EC713}
        name           =    "MS Sans Serif"
        charset        =    0
        weight         =    700
        size           =    9.75
        underline      =    0    'False
        italic         =    0    'False
        strikethrough  =    0    'False
    EndProperty
    AlignSet           =    -1   'True
    Style              =    1
    SimpleText         =    ""
    i1                 =    "browser2.frx":0000
  End
End
Attribute VB_Name = "BrowserForm"
Attribute VB_Creatable = False
Attribute VB_Exposed = False
```

Adding the New Controls

The first new control we will add to the form is the **OpenBtn** command button. When this button is clicked, we want to activate the common dialogs control by sending it the OpenFile command. as shown in Listing 12.8.

Listing 12.8   The OpenBtn_Click() Event Procedure from BROWSER2.FRM

```
Private Sub OpenBtn_Click()

  OpenHTMLDialog.Filter = "HTML(*.HTM)|*.HTM|Text(*.txt)|*.txt|All _
    Files(*.*)|*.*"
  OpenHTMLDialog.DialogTitle = "Open HTML File"
  OpenHTMLDialog.Flags = OFN_READONLY Or OFN_HIDEREADONLY Or OFN_FILEMUSTEXIST
  OpenHTMLDialog.ShowOpen
  If Not Ucase(OpenHTMLDialog.Filename) = Ucase(CurrentFileName) Then
    UpdateHtml OpenHTMLDialog.Filename, TextPicBox, Scrollbar, FileEntryBox
  End If
End Sub
```

The first line of this code sets the **Filter** property of the common dialog control. This property tells the dialog box which types of files are allowed to be displayed. The format goes something like this:

```
Description | Extension | Description | Extension | Description | Extension
```

This format can be carried out as long as you wish. However, for our needs, we are only going to allow three options. Table 12.2 lists the options and Figure 12.6 shows what they will look like when the dialog box is activated.

The second line of code from the **OpenBtn_Click()** event procedure sets the **Dialog Title** property. This property does exactly what its name says, it sets the text at the top of the dialog box to whatever you tell it. In this case, we will set it equal to "Open HTML File."

The next line of code is a little harder to figure out just by looking at it, but is very important. The **Flags** property is used to tell the control how to handle certain situations. Since the common dialog control can be used for many tasks other than opening a file, we won't be able to use most of the flags. But if you want to learn more about them, check out the VB 4 help file, and also look in GLOBCONS.BAS for the section with the commented-out

---

Table 12.2 *The Open File Dialog Box File Type Options*

Description	Extension
HTML (*.HTM)	*.HTM
Text (*.TXT)	*.TXT
All Files (*.*)	*.*

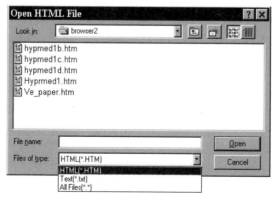

Figure 12.6 *The Open File common dialog box showing the File Options.*

Table 12.3 *Flags Used to Select File Options*

Flag	Meaning
OFN_READONLY	Do not let our program have write access to the file.
OFN_HIDEREADONLY	Hide the check box that gives the user the option to turn write access back on.
OFN_FILEMUSTEXIST	Return a filename only if the specified file actually exists.

title of "File Open | Save Dialog Flags." The three flags we will be using are listed in Table 12.3, along with their meanings.

Notice that we use the **Or** function to string the flags together:

```
OFN_READONLY Or OFN_HIDEREADONLY Or OFN_FILEMUSTEXIST
```

You might think that the **And** function would be the correct choice—but it isn't. As we described in Chapters 7 and 8, the **And** and **Or** functions don't always work the way you might expect. You need to think in binary terms when figuring out where to use them. To simplify things, you could also add the flags together like this:

```
OpenHTMLDialog.Flags = OFN_READONLY + OFN_HIDEREADONLY + OFN_FILEMUSTEXIST
```

However, because it's good to use the same techniques throughout your coding, let's stick with the **Or** function.

Once we have set the required properties, we actually open the dialog box with the **OpenHTMDialog.ShowOpen** command. This brings up the dialog box and pauses execution of our program until the user clicks on OK, or cancels. Once that happens, the **Filename** property of the **OpenHTMLDialog** control is set to equal whatever file the user selected from the dialog box. If no file was chosen and the user clicked Cancel, **Filename** will be set to the last file that was opened by the control. Now that we have our filename, we can call the **UpdateHTML()** routine to update our browser with the new file.

Controlling Navigation

The next button on our form is the one that allows the user to go back to the previous document. Listing 12.9 shows the **BackBtn_Click()** event procedure used to set up and process this button.

Listing 12.9   The BackBtn_Click() Event Procedure from BROWSER2.FRM

```
Private Sub BackBtn_Click()

    DoBackJump TextPicBox, Scrollbar, FileEntryBox
End Sub
```

As you can see, there is not much to this procedure, it simply calls the **DoBackJump()** (Listing 12.10) routine, located in BROWSER2.BAS.

Listing 12.10   The DoBackJump() Subroutine from BROWSER2.BAS

```
Public Sub DoBackJump(TextPicBox As PictureBox, Scrollbar As VScrollBar, _
    FileEntryBox As TextBox)

    If Not LastFileName = "" Then
        UpdateHtml LastFileName, TextPicBox, Scrollbar, FileEntryBox
    End If
End Sub
```

Once again, there is not much to this routine. You may wonder why we didn't just put this code directly into the event procedure from the button. There are two reasons we did it this way. First, the scope of the **LastFileName** variable is limited to the BROWSER2.BAS code module; and second, we will be adding to this code later.

The final command button on our form is the all-important Exit button. We would all like to think that our programs are so wonderful that no one would ever want to exit them, but this just is not the case, and this button is mandatory for an application like this. The code for the **ExitBtn_Click()** event procedure (Listing 12.11) is about as simple and easy as it gets.

Listing 12.11   The ExitBtn_Click() Event Procedure from BROWSER2.FRM

```
Private Sub ExitBtn_Click()
    End
End Sub
```

The sole line of code here simply calls the **End** function that tells VB to shut down this program. We are not using any special databases or messing with palettes in this program, so we don't need to worry about cleaning anything up. We will let VB handle the housekeeping chores.

We added the other group of controls so that users can type the names of files they want to open, and view the current filename. We will use a TextBox control for the text entry and a simple Label control to tell the user what the text entry box is for. We will place the Label control and the TextBox control onto an SSPanel control to tie them together and give us a nice, uniform look across the top of our form.

Of these three controls, the only one that actually has any code associated with it is the TextBox control. In Listing 12.7, you will notice that the TextBox control's **Name** property has been set to **FileEntryBox** to make it easy to keep track of. Now we need to determine when and how to respond to a filename being entered. We could check for the file on each key stroke, or add another button that the user could press that would search for the file. We decided to keep things simple, and respond only when the user presses the Enter key. Listing 12.12 shows the code for the **FileEntryBox_KeyPress()** event procedure.

Listing 12.12   The FileEntryBox_KeyPress() Event Procedure from BROWSER2.FRM

```
Private Sub FileEntryBox_KeyPress(KeyAscii As Integer)

    If KeyAscii = (13) Then
        If Dir(FileEntryBox.Text) = "" Then
            MsgBox "There was an error trying to load the file: " & Chr(10) & _
                FileEntryBox.Text, MB_ICONEXCLAMATION, "HTML Load Error"
        Else
            UpdateHtml FileEntryBox.Text, TextPicBox, Scrollbar, FileEntryBox
        End If
    End If
End Sub
```

The first thing we do here is check to see if the Enter key has been pressed. If it hasn't, then there is no need to waste any more time. **KeyPress()** events send a single argument, **KeyAscii**. **KeyAscii** is just what it sounds like—the ASCII representation of whatever key was pressed. In this case, we are checking for the Enter key, represented by ASCII code 13. If **KeyAscii** returns the value 13, we need to check to see if the text entered by the user is a valid filename. We use the **Dir()** function to check to see if the file actually exists. The **Dir()** function is pretty much identical to the DOS **Dir()** function. You can perform searches for files, check for hidden files, or perform any of the file-related searching operations you can perform at the DOS prompt. Look in the VB help file for more detailed information on this function. For our purposes, we need to know only if the file exists or not. By sending the text entered in the **FileEntryBox**, **Dir()** will look for the file. If it finds the file, **Dir()** returns the filename. If it does not find the file, **Dir()** returns nothing. So we will test for a null return value by checking to see if the return value is equal to "". If a null value is returned, we need to display a message box to indicate that the file cannot be found. If the file exists, the filename is passed on to the **UpdateHTML()** routine.

More User Feedback

One other thing we need to do with the new controls we just added is to give them the ability to update our status bar whenever the user passes the mouse pointer over them. This is done with a single line of code that looks something like this:

```
StatusBar.SimpleText = "Enter whatever text you want displayed here."
```

This code needs to go into the **MouseMove()** event procedures for any controls that you want to display information about, and is also recommended for those that you don't want to display information about. You just need to set the **SimpleText** property equal to a Null string (""). If you don't add these empty string commands, the message from the last control under the mouse pointer will be displayed until another button is passed over, or until the mouse pointer is moved over the **PictureFrame** control. It can be disconcerting to users to see a message that says "Click this button to do such and such" when the mouse pointer has moved to a blank portion of the form. It doesn't take much extra time to fix this situation, so take the time to do it now.

The declaration section for the BROWSER2.BAS code module needs to be updated slightly. We need to add declarations for two global variables that will hold our current and previous filenames. Listing 12.13 shows the updated declaration section.

Listing 12.13　The Declaration Section from BROWSER2.BAS

```
Option Explicit

Type HyperLinkElement
    Left As Long
    Top As Long
    Right As Long
    Bottom As Long
    DestinationSubject As String
End Type

Type AnchorElement
    Name As String
    VPosition As Long
End Type
```

```
#If Win32 Then
    Declare Function mciSendString Lib "winmm.dll" Alias "mciSendStringA" _
        (ByVal lpstrCommand As String, ByVal lpstrReturnString As String, _
        ByVal uReturnLength As Long, ByVal hwndCallback As Long) As Long
#Else
    Declare Function mciSendString Lib "mmsystem" (ByVal lpstrCommand _
        As String, ByVal lpstrReturnString As String, ByVal uReturnLength _
        As Integer, ByVal hwndCallback As Integer) As Long
#End If

Dim HyperLinkArray(1000) As HyperLinkElement
Dim AnchorArray(1000) As AnchorElement
Dim LinkArrayPos As Integer
Dim AnchorArrayPos As Integer
Dim IsLink As Boolean
Dim Dummy As Variant
Dim CurrentFileName As String
Dim LastFileName As String
```

The **MouseClick()** and **ParseHTML()** subroutines need to have the **FileEntryBox** control passed to them so that they can then pass the control on to the **UpdateHTML()** routine (Listing 12.14), which updates the text box with the current filename. Here is what the new calls to **UpdateHTML()** should look like:

```
UpdateHtml LinkSubjectFile, TextPicBox, Scrollbar, FileEntryBox
```

As you can see, the only difference is that the **FileEntryBox** control is being passed as an argument so that the control can be updated.

Listing 12.14   The UpdateHTML() Subroutine from BROWSER2.BAS

```
Public Sub UpdateHtml(ByVal FileToLoad As String, TextPicBox As PictureBox, _
    Scrollbar As VScrollBar, FileEntryBox As TextBox)
Dim Text As String

    If Not FileToLoad = "RESIZE" Then
        Text = LoadHTMLFile(FileToLoad)
        LastFileName = CurrentFileName
        CurrentFileName = FileToLoad
        FileEntryBox.Text = FileToLoad
    Else
        Text = LoadHTMLFile(CurrentFileName)
    End If
    ParseText Text, TextPicBox, Scrollbar
End Sub
```

This code is very similar to the code we used before, except that now we check for the "RESIZE" string, which we'll discuss in a minute. Notice that

when we now load a new file, we set the **Text** property of our **FileEntryBox**
text box equal to the string **FileToLoad**, which, of course, is our filename.

Time to Do Some Sizing

We also need to make a small change to the **ParseText()** subroutine (Listing
12.15). Whenever the form is resized, we will need to parse the text again in
order to format it to the new form's size. Figures 12.7 and 12.8 show the same
HTML document laid out on two different sized forms.

Listing 12.15   The ParseText() Subroutine from BROWSER2.BAS

```
Private Sub ParseText(Text As String, TextPicBox As PictureBox, Scrollbar _
    As VScrollBar)

    ' Reset PictureBox
    TextPicBox.Cls
    TextPicBox.CurrentX = 0
```

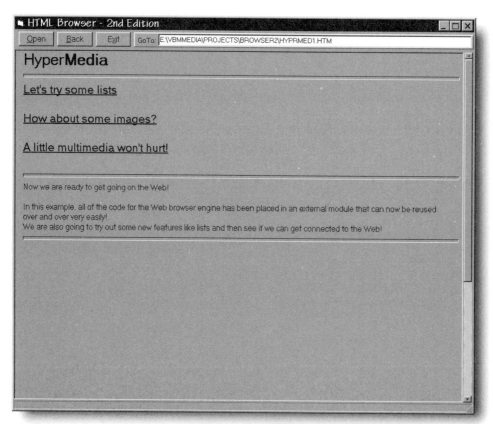

Figure 12.7   *The BROWSER2 project running with the form sized to fill the screen.*

```
   TextPicBox.Top = 0
   TextPicBox.Height = 25000
   Scrollbar.Value = 0
   ' Initialize Arrays
   Erase HyperLinkArray
   LinkArrayPos = 0
   Erase AnchorArray
   AnchorArrayPos = 0
   ' Set base text attributes
   TextPicBox.ForeColor = BLACK
   TextPicBox.FontBold = False
   TextPicBox.FontUnderline = False
   TextPicBox.FontItalic = False
   TextPicBox.FontStrikethru = False
   TextPicBox.FontSize = 12
   ' Check to see if there is any HTML tags in the string
   Screen.MousePointer = 11
   If InStr(Text, "<") Then
      While InStr(Text, "<") ' Don't stop parsing until all tags are gone
         ' Print line up to tag
         PrintLine Left(Text, InStr(Text, "<") - 1), TextPicBox
         ' Pull HTML info from tag and parse
         ParseHTML Mid(Text, InStr(Text, "<") + 1, InStr(Text, ">") - 1 - _
            InStr(Text, "<")), TextPicBox
         ' Strip away text up to the end of the HTML tag
         Text = Right(Text, Len(Text) - InStr(Text, ">"))
         TextPicBox.Refresh
      Wend
   End If
   ' Print remaining string
   PrintLine Text, TextPicBox
   NewLine TextPicBox
   Screen.MousePointer = 0
   TextPicBox.Height = TextPicBox.CurrentY
   Scrollbar.LargeChange = 1000 * TextPicBox.Parent.Height / TextPicBox.CurrentY
End Sub
```

Figure 12.8   *The BROWSER2 project running with the form at its smallest size.*

Now that we have added some useful new controls and provided the user with a method of getting feedback about them, we need to create code that will resize and move the controls whenever the user resizes the form. With complicated forms, this procedure can be very difficult to handle. If you had controls all over the form, it would be difficult to determine which controls should be moved, which ones need to be resized, and which ratio should be used to resize them, not to mention what you might have to do with all the font sizes! Luckily, because our form is relatively simple, we are concerned with resizing or moving only five controls—not too difficult for us novices.

Table 12.4 lists all of the controls that we will have to deal with, the properties that need to be changed, the type of change required, and what the setting is for the new value.

As you can see, many of the values are based on values that were just set in the previous function, so it is important that you keep them in order. You may be able to reorder them if you figure the values out in a different manner, but we will leave that for you to experiment with.

To perform these operations, we need to add code to the **Form_Resize()** event procedure (Listing 12.16).

Listing 12.16 The Form_Resize() Event Procedure from BROWSER2.FRM

```
Private Sub Form_Resize()

    If BrowserForm.WindowState = MINIMIZED Then Exit Sub
    If BrowserForm.Width < 6000 Then BrowserForm.Width = 6000
    If BrowserForm.Height < 4000 Then BrowserForm.Height = 4000
    PictureFrame.Height = BrowserForm.Height - PictureFrame.Top - 810
    Scrollbar.Height = PictureFrame.Height
    Scrollbar.Left = BrowserForm.Width - Scrollbar.Width - 150
    PictureFrame.Width = Scrollbar.Left - PictureFrame.Left - 25
```

Table 12.4 *Controls That Need to Be Resized and/or Moved when a Form_Resize Event Is Triggered*

Control	Property	Action	Value
PictureFrame	Height	Resize	BrowserForm.Height - PictureFrame.Top - 810
Scrollbar	Height	Resize	PictureFrame.Height
Scrollbar	Left	Move	BrowserForm.Width - Scrollbar.Width - 150
PictureFrame	Width	Resize	Scrollbar.Left - PictureFrame.Left - 25
TextPicBox	Width	Resize	PictureFrame.Width - 400
SSPanel1	Width	Resize	BrowserForm.Width - SSPanel1.Left - 120
FileEntryBox	Width	Resize	SSPanel1.Width - FileEntryBox.Left - 75

```
    TextPicBox.Width = PictureFrame.Width - 400
    SSPanel1.Width = BrowserForm.Width - SSPanel1.Left - 120
    FileEntryBox.Width = SSPanel1.Width - FileEntryBox.Left - 75
    If TextPicBox.CurrentY > 0 Then
        UpdateHtml "RESIZE", TextPicBox, Scrollbar, FileEntryBox
    End If
End Sub
```

The first line of this code checks to see whether or not the form is mini-mized. If it is, we know that there is no need to resize the form. In fact, trying to resize a minimized form will result in an error, so it's definitely good to include this line of code. The next two lines of code will verify if the form is too small. If the form is made much smaller than the values given here, you may not be able to see any of the document, so we need to limit the size; if the user tries to make the form smaller than the minimum size, the form will be set to its default size.

After all the controls have been properly placed and sized, we need to call the **UpdateHTML()** routine so that the document will properly fit in the re-sized **TextPicBox** control. You may notice that we are sending the string "RESIZE," in place of a filename. This tells the **UpdateHTML()** function (back in Listing 12.14) that a resize event has occurred, and that we need to use the buffered document string instead of loading a new file.

That's it for the BROWSER2.VBP project. Now we are going to move on to our final project of this chapter. We will be adding support for a multiple document history list, improve on our simple status bar, add support for the HTML lists tags, and last—but certainly not least—we will be adding support for inline images!

Taking the Final Step Toward Our HTML Document Browser

By now, we have a pretty complete HTML document browser. We'll put the icing on the cake in our next project by adding a few new features that will really make our browser stand out. Check out Figure 12.9 to see what our finished HTML document browser looks like.

Our first task will be to change our buttons from generic command buttons to the Sheridan command button that ships with VB 4. This button supports images and text, so it will allow us to use iconic graphics instead of text. We could also show graphics and text, or give the user an option to display either or both.

Next, we'll add support for inline images. This is not as difficult as it sounds if you plan out what you need to do with the images. We will show you how

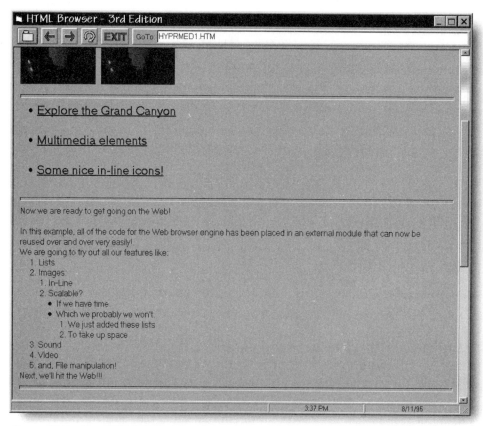

Figure 12.9   The BROWSER3 project at run-time.

to place images exactly where you need them. We'll also suggest ideas for how you can improve on our system to add features like wrap-around text and scaling.

We also need to add support for the HTML tags that display lists. We will support ordered (numbered) as well as unordered (bulleted) lists that can have nested lists within them. These tags are frequently used on many Web pages, so it is important that we support them.

In the previous chapter, we used a very simple system for letting the user go back and forth between the current document and the previous one. Well, now we'll add support for a multiple document history list that will store an almost unlimited number of previous documents and allow the user to step backwards and forwards through them.

Individually, these changes are relatively easy to make; but as a group, they amount to a pretty serious upgrade. So stay focused, and let's dive in.

Putting the Final Touches on Our HTML Browser

This project builds on the previous project by adding another HTML tag, implementing inline images, and creating graphical buttons.

1. Copy the form and code modules from the BROWSER2 project. This project was created earlier in this chapter and can be found on the companion CD-ROM in the \VBMAGIC\BROWSER2 subdirectory.
2. Open a new VB project file called BROWSER3.VBP.
3. Add the files copied from the BROWSER2 project and rename them to match the main filename.
4. Add the declarations section for the main code module BROWSER3.BAS (Listing 12.17).
5. Modify the main form (Figure 12.10) by adding the new controls and their respective code (Listings 12.18, 12.19, and 12.22).
6. Modify the BROWSER2.BAS code module by updating the **DoDocJump()** and **UpdateHTML()** routines (Listings 12.20 and 12.21).
7. Add the code to support the new HTML list features (Listings 12.23 and 12.24).
8. Add the remaining code required to support inline images and a few other new user interface controls (Listings 12.25 through 12.28).

 You'll find this project in the subdirectory \VBMAGIC\BROWSER3 in the files BROWSER3.VBP, BROWSER3.FRM, BROWSER3.BAS, and GLOBCONS.BAS. You will also need the HTML files and related media files.

Creating the Form for the Final HTML Document Browser

Once again, we need to follow the steps for copying and renaming files that we used with the previous two projects. But this time we need to copy from BROWSER2.* to BROWSER3.*.

Let's start changing this project by updating the main form with the new controls. To do this, first delete the three command buttons. Even after you delete a control, the code for the control is still kept around. Therefore, we can now add the new SSCommand controls, assign them the same names as the command buttons we deleted, and the old code will still work. Figure 12.11 shows a close-up of the new SSCommand buttons, and lists their functions.

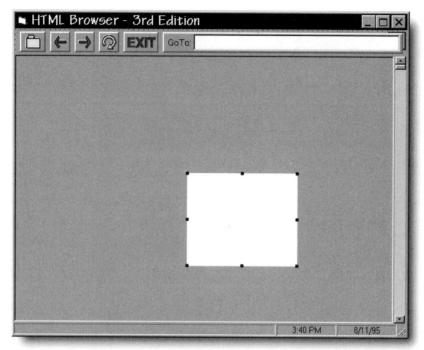

Figure 12.10   *The BROWSER3 project at design-time.*

The open and exit buttons perform exactly the same tasks as they did in the previous version of the browser. The back and forward buttons are used to traverse the document history list. The refresh button reloads and redisplays the current document.

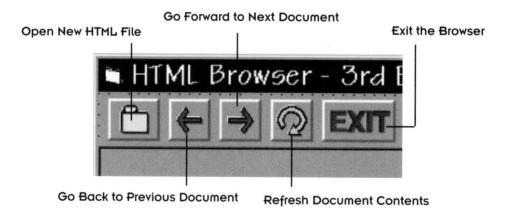

Figure 12.11   *The new SSCommand buttons on the BROWSER3 project's main form.*

The buttons we are using are not standard Microsoft buttons, rather, they are customized buttons made by a control vendor named Sheridan who has let Microsoft include their control with VB 4. To add the SSCommand button to the ToolBox, click on Tools|Custom Controls (Ctrl-T), which opens the Custom Controls dialog box. Here you will see all of the controls available to you. If it is not chosen already, pick the control labeled "Sheridan 3D Controls," then click on OK. These controls should already be loaded, since we used the SSPanel control from Sheridan 3D Controls OCX earlier in this chapter.

Place five of the controls on the form and position them where you feel they are appropriate. Now, erase any text from their **Caption** properties and set their **Name** properties accordingly. Next, you need to load in the images that will be displayed for each button. This is done by clicking on the options icon in the properties browser located next to the **Picture** property, as shown in Figure 12.12.

Figure 12.12   *Setting the **Picture** property for our new button controls.*

The bitmap icons for the buttons are located in the VBMAGIC\BROWSER3 subdirectory on the companion CD-ROM. They are named OPEN.BMP, BACK.BMP, FORWARD.BMP, REFRESH.BMP, and EXIT.BMP. You can probably guess which ones go with which button. Don't worry about adding the code for the two new buttons, **Forward** and **Refresh**—we will get to those in a minute. Let's finish up the changes to our main form before moving on to the code.

The next change we need to make to the layout of our browser's interface is to add more functionality to our status bar. Here is where the real advantages of using the StatusBar custom control come to light. We are going to add two more panels for displaying the current date and time. If you look back at Figures 12.9 and 12.10, you will see, down at the bottom of the form, that two new display panels appear on the right side of the status bar. You may also notice that the panels display the date and time, even at design-time. This is a useful feature that helps you visualize how things will look without having to run the program.

The date and time displays are built-in features of the StatusBar control. Along with them, the StatusBar control can also automatically keep track of the status of the Caps Lock, Scroll Lock, Num Lock, and Insert key states. This is an incredibly fast way to add word processor-like features to a program that needs to keep track of these keys. The easiest way to add panels to the StatusBar control is to open its Properties dialog box. You can do this by right-button clicking on the control and choosing Properties, or by clicking on the Custom property in the properties window. Once you complete either of those procedures, you will be greeted with the Properties dialog box. This dialog box gives you a more organized method for customizing controls, as shown in Figure 12.13. Similar types of properties are separated and put onto

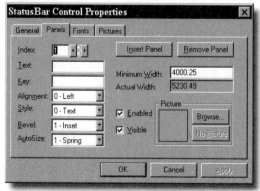

Figure 12.13 *The Properties Dialog Box for the StatusBar custom control.*

individual pages of a property sheet. For example, all the properties related to fonts are put on one page, all the properties that deal with colors are on another.

For our control, we want to pick the **Panels** tab. Here you will find everything you need to customize, add, edit, and delete panels on the status bar. Start by clicking on the Insert Panel button twice and clicking on Apply. Now you will see three panels on the status bar instead of one. Table 12.5 shows you which properties you will need to edit for each panel.

The **Alignment** property works the same with a text box or a label control. To use it, simply set it to the object type you need. The **Style** property is used to set the style for the panel: plain text panel, time, or date panel, as is the case for our new panels. The **AutoSize** property tells VB what to do with the size of the control when the form, and therefore the status bar, is resized. There are three possible settings:

- **0-None** Indicates that you need to set the size of the control if you want the panel to be resized when the form is.
- **1-Spring** Tells VB to divide extra space beyond what is needed by the individual panels and split up the extra space between them. (This is the setting we will use for our project.)
- **2-Content** Tells VB to resize the panels to fit whatever text is inside them.

You may notice that when you enter a value for the **Minimum Width** property, something strange happens; VB changes the value slightly either up or down. The documentation says nothing of this, and we haven't been able to figure out why VB does it, but it does not seem to make much difference, so we won't worry about it here.

Since we changed the number of panels, we have to change how we address the **Text** property. In the previous two projects, we simply set the **StatusBar.SimpleText** property equal to whatever we wanted, or equal to the destination subject of a link the mouse pointer was on. Now, we have to

---

Table 12.5 *Properties Used with the Panel Control*

	Panel 1	Panel 2	Panel 3
Alignment	0-Left	1-Center	1-Center
Style	0-Text	5-Time	6-Date
AutoSize	1-Spring	1-Spring	1-Spring
Maximum Width	4000	750	750

change that call a little bit to tell VB we want to change the **Text** property of the first panel.

Here is what the code looked like before:

```
StatusBar.SimpleText = HyperLinkArray(Index).DestinationSubject
```

Here is what the code looks like now:

```
StatusBar.Panels(1).Text = HyperLinkArray(Index).DestinationSubject
```

If you forget to make this slight change, you won't get any more updates. And you won't get an error either—VB would just ignore the request.

Adding File History Capabilities

Now that we have updated the form, we need to start adding code for the new features that we want to implement. Since some of our new controls are going to be used for descending and ascending through a file list, let's start with that code.

We've chosen to implement our file list using a dynamic array, so that the list can be expanded as long as memory is available. We will use a single-dimensioned array to hold the filenames, and an integer variable to store the current file number. We also need a Boolean variable so that we can keep track of whether the document we are loading is a new one, or a previously loaded one that we are backing up to. Listing 12.17 shows the declaration section from the BROWSER3.BAS code module where our new data structure is set up.

Listing 12.17   The Declarations Section from BROWSER3.BAS

```
Option Explicit

Type HyperLinkElement
    Left As Long
    Top As Long
    Right As Long
    Bottom As Long
    DestinationSubject As String * 50
End Type

Type AnchorElement
    Name As String * 50
    VPosition As Long
End Type
```

```
#If Win32 Then
    Declare Function mciSendString Lib "winmm.dll" Alias "mciSendStringA" _
        (ByVal lpstrCommand As String, ByVal lpstrReturnString As String, ByVal _
        uReturnLength As Long, ByVal hwndCallback As Long) As Long
#Else
    Declare Function mciSendString Lib "mmsystem" (ByVal lpstrCommand _
        As String, ByVal lpstrReturnString As String, ByVal uReturnLength _
        As Integer, ByVal hwndCallback As Integer) As Long
#End If

Dim HyperLinkArray(100) As HyperLinkElement
Dim AnchorArray(100) As AnchorElement
Dim LinkArrayPos As Integer
Dim AnchorArrayPos As Integer
Dim IsLink As Boolean
Dim TextBuffer As String
Dim Dummy As Variant
Dim ImageHeight As Long
Dim ListNumber() As Integer
Dim CurrentLevel As Integer
Dim FileHistory() As String * 50
Dim CurrentFileNumber As Integer
Dim NewLink As Boolean
```

The dynamic array is named **FileHistory()**. We gave it a maximum string length of 50 characters to reduce memory requirements. **CurrentFileNumber** is the variable that keeps track of the file in the array we are presently using. There are a few other new declarations here, but they are needed mainly so that we can support inline images and HTML lists. We'll talk about these variables later. The **NewLink** variable is used to keep track of documents that have previously been viewed by the user, and that are already on our list.

When new documents are loaded, we need to tack an element onto the end of our dynamic array and fill in our new filename, while incrementing our file number variable, **CurrentFileNumber**. When the user clicks the back button, we decrement **CurrentFileNumber** and read in the element in the **FileHistory()** array that is at that location. When the user clicks the forward button, we increment **CurrentFileNumber** and read in the string at that element location. If a user goes backwards, but then goes off on another course, we erase everything that was in the **FileHistory()** array after our present location and start reading in new filenames.

Listings 12.18 and 12.19 show the code from the **BackBtn_Click()** and **ForwardBtn_Click()** event procedures, respectively. These procedures both call the **DoDocJump()** routine that resides in the BROWSER3.BAS code module. The only difference in the calls is that the first argument sent is different. This argument tells the **DoDocJump()** routine (Listing 12.20) which direction to go, forward or backward.

Listing 12.18   The BackBtn_Click() Event Procedure from BROWSER3.FRM

```
Private Sub BackBtn_Click()

    DoDocJump -1, TextPicBox, Scrollbar, PictureBuffer, FileEntryBox
End Sub
```

Listing 12.19   The ForwardBtn_Click() Event Procedure from BROWSER3.FRM

```
Private Sub ForwardBtn_Click()

    DoDocJump 1, TextPicBox, Scrollbar, PictureBuffer, FileEntryBox
End Sub
```

Listing 12.20   The DoDocJump() Subroutine from BROWSER3.BAS

```
Public Sub DoDocJump(Direction As Integer, TextPicBox As PictureBox, Scrollbar _
        As VScrollBar, PictureBuffer As PictureBox, FileEntryBox As TextBox)
    If Direction > 0 Then
        If UBound(Filehistory, 1) < CurrentFileNumber + 1 Then Exit Sub
        CurrentFileNumber = CurrentFileNumber + 1
        NewLink = False
        UpdateHtml Filehistory(CurrentFileNumber), TextPicBox, Scrollbar, _
            PictureBuffer, FileEntryBox
    Else
        If LBound(Filehistory, 1) > CurrentFileNumber - 1 Then Exit Sub
        CurrentFileNumber = CurrentFileNumber - 1
        NewLink = False
        UpdateHtml Filehistory(CurrentFileNumber), TextPicBox, Scrollbar, _
            PictureBuffer, FileEntryBox
    End If
End Sub
```

The **DoDocJump()** routine does almost all the work of traversing our file history. It checks to see if the direction value is positive or negative. If it is positive, we go forward; otherwise, we go backward. No matter which way we go, we need to check if the requested direction will put us on an element that does not exist. In other words, if we just opened our first file and press the forward or backward button, we don't want the **DoDocJump()** routine trying to traverse files that have not been loaded yet. So, we use the **Lbound()** and **Ubound()** functions to see if the element is within the bounds of our array. Next, we either increment or decrement the **CurrentFileNumber** variable and load the requested file.

We also need to set the **NewLink** flag to **False** so that the document to which we went forward or backward is not put into the file list again. Listing 12.21 shows the **UpdateHTML()** routine from BROWSER3.BAS and how it uses the **NewLink** variable to decide whether to add the document it is loading to the document list.

Listing 12.21   The UpdateHTML() Subroutine from BROWSER3.BAS

```
Public Sub UpdateHtml(ByVal FileToLoad As String, TextPicBox As PictureBox, _
    Scrollbar As VScrollBar, PictureBuffer As PictureBox, FileEntryBox _
    As TextBox)

    CurrentLevel = 0
    Erase ListNumber
    TextPicBox.Picture = LoadPicture()
    If Not FileToLoad = "RESIZE" Then
        TextBuffer = LoadHTMLFile(FileToLoad)
        If NewLink = False Then
            NewLink = True
        Else
            If Not CurrentFileNumber = -1 Then
                If UCase(Filehistory(CurrentFileNumber)) = UCase(FileToLoad) Then _
                    ParseText TextPicBox, Scrollbar, PictureBuffer: Exit Sub
            End If
            CurrentFileNumber = CurrentFileNumber + 1
            ReDim Preserve Filehistory(CurrentFileNumber)
            Filehistory(CurrentFileNumber) = FileToLoad
            FileEntryBox.Text = FileToLoad
        End If
    End If
    ParseText TextPicBox, Scrollbar, PictureBuffer
End Sub
```

UpdateHTML() also contains the code that resizes the **FileHistory()** array and adds new documents to the list. If **NewLink** is **False**—as it would be if we hit the back button—we simply reset **NewLink** to **True**, and proceed to load our document. However, if **NewLink** is **True**, we know that we are dealing with a brand new file, and need to add it to the list at a point that is one greater than our present location in the list of files. Before we proceed, we check to see if the file being requested is the same as the open one. If it is, we simply reload the file without updating the file history list. This technique eliminates the problem of having the same filename reside next to itself in the history list.

Now that we have passed all the tests, we can go ahead and increment our current file number variable, redimension the **FileHistory()** array, and add the document to the list.

Our other new button, the refresh button, is easy to implement, because we already have the code ready for it. How did we do that? Think about it for a minute: What are we doing when we resize the form? We refresh the document. So, we can just transfer a line of code from the **Form_Resize()** event procedure into the **RefreshBtn_Click()** event procedure, and our refresh button will be ready to go! Listing 12.22 shows the simple code needed.

Listing 12.22   The RefreshBtn_Click() Event Procedure from BROWSER3.FRM

```
Private Sub RefreshBtn_Click()
   If TextPicBox.CurrentY > 0 Then
      UpdateHtml "RESIZE", TextPicBox, Scrollbar, PictureBuffer, FileEntryBox
   End If
End Sub
```

The only line we added was our standard **If..Then** statement that checks to see if any information has been displayed.

That's all we need to implement our file history features. Now let's see how we can add a new HTML tag to support lists.

Processing HTML Lists

The HTML list tags provide a very effective way of displaying certain types of information. If you have a group of items that you want enumerated and neatly displayed, the list tags are a must. Since they were first supported by Web browsers such as Netscape and Mosaic, it's hard to find a Web page on the Internet that doesn't make use of them.

There are two types of lists in HTML—*ordered* and *unordered*. *Ordered* lists are numbered lists that typically start with the first item labeled with a "1" and each other item is incremented. Here's an example:

```
1. This is item 1
2. This is item 2
3. This is item 3
```

Unordered lists look more like bulleted lists where numbering is not important as shown here:

```
• This is item 1
• This is item 2
• This is item 3
```

In HTML, an ordered list is created using the **<OL>** tag and an unordered list is created using the **<UL>** tag. And, of course, these list tags must be terminated with the **</OL>** and **</UL>** tags, respectively. Individual list elements within these tags are preceded by the **<LI>** tag. Let's look at a few examples. This HTML creates an ordered list with these three items:

```
<OL>
<LI>This is item 1
<LI>This is item 2
<LI>This is item 3
</OL>
```

If you wanted to turn this into an unordered list, you would just change the **<OL>** tags to **<UL>** tags:

```
<UL>
<LI>This is item 1
<LI>This is item 2
<LI>This is item 3
</UL>
```

Notice how the **<LI>** tag is used to define a list element for either type of list. Simple ordered and unordered lists are used to write in HTML and the resulting HTML code is easy to parse. The bigger challenge comes from trying to process nested lists, which HTML supports. For example, you can use HTML to compose nested lists like this:

```
<OL>
<LI>This is item 1
<LI>This is item 2
   <OL>
   <LI>This is nested item 1
   <LI>This is nested item 2
   <LI>This is nested item 3
   </OL>
<LI>This is item 3
</OL>
```

In this case, the outer list includes three elements; however, a second list (inner list) is nested between the second and third elements of the outer list.

To support this feature, our new HTML parser must be able to detect nested list tags and display the list elements correctly. We can accomplish this by using a dynamic array to store the current element location for each level of recursion. We will also need a variable to keep track of our current level. Listing 12.23 shows the updated **ParseHTML()** routine with the new code to handle the HTML list tags.

Listing 12.23   The ParseHTML() Subroutine from BROWSER3.BAS

```
Private Sub ParseHTML(HTML, TextPicBox As PictureBox, PictureBuffer As PictureBox)
Dim TempColor As Long
Dim TempFontSize As Integer
Dim TempUnderline As Boolean
Dim LinkSubject As String
Dim LinkSubjectFile As String
Dim LinkSubjectLink As String
Dim LinkType As String
Dim HRSize As Integer
Dim HRScale As Double
```

```
' Switch to all uppercase and pull off first two characters
Select Case (Left(UCase(HTML), 2))
    Case "BR"              'Line Break
        NewLine TextPicBox
    Case "P", "/P"         'End Paragraph
        If TextPicBox.CurrentX > 0 Then NewLine TextPicBox
        NewLine TextPicBox
    Case "HR"              'Horizontal Rule
        If TextPicBox.CurrentX > 0 Then NewLine TextPicBox
        TextPicBox.ScaleMode = 3
        ' Check for 'SIZE' tag within HTML
        If InStr(UCase(HTML), "SIZE=") Then
            HRSize = Val(Right(HTML, Len(HTML) - InStr(HTML, "SIZE=") - 4))
        Else
            HRSize = 1
        End If
        TempColor = TextPicBox.ForeColor ' Store previous foreground(font) color
        TextPicBox.ForeColor = vbBlack
        ' Draw horizontal and vertical portions of black section of rectangle
        TextPicBox.Line (0, (TextPicBox.CurrentY + _
            (TextPicBox.TextHeight("A") / 2)))- (TextPicBox.ScaleWidth - 1, _
            (TextPicBox.CurrentY + (TextPicBox.TextHeight("A") / 2)))
        TextPicBox.Line (0, TextPicBox.CurrentY)-(0, TextPicBox.CurrentY + _
            1 + HRSize)
        TextPicBox.ForeColor = vbWhite
        ' Draw horizontal and vertical portions of white section of rectangle
        TextPicBox.Line (1, (TextPicBox.CurrentY))-(TextPicBox.ScaleWidth - 1, _
            (TextPicBox.CurrentY))
        TextPicBox.Line (TextPicBox.ScaleWidth - 1, TextPicBox.CurrentY - _
            HRSize)- (TextPicBox.ScaleWidth - 1, TextPicBox.CurrentY)
        TextPicBox.ForeColor = TempColor ' Reset to old color
        TextPicBox.CurrentY = TextPicBox.CurrentY + _
            TextPicBox.TextHeight("A") / 2
        TextPicBox.ScaleMode = 1
        TextPicBox.CurrentX = 0
    Case "A "      'Begin Link or Anchor
        ' If there are quotation marks present, then we know
        ' that the link subject is the string between the quotation marks.
        ' Else take everything from the right of the equal sign
        ' up to, but not including, the next space encountered.
        If InStr(HTML, Chr$(34)) Then
            LinkSubject = Right(HTML, ((Len(HTML) - InStr(HTML, Chr$(34)))))
            If InStr(HTML, Chr$(34)) Then
                LinkSubject = Left(LinkSubject, InStr(LinkSubject, Chr$(34)) - 1)
            End If
        Else
            LinkSubject = Right(HTML, ((Len(HTML) - InStr(HTML, Chr$(61)))))
            If InStr(LinkSubject, Chr$(32)) Then
                LinkSubject = Left(LinkSubject, InStr(LinkSubject, Chr$(32)) - 1)
            End If
        End If
        ' The link type is the variable before the subject.
        ' So, lets grab the characters between up to the
```

```
    ' equal sign first, then strip off everything up
    ' to the final space.
    LinkType = Left(HTML, InStr(HTML, Chr$(61)) - 1)
    While InStr(LinkType, Chr$(32))
      LinkType = Right(LinkType, ((Len(LinkType) - InStr(LinkType, _
        Chr$(32)))))
    Wend
    Select Case LinkType
      Case "HREF" ' Hypermedia Jump
        If Not IsLink Then
          TempColor = TextPicBox.ForeColor
          TempUnderline = TextPicBox.Font.Underline
          TextPicBox.ForeColor = vbBlue
          TextPicBox.Font.Underline = True
          HyperLinkArray(LinkArrayPos).DestinationSubject = LinkSubject
          HyperLinkArray(LinkArrayPos).Top = TextPicBox.CurrentY
          HyperLinkArray(LinkArrayPos).Left = TextPicBox.CurrentX
          IsLink = True
        End If
      Case "NAME" ' Anchor
        AnchorArray(AnchorArrayPos).Name = UCase(LinkSubject)
        AnchorArray(AnchorArrayPos).VPosition = TextPicBox.CurrentY
        AnchorArrayPos = AnchorArrayPos + 1
    End Select
  Case "/A"        'End link
    If IsLink Then
      HyperLinkArray(LinkArrayPos).Bottom = TextPicBox.CurrentY + _
        TextPicBox.TextHeight("A")
      HyperLinkArray(LinkArrayPos).Right = TextPicBox.CurrentX
      LinkArrayPos = LinkArrayPos + 1
      TextPicBox.ForeColor = TempColor
      TextPicBox.Font.Underline = TempUnderline
      IsLink = False
    End If
  Case "IM"        'Image
    ' If there are quotation marks present, then we know
    ' that the image name is the string between the quotation marks.
    ' Else take everything from the right of the equal sign
    ' up to, but not including, the next space encountered.
    If InStr(HTML, Chr$(34)) Then
      LinkSubject = Right(HTML, ((Len(HTML) - InStr(HTML, Chr$(34)))))
      LinkSubject = Left(LinkSubject, InStr(LinkSubject, Chr$(34)) - 1)
    Else
      LinkSubject = Right(HTML, ((Len(HTML) - InStr(HTML, Chr$(61)))))
      If InStr(LinkSubject, Chr$(32)) Then
        LinkSubject = Left(LinkSubject, InStr(LinkSubject, Chr$(32)) - 1)
      End If
    End If
    If Dir(LinkSubject) = "" Then
      PictureBuffer.Picture = LoadPicture(App.Path & "\missing.bmp")
      TextPicBox.PaintPicture PictureBuffer.Picture, _
        TextPicBox.CurrentX, TextPicBox.CurrentY
      TextPicBox.CurrentX = TextPicBox.CurrentX + PictureBuffer.Width + _
        TextPicBox.TextWidth("A")
```

```
            If ImageHeight < PictureBuffer.Height - _
                TextPicBox.TextHeight("A") / 2 Then
              ImageHeight = PictureBuffer.Height - _
                TextPicBox.TextHeight("A") / 2
            End If
            PictureBuffer.Picture = LoadPicture()
         Else
            PictureBuffer.Picture = LoadPicture(LinkSubject)
            TextPicBox.PaintPicture PictureBuffer.Picture, _
               TextPicBox.CurrentX, TextPicBox.CurrentY
            TextPicBox.CurrentX = TextPicBox.CurrentX + PictureBuffer.Width + _
               TextPicBox.TextWidth("A")
            If ImageHeight < PictureBuffer.Height - _
                TextPicBox.TextHeight("A") / 2 Then
              ImageHeight = PictureBuffer.Height - _
                TextPicBox.TextHeight("A") / 2
            End If
            PictureBuffer.Picture = LoadPicture()
         End If
      Case "UL"        ' Un-ordered List
         CurrentLevel = CurrentLevel + 1
         ReDim Preserve ListNumber(CurrentLevel)
         ListNumber(CurrentLevel) = 0
      Case "OL"        ' Ordered List
         CurrentLevel = CurrentLevel + 1
         ReDim Preserve ListNumber(CurrentLevel)
         ListNumber(CurrentLevel) = 1
      Case "/U", "/O"        'End Current List Level
         If CurrentLevel > 0 Then
            If TextPicBox.CurrentX > 0 Then NewLine TextPicBox
            CurrentLevel = CurrentLevel - 1
         End If
      Case "LI"              'New List Item
         If TextPicBox.CurrentX > 0 Then NewLine TextPicBox
         TextPicBox.CurrentX = CurrentLevel * 300
         If ListNumber(CurrentLevel) = 0 Then
            TextPicBox.CurrentY = TextPicBox.CurrentY + _
               TextPicBox.TextHeight("A") / 2
            TextPicBox.Circle Step(0, 0), 50, vbBlack
            TextPicBox.CurrentY = TextPicBox.CurrentY - _
               TextPicBox.TextHeight("A") / 2
            TextPicBox.CurrentX = TextPicBox.CurrentX + 200
         Else
            TextPicBox.Print ListNumber(CurrentLevel) & ". ";
            ListNumber(CurrentLevel) = ListNumber(CurrentLevel) + 1
         End If
      Case "H1"        'Heading 1
         If TextPicBox.CurrentX > 0 Then NewLine TextPicBox
         TextPicBox.Font.Size = 24
      Case "H2"        'Heading 2
         If TextPicBox.CurrentX > 0 Then NewLine TextPicBox
         TextPicBox.Font.Size = 21
      Case "H3"        'Heading 3
         If TextPicBox.CurrentX > 0 Then NewLine TextPicBox
```

```
            TextPicBox.Font.Size = 18
        Case "H4"          'Heading 4
            If TextPicBox.CurrentX > 0 Then NewLine TextPicBox
            TextPicBox.Font.Size = 15
        Case "H5"          'Heading 5
            If TextPicBox.CurrentX > 0 Then NewLine TextPicBox
            TextPicBox.Font.Size = 9
        Case "H6"          'Heading 6
            If TextPicBox.CurrentX > 0 Then NewLine TextPicBox
            TextPicBox.Font.Size = 6
        Case "/H"          'Bold On
            If TextPicBox.CurrentX > 0 Then NewLine TextPicBox
            TextPicBox.Font.Size = 12
        Case "B"           'Bold On
            TextPicBox.Font.Bold = True
        Case "/B"          'Bold Off
            TextPicBox.Font.Bold = False
        Case "U"           'Underline On
            TextPicBox.Font.Underline = True
        Case "/U"          'Underline Off
            TextPicBox.Font.Underline = False
        Case "I"           'Italic On
            TextPicBox.Font.Italic = True
        Case "/I"          'Italic Off
            TextPicBox.Font.Italic = False
        End Select
End Sub
```

Let's cut out the section we want to look at so that we can reference it easier:

```
        -
        -
        -
    Case "UL"          ' Un-ordered List
        CurrentLevel = CurrentLevel + 1
        ReDim Preserve ListNumber(CurrentLevel)
        ListNumber(CurrentLevel) = 0
    Case "OL"          ' Ordered List
        CurrentLevel = CurrentLevel + 1
        ReDim Preserve ListNumber(CurrentLevel)
        ListNumber(CurrentLevel) = 1
    Case "LI"               'New List Item
        If TextPicBox.CurrentX > 0 Then NewLine TextPicBox
        TextPicBox.CurrentX = CurrentLevel * 300
        If ListNumber(CurrentLevel) > 0 Then
            TextPicBox.Print ListNumber(CurrentLevel) & ". ";
            ListNumber(CurrentLevel) = ListNumber(CurrentLevel) + 1
        Else
            TextPicBox.CurrentY = TextPicBox.CurrentY + _
                TextPicBox.TextHeight("A") / 2
            TextPicBox.Circle Step(0, 0), 50, vbBlack
```

```
        TextPicBox.CurrentY = TextPicBox.CurrentY - _
            TextPicBox.TextHeight("A") / 2
        TextPicBox.CurrentX = TextPicBox.CurrentX + 200
    End If
Case "/U", "/O"        'End Current List Level
    If CurrentLevel > 0 Then
        If TextPicBox.CurrentX > 0 Then NewLine TextPicBox
        CurrentLevel = CurrentLevel - 1
    End If
  .
  .
  .
```

Whenever we start a new list, we first increment the **CurrentLevel** variable by one. Then, we perform a **ReDim** function with the **Preserve** option (so we don't erase any old data) to make room in the array for the additional information. Since the **CurrentLevel** variable is set to zero when the document is loaded, we have now redimensioned the array to be two elements deep. We really only need a single unit, so we will just ignore the zero element of the array.

Next, we set the value of our array element. If it is an ordered list, we set it to 1; if it is an unordered list, we set it to zero. This gives us an easy way to check what type of list we have when we hit a **<LI>** tag. That's it for starting a list—pretty simple, right?

Now when we parse out a **<LI>** tag, we have an array all set up and ready to go with the initial values set. We check to see if we are at the side of the page farthest left by testing the expression **TextPicBox.CurrentX > 0**. If this condition is true, we call the **NewLine()** routine to drop us down a line. Then, we need to indent the line. Because each nested level of lists must be indented more than the previous one, we multiply our indentation amount (400 twips) by the **CurrentLevel** variable, thereby indenting each nested level of lists 400 twips further than the one before it. Now, we check the value stored in our array to determine the level we are at by evaluating **ListNumber(CurrentNumber)**. If it's greater than zero, we know that we have an ordered list; if not, we have an unordered list.

For an ordered list, we simply print the **ListNumber(CurrentNumber)** value, then increment it by one. If we have an unordered list, we need to display a bullet before we display the text associated with the list element. We accomplish this by using the **Circle()** function to draw a small filled circle in the middle of the current line. Before actually drawing the circle, we need to move to the center of the line by adding half the line height to the **TextPicBox.CurrentY** property. Then, we call the **Circle()** function, using the **Step** argument to tell it to use the coordinates we send it in reference to our current location, instead of using absolute values. **Circle()** takes four arguments: X and Y location, radius, and color. Make sure the **FillStyle** property for the **TextPicBox** is set to **0-Solid**, otherwise the circle will be drawn as an outline, instead of filled. After the bullet is drawn, we need to reset the **CurrentX** and **CurrentY** properties of the **TextPicBox** control so that when the list item text is displayed, it is centered with the bullet.

When we hit a termination tag for a list, we check to make sure there are lists available to delete, then we redimension our list array to get rid of the old list. Don't forget to use the **Preserve** argument to preserve any other lists that may be still active.

Wait a minute—we have just one more thing to add. Due to the new variables and arrays we have introduced, we need to create an initialization function that will correctly set up all the variables for us. Create a subroutine in the BROWSER3.BAS code module called **InitializeBrowser()**, and add the code from Listing 12.24. This routine will be called from the **Form_Load()** event procedure every time the browser is run.

Listing 12.24   The InitializeBrowser() Subroutine from BROWSER3.BAS

```
Sub InitializeBrowser()
   NewLink = True
   CurrentFileNumber = -1
   CurrentLevel = 0
   ReDim Filehistory(0)
End Sub
```

Finally, Let's See Some Images!

Last, but not least, let's add support for inline images. Thanks to a new graphics method named **PaintPicture**, the task of adding images to our HTML browser will be relatively simple.

The first thing we need to do is add one more control to our browser's main form. If you look back at Figure 12.10, you will see a small white rectangle in the middle of the image. This is a PictureBox control that is used as an intermediate buffer for our images. Set the **Name** property of the new PictureBox to **PictureBuffer**, and set the **Visible** property to False so that the control does not show up when the browser is running. You should also verify that the **AutoRedraw** property is set to False. (No need to waste memory for an image that won't be displayed—all we want is the data and the dimensions.) Most importantly, set the **AutoSize** property to True so that when an image is loaded into the buffer, the PictureBox will resize itself to fit the image perfectly. By using this method, we can easily get the dimensions of the image for easy transfer to our display.

Let's look at the code from the **ParseHTML()** subroutine that handles the image display:

```
-
-
-
Case "IM"      'Image
   ' If there are quotation marks present, then we know
   ' that the image name is the string between the quotation marks.
   ' Else take everything from the right of the equal sign
   ' up to, but not including, the next space encountered.
   If InStr(HTML, Chr$(34)) Then
      LinkSubject = Right(HTML, ((Len(HTML) - InStr(HTML, Chr$(34)))))
      LinkSubject = Left(LinkSubject, InStr(LinkSubject, Chr$(34)) - 1)
   Else
      LinkSubject = Right(HTML, ((Len(HTML) - InStr(HTML, Chr$(61)))))
      If InStr(LinkSubject, Chr$(32)) Then
         LinkSubject = Left(LinkSubject, InStr(LinkSubject, Chr$(32)) - 1)
      End If
   End If
   If Dir(LinkSubject) = "" Then
      PictureBuffer.Picture = LoadPicture(App.Path & "\missing.bmp")
   Else
      PictureBuffer.Picture = LoadPicture(LinkSubject)
   End If
   TextPicBox.PaintPicture PictureBuffer.Picture, TextPicBox.CurrentX, _
      TextPicBox.CurrentY
   TextPicBox.CurrentX = TextPicBox.CurrentX + PictureBuffer.Width + _
      TextPicBox.TextWidth("A")
   If ImageHeight < PictureBuffer.Height - TextPicBox.TextHeight("A") / 2 Then
      ImageHeight = PictureBuffer.Height - TextPicBox.TextHeight("A") / 2
   End If
   PictureBuffer.Picture = LoadPicture()
-
-
-
```

The code left in the **<IM>** tag location remains unchanged. We still need to parse out the image filename from the HTML text. Once we have the filename safely stored in the variable **LinkSubject**, we need to load it into our buffer. Next, we use the **Dir()** function again, sending it **LinkSubject** as its sole argument. If **Dir()** returns nothing, the image is missing. If **Dir()** returns our filename back to us, the file was found and we can proceed with the load operation. Either way, the process is almost the same. But if the image is missing, we will supply and load an image called MISSING.BMP, which will be displayed in the place of any missing bitmaps.

Next, we use the **LoadPicture()** function to place the requested image into the **PictureBuffer** PictureBox. Once the buffer has been filled, we use the **PaintPicture** method to copy the image onto our display form. **PaintPicture**, basically a wrapper for the **BitBlt()** and **StretchBlt()** API functions, is new to VB 4. There are a total of ten arguments that can be passed that tell **PaintPicture** how to display the image. Everything from scaling to placement to ROP code can be passed. In fact, many of the graphics projects we developed earlier in the book could be redone using the **PaintPicture** method. We decided to show you how to do it at a lower level, so that you can build on the mechanism yourself. Because using **BitBlt()** and **StretchBlt()** allows you a little more flexibility, they are worth learning. For this situation, we only need to send three arguments to the **PaintPicture** method; destination, horizontal location, and vertical location:

```
TextPicBox.PaintPicture PictureBuffer.Picture, TextPicBox.CurrentX, _
    TextPicBox.CurrentY
```

That's it, the image is now transferred! Now we need to position our input coordinates so that we can continue printing on the other side of the image:

```
TextPicBox.CurrentX = TextPicBox.CurrentX + PictureBuffer.Width + _
    TextPicBox.TextWidth("A")
```

The horizontal location (**TextPicBox.CurrentX**) is simply the current location plus the width of the image, plus a little extra as a spacer. The vertical location does not need to be changed, but we do need to save the height of the image so that when we have to drop down to the next line, we drop down below the image, not below the current text line, which would allow text to write over our image. If you look back at the Declaration section of our code module (Listing 12.21), you will notice that we declared an integer variable called **ImageHeight**. We will use this variable to store the height of the image.

```
If ImageHeight < PictureBuffer.Height - TextPicBox.TextHeight("A") / 2 Then
    ImageHeight = PictureBuffer.Height - TextPicBox.TextHeight("A") / 2
End If
```

We can't just save the image height blindly, however. After all, what would happen if there were two images on one line, and the first image was taller than the second? Well, the height of the second image would be saved and the next line of text would be printed over the first. That's no good. So, we need to check and see if the height of our current image is greater than the present value of **ImageHeight** before we save it. This means that we also have to make a small change to the **NewLine()** function, shown in Listing 12.25.

Listing 12.25   The NewLine() Subroutine from BROWSER3.BAS

```
Private Sub NewLine(TextPicBox As PictureBox)

    If ImageHeight > 0 Then
        TextPicBox.CurrentY = TextPicBox.CurrentY + ImageHeight
        ImageHeight = 0
    End If
    TextPicBox.Print
End Sub
```

As you can see, all we added was an **If..Then** statement that checks to see if **ImageHeight** is greater than zero. If it is, we increase **TextPicBox.CurrentY** by **ImageHeight** before performing our **Print** method.

Odds and Ends

That's about it for the HTML document browser, although there are a couple more things we need to add. First, the scroll bar works, but we didn't like the way it didn't update the display while you drag the bar up and down. To remedy this, you simply have to add a line of code to the **ScrollBar_Scroll()** (Listing 12.26) event procedure that calls the **ScrollBar_Change()** event procedure. That way, whenever the bar is being moved, it will constantly be triggering change events that will update the display.

Listing 12.26   The ScrollBar_Scroll() Event Procedure from BROWSER3.FRM

```
Private Sub Scrollbar_Scroll()
    ScrollBar_Change
End Sub
```

One other little feature that we wanted to include is the ability to use the keyboard to navigate through documents. For instance, we want to be able to use the Up and Down arrow keys to perform small steps, and the Page Up and Page Down keys to do large jumps. To accomplish this, we'll use the main form as our keystroke watcher by setting its **KeyPreview** property to **True**. This property tells VB that whenever any keys are pressed, to let the form look at them before handing them off to whichever control is active. Listing 12.28 shows the **Form_KeyDown()** event procedure. **KeyDown** procedures receive KeyCodes that represent almost all of the keys of a 102-key keyboard. They are not necessarily ASCII codes, so VB has built-in constants that represent certain keys. For example, **vbKeyHome** represents the Home key, **vbKeyF1** represents the F1 key, and **vbKeyNext** represents the Page Down key.

Listing 12.27 The Form_KeyDown() Event Procedure from BROWSER3.FRM

```
Private Sub Form_KeyDown(KeyCode As Integer, Shift As Integer)

    Select Case KeyCode
        Case vbKeyHome
            Scrollbar.Value = Scrollbar.Min
        Case vbKeyUp
            If (Scrollbar.Value - Scrollbar.SmallChange) < Scrollbar.Min Then
                Scrollbar.Value = Scrollbar.Min
            Else
                Scrollbar.Value = Scrollbar.Value - Scrollbar.SmallChange
            End If
        Case vbKeyDown
            If (Scrollbar.Value + Scrollbar.SmallChange) > Scrollbar.Max Then
                Scrollbar.Value = Scrollbar.Max
            Else
                Scrollbar.Value = Scrollbar.Value + Scrollbar.SmallChange
            End If
        Case vbKeyPrior
            If (Scrollbar.Value - Scrollbar.LargeChange) < Scrollbar.Min Then
                Scrollbar.Value = Scrollbar.Min
            Else
                Scrollbar.Value = Scrollbar.Value - Scrollbar.LargeChange
            End If
        Case vbKeyNext
            If (Scrollbar.Value + Scrollbar.LargeChange) > Scrollbar.Max Then
                Scrollbar.Value = Scrollbar.Max
            Else
                Scrollbar.Value = Scrollbar.Value + Scrollbar.LargeChange
            End If
    End Select
End Sub
```

Also, don't forget to go into each visible control's **MouseMove()** event procedure and add a line of code that sets the StatusBar's first panel so that it gives the user some feedback about the control. For example, Listing 12.28 shows the **MouseMove()** procedure for the refresh button.

Listing 12.28 The RefreshBtn_MouseMove() Event Procedure
from BROWSER3.FRM

```
Private Sub RefreshBtn_MouseMove(Button As Integer, Shift As Integer, X As
Single, Y As Single)
    If StatusBar.Panels(1).Text = "Click here to refresh the current document."
Then Exit Sub
    StatusBar.Panels(1).Text = "Click here to refresh the current document."
End Sub
```

Upgrading the HTML Browser

When we started this book, a browser like the one we just finished might have been pretty hot, but nowadays HTML is changing so rapidly that you'll want to add more features just to remain up-to-date with the latest standard. In fact, you might want to jump in and start adding some of the newer HTML 3 and Netscape features such as backgrounds, tables, scaleable images, different text colors, and so on. Our browser handles most of the HTML 2 tags, so upgrading to the HTML 3 level shouldn't take you too long, especially if you are familiar with HTML 3. (If you need a review of HTML 3, be sure to read Appendix A.)

To help you get started adding HTML 3 tags, here are some design and implementation suggestions:

- **Backgrounds** Before parsing any text, get the image for the background and paint it repeatedly across the **TextPicBox** control.

- **ImageMaps** Create an array of a user-defined structure of variables that would hold the dimensions and placement of images. Then, when an ImageMap is clicked on, load a file that contains the link data. Parse it until you find one that matches the coordinates of the mouse click relative to the origin of the image.

- **Tables** Tables might be one of the more difficult features to add because there are so many options and variables to work with. Once again, though, you could develop an array that stored pertinent information, such as bounding box information, border type, border thickness, and so on.

- **Scaleable Images** Unlike tables, this feature would not be difficult to add at all. Simply parse out **Width** and **Height** variables from the HTML text before the **SRC** text, and use the scaling function of the **PaintPicture** method to scale the image when you transfer it to the display from the buffer.

- **Different Text Colors** This HTML 3 feature would also be fairly easy to implement. At the beginning of HTML 3 documents, colors are sometimes supplied for standard text and link text. You could capture these values in a variable, and use them instead of the standard colors used in our projects.

- **New Tags** The big advantage you have by building your own HTML document browser is that you can use your own HTML tags. If you have a great idea for an extension to the HTML protocol but can't get Netscape to add it, then do it yourself!

Connecting to the Web

To complete the browser, we'll want to add the necessary code to communicate with the World Wide Web. Typically, this involves implementing special Internet communication protocols to send and receive data. To handle some of the low-level details of programming Internet connections under Windows, a special API has been developed called Winsock. Fortunately, we won't need to write any low-level code to handle the Internet communications, because we have a custom control to do the work for us. In Chapter 18 we'll show you how to use this control to add the missing link required to make our own HTML engine a Web browser (minus GIF image support). If you are interested in learning more about Internet programming, we recommend you get a copy of the book *Developing for the Internet with Winsock* by Dave Roberts (Coriolis Group Books).

Optimization Notes

One other item we need to talk about is optimizing the code in these projects for speed and robustness. We decided to code these projects in a fairly straightforward manner, trying to not get bogged down in the finer details of programming a project of this magnitude. We could write an entire book about how to design, build, and optimize an HTML document browser. But with only a couple of chapters, we did not use methods that would take three chapters to execute. One of the concessions we made was to not include information on how to buffer the HTML text. The method we used to display the text and images, by which it is all printed to a PictureBox at one time, is valid, but not very practical for a full-blown commercial product. It is acceptable to use this technique with the HyperMedia projects because the amount of text in one document is usually not very large, and therefore, the size of the PictureBox needed to display the information is reasonable. However, when you start dealing with large HTML documents that include inline images and nested lists, the size of the PictureBoxes required becomes large very fast. And since VB stores the information in a PictureBox as a bitmap, the memory demands can rapidly become gargantuan. We recommend using an array to store the individual lines of text in, and display only the lines that would be visible. This would tremendously cut down on overhead memory, but it would also take a couple chapters to explain properly. Needless to say, we will let you tackle that project on your own.

Good luck!

Animation is one of the more challenging, but fun, areas of multimedia. This chapter begins our extensive animation adventure that will provide you with numerous exciting programming projects.

The Magic of Animation

Animation packs a potent punch when it's used right. Here's an amazing fact: Last year video games generated more income than movies in the U.S. What was their big attraction?—dazzling interactive animation. If you want your multimedia apps to really grab your user's attention, don't underestimate the power of pictures in motion.

The animation used in interactive multimedia comes in two basic forms:

- Movies or video clips
- Graphical simulations

With an animation authoring tool, such as Autodesk's Animator Studio or Macromedia's Director, you can create animated movies that illustrate anything from the formation of solar systems to the proper way to swing a tennis racket. To play them back, you can load them up with our old friend the Media Control Interface (MCI) and let them fly. You can also use MCI commands to pause them, to rewind them, or to skip to specific frames. Playback is a snap—the hard part is creating the animation in the first place. And since this book is not about how to create multimedia elements, but how to use them in multimedia products that you develop, we'll skip the complex subject of animation authoring. In fact, we'll skip this *frame-based* type of animation entirely, until we talk about Video for Windows in Chapter 19.

In this chapter, we'll introduce you to some basic graphics animation techniques, including flip book animation. These are the techniques that game developers use to create fast action adventures. We'll continue our graphics animation adventures in Chapter 14 as we show you how to create fast, smooth, flicker-free animation using some of the new Windows 95 tools.

Exploring Flip Books

Although they often resemble other types of pre-recorded, frame-based animation, flip books give you a little more control at the cost of smaller size. The principle is simple. To create a paper flip book, each frame of the animation is drawn on a separate page. To view the result, you drag your thumb across the edges of the pages, flipping them past quickly enough that the figures in the drawings appear to move. To create a VB flip book, each frame of the animation is placed in a separate Picture Box or Image control. You position the controls in a stack, then use the **Visible** property to quickly cycle through them, displaying one at a time.

The Flip Book

In this simple experiment, we'll use an array of Image controls to turn the pages of an animated book. Follow these steps:

1. Add the SPIN.OCX custom control to your new project.
2. Create the form FLIPBOOK.FRM.
3. Create a **Timer()** event procedure (Listing 13.1).
4. Add the necessary event procedures to the spin control (Listing 13.2).
5. Add the **Form_Load()** event procedure and the declarations section (Listings 13.3 and 13.4) to the form.

 You'll find this project in the subdirectory \VBMAGIC\FLIPBOOK in the files FLIPBOOK.VBP and FLIPBOOK.FRM. You'll also need the VB custom control SPIN.OCX. All of the artwork for the project is in the file FLIPBOOK.BMP.

Running the Program

Figure 13.1 shows what the flip book looks like when you run the program. Try clicking on the spin button. The page will turn either to the left or to the right, depending on which side of the spin button you choose. To reverse the process while the page is turning, click the opposite button.

Creating the Form

Start a new VB project and name the form FlipBook. Place an Image control on the form, set its **Name** property to DictionaryImage, and the **Stretch** property to False. This will be the first frame of the animation, so set its **Visible** property to True. The next step is to set the **Picture** property. Usually you do this by selecting **Picture** in the Properties window to display the Load Picture dialog box, and then select a bitmap or metafile. But there is another way—you can also paste pictures into the control from the Clipboard.

Run the Windows 95 Paint program and load the file FLIPBOOK.BMP from the companion CD-ROM. This file contains a series of pictures that illustrate the turning of pages in a book, as shown in Figure 13.2.

Follow these steps to copy each frame from the Paintbrush file to an Image control:

1. Use Paint's Pick tool (the top-right button that looks like scissors with a rectangle) to outline the first picture, the one in which the book's pages lay flat. You'll need to precisely align the upper-left corners of all the pictures, which means that you'll need to line up the Pick Tool's bounding box (the dashed outline) just outside the image, against the top and left edges. The bottom and right edges don't require such careful alignment, just make sure the bounding box completely encloses the picture. The size of each frame may vary, but the upper-left corners must match.

2. Once you've selected the picture, choose Edit|Copy from the Paint menu bar to copy the image to the Clipboard.

Figure 13.1   *This figure shows the flip book at runtime.*

Figure 13.2 *These pictures are found in FLIPBOOK.BMP.*

3. Click on the Image control to select it (the handles should appear around its edges).
4. Choose Edit|Paste from the VB menu bar to copy the image to the Image control. The **Picture** property will now contain (Bitmap). The control should automatically resize itself to fit the picture clip. If it doesn't, make sure the **Stretch** property is set to False.

Add another image control to the form, and set its **Name** property to DictionaryImage. VB will display a message box telling you that you already have a control named DictionaryImage and will ask if you wish to create a control array. Answer yes. Set the **Visible** property of this and all subsequent image controls to False. Then use the copy and paste operations described in the previous steps to transfer the next image to the control. Place the second Image control directly over the first. To align them, set their **Top** and **Left** properties to identical values. Setting the same property for multiple controls is easy; simply select both controls by clicking and holding the mouse button in the form client area, then drag the selection box around them. When you release the mouse button, the Properties windows will display a property list whose settings will affect all selected controls. After you set the **Top** and **Left** properties, deselect the controls by clicking the form anywhere outside the selection.

The bitmap file contains 16 progressions of the dictionary pages. In the sample program, we have only used 12. You can use as few or as many images as you wish. For each picture clip, add one image control to the form and repeat the steps we've discussed. You might find it easier to align the controls after you've added them all.

We'll need two more controls to animate the dictionary, a Timer and a spin button. You can place the Timer anywhere on the form; it will disappear at runtime. Set its **Enabled** property to False, and its **Interval** to 56 (the fastest meaningful value).

Place the spin button anywhere near—but not overlapping—the stack of image controls, and set its **Orientation** property to 1 - Horizontal.

Coding the Event Procedures

To make the dictionary look as if its page is turning, we have to cycle through the image controls, displaying one at a time. We can't just run through them with a **For** loop though, because they would change too quickly. Instead, we'll use the Timer control to set a more reasonable pace. The **Interval** of 56 milliseconds should produce a rate of about 18 frames per second. In reality, it probably won't, because Windows can't always handle **Timer** events that quickly. Actually, the standard Timer is not accurate enough for most time-critical applications, but it works well enough for many types of animation.

With each tick, the Timer will hide the current image and display either the next or previous image in the series. Take a look at Listing 13.1 to see how this works.

Listing 13.1   The Timer1_Timer() Event Procedure from FLIPBOOK.FRM

```
Private Sub Timer1_Timer()

    DictionaryImage(FrameCounter).Visible = False
    If TurnForward Then
        FrameCounter = (FrameCounter + 1) Mod 12
    Else
        FrameCounter = (FrameCounter + 11) Mod 12
    End If
    DictionaryImage(FrameCounter).Visible = True
    If FrameCounter = 0 Then
        Timer1.Enabled = False
    End If
End Sub
```

When the form-level Boolean variable **FrameCounter** reaches zero, the Timer disables itself. The form level variable **TurnForward** will contain either **True** or **False**, and will be set by the **Spin1_SpinUp()** or **Spin1_SpinDown()** event procedures as shown in Listing 13.2.

Listing 13.2   The Spin1_SpinDown() and Spin1_SpinUp() Event Procedures from FLIPBOOK.FRM

```
Sub Spin1_SpinDown ()
    TurnForward = False
    Timer1.Enabled = True
```

```
End Sub
Sub Spin1_SpinUp ()
   TurnForward = True
   Timer1.Enabled = True
End Sub
```

When you click on the spin button, one of these two event procedures will set **TurnForward** to the appropriate direction and enable the Timer.

Finishing the Form's Code

The **Form_Load()** event procedure shown in Listing 13.3 disables the Timer, and initializes the two form level variables shown in Listing 13.4.

Listing 13.3   The Form_Load() Event Procedure from FLIPBOOK.FRM

```
Sub Form_Load ()
   Timer1.Enabled = False
   TurnForward = True
   FrameCounter = 1
End Sub
```

Listing 13.4   The Declarations Section from FLIPBOOK.FRM

```
Option Explicit
Dim TurnForward As Boolean
Dim FrameCounter As Integer
```

Adventures with Sprite Animation

The most interactive form of animation lets the user move objects around on the screen, usually to do something like shoot alien monsters or scramble up or down ladders. In video games, you often find that you can move objects in different directions at varying speeds, and that other objects, sometimes quite a few of them, whiz around the screen at the same time. If the authors of these games had to create completely rendered frames for every possible combination of background and moving objects, they would find themselves buried in artwork. Every flick of the joystick would need to send the blting engine off on another path, spitting out screen-sized images quickly enough to simulate motion.

Film animators solved a similar problem, decades before the invention of video games—actually, decades before the invention of video. They call their solution *cel animation*, which comes from the term *celluloid animation*. A feature-length animated movie requires thousands of drawings. Each second of screen time requires twelve images (in most animation, each frame is photographed twice to produce the standard film speed of 24 frames per second). That's 720 frames per minute. Animated feature films tend to run about 100 minutes, for a total of 72,000 drawings. But most of the stuff in each frame doesn't move, or when it does, it just scrolls (*pans* in film language) right or left, up or down. So why redraw the background over and over again, hundreds of times for each scene? Instead, the background is drawn once. The characters are then painted on to clear acetate sheets (before the invention of plastics, they were painted on celluloid), which the camera operator lays over the background to compose each frame. This labor-saving method revolutionized animation, and later made it practical to produce television shows like *Rocky and Bullwinkle* or *The Simpsons*, because once the cels of a TV cartoon are painted, they can be reused for other scenes and future episodes.

In computer animation, cels become *sprites*, bitmapped graphical objects that move around on the screen independently of the background—and each other. Just as cels make it practical to produce animated film, sprites make it practical to do real-time computer animation, which means that instead of just playing back pre-recorded animated clips, we can make animated graphics that respond to user activity.

Sprites Over Easy

In this brief project, we'll use the simplest method to move a bitmap around on the screen—with no API function calls.

1. Create a new form named SPRITE1.FRM.
2. Add the code shown in Listing 13.5 to the form.

> *You'll find this project in the subdirectory \VBMAGIC\SPRITE1 in the files SPRITE1.VBP, SPRITE1.FRM, and SPRITE1.FRX.*

Start a new project and place a Timer and an Image control on the form, as shown in Figure 13.3. Set the **Picture** property of the form by loading a bitmap. (Try the file HIBISC2.BMP on the companion CD-ROM.) This will become the background image. If you wish, resize the form so its dimensions match the size of the background bitmap. Set the Timer **Interval** property to 56 or some similar value, and set its **Enabled** property to True. Set the **Stretch** property of the Image control to False and load an image into its **Picture** property. You'll find a set of four bitmap files in the \VBMAGIC\SPRITE1 subdirectory with the names MOTH1.DIB through MOTH4.DIB. You may load any of these images into the **Picture** property of the Image control, or

Figure 13.3 *The SPRITE1.FRM form at design time.*

you may use any other picture you wish.

You'll find all the code for this project in Listing 13.5.

Listing 13.5 SPRITE1.FRM

```
VERSION 4.00
Begin VB.Form Form1
   Caption         =   "Sprite Animation Project 1"
   ClientHeight    =   4395
   ClientLeft      =   2280
   ClientTop       =   2655
   ClientWidth     =   6600
   BeginProperty Font
      name         =   "MS Sans Serif"
      charset      =   0
      weight       =   700
      size         =   8.25
      underline    =   0   'False
      italic       =   0   'False
      strikethrough =  0   'False
   EndProperty
   Height          =   4905
   Left            =   2220
   LinkTopic       =   "Form1"
   Picture         =   "sprite1.frx":0000
   ScaleHeight     =   293
   ScaleMode       =   3   'Pixel
   ScaleWidth      =   440
   Top             =   2205
   Width           =   6720
   Begin VB.Timer Timer1
      Interval     =   50
      Left         =   684
      Top          =   2196
```

```
      End
      Begin VB.Image Image1
         Height          =    1200
         Left            =    1320
         Picture         =    "sprite1.frx":2006E
         Top             =    1545
         Width           =    1200
      End
   End
End
Attribute VB_Name = "Form1"
Attribute VB_Creatable = False
Attribute VB_Exposed = False

Option Explicit

Dim Forward As Integer
Dim Down As Integer

Private Sub Timer1_Timer()
Dim NewLeft As Integer
Dim NewTop As Integer

   If (((Image1.Left + Image1.Width) > Form1.ScaleWidth) And Forward) Or _
         ((Image1.Left < 0) And Not Forward) Then
      Forward = Not Forward
   End If
   If Forward Then
      NewLeft = Image1.Left + 10
   Else
      NewLeft = Image1.Left - 10
   End If
   If (((Image1.TOP + Image1.Height) > Form1.ScaleHeight) And Down) Or _
         ((Image1.TOP < 0) And Not Down) Then
      Down = Not Down
   End If
   If Down Then
      NewTop = Image1.TOP + 7
   Else
      NewTop = Image1.TOP - 7
   End If
   Image1.Move NewLeft, NewTop
End Sub
```

The **Timer1_Timer()** event procedure uses the **Move** method of the Image control to change its position with each tick. The variables just keep track of position and direction. When you run this program, the Image control (with its contents, of course) will bounce around the screen—not too complicated, but it's not too exciting, either. Let's face it, there are a lot of things lacking here:

- The sprite and its host image control cut a rectangular block out of the background.

- The image moves in a slow, jerky motion.
- The sprite looks dead.

Let's explore how we can address these shortcomings.

Animating Sprites with BitBlt()

Image and Picture Box controls will work when we want to move sprites around on a plain background, and when we don't care much about smoothness of motion. But to get anywhere near the quality of game animation, we're going to need the power of the Windows GDI functions.

A faster way to perform sprite animation would be to blt our sprites to the device context holding the background image. This will introduce a new problem: How do we restore the background once we've poked a hole in it? We'll also show you how to perform a *transparent* blt, which will enable us to display the sprite without its white, rectangular background. We'll also cycle between two versions of the sprite to breathe a little life into our moth from the previous project.

Blt Animation

This project shows you how to produce faster and smoother animation by using blting techniques. Here are the steps to follow:

1. Create a form named SPRITE2.FRM.
2. Make special versions of the sprite bitmaps to help us perform the transparent bitblt.
3. Fill in the code for the **Paint** event (Listing 13.6).
4. Set up the **Timer** event (Listing 13.7).
5. Finish the declarations and initializations (Listing 13.8) and add the MINMAX.BAS code (Listing 13.9).

You'll find this project in the subdirectory \VBMAGIC\SPRITE2 in the files SPRITE2.VBP, SPRITE2.FRM, SPRITE2.FRX, and MINMAX.BAS. The original bitmaps are in the files HIBISC2.BMP, MOTHSPT1.BMP, MOTHSPT4.BMP, MOTHMSK1.BMP, and MOTHMSK4.BMP in the same directory.

Running the Program

When you run this program, the moth will fly around AnimationPicture's client area, as shown in Figure 13.4. You can hide the sprites and masks by stopping the program and changing their **Visible** properties to False. We'll set them to **AutoRedraw** when we create the program so they'll behave as memory device contexts. Because we've omitted two of the four versions of the sprite bitmap, the animation won't be too smooth, but that's the least of our problems.

You'll notice that the animation flickers badly. Each update of the sprite triggers three blts to the screen. On some systems you'll be able to detect the separate steps as the mask appears, followed by the sprite, then by the restoration of the background—especially if Windows is busy handling events triggered by other applications. We'll show you how to fix these problems a little later.

Creating the Form

In this version of the sprite project, we'll stop drawing on the form and use it as just the container. Place six Picture Boxes on the form. Set the **ScaleMode** property of the form and all six Picture Boxes to 3 - Pixel, then set the **Name** property of the first picture box to AnimationPicture. Use the Load Picture

Figure 13.4 *The SPRITE2 animation program running.*

dialog box to load the background bitmap and assign it to the **Picture** property. In the sample program, we have loaded the file HIBISC2.BMP. This will become the largest Picture Box, and will become the stage for the animation. Set its **AutoRedraw** property to False, and if you wish, set its **AutoSize** property to True (the Picture Box will automatically resize itself to the dimensions of the loaded bitmap). Figure 13.5 shows how the completed form should look.

From two of the remaining five pictures, create a control array called SpritePicture, and from two more, create the control array MaskPicture. These four smaller pictures will hold the sprite images and their *masks* (more on masks later). Set the **AutoRedraw** and **AutoSize** properties of all four of these Picture Boxes to True.

Name the last Picture Box BufferPicture, and once again, set its **AutoRedraw** property to True. Its **AutoSize** property is irrelevant. Once we've finished loading the sprite bitmaps into the SpritePicture and MaskPicture Picture Boxes, we'll want to make sure that BufferPicture is at least as large as they are. To be safe, we've drawn this control a little larger than it needs to be.

Preparing the Sprites—Transparent Bitmaps

In the previous project, the Image control that contained the sprite bitmap cut a rectangular swatch out of the background. It's pretty hard to create the illusion that the sprite belongs to the background when it always appears

Figure 13.5   *The SPRITE2.FRM form being built at design-time.*

against its own white mat. But there is a way to trim it neatly around the edges and display just the moth itself. To do that we need a couple of raster operations and two modified versions of the sprite bitmap.

In effect, we want the sprite bitmap to work like an animation cel. The moth should overlay the background, while the "blank" area that surrounds it should become transparent, allowing the background to show through. This is easier than you might think.

The first thing we need to do is decide which color in the original sprite bitmap will become transparent. The moth bitmaps are drawn on a white background, so let's assume that white pixels are transparent. We can't just blt the sprite to the background in a single operation because any raster operation we use will either blend the images in some way, ignore the sprite bitmap entirely, or transfer the entire rectangle. The problem is that we need the sprite's own background and foreground to behave differently when we combine them with the background image; the background of the sprite must not appear at all, while the sprite's foreground shape must opaquely cover the background image. Clearly, we need to prepare the sprite and the background image in a way that they can be combined without disrupting each other.

Bear with us while we work backwards. Imagine that the white pixels of the sprite bitmap have been changed to black, which means they reference palette entry &H00 in an identity palette, and that an area in the shape of the moth has been colored black in the background image. If we could get this far, we could use an **Or** raster operation (**SRCPAINT**) to align and combine the images, because wherever we combined the black pixels in the sprite with the colored pixels in the background, the background pixels would determine the colors of the combined bitmaps; and wherever we combined the black pixels of the background with the colored pixels in the sprite, the sprite's pixels would determine the colors. (Remember, when you **Or** any value with &H00, you get the original value.)

That's fine. But, if we can't blt the moth shape on to the background in the first place, how are we supposed to punch a moth-shaped hole? The answer to that question begins with yet another variation of the original sprite. Use your imagination again, and think what happens when you use an **And** raster operation (**SRCAND**) to blt a monochrome (black and white) bitmap on to a colored background. This time, the pixels in the monochrome bitmap that reference palette entry **&H00** (black in the system default palette and all identity palettes) will force the colored pixels in the background to turn black, and the pixels that reference palette entry **&HFF** (white in the system default palette and all identity palettes) will leave the background pixels set to their original colors. So, if we begin with a monochrome version of the sprite in which the moth is colored completely black, and the surrounding pixels are colored white, their original color, then the **SRCAND** raster operation will paint a black silhouette of the moth on to the background. This monochrome version of the sprite bitmap is called a *mask*.

That's all there is to it. You take your original bitmap with its white background and make two new copies of it. Change the background of one from white to black; and in the other, leave the white background as it is, but change all the other pixels—the ones that depict the sprite itself—to black.

Working forward this time, you first blt the monochrome mask on to the background with the **SRCAND** raster operation to punch the black silhouette. Then you blt the sprite, the version with the black background, to the same position with the **SRCPAINT** raster operation.

Converting Bitmaps to Sprites and Masks

To create the sprites and masks for this project, we used Adobe Photoshop. The sprite was easy—we flood-filled the white areas with black and saved them under new names. To make the masks we started again with the original bitmaps, changed their color mode to RGB (true color), and tweaked the threshold curve and contrast until we produced solid monochrome versions. We then saved these in 8-bit Windows bitmap format, again under new names. Next, we opened each mask in Microsoft's BitEdit and converted them back to the palette RAINBOW.DIB that ships with VB (usually located in the \VB program directory). This last step produced monochrome bitmaps that contained identity palettes, so that the images would be compatible with the other versions of the sprites and with the background, which we also converted to the RAINBOW.DIB palette.

Converting bitmaps to sprites and masks can be tedious work. We'll deal with that in the next project. For now, you'll find the results of our efforts in the files MOTHSPT1.BMP and MOTHSPT4.BMP. (We skipped versions 2 and 3—too much work!) Use the Load Picture dialog box to load these into the two SpritePicture and two MaskPicture Picture Box controls. When you're done, the form should appear as in Figure 13.6.

The Paint Event

Now that we have all our bitmaps in place, let's put together the code to display the sprite. Besides the two blt operations that will transfer the mask and sprite to the background, we'll need a way to save the contents of the

Figure 13.6 *SPRITE2.FRM with all of the bitmaps loaded.*

background at the sprite position so we can later restore it. That's why we have an extra Picture Box control called BufferPicture. Take a look at Listing 13.6.

Listing 13.6 The AnimationPicture_Paint() Event Procedure from SPRITE2.FRM

```
Private Sub AnimationPicture_Paint()
Dim Dummy As Long
Dim SrcWidth As Integer
Dim CurrentX As Integer

    If Forward Then
        SrcWidth = SpritePicture(CurrentSpriteCel).ScaleWidth
        CurrentX = CurrentLeft
    Else
        SrcWidth = -SpritePicture(CurrentSpriteCel).ScaleWidth
        CurrentX = CurrentLeft + SpritePicture(CurrentSpriteCel).ScaleWidth - 1
    End If

    Dummy = BitBlt(AnimationPicture.hDC, OldLeft, OldTop, _
        SpritePicture(CurrentSpriteCel).ScaleWidth, _
        SpritePicture(CurrentSpriteCel).ScaleHeight, BufferPicture.hDC, _
        0, 0, SRCCOPY)
    Dummy = BitBlt(BufferPicture.hDC, 0, 0, _
        SpritePicture(CurrentSpriteCel).ScaleWidth, _
        SpritePicture(CurrentSpriteCel).ScaleHeight, AnimationPicture.hDC, _
        CurrentLeft, CurrentTop, SRCCOPY)
```

```
   Dummy = StretchBlt%(AnimationPicture.hDC, CurrentX%, CurrentTop%, SrcWidth%, _
      SpritePicture(CurrentSpriteCel).ScaleHeight, _
      MaskPicture(CurrentSpriteCel).hDC, 0, 0, _
      SpritePicture(CurrentSpriteCel).ScaleWidth, _
      SpritePicture(CurrentSpriteCel).ScaleHeight, SRCAND)
   Dummy = StretchBlt%(AnimationPicture.hDC, CurrentX%, CurrentTop%, SrcWidth%, _
      SpritePicture(CurrentSpriteCel).ScaleHeight, _
      SpritePicture(CurrentSpriteCel).hDC, 0, 0, _
      SpritePicture(CurrentSpriteCel).ScaleWidth, _
      SpritePicture(CurrentSpriteCel).ScaleHeight, SRCPAINT)
   OldLeft = CurrentLeft
   OldTop = CurrentTop
   ' This next statement is optional.
   BufferPicture.Refresh
End Sub
```

First of all, since the moth flies back and forth across the Picture Box, we'll want to display it so it always faces the direction it's flying. Rather than drawing a set of mirror image sprite and mask bitmaps, we can use the **StretchBlt()** function to draw a horizontally inverted version of the moth whenever it's moving from right to left. The **If** statement at the top of this procedure sets a working variable called **SrcWidth** to either the positive or negative value of the sprite width. When you pass a negative width to **StretchBlt()**, it draws the image backwards. When we flip the sprite, we also need to start drawing at the right edge of the imaginary square that bounds the sprite. This is because the blt function will draw the image to the left of the position we pass as the destination X, the second argument of the blt function. So unless we compensate, the sprite will flip to the left, effectively causing the moth to leap a distance equal to its total width when we switch from forward to backward motion, as shown in Figure 13.7. We'll use the variable **CurrentX** as shorthand for the expression that determines the proper starting position for the blt. When the moth is flying toward the right, **CurrentX** will equal the left position of the imaginary bounding square; when the moth is flying toward the left, **CurrentX** will equal the position of the square's right edge.

The first **BitBlt()** restores the background by copying the contents of BufferPicture back to the position currently occupied by the sprite, effectively erasing the sprite. The second **BitBlt()** saves the portion of the background that lies under the next sprite position by copying it to BufferPicture. The two calls to **StretchBlt()** copy the mask and sprite to the background. **StretchBlt()** is slower than **BitBlt()**, but **StretchBlt()** enables us to mirror the sprite bitmaps at runtime.

After we've drawn the sprite, we copy **CurrentLeft** and **CurrentTop** to **OldLeft** and **OldTop**, respectively. The last line of the **Paint()** event procedure

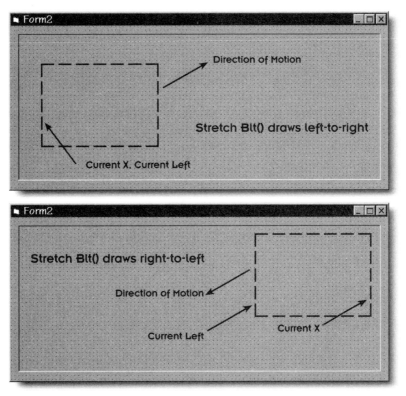

Figure 13.7   *The sprite is drawn in an imaginary rectangle, a bounding box, that moves across the client area. When it moves from left to right, we start the StretchBlt() at the left edge, and when it moves from right to left, we start the blt at the right edge.*

performs an optional call to the **Refresh** method for BufferPicture. Since the **AutoRedraw** property of BufferPicture is set to True, this Picture Box acts like a memory device context. In other words, the two **BitBlt()** operations copy the saved background rectangles to and from the VB persistent bitmap, which is in a memory device context. By calling the **Refresh** method, we force VB to copy the contents of the persistent bitmap to the screen device context of the control so we can see what it's doing. We don't *need* to see it—it will work correctly either way; it's just a handy way to watch what's happening.

Programming the Timer

Just as in the previous project, the job of setting the sprite position will be assigned to the Timer control, as shown in Listing 13.7.

Listing 13.7 The Timer1_Timer() Event Procedure from SPRITE2.FRM

```
Private Sub Timer1_Timer()
Dim Limit As Single

    CurrentSpriteCel = (CurrentSpriteCel + 1) Mod 2
    If (((CurrentLeft + SpritePicture(CurrentSpriteCel).ScaleWidth) >= _
        AnimationPicture.ScaleWidth) And Forward) Then
        Forward = False
    ElseIf ((CurrentLeft <= 0) And Not Forward) Then
        Forward = True
    End If
    If Forward Then
        Limit = AnimationPicture.ScaleWidth - _
            SpritePicture(CurrentSpriteCel).ScaleWidth
        CurrentLeft = MinSingle(CurrentLeft + 20, Limit)
    Else
        Limit = SpritePicture(CurrentSpriteCel).ScaleWidth
        CurrentLeft = MaxSingle(CurrentLeft - 20, 0)
    End If
    If (((CurrentTop + SpritePicture(CurrentSpriteCel).ScaleHeight) >= _
        AnimationPicture.ScaleHeight) And Down) Or ((CurrentTop <= 0) _
        And Not Down) Then
        Down = Not Down
    End If
    If Down Then
        Limit = AnimationPicture.ScaleHeight - _
            SpritePicture(CurrentSpriteCel).ScaleHeight
        CurrentTop = MinSingle(CurrentTop + 7, Limit)
    Else
        CurrentTop = MaxSingle(CurrentTop - 7, 0)
    End If

    'AnimationPicture.Refresh
    AnimationPicture_Paint
End Sub
```

It's easy to become distracted by all the activity in this procedure. None of it has anything to do with the process of displaying transparent sprites. We handled all that in the **Paint** event. The **Timer** event is responsible for four clerical tasks:

- cycling between the two versions of the sprite
- changing the vertical and horizontal position of the sprite relative to the background
- reversing the direction of motion when the sprite bumps into one of the edges of the background
- calling the **AnimationPicture_Paint()** event procedure to update the display.

We've included two lines that perform similar functions. To update the image in **AnimationPicture**, we can either call **AnimationPicture_Paint()** directly, like any other procedure, or invoke the **Refresh** method, which will send a Paint message to the control. When VB detects the Paint message, it will automatically recopy some or all of the background image to the screen, then execute the **Paint()** event procedure. The advantage of the **Refresh** method is that it will properly clean up the image after it has been covered and re-exposed by another window. The disadvantage is that it tends to be slower than simply executing a **AnimationPicture_Paint()** event. Depending on available system resources, these two approaches can look similar on-screen, or quite different. Try them both.

Declarations and Initializations

Before we can start up the program, we need to do some initialization. First of all, it's always wise to initialize global or form level variables like **Forward**, **Down**, **CurrentLeft**, and **CurrentTop**. Even more importantly, the BufferPicture is empty—or rather, it contains a plain white bitmap. The first time the **AnimationPicture_Paint()** event procedure runs, it will copy that white block over the upper-left corner of the background, leaving a permanent hole. To prevent that from happening, we'll initialize the background buffer by calling the **BitBlt()** function from the **Form_Activate()** event procedure. Listing 13.8 contains the declarations from SPRITE2.FRM, along with the **Form_Load()** and **Form_Activate()** event procedures.

Listing 13.8 The Declarations Section and the Form_Load() and Form_Activate() Event Procedures from SPRITE2.FRM

```
Option Explicit

Option Explicit

#If Win32 Then
   Private Declare Function BitBlt Lib "gdi32" (ByVal hDestDC As Long, _
      ByVal X As Long, ByVal Y As Long, ByVal nWidth As Long, _
      ByVal nHeight As Long, ByVal hSrcDC As Long, ByVal XSrc As Long, _
      ByVal YSrc As Long, ByVal dwRop As Long) As Long
   Private Declare Function StretchBlt Lib "gdi32" (ByVal hDC As Long, _
      ByVal X As Long, ByVal Y As Long, ByVal nWidth As Long, _
      ByVal nHeight As Long, ByVal hSrcDC As Long, _
      ByVal XSrc As Long, ByVal YSrc As Long, ByVal nSrcWidth As Long, _
      ByVal nSrcHeight As Long, ByVal dwRop As Long) As Long
#Else
   Private Declare Function BitBlt Lib "GDI" (ByVal hDestDC As Integer, _
      ByVal X As Integer, ByVal Y As Integer, ByVal nWidth As Integer, _
```

```
        ByVal nHeight As Integer, ByVal hSrcDC As Integer, ByVal XSrc As Integer, _
        ByVal YSrc As Integer, ByVal dwRop As Long) As Integer
    Private Declare Function StretchBlt Lib "GDI" (ByVal hDC As Integer, _
        ByVal X As Integer, ByVal Y As Integer, ByVal nWidth As Integer, _
        ByVal nHeight As Integer, ByVal hSrcDC As Integer, _
        ByVal XSrc As Integer, ByVal YSrc As Integer, ByVal nSrcWidth As Integer, _
        ByVal nSrcHeight As Integer, ByVal dwRop As Long) As Integer
#End If

Const SRCCOPY = &HCC0020
Const SRCAND = &H8800C6
Const SRCPAINT = &HEE0086

Dim Forward As Boolean
Dim Down As Boolean
Dim CurrentLeft As Integer
Dim CurrentTop As Integer
Dim OldLeft As Integer
Dim OldTop As Integer
Dim CurrentSpriteCel As Integer

Private Sub Form_Load()
    Forward = True
    Down = True
    CurrentLeft = 0
    CurrentTop = 0
End Sub

Private Sub Form_Activate()
Dim Dummy As Integer

    Dummy = BitBlt(BufferPicture.hDC, 0, 0, _
        SpritePicture(CurrentSpriteCel).ScaleWidth, _
        SpritePicture(CurrentSpriteCel).ScaleHeight, AnimationPicture.hDC, _
        CurrentLeft, CurrentTop, SRCCOPY)
End Sub
```

Now for the MINMAX Code Module

The code module MINMAX.BAS, shown in Listing 13.9, contains some miscellaneous functions, all of which return either the lesser or greater of two values in the various numeric formats **Integer**, **Long** integer, and **Single** precision real.

Listing 13.9　MINMAX.BAS

```
Option Explicit
Function MaxInt (A As Integer, B As Integer) As Integer
    If A > B Then
        MaxInt = A
    Else
        MaxInt = B
```

```
      End If
End Function
Function MaxLong (A As Long, B As Long) As Long
   If A > B Then
      MaxLong = A
   Else
      MaxLong = B
   End If
End Function
Function MaxSingle (A As Single, B As Single) As Single
   If A > B Then
      MaxSingle = A
   Else
      MaxSingle = B
   End If
End Function
Function MinInt (A As Integer, B As Integer) As Integer
   If A < B Then
      MinInt = A
   Else
      MinInt = B
   End If
End Function
Function MinLong (A As Long, B As Long) As Long
   If A < B Then
      MinLong = A
   Else
      MinLong = B
   End If
End Function
Function MinSingle (A As Single, B As Single) As Single
   If A < B Then
      MinSingle = A
   Else
      MinSingle = B
   End If
End Function
```

In the next version of the sprite program we'll begin to tackle flicker. But first, let's find an easier way to convert bitmaps to sprites and masks.

Making Masks and Sprites Automatically

To keep things from getting too mixed up, let's take a break from sprite animation and concentrate on sprite creation—in other words, the conversion of bitmaps into transparent sprites and masks. Let's explore how we can convert an 8-bit bitmap with a white background into a monochrome mask (still 8-bits, but only two colors) and a sprite with a black background. We'll use the code we develop here for the sprite animation program that we're going to create in the next chapter.

The Animation Mask Maker

This project creates an animation mask for a sprite animation. Here are the steps to follow:

1. Create a form named MAKEMASK.FRM with three Picture Boxes.
2. Write the **LoadBitmapOption_Click()** event procedure (Listing 13.10).
3. Create the code module MAKEMASK.BAS, and write the general functions **ConvertImageToSprite()** and **ConvertImageToMask()** (Listings 13.11 and 13.12).
4. Fill in the remaining event procedures and declarations in MAKEMASK.FRM (Listing 13.13).

 You'll find this project in the subdirectory \VBMAGIC\MAKEMASK in the files MAKEMASK.VBP, MAKEMASK.FRM, and MAKEMASK.BAS, along with DIB.BAS and PALETTE2.BAS. You'll also need the Common Dialog custom control, located in the file CMDIALOG.OCX, which the VB setup program should have copied to your \WINDOWS\SYSTEM subdirectory.

Running the Program

Run MAKEMASK.EXE, or load and run the project MAKEMASK.VBP. Figure 13.8 shows the program. This program has only one form. Choose File | Load Bitmap from the menu bar, and use the Load Sprite Bitmap dialog box to select an 8-bit bitmap. To produce a usable sprite, you must begin with a bitmap based on an identity palette. This will ensure that the first and last entries in the logical palette contain black and white, respectively. For best performance, an animation background and its sprites should share a common palette.

Figure 13.8 *The animation mask program at runtime.*

The image you load will appear in the first of the three Picture Boxes. When you choose File | Make Mask from the form's menu, the program generates two alternative versions of the bitmap, a monochrome mask and a sprite with a black background, and displays them in the second and third Picture Boxes, respectively (see Figure 13.8). This program only demonstrates the conversion functions—it does not save the new images as bitmap files. In fact, that would defeat the purpose, since the idea of writing these functions is to generate the mask and sprite bitmaps at runtime. We'll put this code to work in the next version of the sprite animation program.

To close the program and release all its resources, choose File | Quit from the form's menu, or use the form's Control menu.

Creating the Form

Set the **Name** property of the form to MakeMask. Place three Picture Box controls in a row on the form, and name them BitmapPictureBox, MaskPictureBox, and SpritePictureBox. Set all their **AutoRedraw** and **AutoSize** properties to False, and their **ScaleMode** properties to 3 - Pixel.

Add a Common Dialog control to the form. Set its **Name** property to LoadBitmapDialog. Set the **DialogTitle** property to "Load Sprite Bitmap," and set the **Filter** property to "Pictures | *.BMP;*.DIB;*.ICO".

Next, choose Window | Menu Design from the VB menu bar to open the Menu Design window. Add a File menu to the form with three suboptions: Load Bitmap, Make Mask, and Quit. Set the **Name** property of the File menu to FileMenu. Set the **Name** properties of the three suboptions to LoadBitmapOption, MakeMaskOption, and QuitOption, respectively.

Loading the Bitmap File into Memory

In Chapters 7 and 8, we looked at the structure of device independent bitmaps (DIBs) and how to construct them and read them from files. In this project, we'll reuse that knowledge—and even some of the code we originally developed for the dissolve program. Once we get the pixel data out of the DIB file and into memory, we can change it. In this case, we wish to make two alternate versions, one with a normally colored sprite on a black background, and one monochrome version in which the sprite is colored completely black, while its background remains pure white.

For the code module DIB.BAS we wrote a general procedure called **ReadBitmapFile()** (Listing 8.16 in Chapter 8), which would open a bitmap file, read its header information, and transfer its pixel data to a byte array. In this program, we'll call that procedure from the Load Bitmap menu option, as shown in Listing 13.10.

Listing 13.10　The LoadBitmapOption_Click() Event Procedure from MAKEMASK.FRM

```
Private Sub LoadBitmapOption_Click()
Dim RetValue As Integer
Dim SpritePalette As LOGPALETTE

    If PictureLoaded Then
      . Form_QueryUnload 0, 0
        CleanUp
    End If
    LoadBitmapDialog = 1
    If Len(LoadBitmapDialog.FileName) > 0 Then
        ReadBitmapFile LoadBitmapDialog.FileName, bmBitmapFileHeader, _
            bmBitmapInfo, BitmapPixelData
        If bmBitmapInfo.bmiHeader.biBitCount <> 8 Then
            MsgBox "Please load an 8-bit image.", 16, "Load Error"
        Else
            ConstructPaletteFromColorTable bmBitmapInfo.bmiColors(), SpritePalette
            hSpritePal = CreatePalette(SpritePalette)
            RetValue = SelectPalette(BitmapPictureBox, hSpritePal, False)
            RetValue = SelectPalette(SpritePictureBox, hSpritePal, False)
            RetValue = SelectPalette(MaskPictureBox, hSpritePal, False)
            RetValue = RealizePalette(SpritePictureBox)
            PictureLoaded = True
            BitmapPictureBox.Refresh
        End If
    End If
End Sub
```

This event procedure first checks whether a bitmap has already been loaded, and if so, calls the **Form_QueryUnload()** event procedure and the general procedure **CleanUp()** to dispose of the palette used by the previous image.

After calling **ReadBitmapFile()**, the procedure checks the **biBitCount** field in the **BITMAPINFOHEADER** to make certain that the DIB file contains an 8-bit (256 color) bitmap. If so, it creates the palette, selects it into the device contexts of all three Picture Boxes, and realizes it. It then sets the form level variable **PictureLoaded** to **True** and calls **BitmapPictureBox.Refresh** to display the bitmap.

Once we have the pixel data in a global Byte array, we can get to work on it.

Converting the Pixel Data

Now we need a function that can duplicate and convert the bitmap pixel data. Actually, we'll write two functions, one called **ConvertImageToSprite()** and one called **ConvertImageToMask()**. We'll need these functions for our next sprite animation project, so we'll place them in a code module, which for now we'll call MAKEMASK.BAS (later this will become SPRITE.BAS).

Here's what we're going to do. To make the sprite, we'll first copy the pixel data. Then we'll step through it pixel by pixel (byte by byte), looking for any pixel set to &HFF (which references white in the system palette or any identity palette) and changing it to **&H00** (which references black). For the mask, we'll make a second copy of the original, and step through it changing any pixel with a value less than &HFF to &H00. Let's begin with **ConvertImageToSprite()**, which is shown in listing 13.11.

Listing 13.11 The ConvertImageToSprite() Subroutine from MAKEMASK.BAS

```
Sub ConvertImageToSprite(bmInfo As BITMAPINFO, BitmapPixelData() As Byte,
SpritePixelData() As Byte)
Dim LastLine As Integer
Dim LineCounter As Integer
Dim ColumnCounter As Integer
Dim LastColumn As Integer
Dim PaddedLineWidth As Integer
Dim ColorTableIndex As Integer
Dim PixelIndex As Long

    ' Copy the original bitmap pixels to another buffer,
    ' which will become the sprite pixel data.
    SpritePixelData = BitmapPixelData

    LastLine = bmInfo.bmiHeader.biHeight - 1
    LastColumn = bmInfo.bmiHeader.biWidth - 1
    PaddedLineWidth = (LastColumn \ 4 + 1) * 4
    For LineCounter = 0 To LastLine
        For ColumnCounter = 0 To LastColumn
            PixelIndex = CLng(LineCounter) * PaddedLineWidth + ColumnCounter
            ColorTableIndex = SpritePixelData(PixelIndex)
            With bmInfo.bmiColors(ColorTableIndex)
                If (.rgbRed = 255) And (.rgbBlue = 255) And (.rgbGreen = 255) Then
                    SpritePixelData(PixelIndex) = 0
                End If
            End With
        Next ColumnCounter
    Next LineCounter
End Sub
```

The first block of code following the local variable declarations creates a new Byte array block, the same size as the one holding the original bitmap pixel data.

Next, we need to find out the dimension of the image so we can set up a pair of **For..Next** loops that will step through the entire bitmap one pixel at a time. **LastLine** and **LastColumn** are integers that store the number of rows and columns, respectively. We subtract one because our arrays are all zero-based. Before we examine any data, we need to know what length each row is padded to. This occurs because different bitmaps will have different widths, and each one may have anywhere from one to three bytes of padding tacked on to the end of the line, so we need to find the next number, greater than our **LastLine**, that is divisible by four. Here is the line that accomplishes this:

```
PaddedLineWidth = (LastColumn \ 4 + 1) * 4
```

This set of functions uses the integer division function "\" to find the integer part of the division of **LastColumn** by 4. Next we add 1 to it and multiply it back up by 4. This gives us a number that is the next greatest number divisible by four—our padded line width.

Now, we start two **For..Next** loops. The first loop will step through each row, and the nested loop will step through each column. This way, every single pixel in the image will be accessed. Here is the code that is run for each pixel:

```
With bmInfo.bmiColors(ColorTableIndex)
    If (.rgbRed = 255) And (.rgbBlue = 255) And (.rgbGreen = 255) Then
        SpritePixelData(PixelIndex) = 0
    End If
End With
```

We use the **With** statement so that we only need to access **bmInfo.bmiColors(ColorTableIndex)** once, instead of three times. The **If..Then** statement then checks to see if the pixel we have landed on is equal to white. If it is, we set the corresponding pixel in our **SpritePixelData()** byte array to black (0).

Next, we need to do it all over again to create the mask. We copied the contents of the **ConvertImageToSprite()** subroutine into a new subroutine called **ConvertImageToMask()** as shown in listing 13.12.

Listing 13.12   The ConvertImageToMask() Subroutine from MAKEMASK.BAS

```
Sub ConvertImageToMask(bmInfo As BITMAPINFO, BitmapPixelData() As Byte, _
    MaskPixelData() As Byte)
Dim LastLine As Integer
Dim LineCounter As Integer
Dim ColumnCounter As Integer
Dim LastColumn As Integer
Dim PaddedLineWidth As Integer
Dim ColorTableIndex As Integer
Dim PixelIndex As Long

    ' Copy the original bitmap pixels to another buffer,
    ' which will become the Mask pixel data.
    MaskPixelData = BitmapPixelData
```

```
    LastLine = bmInfo.bmiHeader.biHeight - 1
    LastColumn = bmInfo.bmiHeader.biWidth - 1
    PaddedLineWidth = (LastColumn \ 4 + 1) * 4
    For LineCounter = 0 To LastLine
        For ColumnCounter = 0 To LastColumn
            PixelIndex = CLng(LineCounter) * PaddedLineWidth + ColumnCounter
            ColorTableIndex = MaskPixelData(PixelIndex)
            With bmInfo.bmiColors(ColorTableIndex)
                If (.rgbRed <> 255) Or (.rgbBlue <> 255) Or (.rgbGreen <> 255) Then
                    MaskPixelData(PixelIndex) = 0
                Else
                    MaskPixelData(PixelIndex) = 255
                End If
            End With
        Next ColumnCounter
    Next LineCounter
End Sub
```

Finishing the Code in the Form Module

The remaining code in MAKEMASK.FRM performs the housekeeping tasks, such as painting the Picture Boxes and disposing of the palette when the program is terminated. By now, you're pretty familiar with this stuff, so we'll skip the detailed analysis. Listing 13.13 contains the complete listing of MAKEMASK.FRM, including the event procedures we just discussed.

Listing 13.13   MAKEMASK.FRM

```
VERSION 4.00
Begin VB.Form MakeMask
    Caption         =   "Convert a Bitmap to a Sprite & Mask"
    ClientHeight    =   2370
    ClientLeft      =   870
    ClientTop       =   1860
    ClientWidth     =   8535
    BeginProperty Font
        name            =   "MS Sans Serif"
        charset         =   0
        weight          =   700
        size            =   8.25
        underline       =   0   'False
        italic          =   0   'False
        strikethrough   =   0   'False
    EndProperty
    ForeColor       =   &H80000008&
    Height          =   3225
    Left            =   810
    LinkTopic       =   "Form1"
    ScaleHeight     =   158
    ScaleMode       =   3   'Pixel
    ScaleWidth      =   569
```

```
Top              =    1065
Width            =    8655
Begin VB.PictureBox BitmapPictureBox
   Appearance    =    0    'Flat
   BackColor     =    &H80000005&
   ForeColor     =    &H80000008&
   Height        =    1815
   Left          =    120
   ScaleHeight   =    1785
   ScaleWidth    =    2625
   TabIndex      =    2
   Top           =    120
   Width         =    2655
End
Begin VB.PictureBox MaskPictureBox
   Appearance    =    0    'Flat
   BackColor     =    &H80000005&
   ForeColor     =    &H80000008&
   Height        =    1815
   Left          =    2880
   ScaleHeight   =    119
   ScaleMode     =    3    'Pixel
   ScaleWidth    =    183
   TabIndex      =    1
   Top           =    120
   Width         =    2775
End
Begin VB.PictureBox SpritePictureBox
   Appearance    =    0    'Flat
   BackColor     =    &H80000005&
   ForeColor     =    &H80000008&
   Height        =    1815
   Left          =    5760
   ScaleHeight   =    119
   ScaleMode     =    3    'Pixel
   ScaleWidth    =    175
   TabIndex      =    0
   Top           =    120
   Width         =    2655
End
Begin MSComDlg.CommonDialog LoadBitmapDialog
   Left          =    -15
   Top           =    1815
   _Version      =    65536
   _ExtentX      =    847
   _ExtentY      =    847
   _StockProps   =    0
   DialogTitle   =    "Load Sprite Bitmap"
   Filter        =    "Pictures|*.BMP;*.DIB;*.ICO"
End
Begin VB.Label Label3
   Alignment     =    2    'Center
   Appearance    =    0    'Flat
```

```
      BackColor       =   &H80000005&
      BackStyle       =   0   'Transparent
      Caption         =   "Sprite"
      ForeColor       =   &H80000008&
      Height          =   228
      Left            =   6324
      TabIndex        =   5
      Top             =   2040
      Width           =   1488
   End
   Begin VB.Label Label2
      Alignment       =   2   'Center
      Appearance      =   0   'Flat
      BackColor       =   &H80000005&
      BackStyle       =   0   'Transparent
      Caption         =   "Mask"
      ForeColor       =   &H80000008&
      Height          =   264
      Left            =   3372
      TabIndex        =   4
      Top             =   2028
      Width           =   1560
   End
   Begin VB.Label Label1
      Alignment       =   2   'Center
      Appearance      =   0   'Flat
      BackColor       =   &H80000005&
      BackStyle       =   0   'Transparent
      Caption         =   "Original Bitmap"
      ForeColor       =   &H80000008&
      Height          =   264
      Left            =   588
      TabIndex        =   3
      Top             =   2040
      Width           =   1356
   End
   Begin VB.Menu FileMenu
      Caption         =   "&File"
      Begin VB.Menu LoadBitmapOption
         Caption         =   "&Load Bitmap"
      End
      Begin VB.Menu MakeMaskOption
         Caption         =   "&Make Mask"
      End
      Begin VB.Menu SaveMaskOption
         Caption         =   "&Save Mask"
         Enabled         =   0   'False
      End
      Begin VB.Menu QuitOption
         Caption         =   "&Quit"
      End
   End
End
```

```
Attribute VB_Name = "MakeMask"
Attribute VB_Creatable = False
Attribute VB_Exposed = False
Option Explicit

Dim bmBitmapFileHeader As BITMAPFILEHEADER
Dim bmBitmapInfo As BITMAPINFO
Dim hSpritePal As Integer
Dim PictureLoaded As Integer

Dim BitmapPixelData() As Byte
Dim MaskPixelData() As Byte
Dim SpritePixelData() As Byte

Private Sub BitmapPictureBox_Paint()
Dim RetValue As Long
Dim lpBitmapPixelData As Long

    If PictureLoaded Then
        RetValue = SelectPalette(BitmapPictureBox.hdc, hSpritePal, False)
        RetValue = RealizePalette(BitmapPictureBox.hdc)
        RetValue = SetDIBitsToDevice(BitmapPictureBox.hdc, 0, 0, _
            bmBitmapInfo.bmiHeader.biWidth, bmBitmapInfo.bmiHeader.biHeight, _
            0, 0, 0, bmBitmapInfo.bmiHeader.biHeight, BitmapPixelData(0), _
            bmBitmapInfo, DIB_RGB_COLORS)
    End If
End Sub

Private Sub CleanUp()
Dim RetValue As Integer

    If hSpritePal <> 0 Then
        RetValue = DeleteObject(hSpritePal)
        hSpritePal = 0
    End If
    PictureLoaded = False
End Sub

Private Sub Form_Load()
    PictureLoaded = False
End Sub

Private Sub Form_QueryUnload(Cancel As Integer, UnloadMode As Integer)
Dim RetValue As Integer

    RetValue = SelectPalette(BitmapPictureBox.hdc, DEFAULT_PALETTE, False)
    RetValue = SelectPalette(SpritePictureBox.hdc, DEFAULT_PALETTE, False)
    RetValue = SelectPalette(MaskPictureBox.hdc, DEFAULT_PALETTE, False)
End Sub

Private Sub Form_Unload(Cancel As Integer)
    CleanUp
End Sub
```

```
Private Sub LoadBitmapOption_Click()
Dim RetValue As Integer
Dim SpritePalette As LOGPALETTE

    If PictureLoaded Then
        Form_QueryUnload 0, 0
        CleanUp
    End If
    LoadBitmapDialog = 1
    If Len(LoadBitmapDialog.FileName) > 0 Then
        ReadBitmapFile LoadBitmapDialog.FileName, bmBitmapFileHeader, _
            bmBitmapInfo, BitmapPixelData
        If bmBitmapInfo.bmiHeader.biBitCount <> 8 Then
            MsgBox "Please load an 8-bit image.", 16, "Load Error"
        Else
            ConstructPaletteFromColorTable bmBitmapInfo.bmiColors(), SpritePalette
            hSpritePal = CreatePalette(SpritePalette)
            RetValue = SelectPalette(BitmapPictureBox, hSpritePal, False)
            RetValue = SelectPalette(SpritePictureBox, hSpritePal, False)
            RetValue = SelectPalette(MaskPictureBox, hSpritePal, False)
            RetValue = RealizePalette(SpritePictureBox)
            PictureLoaded = True
            BitmapPictureBox.Refresh
        End If
    End If
End Sub

Private Sub MakeMaskOption_Click()
    MousePointer = 11
    ConvertImageToMask bmBitmapInfo, BitmapPixelData, MaskPixelData
    ConvertImageToSprite bmBitmapInfo, BitmapPixelData, SpritePixelData
    BitmapPictureBox.Refresh
    MaskPictureBox.Refresh
    SpritePictureBox.Refresh
    MousePointer = 0
End Sub

Private Sub MaskPictureBox_Paint()
Dim RetValue As Long
Dim lpMaskPixelData As Long

    If PictureLoaded Then
        RetValue = SelectPalette(MaskPictureBox.hdc, hSpritePal, False)
        RetValue = RealizePalette(MaskPictureBox.hdc)
        RetValue = SetDIBitsToDevice(MaskPictureBox.hdc, 0, 0, _
            bmBitmapInfo.bmiHeader.biWidth, bmBitmapInfo.bmiHeader.biHeight, _
            0, 0, 0, bmBitmapInfo.bmiHeader.biHeight, MaskPixelData(0), _
            bmBitmapInfo, DIB_RGB_COLORS)
    End If
End Sub

Private Sub QuitOption_Click()
    Unload MakeMask
    End
End Sub
```

```
Private Sub SaveMaskOption_Click()
    'SavePicture MaskPictureBox.Image, App.Path & "\TestMask.bmp"
End Sub

Private Sub SpritePictureBox_Paint()
Dim RetValue As Integer
Dim lpSpritePixelData As Long

    If PictureLoaded Then
        RetValue = SelectPalette(SpritePictureBox.hdc, hSpritePal, False)
        RetValue = RealizePalette(SpritePictureBox.hdc)
        RetValue = SetDIBitsToDevice(SpritePictureBox.hdc, 0, 0, _
          bmBitmapInfo.bmiHeader.biWidth, bmBitmapInfo.bmiHeader.biHeight, _
          0, 0, 0, bmBitmapInfo.bmiHeader.biHeight, SpritePixelData(0), _
          bmBitmapInfo, DIB_RGB_COLORS)
    End If
End Sub
```

Now that we've created masked sprites, we need to find a way to speed them up and reduce the flicker. In the next chapter, we'll use the new bitmap conversion functions we created for the MAKEMASK project to load and prepare all four versions of the moth sprite, which will make for much smoother animation.

Our latest adventure with animation will help you create smooth-motion images with a minimum of new code.

Better Animation

The animation effects we created in Chapter 13 weren't as smooth as we really want. Besides the jerky motion, the other major flaw we discovered was the flickering caused by the multiple, overlapping bitblts.

In this chapter, we are going to explore a few ways we can create faster, smoother animation. We'll develop one more animation project, but this time we'll use a few tricks to enhance the animation.

Creating Flicker-Free Animation

The easiest way to solve our flicker problems would be to create a compatible bitmap and memory device context, perform all the updates there, then copy the entire bitmap to the screen device context with one **BitBlt()**. But blts take time, so what we gain in image stability, we will likely lose in speed.

Another approach would be to work on just the parts of the screen that are affected by each change in the sprite position. For this approach, all you need to do is place those portions of the screen in a separate memory device context. Take a look at Figure 14.1. Each time we move the sprite, we need

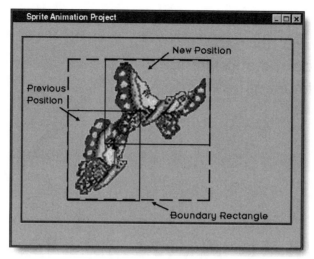

Figure 14.1 *The previous and new positions of the sprite occupy a bounding rectangle.*

to erase it from the background and redraw it in its new position. No matter which direction it's traveling—up, down, right, or left—its two positions define a bounding rectangle. The only part of the background bitmap that changes is that small section. So instead of transferring the whole image with each tick of the Timer, we could work just on this smaller piece, then copy it into position on the background.

For each position change of the sprite, you must complete these six steps:

1. Copy the bounding rectangle—the one that includes the previous position and the new position—from the screen to a buffer device context.
2. Erase the sprite from this small section of the background by restoring the sprite-sized chunk we saved before we last bltted the sprite (see step 3).
3. Save the sprite-sized rectangle that we're about to cover with the new sprite (see step 2).
4. Copy the mask to the sprite's new position in the bounding rectangle.
5. Copy the sprite to its new position, over the mask.
6. Copy the whole bounding rectangle back to its original position on the background.

 *In the \VBMAGIC\SPRITE3 subdirectory, you'll find a program called SPRITE3.VBP that uses this method to display and move the moth sprite. We won't cover this project in detail here, but you may want to take a look at its key procedure, the one that does all this copying, the **AnimationPicture_Paint()** event procedure, which is shown in Listing 14.1.*

Listing 14.1 The AnimationPicture_Paint() Event Procedure from SPRITE3.FRM

```
Private Sub AnimationPicture_Paint()
Dim Dummy As Long
Dim SpriteWidth As Integer
Dim SpriteHeight As Integer
Dim CurrentX As Integer
Dim OffscreenCompositeWidth As Integer
Dim OffscreenCompositeHeight As Integer

    If Forward Then
        SpriteWidth = bmBitmapInfo.bmiHeader.biWidth
        CurrentX = CurrentLeft
    Else
        SpriteWidth = -bmBitmapInfo.bmiHeader.biWidth
        CurrentX = CurrentLeft + bmBitmapInfo.bmiHeader.biWidth - 1
    End If
    SpriteHeight = bmBitmapInfo.bmiHeader.biHeight
    OffscreenCompositeWidth = Abs(SpriteWidth) + Abs(CurrentLeft - OldLeft)
    OffscreenCompositeHeight = SpriteHeight + Abs(CurrentTop - OldTop)
    ' Copy bounding rectangle of old and new positions to offscreen
    ' composite buffer.
    Dummy = BitBlt(OffscreenCompositePicture.hdc, 0, 0, OffscreenCompositeWidth, _
        OffscreenCompositeHeight, AnimationPicture.hdc, MinInt(OldLeft, _
        CurrentLeft), MinInt(OldTop, CurrentTop), SRCCOPY)
    ' Restore previously covered area by copying hold buffer to composite buffer.
    Dummy = BitBlt(OffscreenCompositePicture.hdc, MaxInt(0, OldLeft - _
        CurrentLeft), MaxInt(0, OldTop - CurrentTop), Abs(SpriteWidth), _
        SpriteHeight, BufferPicture.hdc, 0, 0, SRCCOPY)
    ' Copy area that will become next position from composite buffer to
    ' hold buffer.
    Dummy = BitBlt(BufferPicture.hdc, 0, 0, Abs(SpriteWidth), SpriteHeight, _
        OffscreenCompositePicture.hdc, MaxInt(0, CurrentLeft - OldLeft), _
        MaxInt(0, CurrentTop - OldTop), SRCCOPY)
    ' Copy Mask and Sprite to composite buffer.
    Dummy = StretchDIBits(OffscreenCompositePicture.hdc, MaxInt(CurrentX - _
        CurrentLeft, CurrentX - OldLeft), MaxInt(0, CurrentTop - OldTop), _
        SpriteWidth, SpriteHeight, 0, 0, Abs(SpriteWidth), SpriteHeight, _
        MaskPixelData(CurrentSpriteCel).TheBytes(0), bmBitmapInfo, _
        DIB_RGB_COLORS, SRCAND)
    Dummy = StretchDIBits(OffscreenCompositePicture.hdc, MaxInt(CurrentX - _
        CurrentLeft, CurrentX - OldLeft), MaxInt(0, CurrentTop - OldTop), _
        SpriteWidth, SpriteHeight, 0, 0, Abs(SpriteWidth), SpriteHeight, _
        SpritePixelData(CurrentSpriteCel).TheBytes(0), bmBitmapInfo, _
        DIB_RGB_COLORS, SRCPAINT)
    ' Copy composite buffer to screen DC.
    Dummy = BitBlt(AnimationPicture.hdc, MinInt(OldLeft, CurrentLeft), _
        MinInt(OldTop, CurrentTop), OffscreenCompositeWidth, _
        OffscreenCompositeHeight, OffscreenCompositePicture.hdc, 0, 0, SRCCOPY)

    OldLeft = CurrentLeft
    OldTop = CurrentTop
```

```
BufferPicture.Refresh
 'OffscreenCompositePicture.Refresh
End Sub
```

For all the bltting it does, this **Paint** event doesn't handle the most basic responsibility of any **Paint** event—to restore the screen after it has been uncovered by another window. To plug that hole, we could create a memory device context, perform all this work on that copy, then blt the results to the screen—which would put us right back where we started. Only now, instead of five blts, we would be up to seven. Before this gets any more out of hand, we had better simplify things.

Animation with Flicker-Free Sprites

In this sprite animation project, we'll make three major revisions to the project in Chapter 13. First, we'll start a code module called SPRITE4.BAS, which you can expand on your own into a reuseable, general-purpose sprite animation module. Next, we'll use the functions **ConvertImageToMask()** and **ConvertImageToSprite()** to construct masks and sprites at runtime. And finally, we'll write a general procedure called **MoveSprite()** that will perform flicker-free sprite animation with the bare minimum of calls to **BitBlt()** and **StretchDIBits()**.

1. Start a new project and create the form.
2. Fill in the **Form_Load()** event procedure (Listing 14.2).
3. Write the **MoveSprite()** general procedure (Listing 14.3).
4. Fill in the rest of code in the form and code modules (Listings 14.4 and 14.5).

You'll find this project in the subdirectory \VBMAGIC\SPRITE4 in the files SPRITE4.VBP, SPRITE4.FRM, SPRITE4.BAS, DIB.BAS, MINMAX.BAS, and PALETTE2.BAS. The project also uses five bitmap files: KAIBAB.BMP and MOTH1.DIB through MOTH4.DIB.

Running the Program

Run SPRITE4.EXE, or load and run the project SPRITE4.VBP. During the **Load** event, the program will read the four moth bitmaps and convert them to six masks and six sprites. This step will take some time. When the animation finally does begin, click on either of the check boxes, labeled Reversible and

Figure 14.2 *The SPRITE4 project running with smooth, flicker-free animation.*

Flippable, to change the orientation of the sprite, depending on which direction it's flying. From four drawings, we get sixteen variations, all thanks to **StretchDIBits()**. Figure 14.2 shows the program at runtime.

Creating the Form

To demonstrate the SPRITE4.BAS code module, we'll create a form called SpriteAnimationForm with one Picture Box control, a timer control, and two Check Box controls. Once again, set the **Name** property of the picture box to AnimationPicture. Set its **AutoRedraw** and **AutoSize** properties to False, and set its **ScaleMode** to 3 - Pixel. Do not set the form's **Picture** property—we'll load the background at runtime.

Set the **Enabled** property of Timer1 (we'll keep the default name) to False, and set its **Interval** property to 56 milliseconds. Change the **Name** property of the first check box to ReverseBox, set its caption to "Reversible," and set its **Value** property to 1 - Checked. Name the second check box FlipBox, set its caption to "Flippable," and set its **Value** property to 0 - Unchecked.

The Form_Load() Event Procedure

To understand what we're going to need in SPRITE4.BAS in the way of declarations and general procedures, let's begin with the **Form_Load()** event procedure, which is where we'll call the code that loads all the bitmaps. The code for this procedure is shown in Listing 14.2.

Listing 14.2 The Form_Load() Event Procedure from SPRITE4.FRM

```
Private Sub Form_Load()
Dim RetValue As Integer

    SpriteAnimationForm.Show
    Forward = True
    Down = True
    CurrentLeft = 0
    CurrentTop = 0
    ReDim SpriteBitmapFiles(6)
    ReDim SpriteData(6, 2)
    SpriteBitmapFiles(1) = App.Path & "\Moth1.DIB"
    SpriteBitmapFiles(2) = App.Path & "\Moth2.DIB"
    SpriteBitmapFiles(3) = App.Path & "\Moth3.DIB"
    SpriteBitmapFiles(4) = App.Path & "\Moth4.DIB"
    SpriteBitmapFiles(5) = App.Path & "\Moth3.DIB"
    SpriteBitmapFiles(6) = App.Path & "\Moth2.DIB"
    Screen.MousePointer = 11 ' Hourglass
    NumberOfSpriteCels = LoadAndPrepareSprites(6)
    hBackgroundDC = MakeBackgroundShadow(App.Path & "\Kaibab.BMP", _
        AnimationPicture, hSpritePal)
    Screen.MousePointer = 0
    If hBackgroundDC <> 0 Then
        OpenSprites AnimationPicture, hSpritePal
        Timer1.Enabled = True
    Else
        MsgBox "Unable to load background image.", 16, "File Error"
        Unload SpriteAnimationForm
        End
    End If
End Sub
```

In the array **SpriteBitmapFiles**, which we'll declare in SPRITE4.BAS, we specify the filenames of the sprite bitmaps. To produce a complete motion cycle, from wings closed to wings spread and back again, we need to duplicate the second and third bitmaps. Obviously, you could optimize the program so it wouldn't need to create two sets of masks and sprites for images two and three. For the sake of simplicity, we've sacrificed some memory.

The function **LoadAndPrepareSprites()** (see Listing 14.4), which will become part of SPRITE4.BAS, will take as its sole argument the number of sprite bitmaps. It will call the bitmap conversion functions, and return the number of sprites it successfully created. The data for those sprites and for their masks will be stored in the array **SpriteData**, which, like **SpriteBitmapFiles**, is declared in SPRITE4.BAS, but redimensioned in this **Form_Load()** event procedure.

After we prepare the sprites, we call another general function, also located in SPRITE4.BAS, called **MakeBackgroundShadow()** (see Listing 14.4). This function will create a memory device context and bitmap compatible with the AnimationPicture control, which we pass to it as an argument. It will then load the background bitmap from its file, transfer it to the memory device context, and create its palette. The return value of the function is the handle to the memory device context, which we assign to **hBackgroundDC**. The handle to the palette is returned by assigning it to the variable passed in the third argument, in this case, **hSpritePal**.

If **MakeBackgroundShadow()** manages to locate and load the background image, **Form_Load()** calls one more general procedure in SPRITE4.BAS, **OpenSprites()** (see Listing 14.5). This procedure creates the other memory device context used by the program, the scratch pad referenced by **hOffscreen-CompositeDC**.

And finally, with all the bitmaps in place, we kick in the Timer.

Programming the New SpriteMove() Procedure

The most significant difference between the **Timer** event in SPRITE4.FRM, which appears in the complete listing of the form (Listing 14.5), and the version in SPRITE2.FRM (Chapter 13) is the call to the new general procedure **MoveSprite()**, another addition to SPRITE4.BAS.

In previous versions of the sprite project, we handled the blting in the **AnimationPicture_Paint()** event procedure. But, as always, to create a general-purpose library, we need to move that code out of the event procedure in the form module and into a general procedure in the code module. **MoveSprite()** is shown in Listing 14.3

Listing 14.3 The MoveSprite() General Procedure from SPRITE4.BAS

```
Sub MoveSprite(OldLeft As Integer, OldTop As Integer, NewLeft As Integer, _
    NewTop As Integer, ByVal HorizontallyReversible As Boolean, ByVal _
    VerticallyReversible As Boolean, bmBitmapInfo As BITMAPINFO, _
    SpritePixelData() As Byte, MaskPixelData() As Byte, ResultPicture As _
    PictureBox, hAnimationPalette As Long)
Dim Dummy As Long
Dim RetValue As Long
Dim SpriteWidth As Integer
Dim SpriteHeight As Integer
Dim CurrentX As Integer
Dim CurrentY As Integer
Dim OffscreenCompositeWidth As Integer
Dim OffscreenCompositeHeight As Integer
Dim CompositeXOffset As Integer
Dim CompositeYOffset As Integer

    If NewLeft > OldLeft Then
        SpriteWidth = bmBitmapInfo.bmiHeader.biWidth
```

```
      CurrentX = NewLeft
      OffscreenCompositeWidth = MinInt((SpriteWidth + NewLeft - OldLeft), _
         (ResultPicture.ScaleWidth - OldLeft))
   Else
      If HorizontallyReversible Then
         SpriteWidth = -bmBitmapInfo.bmiHeader.biWidth
         CurrentX = NewLeft + bmBitmapInfo.bmiHeader.biWidth - 1
      Else
         SpriteWidth = bmBitmapInfo.bmiHeader.biWidth
         CurrentX = NewLeft
      End If
      OffscreenCompositeWidth = MinInt(OldLeft + Abs(SpriteWidth), _
         (Abs(SpriteWidth) + OldLeft - NewLeft))
   End If
   If HorizontallyReversible Then
      CompositeXOffset = MaxInt(CurrentX - NewLeft, CurrentX - OldLeft)
   Else
      CompositeXOffset = MaxInt(0, NewLeft - OldLeft)
   End If

   If NewTop > OldTop Then
      SpriteHeight = bmBitmapInfo.bmiHeader.biHeight
      CurrentY = NewTop
      OffscreenCompositeHeight = MinInt((SpriteHeight + NewTop - OldTop), _
         (ResultPicture.ScaleHeight - OldTop))
   Else
      If VerticallyReversible Then
         SpriteHeight = -bmBitmapInfo.bmiHeader.biHeight
         CurrentY = NewTop + bmBitmapInfo.bmiHeader.biHeight - 1
      Else
         SpriteHeight = bmBitmapInfo.bmiHeader.biHeight
         CurrentY = NewTop
      End If
      OffscreenCompositeHeight = MinInt((OldTop + Abs(SpriteHeight)), _
         (Abs(SpriteHeight) + OldTop - NewTop))
   End If
   If VerticallyReversible Then
      CompositeYOffset = MaxInt(CurrentY - NewTop, CurrentY - OldTop)
   Else
      CompositeYOffset = MaxInt(0, NewTop - OldTop)
   End If
   Dummy = SelectPalette(hOffscreenCompositeDC, hAnimationPalette, False)
   Dummy = RealizePalette(hOffscreenCompositeDC)
   ' Copy bounding rectangle of old and new positions to offscreen
   ' composite buffer.
   Dummy = BitBlt(hOffscreenCompositeDC, 0, 0, OffscreenCompositeWidth, _
      OffscreenCompositeHeight, hBackgroundDC, MinInt(OldLeft, NewLeft), _
      MinInt(OldTop, NewTop), SRCCOPY)
   ' Copy Mask and Sprite to composite buffer.
   Dummy = StretchDIBits(hOffscreenCompositeDC, CompositeXOffset, _
      CompositeYOffset, SpriteWidth, SpriteHeight, 0, 0, Abs(SpriteWidth), _
      Abs(SpriteHeight), MaskPixelData(0), bmBitmapInfo, DIB_RGB_COLORS, SRCAND)
```

```
    Dummy = StretchDIBits(hOffscreenCompositeDC, CompositeXOffset, _
       CompositeYOffset, SpriteWidth, SpriteHeight, 0, 0, Abs(SpriteWidth), _
       Abs(SpriteHeight), SpritePixelData(0), bmBitmapInfo, DIB_RGB_COLORS, _
       SRCPAINT)
    ' Copy composite buffer to screen DC.
    Dummy = BitBlt(ResultPicture.hdc, MinInt(OldLeft, NewLeft), MinInt(OldTop, _
       NewTop), OffscreenCompositeWidth, OffscreenCompositeHeight, _
       hOffscreenCompositeDC, 0, 0, SRCCOPY)

    OldLeft = NewLeft
    OldTop = NewTop
End Sub
```

This procedure begins by calculating the positions and dimensions for the next screen update. The arguments **HorizontallyReversible** and **VerticallyReversible** specify whether the sprite should be inverted when it is moving from right to left, or from bottom to top. (We've assumed that the original bitmaps are drawn to appear correct when the sprite is moving from left to right or from top to bottom.) The moth sprite looks pretty silly when you let it fly upside-down, but many other types of sprites need to be flipped vertically. Just as it will reverse a bitmap horizontally when you pass it a negative width, **StretchDIBits()** will flip a bitmap vertically when you pass it a negative value in the **nDestHeight** argument.

The blt operations in this procedure are simpler than those in the **AnimationPicture_Paint()** event procedure in SPRITE3.FRM. Instead of fiddling with so many little patches of background bitmap, this procedure uses a reserved copy of the background, stored in a memory device context referenced by the handle in **hBackgroundDC**. With each tick of the timer, **MoveSprite()** transfers a clean copy of the bounding rectangle from this pristine bitmap to **hOffscreenCompositeDC**, replacing the previous sprite at its previous position with the new sprite at its new position. This eliminates the two steps that reserve and restore the rectangular section of the bitmap covered by the sprite. The only thing we need from the previous instance of the sprite is its location, which in combination with the new position, determines the dimensions and location of the bounding rectangle. Now we can update the sprite in only four steps:

1. Copy the bounding rectangle—the one defined by the previous position and the new position—from the uncontaminated memory device context to a scratch pad device context (in this case, the offscreen composite device context).

2. Copy the mask to the sprite's new position in the clean bounding rectangle.

3. Copy the sprite to its new position, covering the mask.

4. Copy the whole bounding rectangle to the screen device context (in this case, AnimationPicture), simultaneously erasing the previous instance of the sprite and replacing it with the next one.

Because it shadows the entire background bitmap, this method uses more memory than the six-step version, but it requires fewer blts, which *may* improve performance. We emphasize "may," because Windows sometimes defies intuition. The performance of blt operations depends on several factors, including display hardware, display drivers, the availability of runtime resources, planetary alignment, fashion trends, and other unpredictable factors. It is, however, safe to assume that performance will not get any worse, and it rarely hurts to simplify code.

There is one significant performance factor you *can* control—the palette. This version of the program uses the identity palette from the background bitmap. You may recall from Chapter 6 that when the Palette Manager realizes an identity palette, it assumes a one-to-one mapping between the system palette and the logical palette, which eliminates the foreground mapping. **StretchDIBits()** must map the colors of the DIB as it copies the pixels to the device context. It does this by looking up the color referenced by each DIB pixel in the color table belonging to the DIB, then looking for the closest matching color in the currently realized logical palette. If the realized palette is not an identity palette, **StretchDIBits()** must then look up the correct pixel value in the foreground mapping table to reference the chosen color in the system palette. By realizing an identity palette, you save **StretchDIBits()** a step, for which it rewards you with speedier service.

The Program Listings

We've covered most of the libraries used in this project in previous chapters. Here are the complete listings of SPRITE4.FRM and SPRITE4.BAS.

Listing 14.4 SPRITE4.FRM

```
VERSION 4.00
Begin VB.Form SpriteAnimationForm
   Caption         =   "Sprite Animation Project 4"
   ClientHeight    =   5430
   ClientLeft      =   1305
   ClientTop       =   1965
   ClientWidth     =   6420
   BeginProperty Font
      name            =   "MS Sans Serif"
      charset         =   0
      weight          =   700
```

```
      size            =    8.25
        underline     =    0    'False
        italic        =    0    'False
        strikethrough =    0    'False
     EndProperty
     Height           =    5880
     Left             =    1245
     LinkTopic        =    "Form1"
     LockControls     =    -1   'True
     ScaleHeight      =    362
     ScaleMode        =    3    'Pixel
     ScaleWidth       =    428
     Top              =    1575
     Width            =    6540
     Begin VB.CheckBox FlipBox
        Caption       =    "Flippable"
        Height        =    288
        Left          =    3390
        TabIndex      =    2
        Top           =    5055
        Width         =    1428
     End
     Begin VB.CheckBox ReverseBox
        Caption       =    "Reversible"
        Height        =    300
        Left          =    1335
        TabIndex      =    1
        Top           =    5055
        Value         =    1    'Checked
        Width         =    1392
     End
     Begin VB.Timer Timer1
        Enabled       =    0     'False
        Interval      =    56
        Left          =    216
        Top           =    3348
     End
     Begin VB.PictureBox AnimationPicture
        Height        =    4785
        Left          =    168
        ScaleHeight   =    315
        ScaleMode     =    3    'Pixel
        ScaleWidth    =    394
        TabIndex      =    0
        Top           =    144
        Width         =    5970
     End
  End
End
Attribute VB_Name = "SpriteAnimationForm"
Attribute VB_Creatable = False
Attribute VB_Exposed = False
Option Explicit
```

```
Dim Forward As Boolean
Dim Down As Boolean
Dim CurrentLeft As Integer
Dim CurrentTop As Integer
Dim OldLeft As Integer
Dim OldTop As Integer
Dim CurrentSpriteCel As Integer
Dim hSpritePal As Long
Dim hBackgroundDC As Long

Private Sub AnimationPicture_Paint()
Dim RetValue As Integer

    RetValue = SelectPalette(AnimationPicture.hdc, hSpritePal, False)
    RetValue = RealizePalette(AnimationPicture.hdc)
    RetValue = BitBlt(AnimationPicture.hdc, 0, 0, AnimationPicture.ScaleWidth, _
        AnimationPicture.ScaleHeight, hBackgroundDC, 0, 0, SRCCOPY)
End Sub

Private Sub Form_Load()
Dim RetValue As Integer

    SpriteAnimationForm.Show
    Forward = True
    Down = True
    CurrentLeft = 0
    CurrentTop = 0
    ReDim SpriteBitmapFiles(6)
    ReDim SpriteData(6, 2)
    SpriteBitmapFiles(1) = App.Path & "\Moth1.DIB"
    SpriteBitmapFiles(2) = App.Path & "\Moth2.DIB"
    SpriteBitmapFiles(3) = App.Path & "\Moth3.DIB"
    SpriteBitmapFiles(4) = App.Path & "\Moth4.DIB"
    SpriteBitmapFiles(5) = App.Path & "\Moth3.DIB"
    SpriteBitmapFiles(6) = App.Path & "\Moth2.DIB"
    Screen.MousePointer = 11 ' Hourglass
    NumberOfSpriteCels = LoadAndPrepareSprites(6)
    hBackgroundDC = MakeBackgroundShadow(App.Path & "\kaibab.BMP", _
        AnimationPicture, hSpritePal)
    Screen.MousePointer = 0
    If hBackgroundDC <> 0 Then
        OpenSprites AnimationPicture, hSpritePal
        Timer1.Enabled = True
    Else
        MsgBox "Unable to load background image.", 16, "File Error"
        Unload SpriteAnimationForm
        End
    End If
End Sub

Private Sub Form_QueryUnload(Cancel As Integer, UnloadMode As Integer)
    Timer1.Enabled = False
    CloseSprites AnimationPicture
End Sub
```

```
Private Sub Form_Unload(Cancel As Integer)
Dim RetValue As Integer

    RetValue = DeleteObject(hSpritePal)
End Sub

Private Sub Timer1_Timer()
Dim Limit As Single
Dim SpriteWidth As Single

    SpriteWidth = bmSpriteInfo.bmiHeader.biWidth
    CurrentSpriteCel = CurrentSpriteCel Mod NumberOfSpriteCels + 1
    If (((CurrentLeft + SpriteWidth) >= AnimationPicture.ScaleWidth) _
        And Forward) Then
        Forward = False
    ElseIf ((CurrentLeft <= 0) And Not Forward) Then
        Forward = True
    End If
    If Forward Then
        Limit = AnimationPicture.ScaleWidth - SpriteWidth
        CurrentLeft = MinSingle(CurrentLeft + 20, Limit)
    Else
        Limit = bmSpriteInfo.bmiHeader.biWidth
        CurrentLeft = MaxSingle(CurrentLeft - 20, 0)
    End If
    If (((CurrentTop + bmSpriteInfo.bmiHeader.biHeight) >= _
        AnimationPicture.ScaleHeight) And Down) Or ((CurrentTop <= 0) And _
        Not Down) Then
        Down = Not Down
    End If
    If Down Then
        Limit = AnimationPicture.ScaleHeight - bmSpriteInfo.bmiHeader.biHeight
        CurrentTop = MinSingle(CurrentTop + 7, Limit)
    Else
        CurrentTop = MaxSingle(CurrentTop - 7, 0)
    End If
    MoveSprite OldLeft, OldTop, CurrentLeft, CurrentTop, (ReverseBox.Value = 1), _
        (FlipBox.Value = 1), bmSpriteInfo, SpriteData(CurrentSpriteCel, _
        2).TheBytes, SpriteData(CurrentSpriteCel, 1).TheBytes, AnimationPicture, _
        hSpritePal
End Sub
```

Listing 14.5   The SPRITE4.BAS Code Module

```
Attribute VB_Name = "SPRITE41"
Option Explicit

Dim hOffscreenCompositeDC As Long
Dim hOffscreenCompositeBitmap As Long
Dim hOldOffscreenCompositeBitmap As Long
Dim hBackgroundPixelData As Long

Dim BackgroundPixelData As PixelData
Dim hBackgroundDC As Long
```

```
Dim hBackgroundBitmap As Long
Dim hOldBackgroundBitmap As Long
Dim hBitmapPixelData As Long

Dim bmBackgroundBitmapFileHeader As BITMAPFILEHEADER
Global bmBackgroundBitmapInfo As BITMAPINFO
Dim bmSpriteFileHeader As BITMAPFILEHEADER
Global bmSpriteInfo As BITMAPINFO

Global SpriteBitmapFiles() As String
Global SpriteData() As PixelData
Global NumberOfSpriteCels As Integer

Sub CloseSprites(ResultPicture As PictureBox)
Dim RetValue As Long

    RetValue = SelectPalette(ResultPicture.hdc, DEFAULT_PALETTE, False)
    RetValue = SelectObject(hOffscreenCompositeDC, hOldOffscreenCompositeBitmap)
    RetValue = SelectPalette(hOffscreenCompositeDC, DEFAULT_PALETTE, False)
    RetValue = DeleteDC(hOffscreenCompositeDC)
    RetValue = DeleteObject(hOffscreenCompositeBitmap)
    RetValue = SelectObject(hBackgroundDC, hOldBackgroundBitmap)
    RetValue = SelectPalette(hBackgroundDC, DEFAULT_PALETTE, False)
    RetValue = DeleteDC(hBackgroundDC)
    RetValue = DeleteObject(hBackgroundBitmap)
End Sub

Sub ConvertImageToMask(bmInfo As BITMAPINFO, BitmapPixelData() As Byte, _
    MaskPixelData() As Byte)
Dim LastLine As Integer
Dim LineCounter As Integer
Dim ColumnCounter As Integer
Dim LastColumn As Integer
Dim PaddedLineWidth As Integer
Dim ColorTableIndex As Integer
Dim PixelIndex As Long

    ' Copy the original bitmap pixels to another buffer,
    ' which will become the Mask pixel data.
    MaskPixelData = BitmapPixelData

    LastLine = bmInfo.bmiHeader.biHeight - 1
    LastColumn = bmInfo.bmiHeader.biWidth
    PaddedLineWidth = ((LastColumn - 1) \ 4 + 1) * 4
    For LineCounter = 0 To LastLine
        For ColumnCounter = 0 To LastColumn - 1
            PixelIndex = CLng(LineCounter) * PaddedLineWidth + ColumnCounter
            ColorTableIndex = MaskPixelData(PixelIndex)
            With bmInfo.bmiColors(ColorTableIndex)
                If (.rgbRed <> 255) Or (.rgbBlue <> 255) Or (.rgbGreen <> 255) Then
                    MaskPixelData(PixelIndex) = 0
                Else
                    MaskPixelData(PixelIndex) = 255
                End If
```

```
            End With
        Next ColumnCounter
    Next LineCounter
End Sub


Sub ConvertImageToSprite(bmInfo As BITMAPINFO, BitmapPixelData() As Byte, _
    SpritePixelData() As Byte)
Dim LastLine As Integer
Dim LineCounter As Integer
Dim ColumnCounter As Integer
Dim LastColumn As Integer
Dim PaddedLineWidth As Integer
Dim ColorTableIndex As Integer
Dim PixelIndex As Long

    ' Copy the original bitmap pixels to another buffer,
    ' which will become the sprite pixel data.
    SpritePixelData = BitmapPixelData

    LastLine = bmInfo.bmiHeader.biHeight - 1
    LastColumn = bmInfo.bmiHeader.biWidth
    PaddedLineWidth = ((LastColumn - 1) \ 4 + 1) * 4
    For LineCounter = 0 To LastLine
        For ColumnCounter = 0 To LastColumn - 1
            PixelIndex = CLng(LineCounter) * PaddedLineWidth + ColumnCounter
            ColorTableIndex = SpritePixelData(PixelIndex)
            With bmInfo.bmiColors(ColorTableIndex)
                If (.rgbRed = 255) And (.rgbBlue = 255) And (.rgbGreen = 255) Then
                    SpritePixelData(PixelIndex) = 0
                End If
            End With
        Next ColumnCounter
    Next LineCounter
End Sub


Function LoadAndPrepareSprites(SpritesToLoad As Integer) As Integer
Dim SpriteCounter As Integer
Dim MsgString As String
Dim RetValue As Long

    SpriteCounter = 1
    Do While SpriteCounter <= SpritesToLoad
        ReadBitmapFile SpriteBitmapFiles(SpriteCounter), bmSpriteFileHeader, _
            bmSpriteInfo, SpriteData(SpriteCounter, 1).TheBytes
        If bmSpriteInfo.bmiHeader.biBitCount <> 8 Then
            MsgString = "File " & SpriteBitmapFiles(SpriteCounter) & " has " & _
                Str$(bmSpriteInfo.bmiHeader.biBitCount) & " bit pixels." & _
                Chr$(13) & Chr$(10)
            MsgString = MsgString & "Please load only 8-bit images."
            MsgBox MsgString, 16, "Load Error"
            LoadAndPrepareSprites = False
```

```
        Else
            ConvertImageToSprite bmSpriteInfo, SpriteData(SpriteCounter, _
                1).TheBytes, SpriteData(SpriteCounter, 2).TheBytes
            ConvertImageToMask bmSpriteInfo, SpriteData(SpriteCounter, _
                1).TheBytes, SpriteData(SpriteCounter, 1).TheBytes
            SpriteCounter = SpriteCounter + 1
        End If
    Loop
    LoadAndPrepareSprites = SpriteCounter - 1
End Function

Function MakeBackgroundShadow(FileName As String, ResultPicture As PictureBox, _
    ByVal hAnimationPalette As Long)
Dim RetValue As Long
Dim SpritePalette As LOGPALETTE

    ReadBitmapFile FileName, bmBackgroundBitmapFileHeader, _
        bmBackgroundBitmapInfo, BackgroundPixelData.TheBytes
    If Len(BackgroundPixelData) > 0 Then
        hBackgroundDC = CreateCompatibleDC(ResultPicture.hdc)
        ConstructPaletteFromColorTable bmBackgroundBitmapInfo.bmiColors(), _
            SpritePalette
        hAnimationPalette = CreatePalette(SpritePalette)
        RetValue = SelectPalette(hBackgroundDC, hAnimationPalette, False)
        RetValue = SelectPalette(ResultPicture.hdc, hAnimationPalette, False)
        RetValue = RealizePalette(hBackgroundDC)
        hBackgroundBitmap = CreateDIBitmap(ResultPicture.hdc, _
            bmBackgroundBitmapInfo.bmiHeader, CBM_INIT, _
            BackgroundPixelData.TheBytes(0), bmBackgroundBitmapInfo, _
            DIB_RGB_COLORS)
        hOldBackgroundBitmap = SelectObject(hBackgroundDC, hBackgroundBitmap)
        MakeBackgroundShadow = hBackgroundDC
    Else
        hBackgroundDC = 0
    End If
End Function

Sub MoveSprite(OldLeft As Integer, OldTop As Integer, NewLeft As Integer, _
    NewTop As Integer, ByVal HorizontallyReversible As Boolean, ByVal _
    VerticallyReversible As Boolean, bmBitmapInfo As BITMAPINFO, _
    SpritePixelData() As Byte, MaskPixelData() As Byte, ResultPicture As _
    PictureBox, hAnimationPalette As Long)
Dim Dummy As Long
Dim RetValue As Long
Dim SpriteWidth As Integer
Dim SpriteHeight As Integer
Dim CurrentX As Integer
Dim CurrentY As Integer
Dim OffscreenCompositeWidth As Integer
Dim OffscreenCompositeHeight As Integer
Dim CompositeXOffset As Integer
Dim CompositeYOffset As Integer
```

```
If NewLeft > OldLeft Then
   SpriteWidth = bmBitmapInfo.bmiHeader.biWidth
   CurrentX = NewLeft
   OffscreenCompositeWidth = MinInt((SpriteWidth + NewLeft - OldLeft), _
      (ResultPicture.ScaleWidth - OldLeft))
Else
   If HorizontallyReversible Then
      SpriteWidth = -bmBitmapInfo.bmiHeader.biWidth
      CurrentX = NewLeft + bmBitmapInfo.bmiHeader.biWidth - 1
   Else
      SpriteWidth = bmBitmapInfo.bmiHeader.biWidth
      CurrentX = NewLeft
   End If
   OffscreenCompositeWidth = MinInt(OldLeft + Abs(SpriteWidth), _
      (Abs(SpriteWidth) + OldLeft - NewLeft))
End If
If HorizontallyReversible Then
   CompositeXOffset = MaxInt(CurrentX - NewLeft, CurrentX - OldLeft)
Else
   CompositeXOffset = MaxInt(0, NewLeft - OldLeft)
End If


If NewTop > OldTop Then
   SpriteHeight = bmBitmapInfo.bmiHeader.biHeight
   CurrentY = NewTop
   OffscreenCompositeHeight = MinInt((SpriteHeight + NewTop - OldTop), _
      (ResultPicture.ScaleHeight - OldTop))
Else
   If VerticallyReversible Then
      SpriteHeight = -bmBitmapInfo.bmiHeader.biHeight
      CurrentY = NewTop + bmBitmapInfo.bmiHeader.biHeight - 1
   Else
      SpriteHeight = bmBitmapInfo.bmiHeader.biHeight
      CurrentY = NewTop
   End If
   OffscreenCompositeHeight = MinInt((OldTop + Abs(SpriteHeight)), _
      (Abs(SpriteHeight) + OldTop - NewTop))
End If
If VerticallyReversible Then
   CompositeYOffset = MaxInt(CurrentY - NewTop, CurrentY - OldTop)
Else
   CompositeYOffset = MaxInt(0, NewTop - OldTop)
End If
Dummy = SelectPalette(hOffscreenCompositeDC, hAnimationPalette, False)
Dummy = RealizePalette(hOffscreenCompositeDC)
' Copy bounding rectangle of old and new positions to offscreen
' composite buffer.
Dummy = BitBlt(hOffscreenCompositeDC, 0, 0, OffscreenCompositeWidth, _
   OffscreenCompositeHeight, hBackgroundDC, MinInt(OldLeft, NewLeft), _
   MinInt(OldTop, NewTop), SRCCOPY)
' Copy Mask and Sprite to composite buffer.
Dummy = StretchDIBits(hOffscreenCompositeDC, CompositeXOffset, _
   CompositeYOffset, SpriteWidth, SpriteHeight, 0, 0, Abs(SpriteWidth), _
   Abs(SpriteHeight), MaskPixelData(0), bmBitmapInfo, DIB_RGB_COLORS, SRCAND)
```

```
    Dummy = StretchDIBits(hOffscreenCompositeDC, CompositeXOffset, _
        CompositeYOffset, SpriteWidth, SpriteHeight, 0, 0, Abs(SpriteWidth), _
        Abs(SpriteHeight), SpritePixelData(0), bmBitmapInfo, DIB_RGB_COLORS, _
        SRCPAINT)
    ' Copy composite buffer to screen DC.
    Dummy = BitBlt(ResultPicture.hdc, MinInt(OldLeft, NewLeft), MinInt(OldTop, _
        NewTop), OffscreenCompositeWidth, OffscreenCompositeHeight, _
        hOffscreenCompositeDC, 0, 0, SRCCOPY)

    OldLeft = NewLeft
    OldTop = NewTop
End Sub

Sub OpenSprites(ResultPicture As PictureBox, hAnimationPalette As Long)
Dim RetValue As Integer

    hOffscreenCompositeDC = CreateCompatibleDC(ResultPicture.hdc)
    hOffscreenCompositeBitmap = CreateCompatibleBitmap(ResultPicture.hdc, _
        ResultPicture.ScaleWidth, ResultPicture.ScaleHeight)
    RetValue = SelectPalette(hOffscreenCompositeDC, hAnimationPalette, False)
    RetValue = RealizePalette(hOffscreenCompositeDC)
    hOldOffscreenCompositeBitmap = SelectObject(hOffscreenCompositeDC, _
        hOffscreenCompositeBitmap)
End Sub
```

Let's also take a look at the DIB.BAS module (Listing 14.6). It hasn't changed from the last few times we used it, but the functions it performs are very important, and the declaration section, in particular, holds many of the palette and image manipulation API function declarations.

Listing 14.6   The DIB.BAS Code Module

```
Attribute VB_Name = "DIB"
Option Explicit

Type PixelData
    TheBytes() As Byte
End Type

Type BITMAPINFOHEADER
    biSize          As Long
    biWidth         As Long
    biHeight        As Long
    biPlanes        As Integer
    biBitCount      As Integer
    biCompression   As Long
    biSizeImage     As Long
    biXPelsPerMeter As Long
    biYPelsPerMeter As Long
    biClrUsed       As Long
    biClrImportant  As Long
End Type
```

```
Type RGBQUAD
    rgbBlue         As Byte
    rgbGreen        As Byte
    rgbRed          As Byte
    rgbReserved     As Byte
End Type

Type BITMAPINFO
    bmiHeader       As BITMAPINFOHEADER
    bmiColors(0 To 255)  As RGBQUAD
End Type

Type INDEXBITMAPINFO
    bmiHeader As BITMAPINFOHEADER
    bmiColorIndexes(0 To 255) As Integer
End Type

Type BITMAPFILEHEADER
    bfType          As Integer
    bfSize          As Long
    bfReserved1     As Integer
    bfReserved2     As Integer
    bfOffBits       As Long
End Type

Global Const SRCCOPY = &HCC0020
Global Const SRCPAINT = &HEE0086
Global Const SRCAND = &H8800C6
Global Const SRCINVERT = &H660046
Global Const SRCERASE = &H440328
Global Const NOTSRCCOPY = &H330008
Global Const NOTSRCERASE = &H1100A6
Global Const MERGECOPY = &HC000CA
Global Const MERGEPAINT = &HBB0226
Global Const PATCOPY = &HF00021
Global Const PATPAINT = &HFB0A09
Global Const PATINVERT = &H5A0049
Global Const DSTINVERT = &H550009
Global Const BLACKNESS = &H42&
Global Const WHITENESS = &HFF0062
Global Const BLACKONWHITE = 1
Global Const WHITEONBLACK = 2
Global Const COLORONCOLOR = 3
Global Const BI_RGB = 0&
Global Const BI_RLE8 = 1&
Global Const BI_RLE4 = 2&
Global Const TRANSPARENT = 1
Global Const OPAQUE = 2

Global Const CBM_INIT = &H4&

#If Win32 Then
    Public Declare Function CreateCompatibleDC Lib "gdi32" (ByVal hdc As Long) _
        As Long
```

```
    Public Declare Function DeleteDC Lib "gdi32" (ByVal hdc As Long) As Long
    Public Declare Function CreateCompatibleBitmap Lib "gdi32" _
        (ByVal hdc As Long, ByVal nWidth As Long, _
        ByVal nHeight As Long) As Long
    Public Declare Function CreateDIBitmap Lib "gdi32" (ByVal hdc As Long, _
        lpInfoHeader As BITMAPINFOHEADER, ByVal dwUsage As Long, _
        lpInitBits As Any, lpInitInfo As BITMAPINFO, ByVal wUsage As Long) _
        As Long
    Public Declare Function CreateDIBitmapByPal Lib "gdi32" Alias _
        "CreateDIBitmap" (ByVal hdc As Long, lpInfoHeader As BITMAPINFOHEADER, _
        ByVal dwUsage As Long, ByVal lpInitBits As String, _
        lpInitInfo As INDEXBITMAPINFO, ByVal wUsage As Long) As Long
    Public Declare Function DeleteObject Lib "gdi32" (ByVal hObject As Long) _
        As Long
    Public Declare Function SelectObject Lib "gdi32" (ByVal hdc As Long, _
        ByVal hObject As Long) As Long
    Public Declare Function BitBlt Lib "gdi32" (ByVal hDestDC As Long, ByVal x _
        As Long, ByVal y As Long, ByVal nWidth As Long, ByVal nHeight As Long, _
        ByVal hSrcDC As Long, ByVal XSrc As Long, ByVal YSrc As Long, ByVal _
        dwRop As Long) As Long
   Public Declare Function SetDIBitsToDevice Lib "gdi32" (ByVal hdc As Long, _
        ByVal x As Long, ByVal y As Long, ByVal dx As Long, ByVal dy As Long, _
        ByVal SrcX As Long, ByVal SrcY As Long, ByVal Scan As Long, ByVal _
        NumScans As Long, Bits As Any, BitsInfo As BITMAPINFO, ByVal wUsage _
        As Long) As Long
    Public Declare Function StretchDIBits Lib "gdi32" (ByVal hdc As Long, ByVal _
        x As Integer, ByVal y As Integer, ByVal dx As Integer, ByVal dy As _
        Integer, ByVal SrcX As Integer, ByVal SrcY As Integer, ByVal wSrcWidth _
        As Integer, ByVal wSrcHeight As Integer, lpBits As Any, lpBitsInfo As _
        BITMAPINFO, ByVal wUsage As Integer, ByVal dwRop As Long) As Integer
#Else
    Public Declare Function CreateCompatibleDC Lib "GDI" (ByVal hdc As Integer) _
        As Integer
    Public Declare Function DeleteDC Lib "GDI" (ByVal hdc As Integer) As Integer
    Public Declare Function CreateCompatibleBitmap Lib "GDI" (ByVal hdc As _
        Integer, ByVal nWidth As Integer, ByVal nHeight As Integer) As Integer
    Public Declare Function CreateDIBitmap Lib "GDI" (ByVal hdc As Integer, _
        lpInfoHeader As BITMAPINFOHEADER, ByVal dwUsage As Long, ByVal _
        lpInitBits As String, lpInitInfo As BITMAPINFO, ByVal wUsage As Integer) _
        As Integer
    Public Declare Function DeleteObject Lib "GDI" (ByVal hObject As Integer) _
        As Integer
    Public Declare Function SelectObject Lib "GDI" (ByVal hdc As Integer, ByVal _
        hObject As Integer) As Integer
    Public Declare Function BitBlt Lib "GDI" (ByVal hDestDC As Integer, ByVal x _
        As Integer, ByVal y As Integer, ByVal nWidth As Integer, ByVal nHeight _
        As Integer, ByVal hSrcDC As Integer, ByVal XSrc As Integer, ByVal YSrc _
        As Integer, ByVal dwRop As Long) As Integer
    Public Declare Function SetDIBitsToDevice Lib "GDI" (ByVal hdc As Integer, _
        ByVal DestX As Integer, ByVal DestY As Integer, ByVal nWidth As Integer, _
        ByVal nHeight As Integer, ByVal SrcX As Integer, ByVal SrcY As Integer, _
        ByVal nStartScan As Integer, ByVal nNumScans As Integer, ByVal lpBits As _
        Long, lpBitsInfo As BITMAPINFO, ByVal wUsage As Integer) As Integer
```

```
    Public Declare Function StretchDIBits Lib "GDI" (ByVal hdc As Integer, _
        ByVal DestX As Integer, ByVal DestY As Integer, ByVal nDestWidth As _
        Integer, ByVal nDestHeight As Integer, ByVal SrcX As Integer, ByVal SrcY _
        As Integer, ByVal nSrcWidth As Integer, ByVal nSrcHeight As Integer, _
        ByVal lpBits As Long, lpBitsInfo As BITMAPINFO, ByVal wUsage As Integer, _
        ByVal dwRop As Long) As Integer
#End If

Private Function MinLong(A As Long, B As Long)
    If A < B Then
        MinLong = A
    Else
        MinLong = B
    End If
End Function

Sub ReadBitmapFile(ByVal FileName As String, bmFileHeader As BITMAPFILEHEADER, _
    bmInfo As BITMAPINFO, PixelData() As Byte)

    Open FileName For Binary As #1
    ' Read the header structures.
    Get #1, 1, bmFileHeader
    Get #1, , bmInfo
    ' Read the pixel data
    ReDim PixelData(bmInfo.bmiHeader.biSizeImage)
    Get #1, , PixelData
    Close #1
End Sub
```

Enhancing the Sprite Animation

As always, you can improve upon the animation techniques we've used. The first, and most complex, improvement would be to translate all the masks and sprites into device-dependent bitmaps at the outset. To do this, you would have to create a memory device context and device compatible bitmap for each image, then transfer the DIBs to them with **StretchDIBit()**. For the moth sprite, you would want at least 16 memory device contexts: a sprite and a mask for each of the four versions, plus mirror images of each. By pre-translating the DIBs into DDBs, you could dramatically improve the performance of the animation.

Another useful enhancement you might want to try out would be to enable the functions **ConvertImageToSprite()** and **ConvertImageToMask()** to accept the RGB value of the transparent color as an argument, instead of assuming that the transparent pixels are always pure white. That way, you could use white in your sprites as an opaque color.

Finally, for all our emphasis on interactivity, these demonstration programs don't offer much. Try using other events to control the motion of the sprites.

You could, for example, limit the timer to cycling the sprite images, and use the **MouseMove** event to control the moth's position on the screen.

Now that you know how to display and move sprites, you can expand the construction set we've developed in this chapter to add all kinds of interesting motion to your VB programs.

Introducing the Latest Animation Technology

When we were first developing a strategy for writing this book, we were really excited by what was then a new technology—WinG. We thought we would be able to talk about WinG and be on the forefront of animation technology—yeah, right. Soon after we started the book, we found out that WinG was being replaced by built-in commands in Windows 95. Specifically, there is a Windows 95 API call named **CreateDibSection()** that is used to create very fast offscreen buffers that can be directly accessed by your image manipulation routines and quickly blted onscreen.

Well, now that technology may not be such a big deal anymore, either. The new kid on the block is called **DirectDraw**. It is a part of the Windows 95 Games Software Development Kit (SDK). This technology is as hot as it gets! DirectDraw gives programmers access to screen memory directly instead of going through the GDI. The Games SDK also features a couple of other APIs that will help put Windows 95 on top of the gaming world:

DirectSound This is the 32-bit replacement for WaveMix. It allows for the real-time mixing of as many sounds as your machine can handle. It also can be used to do real-time manipulation of waveforms.

DirectPlay This API will aid in the development of networked games under Widows 95. DirectPlay provides a transport-independent, protocol independent, and online service independent way for games developed for Windows to communicate with each other. In other words, future Windows 95 games will be able to easily access any number of on-line services, Internet protocols, or modem connections to connect up to other players, or game servers.

AutoPlay This API has already been implemented, and you probably already saw it if you put the Windows 95 CD into your machine. AutoPlay is a feature that will save users a few steps when setting up or running applications off of a CD. Windows 95 has the ability to realize when a new CD has been placed into the machine. Once the format has been recognized, it looks for a file in the CD's root directory called AUTORUN.INF. This file is a simple text file that tells Windows 95 which application to launch when the CD is loaded. Not very exciting, but for those users who don't know the difference between an INI file and a Registry entry, it makes life very simple.

It is difficult to describe how DirectDraw works because it is so new, but let us tell you that it does work, and works well. A demo program called ROIDS that ships with the Games SDK called ROIDs is amazing. This a very simple game is based on the old asteroids game. When you start up the game, it does not look so incredible, but when you start playing, you will see the benefits of DirectDraw immediately. The animation speed is incredible! When you blast the large "asteroids," they break in to many smaller asteroids (sound familiar?). Before you know it, there are a couple hundred sprites flying around your screen, and the frame rate has barely dropped. At one point, using a DX2/66 with an off-the-shelf 1MB VESA display card, we counted over 200 sprites flying around the screen at over 50 frames per second. Even most DOS games can't do that!

Now that we have gotten you all pumped up about the Direct technologies, we have to tell you that they are not very VB-friendly. This technology was designed to be used with lower-level languages like C++ that support callback functions. We don't think that any of the "Direct" technologies will be compatible with VB, unless someone builds an OCX that can be used with VB, and will handle all the callbacks for you.

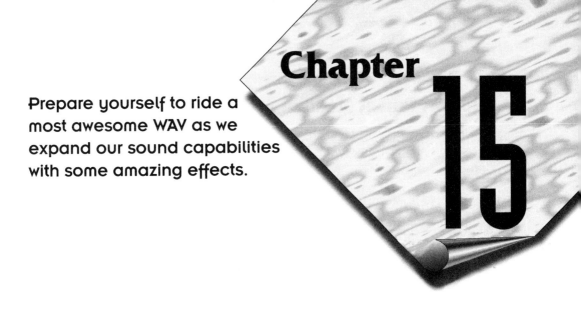

Prepare yourself to ride a most awesome WAV as we expand our sound capabilities with some amazing effects.

Exploring Waveform Audio

W e've told you that multimedia is a visual medium. But what about sound? You certainly don't want to underestimate its value when it comes to creating entertaining or educational multimedia applications. After all, imagine what it would be like to see Steven Spielberg's latest action adventure movie, without sound. You'd be missing out—after all, it's the roar of the Tyrannosaurus Rex that makes you cling to your seat.

In this chapter, we'll start you on the road to mastering the basics of digital audio. We'll discuss the technologies that are involved in digital audio, including redbook audio, MIDI, pulse code modulation, and digital sampling. For our first project, we'll create a VB application that will let us experiment with WAV files. This project illustrates how low-level Windows API calls can be used to play sounds and add echo effects. The overall goal is to show you how waveform data can be manipulated at the byte level.

In the second part of the chapter, we'll show you how to manipulate WAV files as they are being played in real time. We'll do this by using the real-time waveaudio mixer called WaveMix.

Audio: A Potent Medium

Movie and television producers spend a small fortune on their soundtracks. The sound production often can nearly equal the cost of the visual work. But, sitting in a dark theater, watching twenty-feet-high and forty-feet-wide pictures, you probably aren't entirely aware of all the things you hear—the low tones that trigger your anxiety, the reverberating footsteps, and the rhythm of the musical soundtrack.

Few people realize that most of what they hear in a movie theater, on a music CD, or on television, has been carefully fabricated. In the movies, a gunshot may reverberate from cliff to canyon, but when you record the sound of a gunshot, all you usually catch on tape is a popping noise, no more impressive sounding than a kid's capgun. From there, the sound engineers craft that recording; to give it weight, they filter out noise, stretch its duration, and mix in low frequency subharmonics. To locate it in space, whether the ringing confines of an underground garage or an echoing Rocky Mountain pass, they adjust the volume, balance, and Surround Sound™ effects, and run it through a digital effects processor, to add reverberation.

If we're going to produce multimedia that is powerful enough to draw people away from their televisions, we had better learn the methods of sound production and learn how to create the tools necessary for applying them to our projects.

Checking Out the Options

Unfortunately, VB provides no intrinsic support for sound. But as you learned in Chapter 3, that won't hold us back at all. In fact, the Windows multimedia system has so many sound options, it can be hard to decide which to use. Let's sort them out.

Redbook Audio

When you pop a music CD into your Discman™ and press the Play button, you're listening to redbook audio. The specifications for the various data formats available on compact disk come in color-coded books; the cover of the standard audio specification is red, hence "redbook audio." With the MCI, you can play audio CDs on your CD-ROM drive. That's how the Windows Media Player works. Just plug the analog audio output of your CD-ROM drive into any amplifier; you don't even need a sound card. If both the Microsoft MSCDEX.EXE CD driver and the Windows [MCI] CD Audio drivers are loaded, you can use the Media Player—or the Windows 95 CD player—to operate the drive and listen to your favorite tunes. If you have an internal CD-ROM drive and a sound card, you may have connected the drive to the card with a thin, three-wire audio cable. This cable does nothing more than act as an external audio cable. It simply connects the analog audio outputs of the drive to the line-level analog inputs of the mixer/amplifier on the sound card.

Redbook audio is digital, and many sound cards can play and record digital audio at the same 16-bit, 44.1 kHz sampling rate that redbook uses. However, no standard drivers—and as far as I know, no commercially available CD-ROM drives or sound cards—will let you read the digital sound data on the redbook audio tracks. You may use the MCI driver to select tracks, query the drive for timing or other information, play tracks, or manipulate the disk in a variety of other ways. But the conversion of the digital audio into an analog signal is handled entirely by the digital to analog converter (DAC) inside the drive.

Does this mean we can't use redbook audio in our multimedia projects? Not by a long shot. Although the mastering process is different, redbook audio and CD-ROM data can, and often do, co-habitate on the same disk. That's how titles like Microsoft/Voyager's *Multimedia Beethoven* or 7th Level's *Tuneland with Howie Mandel* work. In Chapter 17 we'll take a closer look at the MCI string commands, and how we can use them to monitor and control audio CDs.

MIDI

The musical instrument digital interface (MIDI) actually makes no sound at all. MIDI is just a protocol that enables computers, synthesizers, keyboards, and other musical devices to communicate with each other. Almost every PC sound card available today includes some kind of built-in synthesizer. To play music on it, though, you have to send it messages that tell it which instrument sound (known as a *patch)* to use and which note to play. You'll also need to provide information for volume control and other sound qualities. MIDI is a specification that defines both the serial interface used by instruments to communicate with each other, and the message codes that travel over those links.

MIDI is the most economical type of multimedia sound. For example, to hold a single synthesizer note for an hour would require just 6 bytes—a 3 byte message to start the note, and a 3 byte message to stop it. In contrast, one hour of the lowest-fidelity waveform data would fill 39,690,000 bytes! MIDI enables you to store lengthy musical passages in just a few kilobytes or tens of kilobytes. Another advantage is that it allows you to change music on the fly. For example, you can transpose an entire piece to another key just by adding or subtracting a constant from all the note numbers. You can also change the playback speed of MIDI music without affecting its pitch.

The major disadvantage of MIDI is that the quality of sound it produces depends entirely on the synthesizer on which it is played, whether it be a sound card or an external synthesizer. Even two cards that use the same synthesizer chip can have different sounds programmed into it.

We'll examine MIDI in more detail in the next chapter.

Waveform Audio

Waveform audio is the workhorse of PC multimedia sound. With waveform audio, you can do anything within the practical limitations of memory, disk storage, processor speed, and the capabilities of your sound card. Depending on your needs, you shouldn't necessarily skip MIDI and redbook audio altogether; waveform audio offers the most general-purpose sound system. You can record and play music, sound effects, narration—anything you could do with a tape recorder, you can do with waveform audio.

Like CD audio, waveform audio is a digital medium. Unlike CD audio, however, it supports a variety of formats, from 8-bit monophonic at a sampling rate of 11,025 samples per second (11,025 bytes per second) to 16-bit stereo at a rate of 44,100 samples per second (176,400 bytes per second!). And, also unlike CD audio, you can read and write it, store and retrieve it, and, in short, manipulate it to your heart's content.

The waveform data format you choose—in other words, the sampling rate, number of channels (mono versus stereo), and bit resolution (8 versus 16)—should depend not only on the capabilities of the sound card on which you develop your presentations, but on the capabilities of the sound cards on which they must eventually play.

Digital Audio Basics

Waveform audio is stored in a format known as *pulse code modulation*, or PCM, which is the ten-dollar term for the seven-and-a-half-dollar term *digital sampling*. The principle is actually pretty simple.

Sound consists of a pressure wave moving through a medium, such as air. For each wave pulse there is a traveling zone of compressed air, trailed by a zone of rarefied air. To represent sound electronically, the compression is represented by a positive voltage and the rarification by a negative voltage. The voltage level determines the amplitude of the wave. A pure sine wave forms a nice rolling voltage, gradually switching from a positive value to a negative value of the same degree, and back again, as illustrated in the top portion of Figure 15.1. But most sounds aren't so pure. They include numerous sine waves, and possibly other waveforms, all added together to form an irregular pattern, as shown in the bottom portion of Figure 15.1.

To represent an analog waveform digitally, the voltage levels of the wave are sampled at regular intervals and stored as numbers. Audible frequencies range from about 50 Hz (cycles per second) to over 20,000 Hz. So, to record a meaningful digital representation, you need to sample the waveform frequently. In fact, it was proven mathematically in 1948, by Claude Shannon of Bell Laboratories, that you can accurately represent any analog signal with a digital sampling rate equal to twice the maximum frequency contained in the source. That's why CD audio is recorded at a frequency of 44.1 kHz—twice the maximum audible frequency (at least to humans).

You needn't preserve the full fidelity of the original analog signal, however. By sampling at lower rates, you don't lose the sound entirely, just the higher frequencies. This can produce the "AM radio" effect—the conversion of rich, full-bodied sound into tinny, cracker-box sound.

Sampling rate isn't the only factor that determines fidelity. The resolution of the sample—that is, the number of bits per sample—can also have a major impact. 8-bit samples, regardless of the sampling rate, cannot accurately represent sound. The human brain, by way of its audio sensors—ears—can distinguish very subtle differences in amplitude and frequency. With only 256 recordable levels, many of the subtler elements of a complex sound disappear. This loss is called *aliasing*. This is the audio equivalent of the stairstep aliasing that appears when you blow up bitmap images, or the color banding you often see when you convert a true color image to an 8-bit palette—especially in broad areas of graduated color, such as a clear blue sky. On the

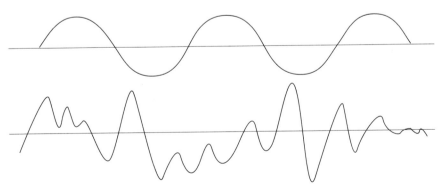

Figure 15.1 *A pure and a not-so-pure sound waveform.*

other hand, 16-bit sampling can differentiate over 65,000 signal levels, which makes it possible to represent a sound with much greater fidelity, while only doubling the storage demand.

Whatever the sampling rate and bit resolution of the digital waveform, the format of the data is simple. In 8-bit samples, each byte represents an amplitude. If the sample contains two channels of audio—in other words, stereo—the left channel is recorded in the even-numbered bytes, beginning with byte zero, and the right channel is recorded in the odd-numbered bytes, beginning with byte one. 8-bit values have no sign, so a value of 128 represents the *baseline* of the data. Values higher than 128 represent positive amplitudes, and values lower than 128 represent negative amplitudes. Since 8 bits represent an even number of possible values, the choice of 128 as the baseline is arbitrary; although 127 would work just as well, 128 is the standard.

In 16-bit wave files, each sample occupies two bytes, which happen to represent an ordinary signed integer. Amplitudes range in value from -32,768 to 32,767. In stereo 16-bit wave files, every other pair of bytes contains the data for one channel. So, bytes zero and one contain the first sample of the left channel, bytes two and three contain the first sample of the right channel, bytes four and five contain the second sample of the left channel, and so on.

The best way to understand waveform audio, and to appreciate its simplicity, is to fiddle with it. In the next project, we'll expand on the code we developed in Chapter 4 to read, play, and modify waveform data (WAV) files with the low-level audio API functions.

Playing and Modifying Wave Data

In the last section of Chapter 5, we used the multimedia I/O functions and the low-level audio functions to read and play a brief waveaudio file. We'll use some simple audio processing techniques to adjust the overall loudness, or *level*, of a sample, and to add echo effects. Here are the steps to follow:

1. Create the form WAVPLAY2.FRM and add the property listing (Listing 15.1).
2. Copy WAVEPLAY.BAS to WAVPLAY2.BAS.
3. Update the **OpenWaveFile()** and **WaveOut()** routines in WAVPLAY2.BAS (Listings 15.2 and 15.3).
4. Add the **DeviceCapsOption_Click()** event procedure to WAVPLAY2.FRM (Listing 15.4).

5. Add the general functions **WaveFormatStringFromConstant()** and **WaveFunctionStringFromConstant()** to WAVPLAY2.BAS (Listings 15.5 and 15.6).

6. Add the general procedure **ChangeLevel()** to WAVPLAY2.BAS (Listing 15.7).

7. Add the general function **WaveFormatConstantFromFormat()** to WAVPLAY2.BAS (Listing 15.8).

8. Add the general procedure **AddEcho()** to WAVPLAY2.BAS (Listing 15.9).

9. Finish the declarations for WAVPLAY2.BAS (Listing 15.10).

10. Complete the code in WAVPLAY2.FRM (Listing 15.11).

You'll find this project in the subdirectory \VBMAGIC\WAVPLAY2 in the files WAVPLAY2.VBP, WAVPLAY2.FRM, WAVPLAY2.BAS, GLBLMEM2.BAS, GLOBCONS.BAS, and MINMAX.BAS. It also uses the Common Dialog custom control.

Running the Program

When you run the program, your screen should look similar to Figure 15.2. Choose File | Get Device Capabilities to display information about your sound card and its driver. You can use this information to decide whether any particular

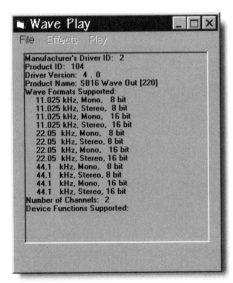

Figure 15.2   *The WAVPLAY project at runtime.*

WAV file will play on your card. Next, choose File | Open Wave File to display the Open Wave File dialog box. Use this dialog box to choose a WAV file, then select Play.

You have two options when it comes to adding special effects to your audio files; choose Effects | Change Volume or Effects | Add Echo. When the mouse pointer changes back to an arrow, select Play again to hear the result of the effects option. The Change Volume option is hard-coded to reduce the amplitude of the WAV file by 50 percent. The Add Echo option will repeatedly echo the sound at a period of one second, with a decay factor of 50 percent per iteration. As you'll soon see, you can easily change these parameters.

Creating the Form

The form for this project requires only two controls: a Picture Box and a Common Dialog. For the Picture Box, keep the default **Name** of Picture1. For the second, set the **Name** property to FileOpenDialog. All the features of this program will be activated from menu options. See Listing 15.1 for the property settings in WAVPLAY2.FRM.

Listing 15.1   The Property Listing of WAVPLAY2.FRM

```
VERSION 4.00
Begin VB.Form WavePlay
   Caption          =    "Wave Play"
   ClientHeight     =    5220
   ClientLeft       =    1215
   ClientTop        =    1860
   ClientWidth      =    4935
   BeginProperty Font
      name          =    "MS Sans Serif"
      charset       =    0
      weight        =    700
      size          =    8.25
      underline     =    0      'False
      italic        =    0      'False
      strikethrough =    0      'False
   EndProperty
   Height           =    6075
   Left             =    1155
   LinkTopic        =    "Form1"
   ScaleHeight      =    5220
   ScaleWidth       =    4935
   Top              =    1065
   Width            =    5055
   Begin VB.PictureBox Picture1
      AutoRedraw     =    -1   'True
      Height         =    4455
      Left           =    240
```

```
            ScaleHeight     =   4395
            ScaleWidth      =   4395
            TabIndex        =   0
            Top             =   120
            Width           =   4455
         End
         Begin MSComDlg.CommonDialog FileOpenDialog
            Left            =   0
            Top             =   4680
            _Version        =   65536
            _ExtentX        =   847
            _ExtentY        =   847
            _StockProps     =   0
            DialogTitle     =   "Open Wave File"
            FileName        =   "*.wav"
            Filter          =   "Wave Audio|*.wav"
         End
         Begin VB.Menu FileMenu
            Caption         =   "File"
            Begin VB.Menu DeviceCapsOption
               Caption         =   "Get Device Capabilities"
            End
            Begin VB.Menu OpenOption
               Caption         =   "Open Wave File"
            End
            Begin VB.Menu QuitOption
               Caption         =   "Quit"
            End
         End
         Begin VB.Menu EffectsMenu
            Caption         =   "Effects"
            Begin VB.Menu VolumeOption
               Caption         =   "Change Volume"
            End
            Begin VB.Menu EchoOption
               Caption         =   "Add Echo"
            End
         End
         Begin VB.Menu PlayOption
            Caption         =   "Play"
         End
      End
Attribute VB_Name = "WavePlay"
Attribute VB_Creatable = False
Attribute VB_Exposed = False
```

The Code Module

All the code that reads, plays, and processes WAV files is located in the code module WAVPLAY2.BAS. To create this file, we'll begin with a copy of WAVEPLAY.BAS, which we developed for the program MCIPLAY.VBP, back in Chapter 5.

The **OpenWaveFile()** (Listing 15.2) routine hasn't changed much, but we will show it to you once again, to refresh your memory.

Listing 15.2 TheOpenWaveFile() General Procedure from WAVPLAY2.BAS

```
Public Function OpenWaveFile(ByVal FileNameAndPath As String) As Boolean
Dim MMCKInfoParent As MMCKINFO
Dim MMCkInfoChild As MMCKINFO
Dim hmmio As Long
Dim ErrorCode As Long
Dim BytesRead As Long

    OpenWaveFile = False

    hmmio = mmioOpen(FileNameAndPath, ByVal 0&, MMIO_READ)
    If hmmio <> 0 Then
        ' Find WAVE Parent Chunk
        MMCKInfoParent.fccType.Chars = "WAVE"
        ErrorCode = mmioDescend(hmmio, MMCKInfoParent, ByVal 0&, MMIO_FINDRIFF)
        If ErrorCode = 0 Then
            ' Find fmt Chunk
            MMCkInfoChild.ckid.Chars = "fmt "
            ErrorCode = mmioDescend(hmmio, MMCkInfoChild, MMCKInfoParent, _
                MMIO_FINDCHUNK)
            If ErrorCode = 0 Then
                ' Read PCM Wave Format Record
                BytesRead = mmioRead(hmmio, PCMWaveFmtRecord, MMCkInfoChild.ckSize)
                If BytesRead > 0 Then
                    ErrorCode = waveOutOpen(hWaveOut, WAVE_MAPPER, _
                        PCMWaveFmtRecord, 0&, 0&, WAVE_FORMAT_QUERY)
                    If ErrorCode = 0 Then
                        ' Ascend back one level in the RIFF file.
                        ErrorCode = mmioAscend(hmmio, MMCkInfoChild, 0)
                        If ErrorCode = 0 Then
                            ' Read data chunk.
                            MMCkInfoChild.ckid.Chars = "data"
                            ErrorCode = mmioDescend(hmmio, MMCkInfoChild, _
                                MMCKInfoParent, MMIO_FINDCHUNK)
                            If ErrorCode = 0 Then
                                ReDim WaveBuffer(MMCkInfoChild.ckSize - 1)
                                BytesRead = mmioRead(hmmio, WaveBuffer(0), _
                                    MMCkInfoChild.ckSize)
                                If BytesRead > 0 Then
                                    ' Get a pointer to the Wave data and fill
                                    ' in Wave Header.
                                    WaveHeader.lpData = lparraycpy(WaveBuffer(0), _
                                        WaveBuffer(0))
                                    WaveHeader.dwBufferLength = BytesRead
                                    WaveHeader.dwFlags = 0&
                                    WaveHeader.dwLoops = 0&
                                    OpenWaveFile = True
                                Else
```

```
                              MsgBox "Couldn't read wave data.", MB_ICONSTOP, _
                                  "RIFF File Error"
                              End If
                          Else
                              MsgBox "Couldn't find data chunk.", MB_ICONSTOP, _
                                  "RIFF File Error"
                          End If
                      Else
                          MsgBox "Couldn't ascend from fmt chunk.", MB_ICONSTOP, _
                              "RIFF File Error"
                      End If
                  Else
                      MsgBox "Format not supported by Wave device.", MB_ICONSTOP, _
                          "Wave Data Error"
                  End If
              Else
                  MsgBox "Couldn't read wave format record.", MB_ICONSTOP, _
                      "RIFF File Error"
              End If
          Else
              MsgBox "Couldn't find fmt chunk.", MB_ICONSTOP, "RIFF File Error"
          End If
      Else
          MsgBox "Couldn't find WAVE parent chunk.", MB_ICONSTOP, _
              "RIFF File Error"
      End If
      ' Close WAVE file.
      ErrorCode = mmioClose(hmmio, 0)
  Else
      MsgBox "Couldn't open file.", MB_ICONSTOP, "RIFF File Error"
  End If
End Function
```

Like the changes to **OpenWaveFile()**, the modifications to **WaveOut()** are short and simple. We only need to take out one line of code, at the bottom of the listing, that erased the byte array. Now that we need to keep the data around for manipulation, we no longer need to erase it. That's it. Take a look at the resulting code in Listing 15.3.

Listing 15.3   The WaveOut() General Function from WAVPLAY2.BAS

```
Sub WaveOut()
Dim ReturnCode As Long

    ' Open the wave device.
    ReturnCode = waveOutOpen(hWaveOut, WAVE_MAPPER, PCMWaveFmtRecord, 0&, 0&, 0&)
    If ReturnCode = 0 Then
        ' Prepare the wave output header.
        ReturnCode = waveOutPrepareHeader(hWaveOut, WaveHeader, Len(WaveHeader))
        If ReturnCode = 0 Then
            ' Write the wave data to the output device.
```

```
        ReturnCode = waveOutWrite(hWaveOut, WaveHeader, Len(WaveHeader))
        ' Wait until it's finished playing.
        If ReturnCode = 0 Then
            Do Until (WaveHeader.dwFlags And WHDR_DONE)
                DoEvents
            Loop
        End If
        ' Unprepare the wave output header.
        ReturnCode = waveOutUnprepareHeader(hWaveOut, WaveHeader, _
            Len(WaveHeader))
        If ReturnCode <> 0 Then
            MsgBox "Unable to Unprepare Wave Header", MB_ICONSTOP, "Wave Error"
        End If
        WaveHeader.dwFlags = 0
        ' Close the wave device.
        ReturnCode = waveOutClose(hWaveOut)
        If ReturnCode <> 0 Then
            MsgBox "Unable to Close Wave Device", MB_ICONSTOP, "Wave Error"
        End If
    Else
        ' Couldn't prepare the header, so close the device.
        MsgBox "Unable to Prepare Wave Header", 0, "Wave Error"
        ReturnCode = waveOutClose(hWaveOut)
        If ReturnCode <> 0 Then
            MsgBox "Unable to Close Wave Device", MB_ICONSTOP, "Wave Error"
        End If
    End If
Else
    ' Couldn't open the device so do nothing.
    MsgBox "Unable to Open Wave Device", MB_ICONSTOP, "Wave Error"
End If
End Sub
```

Checking the Capabilities of Your Sound Card

Although Windows supports device independence, it can't magically grant missing capabilities to hardware devices. The first generation of sound cards supported only 8-bit monophonic sample playback and recording at maximum sampling rates of 22.05 kHz. Hundreds of thousands of computers are still equipped with these cards, so if we plan to write commercial multimedia titles, we had better support them. The Windows multimedia API provides a function called **waveOutGetDevCaps()** with which we can query the device driver for information about the waveaudio device built into the installed sound card. (Other functions ask for MIDI and mixer information.)

To get the device capabilities, you must first declare a structure of type **WAVEOUTCAPS**:

```
Type WAVEOUTCAPS
        wMid As Integer
        wPid As Integer
```

```
        vDriverVersion As Long
        szPname As String * 32
        dwFormats As Long
        wChannels As Integer
        dwSupport As Long
End Type
```

Here's a brief rundown of these fields:

- **wMid** holds the manufacturer's ID for the device driver.
- **wPid** holds the product ID (the manufacturer's ID for the sound card).
- **vDriverVersion** is a long integer field that specifies the version number of the device driver. The high-order byte contains the major version number, while the low-order byte contains the minor version (or release) number.
- **szPName** contains the name of the product.
- **dwFormats** is a flag field, in which each bit represents a waveform audio format. For the list of available formats, see Table 15.1.
- **wChannels** is an integer field that contains a value of either 1 or 2, to indicate support for just monophonic output, or for both mono and stereo.
- **dwSupport**, another flag field, indicates whether the device supports any of the extended wave output capabilities, as listed in Table 15.2. If

Table 15.1 *The Standard Wave Format Constants*

Constant Name	Sampling Rate	Bit Resolution	Channels	Hexadecimal Value
WAVE_FORMAT_1M08	11.025 kHz	8	Mono	&H00000001
WAVE_FORMAT_1S08	11.025 kHz	8	Stereo	&H00000002
WAVE_FORMAT_1M16	11.025 kHz	16	Mono	&H00000004
WAVE_FORMAT_2M08	22.05 kHz	8	Mono	&H00000010
WAVE_FORMAT_2S08	22.05 kHz	8	Stereo	&H00000020
WAVE_FORMAT_2M16	22.05 kHz	16	Mono	&H00000040
WAVE_FORMAT_2S16	22.05 kHz	16	Stereo	&H00000080
WAVE_FORMAT_4M08	44.1 kHz	8	Mono	&H00000100
WAVE_FORMAT_4S08	44.1 kHz	8	Stereo	&H00000200
WAVE_FORMAT_4M16	44.1 kHz	16	Mono	&H00000400
WAVE_FORMAT_4S16	44.1 kHz	16	Stereo	&H00000800

Table 15.2 *The Constants That Indicate Support for Optional Wave Output Capabilities*

Constant Name	Value
WAVECAPS_PITCH	&H00000001
WAVECAPS_PLAYBACKRATE	&H00000002
WAVECAPS_VOLUME	&H00000004
WAVECAPS_LRVOLUME	&H00000008

it does, you can call the three **waveOut** functions that control these features: **waveOutSetPitch()**, **waveOutSetPlaybackRate()**, and **waveOutSetVolume()**, along with the three corresponding query functions: **waveOutGetPitch()**, **waveOutGetPlaybackRate()**, and **waveOutGetVolume()**.

To retrieve the device information, pass the address of a **WAVEOUTCAPS** data structure to **waveOutGetDevCaps()**, as shown in Listing 15.4. Here's the function declaration:

```
Win32:
Declare Function waveOutGetDevCaps Lib "winmm.dll" Alias "waveOutGetDevCapsA" _
    (ByVal uDeviceID As Long, lpCaps As WAVEOUTCAPS, ByVal uSize As Long) As Long

Win16:
Declare Function waveOutGetDevCaps Lib "MMSystem" (ByVal wDeviceID As Integer, _
    lpCaps As WAVEOUTCAPS, ByVal wSize As Integer) As Integer
```

The first argument, **wDeviceID**, specifies the waveaudio output device to query. It's possible to install more than one waveaudio device in a single computer. Each device is given a number, starting with device number 0.

In the second argument, **lpCaps**, we must pass a pointer to the **WAVEOUTCAPS** structure, which we do by omitting the **ByVal** keyword. And in the third argument, **wSize**, we pass the size of the **WAVEOUTCAPS** record.

Listing 15.4 The DeviceCapsOption_Click() Event Procedure from WAVPLAY2.FRM

```
Private Sub DeviceCapsOption_Click()
Dim Result As Long
Dim CapsRecord As WAVEOUTCAPS
Dim MajorVersion As Integer
Dim MinorVersion As Integer
```

```
Dim ProductName As String
Dim Counter As Integer

    Result = waveOutGetDevCaps(0, CapsRecord, Len(CapsRecord))
    If Result = 0 Then
        Picture1.Cls
        Picture1.Print "Manufacturer's Driver ID: "; CapsRecord.wMid
        Picture1.Print "Product ID: "; CapsRecord.wPid
        MajorVersion = CapsRecord.vDriverVersion \ 256
        MinorVersion = CapsRecord.vDriverVersion Mod 256
        Picture1.Print "Driver Version: "; MajorVersion; "."; MinorVersion _
            'Str$(CapsRecord.vDriverVersion)
        ProductName = Left$(CapsRecord.szPname, InStr(CapsRecord.szPname, _
            Chr$(0)) - 1)
        Picture1.Print "Product Name: "; ProductName
        Picture1.Print "Wave Formats Supported:"
        For Counter = 0 To 11
            If CapsRecord.dwFormats And 2 ^ Counter Then
                Picture1.Print "   "; WaveFormatStringFromConstant(2 ^ Counter)
            End If
        Next Counter
        Picture1.Print "Number of Channels: "; Str$(CapsRecord.wChannels)
        Picture1.Print "Device Functions Supported:"
        For Counter = 0 To 4
            If CapsRecord.dwSupport And 2 ^ Counter Then
                Picture1.Print "   "; WaveFunctionStringFromConstant(2 ^ Counter)
            End If
        Next Counter
    End If
End Sub
```

This event procedure calls two support functions located in WAVPLAY2.BAS,
WaveFormatStringFromConstant(), shown in Listing 15.5, and
WaveFunctionStringFromConstant(), shown in Listing 15.6.

Listing 15.5   The WaveFormatStringFromConstant() General Function from WAVPLAY2.BAS

```
Function WaveFormatStringFromConstant(FormatNumber As Long)
Dim Result As String

    Select Case FormatNumber
        Case WAVE_FORMAT_1M08
            Result = "11.025 kHz, Mono,    8 bit"
        Case WAVE_FORMAT_1S08
            Result = "11.025 kHz, Stereo,  8 bit"
        Case WAVE_FORMAT_1M16
            Result = "11.025 kHz, Mono,   16 bit"
        Case WAVE_FORMAT_1S16
            Result = "11.025 kHz, Stereo, 16 bit"
        Case WAVE_FORMAT_2M08
            Result = "22.05  kHz, Mono,    8 bit"
```

```
      Case WAVE_FORMAT_2S08
         Result = "22.05  kHz, Stereo, 8 bit"
      Case WAVE_FORMAT_2M16
         Result = "22.05  kHz, Mono,   16 bit"
      Case WAVE_FORMAT_2S16
         Result = "22.05  kHz, Stereo, 16 bit"
      Case WAVE_FORMAT_4M08
         Result = "44.1   kHz, Mono,   8 bit"
      Case WAVE_FORMAT_4S08
         Result = "44.1   kHz, Stereo, 8 bit"
      Case WAVE_FORMAT_4M16
         Result = "44.1   kHz, Mono,   16 bit"
      Case WAVE_FORMAT_4S16
         Result = "44.1   kHz, Stereo, 16 bit"
      Case Else
         Result = "Invalid Wave Format"
   End Select
   WaveFormatStringFromConstant = Result
End Function
```

Listing 15.6   The WaveFunctionStringFromConstant() General Function from WAVPLAY2.BAS

```
Function WaveFunctionStringFromConstant(FunctionNumber As Long)
Dim Result As String

   Select Case FunctionNumber
      Case WAVECAPS_PITCH
         Result = "Pitch Control"
      Case WAVECAPS_PLAYBACKRATE
         Result = "Playback Rate Control"
      Case WAVECAPS_VOLUME
         Result = "Volume Control"
      Case WAVECAPS_LRVOLUME
         Result = "Separate Left-Right Volume Control"
      Case WAVECAPS_SYNC
         Result = "Synchronization"
      Case Else
         Result = "Invalid Function"
   End Select
   WaveFunctionStringFromConstant = Result
End Function
```

Modifying Wave Data with the ChangeLevel() Procedure

One of the simplest things you can do to waveform sample data is change its overall playback volume, known as its *amplitude*. Each 8- or 16-bit sample represents an amplitude level. To change the overall amplitude, we can multiply each sample by some constant adjustment factor. To increase the amplitude, we raise the peaks of the waves by increasing the positive values, and lower their troughs by decreasing the negative values; to decrease the amplitude, we do just the opposite. The only complicating factor is the number of different, incompatible waveform formats, for example, to handle all twelve standard waveform formats, we need to handle four cases. Here's why: The sampling rate doesn't make any difference when it comes to amplitude scaling, so all we need consider are the bit resolution and the number of channels, which gives us four cases. In fact, because the two channels in stereo sample data work just like two monaural (affecting only one ear) channels, we could get away with just two cases, one for 8-bit samples and one for 16-bit. However, for more advanced effects, such as reverb and echo (which we'll discuss soon), we will often need to account for the number of channels. Take a look at Listing 15.7 to see how we handled this situation.

Listing 15.7 The ChangeLevel() General Procedure from WAVPLAY2.BAS

```
Sub ChangeLevel(LevelChange As Integer)
Dim Position As Long
Dim LevelFactor As Single
Dim TempValue As Integer
Dim MonoEightBitSample As MonoEightBitSamples
Dim StereoEightBitSample As StereoEightBitSamples
Dim MonoSixteenBitSample As MonoSixteenBitSamples
Dim StereoSixteenBitSample As StereoSixteenBitSamples
Dim Templong As Long

    LevelFactor = 1 + LevelChange / 100
    Select Case WaveFormatConstantFromFormat(PCMWaveFmtRecord)
       Case WAVE_FORMAT_1M08, WAVE_FORMAT_2M08, WAVE_FORMAT_4M08 ' Mono 8-bit
          For Position = 0 To (WaveHeader.dwBufferLength - 1)
             MonoEightBitSample.Char = WaveBuffer(Position)
             TempValue = (MonoEightBitSample.Char - 128) * LevelFactor
             MonoEightBitSample.Char = MaxInt(MinInt(TempValue, 127), -128) + 128
             WaveBuffer(Position) = MonoEightBitSample.Char
          Next Position
       Case WAVE_FORMAT_1S08, WAVE_FORMAT_2S08, WAVE_FORMAT_4S08 ' Stereo 8-bit
          For Position = 0 To (WaveHeader.dwBufferLength - 2) Step 2
             StereoEightBitSample.LeftChar = WaveBuffer(Position)
             StereoEightBitSample.RightChar = WaveBuffer(Position + 1)
             TempValue = (StereoEightBitSample.LeftChar - 128) * LevelFactor
             StereoEightBitSample.LeftChar = MaxInt(MinInt(TempValue, 127), _
                -128) + 128
             TempValue = (StereoEightBitSample.RightChar - 128) * LevelFactor
             StereoEightBitSample.RightChar = MaxInt(MinInt(TempValue, 127), _
                -128) + 128
             WaveBuffer(Position) = StereoEightBitSample.LeftChar
             WaveBuffer(Position + 1) = StereoEightBitSample.RightChar
          Next Position
       Case WAVE_FORMAT_1M16, WAVE_FORMAT_2M16, WAVE_FORMAT_4M16 ' Mono 16-bit
          For Position = 0 To (WaveHeader.dwBufferLength - 2) Step 2
             MonoSixteenBitSample.Sample = CLng(WaveBuffer(Position + 1)) * 256 _
                + WaveBuffer(Position)
```

```
                If MonoSixteenBitSample.Sample > 32767 Then _
                    MonoSixteenBitSample.Sample = MonoSixteenBitSample.Sample - 65535
                MonoSixteenBitSample.Sample = _
                    MaxLong(MinLong(MonoSixteenBitSample.Sample * LevelFactor, _
                    32767), -32768)
                If MonoSixteenBitSample.Sample < 0 Then MonoSixteenBitSample.Sample _
                    = 65535 + MonoSixteenBitSample.Sample
                WaveBuffer(Position + 1) = MonoSixteenBitSample.Sample \ 256
                WaveBuffer(Position) = MonoSixteenBitSample.Sample Mod 256
            Next Position
        Case WAVE_FORMAT_1S16, WAVE_FORMAT_2S16, WAVE_FORMAT_4S16 ' Stereo 16-bit
            For Position = 0 To (WaveHeader.dwBufferLength - 4) Step 4
                'Left Channel
                StereoSixteenBitSample.LeftSample = CLng(WaveBuffer(Position + 1)) _
                    * 256 + WaveBuffer(Position)
                If StereoSixteenBitSample.LeftSample > 32767 Then _
                    StereoSixteenBitSample.LeftSample = _
                    StereoSixteenBitSample.LeftSample - 65535
                StereoSixteenBitSample.LeftSample = _
                    MaxLong(MinLong(StereoSixteenBitSample.LeftSample * _
                    LevelFactor, 32767), -32768)
                If StereoSixteenBitSample.LeftSample < 0 Then _
                    StereoSixteenBitSample.LeftSample = 65535 + _
                    StereoSixteenBitSample.LeftSample
                WaveBuffer(Position + 1) = StereoSixteenBitSample.LeftSample \ 256
                WaveBuffer(Position) = StereoSixteenBitSample.LeftSample Mod 256
                'Right Channel
                StereoSixteenBitSample.RightSample = CLng(WaveBuffer(Position + 3)) _
                    * 256 + WaveBuffer(Position + 2)
                If StereoSixteenBitSample.RightSample > 32767 Then _
                    StereoSixteenBitSample.RightSample = _
                    StereoSixteenBitSample.RightSample - 65535
                StereoSixteenBitSample.RightSample = _
                    MaxLong(MinLong(StereoSixteenBitSample.RightSample * _
                    LevelFactor, 32767), -32768)
                If StereoSixteenBitSample.RightSample < 0 Then _
                    StereoSixteenBitSample.RightSample = 65535 + _
                    StereoSixteenBitSample.RightSample
                WaveBuffer(Position + 3) = StereoSixteenBitSample.RightSample \ 256
                WaveBuffer(Position + 2) = StereoSixteenBitSample.RightSample _
                    Mod 256
            Next Position
    End Select
End Sub
```

If we isolate one case, the code looks much simpler:

```
LevelFactor = 1 + LevelChange / 100
    Select Case WaveFormatConstantFromFormat(PCMWaveFmtRecord)
        Case WAVE_FORMAT_1M08, WAVE_FORMAT_2M08, WAVE_FORMAT_4M08 ' Mono 8-bit
            For Position = 0 To (WaveHeader.dwBufferLength - 1)
                MonoEightBitSample.Char = WaveBuffer(Position)
                TempValue = (MonoEightBitSample.Char - 128) * LevelFactor
```

```
        MonoEightBitSample.Char = MaxInt(MinInt(TempValue, 127), -128) + 128
        WaveBuffer(Position) = MonoEightBitSample.Char
    Next Position
```

For 8-bit, monaural sample data, the function reads through our WAV data array byte by byte. For each sample, it shifts the value to a zero baseline by subtracting 128, multiplying the value by the level adjustment factor, shifting it back to a 128 baseline, and rewriting the sample to its position in the byte array. The 16-bit samples are even easier to handle because their values are already signed integers, so all we have to do is multiply them by the **LevelFactor**.

As a case *selector*, we feed the wave format information to another general function called **WaveFormatConstantFromFormat()**, shown in Listing 15.8. This function uses the sampling rate, bit resolution, and number of channels stored in a record of type **PCMWAVEFORMAT** to derive one of the twelve standard wave format constants.

Listing 15.8   The WaveFormatConstantFromFormat() General Function from WAVPLAY2.BAS

```
Function WaveFormatConstantFromFormat(ThePCMWaveFormatRecord As PCMWAVEFORMAT) _
    As Long
Dim SampleRateFactor As Long
Dim ResolutionFactor As Long
Dim ChannelsFactor As Long

    SampleRateFactor = (Log(ThePCMWaveFormatRecord.wf.nSamplesPerSec \ 11025) / _
        Log(2)) * 4
    ResolutionFactor = (ThePCMWaveFormatRecord.wBitsPerSample \ 8 - 1) * 2
    ChannelsFactor = ThePCMWaveFormatRecord.wf.nChannels - 1
    WaveFormatConstantFromFormat = 2 ^ (SampleRateFactor + ResolutionFactor +
ChannelsFactor)
End Function
```

Implementing the AddEcho() Procedure

It's a little harder to add echo to waveform audio than it is to adjust the volume, but not *too* much harder. The old-fashioned analog way to create an electronic echo is to take the output of the monitor head on a tape recorder and feed it back to the record head upstream. By adjusting the gain on this feedback loop, an engineer can control the decay rate of the echo—in other words, the change in loudness from one repetition to the next. To change the period of the echo—the delay between repetitions—you have to change the tape speed, because the heads are usually mounted in fixed positions along the tape path.

With a little digital wizardry, we can reproduce the effect of the analog tape loop method, and gain some flexibility in the process. Unlike the tape process, we'll be starting with a complete recording of the original sound, to which we will add echo. For each sample in the waveform recording, we'll pick up an earlier sample, adjust its amplitude, and add the two together. The distance between the two samples will depend on the sampling rate, the number of bytes per sample (a function of both bit resolution and the number of channels), and the time delay we choose. Take a look at the **AddEcho()** procedure in Listing 15.9.

Listing 15.9 The AddEcho() Procedure from WAVPLAY2.BAS

```
Function AddEcho(Delay As Integer, EchoGain As Integer)
Dim EchoPeriod As Long
Dim GainFactor As Single
Dim lpTheWaveSampleData As Long
Dim lpNewWaveSampleData As Long
Dim LastSamplePosition As Long
Dim Position As Long
Dim Dummy As Long
Dim NewBufferLength As Long

Dim MonoEightBitSample As MonoEightBitSamples
Dim PrevMonoEightBitSample As MonoEightBitSamples
Dim StereoEightBitSample As StereoEightBitSamples
Dim PrevStereoEightBitSample As StereoEightBitSamples
Dim MonoSixteenBitSample As MonoSixteenBitSamples
Dim PrevMonoSixteenBitSample As MonoSixteenBitSamples
Dim StereoSixteenBitSample As StereoSixteenBitSamples
Dim PrevStereoSixteenBitSample As StereoSixteenBitSamples
Const TrailingEchoes = 2

    GainFactor = EchoGain / 50
    EchoPeriod = Delay * PCMWaveFmtRecord.wf.nSamplesPerSec \ 1000

    Select Case WaveFormatConstantFromFormat(PCMWaveFmtRecord)
       Case WAVE_FORMAT_1M08, WAVE_FORMAT_2M08, WAVE_FORMAT_4M08 ' Mono 8-bit
          NewBufferLength = WaveHeader.dwBufferLength + EchoPeriod * _
             TrailingEchoes - 1
          ReDim Preserve WaveBuffer(NewBufferLength)
          PrevMonoEightBitSample.Char = 128
          ' Initialize new bytes to midpoint value.
          For Position = WaveHeader.dwBufferLength To NewBufferLength
             WaveBuffer(Position) = PrevMonoEightBitSample.Char
          Next Position
          ' Mix in echo.
          For Position = EchoPeriod To NewBufferLength
             MonoEightBitSample.Char = WaveBuffer(Position)
             ' Retrieve contents of byte at (Position-Period).
             PrevMonoEightBitSample.Char = WaveBuffer(Position - EchoPeriod)
```

```
        WaveBuffer(Position) = ((MonoEightBitSample.Char - 128) + _
            (PrevMonoEightBitSample.Char - 128) * GainFactor) \ 2 + 128
    Next Position
    WaveHeader.dwBufferLength = NewBufferLength + 1
    MsgBox "Completed " + Str$(Position) + " iterations out of " + _
        Str$(WaveHeader.dwBufferLength)
Case WAVE_FORMAT_1S08, WAVE_FORMAT_2S08, WAVE_FORMAT_4S08 ' Stereo 8-bit
    EchoPeriod = EchoPeriod * 2
    NewBufferLength = WaveHeader.dwBufferLength + EchoPeriod * _
        TrailingEchoes - 1
    ReDim Preserve WaveBuffer(NewBufferLength)
    PrevStereoEightBitSample.LeftChar = 128
    PrevStereoEightBitSample.RightChar = 128
    ' Initialize new bytes to midpoint value.
    For Position = WaveHeader.dwBufferLength To NewBufferLength Step 2
        WaveBuffer(Position) = PrevStereoEightBitSample.LeftChar
        WaveBuffer(Position + 1) = PrevStereoEightBitSample.RightChar
    Next Position
    ' Mix in echo.
    For Position = EchoPeriod To NewBufferLength Step 2
        StereoEightBitSample.LeftChar = WaveBuffer(Position)
        StereoEightBitSample.RightChar = WaveBuffer(Position + 1)
        ' Retrieve contents of byte at (Position-Period).
        PrevStereoEightBitSample.LeftChar = WaveBuffer(Position - _
            EchoPeriod)
        PrevStereoEightBitSample.RightChar = WaveBuffer(Position - _
            EchoPeriod + 1)
        WaveBuffer(Position) = ((StereoEightBitSample.LeftChar - 128) + _
            (PrevStereoEightBitSample.LeftChar - 128) * GainFactor) \ 2 + 128
        WaveBuffer(Position + 1) = ((StereoEightBitSample.RightChar - 128) _
            + (PrevStereoEightBitSample.RightChar - 128) * GainFactor) \ 2 _
            + 128
    Next Position
    WaveHeader.dwBufferLength = NewBufferLength + 1
    MsgBox "Completed " + Str$(Position) + " iterations out of " + _
        Str$(WaveHeader.dwBufferLength)
Case WAVE_FORMAT_1M16, WAVE_FORMAT_2M16, WAVE_FORMAT_4M16 ' Mono 16-bit
    EchoPeriod = EchoPeriod * 2
    NewBufferLength = WaveHeader.dwBufferLength + EchoPeriod * _
        TrailingEchoes - 1
    ReDim Preserve WaveBuffer(NewBufferLength + 1)
    ' Mix in echo.
    For Position = EchoPeriod To NewBufferLength Step 2
        MonoSixteenBitSample.Sample = CLng(WaveBuffer(Position + 1)) * 256 _
            + WaveBuffer(Position)
        If MonoSixteenBitSample.Sample > 32767 Then _
            MonoSixteenBitSample.Sample = MonoSixteenBitSample.Sample - 65535
        PrevMonoSixteenBitSample.Sample = CLng(WaveBuffer(Position + 1 - _
            EchoPeriod)) * 256 + WaveBuffer(Position - EchoPeriod)
        If PrevMonoSixteenBitSample.Sample > 32767 Then _
            PrevMonoSixteenBitSample.Sample = _
                PrevMonoSixteenBitSample.Sample - 65535
        MonoSixteenBitSample.Sample = (MonoSixteenBitSample.Sample + _
            PrevMonoSixteenBitSample.Sample * GainFactor) \ 2
```

```
            If MonoSixteenBitSample.Sample < 0 Then MonoSixteenBitSample.Sample _
                = 65535 + MonoSixteenBitSample.Sample
            WaveBuffer(Position + 1) = MonoSixteenBitSample.Sample \ 256
            WaveBuffer(Position) = MonoSixteenBitSample.Sample Mod 256
        Next Position
        WaveHeader.dwBufferLength = NewBufferLength + 1
        MsgBox "Completed " + Str$(Position) + " iterations out of " + _
            Str$(WaveHeader.dwBufferLength)
    Case WAVE_FORMAT_1S16, WAVE_FORMAT_2S16, WAVE_FORMAT_4S16 ' Stereo 16-bit
        EchoPeriod = EchoPeriod * 4
        NewBufferLength = WaveHeader.dwBufferLength + EchoPeriod * _
            TrailingEchoes - 4
        ReDim Preserve WaveBuffer(NewBufferLength)
        For Position = EchoPeriod To NewBufferLength - 4 Step 4
            ' Left Channel
            StereoSixteenBitSample.LeftSample = CLng(WaveBuffer(Position + 1)) _
                * 256 + WaveBuffer(Position)
            If StereoSixteenBitSample.LeftSample > 32767 Then _
                StereoSixteenBitSample.LeftSample = _
                StereoSixteenBitSample.LeftSample - 65535
            PrevStereoSixteenBitSample.LeftSample = CLng(WaveBuffer(Position + _
                1 - EchoPeriod)) * 256 + WaveBuffer(Position - EchoPeriod)
            If PrevStereoSixteenBitSample.LeftSample > 32767 Then _
                PrevStereoSixteenBitSample.LeftSample = _
                PrevStereoSixteenBitSample.LeftSample - 65535
            StereoSixteenBitSample.LeftSample = _
                (StereoSixteenBitSample.LeftSample + _
                PrevStereoSixteenBitSample.LeftSample * GainFactor) \ 2
            If StereoSixteenBitSample.LeftSample < 0 Then _
                StereoSixteenBitSample.LeftSample = 65535 + _
                StereoSixteenBitSample.LeftSample
            WaveBuffer(Position + 1) = StereoSixteenBitSample.LeftSample \ 256
            WaveBuffer(Position) = StereoSixteenBitSample.LeftSample Mod 256
            ' Right Channel
            StereoSixteenBitSample.RightSample = CLng(WaveBuffer(Position + 3)) _
                * 256 + WaveBuffer(Position + 2)
            If StereoSixteenBitSample.RightSample > 32767 Then _
                StereoSixteenBitSample.RightSample = _
                StereoSixteenBitSample.RightSample - 65535
            PrevStereoSixteenBitSample.RightSample = CLng(WaveBuffer(Position _
                + 3 - EchoPeriod)) * 256 + WaveBuffer(Position + 2 - EchoPeriod)
            If PrevStereoSixteenBitSample.RightSample > 32767 Then _
                PrevStereoSixteenBitSample.RightSample = _
                PrevStereoSixteenBitSample.RightSample - 65535
            StereoSixteenBitSample.RightSample = _
                (StereoSixteenBitSample.RightSample + _
                PrevStereoSixteenBitSample.RightSample * GainFactor) \ 2
            If StereoSixteenBitSample.RightSample < 0 Then _
                StereoSixteenBitSample.RightSample = 65535 + _
                StereoSixteenBitSample.RightSample
            WaveBuffer(Position + 3) = StereoSixteenBitSample.RightSample \ 256
            WaveBuffer(Position + 2) = StereoSixteenBitSample.RightSample Mod 256
        Next Position
        WaveHeader.dwBufferLength = NewBufferLength
```

```
        MsgBox "Completed " + Str$(Position) + " iterations out of " + _
            Str$(WaveHeader.dwBufferLength)
    End Select
End Function
```

This procedure takes two arguments: the echo **Delay** in milliseconds, and the **EchoGain** given as a whole percentage (here we use 50 for a fifty percent dropoff rate, rather than 0.5).

Just as in the **ChangeLevel()** procedure, the sampling rate is irrelevant, except to determine the **EchoPeriod**. So, we can divide all twelve standard waveform data formats into just four cases, based on bit resolution and number of channels.

We need some room at the end of the sound for the trailing echoes, so the first thing we do in each of the four cases is to extend the sample data. We have arbitrarily set the value of **TrailingEchoes** to **2**. The number you use will depend on how much memory you're willing to commit to the waveform sample data, and how much you *attenuate* (reduce the amplitude of) the feedback sample with each iteration. With only two extra iterations, you'll often hear a distinct cutoff before the sound entirely fades away. If you wish, increase the value of **TrailingEchoes** until you get the effect you want (you may wish to pass this value in as another argument of the procedure). To pad the waveform sample data in preparation for the echo, we simply perform a **ReDim Preserve** function to reset the size of our buffer to be equal to the current size, plus the size of the echo delay multiplied by the number of echoes.

There is no need to change the sample data prior to the first echo, so the **For** loops that mix in the echo effect begin not at the first byte in the sample, but at an offset equal to the echo period, as in this line from the stereo 16-bit format case:

```
For Position = EchoPeriod To NewBufferLength - 4 Step 4
```

When you mix waveform sample data, you need to decide whether to attenuate the overall amplitude of the sample to avoid exceeding the limits of the 8- or 16-bit integer values, or to *clip* the sample at those limits. Clipping is the effect that occurs when you flatten out the top or bottom of a waveform. In **AddEcho()**, we have averaged the two samples, which scales them to prevent the mixed result from exceeding the amplitude limits. This will not always sound right. Imagine that you're processing a sound with a steady amplitude—some loud, continuous noise, like a train clattering along its tracks. If that sound already peaks near the limits of the amplitude range, then the averaging method will cause the original sound to suddenly drop its amplitude by half when the first echo begins.

For a more accurate sound, you should use the clipping method. Here's the code for 8-bit clipping:

```
TempValue% = ((MonoEightBitSample.Char - 128) + (PrevMonoEightBitSample.Char - _
    128) * GainFactor) \ 2 + 128
MonoEightBitSample.Char = MinInt(MaxInt(TempValue%, 0), 255)
```

And this code is for 16-bit clipping:

```
TempValue% = (MonoSixteenBitSample.Sample + PrevMonoSixteenBitSample.Sample * _
    GainFactor) \ 2
MonoSixteenBitSample.Sample = MinInt(MaxInt(TempValue%, -32768), 32767)
```

Clipping will cause popping and other noise, so if you choose this method, make sure the wave samples start out with low enough peak levels, so that clipping will rarely occur. You'll still get better results than you would with averaging.

On a more basic level, the biggest problem with this procedure, and also with **ChangeLevel()**, is speed. Some of the performance problems come from VB's interpreted math processing, which can be much slower than similar processing in Holy Trinity languages. We have optimized this code about as far as it will go with present VB technology. One area that you might be able to find some speed in is the method we used to convert the two bytes of sound information into a single integer.

```
StereoSixteenBitSample.LeftSample = CLng(WaveBuffer(Position + 1)) * 256 + _
    WaveBuffer(Position)
If StereoSixteenBitSample.LeftSample > 32767 Then _
    StereoSixteenBitSample.LeftSample = StereoSixteenBitSample.LeftSample - 65535
```

This code uses a brute force method for performing what should be a very simple operation. In languages like C and Pascal, you could easily convert this type of data; unfortunately, we couldn't find an easy way to do it in VB. If you can find a better way, don't be afraid to hurt our feelings—just use it!

The Declarations for WAVPLAY.BAS

WAVPLAY2.BAS has grown considerably from the version we developed in Chapter 5. To support all these functions, you'll need some API functions, data structures, and variables. You'll find them all in the declarations section of the code module, shown in Listing 15.10.

Listing 15.10 The Declarations Section of WAVPLAY2.BAS

```
Option Explicit

Type FOURCC
        Chars As String * 4
End Type

Type WAVEFORMAT
        wFormatTag As Integer
        nChannels As Integer
        nSamplesPerSec As Long
        nAvgBytesPerSec As Long
        nBlockAlign As Integer
End Type

Type WAVEOUTCAPS
        wMid As Integer
        wPid As Integer
        vDriverVersion As Long
        szPname As String * 32
        dwFormats As Long
        wChannels As Integer
        dwSupport As Long
End Type

Type WAVEHDR
        lpData As Long
        dwBufferLength As Long
        dwBytesRecorded As Long
        dwUser As Long
        dwFlags As Long
        dwLoops As Long
        lpNext As Long
        Reserved As Long
End Type

Type PCMWAVEFORMAT
        wf As WAVEFORMAT
        wBitsPerSample As Integer
End Type

Type MMIOINFO
        dwFlags As Long
        fccIOProc As Long
        pIOProc As Long
        wErrorRet As Long
        htask As Long
        cchBuffer As Long
        pchBuffer As String
        pchNext As String
        pchEndRead As String
        pchEndWrite As String
```

```
        lBufOffset As Long
        lDiskOffset As Long
        adwInfo(4) As Long
        dwReserved1 As Long
        dwReserved2 As Long
        hmmio As Long
End Type

Type MMCKINFO
        ckid As FOURCC          ' chunk ID
        ckSize As Long          ' chunk size
        fccType As FOURCC       ' form type or list type
        dwDataOffset As Long    ' offset of data portion of chunk
        dwFlags As Long         ' flags used by MMIO functions
End Type

#If Win32 Then
    Private Declare Function lparraycpy Lib "kernel32" Alias "lstrcpy" _
        (lpString1 As Any, lpString2 As Any) As Long
    Private Declare Function mmioAscend Lib "winmm.dll" (ByVal hmmio As Long, _
        lpck As Any, ByVal uFlags As Long) As Long
    Private Declare Function mmioClose Lib "winmm.dll" (ByVal hmmio As Long, _
        ByVal uFlags As Long) As Long
    Private Declare Function mmioDescend Lib "winmm.dll" (ByVal hmmio As Long, _
        lpck As Any, lpckParent As Any, ByVal uFlags As Long) As Long
    Private Declare Function mmioOpen Lib "winmm.dll" Alias "mmioOpenA" (ByVal _
        szFileName As String, lpmmioinfo As Any, ByVal dwOpenFlags As Long) As Long
    Private Declare Function mmioRead Lib "winmm.dll" (ByVal hmmio As Long, _
        pch As Any, ByVal cch As Long) As Long
    Private Declare Function waveOutClose Lib "winmm.dll" (ByVal hWaveOut _
        As Long) As Long
    Public Declare Function waveOutGetDevCaps Lib "winmm.dll" Alias _
        "waveOutGetDevCapsA" (ByVal uDeviceID As Long, lpCaps As WAVEOUTCAPS, _
        ByVal uSize As Long) As Long
    Private Declare Function waveOutOpen Lib "winmm.dll" (lphWaveOut As Long, _
        ByVal uDeviceID As Long, lpFormat As PCMWAVEFORMAT, ByVal dwCallback As _
        Long, ByVal dwInstance As Long, ByVal dwFlags As Long) As Long
    Private Declare Function waveOutPrepareHeader Lib "winmm.dll" (ByVal _
        hWaveOut As Long, lpWaveOutHdr As Any, ByVal uSize As Long) As Long
    Private Declare Function waveOutUnprepareHeader Lib "winmm.dll" (ByVal _
        hWaveOut As Long, lpWaveOutHdr As Any, ByVal uSize As Long) As Long
    Private Declare Function waveOutWrite Lib "winmm.dll" (ByVal hWaveOut As _
        Long, lpWaveOutHdr As Any, ByVal uSize As Long) As Long
    Private Declare Function mmioReadToGlobal Lib "winmm.dll" Alias "mmioRead" _
        (ByVal hmmio As Long, ByVal lpBuffer As Long, ByVal cch As Long) As Long
#Else
    Public Declare Function waveOutGetDevCaps Lib "MMSystem" (ByVal wDeviceID _
        As Integer, lpCaps As WAVEOUTCAPS, ByVal wSize As Integer) As Integer
    Private Declare Function waveOutOpen Lib "MMSystem" (lphWaveOut As Integer, _
        ByVal wDeviceID As Integer, lpFormat As Any, dwCallback As Long, _
        ByVal dwCallback As Long, ByVal dwFlags As Long) As Integer
    Private Declare Function waveOutClose Lib "MMSystem" (ByVal hWaveOut As _
        Integer) As Integer
```

```
      Private Declare Function waveOutPrepareHeader Lib "MMSystem" (ByVal _
          hWaveOut As Integer, lpWaveOutHdr As Any, ByVal wSize As Integer) _
          As Integer
      Private Declare Function waveOutUnprepareHeader Lib "MMSystem" (ByVal _
          hWaveOut As Integer, lpWaveOutHdr As Any, ByVal wSize As Integer) _
          As Integer
      Private Declare Function waveOutWrite Lib "MMSystem" (ByVal hWaveOut As _
          Integer, lpWaveOutHdr As Any, ByVal wSize As Integer) As Integer
      Private Declare Function mmioOpen Lib "MMSystem" (ByVal szFileName As _
          String, lpmmioinfo As Any, ByVal dwOpenFlags As Long) As Integer
      Private Declare Function mmioClose Lib "MMSystem" (ByVal hmmio As Integer, _
          ByVal wFlags As Integer) As Integer
      Private Declare Function mmioDescend Lib "MMSystem" (ByVal hmmio As Integer, _
          lpck As Any, lpckParent As Any, ByVal wFlags As Integer) As Integer
      Private Declare Function mmioAscend Lib "MMSystem" (ByVal hmmio As Integer, _
          lpck As Any, ByVal wFlags As Integer) As Integer
      Private Declare Function mmioRead Lib "MMSystem" (ByVal hmmio As Integer, _
          pch As Any, ByVal cch As Long) As Long
      Private Declare Function mmioReadToGlobal Lib "MMSystem" Alias "mmioRead" _
          (ByVal hmmio As Integer, ByVal lpBuffer As Long, ByVal cch As Long) As Long
      Private Declare Function lparraycpy Lib "kernel" Alias "lstrcpy" (lpString1 _
          As Any, lpString2 As Any) As Long
#End If

Global Const WAVE_MAPPER = -1          ' Device ID for Wave Mapper
Global Const MMIO_READ = &H0&
Global Const MMIO_WRITE = &H1&
Global Const MMIO_READWRITE = &H2&

Global Const MMIO_FINDCHUNK = &H10    ' mmioDescend: find a chunk by ID
Global Const MMIO_FINDRIFF = &H20     ' mmioDescend: find a LIST chunk

Global Const WHDR_DONE = &H1          ' done bit

' flags for dwFlags parameter in waveOutOpen() and waveInOpen()
Global Const WAVE_FORMAT_QUERY = &H1

Global Const WAVECAPS_PITCH = &H1              ' Supports pitch control
Global Const WAVECAPS_PLAYBACKRATE = &H2       ' Supports playback rate control
Global Const WAVECAPS_VOLUME = &H4             ' Supports volume control
Global Const WAVECAPS_LRVOLUME = &H8           ' Supports separate left-right
volume control
Global Const WAVECAPS_SYNC = &H10

Global Const WAVE_INVALIDFORMAT = &H0 ' Invalid Format
Global Const WAVE_FORMAT_1M08 = &H1    ' 11.025 kHz, Mono,   8 bit
Global Const WAVE_FORMAT_1S08 = &H2    ' 11.025 kHz, Stereo, 8 bit
Global Const WAVE_FORMAT_1M16 = &H4    ' 11.025 kHz, Mono,   16 bit
Global Const WAVE_FORMAT_1S16 = &H8    ' 11.025 kHz, Stereo, 16 bit
Global Const WAVE_FORMAT_2M08 = &H10   ' 22.05  kHz, Mono,   8 bit
Global Const WAVE_FORMAT_2S08 = &H20   ' 22.05  kHz, Stereo, 8 bit
Global Const WAVE_FORMAT_2M16 = &H40   ' 22.05  kHz, Mono,   16 bit
Global Const WAVE_FORMAT_2S16 = &H80   ' 22.05  kHz, Stereo, 16 bit
Global Const WAVE_FORMAT_4M08 = &H100 ' 44.1   kHz, Mono,   8 bit
```

```
Global Const WAVE_FORMAT_4S08 = &H200 ' 44.1   kHz, Stereo, 8 bit
Global Const WAVE_FORMAT_4M16 = &H400 ' 44.1   kHz, Mono,   16 bit
Global Const WAVE_FORMAT_4S16 = &H800 ' 44.1   kHz, Stereo, 16 bit

Type MonoEightBitSamples
   Char As Byte
End Type

Type StereoEightBitSamples
   LeftChar As Byte
   RightChar As Byte
End Type

Type MonoSixteenBitSamples
   Sample As Long
End Type

Type StereoSixteenBitSamples
   LeftSample As Long
   RightSample As Long
End Type

Dim WaveBuffer() As Byte
Dim hWaveOut As Long
Dim WaveHeader As WAVEHDR
Global PCMWaveFmtRecord As PCMWAVEFORMAT
```

Completing the Form-Level Code

We've already covered the longest procedure in the form module, **DeviceCapsOption_Click()**. The other event procedures delegate most of their responsibilities to the general functions and procedures in the code module. You'll find all the code from WAVPLAY2.FRM in Listing 15.11.

Listing 15.11 WAVPLAY2.FRM

```
Option Explicit

Private Sub DeviceCapsOption_Click()
Dim Result As Long
Dim CapsRecord As WAVEOUTCAPS
Dim MajorVersion As Integer
Dim MinorVersion As Integer
Dim ProductName As String
Dim Counter As Integer

   Result = waveOutGetDevCaps(0, CapsRecord, Len(CapsRecord))
   If Result = 0 Then
      Picture1.Cls
      Picture1.Print "Manufacturer's Driver ID: "; CapsRecord.wMid
      Picture1.Print "Product ID: "; CapsRecord.wPid
      MajorVersion = CapsRecord.vDriverVersion \ 256
```

```
        MinorVersion = CapsRecord.vDriverVersion Mod 256
        Picture1.Print "Driver Version: "; MajorVersion; "."; MinorVersion _
            'Str$(CapsRecord.vDriverVersion)
        ProductName = Left$(CapsRecord.szPname, InStr(CapsRecord.szPname, _
            Chr$(0)) - 1)
        Picture1.Print "Product Name: "; ProductName
        Picture1.Print "Wave Formats Supported:"
        For Counter = 0 To 11
            If CapsRecord.dwFormats And 2 ^ Counter Then
                Picture1.Print "    "; WaveFormatStringFromConstant(2 ^ Counter)
            End If
        Next Counter
        Picture1.Print "Number of Channels: "; Str$(CapsRecord.wChannels)
        Picture1.Print "Device Functions Supported:"
        For Counter = 0 To 4
            If CapsRecord.dwSupport And 2 ^ Counter Then
                Picture1.Print "    "; WaveFunctionStringFromConstant(2 ^ Counter)
            End If
        Next Counter
    End If
End Sub

Private Sub EchoOption_Click()
Dim Dummy As Integer

    Screen.MousePointer = 11
    PlayOption.Enabled = False
    Dummy = AddEcho(500, 50)
    PlayOption.Enabled = True
    Screen.MousePointer = 0
End Sub

Private Sub Form_Load()
    PlayOption.Enabled = False
    VolumeOption.Enabled = False
    EchoOption.Enabled = False
    EffectsMenu.Enabled = False
    End Sub

Private Sub OpenOption_Click()
    PlayOption.Enabled = False
    VolumeOption.Enabled = False
    EchoOption.Enabled = False
    EffectsMenu.Enabled = False
    FileOpenDialog.Action = 1
    If OpenWaveFile(FileOpenDialog.filename) Then
        PlayOption.Enabled = True
        VolumeOption.Enabled = True
        EchoOption.Enabled = True
        EffectsMenu.Enabled = True
        Picture1.Cls
        Picture1.Print "Format: "; WaveFormatConstantFromFormat(PCMWaveFmtRecord)
        Picture1.Print "    Sample Rate: "; PCMWaveFmtRecord.wf.nSamplesPerSec; _
            " Hz"
```

```
     Picture1.Print "     Resolution: "; PCMWaveFmtRecord.wBitsPerSample
     Picture1.Print "     Channels: "; PCMWaveFmtRecord.wf.nChannels
   End If
End Sub

Private Sub PlayOption_Click()

   WaveOut
End Sub

Private Sub QuitOption_Click()
   Unload WavePlay
   End
End Sub

Private Sub VolumeOption_Click()

   Screen.MousePointer = 11
   PlayOption.Enabled = False
   ChangeLevel -50
   PlayOption.Enabled = True
   Screen.MousePointer = 0
End Sub
```

Real-Time Audio Effects

In the previous project, we explored ways to manipulate waveform data at the byte level. By using the low-level sound functions in the multimedia API, we were able to load a WAV file into memory and trigger instant replay. On the other hand, while we were also able to modify the individual digital sample values to change the overall amplitude of the recording and to add echo effects, those operations were anything but instantaneous.

Imagine what we could do if we could manipulate wave data on the fly. We could combine WAV files to produce effects for the ears that are as compelling and interactive as sprite animation is to the eyes. But clearly, based on our experience, it wouldn't be possible in VB to do something even so basic as mixing multiple WAV files in real time. VB just doesn't have the horsepower to do it—not by itself, that is.

Introducing WaveMix

As Microsoft continues to expand and refine the multimedia features of Windows, they have occasionally tossed us new components with which to tinker. One of the hottest libraries around lately is a real-time waveaudio mixer, known appropriately as *WaveMix*. Although Microsoft officials are quick to remind us that this is not a *supported product*, the author of the library, Angel Diaz, has been answering all sorts of questions by way of CompuServe (GO

WINMM). There are two consequences to using an unsupported product. First, because it is a work in progress, it may have bugs. And second, future releases may not provide complete backward compatibility. But WaveMix is so useful and easy to use, it's worth tolerating these minor inconveniences.

At the time of this writing, the 32-bit version of WaveMix was still in development, and we included the C source code for it on the CD-ROM in the \WAVEMIX subdirectory. We tried to get the new 32-bit DLL to work, but it is still pretty buggy. This is likely why Microsoft is not distributing a compiled version of the DLL; they probably want one of you out there to fix the problems, and share the result with them!

WaveMix is contained entirely in a single file called WAVEMIX.DLL. Although it works fine alone, WAVEMIX.DLL can be configured by setting various constants in a file called WAVEMIX.INI, an unusual feature for a DLL.

Cutting Edge Sound Mixing

If you really want to be on the cutting edge of sound mixing and playback, you need to check out the DirectSound technology being developed by Microsoft. DirectSound is the future of WaveMix. DirectSound takes over where WaveMix leaves off. It allows you to mix an unlimited number of WAV tracks in real-time. You can even play sounds from two different applications at once—something impossible and undreamed-of with WaveMix and the Windows 3.1 sound system. Another cool trick that DirectSound makes possible is audio streaming, which allows you to perform real-time effects like echo and reverb, and you can also change the speed of the playback with very high precision.

Unfortunately, DirectSound and the other DirectX technologies; DirectDraw and DirectPlay, don't work too well with VB. They are designed to work with lower-level languages like C++, because they make heavy use of callbacks.

If a custom control ever comes out that lets you use any of these technologies, jump on it! You won't regret it.

Mixing Waves in Real Time

The WaveMix API consists of 12 functions. In this project, we'll use most of them. Follow these steps to see just how useful this product can be:

1. Install WAVEMIX.DLL and test it out.
2. Create a form with seven Command Buttons.

> 3. Add the API declarations to the WAVEMIX.BAS code module (Listing 15.12).
> 4. Add the event procedures to WAVEMIX.FRM.
>
> *You'll find this project in the subdirectory \VBMAGIC\WAVEMIX in the files WAVEMIX.VBP, WAVEMIX.FRM, and WAVEMIX.BAS. You'll also need WAVEMIX.DLL and WAVEMIX.INI, which are located in the directory \WAVEMIX. The sample WAV files 1.WAV through 7.WAV are supplied by Microsoft with the WAVEMIX.DLL. They, too, are located in the \WAVEMIX directory.*

Installing and Testing WaveMix

Before you can run the demonstration program, you have to install the WaveMix DLL. This couldn't be much simpler. Copy the files WAVEMIX.DLL and WAVEMIX.INI from the directory \WAVEMIX on the companion CD-ROM into your \WINDOWS\SYSTEM directory. That's it.

Next, load and run WAVEMIX.VBP into the 16-bit version of VB 4. The program displays a simple form with seven Command Buttons, as shown in Figure 15.3.

To play any of the seven sounds individually, simply click on a button. To play more than one sound simultaneously, click on several of the buttons. If you click on the same button repeatedly, the WAV file attached to that button will be queued up to play once for each click.

To stop the program, use the Control menu, or the Quit option on the form's own File menu. If you stop the program with the VB End button or menu option, the waveaudio device driver will become locked. If this happens, the only way to reactivate the waveaudio device is to restart Windows.

Create the Form

For this project we'll need just one form. In the sample program on the companion CD-ROM, I have named it WaveMixForm, but because we won't reference the form name anywhere in the program, you may name it whatever you wish.

Figure 15.3   *The WAVEMIX project at runtime.*

Place a Command Button on the form and set its **Name** property to PlayWaveButton. Then add six more Command Buttons with the same name. When you add the second button, VB will ask you if you wish to create a control array. Click on the Yes button, then add the five remaining buttons. Set the button captions to "1" through "7."

We'll also need a File menu with one option: Quit. If you wish, you can dispense with the File menu and place the Quit option directly on the menu bar. Set the **Name** property of the Quit option to QuitOption.

The WaveMix API

In some ways, the WaveMix API resembles the GDI, although it's much simpler. You prepare to play waveaudio through the mixer by calling a function that returns a handle to a mixer *session*. You then use that handle to open *channels* and *waves*, which is a little like creating a GDI device context and selecting in drawing objects and bitmaps. When you're done playing sound, you have to close the channels and waves, and release the *session*.

A complete session with WaveMix actually requires at least eight steps, four to set things up, one to play the WAV clip, and three to shut down:

1. Call either **WaveMixInit()** or **WaveMixConfigureInit()** to initialize the DLL and acquire a handle to a mix session.
2. Call **WaveMixOpenWave()** to open a WAV file. If you're working in a low-level language like C++, you can also open wave resources. Or if you wish, you may open waves you've loaded into memory with the multimedia I/O functions.
3. Call **WaveMixOpenChannel()** to open one or more of the eight available mixer channels.
4. Call **WaveMixActivate()** to grab the waveaudio output device. This function enables your application to share the device with other applications.
5. Call **WaveMixPlay()** to feed a WAV to a channel.
6. Call **WaveMixCloseChannel()** to close one or more open channels.
7. Call **WaveMixFreeWave()** to release a WAV file or resource.
8. Call **WaveMixCloseSession()** to end the mixer session.

Along with these essential functions, the API includes three others. The first function, **WaveMixFlushChannel()**, will clear the queue of WAVs waiting to play on the specified channel, and will stop the WAV that is currently playing. You can flush a single channel, or all open channels with a single call.

WaveMixPump() works like a specialized version of the VB function **DoEvents**. WaveMix works by slicing off and adding together small chunks of sample data from each of the open channels. It passes these mixed chunks to the waveaudio device via the device driver's queue. WaveMix has to perform all that arithmetic at least as fast as the waveaudio device can play it. At sampling rates that begin at 11.025 kHz, that's quite a juggling act! If your program does a lot of processing, however, WaveMix will not get enough processor time to prepare these buffers, and the device driver's queue will empty, causing playback interruptions. To keep WaveMix from falling behind, scatter calls to **WaveMixPump()** throughout your program.

The last function, **WaveMixGetInfo()**, will retrieve some basic information about the WaveMix DLL, including its version number, its compilation date, and a list of supported wave formats.

The declarations for all twelve WaveMix functions, along with their required data structures and constants, appear in Listing 15.12.

Listing 15.12   WAVEMIX.BAS

```
Option Explicit

Type MIXCONFIG
    wSize As Integer
    dwFlags As Long
    wChannels As Integer
    wSamplingRate As Integer '(11=11025, 22=22050, 44=44100 Hz)
End Type

Type MIXPLAYPARAMS
    wSize As Integer
    hMixSession As Integer
    iChannel As Integer
    lpMixWave As Long
    hWndNotify As Integer
    dwFlags As Long
    wLoops As Integer ' = &HFFFF means loop forever
End Type

Type WAVEMIXINFO
    wSize As Integer
    Version As Integer
    Date As String * 12
    dwFormats As Long
End Type

Declare Function WaveMixInit Lib "WaveMix.DLL" () As Integer
Declare Function WaveMixConfigureInit Lib "WaveMix.DLL" _
    (lpConfig As MIXCONFIG) As Integer
Declare Function WaveMixActivate Lib "WaveMix.DLL" (ByVal hMixSession As _
    Integer, ByVal fActivate As Integer) As Integer
```

```
Declare Function WaveMixOpenWave Lib "WaveMix.DLL" (ByVal hMixSession As _
    Integer, ByVal szWaveFilename As String, ByVal hInst As Integer, ByVal _
    dwFlags As Long) As Long
Declare Function WaveMixOpenChannel Lib "WaveMix.DLL" (ByVal hMixSession As _
    Integer, ByVal iChannel As Integer, ByVal dwFlags As Long) As Integer
Declare Function WaveMixPlay Lib "WaveMix.DLL" (lpMixPlayParams As _
    MIXPLAYPARAMS) As Integer
Declare Function WaveMixFlushChannel Lib "WaveMix.DLL" (ByVal hMixSession As _
    Integer, ByVal iChannel As Integer, ByVal dwFlags As Long) As Integer
Declare Function WaveMixCloseChannel Lib "WaveMix.DLL" (ByVal hMixSession As _
    Integer, ByVal iChannel As Integer, ByVal dwFlags As Long) As Integer
Declare Function WaveMixFreeWave Lib "WaveMix.DLL" (ByVal hMixSession As _
    Integer, ByVal lpMixWave As Long) As Integer
Declare Function WaveMixCloseSession Lib "WaveMix.DLL" (ByVal hMixSession As _
    Integer) As Integer
Declare Sub WaveMixPump Lib "WaveMix.DLL" ()
Declare Function WaveMixGetInfo Lib "WaveMix.DLL" _
    (lpWaveMixInfo As WAVEMIXINFO) As Integer


' Wave Format Constants for WAVEMIXINFO
Global Const WAVE_FORMAT_1M08 = &H1    ' 11.025 kHz, Mono,   8 bit
Global Const WAVE_FORMAT_1S08 = &H2    ' 11.025 kHz, Stereo, 8 bit
Global Const WAVE_FORMAT_1M16 = &H4    ' 11.025 kHz, Mono,   16 bit
Global Const WAVE_FORMAT_1S16 = &H8    ' 11.025 kHz, Stereo, 16 bit
Global Const WAVE_FORMAT_2M08 = &H10   ' 22.05  kHz, Mono,   8 bit
Global Const WAVE_FORMAT_2S08 = &H20   ' 22.05  kHz, Stereo, 8 bit
Global Const WAVE_FORMAT_2M16 = &H40   ' 22.05  kHz, Mono,   16 bit
Global Const WAVE_FORMAT_2S16 = &H80   ' 22.05  kHz, Stereo, 16 bit
Global Const WAVE_FORMAT_4M08 = &H100  ' 44.1   kHz, Mono,   8 bit
Global Const WAVE_FORMAT_4S08 = &H200  ' 44.1   kHz, Stereo, 8 bit
Global Const WAVE_FORMAT_4M16 = &H400  ' 44.1   kHz, Mono,   16 bit
Global Const WAVE_FORMAT_4S16 = &H800  ' 44.1   kHz, Stereo, 16 bit


' Flag values for MIXPLAYPARAMS.
Global Const WMIX_QUEUEWAVE = &H0
Global Const WMIX_CLEARQUEUE = &H1
Global Const WMIX_USELRUCHANNEL = &H2
Global Const WMIX_HIGHPRIORITY = &H4
Global Const WMIX_WAIT = &H8


' Flag values for MIXCONFIG.
Global Const WMIX_CONFIG_CHANNELS = &H1
Global Const WMIX_CONFIG_SAMPLINGRATE = &H2


' Flag values for WaveMixOpenWave().
Global Const WMIX_FILE = &H1
Global Const WMIX_RESOURCE = &H2
Global Const WMIX_MEMORY = &H4


' Flag values for WaveMixOpenChannel().
Global Const WMIX_OPENSINGLE = 0   ' Opens the single channel specified by
                                   ' iChannel.
Global Const WMIX_OPENALL = 1      ' Opens all the channels, iChannel is ignored.
Global Const WMIX_OPENCOUNT = 2    ' Opens iChannel Channels (e.g. if iChannel =
```

```
                                          ' 4 will create channels 0-3).
' Flag values for WaveMixFlushChannel() and WaveMixCloseChannel().
Global Const WMIX_ALL = &H1          ' Stops sound on all the channels, iChannel
                                     ' is ignored.
Global Const WMIX_NOREMIX = &H2      ' Prevents the currently submitted blocks
                                     ' from being remixed to exclude the new
                                     ' channel.
```

Note: *Microsoft's preliminary documentation for WaveMix is located in the file WAVEMIX.TXT, in the \WAVEMIX subdirectory on the companion CD-ROM. In this directory you will also find a file named MIXDESCR.DOC, a brief document in Word for Windows format that discusses the mixer's theory of operation.*

Adding the Event Procedures to the Form Module

In this demonstration program, we'll handle the four steps that open and prepare a WaveMix session in the **Form_Load()** event procedure, as shown in Listing 15.13.

Listing 15.13   The Form_Load() Event Procedure from WAVEMIX.FRM

```
Sub Form_Load ()
    Dim Counter As Integer
    Dim RetValue As Integer
    WaveMixConfiguration.wSize = Len(WaveMixConfiguration)
    WaveMixConfiguration.dwFlags = WMIX_CONFIG_CHANNELS Or _
        WMIX_CONFIG_SAMPLINGRATE
    WaveMixConfiguration.wChannels = 2
    WaveMixConfiguration.wSamplingRate = 11
    hThisMixSession = WaveMixConfigureInit(WaveMixConfiguration)
    WaveFiles(1) = App.Path & "\1.wav"
    WaveFiles(2) = App.Path & "\2.wav"
    WaveFiles(3) = App.Path & "\3.wav"
    WaveFiles(4) = App.Path & "\4.wav"
    WaveFiles(5) = App.Path & "\5.wav"
    WaveFiles(6) = App.Path & "\6.wav"
    WaveFiles(7) = App.Path & "\7.wav"
    For Counter = 1 To 7
        lpMixWaves(Counter) = WaveMixOpenWave(hThisMixSession, _
            WaveFiles(Counter), 0, WMIX_FILE)
    Next Counter
    RetValue = WaveMixOpenChannel(hThisMixSession, 0, WMIX_ALL)
    If RetValue Then
        MsgBox "Unable to open channels.", 16, "WaveMix Error"
        Unload WaveMixForm
        End
    End If
    RetValue = WaveMixActivate(hThisMixSession, True)
End Sub
```

In this procedure we're calling **WaveMixConfigureInit()**, which takes one argument, a structure of type **MIXCONFIG**. The alternative function, **WaveMixInit()**, takes no argument, but instead gets its initialization data from the WAVEMIX.INI file, which must be located in the same directory as WAVEMIX.DLL, usually \WINDOWS\SYSTEM.

In the call to **WaveMixOpenWave()**, we use the constant **WMIX_FILE** to indicate that we want the DLL to open the WAV data files for us, rather than look for WAV resources or for copies pre-loaded into memory. Since we can't load resources in VB, the third parameter of this function, **hInst**, will always be **0**.

Rather than open seven channels one by one, we call **WaveMixOpenChannel()** with the **WMIX_ALL** flag, which opens all eight mixer channels. We have only seven WAV files to play, so the eighth channel will remain idle; if you wish, you can add a WAV file of your own. In this case, the function will ignore its second argument, **iChannel**, which normally specifies the channel to open.

Finally, we call **WaveMixActivate()** to turn on the mixer session.

Playing the Waves

We'll feed the WAVs to the mixer channels in the **PlayWaveButton_Click()** event procedure, as shown in Listing 15.14.

Listing 15.14 The PlayWaveButton_Click() Event Procedure from WAVEMIX.FRM

```
Sub PlayWaveButton_Click (Index As Integer)
Dim RetValue As Integer
Dim MixPlayParameters As MIXPLAYPARAMS
    MixPlayParameters.wSize = Len(MixPlayParameters)
    MixPlayParameters.hMixSession = hThisMixSession
    MixPlayParameters.iChannel = Index
    MixPlayParameters.lpMixWave = lpMixWaves(Index + 1)
    MixPlayParameters.hWndNotify = 0
    MixPlayParameters.dwFlags = WMIX_HIGHPRIORITY
    MixPlayParameters.wLoops = 0
    RetValue = WaveMixPlay(MixPlayParameters)
End Sub
```

Instead of a long list of parameters, **WaveMixPlay()** takes a single argument, a pointer to a structure of type **MIXPLAYPARAMS**, which contains the actual control parameters. In the **MixPlayParameters** record we associate a WAV with a channel. There is no relationship between the order in which you open WAVs and the order in which you open channels. WAVs are assigned to channels only in the call to **WaveMixPlay()**. In fact, you may feed the same wave to multiple channels. You may also feed multiple WAVs to the same channel; WaveMix will play them in the order submitted.

Besides the handle to the session, the channel number, and the pointer to the open WAV sample data, the structure holds three other parameters. The **hWndNotify** field can accept a handle to a window. When it has finished playing the submitted WAV, WaveMix will send a notification message to the window specified by that handle. However, because we haven't added any custom controls, we cannot intercept that message from a VB program, and we set the handle to NULL (zero).

The fifth field, **dwFlags**, specifies how the newly submitted WAV should affect the queue for the channel and the waveaudio device. There are five flag constants:

- **WMIX_QUEUEWAVE** will simply add the new WAV to the existing queue.
- **WMIX_CLEARQUEUE** will clear the queue before submitting the new waveform data.
- **WMIX_HIGHPRIORITY**—the flag used in the sample program—causes WaveMix to cancel and remix the data already submitted to the device driver, which can prevent a noticeable delay between the call to **WaveMixPlay()** and actual playback on the device.
- **WMIX_USELRUCHANNEL** causes WaveMix to play the WAV on the first available, least recently used, channel. The documentation says that you should use this flag in combination with either **WMIX_QUEUEWAVE** *or* **WMIX_CLEARQUEUE**, but not both.
- **WMIX_WAIT** will queue the WAV, but will not begin playback until the next time **WaveMixPlay()** is called without the wait flag. You can use this feature to queue up several WAVs for simultaneous playback.

To prevent a playback delay when you resubmit a WAV to the same channel, you have two options. You can combine the flags **WMIX_CLEARQUEUE** and **WMIX_HIGHPRIORITY** as shown here:

```
MixPlayParameters.dwFlags = WMIX_HIGHPRIORITY Or WMIX_CLEARQUEUE
```

You may also use the function **WaveMixFlushChannel()** to clear the channel before you submit the next WAV:

```
RetValue = WaveMixFlushChannel(hThisMixSession, Index, WMIX_NOREMIX)
```

You may ask WaveMix to repeat a WAV by setting the **wLoops** field. To force the WAV to loop indefinitely, set this field to &HFFFF, which causes the WAV to repeat until you flush, preempt, or close the channel.

Completing the Form Module

The remaining code in the form module includes a handful of declarations, and the housekeeping event procedures, as shown in Listing 15.15.

Listing 15.15 The Remaining Declarations and Event Procedures from WAVEMIX.FRM

```
Option Explicit

Dim WaveMixConfiguration As MIXCONFIG
Dim hThisMixSession As Integer
Dim WaveFiles(7) As String
Dim lpMixWaves(7) As Long

Sub Form_Activate ()
Dim RetValue As Integer
    RetValue = WaveMixActivate(hThisMixSession, True)
End Sub

Sub Form_Deactivate ()
Dim RetValue As Integer
    RetValue = WaveMixActivate(hThisMixSession, False)
End Sub

Sub Form_Unload (Cancel As Integer)
Dim Counter As Integer
Dim RetValue As Integer
    RetValue = WaveMixCloseChannel(hThisMixSession, 0, WMIX_ALL)
    For Counter = 1 To 7
        lpMixWaves(Counter) = WaveMixFreeWave(hThisMixSession, lpMixWaves(Counter))
    Next Counter
    RetValue = WaveMixCloseSession(hThisMixSession)
End Sub

Sub QuitOption_Click ()
    Unload WaveMixForm
    End
End Sub
```

Recording Waveaudio

Besides all the playback features we've covered in this chapter and in Chapters 3 and 4, the multimedia system also supports WAV recording. For many of the **waveOut** functions, you will find corresponding **waveIn** functions.

However, because of VB's inability to support callback functions, the easiest way to record WAV data is to use the MCI.

Using MCI to Record Waveaudio

In this brief project, we'll use the API function **mciSendString()** to record waveaudio. Follow these steps to see how this works:

1. Create a simple form with three Command Buttons.
2. Add the form code, including the declarations for **mciSendString()** and a few variables (Listing 15.16).

> *You'll find this program in the subdirectory \VBMAGIC\WAVERCD in the files WAVERCRD.VBP and WAVERCRD.FRM.*

Running the Program

When you run WAVERCRD.VBP, it will display a small form with three Command Buttons, as shown in Figure 15.4.

Make sure you have some kind of input audio source ready, such as a microphone or an audio CD in your CD-ROM drive. You may need to select an input source using the mixer application that came with your sound card. For specific instructions, consult the user guide for your sound card.

When your input source is ready, click on the Record Command Button to begin recording. Wait a few seconds, then click on the Command Button labeled Stop and Save. You may then click on the Play Command Button to replay your recording.

Figure 15.4 *The WAVERCD project at runtime.*

Creating the Form

Place three Command Buttons on a new form, and name them RecordButton, StopButton, and PlayButton. The complete property list, declarations section, and program code for this project appears in Listing 15.16.

Listing 15.16 WAVERCRD.FRM

```
VERSION 2.00
Begin Form WaveRecordForm
   Caption          =   "Wave Recording"
   ClientHeight     =   3156
   ClientLeft       =   876
   ClientTop        =   1524
   ClientWidth      =   3072
   Height           =   3576
   Left             =   828
   LinkTopic        =   "Form1"
   ScaleHeight      =   3156
   ScaleWidth       =   3072
   Top              =   1152
   Width            =   3168
   Begin CommandButton StopButton
      Caption          =   "&Stop and Save"
      Height           =   552
      Left             =   720
      TabIndex         =   2
      Top              =   1380
      Width            =   1572
   End
   Begin CommandButton PlayButton
      Caption          =   "&Play"
      Height           =   552
      Left             =   720
      TabIndex         =   1
      Top              =   2340
      Width            =   1692
   End
   Begin CommandButton RecordButton
      Caption          =   "&Record"
      Height           =   552
      Left             =   660
      TabIndex         =   0
      Top              =   360
      Width            =   1692
   End
End
Option Explicit
Declare Function mciSendString Lib "MMSystem" (ByVal lpstrCommand As String, _
   ByVal lpstrReturnString As String, ByVal wReturnLength As Integer, ByVal _
   hCallback As Integer) As Long
```

```
Dim CommandString As String
Dim ReturnString As String * 255
Dim RetValue As Long
Sub PlayButton_Click ()
    Dim CommandString As String
    CommandString = "play " & App.Path & "\TestFile.Wav"
    RetValue = mciSendString(CommandString, ReturnString, 256, 0)
    End Sub
Sub RecordButton_Click ()
    RetValue = mciSendString("Open New type WaveAudio alias wave", _
        ReturnString, 256, 0)
    RetValue = mciSendString("set wave bitpersample 8", ReturnString, 256, 0)
    RetValue = mciSendString("set wave samplespersec 11025", ReturnString, _
        256, 0)
    RetValue = mciSendString("set wave channels 2", ReturnString, 256, 0)
    RetValue = mciSendString("record wave", ReturnString, 256, 0)
    End Sub
Sub StopButton_Click ()
    Dim CommandString As String
    RetValue = mciSendString("stop wave", ReturnString, 256, 0)
    CommandString = "save wave " & App.Path & "\TestFile.Wav"
    RetValue = mciSendString(CommandString, ReturnString, 256, 0)
    RetValue = mciSendString("close wave", ReturnString, 256, 0)
    End Sub
```

With a handful of MCI commands, and the functions we explored earlier in this chapter and in Chapters 4 and 5, you can create your own complete WAV recording and editing system. Now that we have covered WAV audio pretty thouroughly, let's move on to MIDI.

Learn how to use MIDI to
successfully add music to
your programs.

Using the Musical Instrument Digital Interface

At the 1982 convention of the National Association of Music Manufacturers, a revolution started in the electronic music industry. Korg and Kawai, two of the largest makers of electronic musical instruments, drove the Golden Spike of the music industry when they linked together their instruments with the new Musical Instrument Digital Interface (MIDI). The music industry has never looked back. MIDI now occupies a prominent place and has appeared in hundreds of thousands of recordings and live performances. Almost any electronic device, from the humblest portable keyboards to 48-channel studio mixers, includes a set of MIDI ports.

These simple five pin connectors offer some of the most thrilling opportunities for budding multimedia moguls. But, along with its phenomenal benefits, MIDI has also opened the door to corridors of confusion. Before you can fully appreciate MIDI's potential, you need to grasp some MIDI fundamentals. Let's take a closer look at what MIDI does and how it works, and then we'll explore how to access MIDI devices from our VB apps.

Everything You Need to Know about MIDI

Most MIDI devices—electronic keyboards, modular synthesizers, audio mixers, drum machines, and so on—are external. They talk to each other over a three-wire cable. You might not realize it, but your sound card includes a MIDI compatible synthesizer. This MIDI device lives inside your computer and talks directly to your computer's bus. Most sound cards let you hook up additional MIDI devices through a set of MIDI ports known as *In*, *Out*, and *Through*.

MIDI is actually a real-time interactive network. In theory, any device that includes at least one MIDI In and one MIDI Out port can talk to any other MIDI device. Many MIDI devices also offer a MIDI Through port to pass along data that comes in the MIDI In port. MIDI devices are not limited to three ports, however. In fact, many products provide several ports in various combinations of the three types.

The Musical Connection

When most people hear the term "MIDI," they think of musical applications. After all, the letter "M" in MIDI stands for Musical. But as we explore MIDI's musical features, keep in mind that it has grown far beyond its original specifications.

At the hardware level, MIDI provides a simple asynchronous serial interface that transmits data in ten bit chunks at a rate of 31.25 kilobaud (31,250 bits per second). The ten bits include a start bit, eight data bits, and a stop bit. Although we won't be dealing with many hardware issues in this chapter, you'll want to remember the transmission rate when you create your MIDI apps.

The data that travels through the MIDI cable controls electronic musical instruments—synthesizers. Before MIDI, in the late 1970s, as these instruments began to acquire the sophistication of digital electronics, their manufacturers developed various proprietary systems for interconnecting their products. Their main goal was to create integrated musical workshops so that musicians could compose and play music on several instruments simultaneously. This required at least one synthesizer, along with a device that could record what was played as a *sequence* of control events, or keypresses, just like a player piano roll. With such a system, you could later substitute a different note, change the duration of a note, or eliminate a note entirely without recording the entire passage again. And because you were only recording keystrokes (rather than analog waveforms), you could even change the tempo of the music without changing its pitch, or transpose the pitch without changing the tempo. These recording devices became known as *sequencers.* Once that problem was solved, it didn't take long for most manufacturers to recognize the need for a standard protocol to link sequencers and synthesizers. That's how MIDI was born. Figure 16.1 shows a typical MIDI hardware setup.

Once you can make a sequencer talk to a synthesizer, you can make synthesizers talk to each other. If you plug the MIDI Out port of one instrument into the MIDI In port of a second instrument, you can play the second synthesizer from the keyboard of the first. Most manufacturers now offer their major models in two versions, one with a keyboard, and one without. Keyboardless versions are usually called *synthesizer modules* and they often come in "rack mount" cabinets. In the pre-MIDI era, keyboard players, like Rick Wakeman and Keith Emerson, often appeared on stage in synthesizer pods, surrounded by walls of keyboards. Like space aliens in their cockpits, they flailed around from instrument to instrument, which made for a flashy performance, but created a setup nightmare. Today, performing keyboardists may play one or two keyboards on stage, while controlling dozens of instruments stacked on racks, neatly out of the way.

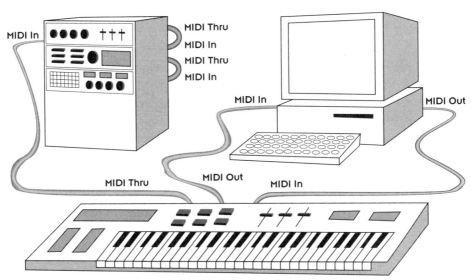

Figure 16.1   *A typical MIDI hardware setup.*

A Look at MIDI Messages

MIDI devices communicate by sending each other messages. Messages are divided into two general categories—*channel* and *system*—and into five types—*voice, mode, system common, system real-time,* and *system exclusive.*

The first category, *channel messages,* includes *voice messages* and *mode messages.* These messages are grouped into the channel message category because they are transmitted on individual channels rather than globally to all devices in the MIDI network. To understand how MIDI devices identify channels, let's take some time to review the structure of a MIDI message.

As shown in Figure 16.2, a MIDI message includes a *status byte* and up to two *data bytes.* It's easy to identify a status byte because all status bytes have their most significant bit set to 1. Conversely, the most significant bit of any data byte is set to 0. This convention holds for all standard MIDI messages and not just channel messages. Therefore, the data in each byte must be encoded in the seven remaining bits.

MIDI devices transmit all messages on the same cable, regardless of their channel assignments. In the early days of MIDI, musicians and recording engineers were accustomed to 48 track audio mixers, tangled patch panels, and fat umbilical cords stuffed with wire. These folks had a hard time understanding that they didn't need a separate cable for each MIDI channel. The four low-order bits of each status byte identify which channel it belongs to. Four bits produce 16 possible combinations, so MIDI supports 16 channels over a single cable string. (Keep in mind that although MIDI users and vendors number the channels from 1 through 16, internally they are numbered 0 through 15.) The three remaining bits identify the message. Three bits encode eight possible combinations, so channel messages could come in eight flavors, but they don't. A status byte with all four high-order bits set to 1 indicates a system common message—the second general category, which we'll get to after we tackle the channel messages. So, there are only seven channel messages.

Figure 16.2   *How MIDI messages are structured.*

The Channel Voice Messages

Most of the channel messages are voice messages, as shown in Table 16.1. Voice messages:

- Instruct the receiving instrument to assign particular sounds to its *voices*
- Turn notes on and off
- Send *controller* signals that can alter how the currently active note sounds

A *voice* is the portion of the synthesizer that produces sound. Most modern synthesizers have several voices—that is, they have several circuits that work independently and simultaneously to produce sounds of different *timbre* and *pitch*. Timbre is the sound that the instrument will imitate, such as a flute, cello, or helicopter. Pitch is the musical note that the instrument plays. To play two notes together, the synthesizer uses two voices. Those voices may play two notes with the same timbre, or may play two notes of different timbres. A Control Change message *modulates* the current note by altering its pitch, volume, or timbre to produce various effects, such as vibrato or tremolo.

Voice messages are followed by either one or two data bytes. A Note On message, for example, is followed by two bytes, one to identify the note, and one to specify the *velocity*. The velocity specifies how the note should sound. For example, if the synthesizer's voice is set to sound like a piano, the velocity could determine how loudly the note should be played. (In the keyboard world, the faster you strike a piano key, the louder it plays.) To play note number 80 with maximum velocity on channel 13, the MIDI device would send the following three hexadecimal byte values:

&H9C &H50 &H7F

Table 16.1 *MIDI Channel Voice Messages*

Voice Message	Status Byte Hex Value	Number of Data Bytes
Note Off	&H8x	2
Note On	&H9x	2
Polyphonic Aftertouch	&HAx	2
Control Change	&HBx	2
Program Change	&HCx	1
Aftertouch	&HDx	1
Pitch Bend	&HEx	1 or 2

To turn off the note, it would send either the Note Off message:

&H8C &H50 &H00

or the Note On message with a velocity of 0:

&H9C &H50 &H00

> **Note:** *The Note Off channel voice message accepts a velocity because some synthesizers can use the* release velocity *to determine how a note should decay once it has been shut off. Almost any instrument will accept a Note On message with a velocity of 0 in lieu of a Note Off message.*

Often, you will hear musicians and synthesizer technicians use the term *patches*. Each synthesizer make and model offers unique controls for designing and setting timbres. A patch is the control settings that define a particular timbre. The actual contents of a patch depend on the particular instrument, so rather than sending the whole patch to the instrument through MIDI (although this is also possible), the Program Change voice message sends a number from 0 to 127, in order to select a patch already stored in the instrument's own *voice bank* memory. For example, to set the instrument on channel 13 to its patch 104, you would send it the MIDI message:

&HCC &H68

Four of the channel voice messages—Control Change, Polyphonic Aftertouch, Aftertouch, and Pitch Bend—signal a *controller* change. For example, when a saxophone player blows harder, his instrument may sound harsher. By cleverly programming the synthetic saxophone, a keyboard musician can use a slider, foot pedal, or some other device to simulate the breath control of a sax player. Let's take a look at these voice message types.

Pitch Bend was so common on synthesizers when the MIDI specification was created, that it was given its own MIDI message (&HEx). This message signals the synthesizer to raise or lower the pitch of currently active notes on the channel. Pitch Bend messages do not contain note values. The value of the Pitch Bend message bytes reflects the degree to which the pitch bend controller (usually a wheel or lever beside the keyboard) has been moved up or down. The degree to which the pitch changes is up to the instrument itself.

Like Pitch Bend, *Aftertouch* was considered valuable and common enough to be granted its own MIDI message types. The first type of Aftertouch, known as *Polyphonic Aftertouch* (&HAx), transmits a value on a particular channel, for a particular note, that indicates the degree of pressure on the key after it has been struck. Many electronic keyboards now support this feature, which enables keyboard players to get some of the control that other musicians get by changing the pressure on their mouthpieces or bows. The other Aftertouch control message (&HDx) is used when an instrument supports aftertouch, but not on individual notes. In other words, a change in pressure on one key will affect all the notes currently playing on the channel.

The creators of the MIDI specification realized that other types of controllers were found on some instruments, and that more would follow. So, they created one general purpose channel voice message (&HBx) to handle them. The first data byte of the Control Change message selects the controller type, and the second byte specifies its current value. You'll find a complete listing of the pre-defined controller types in the *MIDI 1.0 Detailed Specification* (see the bibliography). Actually, the Control Change message supports only 121 controllers, numbered 0 through 120. The remaining 7 values are reserved for the Channel Mode Messages.

The Channel Mode Messages

Mode messages determine how an instrument will process MIDI voice messages. Now that you understand how to send MIDI channel voice messages, you'll have an easier time understanding how to send channel mode messages. Unfortunately, some of the modes themselves have caused more confusion than any other aspect of MIDI.

Channel Mode messages are a special case of the Control Change message. They always begin with a status byte containing the value &HBx, where x is the channel number. The difference between a Control Change message and a Channel Mode message, which share the same status byte value, is in the first data byte. Data byte values 121 through 127 have been reserved in the Control Change message for the channel mode messages. These are listed in Table 16.2.

Of these messages, the least understood—and therefore most creatively interpreted by instrument manufacturers—are Omni Mode On, Omni Mode Off, Mono Mode On, and Poly Mode On. Actually, modes are independent of the mode messages; the messages just change the mode on the fly. The intent of these modes is to determine how an instrument responds to incoming channel voice messages.

Omni Mode means that the instrument responds to messages on all 16 channels. So, if Note On messages are transmitted on all channels, the instrument

Table 16.2 *The Channel Mode Messages*

First Data Byte Value	Description	Meaning of Second Data Byte
&H79	Reset All Controllers	None; set to 0
&H7A	Local Control	0 = Off; 127 = On
&H7B	All Notes Off	None; set to 0
&H7C	Omni Mode Off	None; set to 0
&H7D	Omni Mode On	None; set to 0
&H7E	Mono Mode On (Poly Mode Off)	0 means that the number of channels used is determined by the receiver; all other values set a specific number of channels, beginning with the current *basic channel*
&H7F	Poly Mode On (Mono Mode Off)	None; set to 0

in Omni Mode will attempt to play them all, up to the maximum number of voices available. Some synthesizers, *monophonic* instruments, can only play one note at a time. Others, known as *polyphonic* instruments, can play 8, 16, 32, or other numbers of simultaneous notes. If a device with only 8 voices receives 15 simultaneous Note On messages, it will play only the first or last 8.

For most real-world applications, Omni Mode isn't discerning enough. (In fact, it isn't discerning at all.) Most polyphonic instruments can play not only a multitude of simultaneous notes, they can also play them with a variety of patches. So, one synthesizer can sound like a whole band. In Poly Mode, each channel is assigned a patch. All notes on each channel play with the same timbre. For example, you could set channel 1 to play bass, channel 2 to play piano, and channel 3 to play drums. In Mono Mode, only one note can play at a time on each channel. Poly Mode has some powerful capabilities, but we don't have room to discuss them here. For detailed coverage of MIDI modes, order a copy of the *MIDI 1.0 Detailed Specification*.

The System Messages

The second general category of MIDI messages are the *system messages*, which include *system common messages*, *system real-time messages*, and *system exclusive messages*. These messages carry information that is not channel-specific, such as timing signals for synchronization, positioning information in prerecorded MIDI sequences, and detailed setup information for the destination device.

Table 16.3 *The MIDI System Common Messages*

System Common Message	Status Byte Hex Value	Number of Data Bytes
MIDI Time Code	&HF1	1
Song Position Pointer	&HF2	2
Song Select	&HF3	1
Tune Request	&HF6	None

There are four types of system common messages, as shown in Table 16.3.

The six system real-time messages, listed in Table 16.4, primarily affect sequencer playback and recording. These messages have no data bytes.

The third type of system message, the system exclusive message, is used to transfer data between devices. For example, you may wish to store patch setups for an instrument on a computer using a *patch librarian* program. You can then transfer those patches to the synthesizer by means of a system exclusive message. The name *system exclusive* means that these are messages exclusively for a particular device, or type of device, rather than universal messages that all MIDI compatible products should recognize. A system exclusive message is just a stream of bytes, all with their high bits set to 0, bracketed by a pair of system exclusive start and end messages (&HF0 and &HF7).

The MIDI Offspring

Since the introduction of the MIDI protocol, four other MIDI standards have appeared:

- MIDI Show Control 1.0
- MIDI Machine Control 1.0
- Standard MIDI Files 1.0
- General MIDI System, Level 1

Table 16.4 *The MIDI System Real-Time Messages*

System Real Time Message	Status Byte Hex Value
Timing Clock	&HF8
Start Sequence	&HFA
Continue Sequence	&HFB
Stop Sequence	&HFC
Active Sensing	&HFE
System Reset	&HFF

The MIDI Show Control and MIDI Machine Control standards specify a set of system-exclusive messages that can control various types of non-musical equipment. The Show Control focuses specifically on stage lighting and sound control systems, although it is designed to control just about any kind of performance system, including mechanical stages. The Machine Control standard specifies system exclusive messages to operate audio and video recorders.

The biggest problem that surfaced after the widespread adoption of the MIDI protocol was in sequencer file formats. Shortly after the introduction of the first MIDI-equipped synthesizers, several sequencer programs appeared. Sequencer programs allow musicians and composers to record and playback MIDI information. With a sequencer, one person can compose and play an entire symphony, using nothing more than a computer and a few synthesizers. All these programs, no matter which platform they supported, adhered to the MIDI communication protocol. They had to, or they wouldn't work. But the files in which they stored their data were another matter. Each software developer created its own proprietary format, which meant that you couldn't create a music sequence with one program and play it back with another. So in 1988, The International MIDI Association published the second component of the MIDI standard, *Standard MIDI Files 1.0*. Standard MIDI files are built from *chunks*, which contain some header information and a series of data bytes. Sound familiar? Although not identical, MIDI standard files and RIFF files have quite a bit in common. In fact, a Windows MIDI file is actually a standard MIDI file embedded in a RIFF chunk.

Standard MIDI files made it possible for musicians to share their files, regardless of hardware and software platforms. But this new standard brought to light another problem. The *tracks* in a MIDI sequencer file may specify a program number, which determines the instrument sound, or patch, with which that track should be played. But every instrument has its own assortment of patches. So, while program number 30 on one synthesizer might be a brass section patch, the same program number on another instrument could be a tympani drum, or a sci-fi phaser gun. Playback of a standard MIDI file might produce all the right notes, however, they may be on all the wrong instruments. The General MIDI System standard attempts to solve this problem by offering a standard program list, consisting of the 128 most common patch types, from pianos to gunshots (literally—General MIDI program 1 is 'Acoustic Grand Piano,' and program 128 is 'Gunshot'). General MIDI also specifies a layout for percussion instruments, called the General MIDI Percussion Map. Percussion is a special case, because non-melodic percussion sounds, such as drums, cymbals, and cowbells, need to occupy only one note position, so you can theoretically fit up to 128 separate percussion sounds in one patch. General MIDI includes 47 percussion sounds, and specifies that percussion should be transmitted on MIDI channel 10.

General MIDI is considered a *system* rather than a *specification,* because not all instruments need to comply. In fact, that would defeat the purpose of programmable synthesizers, which enable artists to continually invent new sounds. Some synthesizer modules are designed specifically for use as General MIDI devices, and come pre-programmed with compliant patches. Other synthesizers support a General MIDI mode, but also provide a separate programmable patch bank. And some instruments don't support General MIDI at all, unless you program and arrange the patches yourself.

MIDI and Windows

The Windows Multimedia System fully supports MIDI. Besides the standard MCI commands that enable us to play (but not record) MIDI files, there are 29 low-level MIDI functions in the API, with which we can send and receive MIDI messages over any of the 16 channels. To use these functions, you'll need either a sound card equipped with MIDI ports, or a dedicated MIDI adapter.

MIDI Connections

Most sound cards today provide a combination joystick/MIDI port in the form of a 15-pin connector. To use this port for MIDI, you'll need an adapter cable, usually available from the card's manufacturer, to convert the 15-pin connector to either two or three 5-pin DIN connectors, as shown in Figure 16.3. If your adapter cable provides three MIDI ports, there will be one of each type (In, Out, and Through). If only two are present, they will likely be In and Out ports.

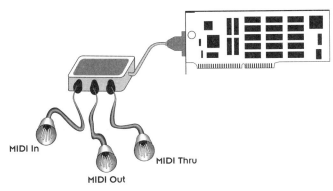

Figure 16.3   A typical sound card with its MIDI adapter cable attached.

Three of the most common brands of PC sound cards, The Creative Labs Soundblaster series, the Media Vision Pro Audio Spectrum series, and the Advanced Gravis Ultrasound, all use the same type of MIDI cable. The professional level Multisound card from Turtle Beach Systems has no joystick port, but provides a 9-pin connector to which you may attach a special MIDI cable, available from the manufacturer.

It's important not to confuse the on-board synthesizer on your sound card with the card's MIDI capabilities. You don't need a sound card at all to use the MIDI multimedia functions. You can just install a MIDI port adapter, such as the Roland MPU-401, which would enable you to exchange MIDI data with any external MIDI device, including synthesizers, drum machines, sequencers, even other computers. The synthesizer on your sound card acts like any other MIDI device; you play notes on it by sending it MIDI messages. How your on-board synthesizer responds to MIDI depends partly on the settings in the Windows MIDI Mapper.

The Windows MIDI Mapper

For some reason, the Windows MIDI Mapper has inspired just about as much fear and loathing as any other Windows feature. That could be because Microsoft slipped it in with little fanfare, and even less explanation. However, the purpose and operation of the MIDI Mapper is really pretty simple.

With Windows 3.1, the MIDI Mapper helped achieve some level of device independence between MIDI devices. For example, not all sound cards' internal patches are organized according to General MIDI guidelines. The Patch Maps section of the Windows 3.1 MIDI Mapper provides a way to map General MIDI patch numbers to the actual patches in the sound card, as shown in Figure 16.4.

The Key Maps dialog box from Windows 3.1, shown in Figure 16.5, is used to remap notes. Why would you need to do this, you ask? There are two reasons. The MIDI 1.0 Detailed Specification places middle C at note 60 (&H3C). Some older devices, especially those not specifically designed to support MIDI, may use a different note position mapping. You can use the Key Maps dialog box to remap the device's own note positions to the standard configuration.

You can also use the Key Maps dialog box to map percussion instruments to the General MIDI layout. For example, in General MIDI, note 35 is an Acoustic Bass Drum. Some devices place that instrument at note 47, one octave higher, so the Key Map can be used to remap it.

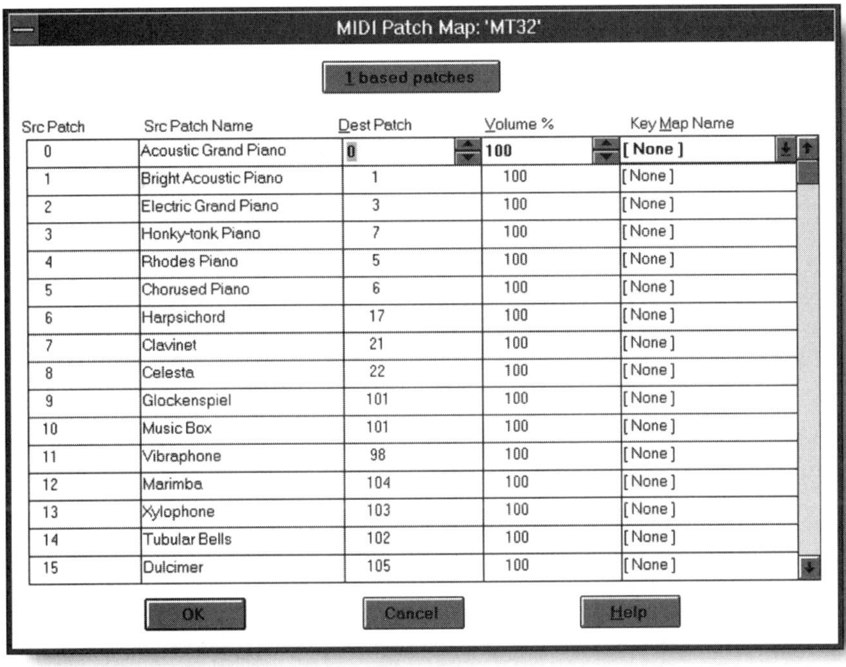
MIDI Patch Map: 'MT32'

1 based patches

Src Patch	Src Patch Name	Dest Patch	Volume %	Key Map Name
0	Acoustic Grand Piano	0	100	[None]
1	Bright Acoustic Piano	1	100	[None]
2	Electric Grand Piano	3	100	[None]
3	Honky-tonk Piano	7	100	[None]
4	Rhodes Piano	5	100	[None]
5	Chorused Piano	6	100	[None]
6	Harpsichord	17	100	[None]
7	Clavinet	21	100	[None]
8	Celesta	22	100	[None]
9	Glockenspiel	101	100	[None]
10	Music Box	101	100	[None]
11	Vibraphone	98	100	[None]
12	Marimba	104	100	[None]
13	Xylophone	103	100	[None]
14	Tubular Bells	102	100	[None]
15	Dulcimer	105	100	[None]

OK Cancel Help

Figure 16.4 *The Windows 3.1 MIDI Patch Map dialog box allows you to map General MIDI patch numbers to the actual patches in the sound card.*

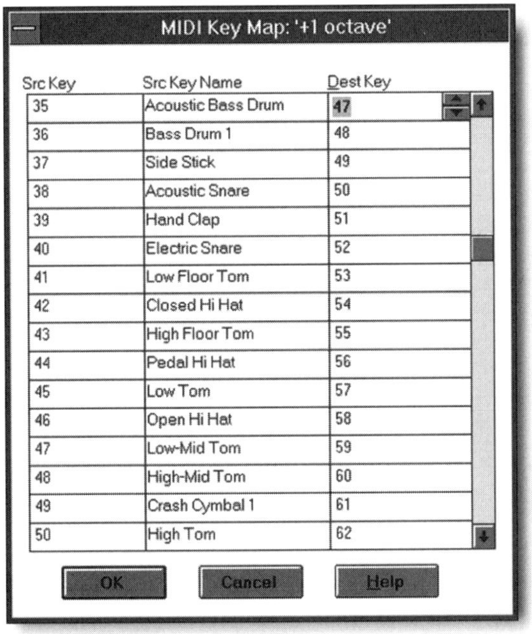
MIDI Key Map: '+1 octave'

Src Key	Src Key Name	Dest Key
35	Acoustic Bass Drum	47
36	Bass Drum 1	48
37	Side Stick	49
38	Acoustic Snare	50
39	Hand Clap	51
40	Electric Snare	52
41	Low Floor Tom	53
42	Closed Hi Hat	54
43	High Floor Tom	55
44	Pedal Hi Hat	56
45	Low Tom	57
46	Open Hi Hat	58
47	Low-Mid Tom	59
48	High-Mid Tom	60
49	Crash Cymbal 1	61
50	High Tom	62

OK Cancel Help

Figure 16.5 *The Windows 3.1 MIDI Key Maps dialog box allows you to remap notes and to map percussion instruments to the General MIDI system.*

The Windows 3.1 MIDI Mapper also includes the MIDI Setups dialog box, shown in Figure 16.6, which enables you to remap channels and select patch maps for each channel individually. The patch map is device-specific. In other words, if you play all music on one instrument, whether the on-board synthesizer on your sound card, or a single external instrument connected to your MIDI Out port, the patch map would be the same on all channels. If you connect multiple instruments into the MIDI chain, by linking the Through port of each instrument to the In port of the next, then you may need a separate patch map for each one. In this case, you would use the MIDI Mapper to assign the patch map to the channel or channels on which the corresponding instrument is waiting for MIDI messages. This may seem complicated, but it really simplifies things when it comes time to play music. By mapping all instruments to the General MIDI patch numbers, you can send MIDI messages that select the correct patches on each instrument without considering each instrument's unique patch layout. So, device-*specific* MIDI Setups produce device-*independent* operation.

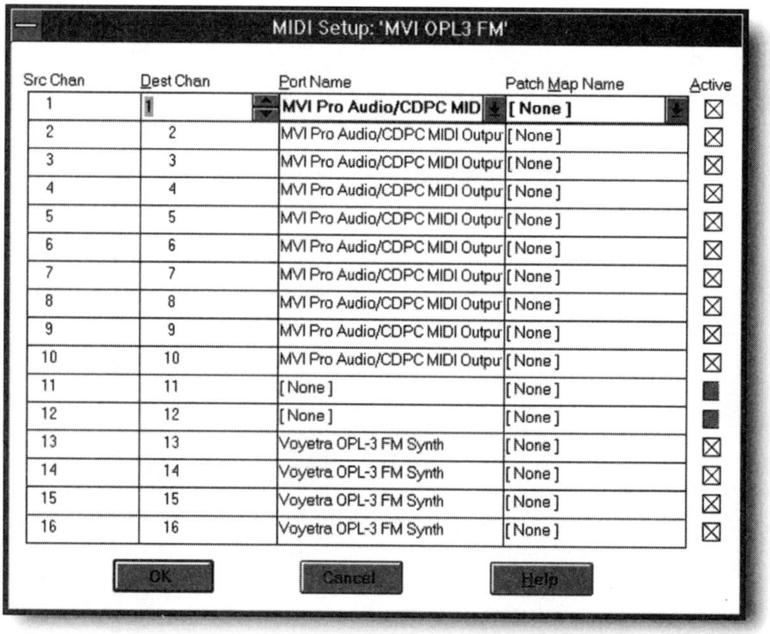

Figure 16.6   *The Windows 3.1 MIDI Mapper Setup dialog box allows you to assign a patch map to each MIDI channel.*

The construction of a complete MIDI setup under Windows 3.1 is a three step process:

1. Create the necessary key maps.
2. Create the patch maps, using the appropriate key maps if needed.
3. Create the MIDI Setup, assigning Source Channels to Destination Channels, Ports, and Patch Maps.

The installation program for your sound card's drivers should have installed the Windows 3.1 MIDI drivers and any required MIDI Mapper setups.

If you look at the setup shown in Figure 16.6, you'll notice that the activated channels are divided into two groups. Channels 1 through 10 are set to MVI Pro Audio/CDPC MIDI Output, while channels 13 through 16 are set to Voyetra OPL-3 FM Synth. The setting on the first ten channels causes them to send their output to an external MIDI device, completely bypassing the on-board synthesizer. The second group of channels do just the opposite; they send all messages to the internal device, the OPL-3 FM synthesizer chip. These groupings reflect Microsoft's own contribution to the standardization of MIDI files and devices, at least as far as Windows 3.1 is concerned!

Windows 95 clearly makes life much easier on us. We no longer have to worry about the MIDI Mapper, because Windows 95 knows which type of audio card is installed, so it figures out how to map the channels and patches to match the card's capabilities. You do have the option of selecting which instrument to play through. On one of our systems, we installed a Creative Labs AWE 32 sound card. After Windows 95 recognized the card and set it up, we can go into the MIDI page of the Multimedia Properties dialog box, where we have three options for MIDI output, as shown in Figure 16.7.

If the default setting does not work well for you, then you can try the others. If that fails to give you the desired results, you can custom-build your own output scheme. Windows 95 will probably set things up pretty well on its own, but this is where you want to go if you have problems. To set up your own instrument configuration, click on the Custom Configuration radio button and click on Configure. You will be presented with the MIDI Configuration dialog box, as shown in Figure 16.8. Here, you custom-pick the output device for each channel.

Windows recognizes two general types of synthesizers: *Base-Level* and *Extended-Level*. These two categories reflect the capabilities of the devices. A Base-Level device can play at least three distinct, simultaneous patches, each assigned to its own channel, with at least six simultaneous notes. The notes may be distributed in any way across the three channels. So, at one point

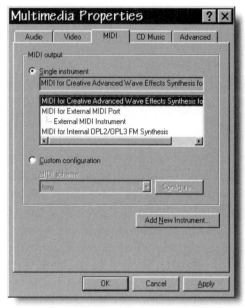

Figure 16.7 *The Multimedia Properties dialog box from Windows 95.*

during playback, one channel can be used to play a single note, the second channel can play two notes, and the third channel can play three notes. Then, later in the same sequence, the voices can shift, so the first channel can play four notes, while the third channel plays the remaining two notes. This is called *dynamic voice allocation*. In addition to the minimum of six simultaneous

Figure 16.8 *The MIDI Configuration properties dialog box from Windows 95.*

melodic notes, a Base-Level device must also support a minimum of three simultaneous percussion notes. The melodic parts are played from MIDI channels 13, 14, and 15, while percussion is played from channel 16.

Extended-Level MIDI devices can play at least nine distinct and simultaneous patches, on nine separate channels, with a minimum of sixteen simultaneous, dynamically allocated notes. The percussion channel should support an additional sixteen simultaneous notes. The melodic voices play on channels 1 through 9, with percussion on channel 10. Channels 11 and 12 are unassigned.

Most of the popular sound cards available today, especially those based on the OPL FM synthesizer chips, meet or exceed the Base-Level requirements. Only a few products meet the Extended-Level specification. Some of the cards that act as if they were Extended-Level devices fail to comply fully with the guidelines, usually by offering fewer than the 32 recommended voices.

To provide device-independent support for MIDI sequencer files, Microsoft recommends that any Windows compatible file should contain two versions of the sequence: one that will play on a Base-Level device and one that will play on an Extended-Level device. The file CANYON.MID, which comes with Windows 95 is an example of such a file. The MIDI playback system will pump out data on all 14 assigned channels, but if the MIDI Setup is correct, as it should be with Windows 95, only one set of tracks will play on any given device. You may run into a situation where both the base-level and extended-level tracks are being played back at the same time. Depending on the MIDI file, you may not notice it at all. With other files, you may distinctly hear two separate tracks. When we were working on the projects for this chapter, we ran into this problem. The solution is to set up a custom MIDI configuration using the Windows 95 MIDI configuration editor (see Figure 16.8). Simply highlight each channel, one at a time, and make sure that channels 1 through 10 are pointing to an available device. Set channels 11 through 16 to None so that their tracks will not be output, and there you have it. Now only the extended-level tracks will be heard. If you only have base-level MIDI support on your sound card, then you probably won't have to worry about anything, because the hardware will ignore the extended-level information.

Sending MIDI Messages

You've seen in Chapter 4 how to play a MIDI file with MCI commands. It's as simple as sending the string "Play filename.MID" with either the **mciExecute()** or **mciSendString()** functions. But now that you know something about MIDI messages and where they go, let's use the low-level MIDI API functions to send some messages directly to the device. We'll begin with a simple experiment so you can see how the functions work. Then we'll explore the VB MIDI Piano, a nifty little program created by MIDI programming wizard Arthur Edstrom, of Artic Software, Inc.

Sending MIDI Messages

It takes only a handful of API functions to open and use a MIDI device. In this project we'll try them out. Here are the steps to follow:

1. Open a code module and declare the **midiOut** API functions (Listing 16.1).
2. Create the form and fill in the form code (Listing 16.2).

You'll find this project in the subdirectory \VBMAGIC\MIDIOUT1 in the files MIDIOUT1.VBP, MIDIOUT1.FRM, and MIDI1.BAS.

Running the Program

When you run the program, it will display a small form with two Command Buttons, as shown in Figure 16.9.

Click on the button labeled Open MIDI Device. Its label will then change to Close MIDI Device. Click on the Send Note button once to turn on a note, and again to turn it off. If you hear nothing, make sure the MIDI channel is set properly for your sound card or external MIDI device. Don't forget to check all your volume settings, including those in your multimedia mixer program and on any physical devices, such as the amplifier controls and the output level of an external synthesizer.

When you're done testing, click on the Close MIDI Device button and end the program.

Declaring the midiOut API Functions

We'll place the four API function declarations in their own code module, called MIDI1.BAS, shown in Listing 16.1. This code module will contain no functions or procedures.

Figure 16.9 *The MIDIOUT1 project main form at run-time.*

Listing 16.1 MIDI1.BAS

```
Option Explicit

#If Win32 Then
   Public Declare Function midiOutClose Lib "winmm.dll" _
      (ByVal hMidiOut As Long) As Long
   Public Declare Function midiOutOpen Lib "winmm.dll" (lphMidiOut As Long, _
      ByVal uDeviceID As Long, ByVal dwCallback As Long, _
      ByVal dwInstance As Long, ByVal dwFlags As Long) As Long
   Public Declare Function midiOutShortMsg Lib "winmm.dll" (ByVal hMidiOut _
      As Long, ByVal dwMsg As Long) As Long
#Else
   Public Declare Function midiOutOpen Lib "MMSystem" (hMidiOut As Integer, _
      ByVal DeviceId As Integer, ByVal dwCallback As Long, _
      ByVal dwInstance As Long, ByVal dwFlags As Long) As Integer
   Public Declare Function midiOutShortMsg Lib "MMSystem" (ByVal hMidiOut _
      As Integer, ByVal MidiMessage As Long) As Integer
   Public Declare Function midiOutClose Lib "MMSystem" (ByVal hMidiOut _
      As Integer) As Integer
#End If

Global Const MIDI_MAPPER = -1
```

Let's take a look at how these functions work.

The **midiOutOpen()** function takes five arguments. In the first argument, **hMidiOut**, we pass an long integer variable, which the function will fill with a handle to the device. The second argument, **DeviceId**, specifies which MIDI device to open. Most systems have only one MIDI device, and its **DeviceId** is 0. To select the MIDI Mapper, pass the constant **MIDI_MAPPER**, which has a decimal value of -1.

The arguments **dwCallback** and **dwInstance** specify either the address of a callback function, or a handle for a window callback. As I explained in earlier chapters, VB does not support callbacks, so we'll set both these arguments to NULL (0). Later in this chapter, when we talk about MIDI input, I'll show you how to use a custom control to service window callbacks. The fifth argument, **dwFlags**, also relates to callbacks. Its only defined flags are **CALLBACK_WINDOW** and **CALLBACK_FUNCTION**.

The function **midiOutShortMsg()** requires only two arguments. The first, as usual, takes the handle set by **midiOutOpen()**. In the second argument, we pass the MIDI message as a four byte long integer. The least significant byte contains the status byte, the actual MIDI command. The next higher-order byte contains the first data byte, if needed. And the third byte contains the second data byte, if needed. The highest-order byte is always set to &H00.

The third and last function declared for this project, **midiOutClose()**, takes nothing but the handle to the device.

All three of these functions return integer values that indicate error conditions. If no error occurs, they return 0.

Creating the Form Module

If you're creating this program from the ground up, start with a small form. Place two Command Buttons on it. Set their **Name** properties to OpenButton and SendMessageButton. Set their initial **Caption** properties to Open MIDI Device and Send Note, respectively. Then place a Text Box on the form. Name it ChannelText, and give it an initial **Text** property value of 16. You may also want to place a Label beside the Text Box, as we did in the sample program on the companion CD. Next, we can fill in the code.

This bare-bones program requires only four event procedures and a handful of variables, as shown in Listing 16.2.

Listing 16.2 The Code and Declarations from MIDIOUT1.FRM

```
Option Explicit

Dim NoteToggle As Boolean
Dim hMidiOut As Long
Dim MidiDeviceOpen As Boolean
Dim MidiChannel As Integer

Sub Form_Load ()
   MidiDeviceOpen = False
End Sub
Sub Form_Unload (Cancel As Integer)
Dim RetValue As Long

   RetValue = midiOutClose(hMidiOut)
End Sub
Sub OpenButton_Click ()
Dim RetValue As Long

   If MidiDeviceOpen Then
      RetValue = midiOutClose(hMidiOut)
      OpenButton.Caption = "Open MIDI Device"
   Else
      RetValue = midiOutOpen(hMidiOut, MIDI_MAPPER, 0, 0, 0)
      OpenButton.Caption = "Close MIDI Device"
   End If
   MidiDeviceOpen = Not MidiDeviceOpen
End Sub
Sub SendMessageButton_Click ()
Dim RetValue As Long
Dim MidiShortMessage As Long
   MidiChannel = (Abs(Val(ChannelText.Text)) - 1) Mod 16
   NoteToggle = Not NoteToggle
```

```
     If NoteToggle Then
        ' Note On = &H9x, where x = channel
        ' Middle C = &H3C
        ' Velocity of 64 = &H40
        MidiShortMessage = &H403C90 + MidiChannel
        SendMessageButton.Caption = "Stop Note"
     Else
        ' Note On = &H9x, where x = channel
        ' Middle C = &H3C
        ' Velocity of 0 = Note Off = &H00
        MidiShortMessage = &H3C90 + MidiChannel
        SendMessageButton.Caption = "Send Note"
     End If
     RetValue = midiOutShortMsg(hMidiOut, MidiShortMessage)
End Sub
```

Most of the action takes place in the **SendMessageButton_Click()** event procedure. After we make sure we're transmitting on a valid MIDI channel, we set **NoteToggle**, which determines whether we're about to turn a note on or off. If **NoteToggle** is True, we send a Note On message, &H9x. By adding the channel number of 0 to 15 to the long integer, we affect only the four low-order bits of the lowest-order byte. The second byte is set to &H3C, which will select Middle C, and the third byte is set to the median velocity, &H40. To turn off the note, we can cheat by retransmitting the Note On message with a velocity of 0.

The Visual Basic MIDI Piano

This program, contributed by Arthur Edstrom of Artic Software, Inc., was written as a tutorial for all the folks hanging around in the Visual Basic forum on CompuServe (GO MSBASIC) who expressed an interest in VB MIDI programming. Here are the steps to follow to create this program:

1. Create the form (Listing 16.3).
2. Add the form code (Listing 16.4).
3. Add a code module (Listing 16.5) with function declarations and three general procedures.

You'll find this project in the directory \VBMAGIC\VBPIANO in the files PIANO.VBP, ABOUTBX1.FRM, PIANO2.FRM, PIANO.BAS, MIDPIANO.WAV, and PATCH.INI.

Figure 16.10   *The About Box from the VB MIDI Piano program.*

Playing the Visual Basic MIDI Piano

When you run the program, it will first play a welcome message from the program's author, and display its About Box, as shown in Figure 16.10.

After this splash screen disappears, the program will display its main form, a piano keyboard with several scroll bars, as shown in Figure 16.11.

Use the scroll bars to select the MIDI channel and set the volume (or in MIDI terms, the *velocity*). You may also shift the octave of the keyboard up or down, change the current patch, and if your sound card supports stereo, set the left-to-right balance, known as the *pan*.

You can press and hold several notes in succession by holding down the mouse button and dragging the pointer across the piano keyboard. To activate selected notes, hold the button and drag off the keyboard, then back on again over the keys of your choice. To release all the currently active notes,

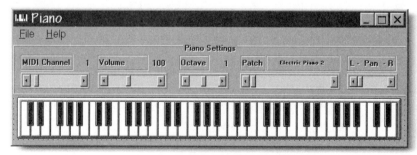

Figure 16.11   *The PIANO2.FRM form from the VB MIDI Piano program.*

release the mouse button while the pointer is over the piano keyboard, or release the mouse button and press it again over another key.

Creating the Main Form

Although you could burn a lot of time designing a bitmap keyboard with sprites to indicate keypresses, Arthur has found a much simpler, and very attractive, alternative. The keys are actually a control array called **PanelWhite()**, consisting of 65 SSPanel controls. (The Toolbox button for the SSPanels will appear when you activate the 'Sheridan 3D Controls' in the Custom Controls dialog box.) To color the keys, the **BackColor** property is set either to pure black (&H000000) or pure white (&HFFFFFF). On all keys, the **BorderWidth** property is set to 2, the **BevelOuter** is set to 2 - Raised, and **RoundedCorners** is set to True. The **BevelWidth** property is set on the black keys to 1, and on the white keys to 2. To indicate a keypress, the program changes **BevelOuter** to 0 - None.

The remaining controls consist of Scroll Bars and Labels, set in SSPanel controls to get the 3D effect. For a complete list of the non-keyboard controls and their properties, see Listing 16.3.

Listing 16.3   The Non-Keyboard Controls from PIANO2.FRM

```
VERSION 4.00
Begin VB.Form Piano
   Appearance      =   0   'Flat
   BackColor       =   &H00C0C0C0&
   BorderStyle     =   1   'Fixed Single
   Caption         =   "Piano"
   ClientHeight    =   2385
   ClientLeft      =   1245
   ClientTop       =   2220
   ClientWidth     =   9510
   ClipControls    =   0   'False
   BeginProperty Font
      name         =   "MS Sans Serif"
      charset      =   0
      weight       =   700
      size         =   8.25
      underline    =   0   'False
      italic       =   0   'False
      strikethrough =  0   'False
   EndProperty
   ForeColor       =   &H80000008&
   Height          =   3240
   Icon            =   "piano2.frx":0000
   Left            =   1185
   LinkTopic       =   "Form1"
   MaxButton       =   0   'False
```

```
    ScaleHeight       =    2385
    ScaleWidth        =    9510
    Top               =    1425
    Width             =    9630
    Begin Threed.SSPanel Panel3D3
        Height            =    975
        Left              =    90
        TabIndex          =    20
        Top               =    1290
        Width             =    9315
        _Version          =    65536
        _ExtentX          =    16431
        _ExtentY          =    1720
        _StockProps       =    15
        ForeColor         =    8421504
        BevelWidth        =    3
        BorderWidth       =    0
        Outline           =    -1    'True
        Font3D            =    3
        Alignment         =    6
        Autosize          =    3
        Begin Threed.SSPanel PanelWhite
            DragIcon          =    "piano2.frx":030A
            DragMode          =    1    'Automatic
            Height            =    585
            Index             =    61
            Left              =    8640
            TabIndex          =    82
            Top               =    90
            Width             =    165
            _Version          =    65536
            _ExtentX          =    291
            _ExtentY          =    1032
            _StockProps       =    15
            ForeColor         =    8421504
            BackColor         =    0
            BorderWidth       =    2
            Outline           =    -1    'True
            Font3D            =    3
            Alignment         =    6
            Autosize          =    3
        End
    Begin Threed.SSFrame SSFrame4
        Height            =    1245
        Left              =    0
        TabIndex          =    0
        Top               =    0
        Width             =    9585
        _Version          =    65536
        _ExtentX          =    16907
        _ExtentY          =    2196
        _StockProps       =    14
        Caption           =    "Piano Settings"
        ForeColor         =    0
```

```
Alignment        =    2
ShadowColor      =    1
Font3D           =    3
ShadowStyle      =    1
Begin Threed.SSPanel SSPanel6
   Height           =    375
   Left             =    2070
   TabIndex         =    18
   Top              =    720
   Width            =    1695
   _Version         =    65536
   _ExtentX         =    2990
   _ExtentY         =    661
   _StockProps      =    15
   Caption          =    "SSPanel6"
   ForeColor        =    8421504
   BorderWidth      =    2
   BevelInner       =    1
   Font3D           =    3
   Alignment        =    6
   Autosize         =    3
   Begin VB.HScrollBar HScrollVolume
      Height           =    255
      LargeChange      =    10
      Left             =    60
      Max              =    127
      TabIndex         =    19
      Top              =    60
      Value            =    50
      Width            =    1575
   End
End
Begin Threed.SSPanel SSPanel5
   Height           =    375
   Left             =    5520
   TabIndex         =    16
   Top              =    720
   Width            =    2415
   _Version         =    65536
   _ExtentX         =    4260
   _ExtentY         =    661
   _StockProps      =    15
   Caption          =    "SSPanel5"
   ForeColor        =    8421504
   BorderWidth      =    1
   BevelInner       =    1
   Font3D           =    3
   Alignment        =    6
   Autosize         =    3
   Begin VB.HScrollBar HScrollPatch
      Height           =    285
      LargeChange      =    10
      Left             =    45
      Max              =    127
```

```
               TabIndex          =    17
               Top               =    45
               Value             =    1
               Width             =    2325
         End
   End
   Begin Threed.SSPanel SSPanel2
         Height               =    375
         Left                 =    180
         TabIndex             =    14
         Top                  =    720
         Width                =    1680
         _Version             =    65536
         _ExtentX             =    2963
         _ExtentY             =    661
         _StockProps          =    15
         Caption              =    "SSPanel2"
         ForeColor            =    8421504
         BorderWidth          =    1
         BevelInner           =    1
         Font3D               =    3
         Alignment            =    6
         Autosize             =    3
         Begin VB.HScrollBar HScrollMIDIChannel
               Height             =    285
               Left               =    45
               Max                =    15
               TabIndex           =    15
               Top                =    45
               Value              =    1
               Width              =    1590
         End
   End
   Begin Threed.SSPanel VolumeLabel
         Height               =    225
         Left                 =    3345
         TabIndex             =    13
         Top                  =    390
         Width                =    375
         _Version             =    65536
         _ExtentX             =    661
         _ExtentY             =    397
         _StockProps          =    15
         Caption              =    "100"
         ForeColor            =    0
         BorderWidth          =    1
         BevelOuter           =    0
         Font3D               =    3
         Alignment            =    4
         Autosize             =    3
   End
   Begin Threed.SSPanel MidiChannelOutLabel
         Height               =    225
         Left                 =    1575
```

```
      TabIndex          =    12
      Top               =    390
      Width             =    300
      _Version          =    65536
      _ExtentX          =    529
      _ExtentY          =    397
      _StockProps       =    15
      Caption           =    "1"
      ForeColor         =    0
      BorderWidth       =    1
      BevelOuter        =    0
      Font3D            =    3
      Alignment         =    4
      Autosize          =    3
   End
   Begin Threed.SSPanel SSPanel10
      Height            =    375
      Left              =    8100
      TabIndex          =    11
      Top               =    300
      Width             =    1185
      _Version          =    65536
      _ExtentX          =    2090
      _ExtentY          =    661
      _StockProps       =    15
      Caption           =    "L -   Pan  - R"
      ForeColor         =    0
      BorderWidth       =    0
      BevelOuter        =    1
      BevelInner        =    2
      FloodShowPct      =    0      'False
      Font3D            =    3
      Autosize          =    3
   End
   Begin Threed.SSPanel SSPanel9
      Height            =    375
      Index             =    0
      Left              =    2070
      TabIndex          =    10
      Top               =    300
      Width             =    1230
      _Version          =    65536
      _ExtentX          =    2170
      _ExtentY          =    661
      _StockProps       =    15
      Caption           =    "Volume"
      ForeColor         =    0
      BorderWidth       =    0
      BevelOuter        =    1
      BevelInner        =    2
      FloodShowPct      =    0      'False
      Font3D            =    3
      Alignment         =    1
      Autosize          =    3
   End
```

```
Begin Threed.SSPanel PatchLabel
    Height          =     375
    Left            =     6150
    TabIndex        =     9
    Top             =     300
    Width           =     1785
    _Version        =     65536
    _ExtentX        =     3149
    _ExtentY        =     661
    _StockProps     =     15
    Caption         =     "Electric Piano 2 "
    ForeColor       =     0
    BeginProperty Font {FB8F0823-0164-101B-84ED-08002B2EC713}
        name            =     "Small Fonts"
        charset         =     0
        weight          =     700
        size            =     6
        underline       =     0      'False
        italic          =     0      'False
        strikethrough   =     0      'False
    EndProperty
    BorderWidth     =     0
    BevelOuter      =     1
    BevelInner      =     2
    Font3D          =     3
    Autosize        =     3
End
Begin Threed.SSPanel SSPanel8
    Height          =     375
    Left            =     5535
    TabIndex        =     8
    Top             =     300
    Width           =     615
    _Version        =     65536
    _ExtentX        =     1085
    _ExtentY        =     661
    _StockProps     =     15
    Caption         =     "Patch"
    ForeColor       =     0
    BorderWidth     =     0
    BevelOuter      =     1
    BevelInner      =     2
    Font3D          =     3
    Alignment       =     1
    Autosize        =     3
End
Begin Threed.SSPanel SSPanel7
    Height          =     375
    Left            =     180
    TabIndex        =     7
    Top             =     300
    Width           =     1275
    _Version        =     65536
    _ExtentX        =     2249
```

```
        _ExtentY         =    661
        _StockProps      =    15
        Caption          =    "MIDI Channel "
        ForeColor        =    0
        BorderWidth      =    0
        BevelOuter       =    1
        BevelInner       =    2
        Font3D           =    3
        Alignment        =    1
        Autosize         =    3
    End
    Begin Threed.SSPanel Panel3D1
        Height           =    375
        Left             =    8100
        TabIndex         =    5
        Top              =    720
        Width            =    1215
        _Version         =    65536
        _ExtentX         =    2143
        _ExtentY         =    661
        _StockProps      =    15
        Caption          =    "SSPanel6"
        ForeColor        =    8421504
        BorderWidth      =    2
        BevelInner       =    1
        Font3D           =    3
        Alignment        =    6
        Autosize         =    3
        Begin VB.HScrollBar HScrollPan
            Height           =    255
            LargeChange      =    10
            Left             =    60
            Max              =    127
            TabIndex         =    6
            Top              =    60
            Width            =    1095
        End
    End
    Begin Threed.SSPanel Panel3D2
        Height           =    375
        Left             =    4050
        TabIndex         =    3
        Top              =    720
        Width            =    1200
        _Version         =    65536
        _ExtentX         =    2117
        _ExtentY         =    661
        _StockProps      =    15
        Caption          =    "SSPanel6"
        ForeColor        =    8421504
        BorderWidth      =    2
        BevelInner       =    1
        Font3D           =    3
        Alignment        =    6
```

```
            Autosize        =    3
            Begin VB.HScrollBar HScrollOctave
               Height       =    255
               Left         =    60
               Max          =    4
               TabIndex     =    4
               Top          =    60
               Value        =    2
               Width        =    1080
            End
         End
         Begin Threed.SSPanel SSPanel9
            Height          =    375
            Index           =    1
            Left            =    4050
            TabIndex        =    2
            Top             =    300
            Width           =    735
            _Version        =    65536
            _ExtentX        =    1296
            _ExtentY        =    661
            _StockProps     =    15
            Caption         =    "Octave"
            ForeColor       =    0
            BorderWidth     =    0
            BevelOuter      =    1
            BevelInner      =    2
            FloodShowPct    =    0      'False
            Font3D          =    3
            Alignment       =    1
            Autosize        =    3
         End
         Begin Threed.SSPanel LabelOctave
            Height          =    225
            Left            =    4950
            TabIndex        =    1
            Top             =    390
            Width           =    300
            _Version        =    65536
            _ExtentX        =    529
            _ExtentY        =    397
            _StockProps     =    15
            Caption         =    "1"
            ForeColor       =    0
            BorderWidth     =    1
            BevelOuter      =    0
            Font3D          =    3
            Alignment       =    4
            Autosize        =    3
         End
      End
   End
   Begin VB.Menu File
      Caption         =    "&File"
      Begin VB.Menu Exit
```

```
            Caption          =     "E&xit"
        End
    End
    Begin VB.Menu help
        Caption          =     "&Help"
        Begin VB.Menu About
            Caption          =     "&About"
        End
    End
End
Attribute VB_Name = "Piano"
Attribute VB_Creatable = False
Attribute VB_Exposed = False
Dim NoteCatchCount As Integer
Dim NoteOnCatcher(1024) As Integer
```

Coding the VB MIDI Piano Form Module

The code for the piano program, shown in Listing 16.4, is simple. One difference between this program and the simple experiment we created in MIDIOUT1.MAK is that this code uses decimal values for MIDI messages. In your own programs, use whichever numeric base you wish; the messages will work either way.

Listing 16.4 The Code in PIANO2.FRM

```
Dim NoteCatchCount As Integer
Dim NoteOnCatcher(1024) As Integer
Private Sub About_Click()
    AboutBox1.Show MODAL
End Sub

Private Sub Exit_Click()
    X% = midiOutClose(hMidiOutCopy)
    End
End Sub

Private Sub Form_Load()
    Screen.MousePointer = 11
    Piano.Left = 0
    Piano.TOP = 0

    ' Open Midi Driver
    MidiOutOpenPort

    HScrollMIDIChannel.VALUE = 13
    HScrollPatch.VALUE = 0
    HScrollVolume.VALUE = 100
    HScrollPan.VALUE = 64
    HScrollOctave.VALUE = 2
    Screen.MousePointer = 0
End Sub
```

```
Private Sub Form_Unload(Cancel As Integer)
    X% = midiOutClose(hMidiOutCopy)
    End
End Sub

Private Sub HScrollMIDIChannel_Change()
    ' Change Midi Channel to Vscroll1 value
    MidiChannelOut = HScrollMIDIChannel.VALUE

    ' Display new channel
    MidiChannelOutLabel.Caption = Str$(MidiChannelOut + 1)

    ' Sets the Patch & Volume for the current Midi Channel Out
    HScrollPatch.VALUE = MidiPatch(MidiChannelOut)
    HScrollVolume.VALUE = MidiVolume(MidiChannelOut)
    HScrollPan.VALUE = MidiPan(MidiChannelOut)
    HScrollOctave.VALUE = Octave(MidiChannelOut) / 12
End Sub

Private Sub HScrollOctave_Change()
    LabelOctave.Caption = Str$(HScrollOctave.VALUE)
    Octave(MidiChannelOut) = (HScrollOctave.VALUE * 12)
End Sub

Private Sub HScrollPan_Change()
    MidiPan(MidiChannelOut) = HScrollPan.VALUE

    ' 05-16-92 Pan Midi Out routine
    MidiEventOut = 176 + MidiChannelOut
    MidiNoteOut = 10
    MidiVelOut = MidiPan(MidiChannelOut)
    SendMidiOut
End Sub

Private Sub HScrollPatch_Change()
    ' Sets the Patch for the current Midi Channel Out
    MidiPatch(MidiChannelOut) = HScrollPatch.VALUE
    ReadPatch

    ' 05-15-92 Patch Midi Out routine
    MidiEventOut = &HC0 + MidiChannelOut
    MidiNoteOut = MidiPatch(MidiChannelOut)
    MidiVelOut = 0
    SendMidiOut
End Sub

Private Sub HScrollVolume_Change()
    MidiVelocity = HScrollVolume.VALUE
    MidiVolume(MidiChannelOut) = HScrollVolume.VALUE
    VolumeLabel.Caption = Str$(MidiVelocity)
End Sub

Private Sub PanelWhite_DragDrop(Index As Integer, Source As Control, _
    X As Single, Y As Single)
```

```
    For nn = 0 To NoteCatchCount - 1
        MidiEventOut = 144 + MidiChannelOut
        MidiVelOut = 0
        MidiNoteOut = NoteOnCatcher(nn)
        SendMidiOut
        Piano.PanelWhite(NoteOnCatcher(nn) - Octave(MidiChannelOut)).BevelOuter = 2
    Next nn
    NoteCatchCount = 0
End Sub

Private Sub PanelWhite_DragOver(Index As Integer, Source As Control, _
        X As Single, Y As Single, State As Integer)
    'If still on same note, discard
    If NoteCatchCount > 0 Then
        If NoteOnCatcher(NoteCatchCount - 1) = Index + Octave(MidiChannelOut) Then
            Exit Sub
        End If
    End If

    Piano.PanelWhite(Index).BevelOuter = 0
    MidiEventOut = 144 + MidiChannelOut
    MidiVelOut = MidiVelocity
    MidiNoteOut = Index + Octave(MidiChannelOut)
    SendMidiOut

    'Since drag/drop is being used, we must keep track of the note being played.
    NoteOnCatcher(NoteCatchCount) = MidiNoteOut
    If NoteCatchCount < 750 Then 'Don't let array get out of range
        NoteCatchCount = NoteCatchCount + 1
    End If
End Sub
```

The playing action takes place in the **PanelWhite_DragOver()** event procedure, while the **PanelWhite_DragDrop()** event procedure handles the
Note Off messages.

To enable the user to successively press and hold two or more piano keys,
the program uses drag and drop operations to activate piano keys, instead of
Click or **MouseDown** events. A **DragOver** event occurs whenever you press
the mouse button on a control that has DragMode enabled either because its
DragMode property is set to Automatic, or because one of the control's other
event procedures calls the **Drag** method. The **DragOver** event occurs even
on the control that started the drag operation. This would cause the procedure to repeatedly activate the same note, also repeatedly adding it to the
NoteOnCatcher array until the mouse cursor has moved off the key. So, the
first part of **PanelWhite_DragOver()** checks whether the current control
index is the same as the previous one. If so, it exits the procedure:

```
If NoteCatchCount > 0 Then
        If NoteOnCatcher(NoteCatchCount - 1) = Index + Octave(MidiChannelOut) Then
```

```
        Exit Sub
    End If
  End If
```

The next five lines in **PanelWhite_DragOver()** set up and send the MIDI Note On message:

```
Piano.PanelWhite(Index).BevelOuter = 0
  MidiEventOut = 144 + MidiChannelOut
  MidiVelOut = MidiVelocity
  MidiNoteOut = Index + Octave(MidiChannelOut)
  SendMidiOut
```

The variables **MidiVelocity** and **MidiChannelOut** are set by the HScrollVolume and the HScrollMidiChannel Scroll Bars. **SendMidiOut()** is a general procedure located in the PIANO.BAS code module, which we'll get to shortly.

To handle the simultaneous notes, the program keeps a list of active notes in an array of integers called **NoteOnCatcher**. The variable **NoteCatchCount** is used to keep track of the number of active notes held in the array. The last part of the **PanelWhite_DragOver()** event procedure updates this list:

```
NoteOnCatcher(NoteCatchCount) = MidiNoteOut
  If NoteCatchCount < 750 Then 'Don't let array get out of range
    NoteCatchCount = NoteCatchCount + 1
  End If
```

The **PanelWhite_DragDrop()** event procedure runs through the list, sending Note On messages with 0 velocity to shut off each note, and changing the **BevelOuter** property back to 2 - Raised.

The VB MIDI Piano Code Module

With the exception of the call to the API function **GetPrivateProfileString()**, the code in PIANO.BAS, shown in Listing 16.5, should be familiar to you if you studied the previous project.

Listing 16.5   The Complete Code and Declarations from PIANO.BAS

```
Attribute VB_Name = "PIANO1"
#If Win32 Then
  Public Declare Function midiOutClose Lib "winmm.dll" _
    (ByVal hMidiOut As Long) As Long
  Public Declare Function midiOutOpen Lib "winmm.dll" (lphMidiOut As Long, _
    ByVal uDeviceID As Long, ByVal dwCallback As Long, ByVal dwInstance _
    As Long, ByVal dwFlags As Long) As Long
```

```
    Public Declare Function midiOutShortMsg Lib "winmm.dll" (ByVal hMidiOut _
        As Long, ByVal dwMsg As Long) As Long
    Public Declare Function sndPlaySound Lib "winmm.dll" Alias "sndPlaySoundA" _
        (ByVal lpszSoundName As String, ByVal uFlags As Long) As Long
    Public Declare Function GetPrivateProfileString Lib "kernel32" Alias _
        "GetPrivateProfileStringA" (ByVal lpApplicationName As String, ByVal _
        lpKeyName As Any, ByVal lpDefault As String, ByVal lpReturnedString _
        As String, ByVal nSize As Long, ByVal lpFileName As String) As Long
#Else
    Public Declare Function midiOutOpen Lib "mmsystem.dll" Alias "MidiOutOpen" _
        (hMidiOut As Long, ByVal DeviceId As Integer, ByVal C As Long, ByVal I _
        As Long, ByVal F As Long) As Integer
    Public Declare Function midiOutShortMsg Lib "mmsystem.dll" Alias _
        "MidiOutShortMsg" (ByVal hMidiOut As Integer, ByVal MidiMessage As Long) _
        As Integer
    Public Declare Function midiOutClose Lib "mmsystem.dll" Alias _
        "MidiOutClose" (ByVal hMidiOut As Integer) As Integer
    Public Declare Function GetPrivateProfileString Lib "kernel" (ByVal Sname$, _
        ByVal Kname$, ByVal Def$, ByVal Ret$, ByVal Size%, ByVal Fname$) As Integer
    Public Declare Function sndPlaySound Lib "mmsystem" (ByVal lpsSound _
        As String, ByVal wFlag As Integer) As Integer
#End If

Global MidiEventOut, MidiNoteOut, MidiVelOut As Long
Global hMidiOut As Long
Global hMidiOutCopy As Long
Global MidiOpenError As String

Global Const MODAL = 1
Global Const ShiftKey = 1

' The Patch number array used for current patch for each midi channel
' The Volume array used for each channels volume setting
' TrackChannel is array for the current midi channel that the Track on the mixi
' is set to.
Global MidiPatch(16), MidiVolume(16), TrackChannel(16), MidiPan(16), _
    Octave(16) As Integer

' The current Midi Channel out set on Piano form
Global MidiChannelOut As Integer

' The Velocity (Volume) of notes for current midi channel
Global MidiVelocity As Integer

'Boolean for if CapsLock has been pressed or not
Global CapsLock As Integer

' NoteRepeat used to stop the same key from repeating.  CapsLock detects if it
' is down.
Global NoteRepeat As Integer

Sub MidiOutOpenPort()
    MidiOpenError = Str$(midiOutOpen(hMidiOut, -1, 0, 0, 0))
```

```
      hMidiOutCopy = hMidiOut
End Sub

Sub ReadPatch()
Dim Sname As String, Ret As String, Ext As String

    Ret = String$(255, 0)
    Default1$ = Ret
    Sname = "General MIDI"
    Ext = Str$(MidiPatch(MidiChannelOut))
    filename$ = App.Path & "\PATCH.INI"
    nSize = GetPrivateProfileString(Sname, Ext, Default1$, Ret, Len(Ret), _
        filename$)
    Piano.PatchLabel.Caption = Ret
End Sub

Sub SendMidiOut()
Dim MidiMessage As Long
Dim lowint As Long
Dim highint As Long

    lowint = (MidiNoteOut * 256) + MidiEventOut
    highint = (MidiVelOut * 256) * 256

    MidiMessage = lowint + highint
    X% = midiOutShortMsg(hMidiOutCopy, MidiMessage)
End Sub
```

The function **GetPrivateProfileString()** is a standard Windows API function that reads data from INI files. For a complete description of this function, consult any good Windows API reference. The purpose of this function in this program is to read the list of patch names from the file PATCH.INI.

Receiving MIDI Messages

One of the most difficult multimedia features to use from VB is MIDI input. Unlike WAV audio, which can be recorded with MCI commands, MIDI provides no MCI input support—only low-level functions. And that creates a problem.

All the low-level recording functions in the Windows Multimedia System use callbacks to request buffers or to report activity. In the MIDI functions, the callback function is where incoming MIDI messages are passed to an application. Since VB provides no support for user-definable callback functions, we cannot capture MIDI input from our VB programs—that is, unless we use a custom control.

Windows Callbacks

Many Windows API functions support either of two kinds of callbacks: a *callback function*, or a *window message callback*. In general, callback functions are needed to handle precision timing and synchronous processes, while window message callbacks are used for tasks where response time is less critical.

To use a callback function, you pass the actual memory address of the function to the API function. The API function then calls your callback function when it has completed an operation. This arrangement enables the API function to perform complex processes, then interrupt all other activity on the system when it's ready to return the result.

To use a window message callback, you pass a handle to the window that needs to receive the callback notification. When messages are used for callbacks, the API function simply posts a message to a window. The message is then delivered when it reaches the front of the message queue.

Some functions, like **midiInOpen()**, support either type of callback. But there's a catch. MIDI data is time-critical. The human ear—or more accurately, the human brain—can detect minute variations in time, down to about two milliseconds. This means that if you're going to faithfully record MIDI input, you need precision down to one millisecond.

The multimedia high-resolution timer can provide this kind of precision, but only when you use a callback function. For each MIDI message it receives from the Input port, the MIDI device driver calls the specified callback function, and passes it the MIDI message and an accurate time stamp. When you request a window message callback for the MIDI input device, however, the multimedia system doesn't even bother to time-stamp the callback message. It is assumed in the design of the MIDI API that window message callbacks can't be used for real-time musical event recording. But even with the limitations of window message callbacks, you can still do some impressive things.

The Visual Basic Messenger Custom Control

Since we can't pass callback functions or add our own event procedures to handle callback messages, the only way to receive MIDI messages in VB is to use a custom control. Fortunately, a programmer named James Tyminski has written one and published it as shareware. The *VB Messenger* is a custom control that intercepts all kinds of windows messages, and provides an event procedure where we can insert VB code, just as we do for any of VB's built-in event handlers.

The distribution copy of VB Messenger is located in the directory \SHARWARE\VBMSG. VB Messenger is a shareware product. For information on how to register your copy, see the file README.TXT in the \SHARWARE\VBMSG directory. If you wish, you can register your copy through the CompuServe Shareware Registration Forum (GO SWREG), registration number 961. Shareware registered through this forum will be billed to your CompuServe account.

In our next project, we'll use the VB Messenger to capture incoming MIDI messages. The Messenger control is a 16-bit VBX, so this project will only work in the 16-bit environment. However, the code will easily port to 32-bit when the 32-bit OCX version becomes available.

Receiving MIDI Messages

In this project, we'll use the VB Messenger custom control to intercept a window callback message and trap incoming MIDI messages.

1. Create the form MIDIIN1.FRM.
2. Add the code for the **Form_Load()** and **StartStopButton_Click()** event procedures (Listings 16.6 and 16.7).
3. Add the **VBMsg1_WindowsMessage()** event procedure (Listing 16.8).
4. Fill in the declarations and housekeeping event procedures in the form module (Listing 16.9).
5. Add the code module MIDI2.BAS, and insert the global declarations and the declarations for the MIDI input functions (Listing 16.10).

You'll find this project in the subdirectory \VBMAGIC\MIDIIN1 in the files MIDIIN1.VBP, MIDIIN1.FRM, and MIDI2.BAS. You'll also need the VB Messenger custom control. You'll find it in the \SHARWARE\VBMSG subdirectory. Copy the file VBMSG.VBX to your \WINDOWS\SYSTEM directory.

Running the Program

To run this program, you'll need an external MIDI controller, such as a professional or portable keyboard with a MIDI Out port. Use a standard MIDI cable to connect the MIDI Out port of the instrument to the MIDI In port on your computer's MIDI adapter. (You can find MIDI cables at most music stores.) This program does not discriminate channels, so you can set your external MIDI device to transmit data on any of the 16 MIDI channels.

Run the program and click on the Start button as shown in Figure 16.12. If the program locates any valid MIDI Input devices, it will display their names in the List Box. These names are determined by the manufacturer of the MIDI adapter or sound card, and its driver. Choose the device whose name contains some reference to the MIDI In port. You can then click on the Start button to open the selected device. If the device is valid, "Device Open" appears in the Picture Box at right, indicating that the form window has received an **MM_MIM_OPEN** message from the device driver. When you press the keys of your MIDI controller keyboard, you should see the MIDI Note On and Note Off messages appear in the Picture Box at right. The messages are displayed as three decimal values. The first number in each line displays the value of the status byte. The second and third numbers display the values of the data bytes.

When you are finished, click on the Command Button, now labeled Stop, or use the form's Control menu to select the Close option. If you close the program by selecting the End option from the VB menu, the device driver may lock up. If this happens, you will need to restart Windows to reactivate the MIDI device.

Creating the Form

Create a form named MidiInTest, set its **Caption** to Test MIDI In, and save it under the filename MIDIIN1.FRM. Place a List Box on the form, named MidiDevList. Then add a Command Button, named StartStopButton, and a Picture Box. Set the **ScaleMode** property of the Picture Box to 3 - Pixel.

Finally, add a VB Messenger control to the form. Like a Timer control, the VB Messenger control is invisible at runtime, so you can place it anywhere on

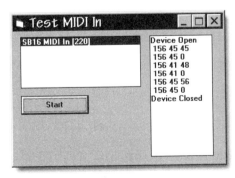

Figure 16.12 *The MIDIIN1 project at runtime.*

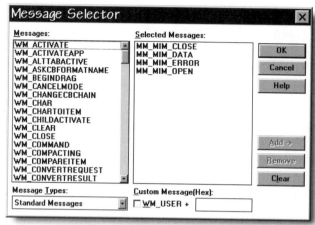

Figure 16.13 *Using the Message Selector dialog box to set up the VB Messenger control at design-time.*

the form. We need to set up this control by telling it which windows messages to detect. First, select the **(Message Selector)** property, then click on the "..." button in the Properties window to open the Message Selector dialog box, shown in Figure 16.13.

In the Message Types list box in the lower-left corner of the dialog box, select Multimedia Messages. Then, from the Messages list box in the upper-left corner, select **MM_MIM_OPEN**, **MM_MIM_CLOSE**, **MM_MIM_ERROR**, and **MM_MIM_DATA**. At runtime, when any of the message types you selected is intercepted, it will trigger the VB Messenger control's **WindowMessage()** event procedure.

Adding the Form Code

The first thing we need to do is query the MIDI device driver for the number of MIDI Input devices and their capabilities. We'll then list that information in the MidiDevList List Box, as shown in Listing 16.6.

Listing 16.6 The Form_Load() Event Procedure from MIDIIN1.FRM

```
Private Sub Form_Load()
Dim NumMidiInDevices As Integer
Dim DevCounter As Integer
Dim RetValue As Integer
Dim DeviceCaps As MIDIINCAPS

    VBMsg1.SubClasshWnd = MidiInTest.hWnd
    StartStopButton.Enabled = False
    NumMidiInDevices = midiInGetNumDevs()
```

```
    For DevCounter = 0 To NumMidiInDevices - 1
        RetValue = midiInGetDevCaps(DevCounter, DeviceCaps, Len(DeviceCaps))
        MidiDevList.AddItem DeviceCaps.szPname
        MidiDevList.ItemData(MidiDevList.NewIndex) = DevCounter
    Next DevCounter
End Sub
```

The first line of the **FormLoad()** event procedure sets the **SubClasshWnd** property of the VB Messenger control to the window handle of the main form, **MidiInTest.hWnd**. To Holy Trinity programmers, subclassing a window or control basically means adding new capabilities to an existing type of object. By adding the ability to respond to MIDI input messages, we are effectively subclassing the form window. By setting this property, we instruct the VB Messenger control to intercept all messages to the specified window that match the types we selected at design time (in the control's Message Selector dialog box).

The API function **midiInGetNumDevs()**, which takes no arguments, returns the number of MIDI Input devices installed in the system. We use that number, captured in the integer variable **NumMidiInDevices** to step through the devices and interrogate them with **midiInGetDevCaps()**. This function takes three arguments: a zero-based device number, a **MIDIINCAPS** record passed by reference, and the size of the **MIDIINCAPS** record. The complete declarations of these functions and the **MIDIINCAPS** structure are listed in Listing 16.10.

Before we can start MIDI input, we need to open the appropriate device, which we do in the **StartStopButton_Click()** event procedure, shown in Listing 16.7.

Listing 16.7   The StartStopButton_Click Event Procedure from MIDIIN1.FRM

```
Private Sub StartStopButton_Click()
Dim RetValue As Integer
Dim NumMidiDevices As Integer

    If Not MidiInActive Then
        RetValue = midiInOpen(hMidiIn, InputDeviceNumber, MidiInTest.hWnd, 0, _
            CALLBACK_WINDOW)
        If RetValue = 0 Then
            RetValue = midiInReset(hMidiIn)
            RetValue = midiInStart(hMidiIn)
            MidiInActive = True
            StartStopButton.Caption = "Stop"
            MidiDevList.Enabled = False
        Else
            MsgBox "Unable to open Midi Device.", 48, "Midi Device Error"
        End If
```

```
    Else
        RetValue = midiInStop(hMidiIn)
        RetValue = midiInClose(hMidiIn)
        MidiInActive = False
        StartStopButton.Caption = "Start"
        MidiDevList.Enabled = True
    End If
End Sub
```

The **midiInOpen()** function takes five arguments:

```
Declare Function midiInOpen Lib "MMSystem" (lphMidiIn As Integer, _
    ByVal uDeviceID As Integer, ByVal dwCallback As Long, _
    ByVal dwInstance As Long, ByVal dwFlags As Long) As Integer
```

The first, **lphMidiIn**, is a variable that the function will set to the handle of the open device. In the second argument, **uDeviceID**, we specify which device to open. The device numbers are zero-based, so the first device is number 0, the second is number 1, and so on. In the third argument, **dwCallback**, we pass either the address of a callback function, or the handle to a window that can receive a message callback. The fourth argument, **dwInstance**, is used when **dwCallback** contains a function address; it is used to pass data to the callback function. Since we can't use a callback function, we always set **dwInstance** to 0. In **dwFlags** we pass a flag that indicates which type of callback to use. In **StartStopButton_Click()** we pass the flag constant **CALLBACK_WINDOW**, which has a value of &H10000.

If we successfully open the device, we call two more functions, **midiInReset()** and **midiInStart()** to reset the device and begin receiving MIDI messages. You can use **midiInStart()** and its sibling, **midiInStop()**, to temporarily suspend MIDI input without closing and reopening the device. When we're ready to shut down the device, we call **midiInStop()** followed by **midiInClose()**. We use the form-level integer variable **MidiInActive** to keep track of whether the device is open or closed. In the **StartStopButton_Click()** event procedure, we open the device if **MidiInActive** is False; otherwise, we close it.

The WindowsMessage Event

The **VBMsg_WindowsMessage()** event procedure, shown in Listing 16.8, is triggered whenever the MIDI device sends the form any of the four windows message types we selected in the VB Messenger control's Message Selector dialog box.

Listing 16.8   The VBMsg1_WindowsMessage() Event Procedure from MIDIIN1.FRM

```
Private Sub VBMsg1_WindowMessage(hWindow As Integer, Msg As Integer, wParam _
    As Integer, lParam As Long, RetVal As Long, CallDefProc As Integer)
Dim MidiDataByte2 As Integer
Dim MidiDataByte1 As Integer
Dim MidiStatusByte As Integer
Dim RetValue As Integer
Dim AreaToScroll As RECT
Dim LineHeight As Integer

    ' Scroll Picture Box 1 line.
    LineHeight = Picture1.TextHeight("A")
    If (Picture1.CurrentY > (Picture1.ScaleHeight - LineHeight)) Then
        AreaToScroll.Top = 0
        AreaToScroll.Left = 0
        AreaToScroll.Right = Picture1.ScaleWidth
        AreaToScroll.Bottom = Picture1.ScaleHeight
        RetValue = ScrollDC(Picture1.hDC, 0, -LineHeight, AreaToScroll, _
            AreaToScroll, 0, ByVal 0&)
        Picture1.Line (0, Picture1.ScaleHeight - LineHeight)- _
            (Picture1.ScaleWidth, Picture1.ScaleHeight), Picture1.BackColor, BF
        Picture1.CurrentX = 0
        Picture1.CurrentY = Picture1.ScaleHeight - LineHeight
    End If
    Select Case Msg
        Case MM_MIM_OPEN
            Picture1.Print "Device Open"
        Case MM_MIM_CLOSE
            Picture1.Print "Device Closed"
        Case Else
            MidiDataByte2 = lParam \ 65536
            MidiDataByte1 = (lParam Mod 65536) \ 256
            MidiStatusByte = lParam Mod 256
            ' Filter out Active Sensing messages, MIDI Status 254.
            If MidiStatusByte <> 254 Then
                Picture1.Print Str$(MidiStatusByte) & Str$(MidiDataByte1) & _
                    Str$(MidiDataByte2)
            End If
    End Select
End Sub
```

This event procedure first uses the Windows API function **ScrollDC()** to scroll the Picture Box, which makes it possible to display a continuously scrolling list of MIDI messages.

In the **Case Else** clause of the **Select Case** statement, we unpack and display the MIDI message, which is passed along with the window message in its **lParam**, a long integer value. The lowest-order byte contains the status byte, the MIDI message code. The second-order byte contains the first data byte, and the third-order byte contains the second data byte. We have filtered out MIDI message 254, which is a MIDI System Real Time Message called Active Sensing. Some MIDI devices continually send this message to announce their presence on the MIDI cable string. Our Roland controller keyboard sends this message about three times per second, which would flood the Picture Box, making it difficult to see any other messages.

Completing the Form Module

Listing 16.9 contains the declarations and remaining event procedures from MIDIIN1.FRM.

Listing 16.9 The Declarations and Remaining Event Code from MIDIIN1.FRM

```
Option Explicit
Declare Function ScrollDC Lib "User" (ByVal hDC As Integer, ByVal dx As Integer, _
    ByVal dy As Integer, lprcScroll As RECT, lprcClip As RECT, _
    ByVal hRgnUpdate As Integer, lprcUpdate As Any) As Integer
Dim hMidiIn As Integer
Dim MidiInActive As Integer
Dim InputDeviceNumber As Integer
Sub Form_Unload (Cancel As Integer)
Dim RetValue As Integer
    RetValue = midiInStop(hMidiIn)
    RetValue = midiInClose(hMidiIn)
End Sub
Sub MidiDevList_Click ()
    InputDeviceNumber = MidiDevList.ItemData(MidiDevList.ListIndex)
    StartStopButton.Enabled = True
End Sub
```

The Code Module

The MIDI2.BAS code module contains nothing but declarations, as shown in Listing 16.10.

Listing 16.10 MIDI2.BAS

```
Option Explicit

Type MIDIINCAPS
    wMid As Integer
    wPid As Integer
    vVersion As Integer
    szPname As String * 128
End Type

Type RECT
    Left As Integer
```

```
      Top As Integer
      Right As Integer
      Bottom As Integer
End Type

Declare Function midiInOpen Lib "MMSystem" (lphMidiIn As Integer, _
    ByVal uDeviceID As Integer, ByVal dwCallback As Long, _
    ByVal dwInstance As Long, ByVal dwFlags As Long) As Integer
Declare Function midiInClose Lib "MMSystem" (ByVal hMidiIn As Integer) As Integer
Declare Function midiInReset Lib "MMSystem" (ByVal hMidiIn As Integer) As Integer
Declare Function midiInStart Lib "MMSystem" (ByVal hMidiIn As Integer) As Integer
Declare Function midiInStop Lib "MMSystem" (ByVal hMidiIn As Integer) As Integer
Declare Function midiInGetNumDevs Lib "MMSystem" () As Integer
Declare Function midiInGetDevCaps Lib "MMSystem" (ByVal wDeviceId As Integer, _
    lpCaps As MIDIINCAPS, ByVal wSize As Integer) As Integer

Global Const CALLBACK_WINDOW = &H10000
Global Const MIDI_MAPPER = -1
Global Const MM_MIM_OPEN = &H3C1
Global Const MM_MIM_CLOSE = &H3C2
```

Beyond MIDI Basics

The API functions we have used in this chapter represent the core of the MIDI programming interface. The multimedia system contains many other functions. Some handle MIDI System Exclusive messages (known in Windows as MIDI Long Messages). Among the others are functions that control playback volume on the internal mixer, translate error codes into string messages, and manage synthesizer patches. With the help of VB Messenger, or a custom control that supports callback functions, you can use the MIDI API to write your own MIDI utilities and sequencers.

You may also wish to review some of the other projects we've explored in earlier chapters, to discover other applications for the VB Messenger custom control—especially the wave audio projects in Chapter 15. Both the standard Windows wave audio functions and the functions in the WaveMix library support callback notifications. With a little help from this handy control, you can increase the utility of these functions.

Join in as we explore the MCI commands that make it possible for you to turn your CD-ROM drive into an audio player.

Working with the Media Control Interface

In Chapter 5 we created a simple test program that we could use to test various MCI command strings. But throughout this book, the only command we've used is **play**. The MCI offers many useful commands, including some that retrieve status information from devices, such as track number, track length, frame number, current position, and a variety of other useful items. In this chapter, we'll try out some of these commands by building an audio CD player with some cool features.

Windows Multimedia's "Simple" Devices

The MCI supports two types of devices: simple devices and compound devices. Up to this point, we've been using compound devices, which consist of a device driver and a data file. The wave audio device is a compound device because without a WAV file, it has nothing to do. Simple devices require no data file, usually because their data is loaded directly into the device on some kind of device-specific medium, such as an audio CD, a video cassette, a video laser disk, or a digital audio tape (DAT). Although the MCI has no control over which data is being played on a simple device, it usually has pretty extensive control over general operation, including rewind, fast forward, play, record, and stop.

Of the compound devices, the most common and easiest to use is a CD-ROM drive. Since CD audio enjoys a widely adopted standard, we can write programs based on MCI commands that will work on any CD, loaded into any CD-ROM drive. Almost all CD-ROM drives come with analog audio outputs. If you have a CD-ROM drive, chances are pretty good you've already used it to play audio disks. If not, check your installation guide for the proper connections to your sound card or external amplifier.

Trying MCI Commands

Before we code anything, let's try a few MCI commands. We'll use the program MCIPlay, which we completed in Chapter 5, to send commands to our CD-ROM drives. Load your favorite disk, then run MCIPLAY3.EXE. Begin by opening the device, as shown in Figure 17.1.

To execute this command, select the mciSendString button. If all goes well, the Error text box should say "The specified command was carried out." If not, then the device may not be available, either because the driver is not installed, or because another application, such as the Media Player, already has opened it.

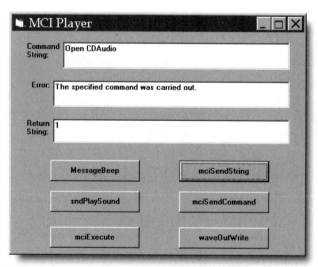

Figure 17.1 *MCIPlay3 with the Open CDAudio command in the Command String text box.*

MCI Player

Command String: status CDAudio number of tracks

Error: The specified command was carried out.

Return String: 13

MessageBeep	mciSendString
sndPlaySound	mciSendCommand
mciExecute	waveOutWrite

Figure 17.2 *The result of an MCI status inquiry.*

To start playing the disk, enter the command "Play CDAudio" in the Command String text box, and again select the mciSendString button. The disk should begin playing.

Next, let's query the device for the number of tracks on the CD. Enter the command "status CDAudio number of tracks" in the Command String text box, then select the mciSendString button. The answer to your query should appear in the Return String text box, as shown in Figure 17.2.

If you send the command "status CDAudio current track," the device will return the number of the current track.

Try a few other commands. For a complete list of available MCI commands, see the Microsoft *Multimedia Programmer's Reference*, or the Waite Group's *Windows API New Testament*. When you're done, be sure to release the device by sending the message "close CDAudio."

Using MCI to Play Redbook Audio

Because just about everyone who works in multimedia has a CD-ROM drive, let's begin this chapter by building a couple of CD player projects that demonstrate the capabilities of the MCI.

One-Step CD Player

We like to listen to music, especially while working on a multimedia project. But we prefer not to mess around with complex gizmos, like over-powered, feature-packed monster CD players. We just want to pop in a CD and have it play. In this project, we'll build a simple CD player that can detect whether a CD is loaded in the drive, and if so, play it. Here are the steps to follow:

1. Create a simple form.
2. Add the declaration for **mciSendString()** (Listing 17.1).
3. Write a general function called **SendMCICommand()** (Listing 17.2).
4. Add the event code shown in Listing 17.3.

You'll find this project in the subdirectory \VBMAGIC\ONESTEP in the files ONESTEP.VBP, ONESTEP.FRM, and ONESTEP.FRX.

Running the One-Step CD Player

When you run ONESTEP.VBP, it will appear as an icon on your desktop. (We have chosen the EAR.ICO icon from the VB icon library.) To play a CD, insert it into the drive. As soon as the program detects that a disk has been loaded, it will issue the **play** command.

To pause the CD, double click on the ONESTEP icon to restore the program window and click on the Pause check box, as shown in Figure 17.3. Click the check box again to resume playback.

To change CDs, simply remove the one that's playing and insert another. Within two or three seconds, the new disk will begin to play.

Use the Control menu, from either the minimized or restored state, to terminate the program. When you close the program, it will stop playback and close the CDAudio device.

Creating the Form

This program uses a simple form with only three controls: a timer, a label, and a check box. Figure 17.4 shows the form at design time. Set the **Name** property of the form to OneStepF1, and set its **Caption** property to "One Step CD Player." Set the **Interval** property of Timer1 to 1000 milliseconds,

Figure 17.3 *ONESTEP.VPB at run time.*

Figure 17.4 *The form ONESTEP.FRM at design time.*

and make sure that **Enabled** is set to True. For Label1, set the **Caption** property to "Now Playing Track:" and set its **Alignment** property to 0 - Left Justify. Finally, set the **Name** property of the check box to PauseCheck, and set its **Caption** property to "&Pause."

Declare the API Function

This program requires only one API function, **mciSendString()**. Add its declaration to the declarations section of ONESTEP.FRM, as shown in Listing 17.1.

Listing 17.1   The Declarations Section of ONESTEP.FRM

```
Option Explicit

#If Win32 Then
    Private Declare Function mciSendString Lib "winmm" Alias "mciSendStringA" _
        (ByVal lpstrCommand As String, ByVal lpstrReturnString As String, _
        ByVal uReturnLength As Long, ByVal hwndCallback As Long) As Long
#Else
    Private Declare Function mciSendString Lib "MMSystem" _
        (ByVal lpstrCommand As String, ByVal lpstrReturnString As String, _
        ByVal wReturnLength As Integer, ByVal hCallback As Integer) As Integer
#End If
```

Encapsulate the API Function

To simplify the calls to **mciSendString()**, we have written a general function called **SendMCICommand()**, shown in Listing 17.2, which will take a command string as its one and only argument, and will return the contents of the return string filled in by the API function.

Listing 17.2   The SendMCICommand General Function from ONESTEP.FRM

```
Private Function SendMCICommand(TheCommand As String) As String
Dim Dummy As Long
Dim ReturnString As String

    ReturnString = String$(128, " ")
    Dummy = mciSendString(TheCommand, ReturnString, 127, 0)
    SendMCICommand = ReturnString
End Function
```

Filling in the Event Code

Now we can fill in the four brief event procedures that make this program tick, shown in Listing 17.3.

Listing 17.3   The Event Code from ONESTEP.FRM

```
Private Sub Form_Load()
Dim ReturnString As String

    ReturnString = SendMCICommand("Open CDAudio")
End Sub

Private Sub Form_QueryUnload(Cancel As Integer, UnloadMode As Integer)
Dim ReturnString As String

    ReturnString = SendMCICommand("stop CDAudio")
    ReturnString = SendMCICommand("close CDAudio")
End Sub

Private Sub PauseCheck_Click()
Dim ReturnString As String

    If PauseCheck.VALUE = 1 Then
       Timer1.Enabled = False
       ReturnString = SendMCICommand("pause CDAudio")
    Else
       Timer1.Enabled = True
       ReturnString = SendMCICommand("play CDAudio")
    End If
End Sub

Private Sub Timer1_Timer()
Dim ReturnString As String

    ReturnString = SendMCICommand("status CDAudio media present")
    If Left$(ReturnString, 4) = "true" Then
       ReturnString = SendMCICommand("status CDAudio mode")
       If Not (Left$(ReturnString, 7) = "playing") Then
          ReturnString = SendMCICommand("play CDAudio")
       Else
          ReturnString = SendMCICommand("status CDAudio current track")
          Label1.Caption = "Now Playing Track: " & Left$(ReturnString, 2)
       End If
    End If
End Sub
```

Once each second, the **Timer1_Timer()** event procedure checks whether a CD is loaded in the drive by sending the message "status CDAudio media present." If it is, the return string will contain the literal string value "true;" otherwise, it will contain "false." The API function **mciSendString()** returns a string with a null terminator between the return value and the blank padding, which prevents the VB **RTrim$()** function from returning a clean string. For this reason, we've instead used the **Left$()** function to grab just the number of characters needed for comparison.

If the drive contains a CD, the **Timer1_Timer()** event procedure sends a second status command to determine whether it is already playing. If not, it sends the play command. If the disk is already playing, it sends a third status command to retrieve the current track number, so we can display it on the form whenever it's restored.

For this simple program, we've used eight MCI commands. That's not too bad when you consider that the CDAudio device supports over three dozen command string combinations. In the next project, we'll try out a few more.

The Smart CD Player

In this project, we'll take greater control over the CDAudio device. We'll even use MCI commands to uniquely identify each CD we load in the drive, so we can store and display their titles. Here are the steps to follow:

1. Create the form (Listing 17.4).
2. Write the **Form_Load()** event procedure (Listing 17.5).
3. Write the **ActivityTimer_Timer()** event procedure (Listing 17.6).
4. Write the **DirectAccess_Click()** event procedure (Listing 17.7).
5. Complete the form code (Listing 17.8).
6. Fill in the code module (Listing 17.9).

 You'll find this project in the subdirectory \VBMAGIC\CDPLAYER in the files CDPLAYER.VBP, CDPLAYER.FRM, CDPLAYER.BAS, and MINMAX.BAS. You'll also need the SPIN.OCX custom control, which the VB Setup program normally installs in your \WINDOWS\SYSTEM directory.

Running the Smart CD Player

When you run the program CDPLAYER.VBP, it will display the form shown in Figure 17.5.

The first time you load a CD into the drive, the program will display <Title Unknown> in the CD Title text box. To assign the correct title, enter it in the text box. The next time you stop or eject the disk, the program will save its title record.

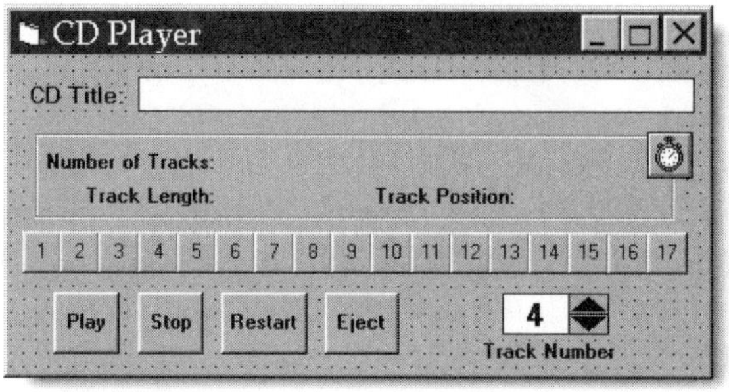

Figure 17.5 *CDPLAYER.FRM at design time.*

Use the spin control to select the starting track, or leave it at the beginning of the disk, and select the Play button to begin playback.

When you load a disk that has been assigned a title, the program will use track and timing information to identify it and display its title. You may edit the title whenever you wish by simply modifying the contents of the text box.

Creating the Form

This simple program has more controls than any other project in this book. For the complete list of controls and their properties, see Listing 17.4.

Listing 17.4   The Form and Control Properties from CDPLAYER.FRM

```
VERSION 4.00
Begin VB.Form CDPlayerF1
   Caption         =   "CD Player"
   ClientHeight    =   2805
   ClientLeft      =   1230
   ClientTop       =   1635
   ClientWidth     =   6420
   BeginProperty Font
      name         =   "MS Sans Serif"
      charset      =   0
      weight       =   700
      size         =   8.25
      underline    =   0    'False
      italic       =   0    'False
      strikethrough =  0    'False
   EndProperty
   ForeColor       =   &H80000008&
   Height          =   3330
   Left            =   1170
   LinkTopic       =   "Form1"
   ScaleHeight     =   2805
   ScaleWidth      =   6420
   Top             =   1170
   Width           =   6540
```

```
Begin VB.CommandButton DirectAccess
   Caption         =   "17"
   BeginProperty Font
      name              =   "MS Sans Serif"
      charset           =   0
      weight            =   400
      size              =   8.25
      underline         =   0      'False
      italic            =   0      'False
      strikethrough     =   0      'False
   EndProperty
   Height          =   375
   Index           =   16
   Left            =   5880
   TabIndex        =   32
   Top             =   1560
   Width           =   375
End
Begin VB.CommandButton DirectAccess
   Caption         =   "16"
   BeginProperty Font
      name              =   "MS Sans Serif"
      charset           =   0
      weight            =   400
      size              =   8.25
      underline         =   0      'False
      italic            =   0      'False
      strikethrough     =   0      'False
   EndProperty
   Height          =   375
   Index           =   15
   Left            =   5520
   TabIndex        =   31
   Top             =   1560
   Width           =   375
End
Begin VB.CommandButton DirectAccess
   Caption         =   "15"
   BeginProperty Font
      name              =   "MS Sans Serif"
      charset           =   0
      weight            =   400
      size              =   8.25
      underline         =   0      'False
      italic            =   0      'False
      strikethrough     =   0      'False
   EndProperty
   Height          =   375
   Index           =   14
   Left            =   5160
   TabIndex        =   30
   Top             =   1560
   Width           =   375
End
```

```
Begin VB.CommandButton DirectAccess
     Caption         =    "14"
     BeginProperty Font
          name            =    "MS Sans Serif"
          charset         =    0
          weight          =    400
          size            =    8.25
          underline       =    0    'False
          italic          =    0    'False
          strikethrough   =    0    'False
     EndProperty
     Height          =    375
     Index           =    13
     Left            =    4800
     TabIndex        =    29
     Top             =    1560
     Width           =    375
End
Begin VB.CommandButton DirectAccess
     Caption         =    "13"
     BeginProperty Font
          name            =    "MS Sans Serif"
          charset         =    0
          weight          =    400
          size            =    8.25
          underline       =    0    'False
          italic          =    0    'False
          strikethrough   =    0    'False
     EndProperty
     Height          =    375
     Index           =    12
     Left            =    4440
     TabIndex        =    28
     Top             =    1560
     Width           =    375
End
Begin VB.CommandButton DirectAccess
     Caption         =    "12"
     BeginProperty Font
          name            =    "MS Sans Serif"
          charset         =    0
          weight          =    400
          size            =    8.25
          underline       =    0    'False
          italic          =    0    'False
          strikethrough   =    0    'False
     EndProperty
     Height          =    375
     Index           =    11
     Left            =    4080
     TabIndex        =    27
     Top             =    1560
     Width           =    375
End
```

```
Begin VB.CommandButton DirectAccess
   Caption         =   "11"
   BeginProperty Font
      name             =   "MS Sans Serif"
      charset          =   0
      weight           =   400
      size             =   8.25
      underline        =   0     'False
      italic           =   0     'False
      strikethrough    =   0     'False
   EndProperty
   Height          =   375
   Index           =   10
   Left            =   3720
   TabIndex        =   26
   Top             =   1560
   Width           =   375
End
Begin VB.CommandButton DirectAccess
   Caption         =   "10"
   BeginProperty Font
      name             =   "MS Sans Serif"
      charset          =   0
      weight           =   400
      size             =   8.25
      underline        =   0     'False
      italic           =   0     'False
      strikethrough    =   0     'False
   EndProperty
   Height          =   375
   Index           =   9
   Left            =   3360
   TabIndex        =   25
   Top             =   1560
   Width           =   375
End
Begin VB.CommandButton DirectAccess
   Caption         =   "9"
   BeginProperty Font
      name             =   "MS Sans Serif"
      charset          =   0
      weight           =   400
      size             =   8.25
      underline        =   0     'False
      italic           =   0     'False
      strikethrough    =   0     'False
   EndProperty
   Height          =   375
   Index           =   8
   Left            =   3000
   TabIndex        =   24
   Top             =   1560
   Width           =   375
End
```

```
Begin VB.CommandButton DirectAccess
   Caption         =   "8"
   BeginProperty Font
      name                 =   "MS Sans Serif"
      charset              =   0
      weight               =   400
      size                 =   8.25
      underline            =   0        'False
      italic               =   0        'False
      strikethrough        =   0        'False
   EndProperty
   Height          =   375
   Index           =   7
   Left            =   2640
   TabIndex        =   23
   Top             =   1560
   Width           =   375
End
Begin VB.CommandButton DirectAccess
   Caption         =   "7"
   BeginProperty Font
      name                 =   "MS Sans Serif"
      charset              =   0
      weight               =   400
      size                 =   8.25
      underline            =   0        'False
      italic               =   0        'False
      strikethrough        =   0        'False
   EndProperty
   Height          =   375
   Index           =   6
   Left            =   2280
   TabIndex        =   22
   Top             =   1560
   Width           =   375
End
Begin VB.CommandButton DirectAccess
   Caption         =   "6"
   BeginProperty Font
      name                 =   "MS Sans Serif"
      charset              =   0
      weight               =   400
      size                 =   8.25
      underline            =   0        'False
      italic               =   0        'False
      strikethrough        =   0        'False
   EndProperty
   Height          =   375
   Index           =   5
   Left            =   1920
   TabIndex        =   21
   Top             =   1560
   Width           =   375
End
```

```
Begin VB.CommandButton DirectAccess
   Caption          =   "5"
   BeginProperty Font
      name             =    "MS Sans Serif"
      charset          =    0
      weight           =    400
      size             =    8.25
      underline        =    0      'False
      italic           =    0      'False
      strikethrough    =    0      'False
   EndProperty
   Height           =   375
   Index            =   4
   Left             =   1560
   TabIndex         =   20
   Top              =   1560
   Width            =   375
End
Begin VB.CommandButton DirectAccess
   Caption          =   "4"
   BeginProperty Font
      name             =    "MS Sans Serif"
      charset          =    0
      weight           =    400
      size             =    8.25
      underline        =    0      'False
      italic           =    0      'False
      strikethrough    =    0      'False
   EndProperty
   Height           =   375
   Index            =   3
   Left             =   1200
   TabIndex         =   19
   Top              =   1560
   Width            =   375
End
Begin VB.CommandButton DirectAccess
   Caption          =   "3"
   BeginProperty Font
      name             =    "MS Sans Serif"
      charset          =    0
      weight           =    400
      size             =    8.25
      underline        =    0      'False
      italic           =    0      'False
      strikethrough    =    0      'False
   EndProperty
   Height           =   375
   Index            =   2
   Left             =   840
   TabIndex         =   18
   Top              =   1560
   Width            =   375
End
```

```
Begin VB.CommandButton DirectAccess
    Caption         =   "2"
    BeginProperty Font
        name            =   "MS Sans Serif"
        charset         =   0
        weight          =   400
        size            =   8.25
        underline       =   0   'False
        italic          =   0   'False
        strikethrough   =   0   'False
    EndProperty
    Height          =   375
    Index           =   1
    Left            =   480
    TabIndex        =   17
    Top             =   1560
    Width           =   375
End
Begin VB.CommandButton DirectAccess
    Caption         =   "1"
    BeginProperty Font
        name            =   "MS Sans Serif"
        charset         =   0
        weight          =   400
        size            =   8.25
        underline       =   0   'False
        italic          =   0   'False
        strikethrough   =   0   'False
    EndProperty
    Height          =   375
    Index           =   0
    Left            =   120
    TabIndex        =   16
    Top             =   1560
    Width           =   375
End
Begin VB.Timer ActivityTimer
    Interval        =   1000
    Left            =   5880
    Top             =   660
End
Begin VB.Frame Frame1
    Height          =   855
    Left            =   240
    TabIndex        =   9
    Top             =   600
    Width           =   5895
    Begin VB.Label Label2
        Alignment       =   1   'Right Justify
        Appearance      =   0   'Flat
        BackColor       =   &H80000005&
        BackStyle       =   0   'Transparent
        Caption         =   "Track Length:"
        ForeColor       =   &H80000008&
```

```
         Height          =    255
         Left            =    480
         TabIndex        =    15
         Top             =    540
         Width           =    1215
      End
      Begin VB.Label TrackLengthLabel
         Appearance      =    0    'Flat
         BackColor       =    &H80000005&
         BackStyle       =    0    'Transparent
         ForeColor       =    &H80000008&
         Height          =    255
         Left            =    1740
         TabIndex        =    14
         Top             =    540
         Width           =    1155
      End
      Begin VB.Label Label3
         Alignment       =    1    'Right Justify
         Appearance      =    0    'Flat
         BackColor       =    &H80000005&
         BackStyle       =    0    'Transparent
         Caption         =    "Track Position:"
         ForeColor       =    &H80000008&
         Height          =    255
         Left            =    3120
         TabIndex        =    13
         Top             =    540
         Width           =    1335
      End
      Begin VB.Label TrackPositionLabel
         Appearance      =    0    'Flat
         BackColor       =    &H80000005&
         BackStyle       =    0    'Transparent
         ForeColor       =    &H80000008&
         Height          =    255
         Left            =    4500
         TabIndex        =    12
         Top             =    540
         Width           =    1215
      End
      Begin VB.Label Label4
         Alignment       =    1    'Right Justify
         Appearance      =    0    'Flat
         BackColor       =    &H80000005&
         BackStyle       =    0    'Transparent
         Caption         =    "Number of Tracks:"
         ForeColor       =    &H80000008&
         Height          =    255
         Left            =    0
         TabIndex        =    11
         Top             =    240
         Width           =    1695
      End
```

```
      Begin VB.Label NumberOfTracksLabel
         Appearance      =   0  'Flat
         BackColor       =   &H80000005&
         BackStyle       =   0  'Transparent
         ForeColor       =   &H80000008&
         Height          =   255
         Left            =   1740
         TabIndex        =   10
         Top             =   240
         Width           =   435
      End
   End
   Begin VB.CommandButton RestartButton
      Appearance      =   0  'Flat
      BackColor       =   &H80000005&
      Caption         =   "Restart"
      Height          =   552
      Left            =   1980
      TabIndex        =   6
      Top             =   2100
      Width           =   792
   End
   Begin VB.CommandButton EjectButton
      Appearance      =   0  'Flat
      BackColor       =   &H80000005&
      Caption         =   "Eject"
      Height          =   552
      Left            =   2940
      TabIndex        =   5
      Top             =   2100
      Width           =   672
   End
   Begin VB.TextBox CDTitleText
      Appearance      =   0  'Flat
      Height          =   315
      Left            =   1200
      TabIndex        =   2
      Top             =   180
      Width           =   5115
   End
   Begin VB.CommandButton StopButton
      Appearance      =   0  'Flat
      BackColor       =   &H80000005&
      Caption         =   "Stop"
      Height          =   552
      Left            =   1200
      TabIndex        =   1
      Top             =   2100
      Width           =   612
   End
   Begin VB.CommandButton PlayButton
      Appearance      =   0  'Flat
      BackColor       =   &H80000005&
      Caption         =   "Play"
```

```
      Height          =     552
      Left            =     420
      TabIndex        =     0
      Top             =     2100
      Width           =     612
   End
   Begin Spin.SpinButton TrackSelectSpin
      Height          =     375
      Left            =     5160
      TabIndex        =     8
      Top             =     2100
      Width           =     375
      _Version        =     65536
      _ExtentX        =     661
      _ExtentY        =     661
      _StockProps     =     73
      ForeColor       =     -2147483630
   End
   Begin VB.Label Label5
      Alignment       =     2  'Center
      Appearance      =     0  'Flat
      BackColor       =     &H80000005&
      BackStyle       =     0  'Transparent
      Caption         =     "Track Number"
      ForeColor       =     &H80000008&
      Height          =     195
      Left            =     4320
      TabIndex        =     7
      Top             =     2520
      Width           =     1335
   End
   Begin VB.Label TrackNumberLabel
      Alignment       =     2  'Center
      Appearance      =     0  'Flat
      BackColor       =     &H80000005&
      BorderStyle     =     1  'Fixed Single
      Caption         =     "4"
      BeginProperty Font
         name            =     "MS Sans Serif"
         charset         =     0
         weight          =     700
         size            =     13.5
         underline       =     0  'False
         italic          =     0  'False
         strikethrough   =     0  'False
      EndProperty
      ForeColor       =     &H80000008&
      Height          =     375
      Left            =     4560
      TabIndex        =     4
      Top             =     2100
      Width           =     615
   End
```

```
    Begin VB.Label Label1
        Alignment       =   1   'Right Justify
        Appearance      =   0   'Flat
        BackColor       =   &H80000005&
        BackStyle       =   0   'Transparent
        Caption         =   "CD Title:"
        BeginProperty Font
            name        =   "MS Sans Serif"
            charset     =   0
            weight      =   700
            size        =   9.75
            underline   =   0   'False
            italic      =   0   'False
            strikethrough =  0  'False
        EndProperty
        ForeColor       =   &H80000008&
        Height          =   315
        Left            =   180
        TabIndex        =   3
        Top             =   225
        Width           =   915
    End
End
Attribute VB_Name = "CDPlayerF1"
Attribute VB_Creatable = False
Attribute VB_Exposed = False
```

Beginning the Form Code

All the event procedures in CDPLAYER.FRM call the API function **mciSendString()** for one reason or another. Let's begin by looking at the **Form_Load()** event procedure, shown in Listing 17.5.

Listing 17.5　The Form_Load() Event Procedure from CDPLAYER.FRM

```
Private Sub Form_Load()
Dim CurrentMode As String

    OpenTitleFile
    mciResult = mciSendString("close CDAudio", ReturnString, 127, 0)
    mciResult = mciSendString("open CDAudio shareable", ReturnString, 127, 0)
    If mciResult <> 0 Then
        MsgBox "Unable to Open CD Audio Device", 16, "MCI Error"
        End
    Else
        mciResult = mciSendString("set CDAudio time format tmsf", _
            ReturnString, 127, 0)
        mciResult = mciSendString("status CDAudio mode", ReturnString, 127, 0)
        CurrentMode = CleanString(ReturnString)
        DiskIdentified = False
        UserWantsToPlay = (CurrentMode = "playing")
        ActivityTimer.Enabled = True
```

```
    End If
End Sub
```

Oddly enough, this event procedure starts by closing the CDAudio device. This is a precautionary measure to cover for the possibility that the device was left open in a previous session—this is particularly helpful when you're debugging a new program that terminates prematurely after opening the device. The variables **mciResult** and **ReturnString** occur frequently in this program, so we decided to declare them as globals in the code module, which we'll discuss later.

After making sure the device is properly closed, the procedure then attempts to reopen it. Most device drivers will return an error if no disk is loaded in the drive, or if another program has the device open, so it's common for the open operation to fail. That's why we chose to trap the error for this particular call to **mciSendString()**. If you wish, you can trap the individual error types and report the specific reason for the failure of the device to open.

If the device opens successfully, we send the command string "set CDAudio time format tmsf" to change the time format, so we can set the playback position in terms of tracks. From this point on, timing and positioning information will appear in this format: track number, minutes, seconds, and frames, in the form tt:mm:ss:ff. For CD audio, the frame count doesn't appear to mean anything. Time format strings are right-padded; that is, 5, 5:00, 5:00:00, and 5:00:00:00 all specify track 5, and 5:1:30 and 5:1:30:00 both specify 1 minute and thirty seconds into track 5.

The last MCI command string we send in the load event, "status CDAudio mode," checks the current status of the drive. It's possible to start the CDPLAYER program while a disk is already playing. Some CD-ROM drives have front panel controls that function even when the drive is under MCI control, which means you can load a disk and start it playing without first loading the CDPLAYER. It's also possible to leave a disk playing by loading another program with CD playback capabilities, such as the Windows Media Player, starting a disk, then exiting the program. If, when CDPLAYER loads, it finds that the CD drive is already playing a disk, it will allow it to continue without interruption.

Finally, we enable the ActivityTimer control, which is where most of the real action takes place in this program. Let's take a look.

The ActivityTimer_Timer() Event Procedure

As you have probably surmised, a device like the CDAudio player is the perfect candidate for an event-driven interface. Each time the device changes status, we can respond to a message, which is represented in VB by an event procedure. When the device locates a track, it could send a "track found" message; when the track starts playing, it could send a "playing" message; and when the track is finished, it could send a "play complete" message. Unfortunately, that's not how the MCI works.

The MCI does support a window callback with a message called **MM_MCINOTIFY**, which we could trap with the VB Messenger custom control (discussed in Chapter 16). But because these messages are posted only when an operation is completed or aborted, it can become extremely confusing to sort them out. And notification messages don't help at all when it comes to monitoring the progress of an operation, such as the current position within a playing track.

Instead of messing around with messages, we'll use a *polling* technique. We'll set a timer control to trigger at 1 second intervals (1000 milliseconds). In the **Timer** event, we'll use the MCI command string "status CDAudio mode" to query the device for its current mode. We'll then use the resulting information to select the appropriate action. Listing 17.6 shows how the **ActivityTimer_Timer()** event procedure works.

Listing 17.6   The ActivityTimer_Timer() Event Procedure from CDPLAYER.FRM

```
Private Sub ActivityTimer_Timer()
Dim CurrentMode As String
Dim TrackPosition
Dim CurrentTrackNumber As String
Dim CurrentPositionHours As Integer
Dim StartPositionHours As Integer
Dim CurrentPositionMinutes As Integer
Dim StartPositionMinutes As Integer
Dim CurrentPositionSeconds As Integer
Dim StartPositionSeconds As Integer
Dim Index As Integer

    mciResult = mciSendString("status CDAudio mode", ReturnString, 127, 0)
    CurrentMode = CleanString(ReturnString)
    Select Case CurrentMode
        ' Insert whatever activity handling you wish in this
        ' Select Case statement.
        Case "not ready"
           UserWantsToPlay = False
           DiskIdentified = False
           'MsgBox "CD Drive Not Ready"
        Case "open"
           UserWantsToPlay = False
           DiskIdentified = False
           'MsgBox "Drive Open"
        Case "paused"
           UserWantsToPlay = False
```

```
        Case "playing", "stopped"
           If Not DiskIdentified Then
               CurrentTitleRecordNumber = GetDiskTitleRecord(DiskTitleRecord)
               If CurrentTitleRecordNumber <> 0 Then
                  CDTitleText.TEXT = DiskTitleRecord.Title
               Else
                  CDTitleText.TEXT = "<Title Unknown>"
               End If
               DiskIdentified = True
           End If
           mciResult = mciSendString("status CDAudio number of tracks", _
               ReturnString, 127, 0)
           NumberOfTracksLabel.Caption = CleanString(ReturnString)
           ' Reset DirectAccess buttons
           For Index = 1 To 17
               If Index > NumberOfTracksLabel.Caption Then
                  DirectAccess(Index - 1).Enabled = False
               Else
                  DirectAccess(Index - 1).Enabled = True
               End If
           Next Index
           mciResult = mciSendString("status CDAudio current track", _
               ReturnString, 127, 0)
           CurrentTrackNumber = CleanString(ReturnString)
           TrackNumberLabel.Caption = CurrentTrackNumber
           mciResult = mciSendString("status CDAudio length track " & _
               CurrentTrackNumber, ReturnString, 127, 0)
           TrackLengthLabel.Caption = Left$(CleanString(ReturnString), 5)

           mciResult = mciSendString("status CDAudio position", _
               ReturnString, 127, 0)
           CurrentPositionHours = Val(Mid$(ReturnString, 4, 2)) \ 60
           CurrentPositionMinutes = Val(Mid$(ReturnString, 4, 2)) Mod 60
           CurrentPositionSeconds = Val(Mid$(ReturnString, 7, 2))

           mciResult = mciSendString("status CDAudio position track " & _
               CurrentTrackNumber, ReturnString, 127, 0)
           StartPositionHours = Val(Mid$(ReturnString, 4, 2)) \ 60
           StartPositionMinutes = Val(Mid$(ReturnString, 4, 2)) Mod 60
           StartPositionSeconds = Val(Mid$(ReturnString, 7, 2))

           TrackPosition = TimeSerial(CurrentPositionHours, _
               CurrentPositionMinutes, CurrentPositionSeconds) - _
               TimeSerial(StartPositionHours, StartPositionMinutes, _
               StartPositionSeconds)
           TrackPositionLabel.Caption = Format$(TrackPosition, "nn:ss")
           ' Restart playback after a track change.
           If (CurrentMode = "stopped") And UserWantsToPlay Then
               mciResult = mciSendString("play CDAudio", ReturnString, 127, 0)
           End If
        Case "seeking"
        'Case "stopped"
        End Select
End Sub
```

In this program, we want to monitor the identity of the disk and the current playback position. In the *open* and *not ready* modes, we can't get any information from the disk, so all we can do is reset our status variables, **UserWantsToPlay** and **DiskIdentified**. In the *seeking* mode, we have to wait until the device locates the requested position, so we do nothing. Most of the action takes place when the device is either *stopped* or *playing*. In these two modes, we can get track and position information. We can then use the information to identify the disk or display its statistics on the form.

If we haven't identified the title of the disk yet, we can call the general function **GetDiskTitleRecord()** (Listing 17.8), located in the code module CDPLAYER.BAS. The integer variable **DiskIdentified** will keep the program from continually looking up the title whenever the **Timer** event fires. After we identify the title, we query the device for track and position information, which we use to display the current track number, the track length in minutes and seconds, and the current position within the track.

Unfortunately, the status command doesn't offer a "position within track" option, so we have to calculate our position within the current track by subtracting the starting position of the track from our current absolute position (our position relative to the beginning of the disk). For this task, we use the VB **TimeSerial()** function to calculate our offset into the track. The MCI tmsf format does not report hours, so we use integer division and the **Mod** operator to split the minutes field into hours and minutes. Notice that the MCI CDAudio driver cannot handle intervals longer than 99 minutes, 59 seconds. Other MCI device drivers, such as the MIDI Sequencer and Videodisc Player, support time formats that include a field for hours.

The frequency of these status messages can have a significant impact on system performance. When you request information from the device, the API function must wait for a response from the driver, which in turn must wait for a response from the CD-ROM drive. Status queries can cause noticeable system pauses. To improve general system performance while CDPLAYER is running, you may wish to reduce the number of status queries by eliminating real-time position tracking ("status CDAudio position") or by increasing the timer **Interval** to decrease MCI activity.

Adding Random Access

You may have noticed a little **For..Next** loop in Listing 17.6. This loop either enables or disables the appropriate button in a control array of command buttons that can be used for direct access to any track. The buttons are created by dropping the first button on the form, sizing it, and naming it

"DirectAccess." Then, perform a copy on the button. You will be asked if you want to create a control array—indicate yes. Then copy the button fifteen more times and line all the buttons up next to each other. Now, go through and set all the **Caption** properties of the buttons so that they number from 1 to 17. Of course, if you wanted to, you could place as many buttons as you want on the form, but 17 seemed like enough, and it fit well onto our form. Figure 17.6 shows the completed CDPLAYER project playing a disc with 13 tracks.

Since we are using a control array, we can use a single code listing to perform the same task for any of the seventeen buttons. Listing 17.7 shows the code from the **DirectAccess_Click()** event procedure.

Listing 17.7   The Declarations and Remaining Event Procedures from CDPLAYER.FRM

```
Private Sub DirectAccess_Click(Index As Integer)
   mciResult = mciSendString("stop CDAudio", ReturnString, 127, 0)
   mciResult = mciSendString("seek CDAudio to " & Str$(Index + 1), _
      ReturnString, 127, 0)
   If UserWantsToPlay Then
      mciResult = mciSendString("play CDAudio", ReturnString, 127, 0)
   End If
End Sub
```

This code is actually very similar to the code executed when the spin control is pressed (Listing 17.8). However, here we do not have to figure out the next or previous track. All we have to do is add one to the **Index** argument, which is the number of the button within the control array.

Finishing the Form Code

The remaining event code in CDPLAYER.FRM sends simple MCI messages to start and stop playback, to close the device, to eject the disk (not supported on all drives), and to select tracks, as shown in Listing 17.8.

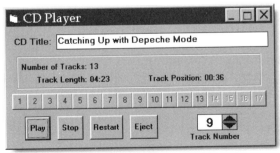

Figure 17.6   *The completed CDPLAYER.VBP playing a disc.*

Listing 17.8 The Declarations and Remaining Event Procedures from CDPLAYER.FRM

```
Option Explicit

Dim UserWantsToPlay As Boolean
Dim DiskIdentified As Boolean
Dim DiskTitleRecord As DiskTitleRecords

Private Sub EjectButton_Click()

    mciResult = mciSendString("stop CDAudio", ReturnString, 127, 0)
    If DiskIdentified Then
      DiskTitleRecord.Title = CDTitleText.TEXT
      SaveDiskTitleRecord DiskTitleRecord, CurrentTitleRecordNumber
    End If
    mciResult = mciSendString("set CDAudio door open", ReturnString, 127, 0)
    UserWantsToPlay = False
End Sub

Private Sub Form_Unload(Cancel As Integer)
Dim mciResult As Integer

    mciResult = mciSendString("close CDAudio", ReturnString, 127, 0)
End Sub

Private Sub PlayButton_Click()
    mciResult = mciSendString("play CDAudio", ReturnString, 127, 0)
    If mciResult = 0 Then
      UserWantsToPlay = True
    End If
End Sub

Private Sub RestartButton_Click()
    mciResult = mciSendString("seek CDAudio to start", ReturnString, 127, 0)
End Sub

Private Sub StopButton_Click()
    mciResult = mciSendString("stop CDAudio", ReturnString, 127, 0)
    UserWantsToPlay = False
    If DiskIdentified Then
      DiskTitleRecord.Title = CDTitleText.TEXT
      SaveDiskTitleRecord DiskTitleRecord, CurrentTitleRecordNumber
    End If
End Sub

Private Sub TrackSelectSpin_SpinDown()
Dim NewPosition As Integer

    NewPosition = MaxInt(Val(TrackNumberLabel.Caption) - 1, 1)
    mciResult = mciSendString("stop CDAudio", ReturnString, 127, 0)
    mciResult = mciSendString("seek CDAudio to " & Str$(NewPosition), _
      ReturnString, 127, 0)
```

```
    If UserWantsToPlay Then
        mciResult = mciSendString("play CDAudio", ReturnString, 127, 0)
    End If
End Sub

Private Sub TrackSelectSpin_SpinUp()
Dim NewPosition As Integer

    NewPosition = MinInt(Val(TrackNumberLabel.Caption) + 1, _
        Val(NumberOfTracksLabel.Caption))
    mciResult = mciSendString("stop CDAudio", ReturnString, 127, 0)
    mciResult = mciSendString("seek CDAudio to " & Str$(NewPosition), _
        ReturnString, 127, 0)
    If UserWantsToPlay Then
        mciResult = mciSendString("play CDAudio", ReturnString, 127, 0)
    End If
End Sub
```

The only noteworthy code in these event procedures is in **TrackSelect-Spin_SpinDown()** and **TrackSelectSping_SpinUp()**. When you reposition the device with a **seek** command, the device driver will halt playback. (At least it does on our systems; this may depend on the device driver version.) We can restart playback with a **play** command, but we don't want to do this arbitrarily, because the user may want to change tracks while the drive is stopped. To manage this problem, we created the variable **UserWantsToPlay** so we could distinguish between the current drive mode and the status selected by the operator. Clicking on the Play button sets **UserWantsToPlay** to True; clicking on the Stop button sets the variable to False. If the drive stops upon seeking, but **UserWantsToPlay** is still True, then we just issue another **play** command.

We ran into another problem that occurred only on a single machine. When we switched tracks while a disc was playing, the player would stop and the current track would jump to the last track on the disc. However, when the disc was stopped, everything worked fine. To fix this, whenever a change in track is called for, we first send a "stop CDAudio" command, then switch the track position, then, if necessary, restart the CD.

The Code Module

The code module, shown in Listing 17.9, contains the global declarations and the code that manages the disk title file, CDTITLES.DAT.

Listing 17.9   CDPLAYER.BAS

```
Attribute VB_Name = "CDPLAYER1"
Option Explicit
```

```
#If Win32 Then        ' Windows 95 Code
    Declare Function mciSendString Lib "winmm.dll" Alias "mciSendStringA" _
        (ByVal lpstrCommand As String, ByVal lpstrReturnString As String, _
        ByVal uReturnLength As Long, ByVal hwndCallback As Long) As Long
#Else                 ' Windows 3.1 Code
    Declare Function mciSendString Lib "MMSystem" (ByVal lpstrCommand As String, _
        ByVal lpstrReturnString As String, ByVal uReturnLength As Integer, _
        ByVal hwndCallback As Integer) As Long
#End If

Type DiskTitleRecords
    IDNumber As Long
    Title As String * 128
End Type

Global mciResult As Long
Global ReturnString As String * 128
Global CDTitleFile As Integer
Global CurrentTitleRecordNumber As Integer


Function CleanString(MessyString As String) As String
    CleanString = Left$(MessyString, InStr(MessyString, Chr$(0)) - 1)
End Function


Function GetDiskTitleRecord(AnyDiskTitleRecord As DiskTitleRecords)
Dim NumberOfTracks As Integer
Dim DiskLength As Long
Dim DiskID As Long
Dim RecordPosition As Integer
Dim Found As Integer

    mciResult = mciSendString("status CDAudio number of tracks", _
        ReturnString, 127, 0)
    NumberOfTracks = Val(CleanString(ReturnString))
    mciResult = mciSendString("set CDAudio time format milliseconds", _
        ReturnString, 127, 0)
    mciResult = mciSendString("status CDAudio length", ReturnString, 127, 0)
    DiskLength = Val(CleanString(ReturnString))
    DiskID = NumberOfTracks * DiskLength
    mciResult = mciSendString("set CDAudio time format tmsf", _
        ReturnString, 127, 0)

    RecordPosition = 0
    Do
        RecordPosition = RecordPosition + 1
        Get CDTitleFile, RecordPosition, AnyDiskTitleRecord
        Found = (DiskID = AnyDiskTitleRecord.IDNumber)
    Loop Until Found Or EOF(CDTitleFile)
    If Found Then
        GetDiskTitleRecord = RecordPosition
    Else
        GetDiskTitleRecord = 0
```

```
            AnyDiskTitleRecord.IDNumber = DiskID
    End If
End Function

Sub OpenTitleFile()
Dim AnyTitleRecord As DiskTitleRecords

    CDTitleFile = 1
    Open App.Path & "\CDTitles.Dat" For Random As CDTitleFile Len = _
        Len(AnyTitleRecord)
End Sub

Sub SaveDiskTitleRecord(AnyDiskTitleRecord As DiskTitleRecords, _
    RecordPosition As Integer)
Dim FileSize As Integer

    If RecordPosition <> 0 Then
        Put CDTitleFile, RecordPosition, AnyDiskTitleRecord
    Else
        FileSize = LOF(CDTitleFile) \ Len(AnyDiskTitleRecord)
        RecordPosition = FileSize + 1
        Put CDTitleFile, RecordPosition, AnyDiskTitleRecord
    End If
End Sub
```

In the general function **GetDiskTitleRecord()**, we temporarily change the time format to milliseconds. We multiply the total length of the disk in milliseconds by the number of tracks, to create a unique *signature* for the disk. Although possible, it's extremely unlikely that any two CDs will have the same signature. For each CD, we store a record with two fields:

```
Type DiskTitleRecords
    IDNumber As Long
    Title As String * 128
End Type
```

We store the signature in the **IDNumber** field, and the CD title in the **Title** field. Each time the user loads a disk in the CD-ROM drive, the **ActivityTimer_Timer()** event procedure (shown in Listing 17.6) calls **GetDiskTitleRecord()**, which calculates the disk's signature and searches CDTITLES.DAT for a record with a matching **IDNumber**. If it finds an existing record, it returns the record position; if not, it returns 0. In the **StopButton_Click()** and **EjectButton_Click()** event procedures (Listing 17.8), we call the **SaveDiskTitleRecord()** general procedure, passing it the current **DiskTitleRecord** and the record position returned by **GetDiskTitleRecord()**. If the record position is not zero, **SaveDiskTitleRecord()** replaces the existing record; if it is zero, **SaveDiskTitleRecord()** appends a new record to the end of the file. The record is replaced every time you stop or eject the disk, allowing you to modify the title any time you wish.

> **Note** : *Pressing the manual eject button on the drive itself will not trigger the* **EjectButton_Click()** *event, which means that it will not rewrite the title record. If your drive does not support automatic eject, you must use the program's Stop button to store the title record before you eject the disk. You may also wish to experiment with the* open *and* not ready *drive modes to trigger file updates.*

Suggested Enhancements

This kind of program is a hacker's wonderland. You can add features to this basic framework to make it do anything you ever imagined you might want from your Discman—except make it portable enough to carry in the next triathlon. Here are a few suggestions:

- Add a second file to hold song titles.
- Replace the binary file system with an Access database.
- Add features to maintain the database, such as a delete option.
- Add random and programmable play ordering.
- Add a musician's practice loop that will repeat the same passage indefinitely.
- Dress up the screen with original artwork and animated buttons.

Don't Underestimate the MCI

Each MCI device supports its own set of commands. Many commands are the same or similar from one device to another, but be careful not to overlook hidden capabilities. Even the innocent-looking **play** command changes from one device to another. For example, in the Videodisc command set, the **play** command can control the speed of playback, and can even order the disc to play in reverse.

The number and type of MCI devices is growing steadily. If you're planning to purchase a laser disc player, a semi-professional VCR, a DAT tape deck, or any other piece of equipment that might be useful in multimedia production, be sure to investigate MCI support. Most of these devices will connect to your computer by way of a serial port, which means they won't require additional IRQs, DMA channels, or I/O addresses.

Don't assume, however, that all MCI devices are created equal. If a manufacturer claims that its product supports MCI, ask for some assurance in the form of a return policy. Not everyone understands just what it means to support MCI. Simple play, stop, and rewind functions won't do you any good when you try to perform step-frame AVI captures.

MCI devices can add a whole new dimension to your multimedia projects, especially those that do not need to run exclusively on a self-contained PC. For museum and kiosk systems, for example, you can really punch up your presentations with separate screens and speakers attached to MCI-controlled videodisc players, VCRs, audio tape players, or any number of other devices. And who knows where MCI and Windows multimedia are headed in the future?

Now we'll learn how we can add much more horsepower to boost our VB multimedia applications with powerful custom controls.

Exploring OCXs and OLE Automation

The Visual Basic development environment's popularity is due, in a large part, to custom controls. With VBXs, and now OCXs, you can easily add powerful and complex features to your applications, with a minimum of code. Think about it: How much work would it take you to create code that would read in a custom image file? Probably about as long as it took us to write this book! Well, maybe not that long. Because VB is not a language that is easily adaptable for writing low-level code, custom controls have greatly helped VB developers add features such as fast animation, low-level graphics, and communications and networking support to their applications.

Over the past couple of years, the number of custom controls available for VB has skyrocketed. You can buy controls that do everything from rendering 3D worlds to connecting to the Internet. Think about what it would take to render a 3D image using only VB. Even if you were a math wizard and could figure out the algorithms needed to render the scene, VB's interpreted math is so slow that it would take an unreasonable amount of time to create the image. However, C and Pascal have very fast math functions. That's where custom controls come in. They allow C/C++ programmers to wrap their best code into small packages that can then be used from within VB. Now, with the advent of the OLE custom controls (OCXs), controls can be used from many languages, including VB 4, C++ 2.0, and future versions of Delphi. You can create code in one language, compile it into an OCX, and use it from within a multitude of other languages. For the moment, VB users cannot create OCXs themselves—but maybe they will be able to in the future!

Since we are using VB 4, we won't be showing you how to create custom controls, but we will talk about how and when to use them. One of the drawbacks of custom controls is the extra memory they consume. If the custom control you want to use was not well optimized by the programmer who originally created it, the control can quickly start to eat up resources. So, when using custom controls, be careful not to use too many on a single form or within a single application. When we used six or seven controls in one application, we already started to notice an impact on memory. Actually, all of the controls in the standard VB repertoire are custom controls; they have just been integrated into the environment. They are also pretty well optimized, so that they use as little resources as possible.

Object Linking and Embedding (OLE) is Microsoft's implementation of a system to share application features between documents. OLE is what allows you to place Excel charts into Word documents. The average user often uses this powerful feature, oblivious of how much work is going on in the background. We are going to give you a simple demonstration of how to implement some of the OLE features in the VB 4 environment, and hopefully teach you along the way a little about how OLE works.

In this chapter, we are going to introduce you to a couple of helpful new OCXs and also show you the basics of OLE Automation. We'll use some controls to build a useful multimedia Web browser that you can actually use to surf the Web.

Working with the Internet FTP Protocol

The FTP protocol is a very important part of the Internet. It is overshadowed by the much more interactive World Wide Web protocol, but is still widely used. We don't have the time or space in this book to go into the details of the FTP protocol, and fortunately don't need to, because we can use a custom control to do the dirty work for us.

The control we'll be using is being developed by Edward Toupin. The version that is included on the companion CD-ROM is yours to use freely. However, it is not the completed product. If you find a function or two that does not work very well, you may be interested in acquiring the full release version of his Internet protocols package. It includes OCXs for many of the Internet protocols, including FTP, GetHost, and SMTP. Read Appendix B if you'd like to find out how to contact the company that sells these controls.

We are going to use the FTP OCX to build a simple FTP application that can be used to download files. Then, we'll use this powerful control to expand the HTML document browser we created in Chapter 12. Our new version will allow us to access the Web.

Building an FTP Application

Let's get started with our FTP app by jumping in and running the program. This will give you an idea of what we need to code. Figure 18.1 shows our simple FTP download program.

We tried to make the form as simple as possible by adding just enough features to give you an idea of how the FTP protocol, and specifically, the FTP OCX, works. When we add the FTP capabilities to our Web document browser, we'll only need to download files. If you want to add file upload capabilities or other features later, you can do so by extending our simple application. We don't think you will have much trouble after you see how useful this easy-to-use control is.

Now that you've seen what the application looks like, let's figure out how this program works. We'll actually be using two new controls for this project. The FTP OCX is pretty self-explanatory. It contains all of the necessary code to connect to remote locations, search through directories, and manipulate remote files. The other control we'll need is the GetHostIP OCX. This control takes the name of a remote location and goes out on the Internet to figure out

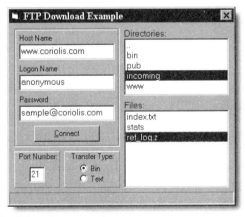

Figure 18.1 *The FTPSAMPL project at runtime.*

the IP address that points to that location. Originally, the Internet was all based on numbers. Web and FTP sites didn't have names, they had numbers—IP addresses. A few years ago, *Domain Names* were implemented, which represented IP addresses. To make this system work, *Domain Name Servers* (DNS) were put online, which store all of the Domain Names and their respective IP addresses. When our GetHostIP OCX sends one of these DNSs a Domain Name, the server sends back an IP address so that we can find the desired site on the Internet. You may have noticed that commercial products like Netscape's Navigator do the same thing. When you go to a new site using Netscape, its status bar will change to indicate the new site. The IP address returned by the DNS is then used by the browser to select the new Web site. This is the exact method we will use with our project.

Jumping on the Internet with the FTP protocol

This project teaches you the basics of creating an FTP application. You can use the application to FTP files on the Internet.

1. Start a new project by invoking the File | New Project command from within VB.

2. Add the FTP custom control and the GetHost control to the Toolbox.

3. Set up the main form and add the required global declarations (Listing 18.1).

4. Add the code for the necessary event procedures: **ConnectBtn_Click()**, **DirList_DblClick()**, and **FileList_DblClick()** (Listings 18.2, 18.4, and 18.5).

5. Add the code for the **GetCurDir()** subroutine (Listing 18.3).

 You'll find this project in the subdirectory \VBMAGIC\FTPSAMPL in the file FTPSAMPL.VBP. You will also need to install the FTP and GETHOST OCXs that are located in the \SHARWARE\TOUPIN subdirectory on the companion CD-ROM. Installation instructions for the OCXs are located in Appendix C.

We need to start this project from scratch, so click on File | New Project. Next, we need to add the new OCXs to our project. You should copy the controls onto your hard drive first. Unlike VB 3, you don't need to place the controls in the WINDOWS\SYSTEM directory anymore. You may want to consider setting up a special directory where you can place your third-party

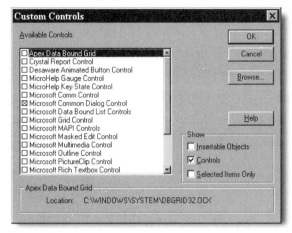

Figure 18.2   *The Custom Controls dialog box.*

custom controls. After copying the controls, you need to tell VB where to find them. Open the Custom Controls dialog box by clicking on Tools|Custom Controls. When the dialog box opens, you should see settings like the ones shown in Figure 18.2.

Now, click on the Browse button. You will be greeted with the standard Windows 95 File Open dialog box. Find the directory where you placed the new custom controls and double click on the FTP.OCX file. Click on the Browse button again and double click on the GETHOST.OCX file. Then click on OK and the new OCXs will be loaded into the ToolBox, ready for you to use.

Adding the Declarations

Next, we need to place all of our controls onto the form. By now, you probably have a pretty good idea of how this process works. Listing 18.1 shows the code from the FTPSAMPL.FRM file that lists all of the controls and their properties.

Listing 18.1   The Controls and Declaration Section from FTPSAMPL.FRM

```
VERSION 4.00
Begin VB.Form Form1
   BorderStyle    =    1   'Fixed Single
   Caption        =    "FTP Download Example"
   ClientHeight   =    4245
   ClientLeft     =    1620
   ClientTop      =    2280
   ClientWidth    =    5415
   Height         =    4755
   Left           =    1560
   LinkTopic      =    "Form1"
```

```
LockControls    =   -1   'True
MaxButton       =   0    'False
MinButton       =   0    'False
ScaleHeight     =   4245
ScaleWidth      =   5415
Top             =   1830
Width           =   5535
Begin VB.ListBox DirList
   BeginProperty Font
      name            =   "MS Sans Serif"
      charset         =   0
      weight          =   400
      size            =   9.75
      underline       =   0    'False
      italic          =   0    'False
      strikethrough   =   0    'False
   EndProperty
   Height          =   1335
   IntegralHeight  =   0    'False
   Left            =   2760
   TabIndex        =   7
   Top             =   360
   Width           =   2535
End
Begin VB.ListBox FileList
   BeginProperty Font
      name            =   "MS Sans Serif"
      charset         =   0
      weight          =   400
      size            =   9.75
      underline       =   0    'False
      italic          =   0    'False
      strikethrough   =   0    'False
   EndProperty
   Height          =   1815
   IntegralHeight  =   0    'False
   ItemData        =   "main.frx":0000
   Left            =   2760
   List            =   "main.frx":0002
   TabIndex        =   6
   Top             =   2040
   Width           =   2535
End
Begin FtpLibCtl.Ftp FtpOCX
   Left            =   4320
   Top             =   1680
   _version        =   65536
   _extentx        =   661
   _extenty        =   661
   _stockprops     =   0
End
Begin Threed.SSPanel SSPanel1
   Height          =   2775
   Left            =   120
```

```
TabIndex        =    0
Top             =    120
Width           =    2535
_Version        =    65536
_ExtentX        =    4471
_ExtentY        =    4895
_StockProps     =    15
BackColor       =    12632256
BorderWidth     =    1
BevelOuter      =    1
BevelInner      =    2
Begin VB.TextBox HostName
   BeginProperty Font
      name            =    "MS Sans Serif"
      charset         =    0
      weight          =    400
      size            =    9.75
      underline       =    0    'False
      italic          =    0    'False
      strikethrough   =    0    'False
   EndProperty
   Height          =    375
   Left            =    120
   TabIndex        =    10
   Text            =    "www.coriolis.com"
   Top             =    360
   Width           =    2295
End
Begin VB.CommandButton ConnectBtn
   Caption         =    "&Connect"
   Height          =    375
   Left            =    480
   TabIndex        =    5
   Top             =    2280
   Width           =    1575
End
Begin VB.TextBox Password
   BeginProperty Font
      name            =    "MS Sans Serif"
      charset         =    0
      weight          =    400
      size            =    9.75
      underline       =    0    'False
      italic          =    0    'False
      strikethrough   =    0    'False
   EndProperty
   Height          =    375
   Left            =    120
   TabIndex        =    3
   Text            =    "sample@coriolis.com"
   Top             =    1800
   Width           =    2295
End
```

```
Begin VB.TextBox LogonName
    BeginProperty Font
        name            =   "MS Sans Serif"
        charset         =   0
        weight          =   400
        size            =   9.75
        underline       =   0       'False
        italic          =   0       'False
        strikethrough   =   0       'False
    EndProperty
    Height          =   375
    Left            =   120
    TabIndex        =   1
    Text            =   "anonymous"
    Top             =   1080
    Width           =   2295
End
Begin VB.Label Label6
    Caption         =   "Host Name"
    Height          =   255
    Left            =   120
    TabIndex        =   11
    Top             =   120
    Width           =   1335
End
Begin VB.Label Label3
    Caption         =   "Password"
    Height          =   255
    Left            =   120
    TabIndex        =   4
    Top             =   1560
    Width           =   1335
End
Begin VB.Label Label2
    Caption         =   "Logon Name"
    Height          =   255
    Left            =   120
    TabIndex        =   2
    Top             =   840
    Width           =   1335
End
End
Begin Threed.SSPanel SSPanel2
    Height          =   855
    Left            =   1320
    TabIndex        =   12
    Top             =   3000
    Width           =   1335
    _Version        =   65536
    _ExtentX        =   2355
    _ExtentY        =   1508
    _StockProps     =   15
    Caption         =   " Transfer Type:"
    BackColor       =   12632256
```

```
      BorderWidth     =   1
      FloodShowPct    =   0     'False
      Alignment       =   6
      Begin VB.OptionButton TextOpt
         Caption         =   "Text"
         Height          =   195
         Left            =   360
         TabIndex        =   14
         Top             =   540
         Width           =   615
      End
      Begin VB.OptionButton BinOpt
         Caption         =   "Bin"
         Height          =   195
         Left            =   360
         TabIndex        =   13
         Top             =   300
         Value           =   -1    'True
         Width           =   615
      End
   End
End
Begin Threed.SSPanel SSPanel4
   Height          =   855
   Left            =   120
   TabIndex        =   15
   Top             =   3000
   Width           =   1095
   _Version        =   65536
   _ExtentX        =   1931
   _ExtentY        =   1508
   _StockProps     =   15
   Caption         =   " Port Number:"
   BackColor       =   12632256
   BorderWidth     =   1
   FloodShowPct    =   0     'False
   Alignment       =   6
   Begin VB.TextBox PortNumber
      Alignment       =   2  'Center
      BeginProperty Font
         name            =   "MS Sans Serif"
         charset         =   0
         weight          =   400
         size            =   9.75
         underline       =   0   'False
         italic          =   0   'False
         strikethrough   =   0   'False
      EndProperty
      Height          =   360
      Left            =   360
      TabIndex        =   16
      Text            =   "21"
      Top             =   360
      Width           =   375
   End
End
```

```
Begin Threed.SSPanel CurDirPanel
    Height          =    285
    Left            =    0
    TabIndex        =    17
    Top             =    3960
    Width           =    5415
    _Version        =    65536
    _ExtentX        =    9551
    _ExtentY        =    503
    _StockProps     =    15
    BackColor       =    12632256
    BeginProperty Font {0BE35203-8F91-11CE-9DE3-00AA004BB851}
        name            =    "MS Sans Serif"
        charset         =    0
        weight          =    400
        size            =    9.76
        underline       =    0    'False
        italic          =    0    'False
        strikethrough   =    0    'False
    EndProperty
    BevelOuter      =    1
    Alignment       =    1
End
Begin MSComDlg.CommonDialog CommDlg
    Left            =    4800
    Top             =    1680
    _Version        =    65536
    _ExtentX        =    847
    _ExtentY        =    847
    _StockProps     =    0
    CancelError     =    -1    'True
    DialogTitle     =    "Download File To:"
End
Begin VB.Label Label5
    AutoSize        =    -1    'True
    Caption         =    "Files:"
    BeginProperty Font
        name            =    "MS Sans Serif"
        charset         =    0
        weight          =    400
        size            =    9.75
        underline       =    0    'False
        italic          =    0    'False
        strikethrough   =    0    'False
    EndProperty
    Height          =    240
    Left            =    2760
    TabIndex        =    9
    Top             =    1800
    Width           =    480
End
Begin VB.Label Label4
    AutoSize        =    -1    'True
    Caption         =    "Directories:"
```

```
    BeginProperty Font
        name            =   "MS Sans Serif"
        charset         =   0
        weight          =   400
        size            =   9.75
        underline       =   0       'False
        italic          =   0       'False
        strikethrough   =   0       'False
    EndProperty
    Height          =   240
    Left            =   2760
    TabIndex        =   8
    Top             =   120
    Width           =   1020
End
Begin GethostLibCtl.GetAdrs GetIPOCX
    Left            =   4440
    Top             =   0
    _version        =   65536
    _extentx        =   661
    _extenty        =   661
    _stockprops     =   0
End
Begin GethostLibCtl.GetName GetNameOCX
    Left            =   4920
    Top             =   0
    _version        =   65536
    _extentx        =   661
    _extenty        =   661
    _stockprops     =   0
End
End
Attribute VB_Name = "Form1"
Attribute VB_Creatable = False
Attribute VB_Exposed = False

Option Explicit

Dim Connected As Boolean

Const cdlOFNHideReadOnly = &H4&
Const cdlOFNOverwritePrompt = &H2&
Const cdOFNLongNames = &H200000
```

Using the FTP Control

The full-blown commercial version of the FTP control we're using with our project will eventually handle all of the Internet connection operations automatically. For now, we'll add in the features we need. The benefit to this approach is that it allows us more flexibility when connecting to a site. Why? Well, without getting into too much detail, every IP address points to a machine that is somewhere on the Internet. Each machine, in turn, can have multiple ports open for access. For example, the FTP protocol uses port 21 as its default port, while port 80 is the Web's default port. If you let the FTP control connect automatically, you might not connect to the correct port, especially if you are using this control in a corporate environment where there might be custom ports set up for internal use.

Enough background, let's add some code to the main form, and make this stuff work!

We will start with the **ConnectBtn**, since it is the most important step. We only need to respond to click events, so let's look at the code for the **CommandBtn_Click()** event (Listing 18.2).

Listing 18.2 The CommandBtn_Click() Event Procedure from FTPSAMPL.FRM

```
Private Sub ConnectBtn_Click()
Dim ReturnValue As Integer
Dim HostIP As String
Dim msg As String

    Screen.MousePointer = 11
    If ConnectBtn.Caption = "&Connect" Then
        If HostName.Text = "" Or LogonName.Text = "" Or Password.Text = "" Then
            MsgBox "You are missing a required entry." & Chr(10) & _
                "Please enter it and try again.", MB_ICONSTOP, "Error!"
        Else
            HostIP = GetIPOCX.GetHostAdrs(HostName.Text)
            If HostIP = "" Then
                MsgBox "Error #" & GetIPOCX.ErrorNum * Chr(10) & _
                    "Could not acquire Host IP Address.", MB_ICONEXCLAMATION, _
                    "FTP Error"
            Else
                If Not PortNumber.Text = 21 And Not PortNumber.Text = 80 Then
                    msg = "Are you sure you want to use Port " & PortNumber.Text & "?"
                    msg = msg & Chr(10) & "Typical Ports settings are:"
                    msg = msg & Chr(10) & "21 - Standard FTP Server Port"
                    msg = msg & Chr(10) & "80 - Standard WWW Server Port"
                    If MsgBox(msg, MB_ICONQUESTION Or MB_YESNO, "Possible Error!") _
                        = IDNO Then
                        Screen.MousePointer = 0
                        Exit Sub
                    End If
                End If
                'FtpOCX.Port = Val(PortNumber.Text)
                ReturnValue = FtpOCX.Logon(HostIP, LogonName.Text, Password.Text, "")
                If Not ReturnValue = 0 Then
                    Connected = True
                    ConnectBtn.Caption = "&Disconnect"
                    curdirpanel.Caption = HostName.Text & "/"
                    GetCurDir
```

```
            Else
                MsgBox "Could not logon to the requested site.", MB_ICONSTOP, _
                    "Error!"
            End If
        End If
    End If
  Else
      FtpOCX.Logout
      Connected = False
      ConnectBtn.Caption = "&Connect"
      curdirpanel.Caption = ""
      FileList.Clear
      DirList.Clear
  End If
  Screen.MousePointer = 0
End Sub
```

This procedure starts off, as usual, by declaring a few variables. The **ReturnValue** variable is a **Long** integer that we will use to store the information returned by our calls to the FTP OCX. The **HostIP** string variable will store the returned IP address that we need to access an FTP site. Finally, we use the **msg String** variable to construct messages for our Message Boxes.

After declaring the variables, we begin by switching the mouse pointer to an hourglass. Then, we check to see if we are connecting or disconnecting. We use the same button for both functions by just changing the **Caption** property of the **ConnectBtn** control back and forth from "&Connect" to "&Disconnect." (Remember, the ampersand character (&) is used to turn the initial letter of the caption into a hot key.)

If the **Caption** property is equal to "&Connect," we know that we want to proceed with a connection. We need to make sure that we have all the required information, including Domain Name, Logon Name, and Password. When accessing an Internet site anonymously, you simply need to send "anonymous" as your logon name, and your email address as your password. We have set some defaults so that you won't have to bother filling in these text boxes every time you run the program. If information is provided in all three text boxes, the user can proceed. If not, we need to display a message box explaining the error. Now we are finally ready to reach out and actually touch the Net!

Our first mission is to take the Domain Name supplied in the **HostName** text box and see if it has an IP address. To accomplish this, we simply call the **GetHostAdrs()** method of the GetHost OCX. This method takes a single argument, our host name, and returns its IP address. If no address can be found, it returns a zero-length string. If the **GetHostArs()** method returns a value, we know we have a valid site name, and we can continue.

Next, we need to check which port number has been requested. If it is not 21 or 80 (the defaults for FTP and the Web, respectively), we need to ask the user if it's all right to use a non-standard port number. If so, proceed. If not, return the mouse pointer to its default state, and exit the procedure.

Now, we are ready to make a connection to our site. First, we have to set the **Port** property of the FTP control equal to the value of the **PortNumber** text box. Next, we call the **Logon()** method of the FTP OCX. This method takes four arguments; the host IP address, the logon name, the password, and the account name. We don't have to worry about the account name, so we just send it a blank string. Next, we need to check the value returned by the **Logon()** method. If it is a zero, we know that an error occurred and we need to display a message box to let the user know. If not, we will set the **Connect** variable to **True**, change the connect button's **Caption** property to "&Disconnect," put the host name in our status panel, and call the **GetCurDir()** subroutine. The **GetCurDir()** routine is used to return the contents of the current directory on the site we are connected to, and display the information appropriately on our two list boxes.

Listing 18.3 shows the code from the **GetCurDir()** subroutine.

Listing 18.3   The GetCurDir() Subroutine from FTPSAMPL.FRM

```
Private Sub GetCurDir()
Dim ReturnString As String
Dim NextLine As String
Dim NextEntry As String
Dim Position As Integer

      ReturnString = FtpOCX.GetDir()
      DirList.AddItem ".."
      While InStr(ReturnString, Chr$(13) & Chr$(10))
         ReturnString = Right(ReturnString, Len(ReturnString) - _
            InStr(ReturnString, Chr$(13) & Chr$(10)) - 1)
         NextEntry = ""
         If ReturnString = "" Then Exit Sub
         NextLine = Left(ReturnString, InStr(ReturnString, Chr$(13) & _
            Chr$(10)) - 1)
         For Position = Len(NextLine) To 0 Step -1
            If Mid(NextLine, Position, 1) = Chr$(32) Then Exit For
            NextEntry = Mid(NextLine, Position, 1) & NextEntry
         Next Position
         If Not UCase(Left(NextLine, 1)) = "D" Then
            FileList.AddItem NextEntry
         Else
            DirList.AddItem NextEntry
         End If
      Wend
End Sub
```

We start this routine by calling the FTP OCX's **GetDir()** method. This will actually go out to the remote site, get the directory, and place it into our **ReturnString** string variable. Much like doing a DOS **Dir()** function, we received a mix of directories and files. We need to now parse through these entries, pick out the directories and the files and place them into the proper list box. We will parse through the entries by searching for the combination of a carriage return followed by a line feed character. When this combination no longer exists, we are finished parsing.

We can dump the first entry—it always returns the size of the current directory, which we don't need. Next, we must figure out how to determine if an entry is a directory or a file. That's not too difficult; if the first letter of an entry is a "d," it is a directory, otherwise, it's a file. Then, we start a **For..Next** loop that will step backward through each entry until it reaches a space in the entry. When we find it, we know we have found the location of the last space, and everything appearing prior to that space is either the directory name or filename we want. Finally, we simply add the name onto the correct list box using the **AddItem** method. When the **GetCurDir()** routine finishes, we will have the full contents of the current directory on the remote site displayed and ready to use. Now, we have to decide what to do with it.

We can start by letting the user search through the directories on the remote site. We can accomplish this by simply switching directories whenever the user double clicks on a directory name in the **DirList** list box, as shown in Listing 18.4.

Listing 18.4   The DirList_DblClick() Event Procedure from FTPSAMPL.FRM

```
Private Sub DirList_DblClick()
Dim ReturnValue As Integer
Dim DirName As String

   If Not Connected Then Exit Sub
   Screen.MousePointer = 11
   DirName = DirList.List(DirList.ListIndex)
   If DirName = ".." Then
      ReturnValue = FtpOCX.ParentDir()
      With curdirpanel
         If InStr(.Caption, "/") < Len(.Caption) Then
            .Caption = Left(.Caption, Len(.Caption) - 1)
            While Not Right(.Caption, 1) = "/"
               .Caption = Left(.Caption, Len(.Caption) - 1)
            Wend
         End If
      End With
   Else
      ReturnValue = FtpOCX.ChangeDir(DirName)
```

```
            curdirpanel.Caption = curdirpanel.Caption & DirName & "/"
         End If
         If Not ReturnValue = 0 Then
            DirList.Clear
            FileList.Clear
            GetCurDir
         End If
         Screen.MousePointer = 0
End Sub
```

This procedure works by calling the **ChangeDir()** method of the FTP control. Then it issues another call to **GetCurDir()** in order to get directory information from the new directory regarding the remote site.

Finally, we will allow the user to download a file by double clicking on a file name in the **FileList** list box, as shown in Listing 18.5.

Listing 18.5   The FileList_DblClick() Event Procedure from FTPSAMPL.FRM

```
Private Sub FileList_DblClick()
Dim ReturnValue As Integer
Dim TransferType As Integer

    If Not Connected Then Exit Sub
    CommDlg.Flags = cdlOFNHideReadOnly Or cdlOFNOverwritePrompt Or cdOFNLongNames
    CommDlg.filename = FileList.List(FileList.ListIndex)
    On Error GoTo LastLine
    CommDlg.ShowSave
    If BinOpt.Value = True Then
       TransferType = 1
    Else
       TransferType = 0
    End If
    Form1.Refresh
    Screen.MousePointer = 11
    ReturnValue = FtpOCX.GetFile(CommDlg.filename, _
       FileList.List(FileList.ListIndex), TransferType)
    Screen.MousePointer = 0
LastLine:
End Sub
```

This procedure starts by opening the Save File dialog box and requesting the user to enter a filename and directory to store the remote file. Here you will notice that we are using an **On Error** function to tell VB to skip to the line of the code marked with **LastLine:** if there is an error. This method is used if the user presses the "Cancel" button instead of picking a filename for saving the download file. Without this capability, the code would still continue, and download the file into nothing.

We also need to check which type of download the user wants to perform (ASCII or Binary). We use the **TransferType** integer variable to store that outcome. Finally, we call the FTP OCXs **GetFile()** method. The **GetFile()** method takes three arguments; the local file name, the remote file name, and the type of transfer.

That's it for our simple FTP demo. Now, we are going to put to use what we learned in our Web Browser project, to allow it access to the World Wide Web.

Accessing the Web

We are now ready to take the Web document browser we created in Chapter 12 to the next level and give it the ability to make links to the World Wide Web. Since we are using custom controls, this won't take much coding, just some careful integration. Run the program BROWSER4.EXE located in the \VBMAGIC\BROWSER4\ subdirectory on the companion CD-ROM. It will look and act identically to the BROWSER3 project from Chapter 12—with one major exception. Now, if you enter the full URL of a Web page, the BROWSER4 application will access and display it! Let's see how this is done.

Adding Web Support to Our HTML Document Browser

This project shows you how to extend the Web documet browser that we created in Chapter 12. Here, we will add the ability to go out on the Web and access HTML files.

1. Copy all the project files from the BROWSER3 project in Chapter 12. Rename the BROWSER3.* files to BROWSER4.*.
2. Add the FTP and GETHOST OCXs to the VB toolbox.
3. Update the **LoadHTMLFile()** function (Listing 18.6).

 You'll find this project in the subdirectory \VBMAGIC\BROWSER4 in the files BROWSER4.VBP, BROWSER4.FRM, BROWSER4.BAS, and GLOBCONS.BAS. You will also need to install the FTP and GETHOST OCXs that are located in the \SHARWARE\TOUPIN subdirectory on the companion CD-ROM. Installation instructions for the OCXs are presented in the FTP.HLP and GETHOST.HLP files.

Looking back at where we left off with the browser projects, all we really need to do is add code to a single function to enable Web access. Since all document jumps need to go through the **LoadHTMLFile()** function, that's where we will place our new code. Listing 18.6 shows the updated **LoadHTMLFile()** function from the BROWSER4 project. We made this a separate project to avoid confusion with Chapter 12's project. However, since we aren't making any dramatic changes to more than one function, we will dispense with the formalities of explaining the entire process of copying the project's files, and launch right into our new browser project.

Listing 18.6   The LoadHTMLFile() Function from BROWSER4.BAS

```
Private Function LoadHTMLFile(Filename As String, FTPOCX As FTP) As String
Dim TempText As String
Dim Fnum As Integer
Dim HostName As String
Dim HostIP As String

    If InStr(UCase(Filename), "HTTP") Then
        Filename = Right(Filename, Len(Filename) - InStr(Filename, "//") + 1)
        HostName = Left(Filename, InStr(Filename, "/") - 1)
        Filename = Right(Filename, Len(Filename) - InStr(Filename, "/"))
        HostIP = GetIPOCX.GetHostAdrs(HostName)

        If HostIP = "" Then
            LoadHTMLFile = "<H2>Error</H2><P> Could not load requested file!"
            Exit Function
        Else
            FTPOCX.Port = 80
            ReturnValue = FTPOCX.Logon(HostIP, "anonymous", _
                "password@coriolis.com", "")
        If Not ReturnValue = 0 Then
            ReturnValue = FTPOCX.GetFile(App.Path & "\HTMLBUFF.HTM", Filename, 1)
            If Not ReturnValue = 0 Then
                Filename = App.Path & "\HTMLBUFF.HTM"
            Else
                LoadHTMLFile = "<H2>Error</H2><P> Could not load requested file!"
                Exit Function
            End If
        Else
            LoadHTMLFile = "<H2>Error</H2><P> Could not load requested file!"
            Exit Function
        End If
    End If
End If

    If Dir(Filename) = "" Then
        MsgBox "There was an error trying to load the file: " & Chr(10) & _
            FileEntryBox.Text, MB_ICONEXCLAMATION, "HTML Load Error"
    Else
        LoadHTMLFile = ""
        ' Acquire number for free file
        Fnum = FreeFile
```

```
      ' Load HTML contents into string
      Open Filename For Input As #Fnum
      ' Loop until end of file
      Do While Not EOF(Fnum)
          ' Read line into temporary string
          Line Input #Fnum, TempText
          ' Add line to document string
          LoadHTMLFile = LoadHTMLFile & TempText
      Loop
   End If

End Function
```

This function takes what we learned in the previous project and condenses it down to just what we need to download Web documents. We start by searching the Filename string to see if it contains the string "HTTP." This string signifies the beginning of a remote HTML link. Next, we need to chop off the "HTTP://" section of the filename, using the **Right()** function. Now, we can pull off the name of the Web site by using the Left function to copy everything up to, but not including, the first "/" character. This information is then stored in the **HostName** variable and then stripped off the **Filename** variable so that all that is left in the **Filename** variable is the directory and filename information for the file we want to download. You may wonder why we aren't pulling off the directory information from the Filename variable. Well, you could if you wanted, but the Web makes life easy on us. As in DOS, we don't actually have to go into a directory to grab a file. We can stay in the root directory and point to the file with the complete directory information, which saves us a step or two in the process.

Now that we have all the information we need, we're ready to continue. First, set the **Port** property of the FTP control to 80 (Web default). Next, log on to the site stored in the HostIP variable. In this case, we won't have any user interaction for user name and password, so you can go ahead and hard code them. If the logon succeeds, go ahead and perform the download. Once again, the user will not have any interaction with the download process, so we can hard code the local location of the file to be downloaded. In this case, we have told the **GetFile()** method to place the incoming file into the HTMLBUFF.HTM file in our applications executable directory. If the download succeeds, set the **Filename** variable equal to the local buffer file and continue with the code that loads local files.

Not too difficult, was it? With the code in its current state, you may run into a few problems accessing pages on the Web. For instance, if the person who set up that site you are browsing used relative filenames instead of absolute filenames, then our browser will not know to look on the remote site. Also—and this is a big one—our browser does not support GIF files in its current state. Adding the capability to read GIFs is trivial if we had a custom control. However, at the time we went to press, there were no OCXs available that could read GIFs. We could explain how to decode GIF files, but that would take up about five chapters and would be so slow under VB that you might wait several seconds for each file to decompress. If you see an OCX on a bulletin board that handles GIFs, you can simply substitute it for the PictureBox we use as an image buffer. It should be really simple.

Creating a Web Browser with the Webster Control

Now that we have spent a couple of chapters and a number of hours learning how to create our own Web browser, we have a custom control to present, called *Webster,* that does it all for you, automatically! Webster is an OCX that is under development by Tanny Bear, from Trafalmador Software. Tanny has graciously allowed us to put a pretty complete beta version of Webster on the companion CD-ROM. If you like the control, and we bet you will, you can contact Trafalmador for information on the commercial release.

Webster is a 32-bit OCX that puts the power of a complete Web browser into a single OCX. It is so simple to use that you can simply place the control onto a form, maximize the controls size to fill the form, and run the program. That's it! When the program starts running as shown in Figure 18.3, it will

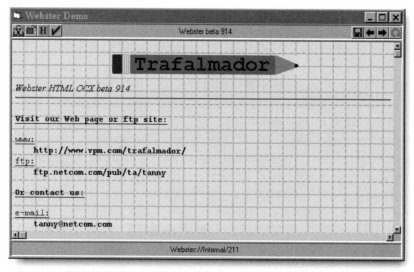

Figure 18.3   *The Webster OCX in action.*

come up with the default HTML file off the hard drive. If you have an Internet connection open, you can simply click on links or use the open option to get directly onto the Web, no programming required!

The beauty of Webster is that it can be customized so easily and can also be used for many other things than just browsing the Web. On the companion CD-ROM, in the SHARWARE\WEBSTER\32BIT directory, you will see a program called VOGON.EXE. This is a little demonstration that comes with the control, which shows you how to use it as a slide show presentation machine.

You also can customize the Webster interface. Figure 18.4 shows the Properties dialog box for Webster. As you can see, it is a very simple matter to add or subtract buttons and capabilities. With a little customized code, we can add new features. For example, we could add a feature that checks requested URLs to see where the user is browsing. If the site is on our restricted list, we can disallow access. Or, we could use Webster as part of an interface to a multimedia application. This versatile control is so new that its uses are just being realized.

If you want to use this control in a 16-bit application, you're in luck. Trafalmador has provided us with a version of Webster that resides in a 16-bit DLL. To use the DLL, you will first need to copy all of the 16-bit Webster files to your WINDOWS\SYSTEM directory. Then, run the REGSVR.EXE program to register the Webster DLL. More in-depth instructions for the install process are located in the README.TXT file that is in the SHARWARE\WEBSTER\16BIT\ directory. Once the DLL has been registered, you can use the OLE container control to manipulate and display Webster. When you place the OLE control on a form, VB immediately pops up the Insert Object dialog box, as shown in Figure 18.5. Pick the Create New radio button, then find "Webster HTML Control" in the Insert Object list box. Now click on OK.

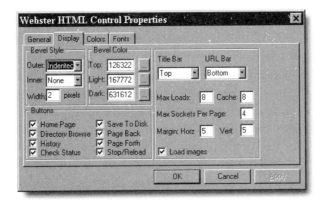

Figure 18.4   Webster's Properties dialog box.

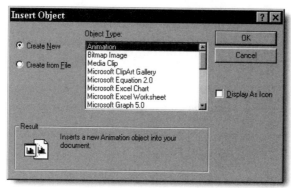

Figure 18.5   *The Insert Object dialog box.*

You should now see the Webster interface inside the OLE control on your form. Press F4 to bring up the properties window. Change the **AutoActivate** property to **1-GetFocus**. This will cause the OLE control, and therefore our Webster interface, to become active on program startup. Go ahead and run the program. You should now see the familiar Webster interface, and it will work just like the 32-bit OCX. Programming with Webster in an OLE control is a little more difficult, but not much. Most of the time, to set properties, you simply need to refer to **Object** property of the OLE control like this:

```
OLE1.Object.PageURL = "FILE:///C:/MYPAGE.HTM"
```

Table 18.1 lists all the methods, events, and properties that Webster currently supports.

Just looking at the exposed properties, methods, and events should make you think about all of the different ways this control could be used. So, what's the catch? One word—BETA. So far, we haven't had too many problems with this software, but it is still missing support for some of the HTML3 tags, and there are a few design quirks here and there. If you plan on using this control for a distributed application, you need to invest in the full commercial package—it's worth every penny.

Now, let's build a project that demonstrates a few of Webster's key features. In the process, we'll add a few new features of our own! Run the WEBSTER1.EXE program that is the the \VBMAGIC\WEBSTER1 subdirectory on the companion CD-ROM. Figure 18.6 shows the two windows that should be displayed. The larger window simply contains the Webster custom control. The smaller form is a floating form that contains a list box that will display all the previous links; you can click on the links to go back to them. Play around with this program for a while, then read on to find out how we built it.

Table 18.1 The Methods, Events, and Properties Supported by the Webster Control

Methods	Properties		
Refresh	BorderStyle	FontListing	MaxPageLoads
SaveToDisk	Font	FontNormal	MarginHorizontal
Cancel	hWnd	FontAddress	MarginVertical
GetContentSize	Enabled	BevelColorTop	LoadImages
GetContentType	BevelStyleInner	BevelColorDark	ShowReferer
GetRedirectedURL	BevelStyleOuter	BevelColorLight	AuthenticName
GetHiddenFlag	BevelWidth	UrlWindowStyle	AuthenticPassword
SetHiddenFlag	FontHeading1	TitleWindowStyle	FromName
DismissPage	FontHeading2	PageURL	BrowserName
GetLinkCount	FontHeading3	PageTitle	ButtonMask
GetLinkURL	FontHeading4	AnchorColor	ProxyServerHTTP
GetContent	FontHeading5	HomePage	ProxyPortHTTP
GetStatus	FontHeading6	DownloadDir	
GetTitle	FontMenu	PagesToCache	**Events**
GetText	FontDir	BackColor	DoClickURL
LoadPage	FontBlockQuote	IgnoreBaseInFile	KeyDown
GetTextSize	FontExample	LoadStatus	LoadComplete
AboutBox	FontPreformatted	ForeColor	
		MaxSockets	

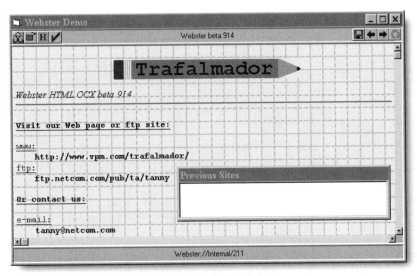

Figure 18.6 The WEBSTER1 project showing both windows.

Going Online with Webster

This project shows you how to use some of the basic features of the Webster OCX.

1. Start a new project by invoking the File | New Project command from within VB.
2. Add the Webster custom control to the VB Toolbox.
3. Set up the main form (Listing 18.7).
3. Set up the secondary form (Listing 18.8).
4. Add the code for the necessary event procedures: **Form_Load()**, **Form_Resize()**, **Form_QueryUnload**, **Webster1_LoadComplete()**, **URLList_Click()**, and **Webster1_DoClickURL()** (Listings 18.9 to 18.14).

You'll find this project in the subdirectory \VBMAGIC\WEBSTER in the files WEBSTER1.VBP, WEBSTER1.FRM, FLOAT.FRM, and GLOBCONS.BAS. You will also need to install the Webster OCX that is located in the \SHARWARE\WEBSTER subdirectory on the companion CD-ROM. Installation instructions for the OCX are located in the README.TXT file.

Setting up the two forms for this project could not be much simpler, since each form has only a single control that is maximized to fill the client space. Listings 18.7 and 18.8 list all of the properties for the two forms and their respective controls that need to be set up ahead of time.

Listing 18.7   The Controls Section from WEBSTER1.FRM

```
VERSION 4.00
Begin VB.Form Form1
    Caption         =   "Webster Demo"
    ClientHeight    =   5475
    ClientLeft      =   195
    ClientTop       =   630
    ClientWidth     =   9480
    Height          =   5925
    Left            =   135
    LinkTopic       =   "Form1"
    LockControls    =   -1  'True
    ScaleHeight     =   5475
    ScaleWidth      =   9480
    Top             =   240
    Width           =   9600
```

```
Begin WebsterLib.Webster Webster1
   Height         =   5460
   Left           =   0
   TabIndex       =   0
   Top            =   0
   Width          =   9495
   _version       =   65537
   _extentx       =   16748
   _extenty       =   9631
   _stockprops    =   100
   BeginProperty fontheading2 {FB8F0823-0164-101B-84ED-08002B2EC713}
      name        =   "Arial"
      charset     =   1
      weight      =   700
      size        =   15.75
      underline   =   0     'False
      italic      =   0     'False
      strikethrough =   0   'False
   EndProperty
   BeginProperty fontheading3 {FB8F0823-0164-101B-84ED-08002B2EC713}
      name        =   "Arial"
      charset     =   1
      weight      =   700
      size        =   13.5
      underline   =   0     'False
      italic      =   0     'False
      strikethrough =   0   'False
   EndProperty
   BeginProperty fontheading5 {FB8F0823-0164-101B-84ED-08002B2EC713}
      name        =   "Arial"
      charset     =   1
      weight      =   700
      size        =   9.75
      underline   =   0     'False
      italic      =   0     'False
      strikethrough =   0   'False
   EndProperty
   BeginProperty fontheading6 {FB8F0823-0164-101B-84ED-08002B2EC713}
      name        =   "Arial"
      charset     =   1
      weight      =   700
      size        =   7.5
      underline   =   0     'False
      italic      =   0     'False
      strikethrough =   0   'False
   EndProperty
   BeginProperty fontmenu {FB8F0823-0164-101B-84ED-08002B2EC713}
      name        =   "Times New Roman"
      charset     =   1
      weight      =   400
      size        =   11.25
      underline   =   0     'False
      italic      =   0     'False
      strikethrough =   0   'False
   EndProperty
```

```
BeginProperty fontdir {FB8F0823-0164-101B-84ED-08002B2EC713}
    name            =   "Courier New"
    charset         =   1
    weight          =   400
    size            =   10.5
    underline       =   0    'False
    italic          =   0    'False
    strikethrough   =   0    'False
EndProperty
BeginProperty fontaddress {FB8F0823-0164-101B-84ED-08002B2EC713}
    name            =   "Arial"
    charset         =   1
    weight          =   400
    size            =   11.25
    underline       =   0    'False
    italic          =   -1   'True
    strikethrough   =   0    'False
EndProperty
BeginProperty fontblockquote {FB8F0823-0164-101B-84ED-08002B2EC713}
    name            =   "Times New Roman"
    charset         =   1
    weight          =   400
    size            =   11.25
    underline       =   0    'False
    italic          =   0    'False
    strikethrough   =   0    'False
EndProperty
BeginProperty fontexample {FB8F0823-0164-101B-84ED-08002B2EC713}
    name            =   "Arial"
    charset         =   1
    weight          =   400
    size            =   11.25
    underline       =   0    'False
    italic          =   0    'False
    strikethrough   =   0    'False
EndProperty
BeginProperty fontpreformatted {FB8F0823-0164-101B-84ED-08002B2EC713}
    name            =   "Courier New"
    charset         =   1
    weight          =   400
    size            =   10.5
    underline       =   0    'False
    italic          =   0    'False
    strikethrough   =   0    'False
EndProperty
BeginProperty fontlisting {FB8F0823-0164-101B-84ED-08002B2EC713}
    name            =   "Courier New"
    charset         =   1
    weight          =   400
    size            =   10.5
    underline       =   0    'False
    italic          =   0    'False
    strikethrough   =   0    'False
EndProperty
```

```
    BeginProperty fontnormal {FB8F0823-0164-101B-84ED-08002B2EC713}
        name            =   "Times New Roman"
        charset         =   1
        weight          =   400
        size            =   11.25
        underline       =   0    'False
        italic          =   0    'False
        strikethrough   =   0    'False
    EndProperty
    End
End
Attribute VB_Name = "Form1"
Attribute VB_Creatable = False
Attribute VB_Exposed = False
```

Listing 18.8   The Controls Section from FLOAT.FRM

```
VERSION 4.00
Begin VB.Form FloatingForm
    BorderStyle     =   1 'Fixed Single
    Caption         =   "Previous Sites"
    ClientHeight    =   870
    ClientLeft      =   195
    ClientTop       =   6555
    ClientWidth     =   5085
    ClipControls    =   0    'False
    ControlBox      =   0    'False
    Height          =   1320
    Left            =   135
    LinkTopic       =   "Form2"
    LockControls    =   -1   'True
    MaxButton       =   0    'False
    MinButton       =   0    'False
    ScaleHeight     =   870
    ScaleWidth      =   5085
    ShowInTaskbar   =   0    'False
    Top             =   6165
    Width           =   5205
    Begin VB.ListBox URLList
        Height          =   840
        IntegralHeight  =   0    'False
        Left            =   0
        TabIndex        =   0
        Top             =   0
        Width           =   5055
    End
End
Attribute VB_Name = "FloatingForm"
Attribute VB_Creatable = False
Attribute VB_Exposed = False
```

Notice that we have disabled all of the buttons that would normally be displayed on the title bar of the floating form. This way, the form will not change size and cannot be closed. Now we have to decide when and how to display the floating form. We decided to have the form display immediately upon program load, and go away only when the program exits. Listings 18.9 and 18.10 show the main forms **Form_Load()** and **Form_QueryUnload()** event procedures where we will handle the opening and closing of the floating form.

Listing 18.9 The Form_Load() Event Procedure from WEBSTER1.FRM

```
Private Sub Form_Load()

    FloatingForm.Show
End Sub
```

Listing 18.10 The Form_QueryUnload() Event Procedure from WEBSTER1.FRM

```
Private Sub Form_QueryUnload(Cancel As Integer, UnloadMode As Integer)

    Unload FloatingForm
End Sub
```

Not much to these procedures. We used the **Unload** routine instead of using the **Hide** method to ensure that VB gives us back the memory used by the form when it is closed. We will, however, use the **Hide** method in the next procedure we need to set up—the **Form_Resize()** event procedure (Listing 18.11). This procedure will accomplish two things. When the form is stretched either width-wise or height-wise, we need the **Webster1** control to resize with it, and fill up the client space on the form. But first, we need to check to see if the form has been minimized. Minimizing a form also calls the **Resize** procedure, so we can use this to make the floating form minimize or restore also. Actually, we don't want the floating form to show up as an icon, or on the Windows 95 Taskbar, so we will use the **Hide** and **Show** methods to make the control disappear and reappear when we need it.

Listing 18.11 The Form_Resize() Event Procedure from WEBSTER1.FRM

```
Private Sub Form_Resize()

    If Form1.WindowState = MINIMIZED Then
        FloatingForm.Hide
    Else
        FloatingForm.Show
        Webster1.Width = Form1.ScaleWidth
        Webster1.Height = Form1.ScaleHeight
    End If
End Sub
```

If you ran the project as it stands now, everything should work fine. Nothing will be displayed in the floating form, but the Webster control should work okay. Let's add the code to fill the list box located on the floating form whenever a new link is activated. Listing 18.12 shows the **Webster1_LoadComplete()** event procedure. This procedure is activated when a new Web page is done downloading, so it's a perfect time to update the list box.

Listing 18.12   The Webster1_LoadComplete() Event Procedure from WEBSTER1.FRM

```
Private Sub Webster1_LoadComplete(URL As String, ByVal Status As Integer)
Dim Index As Integer
Dim Found As Boolean

    Found = False
    For Index = 0 To FloatingForm.URLList.ListCount - 1
        If URL = FloatingForm.URLList.List(FloatingForm.URLList.ListIndex) Then
            Found = True
        End If
    Next Index
    If Not Found Then FloatingForm.URLList.AddItem URL
End Sub
```

As you can see, this code looks at any items currently in the **URLList** list box control that we put on **FloatingForm**. If it does not find a match, it uses the **AddItem** method to add the latest URL onto the end of the item list.

Next, we need to add the code that opens files for our previous URL list when the user clicks on the **URLList** control. We will put the code into the **URLList_Click()** event procedure (Listing 18.13).

Listing 18.13   The URLList_Click() Event Procedure from FLOAT.FRM

```
Private Sub URLList_Click()
Dim Result As Boolean

    Result = Form1.Webster1.DismissPage(Form1.Webster1.PageURL)
    Result = Form1.Webster1.LoadPage(URLList.List(URLList.ListIndex), False)
End Sub
```

The first line tells the **Webster1** control to forget the current page by calling the **Webster1.Dismiss** method with the current page as its only argument. Then, the second line opens the new file by using the **Webster1.LoadPage** method. The first argument is simply the URL we want Webster to load, and the second argument tells Webster whether or not we want the incoming data hidden. We want to see it, obviously, so we set it to **False**.

Go ahead and run the program again. Now, everything should work great. New Web pages will be added to the floating form, and clicking on one of the old ones should bring the form up again.

We want to show you how to use one more feature. If you have been using the shareware version of Netscape Navigator as your Web browser, you may have seen a dialog box that says something like, "Netscape Navigator has expired, you will only be able to open pages on the Netscape site." That message means that any link you attempt to go to must have the string "netscape" in it somewhere. This is an easy way for them to make you do frequent upgrades, without completely killing the software.

We can do something very similar. Maybe this application is only supposed to be used to view company documents that all reside on a single Web site. We can check the URL the user wants to load before it is loaded, to verify which link they are asking for. Webster makes this very easy on us by providing a **DoClickURL()** event procedure. This procedure is activated right after the user clicks on a link, but before the page is actually accessed. We can check the requested URL, and if we don't want to allow access, we simply set the **Cancel** argument to **True**, and nothing will happen. For our demo, the **Webster1_DoClickURL()** event procedure (Listing 18.14) will check to make sure that all links are pointing to a page on the Coriolis Group's Web site, so we need to look for the string "coriolis" within the URL. If it is there, we let the program continue. If it is not there, we display a warning message and set the **Cancel** variable to **False**.

Listing 18.14   The Webster1_DoClickURL() Event Procedure from WEBSTER1.FRM

```
Private Sub Webster1_DoClickURL(SelectedURL As String, Cancel As Boolean)

    If InStr(UCase(SelectedURL), "CORIOLIS") = 0 Then
        MsgBox "Sorry, this browser is limited to looking at the Coriolis" & _
        " Group's Web site only.", MB_ICONEXCLAMATION, "Unauthorized URL"
        Cancel = True
        Exit Sub
    End If

'   If InStr(UCase(SelectedURL), "SEX") > 0 Then
'       MsgBox "Sorry, that topic is off limits at this time.", _
'           MB_ICONEXCLAMATION, "Unauthorized URL"
'       Cancel = True
'       Exit Sub
'   End If

End Sub
```

The commented out section performs a similar function as the first group of code. However, here we are looking for a keyword that we *don't* want access allowed to. In this case, we don't want the user to be able to load any Web pages that have the word "sex" in them. This can be a useful tool, for example, if you were creating a browser for kids, and you didn't want them seeing any illicit Web pages.

As you can see, with just a few lines of code, we were able to add some pretty neat features to the Webster control. It wouldn't take much to add some pretty powerful features of your own, so we recommend experimenting a little, and putting your knowledge of Web browsers that you have learned in this book to some good use.

More Automatic Components

While we are taking advantage of easy-to-use controls, let's take a look at a couple of methods for using OLE automation that could make life easier for us. Actually, OLE does not always necessarily make things easier—it depends on what you want to do with it. If you simply want to add a form to your application that embeds a Word document or an Excel chart into your app, then things will go smoothly for you. However, if you want to add features from a program like Visio or Adobe's Acrobat to your application, then you may have a little more work to do. OLE gives you the ability to use functions and features from other applications without knowing exactly how they were coded. You do need to be careful when you use OLE; it is important to verify that the programs you will be using will be available to people who will be using your application.

Let's do a little project that demonstrates how to use OLE to embed a video window into an application and allow users the capability to control its appearance and position. Using the OLE container, we can specify things like size, border, and caption without much trouble. And we don't need to use any API calls to implement this kind of control.

Compositing a Video Over an Image

In this project, we will show you how to use the OLE container control to display and manipulate a video window.

1. Start a new project by invoking the File | New Project command from within VB.
2. Add the OLE custom control to the Toolbox.

3. Set up the main form (Listing 18.15).

4. Add the code for the necessary event procedures; **Form_Load()**, **List1_DblClick()**, **VidHeight_KeyPress()**, **VidWidth_KeyPress()**, **VidTop_KeyPress()**, **VidLeft_KeyPress()**, **VerbChk_Click()**, and **FileToLoad_KeyPress()** (Listings 18.16 through 18.23).

Listing 18.15 The Controls Section from OLEDEMO.FRM

```
VERSION 4.00
Begin VB.Form OLEDemo
    Caption         =   "OLEDemo"
    ClientHeight    =   6690
    ClientLeft      =   1095
    ClientTop       =   1605
    ClientWidth     =   6270
    Height          =   7140
    Left            =   1035
    LinkTopic       =   "Form1"
    ScaleHeight     =   6690
    ScaleWidth      =   6270
    Top             =   1215
    Width           =   6390
    Begin Threed.SSPanel SSPanel1
        Height          =   1575
        Left            =   120
        TabIndex        =   1
        Top             =   5040
        Width           =   6015
        _Version        =   65536
        _ExtentX        =   10610
        _ExtentY        =   2778
        _StockProps     =   15
        BackColor       =   12632256
        BorderWidth     =   1
        BevelOuter      =   1
        BevelInner      =   2
        Begin VB.TextBox VidLeft
            Height          =   285
            Left            =   4680
            TabIndex        =   12
            Top             =   840
            Width           =   1095
        End
        Begin VB.TextBox VidTop
            Height          =   285
            Left            =   4680
            TabIndex        =   11
            Top             =   1200
            Width           =   1095
        End
```

```
Begin VB.TextBox VidWidth
   Height          =    285
   Left            =    2640
   TabIndex        =    6
   Top             =    840
   Width           =    1095
End
Begin VB.TextBox VidHeight
   Height          =    285
   Left            =    2640
   TabIndex        =    5
   Top             =    1200
   Width           =    1095
End
Begin VB.CheckBox VerbChk
   Alignment       =    1    'Right Justify
   Caption         =    "AutoVerbMenu"
   Height          =    255
   Left            =    120
   TabIndex        =    4
   Top             =    1200
   Width           =    1695
End
Begin VB.ListBox List1
   Height          =    765
   IntegralHeight  =    0    'False
   Left            =    120
   TabIndex        =    3
   Top             =    360
   Width           =    1695
End
Begin VB.TextBox FileToLoad
   BeginProperty Font
      name            =    "MS Sans Serif"
      charset         =    0
      weight          =    400
      size            =    9.75
      underline       =    0    'False
      italic          =    0    'False
      strikethrough   =    0    'False
   EndProperty
   Height          =    375
   Left            =    2040
   TabIndex        =    2
   Top             =    360
   Width           =    3735
End
Begin VB.Label Label6
   AutoSize        =    -1   'True
   Caption         =    "Left:"
   Height          =    195
   Left            =    4080
   TabIndex        =    14
   Top             =    870
```

```
   Width          =    315
End
Begin VB.Label Label5
   AutoSize       =    -1   'True
   Caption        =    "Top:"
   Height         =    195
   Left           =    4080
   TabIndex       =    13
   Top            =    1230
   Width          =    330
End
Begin VB.Label Label1
   AutoSize       =    -1   'True
   Caption        =    "Width:"
   Height         =    195
   Left           =    2040
   TabIndex       =    10
   Top            =    870
   Width          =    465
End
Begin VB.Label Label2
   AutoSize       =    -1   'True
   Caption        =    "Height:"
   Height         =    195
   Left           =    2040
   TabIndex       =    9
   Top            =    1230
   Width          =    510
End
Begin VB.Label Label3
   AutoSize       =    -1   'True
   Caption        =    "Available Verbs:"
   Height         =    195
   Left           =    120
   TabIndex       =    8
   Top            =    120
   Width          =    1140
End
Begin VB.Label Label4
   AutoSize       =    -1   'True
   Caption        =    "File to Load:"
   Height         =    195
   Left           =    2040
   TabIndex       =    7
   Top            =    120
   Width          =    870
End
End
Begin VB.OLE OLE1
   Appearance     =    0    'Flat
   AutoActivate   =    0    'Manual
   AutoVerbMenu   =    0    'False
   BackStyle      =    0    'Transparent
   BorderStyle    =    0    'None
```

```
        Class          =    "avifile"
        Height         =    2655
        Left           =    1080
        OleObjectBlob  =    "main.frx":0000
        SizeMode       =    1    'Stretch
        TabIndex       =    0
        Top            =    720
        Width          =    3615
    End
    Begin VB.Image Image1
        Height         =    4845
        Left           =    120
        Picture        =    "main.frx":14418
        Top            =    120
        Width          =    6000
    End
End
Attribute VB_Name = "OLEDemo"
Attribute VB_Creatable = False
Attribute VB_Exposed = False
```

When you place the OLE control onto the form, you will be asked to insert an OLE object. Choose the "Video Clip" option. This will bring up the Windows 95 video player. You can just close it or open a video to use as the default video.

Now, we need to make things work. Listing 18.16 is the code from the forms **Load** event.

Listing 18.16   The Form_Load() Event Procedure from OLEDEMO.FRM

```
Private Sub Form_Load()

    VidWidth.Text = OLE1.Width
    VidHeight.Text = OLE1.Height
    VidLeft.Text = OLE1.Left
    VidTop.Text = OLE1.Top
    VerbChk.Value = OLE1.AutoVerbMenu

    For I = 1 To OLE1.ObjectVerbsCount - 1
        List1.AddItem OLE1.ObjectVerbs(I)
    Next I

End Sub
```

This code sets all of our text boxes equal to their current values on the OLE object. We also need to find out what types of things, called *verbs*, we can do with the OLE object we are using. Verbs are simply actions that we can perform from within VB, which is not necessarily all the actions that the object we are using can perform when we load the application normally. We can find all the available verbs by calling the **ObjectVerbs()** method, sending as its sole argument the number of the verb we want, starting with the default verb of 0. We can step through the verbs with a **For..Next** loop that terminates when we get up to the **ObjectVerbsCount** property value minus one, since we are using a zero-based system. We will place all the verbs into a list box, so next we'll see what we can do with those. Listing 18.17 is the code from the **List1_DblClick()** event procedure.

Listing 18.17   The List1_DblClick Event Procedure from OLEDEMO.FRM

```
Private Sub List1_DblClick()

   OLE1.DoVerb List1.ListIndex
End Sub
```

We couldn't make this much simpler. We only need to call the OLE control's **DoVerb** method and send it the number of the requested verb.

The OLE object gives us the advantage of being able to stretch its contents to fill the control. In the case of video, this gives us a lot of control over the presentation process. The four size text boxes will dynamically resize the OLE control, as well as the embedded video, whenever the return button is pressed within one of the four controls. Listings 18.18 through 18.21 give the simple code for these controls.

Listing 18.18   The VidWidth_KeyPress() Event Procedure from OLEDEMO.FRM

```
Private Sub VidWidth_KeyPress(KeyAscii As Integer)

   If KeyAscii = 13 Then OLE1.Width = Val(VidWidth.Text)
End Sub
```

Listing 18.19   The VidHeight_KeyPress() Event Procedure from OLEDEMO.FRM

```
Private Sub VidHeight_KeyPress(KeyAscii As Integer)

   If KeyAscii = 13 Then OLE1.Width = Val(VidHeight.Text)
End Sub
```

Listing 18.20   The VidTop_KeyPress() Event Procedure from OLEDEMO.FRM

```
Private Sub VidTop_KeyPress(KeyAscii As Integer)

   If KeyAscii = 13 Then OLE1.Width = Val(VidTop.Text)
End Sub
```

Listing 18.21 The VidLeft_KeyPress() Event Procedure from OLEDEMO.FRM

```
Private Sub VidLeft_KeyPress(KeyAscii As Integer)

   If KeyAscii = 13 Then OLE1.Width = Val(VidLeft.Text)
End Sub
```

The OLE control also can automatically display a menu of available verbs when the user presses the right mouse button anywhere on the OLE control. Use the **AutoVerbMenu** property to decide if the pop-up menu will be displayed or not. We have put this option in the form of a check box (Listing 18.22).

Listing 18.22 The VerbChk_Click() Event Procedure from OLEDEMO.FRM

```
Private Sub VerbChk_Click()

   OLE1.AutoVerbMenu = VerbChk.Value
End Sub
```

The final option we want to offer the user is the ability to load new video files. To make this simple, we used a single text box control that responds to key presses. When the return key is pressed, we try to load the file that is listed in the **FileToLoad** control's **Text** property. Listing 18.23 shows the code that does this work.

Listing 18.23 The FileToLoad_KeyPress() Event Procedure from OLEDEMO.FRM

```
Private Sub FileToLoad_KeyPress(KeyAscii As Integer)

   If KeyAscii = 13 Then
      OLE1.CreateLink FileToLoad.Text, ""
   End If
End Sub
```

Here, we just initiate a **CreateLink** method from the OLE control, sending it the name of the file we want to load.

Go ahead and run the project. You may wonder why we used an image control as a background. Well, this is a neat trick for speeding up video playback. Many times, you may have a video that is displaying a stationary scene with only a limited amount of action occurring in a single place within the frame. We figured: Why make the video codecs do all the work of decompressing and displaying the information about areas of the video that never change? The solution is to create a single image of the video, updating only

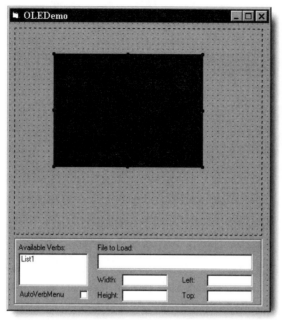

Figure 18.7 *How to place an OLE container over an image control to composite video over a background image.*

the area of the screen where the action takes place. This technique is quite often used to make video run faster, while allowing the image to be larger than a postage stamp. Figure 18.7 illustrates this technique.

Simple, But Effective

The techniques and tricks we showed you in this chapter aren't as complicated as other programming projects we built in other chapters. There have been entire books written about OLE automation and Internet Access. But we wanted you to see how, with these valuable techniques, you can add major features to your own multimedia applications with minimal effort. After all, isn't that what VB is all about?

Learn how to create smooth-motion, eye-catching video on your PC using Visual Basic and some special custom controls.

Developing with PC Video

For better or for worse, video has been a major propellant of the multimedia revolution. The labels of successful multimedia titles often proclaim the number of minutes of video they contain. And, regardless of how much or how little video appears in any particular multimedia product, it's still usually the first thing that most of us want to see. Isn't it amazing that people who spend an average of four hours every day looking at full-color, full-motion television get so excited when they see a tiny, 10-second video clip on their computer screens?

We don't know why PC video gets us so excited. Maybe because it hints at the virtual-reality future in which prerecorded video clips will be replaced by interactive 3D adventures through worlds both real and imaginary. It doesn't really matter—any good salesperson will tell you that you must grab your users' attention, or your message will be lost. When done well, video can get their attention and deliver the message with a single punch.

In this chapter, we'll use the flexible Video for (VfW) Windows that is now built into Windows 95. You'll learn what VfW provides and how you can access its key features using VB and custom controls. In particular, we'll show you how to capture video using a special VB program and then how to play back video using both Windows API calls and a custom control.

Video for Windows

Windows 3.0 did not inherently support video. Microsoft fixed that shortcoming with the release of Video for Windows 1.0. Since that time, VfW has had many new releases and is now a very respectable system for displaying videos. Video for Windows (VfW) is an extension for earlier versions of Windows and is now built into Windows 95. It enables applications to digitize and play video clips captured from conventional analog video sources, such as camcorders, laserdisks, VCRs, and professional video decks. You're probably already thinking of the first blockbuster you'll be creating with this technology—but hold on. Unfortunately, digital video has a long way to go before it will allow you to collaborate with the likes of Steven Spielberg.

The current state of the art barely matches the poor quality pictures we're accustomed to seeing on television. American television has a vertical resolution of 525 lines. Because TV is still an analog system, it's hard to precisely measure horizontal resolution. To some extent, horizontal resolution depends on the TV receiver, but the maximum is equivalent to roughly 700 pixels. If we could play full-screen digital video on our PC monitors, we would be looking at resolutions ranging from 640×480 pixels to over 1600×1200 pixels. Unfortunately, the current standard frame size for most video clips is only 320×200 pixels. It's possible to play full-screen digital video on our screens, but only with assistance from one of several proprietary hardware systems. The other alternative is to have a PC with 32 MB of RAM. Who knows, that may be the standard system in a few months, but for now, hardware assistance is the only way to get full screen AVIs.

Exploring MPEG

If you are interested in using other formats for playing video in addition to VfW, we suggest you explore MPEG. MPEG stands for *Motion Picture Experts Group*. The MPEG group is a committee of people that meet under ISO (International Standards Organization) to generate standards for digital video and audio compression. Actually, the entire MPEG standard simply defines how the video/audio bit stream should be formatted and how it should be decompressed. It is up to the individual programmers to figure out how to compress the data in the first place. But, if they want to be able to be compatible with the rest of the MPEG world, they have to make sure that the compression algorithm they use is compatible with everyone's decompression algorithm.

MPEG has been around for a few years, but it has become popular only recently. This is because of the amount of bandwidth that the bit stream needs to operate properly. Before the Pentium processor was available, your average computer just didn't have enough power to decompress MPEG fast enough without a special video card that had its own hardware-based MPEG decompression chip on it. Now that computers are becoming faster and the decompression algorithms are becoming much more efficient, software-based MPEG playback is more viable. Many new games that feature full-screen video are using MPEG.

All this technological advance is great for us because it means more people are developing MPEG software and working on VfW decompression software. They each want their software to play video faster and smoother and be able to do it with less and less computer. So, keep an eye out for newer MPEG and VfW tools and software so that you will be in a good position to choose the best format for your multimedia project as this technology advances.

Unfortunately, at the time of the printing of this book, no custom OCX controls are available for loading and playing MPEG video clips. You could, of course, write code to perform these tasks; however, you'd need to learn how MPEG compression works and master the art of quickly loading and decompressing MPEG files. If you find an OCX control that will allow you to display MPEG animations, try it out, you may like it. We'll keep our eye out for new MPEG OCX controls and provide information about them on the Coriolis Web site that is dedicated to support this book (www.coriolis.com).

One of the key ideas behind the Windows 95 video system is that it requires no special hardware for playback. To achieve the data throughput necessary to spray bitmaps on the screen fast enough to simulate motion while simultaneously playing synchronized stereo digital audio using nothing but software, something had to be sacrificed—okay, many things had to be sacrificed. Although the current standard frame size for most video clips is 320×200 pixels, Windows 95 also supports three other standard resolutions: 160×120, 240×180, and 640×480 pixels. The problem with the larger dimension is that most PCs can't decompress and display them fast enough to play them smoothly, especially from CD-ROM.

In the future, hardware video decompressors may become as common as sound cards are now. Unfortunately, that will require some kind of standard. Right now it's too early to settle on a video compression standard, because each of the competing systems offers unique advantages. If you've been through the agonizing torture of configuring your own multimedia PC on a pre-Windows 95 system, you know that the last thing we need is a separate card for each video format. Hardware video playback will not become common until either all the best features have been combined into a single standard, or a single card can be manufactured that will support multiple compression standards.

How Digital Video Works

The Windows 95 video system is based on a system called *audio-video interleave*. A basic Windows 95 video file, which carries the extension AVI, contains a series of alternating bitmaps and wave data segments. Unlike bitmap files, the data in an AVI file is usually compressed. In fact, the compression system makes it possible to move the data around fast enough to look like motion pictures. Uncompressed, 60 seconds of 15 frame per second video at 320×200 would fill 178,000,000 bytes! That's almost three megabytes per second—with no sound! Most hard disk drives and controllers could not pump that much data into memory quickly enough to support smooth playback, and no consumer-level CD-ROM drive comes close to that data transfer rate. But compression often reduces the size of an AVI file by a factor of 10 or more. This heavy compression, known as *lossy* compression, noticeably degrades the image quality, but without it, software-only video playback would not be possible on current desktop computers.

The task of the Windows 95 video system is to identify which compression-decompression algorithm, or *codec*, has been used to prepare a particular video clip, then to use that codec to reconstitute the data, separate it into video and audio elements, and feed it to the display system and sound card fast enough that it looks and sounds something like miniature television. This is a monumental task that will tax even the brawniest of PCs.

> **Note:** *For detailed coverage of PC video production and digital video capture, see* How to Digitize Video *by Nels Johnson with Fred Gault and Mark Florence. New York: John Wiley & Sons, Inc., 1994.*

AVI files can get pretty complicated. Windows 95 video supports multiple streams, which means that a single file can contain multiple sound tracks, MIDI music data—even multiple video tracks. Some codecs support 24-bit color, while others use 8-bit color and palettes. Palettes are confusing enough when they apply to nice, quiet, static bitmaps; in digital video files, palettes are utterly unnerving. Each time a scene changes, the palette can change, which means that the palette manager has to perform a quick change, right in the middle of a running video clip. To manage all this data and turn it into something that resembles video requires the services of several special libraries. Together, these libraries make up the Windows 95 video system and its API.

Video for Windows for Programmers

If you combined all the Windows API features we've used so far in this book—from bitblts and ROPs to animation to wave audio—and injected them with steroids, you might end up with something about half as complex as the VfW API. Fortunately, you don't need to grasp all the inner workings of this powerful system to use video in your own multimedia projects. As a matter of fact, in the *Programmer's Guide* from the Video for Windows Development Kit, Microsoft discourages us from peeking too quickly under the hood. Instead, they provide high-level tools in the form of OCXs, VBXs, and *window classes* (for Holy Trinity programmers) that enable us to capture, play, and edit video clips from within our own applications by sending messages or setting properties. After you've grasped the overall design of the video system, if you still feel the need for greater control, you can dive right into the low-level interface. The Developer's Kit includes plenty of sample code to get you started.

Video for Windows comprises six main modules:

- The AVICAP.DLL contains the functions that perform video capture. These functions provide a high-level interface to AVI file I/O and to the video and audio device drivers. The CAPWNDX.VBX primarily calls on the functions in this library.

- The MSVIDEO.DLL handles onscreen video operation with a special set of *DrawDib* functions, which act like a turbo-charged form of **StretchDIBits()**. These functions also support the *Installable Compression Manager* (ICM), which allows them to display frames from compressed video. Both the CAPWNDX.VBX and MCIWNDX.VBX custom controls use functions in this library to display video on the screen.

- The MCIAVI.DRV driver contains the MCI command interpreter for VfW.

- The AVIFILE.DLL supports higher-level file access to AVI files than provided by the standard multimedia I/O (mmio) functions (which we used to play wave audio in Chapters 5 and 15). AVIFILE functions manage AVI files in terms of *video frames* and *data streams*. The purpose of streams is to provide synchronized playback of multiple data channels, such as video, audio soundtrack, MIDI background music, and multilingual narration. You can even write your own file handlers to support other non-standard streams.

- The Installable Compression Manager (ICM) manages the codecs, the drivers that *compress* and *decompress* video data stored in AVI files. Several codecs already exist, including Microsoft Video 1, Intel's Indeo Video, and SuperMac's CinePak. The other modules in VfW access the codecs by way of the ICM.

- The Audio Compression Manager (ACM) provides services similar to the ICM, but works on wave audio data rather than on video. The ACM may be used independently of VfW to provide wave audio compression whenever it is needed. Once you have installed the ACM (done automatically when you install the VfW runtime library), decompression occurs automatically whenever the multimedia system encounters a compressed WAV file. If the ACM is installed on your system, you'll find an applet called Sound Mapper in your Windows Control Panel. Sound Mapper is an interface that enables configuration of the audio codecs and control over the mappings between waveaudio devices and the compression drivers. One of the standard drivers, the Microsoft PCM Converter, is especially interesting because it enables playback of high-resolution, high sample rate WAV files on sound cards with lesser capabilities.

The printed version of the *Programmer's Guide* from the VfW Development Kit is more than 700 pages long! Obviously, we can't cover all the details of VfW in this chapter, so instead we'll focus on the VB support provided by the DK's two custom controls, CAPWNDX.VBX and MCIWNDX.VBX. Before we can get started, you'll need to install the VfW runtime library if you are using Windows 3.x, which will enable your system to play AVI files as well as the VfW Development Kit—no matter which operating system you are using.

Installing the Video for Windows Runtime Library

If you are using Windows 3.x or Windows 95, playing AVI files requires no special hardware. You don't even need a sound card, that is, if you don't mind silent movies. But you do need to install the VfW runtime library, which includes an assortment of files and requires a few additions to your Windows INI files.

The companion CD-ROM for this book includes the \VfW subdirectory, which itself includes several further subdirectories:

```
\VFW
   \RUNTIME
      \VFW11E
      \VFW11A
         \FRN
            \DISK1
         \GER
            \DISK1
         \USA
            \DISK1
      \SETUPSRC
   \VFWDK
```

To install the VfW runtime library, open the Program Manager and select File | Run. Then use the Browse dialog box to locate SETUP.EXE in the subdirectory \VfW\RUNTIME\VFW11E. The runtime libraries will be installed in your \WINDOWS\SYSTEM directory. To activate the VfW drivers, you must restart Windows.

To test the VfW drivers, load the Media Player, then open its Device menu. If the VfW drivers have been correctly installed, you should find an option on this menu called Video for Windows. Select this option to display the Open dialog box. Locate a file with the extension AVI; you'll find several on the companion CD-ROM. Once you have loaded an AVI file, select the play button. The video clip will appear in its own window somewhere on your screen.

With the VfW drivers installed, you can play almost any AVI file. You'll find hundreds of them on clip art disks, on BBSs, and on public networks such as CompuServe and the Internet. To make your own video clips, you'll need a video capture card and either a camcorder or a VCR (or both). Playback quality will vary from clip to clip, depending on the performance of your computer and video display system, and on the frame size, frame rate, and compression method used to prepare each clip. Even the content of the video sequence itself can significantly affect performance; most of the methods used to compress video use a technique called *delta compression*, which works best when there are few changes from one frame to the next. If your system has trouble playing a clip from CD-ROM, try copying the file to your hard drive. CD-ROM drives—even fast ones—are still considerably slower than hard disks.

> **Note:** *If you create products that include AVI files, you'll also need to include the VfW runtime library. The contents of the subdirectories \VfW\RUNTIME\VFW11E, \VfW\RUNTIME\VFW11A\USA\DISK1, ..\FRN\DISK1, and ..\GER\DISK1 are freely redistributable. The source code for the setup program is located in \VfW\RUNTIME\SETUPSRC.*

You may use this source code to incorporate the video runtime setup into your application's own setup program. For more information on runtime redistribution and the setup source, see the file DEV_KIT.TXT in the \VFW\VFWDK subdirectory.

Installing the Video for Windows Development Kit

The Video for Windows Development Kit is almost as easy to install as the runtime library. Open the Program Manager and select File I Run from the menu. Then use the Browse option to locate the program SETUP.EXE in the \VfW\VfWDK subdirectory. Select this program and follow the instructions for installation.

The setup program will create a directory structure with eight subdirectories off the main subdirectory (usually \VfWDK). The \VfWDK\SAMPLES subdirectory will contain 26 subdirectories of its own, one for each sample program. The \VfWDK\TOOLS subdirectory will contain one subdirectory called \DEBUG. The VfW DK will require a total of approximately 13 megabytes of disk space.

The setup program will also create a program group called VfW 1.1 DK, which will include an icon for the ReadMe file, several of the sample programs (including two VB programs), and the Programmer's Guide, a lengthy help file that contains the complete documentation for the Development Kit.

Note: *For more information on the directory structure created by the VfWDK, see the DEV_KIT.TXT file in the \VfW subdirectory.*

Video Capture

The most complex process in PC video is the conversion of analog video into digital data. If you've used a video capture card, you're probably already familiar with VidCap, the VfW capture utility. With VidCap, you can specify the frame size, compression method, and frame rate, along with audio resolution and sampling rate, and a variety of other parameters. You may then select one of four capture techniques: streaming video capture, streaming video capture with MCI control, step-frame capture with MCI control, and single-frame capture. VidCap and its companion utility, VidEdit, are components of the commercial Video for Windows product, available through retail channels, but are also often bundled with video capture hardware—they are not included in the VfW Development Kit. However, with a lot of help from the CAPWNDX.VBX custom control, which does come with the VfW Developer's Kit, we can create a VB program with most of VidCap's capabilities.

One problem with using the CAPWNDX.VBX control is that it is a VBX, and the 32-bit version of VB4 does not support VBXs. At the time of this book's printing, there were no OCX controls available for capturing video, so we are forced to drop down to 16-bit programming. Look for a new release of the VfW Developer's Kit for Windows 95 sometime in the near future. The new developer's kit should have the OCX version of the control we are using in this chapter, and it should not be difficult at all to port the code over to the 32-bit platform.

Capturing Video with the CAPWNDX.VBX Custom Control

You may find that the controls of the VfW capture program, VidCap, are not arranged well for your particular application. Or, you may want to embed video capture capabilities in your own applications, such as a video email system. With the CAPWNDX.VBX custom control, we can build our own video capture utilities. In this project, we'll write a simple video capture program. Here are the steps to follow:

1. Create the form VIDCAP1.FRM.
2. Add the event procedures to the form.

You'll find this project in the subdirectory \VBMAGIC\VIDCAP1, in the files VIDCAP1.VBP and VIDCAP1.FRM. You'll also need the THREED.VBX custom control, usually installed in your \WINDOWS\SYSTEM subdirectory by VB Setup, and the CAPWNDX.VBX, which you should first copy from \VfWDK\BIN to \WINDOWS\SYSTEM.

Running the Video Capture Program

The first thing you need to run this program is a properly installed and tested video capture card. Any card that supports VfW will work. Luckily, this pretty much includes every card on the market. We use the Intel Smart Video Recorder (ISVR) because it supports real-time capture and compression, which saves both time and disk space. Creative Labs makes several video capture cards, including their VideoBlaster series and the VideoSpigot. And don't forget to check out the Pro MovieStudio from Media Vision, and VideoLogic's Captivator. Each card requires unique installation procedures, so follow the documentation carefully.

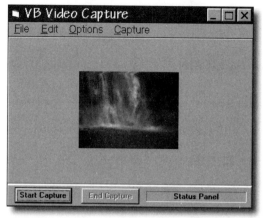

Figure 19.1 *VIDCAP1.FRM at runtime.*

VIDCAP1 has only one VB form. Figure 19.1 shows the form at runtime. To capture a video sequence:

1. Set up your video source (usually either a camcorder or a VCR), and make sure it is properly connected with the appropriate cables to your video capture card and sound card.
2. Run VIDCAP1.EXE.
3. Access the dialog boxes from the Options menu commands that allow you to choose a video format (such as 160×120 pixels) and a video source.
4. To begin capture, either select Capture | Video... from the menu bar, or click on the Start Capture button. If the capture is working, the cursor will change to an hourglass.
5. To end capture, either press Esc or click on the right mouse button.

To replay the captured video sequence:

1. Open the Media Player.
2. Select Option | Video for Windows to display the Open dialog box.
3. Use the Open dialog box to locate and select the file CAPTURE.AVI (set in the sample program to be created in C:\).
4. Click on the Play button.

Creating the Form

The centerpiece of VIDCAP1 is the CAPWNDX.VBX custom control. When you place this control on a form, it appears as a black rectangle. This will become the video preview window. CAPWNDX has no buttons, labels, captions, or scroll bars of its own. To manipulate its features we have to set some properties. CAPWNDX has only two event procedures, **Status()** and **Error()**, and 54 properties, shown in Table 19.1.

Table 19.1 *The Properties List for CAPWNDX.VBX*

Property	Purpose
AudioBits	Specifies 8 or 16 bit audio.
AudioChannels	Specifies 1 for mono or 2 for stereo audio.
AudioRate	Specifies audio sampling rate of 11025, 22050, or 44100 Hz.
CaptureAudio	Set to True to capture audio along with video.
Capture	Set to True to begin capture; False to stop capture.
CaptureHitOK	If set to True, will display a prompt to press Enter before capture begins.
CaptureDOSMem	If True, this property uses memory under 1 MB boundary to buffer capture data (the best choice for large direct-to-disk captures); if False, it uses extended memory to buffer capture (the best choice when the entire sequence will fit in memory).
CaptureUseLimit	Set to True to automatically stop capture after number of seconds specified in CaptureLimit property.
CaptureLimit	Limit captures to the specified number of seconds.
VideoRate	Specifies the frame rate; usually set to 15 or fewer frames, depending on capabilities of host machine and frame dimensions.
SingleFrameOpen	Set to True to prepare for single frame capture.
SingleFrame	Each time this property is set to True, it captures a single frame, appends it to the current capture file, and resets itself to False.
SingleFrameClose	Closes the single frame capture mode.
Yield	Set to True to allow other Windows applications to continue execution during video capture (I wouldn't try this).
CaptureAbort	If Yield is True, then the Esc key will no longer stop video capture; instead, you must set the property to True to end background capture.
CaptureStop	Set to True to stop step-frame capture. MCI commands will then be used to rerun the capture sequence on the source device to capture the audio tracks.
CaptureFile	Specifies the path and filename of the capture file.
CaptureFileSize	Used to preallocate a file large enough to hold the captured sequence; preallocation improves performance.

continued

Table 19.1   *The Properties List for CAPWNDX.VBX (continued)*

Property	Purpose
CaptureSave	Specifies a path and filename to which the capture file will be copied. This allows the maintenance of a permanently preallocated and defragmented capture file, which is then copied to a destination file upon completion of capture. Copy occurs upon assignment of the filename to the property.
DriverNum	Specifies the capture driver to use; zero based.
Connect	Set to True to connect to the capture driver; the connection occurs automatically when capture begins, but to preview video before the capture, you must set Connect to True.
DriverName	Returns a string containing the name of the driver specified in the DriverNum property.
DriverVersion	Returns a string containing the version of the driver specified in the DriverNum property.
MCIDeviceEnable	Set to True to enable MCI capture control; currently requires a Sony VISCA compatible video source.
MCIDeviceName	A string used to specify the MCI device from which to capture.
MCIStartMS	Specifies the starting time for the capture on the source device (in milliseconds).
MCIStepCapture	Set to True to enable step frame capture.
MCIStopMS	Specifies the ending time for the capture on the source device (in milliseconds).
EditCopy	Set to True to copy the current frame to the Clipboard; automatically resets to False after the procedure.
CanOverlay	Read-only; indicates whether the device supports video overlay (display of live analog video to a window on the screen).
Overlay	If set to True, disables preview and displays live video in the capture window.
PalCreate	When set to True, automatically constructs a palette for the video being captured; applies only to 8-bit capture devices.
PalCreateManual	Set to True to add the palette of the current frame to an accumulator; set to False to build a palette from the accumulated color data.
PalNumColors	Specifies the number of colors in the palette created by either PalCreate or PalCreateManual: 2 to 256.
PalNumFrames	Specifies the number of frames examined by PalCreate to produce a palette for the entire sequence; if the sequence includes frequent scene changes, set this number high (defaults to 20 frames).

continued

Table 19.1 *The Properties List for CAPWNDX.VBX (continued)*

Property	Purpose
PalSave	Specifies the path and filename of a file in which to save the palette; copy occurs upon assignment of the filename.
PalOpen	Specifies the path and filename of a palette to use for 8-bit capture.
PreviewRate	Specifies the refresh rate of the preview window when Preview is set to True.
Preview	Set to True to activate Preview, which periodically samples the incoming video stream and displays the frames.
Error	Returns a string containing a description of the latest error.
ErrorNum	Returns the number of the latest error.
Status	Returns a string containing a description of the status of the capture process.
VideoCompressionDlg	Set to True to display a dialog box that enables the user to select the real-time compression method to use during capture. The actual dialog box depends on the current driver and data format.
VideoDisplayDlg	Set to True to display a dialog box that enables the user to choose display options. This dialog box is driver-dependent and is not always available.
VideoFormatDlg	Set to True to display a dialog box that enables the user to choose the video format, such as dimensions and color depth (such as 8-bit or 24-bit). This dialog box is driver-dependent, and is not always available.
VideoSourceDlg	Set to True to display a dialog box that enables the user to choose a video source. This dialog box is driver-dependent, and is not always available.
AutoSize	Set to True to cause the control window to resize itself to the video image; set to False to stretch the video image to fit the control window.
Left	Specifies the position of the left side of the control within the form or other container.
Height	Specifies the height of the control window.
Top	Specifies the position of the top of the control window within the form or other container.
Width	Specifies the width of the control window.
Name	Specifies the VB control name within the application.
Visible	Set to True to display the control; set to False to hide it.
BorderStyle	Set to True to display a single-pixel width border; set to False for no border.

Most of the other controls in this program are menu options, as shown in Listing 19.1.

Listing 19.1   The Controls and Properties from VIDCAP1.FRM

```
VERSION 4.00
Begin VB.Form VidCap1F1
    Appearance      =   0  'Flat
    BackColor       =   &H80000005&
    BorderStyle     =   3  'Fixed Dialog
    Caption         =   "VB Video Capture"
    ClientHeight    =   3960
    ClientLeft      =   2115
    ClientTop       =   3195
    ClientWidth     =   5895
    BeginProperty Font
        name            =   "MS Sans Serif"
        charset         =   1
        weight          =   700
        size            =   8.25
        underline       =   0  'False
        italic          =   0  'False
        strikethrough   =   0  'False
    EndProperty
    ForeColor       =   &H80000008&
    Height          =   4815
    Left            =   2055
    LinkTopic       =   "Form1"
    ScaleHeight     =   3960
    ScaleWidth      =   5895
    Top             =   2400
    Width           =   6015
    Begin Threed.SSPanel Panel3D2
        Align           =   1  'Align Top
        Height          =   3432
        Left            =   0
        TabIndex        =   3
        Top             =   0
        Width           =   5892
        _version        =   65536
        _extentx        =   10398
        _extenty        =   6059
        _stockprops     =   15
        backcolor       =   12632256
        alignment       =   8
        Begin VBX.CAPWND CapWnd1
            AudioBits       =   8
            AudioChannels   =   1
            AudioRate       =   11025
            AutoSize        =   -1  'True
            CaptureAudio    =   -1  'True
            CaptureDOSMem   =   0  'False
            CaptureFile     =   "C:\CAPTURE.AVI"
```

```
       CaptureHitOK    =   0    'False
       CaptureLimit    =   0
       CaptureUseLimit =   0    'False
       Connect         =   0    'False
       DriverNum       =   -1
       Height          =   1872
       Left            =   60
       MCIDeviceEnable =   0    'False
       MCIDeviceName   =   ""
       MCIStartMS      =   0
       MCIStepCapture  =   0    'False
       MCIStopMS       =   0
       Overlay         =   0    'False
       PalNumColors    =   256
       PalNumFrames    =   20
       Preview         =   0    'False
       PreviewRate     =   1
       Top             =   120
       VideoRate       =   15
       Width           =   1992
       Yield           =   0    'False
    End
    Begin MSComDlg.CommonDialog CaptureFileDialog
       Left            =   5340
       Top             =   2940
       _version        =   65536
       _extentx        =   847
       _extenty        =   847
       _stockprops     =   0
       defaultext      =   ".AVI"
       filter          =   "Video (*.avi)|*.avi"
    End
 End
 Begin Threed.SSPanel Panel3D1
    Align           =   2    'Align Bottom
    Height          =   495
    Left            =   0
    TabIndex        =   0
    Top             =   3465
    Width           =   5895
    _version        =   65536
    _extentx        =   10398
    _extenty        =   873
    _stockprops     =   15
    backcolor       =   12632256
    alignment       =   8
    Begin VB.CommandButton EndCaptureButton
       Appearance      =   0    'Flat
       BackColor       =   &H80000005&
       Caption         =   "End Capture"
       Enabled         =   0    'False
       Height          =   372
       Left            =   1800
       TabIndex        =   2
```

```
            Top            =    60
            Width          =    1392
         End
         Begin VB.CommandButton StartButton
            Appearance     =    0   'Flat
            BackColor      =    &H80000005&
            Caption        =    "Start Capture"
            Height         =    372
            Left           =    180
            TabIndex       =    1
            Top            =    60
            Width          =    1392
         End
         Begin Threed.SSPanel StatusPanel
            Height         =    255
            Left           =    3360
            TabIndex       =    4
            Top            =    120
            Width          =    2415
            _version       =    65536
            _extentx       =    4260
            _extenty       =    450
            _stockprops    =    15
            caption        =    "Status Panel"
            backcolor      =    12632256
            bevelouter     =    1
            alignment      =    8
         End
      End
   End
   Begin VB.Menu FileMenu
      Caption        =    "&File"
      Begin VB.Menu LoadPaletteOption
         Caption        =    "&Load Palette"
      End
      Begin VB.Menu SetCapFileOption
         Caption        =    "&Set Capture File"
      End
      Begin VB.Menu Break1
         Caption        =    "-"
      End
      Begin VB.Menu SaveAsOption
         Caption        =    "Save &Captured Video As..."
      End
      Begin VB.Menu SavePaletteOption
         Caption        =    "Save &Palette"
      End
      Begin VB.Menu SaveFrameOption
         Caption        =    "Save Single &Frame"
         Enabled        =    0   'False
      End
      Begin VB.Menu Break2
         Caption        =    "-"
      End
```

```
      Begin VB.Menu ExitOption
         Caption         =   "E&xit"
      End
   End
   Begin VB.Menu EditMenu
      Caption         =   "&Edit"
      Begin VB.Menu CopyOption
         Caption         =   "&Copy Frame"
         Shortcut        =   ^C
      End
      Begin VB.Menu PastePalOption
         Caption         =   "Paste &Palette"
         Enabled         =   0   'False
      End
      Begin VB.Menu Break3
         Caption         =   "-"
      End
      Begin VB.Menu PreferencesOption
         Caption         =   "Pre&ferences"
         Enabled         =   0   'False
      End
   End
   Begin VB.Menu OptionsMenu
      Caption         =   "&Options"
      Begin VB.Menu AudioCaptureOption
         Caption         =   "Capture &Audio"
      End
      Begin VB.Menu Break4
         Caption         =   "-"
      End
      Begin VB.Menu VideoFormatOption
         Caption         =   "&Video Format"
      End
      Begin VB.Menu VideoSourceOption
         Caption         =   "Video &Source"
      End
      Begin VB.Menu VideoDisplayOption
         Caption         =   "Video &Display"
      End
      Begin VB.Menu Break5
         Caption         =   "-"
      End
      Begin VB.Menu PreviewOption
         Caption         =   "&Preview Video"
      End
      Begin VB.Menu OverlayOption
         Caption         =   "&Overlay Video"
      End
   End
   Begin VB.Menu CaptureMenu
      Caption         =   "&Capture"
      Begin VB.Menu SingleFrameOption
         Caption         =   "&Single Frame"
      End
```

```
        Begin VB.Menu FramesOption
            Caption         =    "&Frames..."
            Enabled         =    0    'False
        End
        Begin VB.Menu CaptureVideoOption
            Caption         =    "&Video..."
        End
        Begin VB.Menu PaletteOption
            Caption         =    "&Palette..."
            Enabled         =    0    'False
        End
    End
End
Attribute VB_Name = "VidCap1F1"
Attribute VB_Creatable = False
Attribute VB_Exposed = False
```

Adding the Event Code

The overwhelming bulk of the code in the event procedures sets the properties of the CapWnd1 control, as shown in Listing 19.2. This program has no code module. In fact, it has no general procedures, functions, or even any variables! CapWnd1 is virtually a program in itself.

Listing 19.2   The Event Procedures from VIDCAP1.FRM

```
Option Explicit

Private Sub AudioCaptureOption_Click()
    If Not AudioCaptureOption.Checked Then
        CapWnd1.AudioBits = 8
        CapWnd1.AudioChannels = 1
        CapWnd1.AudioRate = 22050
        CapWnd1.CaptureAudio = True
        AudioCaptureOption.Checked = True
    Else
        CapWnd1.CaptureAudio = False
        AudioCaptureOption.Checked = False
    End If
End Sub

Private Sub CaptureVideoOption_Click()
    CapWnd1.DriverNum = 0
    CapWnd1.Connect = True
    CapWnd1.CaptureLimit = 20 '20 seconds
    CapWnd1.CaptureUseLimit = True
    CapWnd1.VideoRate = 15
    CapWnd1.Capture = True
End Sub

Private Sub CapWnd1_Error()
    If CapWnd1.ErrorNum > 0 Then
```

```
        MsgBox CapWnd1.Error, , "Video Capture Error"
    End If
End Sub

Private Sub CapWnd1_Status()
    StatusPanel.Caption = CapWnd1.Status
End Sub

Private Sub CopyOption_Click()
    CapWnd1.EditCopy = True
End Sub

Private Sub EndCaptureButton_Click()
    CapWnd1.CaptureStop = True
End Sub

Private Sub ExitOption_Click()
    Unload VidCap1F1
    End
End Sub

Private Sub Form_Load()
    CapWnd1.TOP = Panel3D2.Height \ 2 - CapWnd1.Height \ 2
    CapWnd1.Left = Panel3D2.Width \ 2 - CapWnd1.Width \ 2
    CapWnd1.DriverNum = 0
    CapWnd1.Connect = True
    OverlayOption.Enabled = CapWnd1.CanOverlay
End Sub

Private Sub LoadPaletteOption_Click()
    CaptureFileDialog.DefaultExt = ".PAL"
    CaptureFileDialog.Filter = "Palette (*.pal)|*.pal"
    CaptureFileDialog.Action = 1
    CapWnd1.PalOpen = CaptureFileDialog.filename
End Sub

Private Sub OverlayOption_Click()
    If CapWnd1.CanOverlay Then
        If OverlayOption.Checked Then
            CapWnd1.Overlay = False
            OverlayOption.Checked = False
        Else
            CapWnd1.Overlay = True
            OverlayOption.Checked = True
        End If
    End If
End Sub

Private Sub PreviewOption_Click()
    If Not PreviewOption.Checked Then
        CapWnd1.PreviewRate = CapWnd1.VideoRate
        CapWnd1.Preview = True
        PreviewOption.Checked = True
```

```
      Else
         CapWnd1.Preview = False
         PreviewOption.Checked = False
      End If
End Sub

   Private Sub SaveAsOption_Click()
      CaptureFileDialog.DefaultExt = ".avi"
      CaptureFileDialog.Filter = "Video (*.avi)|*.avi"
      CaptureFileDialog.Action = 1
      CapWnd1.CaptureSave = CaptureFileDialog.filename
   End Sub

   Private Sub SavePaletteOption_Click()
      CaptureFileDialog.DefaultExt = ".pal"
      CaptureFileDialog.Filter = "Palette (*.pal)|*.pal"
      CaptureFileDialog.Action = 1
      CapWnd1.PalSave = CaptureFileDialog.filename
   End Sub

   Private Sub SetCapFileOption_Click()
      CaptureFileDialog.DefaultExt = ".AVI"
      CaptureFileDialog.Filter = "Video (*.avi)|*.avi"
      CaptureFileDialog.Action = 1
      CapWnd1.CaptureFile = CaptureFileDialog.filename
   End Sub

   Private Sub SingleFrameOption_Click()
      CapWnd1.SingleFrameOpen = True
      CapWnd1.SingleFrame = True
      CapWnd1.SingleFrameClose = True
   End Sub

   Private Sub StartButton_Click()
      CapWnd1.DriverNum = 0
      CapWnd1.Connect = True
      CapWnd1.CaptureLimit = 20 '20 seconds
      CapWnd1.CaptureUseLimit = True
      CapWnd1.VideoRate = 15
      CapWnd1.Capture = True
   End Sub

   Private Sub VideoDisplayOption_Click()
      CapWnd1.VideoDisplayDlg = True
   End Sub

   Private Sub VideoFormatOption_Click()
      CapWnd1.VideoFormatDlg = True
      CapWnd1.TOP = Panel3D2.Height \ 2 - CapWnd1.Height \ 2
      CapWnd1.Left = Panel3D2.Width \ 2 - CapWnd1.Width \ 2
   End Sub

   Private Sub VideoSourceOption_Click()
      CapWnd1.VideoSourceDlg = True
   End Sub
```

If you can't get what you need from CAPWNDX.VBX, you can resort to the API functions. But realize that this will not be a trivial enterprise. The custom control handles a myriad of details for us, including AVI file access, interaction with the ICM, and screen updates using the high-speed DrawDIB functions. To get all this stuff working, you'll need callback functions and fast memory management. As much as we hate to admit it, the VfW API may lie outside the domain of practical VB programming. To write a more sophisticated capture program or any kind of video editor, you may find it easier to implement the lower-level functions in a lower-level language such as C. You can always pack the complex code into custom controls or DLLs, and use VB to create the user interface, just as we did in VIDCAP1.VBP.

Okay, now back to the 32-bit world!

The Playback's the Thing

We've already used the easiest method to replay a video clip, the MCI Play command. When you play an AVI file with MCI, the driver will open up its own window somewhere on the screen. With a little more work, we can instruct the driver to display the video in a specific window.

Playing Video in a Window with the MCI

In this project, we'll use the **mciSendString()** function to open, position, and play a video clip in a VB form. Here are the steps to follow:

1. Create a form as shown in Figure 19.2.
2. Write the general procedure **PlayVideo()** (Listing 19.3).
3. Add the general procedure **GetWordFrom()** (Listing 19.4) to the form.
4. Fill in the **Form_Click()** event procedure (Listing 19.5) and the declarations section (Listing 19.6) for the form.

 You'll find this project in the subdirectory \VBMAGIC\AVIPLAY1 in the files AVIPLAY1.VBP, AVIPLAY1.FRM, and MINMAX.BAS.

Running the Program

When you run this simple program, it will display a small, blank form. To play the video clip (the filename is hard-coded), click anywhere in the client

Figure 19.2 *AVIPLAY1 at runtime.*

area of the form. The clip will play in the center of the form, as shown in Figure 19.2.

Creating the Form

This form has no controls. Set the **Name** property of the form to AVIPlay1F1, and its **ScaleMode** property to 3 - Pixel.

Adding PlayVideo() General Procedure

The general procedure **PlayVideo()**, shown in Listing 19.3, consists primarily of a series of calls to **mciSendString()**.

Listing 19.3   The PlayVideo() General Procedure from AVIPLAY1.FRM

```
Private Sub PlayVideo(FileName As String, ByVal hWindow As Integer, _
    ByVal DestWidth As Integer, ByVal DestHeight As Integer)
Dim MCIError As Long
Dim CommandString As String
Dim ReturnString As String * 128
Dim DummyString As String
Dim ClipWidth As Integer
Dim ClipHeight As Integer
Dim XPos As Integer
Dim YPos As Integer

    'Open AVI device.
    CommandString = "Open " & FileName & " alias VidClip"
    MCIError = mciSendString(CommandString, ByVal ReturnString, _
        Len(ReturnString) - 1, 0)

    'Set output window.
    CommandString = "Window VidClip handle " & Str$(hWindow)
    MCIError = mciSendString(CommandString, ByVal ReturnString, _
        Len(ReturnString) - 1, 0)

    'Get dimensions of clip in window.
    CommandString = "Where VidClip destination"
```

```
    MCIError = mciSendString(CommandString, ByVal ReturnString, _
        Len(ReturnString) - 1, 0)
    DummyString = GetWordFrom(ReturnString)
    DummyString = GetWordFrom(ReturnString)
    ClipWidth = Val(GetWordFrom(ReturnString))
    ClipHeight = Val(GetWordFrom(ReturnString))
    XPos = MaxInt(0, DestWidth - ClipWidth) \ 2
    YPos = MaxInt(0, DestHeight - ClipHeight) \ 2

    'Re-position clip in center of window.
    CommandString = "Put VidClip destination at " & Str$(XPos) & " " & Str$(YPos)
    CommandString = CommandString & " " & Str$(ClipWidth) & " " & _
        Str$(ClipHeight)
    MCIError = mciSendString(CommandString, ByVal ReturnString, _
        Len(ReturnString) - 1, 0)

    'Play clip.
    MousePointer = 11
    CommandString = "Play VidClip wait"
    MCIError = mciSendString(CommandString, ByVal ReturnString, _
        Len(ReturnString) - 1, 0)
    MousePointer = 0

    'Close the device.
    CommandString = "Close VidClip"
    MCIError = mciSendString(CommandString, ByVal ReturnString, _
        Len(ReturnString) - 1, 0)
End Sub
```

Simply sending the **Play** command would cause the driver to open its own window, play the clip, and close the device. Instead, we'll send the **Open** command, allowing us to send further instructions before we commence playback. It may become unwieldy to repeat the path and filename in every command, so we'll use a shorthand name, **VidClip**, known to MCI as an *alias*. In each subsequent command, we'll use this alias to refer to this instance of the AVI file and device.

After we open the device, we send the **Window** command with its handle parameter to specify the output window, which, in this case, is the handle of AVIPlay1F1. To pass the handle, we need to convert it to a string. The conversion is no problem because handles are just long integer values.

Before we can center the video clip in the window, we need to know its dimensions. The command **Where <devicename> destination** will return a string containing four integer values separated by spaces. These values represent the left, top, width, and height of the clip, positioned relative to the window's client area and scale mode. The Windows API does not recognize VB twips, so make sure the form's **ScaleMode** property is set to 3 - Pixel. To parse out the string and extract the width and height values, we'll create a general function called **GetWordFrom()**, which will pull individual words out of a string, one at a time. We don't need the left and top positions, so we toss them out by assigning them to **DummyString**. Once we have the **ClipWidth** and **ClipHeight**, we can calculate the proper position for the clip within the window. We then send the **Put <devicename> destination at** command with **XPos**, **YPos**, **ClipWidth**, and **ClipHeight** as its arguments (all converted to strings, of course), to center the image.

Finally, we send the **Play <devicename> wait** command to play the clip, followed by the **Close <devicename>** command to close the device and release the driver.

Creating the GetWordFrom() General Function

Listing 19.4 shows the code for the **GetWordFrom()** function.

Listing 19.4   The GetWordFrom() General Function from AVIPLAY1.FRM

```
Private Function GetWordFrom(AnyString As String) As String
Dim TempString As String

    If InStr(AnyString, " ") = 0 Then
       TempString = AnyString
       AnyString = ""
    Else
       TempString = Left$(AnyString, InStr(AnyString, " "))
       AnyString = Mid$(AnyString, InStr(AnyString, " ") + 1)
    End If
    If (InStr(".,?!", Right$(TempString, 1)) > 0) And (Len(TempString) > 1) Then
       AnyString = Right$(TempString, 1) & AnyString
       TempString = Left$(TempString, Len(TempString) - 1)
    End If
    GetWordFrom = TempString
End Function
```

This function works by checking for spaces and pulling off the characters to the left of the space. If there is no space, it simply returns the original string.

Adding the Form_Click() Event Procedure

The only event procedure in this program, **Form_Click()** (Listing 19.5), exists solely to call **PlayVideo()**.

Listing 19.5   The Form_Click Event Procedure from AVIPLAY1.FRM

```
Sub Form_Click ()
 PlayVideo "c:\vbmagic\video\watrfall.avi", AVIPlay1F1.hWnd, _
      AVIPlay1F1.ScaleWidth, AVIPlay1F1.ScaleHeight
End Sub
```

Finally, don't forget to add the declaration for **mciSendString()**, as shown in Listing 19.6.

Listing 19.6 The Declarations Section from AVIPLAY1.FRM

```
Option Explicit

#If Win32 Then
    Private Declare Function mciSendString Lib "winmm.dll" Alias _
        "mciSendStringA" (ByVal lpstrCommand As String, ByVal lpstrReturnString _
        As String, ByVal uReturnLength As Long, ByVal hwndCallback As Long) _
        As Long
#Else
    Private Declare Function mciSendString Lib "MMSystem" (ByVal lpstrCommand _
        As String, ByVal lpstrReturnString As String, ByVal wReturnLength _
        As Integer, ByVal hCallback As Integer) As Long
#End If
```

The MCIWNDX.VBX Custom Control

For the quickest and cleanest way to play AVI files from within a VB program, use the MCIWNDX.VBX custom control, supplied with the VfW DK. Figure 19.3 shows how this control appears on a form.

Like the MCI.OCX included in the Professional Edition of VB, this control will operate any MCI device, but there are some important differences:

- Once again, we must drop down into the 16-bit realm, due to 32-bit VB4s lack of support for VBXs. Look for the OCX version of this control to be available very soon.

- MCI.VBX cannot send complete MCI command strings, so it cannot use all the features offered by all the MCI device drivers. Also, the only return values available to MCI.VBX are those for which control properties have been defined. MCI.VBX cannot support new devices, or newly added features in existing MCI device drivers. MCIWNDX.VBX, on the other hand, can send any valid MCI command string to any MCI device, and can retrieve return strings.

- MCI.VBX offers a set of nine control buttons: Back, Eject, Next, Pause, Play, Prev, Record, Step, and Stop. MCIWNDX.VBX offers only a Play/Stop button and a slider for positioning.

- MCI.VBX does not support window-oriented devices, such as video and animation. MCIWNDX.VBX provides its own display window.

MCIWNDX.VBX has six event procedures, listed in Table 19.2, and 35 properties, listed in Table 19.3.

Table 19.2　*The Event Procedures Supported by MCIWNDX.VBX*

Event Procedure	Purpose
Error()	Occurs whenever an MCI command causes an error.
MediaChange()	Occurs whenever a device is opened or closed; for example, when you change the file to be played, or change the disk in the CD-ROM drive.
ModeChange()	Occurs whenever the mode—open, not ready, playing, stopped, paused, seeking, or recording—of a device changes.
Notify()	Occurs when the notify flag is used with an MCI command to indicate the success or failure of an operation.
PositionChange()	Occurs repeatedly as the file or media position changes during seek, play, or record operations. *Caution: Use the* **WantPosEvent** *property to enable or disable this event, and use the* **TimerFreq** *property to keep the event from firing too frequently.*
SizeChange()	Occurs whenever the display window changes size, such as when the user resizes the video playback window, or when the **AutosizeWindow** property is set to True and activated.

Table 19.3　*The Properties List for MCIWNDX.VBX*

Property	Purpose
Command	Set this string property to the MCI command string you wish to execute. Use this just like any other MCI string command, except that you must omit the alias or device name. The field will clear once the command is executed. The error code will be stored in the **Error** property; the return string will be stored in the **CommandReturn** property.
CommandReturn	Will contain any information returned by the latest MCI command executed.
DeviceID	Returns the ID of the currently open device. Not often used.
Device	A string containing the name of the current device.
FileName	For simple devices, set this string property to a device name, such as "CDAudio." For compound devices, set it to a path and filename. If you set this property to a question mark, the control will display a file open dialog box.
Speed	With this integer property, you can control the playback speed of many MCI devices. Normal speed, or 100 percent, is represented by a value of 1000. Specify lower values for slower operation, higher values for faster speeds.
TimeFormat	Returns the current time format of the open device.
Volume	As in the Speed property, a value of 1000 represents normal audio volume.

continued

Table 19.3 *The Properties List for MCIWNDX.VBX (continued)*

Property	Purpose
End	Returns the end position of the current device element in the current time format.
Length	Returns the length of the current device element in the current time format.
Position	Returns the current position of the device in the current time format.
PositionString	Returns the current position in string format, such as TT:MM:SS:FF.
Start	Returns the starting position of the current device element in the current time format.
Error	Returns the error code of the latest MCI command executed.
ErrorDlg	Set to True if you want the control to display an Error dialog box whenever a command fails.
ErrorString	Returns the current error message as a string.
Mode	Returns the current mode of the device. (See the ModeChange() event in Table 19.2.)
TimerFreq	Determines the number of milliseconds between PositionChange() events; defaults to 500 milliseconds.
WantPosEvent	Set to True to enable PositionChange() events.
AutosizeMovie	Set to True if you want the image stretched (or squished) to fit the current display window.
AutosizeWindow	Set to True if you want the display window to resize itself to match the dimensions of the current device element (animation or video file).
BorderStyle	Set to True for a single pixel border or False for no border.
Zoom	Used to resize a visual device element (animation or video file). Specify integer percentages, such as 100 (default), 200 for double size, 33 for one-third size.
NewDevice	Opens a recordable device, such as wave audio, for recording with no existing device element. Similar to the MCI string command open new wave audio.
Left	Specifies or returns the current left position of the control in its container.
Top	Specifies or returns the current top position of the control in its container.
Height	Specifies or returns the current height of the control.
Width	Specifies or returns the current width of the control.
Menu	Set to True to enable the pop-up control menu.
Playbar	Set to True to display the user controlled play controls (Play/Stop button, Menu button, and position scroll bar). If False, all operation must occur under program control.

continued

Table 19.3   *The Properties List for MCIWNDX.VBX (continued)*

Property	Purpose
Record	Set to True to enable display of recording controls when appropriate. The AVIVideo device does not support recording under MCI control.
Repeat	Set to True to enable automatic repeat. Not supported by all MCI devices.
Name	The VB control instance name.
Enabled	Set to True to enable control at runtime.
Visible	Set to True to display the control at runtime, or False to hide the control.

Playing Video with MCIWNDX.VBX

The MCIWNDX.VBX custom control makes it a breeze to play video when and where you want it. In this very simple program, we'll center the control on a form and display the Playbar to control playback at runtime.

You'll find this project in the subdirectory \VBMAGIC\AVIPLAY2 in the files AVIPLAY2.VBP, AVIPLAY2.FRM, and MINMAX.BAS. You'll also need to copy MCIWNDX.VBX from the subdirectory \VfWDK\BIN to your \WINDOWS\SYSTEM subdirectory.

Creating the AVIPlay2 Form

This project requires nothing more than a form with a simple File menu and a single MCIWNDX.VBX control, as shown in Figures 19.3 and 19.4.

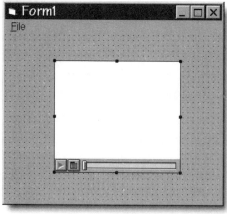

Figure 19.3   *AVIPLAY2 at design-time.*

Figure 19.4 *AVIPLAY2 at runtime.*

The form code includes just four brief event procedures and one general procedure, as shown in Listing 19.7.

Listing 19.7   AVIPLAY2.FRM

```
VERSION 4.00
Begin VB.Form AVIPlay2F1
   Caption        =    "Form1"
   ClientHeight   =    3930
   ClientLeft     =    1650
   ClientTop      =    2640
   ClientWidth    =    5250
   BeginProperty Font
      name        =    "MS Sans Serif"
      charset     =    1
      weight      =    700
      size        =    8.25
      underline   =    0    'False
      italic      =    0    'False
      strikethrough =  0    'False
   EndProperty
   ForeColor      =    &H80000008&
   Height         =    4785
   Left           =    1590
   LinkTopic      =    "Form1"
   ScaleHeight    =    3930
   ScaleWidth     =    5250
   Top            =    1845
   Width          =    5370
   Begin VBX.MCIWND MCIWnd1
      AutosizeMovie  =   -1   'True
      AutosizeWindow =   -1   'True
      ErrorDlg       =    0   'False
```

```
            Filename       =    ""
            Height         =    2625
            Left           =    1200
            Menu           =    -1    'True
            Playbar        =    -1    'True
            Record         =    0     'False
            Repeat         =    0     'False
            Speed          =    1000
            TimeFormat     =    ""
            TimerFreq      =    500
            Top            =    600
            Volume         =    1000
            WantPosEvent   =    -1    'True
            Width          =    3075
            Zoom           =    100
         End
         Begin VB.Menu FileMenu
            Caption        =    "&File"
            Begin VB.Menu OpenOption
               Caption        =    "&Open File"
            End
            Begin VB.Menu QuitOption
               Caption        =    "&Quit"
            End
         End
      End
End
Attribute VB_Name = "AVIPlay2F1"
Attribute VB_Creatable = False
Attribute VB_Exposed = False
Option Explicit

Private Sub MCIWnd1_MediaChange(Media As String)
   ResizeMCIWindow
   AVIPlay2F1.Caption = UCase$(Media)
End Sub


Private Sub MCIWnd1_SizeChange()
   ResizeMCIWindow
End Sub


Private Sub OpenOption_Click()
   MCIWnd1.filename = "?"
End Sub


Private Sub QuitOption_Click()
   End
End Sub


Private Sub ResizeMCIWindow()
   MCIWnd1.Left = MaxInt(0, (AVIPlay2F1.ScaleWidth - MCIWnd1.Width) \ 2)
   MCIWnd1.TOP = MaxInt(0, (AVIPlay2F1.ScaleHeight - MCIWnd1.Height) \ 2)
End Sub
```

Developing More with Video

With the code we've developed in this book and the shareware authoring tools you'll find on the companion CD-ROM, you have a rich toolkit. But don't stop here. These projects are meant to illustrate the basic principles of using video with your VB multimedia programs, but don't be afraid to change them. Create the effects *you* need to drive *your* presentation. Interactive multimedia at its best is not just informative—it's exciting. Visual Basic and the Windows API can deliver the power you need to turn your favorite subject into a multimedia extravaganza.

As you gain more experience using video clips with your multimedia applications, keep an eye out for new custom controls and video capture and playback techniques. Keep in mind that this is a technology in its early stages of development, and is rapidly changing. Windows 95 and 32-bit programming platforms like Visual Basic offer many advantages for developers who are using video, and in the near future, you're likely to see the emergence of many powerful and flexible custom controls for video processing.

Appendix A

HTML 3 Reference Guide

o use one of the HTML-driven multimedia engines or the Web browsers we've created in this book, you'll need to learn HTML. HTML is essentially a basic ASCII *markup language* that can easily be composed and edited with any Windows or DOS editor. In fact, we've included a useful custom HTML editor called Web Spinner on the companion CD-ROM to help you create HTML files.

As you probably know, HTML is the formatting language used by the World Wide Web. The acronym *HTML* stands for *Hypertext Markup Language*. The hypertext part means that an HTML document can contain references to other documents. This is why HTML makes a great platform for developing interactive multimedia applications. You can design HTML documents to link to other HTML documents or video, sound, and animation files. The other advantage to using HTML as a multimedia platform is that you can develop multimedia applications that can access and use the power of the Internet and the World Wide Web. This is a whole new field, one we like to call *virtual media*.

Originally, HTML was designed as a typesetting language for documents that were created using a computer. The "markup" part of its name comes from the days when book and magazine editors made special marks on the authors' manuscripts to instruct typesetters how to format the text. This process was called markup, and the term was adopted when people started inserting formatting instructions into their computer files.

Although we discussed some of the basic features of HTML as we presented our programming projects, we covered only a few of the many HTML tags that are available. This appendix provides a useful guide to most of the HTML features supported by leading Web browsers such as Netscape and Mosaic. You'll want to use this guide as you create HTML documents for the

677

multimedia engine and Web browser presented in this book. But keep in mind that these basic HTML engines developed in this book do not support all the HTML tags introduced by the HTML 3 standard. Of course, you can add the newer tags by studying them in this appendix and adding the necessary support code to the VB programs.

HTML—The Language of the Web

The HTML that we use in this book to create our multimedia and Web documents is actually a subset of a language called *SGML,* which stands for *Standard Generalized Markup Language.* HTML commands are enclosed in angle brackets, **<like this>**. Most commands come in pairs that mark the beginning and end of a part of text. The end command is often identical to the start command, except that it includes a forward slash between the opening bracket and the command name. For example, the title of an HTML document called "Multimedia Adventures" would look like this:

```
<TITLE>Multimedia Adventures/TITLE>
```

Similarly, a word or phrase that you want to display in bold type would be indicated like this:

```
<B>Display this phrase in bold</B>
```

It's not too hard to mark up your text, but all the bracketed tags can make your source text hard to read and proofread. No one has created a true "Web processor," a WYSIWYG word processor that happens to read and write HTML files, but we're bound to see one soon. For now we have to use word processors, text editors, or simple HTML editors that display the tags, not their effects.

Using an HTML Editor

Many people do prefer using an HTML editor over a word processor like Microsoft Word or a simple text editor like Windows Notepad. In fact, we've included some handy HTML editors on the companion CD-ROM, including Web Spinner and HTMLAssistant. It is easier to start writing HTML with an HTML editor than with a basic text editor, because most HTML editors offer some sort of menu of tags. This can help you get acquainted with the HTML tag set.

The other advantage of an HTML editor is that when it inserts tags for you, it inserts both the start and the end tags. This feature greatly reduces the chance that your whole document will end up in the **<H1>** (first level header) style, or that a bold word will become three bold paragraphs.

HTML Basics

All HTML files consist of a mixture of text to be displayed and HTML tags that describe how the text should be displayed. Normally, extra whitespace (spaces, tabs, and line breaks) is ignored, and text is displayed with a single space between each word. Text is always wrapped to fit within a browser's window in the reader's choice of fonts. Line breaks in the HTML source are treated as any other whitespace, that is, they're ignored—and a paragraph break must be marked with a **<P>** tag.

Tags are always set off from the surrounding text by angle brackets, the less-than and greater-than signs. Most tags come in *begin* and *end* pairs, for example, **<I>** ... **</I>**. The end tag includes a slash between the opening bracket and the tag name. There are a few tags that require only a start tag; we'll point out these tags as they come up.

HTML is case insensitive: **<HTML>** is the same as **<html>** or **<hTmL>**. However, many Web servers run on Unix systems, which *are* case sensitive. This will never affect HTML interpretation, but will affect your hyperlinks: My.gif is not the same file as my.gif or MY.GIF.

Some begin tags can take parameters, which come between the tag name and the closing bracket like this: **<DL COMPACT>**. Others, like description lists, have optional parameters. Still others, such as anchors and images, require certain parameters and can also take optional parameters.

The Structure of an HTML Document

All HTML documents have a certain standard structure, but Netscape and most other Web browsers will treat any file that ends in .HTML (.HTM on PCs) as an HTML file, even if it contains no HTML tags. All HTML text and tags should be contained within this tag pair:

```
<HTML> ... </HTML>
```

<HEAD> ... </HEAD> Tag

All HTML documents are divided into a header that contains the title and other information about the document, and a body that contains the actual document text.

While you should not place display text outside the body section, this is currently optional since most Web browsers and HTML readers will format and display any text that's not in a tag. Also, while you can get away with not using the **<HEAD>** tag pair, we recommend you use it.

<BODY> ... </BODY> Tag

The tags that appear within the body of an HTML document do not separate the document into sections. Rather, they're either special parts of the text, like images or forms, or they're tags that say something about the text they enclose, like character attributes or paragraph styles.

Headings and Paragraphs

In some ways, HTML text is a series of paragraphs. Within a paragraph, the text will be wrapped to fit the reader's screen. In most cases, any line breaks that appear in the source file are totally ignored.

Paragraphs are separated either by an explicit paragraph break tag, **<P>**, or by paragraph style commands. The paragraph style determines both the font used for the paragraph and any special indenting. Paragraph styles include several levels of section headers, five types of lists, three different *block formats*, and the normal, or default, paragraph style. Any text outside of an explicit paragraph style command will be displayed in the normal style.

<ADDRESS> ... </ADDRESS> Tag

The last part of the document body should be an **<ADDRESS>** tag pair, which contains information about the author and, often, the document's copyright date and revision history. While the address block is not a required part of the document in the same way that the header or the body is, official style guides urge that all documents have one. In current practice, while most documents use the **<HTML>**, **<HEAD>**, and **<BODY>** tag pairs, almost all documents have address blocks—perhaps because the address block is visible.

The format for using the **<ADDRESS>** tag is as follows:

```
<ADDRESS>Address text goes here</ADDRESS>
```

Comments

Comments can be placed in your HTML documents using a special tag as shown:

```
<!-Comment text goes here->
```

Everything between the <> will be ignored by a browser when the document is displayed.

Header Elements

The elements used in the header of an HTML document include a title section and internal indexing information.

<TITLE> ... </TITLE> Tag

Every document should have a title. The manner in which a title is displayed varies from system to system and browser to browser. The title could be displayed as a window title, or it may appear in a pane within the window. The title should be short—64 characters or less—and should contain just text.

The title should appear in the header section, marked off with a **<TITLE>** tag pair; for example, **<TITLE>**Explore the Grand Canyon**</TITLE>**. Some Web browsers like Netscape are quite easy-going and will let you place the title anywhere in the document, even after the **</HTML>** tag, but future browsers might not be quite so accommodating. Including a title is important because many Web search engines will use the title to locate a document.

The format for using the **<TITLE>** tag is as follows:

```
<TITLE>Title text goes here</TITLE>
```

Other <HEAD> Elements

There are a few optional elements that may only appear in the document's header (**<HEAD>** tag pair). The header elements that browsers use are the **<BASE>** and **<ISINDEX>** tags. Both are empty or solitary tags that do not have a closing **</...>** tag and thus do not enclose any text.

The **<BASE>** tag contains the current document's URL, or Uniform Resource Locator; browsers can use it to find local URLs.

The **<ISINDEX>** tag tells browsers that this document is an index document, which means that the server can support keyword searches based on the document's URL. Searches are passed back to the Web server by concatenating a question mark and one or more keywords to the document URL and then requesting this extended URL. This is very similar to one of the ways that form data is returned. (See the section *Form Action and Method Attributes* for more information.)

HTML includes other header elements, such as **<NEXTID>** and **<LINK>**, which are included in HTML for the benefit of editing and cataloging software. They have no visible effect; browsers simply ignore them.

Normal Text

Most HTML documents are composed of plain, or normal, text. Any text not appearing between format tag pairs is displayed as normal text.

Normal text, like every other type of paragraph style except the preformatted style, is wrapped at display time to fit in the reader's window. A larger or smaller font or window size will result in a totally different number of words on each line, so don't try to change the wording of a sentence to make the line breaks come at appropriate places. It won't work.

*
 Tag*

If line breaks are important, as in postal addresses or poetry, you can use the **
** command to insert a line break. Subsequent text will appear one line down, on the left margin.

The general format for this tag is:

```
<BR CLEAR=[Left|Right]>
```

The section listed between the [] is optional. This is a feature introduced as an HTML enhancement and supported by newer versions of Netscape.

Let's look at an example of how **
** is used. To keep

```
Coriolis Group Books
7339 East Acoma Drive, Suite 7
Scottsdale, Arizona 85260-6912
```

from coming out as

```
Coriolis Group Books 7339 East Acoma Drive, Suite 7 Scottsdale, Arizona
85260-6912
```

you would write:

```
Coriolis Group Books<BR>
7339 East Acoma Drive, Suite 7<BR>
Scottsdale, Arizona 85260-6912<BR>
```

The extended form of the **
** tag allows you to control how text is wrapped. The **CLEAR** argument allows text to be broken so that it can flow to the right or to the left around an image. For example, this tag shows how text can be broken to flow to the left:

```
This text will be broken here.<BR CLEAR=Left>
```

This line will flow around to the right of an image that can be displayed with the **IMG** tag.

<NOBR> Tag

This tag stands for *No Break*. This is another HTML extension supported by Netscape. To keep text from breaking, you can include the **<NOBR>** tag at the beginning of the text you want to keep together.

<WBR> Tag

This tag stands for Word Break. If you use the **<NOBR>** tag to define a section of text without breaks, you can force a line break at any location by inserting the **<WBR>** tag followed by the **
** tag.

<P> Tag

The **
** command causes a line break within a paragraph, but more often we want to separate one paragraph from another. We can do this by enclosing each paragraph in a **<P>** tag pair, starting the paragraph with **<P>** and ending it with **</P>**. The actual appearance of the paragraphs will depend on your reader's Web browser: Paragraph breaks may be shown with an extra line or half line of spacing, a leading indent, or both.

The **</P>** tag is optional; most people include a single **<P>** at the beginning of each paragraph, at the end, or alone on a line between two paragraphs.

Physical and Logical Attributes

Character attribute tags let you emphasize words or phrases within a paragraph. HTML supports two different types of character attributes: physical and logical. Physical attributes include the familiar bold, italic, and underline, as well as a tty attribute for monospaced text.

Logical attributes are different. In keeping with the SGML philosophy of using tags to describe content and not the actual formatting, logical attributes let you describe what sort of emphasis you want to put on a word or phrase, but leave the actual formatting up to the browser. That is, where a word marked with a physical attribute like **<B>**bold**</B>** will always appear in bold type, an **<EM>**emphasized**</EM>** word may be italicized, underlined, bolded, or displayed in color.

Web style guides suggest that you use logical attributes whenever you can, but there's a slight problem: Some current browsers only support some physical attributes, and few or no logical attributes. Since Web browsers simply ignore

Table A.1   *List of Physical Attributes*

Attribute	Tag	Sample	Effect
Bold	\<B\>	Some \<B\>bold\</B\> text	Some **bold** text
Italic	\<I\>	Some \<I\>italicized\</I\> text	Some *italicized* text
Underline	\<U\>	Some \<U\>underlined\</U\> text	Some <u>underlined</u> text
TTY	\<TT\>	Some \<TT\>monospaced (tty)\</TT\> text	Some `monospaced (tty)` text

any HTML tag that they don't *understand*, when you use logical tags, you run the risk that your readers will not see any formatting at all!

The standard format for using any of the physical attributes tags is as follows:

```
<tag>text goes here</tag>
```

You can nest attributes, although the results will vary from browser to browser. For example, some browsers can display bold italic text, while others will only display the innermost attribute. (That is, **<B><I>**bold italic**</I></B>** may show up as bold italic.) If you use nested attributes, be sure to place the end tags in reverse order of the start tags; don't write something like **<B><I>**bold italic**</B></I>**! This may work with some Web browsers, but may cause problems with others.

Table A.2   *List of Logical Attributes*

Attribute	Tag	Use or Interpretation	Typical Rendering
Citation	\<CITE\>	Titles of books and films	Italic
Code	\<CODE\>	Source code fragments	Monospaced
Definition	\<DFN\>	A word being defined	Italic
Emphasis	\<EM\>	Emphasize a word or phrase	Italic
PRE	\<PRE\>	Used for tables and text	Preformatted text
Keyboard	\<KBD\>	Something the user should type, word-for-word	Bold monospaced
Sample	\<SAMP\>	Computer status messages	Monospaced
Strong	\<STRONG\>	Strong emphasis	Bold
Variable	\<VAR\>	A description of something the user should type, like \<filename\>	Italic

Keep in mind that even if current browsers arbitrarily decide that **<EM>** text will be displayed as italic and **<KBD>** text will be displayed as Courier, future browsers will probably defer these attributes to a setting controlled by the user. So, don't conclude that citations, definitions, and variables all look alike and that you should ignore them and use italic.

<BLINK> ... </BLINK>

This is a new enhanced tag supported by Netscape. Text placed between this pair will blink on the screen. This feature is useful for attention-grabbing, but using it too much could get rather annoying. The format for this tag is:

```
<BLINK>This text will blink</BLINK>
```

<CENTER> ... </CENTER>

This HTML enhancement makes some Web page authors feel like they've died and gone to heaven. Any text (or images) placed between this pair is centered between the left and right margins of a page. The format for this tag is:

```
<CENTER>This text will be centered between the left and right margins</CENTER>
```

<FONT> ... </FONT>

This HTML enhancement allows you to control the sizes of the fonts displayed in your documents. The format for this tag is:

```
<FONT SIZE=font-size>text goes here</FONT>
```

where *font-size* must be a number from 1 to 7. A size of 1 produces the smallest font. The default font size is 3. Once the font size has been changed, it will remain in effect until the font size is changed by using another tag.

<BASEFONT>

To give you even greater control over font sizing, a new HTML tag has been added so that you can set the base font for all text displayed in a document. The format for this tag is:

```
<BASEFONT SIZE=font-size>
```

Again, *font-size* must be a number from 1 to 7. A size of 1 produces the smallest font. The default font size is 3. Once the base font size has been defined, you can display text in larger or smaller fonts using the **+** or **-** sign with the **<FONT>** tag. Here's an example of how this works:

```
<BASEFONT SIZE=4>
This text will be displayed as size 4 text.
<FONT SIZE=+2>
This text will be displayed as size 6.
</FONT>
This text will return to the base font size--size 4.
```

Headings

HTML provides six levels of section headers, **<H1>** through **<H6>**. While these are typically short phrases that fit on a line or two, the various headers are actually full-fledged paragraph types. They can even contain line and paragraph break commands.

You are not required to use a **<H1>** before you use a **<H2>**, or to make sure that a **<H4>** follows a **<H3>** or another **<H4>**.

The standard format for using one of the six heading tags is illustrated by this sample:

```
<H1>Text Goes Here</H1>
```

Lists

HTML supports five different list types. All five types can be thought of as a sort of paragraph type. The first four list types share a common syntax, and differ only in how they format their list elements. The fifth type, the *description* list, is unique in that each list element has two parts—a tag and a description of the tag.

All five list types display an element marker—whether it be a number, a bullet, or a few words—on the left margin. The marker is followed by the actual list elements, which appear indented. List elements do not have to fit on a single line or consist of a single paragraph—they may contain **<P>** and **
** tags.

Lists can be nested, but the appearance of a nested list depends on the browser. For example, some browsers use different bullets for inner lists than for outer lists, and some browsers do not indent nested lists. However, Netscape and Lynx, which are probably the most common graphical and text mode browsers, do indent nested lists; the tags of a nested list align with the elements of the outer list, and the elements of the nested list are further indented. For example,

```
 •  This is the first element of the main bulleted list.
     •  This is the first element of a nested list.
     •  This is the second element of the nested list.
 •  This is the second element of the main bulleted list.
```

The four list types that provide simple list elements use the list item tag, **<LI>**, to mark the start of each list element. The **<LI>** tag always appears at the start of a list element, not at the end.

Thus, all simple lists look something like this:

```
<ListType>

<LI>
There isn't really any ListType list, however the OL, UL, DIR, and
MENU lists all follow this format.

<LI>
Since whitespace is ignored, you can keep your source legible by
putting blank lines between your list elements. Sometimes, we like to put the
&lt;li&gt; tags on their own lines, too.              \

<LI>
(If we hadn't used the ampersand quotes in the previous list element,
the "&lt;li&gt;" would have been interpreted as the start of a new
list element.)

</ListType>
```

Numbered List

In HTML, numbered lists are referred to as *ordered lists*. The list type tag is **<OL>**. Numbered lists can be nested, but some browsers get confused by the close of a nested list, and start numbering the subsequent elements of the outer list from 1.

Bulleted List

If a numbered list is an ordered list, what else could an unnumbered, bulleted list be but an unordered list? The tag for an unordered (bulleted) list is **<UL>**. While bulleted lists can be nested, you should keep in mind that the list nesting may not be visible; some browsers indent nested lists; some don't. Some use multiple bullet types; others don't.

Netscape List Extensions

Netscape has added a useful feature called **TYPE** that can be included with unordered and ordered lists. This feature allows you to specify the type of bullet or number that you use for the different levels of indentation in a list.

Unordered List with Extensions

When Netscape displays the different levels of indentation in an unordered list, it uses a solid disk (level 1) followed by a bullet (level 2) followed by a square (level 3). You can use the **TYPE** feature with the **<UL>** tag to override this sequence of bullets. Here's the format:

```
<UL TYPE=Disc|Circle|Square>
```

For example, here's a list defined to use circles as the bullet symbol:

```
<UL TYPE=Circle>
<LI>This is item 1
<LI>This is item 2
<LI>This is item 3
</UL>
```

Ordered List with Extensions

When Netscape displays ordered (numbered) lists, it numbers each list item using a numeric sequence—1, 2, 3, and so on. You can change this setting by using the **TYPE** modifier with the **<OL>** tag. Here's how this feature is used with numbered lists:

```
<OL TYPE=A|a|I|i|1>
```

where **TYPE** can be assigned to any one of these values:

A   Mark list items with capital letters
a   Mark list items with lowercase letters
I   Mark list items with large roman numerals
i   Mark list items with small roman numerals
1   Mark list items with numbers (default)

Wait, there's more. You can also start numbering list items with a number other than 1. To do this, you use the **START** modifier as shown:

```
<OL START=starting-number>
```

where starting-number specifies the first number used. You can use the feature with the **TYPE** tag. For example, the tag

```
<OL TYPE=A START=4>
```

would start the numbered list with the roman numeral IV.

Using Modifiers with List Elements

In addition to supporting the **TYPE** modifier with the **<UL>** and **<OL>** tags, Netscape allows you to use this modifier with the **<LI>** tag to define list elements for ordered and unordered lists. Here's an example of how it can be used with an unordered list:

```
<H2>Useful Publishing Resources</H2>
<UL TYPE=Disc>
<LI>HTML Tips
<LI>Web Page Samples
<LI TYPE=Square>Images
<LI TYPE=Disc>Templates
</UL>
```

In this case, all the list items will have a disc symbol as the bullet, except the third item, *Images*, which will be displayed with a square bullet.

The **TYPE** modifier can be assigned the same values as those used to define lists with the **<UL>** and **<OL>** tags. Once it is used to define a style for a list item, all subsequent items in the list will be changed, unless another **TYPE** modifier is used.

If you are defining **<LI>** list elements for ordered lists **<OL>**, you can also use a new modifier named **VALUE** to change the numeric value of a list item. Here's an example:

```
<H2>Useful Publishing Resources</H2>
<OL>
<LI>HTML Tips
<LI>Web Page Samples
<LI VALUE=4>Images
<LI>Templates
</UL>
```

In this list, the third item would be assigned the number 4 and the fourth item would be assigned the number 5.

Directory and Menu Lists

The directory and menu lists are special types of unordered lists. The menu list, **<MENU>**, is meant to be visually more compact than a standard unordered list; menu list items should all fit on a single line. The directory list, **<DIR>**, is supposed to be even more compact; all list items should be less than 20 characters long, so that the list can be displayed in three (or more) columns.

We're not sure if we've ever actually seen these lists in use, and their implementation is still spotty; current versions of Netscape do not create multiple columns for a **<DIR>** list, and while they let you choose a directory list font and a menu list font, they do not actually use these fonts.

Description List

The description list, or **<DL>**, does not use the **<LI>** tag the way other lists do. Each description list element has two parts, a tag and its description. Each tag begins with a **<DT>** tag, and each description with a **<DD>** tag. These appear at the start of the list element, and are not paired with **</DT>** or **</DD>** tags.

The description list looks a lot like any other list, except that instead of a bullet or a number, the list tag consists of your text. Description lists are intended to be used for creating formats like a glossary entry, where a short tag is followed by an indented definition, but the format is fairly flexible. For example, a long tag will wrap, just like any other paragraph, although it should not contain line or paragraph breaks. (Netscape will indent any **<DT>** text after a line or paragraph, as if it were the **<DD>** text.) Further, you needn't actually supply any tag text; **<DT><DD>** will produce an indented paragraph.

Compact and Standard Lists

Normally, a description list puts the tags on one line, and starts the indented descriptions on the next:

```
Tag 1
Description 1.
Tag 2
Description 2.
```

For a tighter look, you can use a **<DL COMPACT>**. If the tags are very short, some browsers will start the descriptions on the same line as the tags:

```
Tag 1    Description 1
Tag 2    Description 2
```

However, most browsers do not support the compact attribute, and will simply ignore it. For example, with current versions of Windows Netscape, a **<DL COMPACT>** will always look like a **<DL>**, even if the tags are very short.

Inline Images

Using only text attributes, section headers, and lists, you can build attractive-looking documents. The next step is to add pictures.

<IMG ...> Tag

The <IMG> tag is a very useful HTML feature. It lets you insert inline images into your text. This tag is rather different from the tags we've seen so far. Not only is it an empty tag that always appears alone, it has a number of parameters between the opening **<IMG** and the closing **>**. Some of the parameters include the image file name and some optional modifiers. The basic format for this tag is:

```
<IMG SRC="URL" ALT="text"
     ALIGN=top|middle|bottom
     ISMAP>
```

Since HTML 3 has emerged and additional Netscape extensions have been added, this tag has expanded more than any other HTML feature. Here is the complete format for the latest and greatest version of the **<IMG>** tag:

```
<IMG SRC="URL" ALT="text"
     ALIGN=left|right|top|texttop|middle|absmiddle|
           baseline|bottom|absbottom
     WIDTH=pixels
     HEIGHT=pixels
     BORDER=pixels
     VSPACE=pixels
     HSPACE=pixels
     ISMAP>
```

The extended version allows you to specify the size of an image, better control image and text alignment, and specify the size of an image's border.

Every **<IMG>** tag must have a **SRC=** parameter. This specifies a URL, or Uniform Resource Locator, which points to a GIF or JPEG bitmap file. When the bitmap file is in the same directory as the HTML document, the file name is an adequate URL. For example, **<IMG SRC**=MySmilingFace.gif> would insert a picture of a smiling face.

Some people turn off inline images because they have a slow connection to the Web. This replaces all images, no matter what size, with a standard graphic. This isn't so bad if the picture is ancillary to your text, but if you've used small inline images as bullets in a list or as section dividers, the placeholder graphic will usually make your page look rather strange. For this reason, some people avoid using graphics as structural elements; others simply don't worry about people with slow connections; still others include a note at the top of the page saying that all the images on the page are small, and invite people with inline images off to turn them on and reload the page.

Keep in mind that some people use text-only browsers, like Lynx, to navigate the Web. If you include a short description of your image with the **ALT=** parameter, text-only browsers can show something in place of your graphic. For example, **<IMG SRC=**MySmilingFace.gif could be supplemented by the code: **ALT=**"A picture of the author">, so that no one feels left out.

Since the the value assigned to the **ALT** parameter has spaces in it, we have to put it within quotation marks. In general, you can put any parameter value in quotation marks, but you need to do so only if it includes spaces.

Mixing Images and Text

You can mix text and images within a paragraph; an image does not constitute a paragraph break. However, some Web browsers, like earlier versions of Netscape, did not wrap paragraphs around images; they displayed a single line of text to the left or right of an image. Normally, any text in the same paragraph as an image would be lined up with the bottom of the image, and would wrap normally below the image. This works well if the text is essentially a caption for the image, or if the image is a decoration at the start of a paragraph. However, when the image is a part of a header, you may want the text to be centered vertically in the image, or to be lined up with the top of the image. In these cases, you can use the optional **ALIGN=** parameter to specify **ALIGN=top**, **ALIGN=middle**, or **ALIGN=bottom**.

Using Floating Images

With the extended version of the **<IMG>** tag, you can now create "floating" images that will align to the left or right margin of a Web page. Text that is displayed after the image will either wrap around the right-hand or left-hand side of the image. Here's an example of how an image can be displayed at the left margin with text that wraps to the right of the image:

```
<IMG SRC="limage.gif" ALIGN=left>
```

Text will be displayed to the right of the image.

Specifying Spacing for Floating Images

When you use floating images with wrap-around text, you can specify the spacing between the text and the image by using the **VSPACE** and **HSPACE** modifiers. **VSPACE** defines the amount of spacing in units of pixels between the top and bottom of the image and the text. **HSPACE** defines the spacing between the left or right edge of the image and the text that wraps.

Sizing Images

Another useful feature that has been added to the **<IMG>** tag is image sizing. The **WIDTH** and **HEIGHT** modifiers are used to specify the width and height for an image in pixels. Here's an example:

```
<IMG SRC="logo.gif" WIDTH=250 HEIGHT=310>
```

When a browser like Netscape displays an image, it needs to determine the size of the image before it can display a placeholder or bounding box for the image. If you include the image's size using **WIDTH** and **HEIGHT**, a Web page can be built much faster. If the values you specify for **WIDTH** and **HEIGHT** differ from the image's actual width and height, the image will be scaled to fit.

Using Multiple Images per Line

Since an image is treated like a single (rather large) character, you can have more than one image on a single line. In fact, you can have as many images on a line as will fit in your reader's window! If you put too many images on a line, the browser will wrap the line and your images will appear on multiple lines. If you don't want images to appear on the same line, place a **
** or **<P>** between them.

Defining an Image's Border

Typically, an image is displayed with a border around it. This is the border that is set to the color blue when the image is part of an anchor. Using the **BORDER** modifier, you can specify a border width for any image you display. Here's an example that displays an image with a five pixel border:

```
<IMG SRC="logo.gif" BORDER=5>
```

Table A.3　*Summary of <IMG> Parameters*

Parameter	Required?	Settings
SRC	Yes	URL
ALT	No	A text string
ALIGN	No	top, middle, bottom, left, right, texttop, absmiddle, baseline, absbottom
HEIGHT	No	Pixel setting
WIDTH	No	Pixel setting
BORDER	No	Pixel setting
VSPACE	No	Pixel setting
HSPACE	No	Pixel setting
ISMAP	No	None

IsMap Parameter

The optional **ISMAP** parameter allows you to place hyperlinks to other documents in a bitmapped image. This technique is used to turn an image into a clickable map. (See the section *Using Many Anchors in an Image* for more detail.)

Horizontal Rules

The **<HR>** tag draws a horizontal rule, or line, across the screen. It's fairly common to put a rule before and after a form, to help set off the user entry areas from the normal text.

Many people use small inline images for decoration and separation, instead of rules. Although using images in this manner lets you customize your pages, it also takes longer for them to load—and it may make them look horrible when inline images are turned off.

The original **<HR>** tag simply displayed an engraved rule across a Web page. A newer version of the tag has been extended to add additional features including sizing, alignment, and shading. The format for the extended version of **<HR>** is:

```
<HR SIZE=pixels
    WIDTH=pixels|percent
    ALIGN=left|right|center
    NOSHADE>
```

The **SIZE** modifier sets the width (thickness) of the line in pixel units. The **WIDTH** modifier specifies the length of the line in actual pixel units or a percentage of the width of the page. The **ALIGN** modifier specifies the alignment for the line (the default is center) and the **NOSHADE** modifier allows you to display a solid line.

As an example of how some of these new features are used, the following tag displays a solid line, five pixels thick. The line is left justified and spans 80 percent of the width of the page:

```
<HR SIZE=5 WIDTH=80% ALIGN="left" NOSHADE>
```

Hypermedia Links

The ability to add links to other HTML documents or to entirely different sorts of documents is what makes the HTML-driven readers so powerful. The special sort of highlight that your reader clicks on to traverse a hypermedia link is called an anchor, and all links are created with the anchor tag, **<A>**. The basic format for this tag is:

```
<A HREF="URL"
   NAME="text"
   REL=next|previous|parent|made
   REV=next|previous|parent|made
   TITLE="text">

text</A>
```

Links to Other Documents

While you can define a link to another point within the current page, most links are to other documents. Links to points within a document are very similar to links to other documents, but are slightly more complicated, so we will talk about them later. (See the section *Links to Anchors*.)

Each link has two parts: The visible part, or anchor, which the user clicks on, and the invisible part, which tells the browser where to go. The anchor is the text between the **<A>** and **</A>** tags of the **<A>** tag pair, while the actual link data appears in the **<A>** tag.

Just as the **<IMG>** tag has a **SRC=** parameter that specifies an image file, so does the **<A>** tag have an **HREF=** parameter that specifies the hypermedia reference. Thus, **<A HREF=**SomeFile.Type>click here**</A>** is a link to *somefile.type* with the visible anchor *click here*.

Browsers will generally use the linked document's filename extension to decide how to display the linked document. For example, HTML or HTM files will be interpreted and displayed as HTML, whether they come from an http server, an FTP server, or a gopher site. Conversely, a link can be to any sort of file—a large bitmap, sound file, or movie.

Images as Hotspots

Since inline images are in many ways just big characters, there's no problem with using an image in an anchor. The anchor can include text on either side of the image, or the image can be an anchor by itself. Most browsers show an image anchor by drawing a blue border around the image (or around the placeholder graphic). The image anchor may be a picture of what is being linked to, or for reasons we'll explain shortly, it may even just point to another copy of itself:

```
<A HREF=image.gif><IMG SRC=image.gif></A>.
```

Thumbnail Images

One sort of *picture of the link* is called a thumbnail image. This is a tiny image, perhaps 100 pixels in the smaller dimension, which is either a condensed version of a larger image or a section of the image. Thumbnail images can be transmitted quickly, even via slow communication lines, leaving it up to the reader to decide which larger images to request. A secondary issue is aesthetic: Large images take up a lot of screen space, smaller images don't.

Linking an Image to Itself

Many people turn off inline images to improve performance over a slow network link. If the inline image is an anchor for itself, these people can then click on the placeholder graphic to see what they missed.

Using Many Anchors in an Image

The **<IMG>** tag's optional ISMAP parameter allows you to turn rectangular regions of a bitmap image into clickable anchors. Clicking on these parts of the image will activate an appropriate URL. (A default URL is also usually provided for when the user clicks on an area outside of one of the predefined regions.) While forms let you do this a bit more flexibly, the ISMAP approach doesn't require any custom programming—just a simple text file that defines the rectangles and their URLs—and this technique may work with browsers that do not support forms. An example of how to do this can be found on the Web site at:

```
http://wintermute.ncsc.uiuc.edu:8080/map-tutorial/image-maps.html
```

Links to Anchors

When an HREF parameter specifies a filename, the link is to the whole document. If the document is an HTML file, it will replace the current document and the reader will be placed at the top of the new document. Often this is just what you want. But sometimes you'd rather have a link take the reader to a specific section of a document. Doing this requires two anchor tags: one that defines an anchor name for a location, and one that points to that name. These two tags can be in the same document or in different documents.

Defining an Anchor Name

To define an anchor name, you need to use the **NAME** parameter: **<A NAME=**AnchorName**>**. You can attach this name to a phrase, not just a single point, by following the **<A>** tag with a **</A>** tag.

Linking to an Anchor in the Current Document

To then use this name, simply insert an **<A HREF=**...**>** tag as usual, except that instead of a filename, use a **#** followed by an anchor name. For example, **<A HREF=#**AnchorName**>** refers to the example in the previous paragraph.

Names do not have to be defined before they are used; it's actually fairly common for lengthy documents to have a table of contents with links to names defined later in the document. It's also worth noting that while tag and parameter names are not case sensitive, anchor names are; **<A HREF=#**anchorname**>** will not take you to the AnchorName example.

Linking to an Anchor in a Different Document

You can also link to specific places in any other HTML document, anywhere in the world—provided, of course, that it contains named anchors. To do this, you simply add the # and the anchor name after the URL that tells where the document can be found. For example, to plant a link to the anchor named "Section 1" in a file named complex.html in the same directory as the current file, you could use **<A HREF=**"Complex.html#Section 1"**>**. Similarly, if the named anchor was in http://www.another.org/Complex.html, you'd use **<A HREF=**"http://www.another.org/Complex.html#Section 1"**>**.

Using URLs

Just as a complete DOS filename starts with a drive letter followed by a colon, so a full URL starts with a resource type—HTTP, FTP, GOPHER, and so on—

followed by a colon. If the name doesn't have a colon in it, it's assumed to be a local reference, which is a filename on the same file system as the current document. Thus, **<A HREF=**Another.html**>** refers to the file "Another.html" in the same directory as the current file, while **<A HREF=**/html/File.html**>** refers to the file "File.html" in the top-level directory *html*. One thing to note here is that a URL always uses "/" (the Unix-style forward slash) as a directory separator, even when the files are on a Windows machine, which would normally use "\", the DOS-style backslash.

Local URLs can be very convenient when you have several HTML files with links to each other, or when you have a large number of inline images. If you ever have to move them all to another directory, or to another machine, you don't have to change all the URLs.

<BASE> Tag

One drawback of local URLs is that if someone makes a copy of your document, the local URLs will no longer work. Adding the optional **<BASE>** tag to the **<HEAD>** section of your document will help eliminate this problem. While many browsers do not yet support it, the intent of the **<BASE>** tag is precisely to provide a context for local URLs.

The **<BASE>** tag is like the **<IMG>** tag, in that it's a so-called empty tag. It requires an HREF parameter—for example, **<BASE HREF=**http://www.imaginary.org/index.html**>**—which should contain the URL of the document itself. When a browser that supports the **<BASE>** tag encounters a URL that doesn't contain a protocol and path, it will look for it relative to the base URL, instead of relative to the location from which it actually loaded the document. The format for the **<BASE>** tag is:

```
<BASE HREF="URL">
```

Table A.4　*Summary of the <A> Tag Syntax*

To:	Use:
Link to another document	<A HREF="URL">highlighted anchor text</A>
Name an anchor	<A NAME="Anchor Name">normal text</A>
Link to a named anchor in this document	<A href="#Anchor Name">highlighted anchor text</A>
Link to a named anchor in another document	<A href="URL#Anchor Name">highlighted anchor text</A>

Reading and Constructing URLs

Where a local URL is just a file name, a global URL specifies an instance of one of several resource types, which may be located on any Internet machine in the world. The wide variety of resources is reflected in a complex URL syntax. For example, while most URLs consist of a resource type followed by a colon, two forward slashes, a machine name, another forward slash, and a resource name, others consist only of a resource type, a colon, and the resource name.

The resource-type://machine-name/resource-name URL form is used with centralized resources, where there's a single server that supplies the document to the rest of the net, using a particular protocol. Thus, "http://www.another.org/Complex.html" means "use the Hypertext Transfer Protocol to get file complex.html from the main www directory on the machine www.another.org", while "ftp://foo.bar.net/pub/www/editors/README" means "use the File Transfer Protocol to get the file /pub/www/editors/README from the machine foo.bar.net".

Conversely, many resource types are distributed. We don't all get our news or mail from the same central server, but from the nearest one of many news and mail servers. URLs for distributed resources use the simpler form resource-type:resource-name. For example, "news:comp.infosystems.www.providers" refers to the Usenet newsgroup comp.infosystems.www.providers, which, by the way, is a good place to look for further information about writing HTML.

Using www and Actual Machine Names

In the HTTP domain, you'll often see "machine names" like "www.coriolis.com". This usually does not mean there's a machine named www.coriolis.com that you can FTP or Telnet to; "www" is an alias that a Webmaster can set up when he or she registers the server. Using the www alias makes sense, because

Table A.5   *A Partial Table of URL Resource Types*

Resource	Interpretation	Format
HTTP	Hypertext Transfer Protocol	http://machine-name/file-name
FTP	File Transfer Protocol	ftp://machine-name/file-name
GOPHER	Gopher	gopher://machine-name/file-name
NEWS	Internet News	news:group-name
TELNET	Log on to a remote system	telnet://machine-name
MAILTO	Normal Internet e-mail	mailto:user-name@machine-name

machines come and go, but sites (and, we hope, the Web) last for quite a while. If URLs refer to www at the site and not to a specific machine, the server and all the HTML files can be moved to a new machine simply by changing the www alias, without having to update all the URLs.

Using Special Characters

Since < and > have special meanings in HTML, there must be a way to represent characters like these as part of text. While the default character set for the Web is ISO Latin-1, which includes European language characters like _ and § in the range from 128 to 255, it's not uncommon to pass around snippets of HTML in 7-bit email, or to edit them on dumb terminals, so HTML also needs a way to specify high-bit characters using only 7-bit characters.

Two Forms: Numeric and Symbolic

There are two ways to specify an arbitrary character: numeric and symbolic. To include the copyright symbol, ©, which is character number 169, you can use ©. That is, &#, then the number of the character you want to include, and a closing semicolon. The numeric method is very general, but not easy to read.

The symbolic form is much easier to read, but its use is restricted to the four low-bit characters with special meaning in HTML. To use the other symbols in the ISO Latin-1 character set, like ® and the various currency symbols, you have to use the numeric form. The symbolic escape is like the numeric escape, except there's no #. For example, to insert é, you would use é, or &, the character name, and a closing semicolon. You should be aware that symbol names are case sensitive: É is É, not é, while &EAcute; is no character at all, and will show up in your text as &EAcute;!

Preformatted and Other Special Paragraph Types

HTML supports three special "block" formats. Any normal text within a block format is supposed to appear in a distinctive font.

<BLOCKQUOTE> ... </BLOCKQUOTE> Tag

The block quote sets an extended quotation off from normal text. That is, a **<BLOCKQUOTE>** tag pair does not imply indented, single-spaced, and italicized; rather, it's just meant to change the default, plain text font. The format for this tag is:

```
<BLOCKQUOTE>text</BLOCKQUOTE>
```

<PRE> ... </PRE> Tag

Everything in a preformatted block will appear in a monospaced font. The **<PRE>** tag pair is also the only HTML element that pays any attention to the line breaks in the source file; any line break in a preformatted block will be treated just as a **
** elsewhere. Since HTML tags can be used within a preformatted block, you can have anchors as well as bold or italic monospaced text. The format for this tag is:

```
<PRE WIDTH=value>text</PRE>
```

The initial **<PRE>** tag has an optional **WIDTH=** parameter. Browsers won't trim lines to this length; the intent is to allow the browser to select a monospaced font that will allow the maximum line length to fit in the browser window.

<ADDRESS> ... </ADDRESS> Tag

The third block format is the address format: **<ADDRESS>**. This is generally displayed in italics, and is intended for displaying information about a document, such as creation date, revision history, and how to contact the author. Official style guides say that every document should provide an address block. The format for this tag is:

```
<ADDRESS>text</ADDRESS>
```

Many people put a horizontal rule, **<HR>**, between the body of the document and the address block. If you include a link to your home page or to a page that lets the reader send mail to you, you won't have to include a lot of information on each individual page.

Using Tables

Features like lists are great for organizing data; however, sometimes you need a more compact way of grouping related data. Fortunately, some of the newer browsers like Netscape have implemented the proposed HTML 3 specification for tables. Tables can contain a heading and row and column data. Each unit of a table is called a cell and cell data can be text and images.

<TABLE > ... </TABLE> Tag

This tag is used to define a new table. All of the table-specific tags must be placed within the pair **<TABLE>** ... **</TABLE>**, otherwise they will be ignored. The format for the **<TABLE>** tag is:

```
<TABLE BORDER>table text</TABLE>
```

Leaving out the **BORDER** modifier will display the table without a border.

Creating a Table Title

Creating a title or caption for a table is easy with the **<CAPTION>** tag. This tag must be placed within the **<TABLE>** ... **</TABLE>** tags. Here is its general format:

```
<CAPTION ALIGN=top|bottom>caption text</CAPTION>
```

Notice that you can display the caption at the top or bottom of the table. By default, the caption will be displayed at the top of the table.

Creating Table Rows

Every table you create will have one or more rows. (Otherwise it won't be much of a table!) The simple tag for creating a row is:

```
<TR>text</TR>
```

For each row that you want to add, you must place the **<TR>** tag inside the body of the table, between the **<TABLE>** ... **</TABLE>** tags.

Defining Table Data Cells

Within each **<TR>** ... **</TR>** tag pair come one or more **<TD>** tags to define the table cell data. You can think of the cell data as the column definitions for the table. Here is the format for a **<TD>** tag:

```
<TD ALIGN=left|center|right
    VALIGN=top|middle|bottom|baseline
    NOWRAP
    COLSPAN=number
    ROWSPAN=number>
text</TD>
```

The size for each cell is determined by the width or height of the data that is displayed. The **ALIGN** parameter can be used to center or left- or right-justify the data displayed in the cell. The **VALIGN** parameter, on the other hand, specifies how the data will align vertically. If you don't want the text to wrap within the cell, you can include the **NOWRAP** modifier.

When defining a cell, you can manually override the width and height of the cell by using the **COLSPAN** and **ROWSPAN** parameters. **COLSPAN** specifies the number of columns the table cell will span and **ROWSPAN** specifies the number of rows to span. The default setting for each of these parameters is 1.

Defining Headings for Cells

In addition to displaying a table caption, you can include headings for a table's data cells. The tag for defining a heading looks very similar to the **<TD>** tag:

```
<TH ALIGN=left|center|right
    VALIGN=top|middle|bottom|baseline
    NOWRAP
    COLSPAN=number
    ROWSPAN=number>
text</TH>
```

Using Forms

The HTML features presented so far correspond with traditional publishing practices: You create a hypermedia document, and others read it. With HTML forms, however, you can do much more. You can create a form that lets your readers search a database using any criteria they like. Or you can create a form that lets them critique your Web pages. Or—and this is what excites business people—you can use forms to sell things over the Internet.

Forms are easy to create. However, to use them, you'll need a program that runs on your Web server to process the information that the user's client sends back to you. For simple things like a "comments page," you can probably use an existing program. For anything more complex, you'll probably need a custom program. While we will briefly describe the way form data looks to the receiving program, any discussion of form programming is beyond this book's scope.

<FORM> ... </FORM> Tag

All input widgets—text boxes, check boxes, and radio buttons—must appear within a **<FORM>** tag pair. When a user clicks on a submit button or an image map, the contents of all the widgets in the form will be sent to the program that you specify in the **<FORM>** tag. HTML widgets include single- and multi-line text boxes, radio buttons and check boxes, pull-down lists, image maps, a couple of standard buttons, and a hidden widget that might be used to identify the form to a program that can process several forms.

Within your form, you can use any other HTML elements, including headers, images, rules, and lists. This gives you a fair amount of control over your form's appearance, but you should always remember that the user's screen size and font choices will affect the actual appearance of your form.

While you can have more than one form on a page, you cannot nest one form within another.

The basic format for the **<FORM>** tag is as follows:

```
<FORM ACTION="URL"
     METHOD=get|post>
text</FORM>
```

Notice that text can be included as part of the form definition.

Form Action and Method Attributes

Nothing gets sent to your Web server until the user presses a Submit button or clicks on an image map. What happens then depends on the **ACTION**, **METHOD**, and **ENCTYPE** parameters of the **<FORM>** tag.

The ACTION parameter specifies which URL the form data should be sent to for further processing. This is most commonly in the cgi-bin directory of a Web server. If you do not specify an action parameter, the contents will be sent to the current document's URL.

The **METHOD** parameter tells how to send the form's contents. There are two possibilities here: Get and Post. If you do not specify a method, Get will be used. Get and Post both format the form's data identically; they differ only in how they pass the form's data to the program that uses that data.

Get and Post both send the forms contents as a single long text vector consisting of a list of WidgetName=WidgetValue pairs, each separated from its successor by an ampersand. For example:

```
"NAME=Tony Potts&Address=aapotts@coriolis.com"
```

(Any & or = sign in a widget name or value will be quoted using the standard ampersand escape; any bare "&" and any "=" sign can therefore be taken as a separator.) You will not necessarily get a name and value for every widget in the form; while empty text is explicitly sent as a WidgetName= with an empty value, unselected radio buttons and check boxes don't send even their name.

Where Get and Post differ is that the Get method creates a "query URL," which consists of the action URL, a question mark, and the formatted form data. The Post method, on the other hand, sends the formatted form data to the action URL in a special data block. The Web server parses the query URL that a Get method creates and passes the form data to the form processing program as a command line parameter. This creates a limitation on form data length that the Post method does not.

Currently, all form data is sent in plain text. This creates a security problem. The optional **ENCTYPE** parameter offers a possible solution, which only allows you to ratify the plain text default. In the future, however, values may be provided that call for an encrypted transmission.

Widgets

From a users' point of view, there are seven types of Web widgets; all of them are generated by one of three HTML tags. Except for the standard buttons, all widgets must be given a name.

<INPUT> Tag

The **<INPUT>** tag is the most versatile, and the most complex. It can create single-line text boxes, radio buttons, check boxes, image maps, the two standard buttons, and the hidden widget. It's somewhat like the **<IMG>** tag in that it appears by itself, not as part of a tag pair, and has some optional parameters. Of these, the **TYPE=** parameter determines both the widget type and the meaning of the other parameters. If no other parameters are provided, the **<INPUT>** tag generates a text box.

The format for the **<INPUT>** tag is:

```
<INPUT TYPE="text"|"password"|"checkbox"|"radio"|"submit"|"reset"|"hidden"|"image"
       NAME="name"
       VALUE="value"
       SIZE="number"
       MAXLENGTH="number"
       CHECKED>
```

The **TYPE** parameter can be set to one of eight values. We'll look at each of these options shortly. Each input must contain a unique name defined with **NAME**. The **VALUE** parameter specifies the initial value of the input. This value is optional. The **SIZE** parameter defines the size of a text line and **MAXLENGTH** is the maximum size allowed for the returned text.

Table A.6   *Syntax of the Text and Password Input Types*

Attribute	Required?	Format	Meaning
TYPE	No	TYPE="text" *or* TYPE="password"	Determines what type of widget this will be. Default is "text".
NAME	Yes	NAME="WidgetName"	Identifies the widget.
VALUE	No	VALUE="Default text"	You supply default value. Cannot contain HTML commands.
SIZE	No	SIZE=*Cols*	Width (in characters) of a single line text area. Default is 20.
SIZE	No	SIZE=*Cols,Rows*	Height and width (in characters) of a multi-line text area.
MAXLENGTH	No	MAXLENGTH=*Chars*	Longest value a single line text area can return. Default unlimited.

Text Boxes

If the **TYPE=** parameter is set to text (or no parameter is used), the input widget will be a text box. The password input type is just like the text type, except that the value shows only as a series of asterisks. All text areas must have a name. Text areas always report their value, even if it is empty.

Check Boxes and Radio Buttons

Check boxes and radio buttons are created by an **<INPUT>** tag with a checkbox or radio type. Both must have a name and a value parameter, and may be initially checked. The name parameter is the widget's symbolic name, used in returning a value to your Web server, not its onscreen tag. For that, you use normal HTML text next to the **<INPUT>** tag. Since the display tag is not part of the **<INPUT>** tag, Netscape check boxes and radio buttons operate differently from their dialog box kin; you cannot toggle a widget by clicking on its text, you have to click on the widget itself.

Radio buttons are grouped by having identical names. Only one (or none) of the group can be checked at any one time; clicking on a radio button will turn off whichever button in the name group was previously on.

Check boxes and radio buttons return their value only if they are checked.

Table A.7 *Syntax of the Check Box and Radio Types*

Attribute	Required?	Format	Meaning
TYPE	Yes	TYPE=checkbox *or* TYPE=radio	Determines what type of widget this will be. Default is "text".
NAME	Yes	NAME="WidgetName"	A unique identifier for a checkbox; a group identifier for radio buttons.
VALUE	Yes	VALUE="WidgetValue"	The value is sent if the widget is checked.
CHECKED	No	CHECKED	If this attribute is present, the widget starts out checked.

Image Maps

Image maps are created with the **TYPE=**"image" code. They return their name and a pair of numbers that represents the position that the user clicked on; the form handling program is responsible for interpreting this pair of numbers. Since this program can do anything you want with the click position, you are not restricted to rectangular anchors, as with **<IMG ISMAP>**.

Clicking on an image map, like clicking on a Submit button, will send all form data to the Web server.

Submit/Reset Buttons

The submit and reset types let you create one of the two standard buttons. Clicking on a Submit button, like clicking on an image map, will send all form data to the Web server. Clicking on a Reset button resets all widgets in the form to their default values. These buttons are the only widgets that don't need to have names. By default, they will be labeled Submit and Reset; you can specify the button text by supplying a VALUE parameter.

Table A.8 *Syntax of the Image Type*

Attribute	Required?	Format	Meaning
TYPE	Yes	TYPE=image	Determines what type of widget this will be. Default is "text".
NAME	Yes	NAME="WidgetName"	Identifies the widget.
SRC	Yes	SRC="URL"	The URL of a bitmapped image to display.

Table A.9   *Syntax of the Submit and Reset Types*

Attribute	Required?	Format	Meaning
TYPE	Yes	TYPE=submit *or* TYPE=reset	Determines what type of widget this will be. Default is "text".
NAME	No	NAME="WidgetName"	The buttons never return their values, so a name will never be used.
VALUE	No	VALUE="WidgetValue"	The button text. Default is Submit or Reset, respectively.

Hidden Fields

A hidden type creates an invisible widget. This widget won't appear onscreen, but its name and value are included in the form's contents when the user presses the Submit button or clicks on an image map. This feature might be used to identify the form to a program that processes several different forms.

<TextArea> ... </TextArea> Tag

The **<TEXTAREA>** tag pair is similar to a multi-line text input widget. The primary difference is that you always use a <TextArea> tag pair and put any default text between the **<TEXTAREA>** and **</TEXTAREA>** tags. As with **<PRE>** blocks, any line breaks in the source file are honored, which lets you include line breaks in the default text. The ability to have a long, multi-line default text is the only functional difference between a **TEXTAREA** and a multi-line input widget.

The format for the **<TEXTAREA>** tag is:

```
<TEXTAREA NAME="name"
          ROWS="rows"
          COLS="cols"> </TEXTAREA>
```

Table A.10   *Syntax of the Hidden Type*

Attribute	Required?	Format	Meaning
TYPE	Yes	TYPE=hidden	Determines what type of widget this will be. Default is "text".
NAME	Yes	NAME="WidgetName"	Identifies the widget.
VALUE	Yes	VALUE="WidgetValue"	Whatever constant data you might want to include with the form.

Table A.11 *Syntax of the <TEXTAREA> tag*

Attribute	Required?	Format	Meaning
NAME	Yes	NAME="WidgetName"	Identifies the widget.
ROWS	No	ROWS=*Rows*	TextArea height, in characters.
COLS	No	COLS=*Cols*	TextArea width, in characters. Default is 20.

<SELECT> ... </SELECT> Tag

The **<SELECT>** tag pair allows you to present your users with a set of choices. This is not unlike a set of check boxes, yet it takes less room on the screen.

Just as you can use check boxes for 0 to N selections, or radio buttons for 0 or 1 selection, you can specify the cardinality of selection behavior. Normally, select widgets act like a set of radio buttons; your users can only select zero or one of the options. However, if you specify the multiple option, the select widget will act like a set of check boxes, and your users may select any or all of the options.

The format for the **<SELECT>** tag is:

```
<SELECT NAME="name"
        SIZE="rows"
        MULTIPLE>text/option list</SELECT>
```

Within the **<SELECT>** tag pair is a series of **<OPTION>** statements, followed by the option text. These are similar to **<LI>** list items, except that **<OPTION>** text may not include any HTML markup. The **<OPTION>** tag

Table A.12 *Syntax of the <SELECT> tag*

Attribute	Required?	Format	Meaning
NAME	Yes	NAME="WidgetName"	Identifies the widget.
SIZE	No	SIZE=*Rows*	This is the widget height, in character rows. If the size is 1, you get a pull-down list. If the size is greater than 1, you get a scrolling list. Default is 1.
MULTIPLE	No	MULTIPLE	Allows more than one option to be selected.

may include an optional selected attribute; more than one option may be selected if and only if the **\<SELECT\>** tag includes the **MULTIPLE** option.

For example:

```
Which Web browsers do you use?
<SELECT NAME="Web Browsers" MULTIPLE>
<OPTION>Netscape
<OPTION>Lynx
<OPTION>WinWeb
<OPTION>Cello
</SELECT>
```

For more information on creating HTML documents, go to the following World Wide Web sites:

A Beginner's Guide to HTML
http://www.ncsa.uiuc.edu/General/Internet/WWW/HTMLPrimer.html

The HTML Quick Reference Guide
http://kuhttp.cc.ukans.edu/lynx_help/HTML_quick.html

Information on the Different Versions of HTML
http://www.w3.org/hypertext/WWW/MarkUp/MarkUp.html

Composing Good HTML
http://www/willamette.edu/html-composition/strict-html.html

HTML+ Specifications
http://info.cern.ch/hypertext/WWW/MarkUp/HTMLPlus/htmlplus_1.html

HTML Specification Version 3.0
http://www.hpl.hp.co.uk/people/dsr/html3/CoverPage.html

HTML Editors
http://akebono.stanford.edu/yahoo/Computers/World_Wide_Web/HTML_Editors/

Resources for Converting Documents to HTML
http://info.cern.ch/hypertext/WWW/Tools/Filters.html

An Archive of Useful HTML Translators
ftp://src.doc.ic.ac.uk/computing/information-systems/www/tools/translators/

Appendix B

Multimedia Resources

This guide provides information on resource materials that can greatly help you develop Visual Basic multimedia applications. The products section lists software that can be very useful to a multimedia developer. The books section lists reference materials that we found useful when writing this book, which you may be interested in also.

Products

Adobe Premiere V3 ($295)

Adobe Systems, Inc.
1585 Charleston Rd.
P.O. Box 7900
Mountain View, CA 94039-7900
800-833-6687

Adobe Premiere for Windows offers PC users an intuitive, cost-effective way to create digital movies for a variety of uses. It makes it easy to combine video footage, audio recordings, animation, still images, and graphics to create digital movies. The program supports the use of all common media types, including still images in DIB, TIFF, Adobe Photoshop, and PCX formats, sound in AIFF and WAV formats, video content in AVI and QuickTime formats, and animation in Autodesk Animator (FLC/FII) and PICT formats. Adobe Premiere 1.1 for Windows now includes software for capturing live video and audio to a computer, instead of requiring a separate software utility program.

Morphology 101 ($39.95)

Andover Advanced Technologies
239 Littleton Rd., Suite 2A
Westford, MA 01886
800-274-9674

Morphology 101 is the first multimedia product that includes a comprehensive interactive tutorial on professional morphing techniques. The interactive tutorial uses animation to illustrate basic techniques such as point placement and morphing between images of different size and shape. It includes a guide to file formats, compression algorithms, and special effects. Its advanced sections show how to use transition images to bring still images to life, how to do a liquid metal morph, and how to avoid spider webs and ghosting. The clips can be used royalty-free in any computer presentation or application you create, even when those presentations or applications are for resale.

Sound Choice ($69)

Cambium
P.O. Box 296-H
Scarsdale, NY 10583-8796
800-231-1779
FAX 914-472-6729

Sound Choice is a CD-ROM based, MPC clip music library and Windows software package. The royalty-free, impeccably recorded compositions include classical, rock, jazz, contemporary, new age, and more. Each volume contains more than 25 main selections and over 75 pre-edited "bumpers," totaling more than 100 individual clips and 900 music files in CD Audio, six WAV, and two MIDI formats. Three of the WAV formats are state-of-the art ADPCM-compressed, offering superb quality and reduced disk usage.

The powerful software features a scalable, interactive database, and enables you to audition and edit music files. Cross-platform developers can output WAV and device-independent MIDI files for Windows, and AIFF and extended MIDI for Macintosh.

ProVoice for Windows ($595)

First Byte
19840 Pioneer Avenue
Torrance, CA 90503
800-556-6141

ProVoice for Windows allows developers to add synthesized speech to their Windows applications. ProVoice for Windows supports most Windows 95 and Windows 3.1 programming languages through a DLL interface. Your program simply passes text strings to a speech driver, which translates the text into audible speech. All of the necessary tools and examples are provided to facilitate manipulation of the ProVoice speech technology.

1000 of the World's Greatest Sound Effects ($39.95)

Interactive Publishing Corporation
c/o Corporate Mailing Inc.
26 Parsipanny Rd.
Whippany, NY 07981
800-472-8777

1000 of the World's Greatest Sound Effects is a dual-platform CD-ROM sound effects studio that also provides sophisticated sound shaping, editing, and digital recording tools. The product, which contains effects like a roaring tiger, exploding dynamite, and a cruise ship whistle, offers its samples royalty-free. They are recorded in both 8- and high-fidelity 16-bit digital audio formats.

The product's Sound Finder utility categorizes each effect for quick access, testing, and copying. As a bonus, the title also includes Multimedia Sound Studio, which allows the user to play, record, and edit sounds from within the digital domain. It also offers compatibility with MIDI-equipped musical instruments and sequencers, as well as audio CDs. A sophisticated WAV editor provides even greater control over customizing and shaping sounds, while the Attach utility allows sound effects to be activated by system events, for that perfect default alarm.

Director 3.0 ($399)

MacroMedia
600 Townsend Street
San Francisco, CA 94103
800-288-4797

Director is a multimedia application development program for Windows that gives users the power to integrate graphics, motion, digital video, animations, sound, and interactivity into compelling presentations. It has a scene sorter, outliner, drawing tools, and spell checker. Users can then add sound, motion, digital video, and special effects to make their messages stand out. With Director you can also create cross-platform applications that run on either

Windows or Mac. All the data is stored in files that will work on either system, and only the executables are platform-specific.

ImageKnife/VBX, Pro Pack V2.0 ($349)

Media Architects, Inc.
1075 NW Murray Rd. #230
Portland, OR 97229-5501
503-639-2505

ImageKnife is a data-aware custom control for Visual Basic and Visual C++ that provides simple, but comprehensive, image handling including display (with pan and zoom), format conversion (TIFF, BMP, DIB, PCX, GIF, TARGA, and JPEG), and image processing (rotate, sharpen, matrix filter, and so on). ImageKnife supports True Color (24-bit), Super VGA (8-bit), VGA (4-bit), and monochrome images. Its color processing includes color reduction, palette remapping, optimization, and more. The product provides easy multiple image operations (such as compositing and masking), quality printing to Windows graphics-capable devices, and access to image data via a DIB handle or scanline get/put functions. A fully documented browser sample application is included. ImageKnife supports TWAIN-compliant image acquisition devices.

Media-Pedia Video Clips

Media-Pedia Inc.
22 Fisher Avenue
Wellesley, MA 02181
617-235-5617
FAX orders: 800-633-7332

Media-Pedia Video Clips videotape is a collection of over 150 royalty-free video clips with synchronized natural sound effects. It contains more than 50 minutes of professionally shot and selected clips from all decades of the twentieth century, displayed in aerial, time-lapse, slow motion, and point-of-view cinematography. The product is $195 in VHS, $295 in S-VHS and Hi8, $395 in 3/4SP, and $495 in BETACAM SP. Media-Pedia Video Clips on CD-ROM for Windows in AVI format compressed with Intel Indeo video technology is available for an introductory price of $49.

MediaStudio ($349)

Ulead Systems, Inc.
970 W. 190th Street, Ste. 520

Torrance, CA 90502
800-858-5323

MediaStudio unleashes your creativity for producing captivating multimedia business presentations, training materials, and proposals. It unites video, audio, and image editing in one easy-to-use program. Browse through the Album— a visual catalog of all your image, graphic, animation, audio, and video files— to easily locate the clip you need. Transform your images with Image Editor or Morph Editor by adding a splash of color, morphing your images, or applying one of the many special effects including fish eye, whirlpool, and more. Or bump up the volume on your audio track with a comprehensive range of audio filters, bringing it all together in Video Editor. Create video-in-video overlays and special effects, add flying text, then mix in your audio tracks to complete your multimedia production.

Books

The International MIDI Association. *MIDI 1.0 Detailed Specification: Document Version 4.1.1, February, 1990.*

> *Available only from the publisher:*
> *The International MIDI Association*
> *5316 West 57th Street*
> *Los Angeles, CA 90056*
> *818-598-0088*
> *Also available:*
> *Standard MIDI Files 1.0*
> *General MIDI System, Level 1*
> *MIDI Show Control (MSC) 1.0*

Appleman, Daniel. *Visual Basic Programmer's Guide to the Windows API.* Emeryville: Ziff-Davis Press, 1993.

> *Almost all Windows API references are written for C programmers. But not all API functions are useful to VB programmers, and calling many of those that are requires a little VB witchcraft. This indispensable reference covers the Windows API from a VB programmer's perspective. For example, all functions are listed with their proper VB declarations. Appleman also explains some of the peculiar ways in which VB interacts with Windows, so you can make better use of the API. Includes a complete table of the 256 ternary raster operations. A new version of this book will cover the Windows 32-bit API calls.*

Heiny, Loren. *Advanced Graphics Programming Using C/C++*. New York: John Wiley & Sons, Inc., 1993.

> *Although written for C programmers, Heiny's coverage of graphics programming techniques will benefit anyone with an interest in 3D ray tracing, image processing, and polymorphic tweening (morphing, as popularized by the movie* Terminator II *and Michael Jackson's* Black or White *music video).*

Johnson, Nels with Fred Gault and Mark Florence. *How to Digitize Video*. New York: John Wiley & Sons, Inc., 1994.

> *Written by the principals of The San Francisco Canyon Company, creators of QuickTime for Windows, this book contains comprehensive coverage of PC and Macintosh digital video, from the proper way to handle tape cartridges to scaling, frame rates, and compression strategies.*

Microsoft Corporation. *Microsoft Win32 Programmer's Reference: Volumes 1-5*. Redmond: Microsoft Press, 1993.

> *Third-party references are great for sample code and interpretation, but sometimes you need to go directly to the source. If you program in 32-bit Windows, regardless of what other API references you may keep your fingers in, you should own a copy of the original document. Then, when a function fails to work as expected, you can check your code against the documentation in at least two sources. Remember, the documentation for every function, message, and macro you find in a third-party API reference began with the information in these books, Microsoft's original SDK manuals.*

Microsoft Corporation. *Microsoft Windows Multimedia Authoring and Tools Guide*. Redmond: Microsoft Press, 1991.

> *Although it provides few specifics, this volume of Microsoft's Multimedia trilogy offers a thorough overview of multimedia production techniques. Keep in mind that it is a very technical book, but if you want to learn more about topics such as virtual memory, threads, heaps, file systems and file I/O, this is the place to go.*

Microsoft Corporation. *Microsoft Windows Multimedia Programmer's Reference*. Redmond: Microsoft Press, 1991.

> *If you do any extensive multimedia programming, you'll need this guide. None of the other Windows reference guides I've seen includes the Multimedia APIs and messages.*

Microsoft Corporation. *Microsoft Windows Multimedia Programmer's Workbook*. Redmond: Microsoft Press, 1991.

> *The* Programmer's Reference *does not provide examples, but the* Workbook *does. Microsoft could have included a more detailed discussion of the various interfaces, but even so, the* Workbook *may bring you further faster than with the* Programmer's Reference *alone.*

Microsoft Corporation. *Programmer's Guide to Microsoft Windows 95.* Redmond: Microsoft Press, 1995.

> *Third-party references are great for sample code and interpretation, but sometimes you need to go directly to the source. If you program in Windows 95, regardless of what other API references you may keep your fingers in, you should own a copy of this book. It contains a number of chapters that explain the architecture of Windows 95, Win32 limitations in Windows 95, and explains how to create multimedia applications with Win32 API calls.*

Ozer, Jan. *Video Compression for Multimedia*. Boston: Academic Press, 1995.

> *If you plan to do any work with digital video, this is the book to read and use. Video capture is a black art and this guide will walk you through the undocumented techniques of producing high-quality digital and video.*

Richter, Jeffrey. *Advanced Windows: The Developer's Guide to the Win32 API for Windows NT 3.5 and Windows 95*. Redmond: Microsoft Press, 1995.

> *This book is the experienced developer's main source of information on programming in Win32.*

Thompson, Nigel. *Animation Techniques in Win32*. Redmond: Microsoft Press, 1995.

> *This is the book to get if you want to learn more about animation programming under Windows—especially for the 32-bit platform. This recently published book gives solid background on WinG, DIBs, sprite animation, the palette manager, and Windows sound.*

Toohey, John and Edward B. Toupin. *Building OCXs*. Redmond: Microsoft Press, 1995.

> *One of the authors of this book developed the Internet OCX control used in Chapter 18. This guide explains what the new OCXs are all about and shows you how to build your own in C++.*

Appendix C

Using the Companion CD-ROM

The software and demonstration products on the companion CD-ROM are a sampling of many different types of multimedia products. Also on the CD is the sample code from the book, as well as the 16-bit version of the projects from the previous edition of this book.

The files on the CD are split into seven categories, with each category having its own directory.

Directory	Contents
CLIPS	Assorted images, and audio and video clips
SHARWARE	Software that you can sample before buying
TOOLS	Apps for Web access, image manipulation, HTML editing, and so on
VBMAGIC	Sample code for book projects
VFW	Video for Windows runtime and Developer's Kit
WINDOWS	Files needed to run VB software
AUDIO	
VIDEO	Files for demo version of the commercial product:
IMAGES	*Explore the Grand Canyon*
DEM_DATA	
VFWRT	

Installing the VB Programs

We chose not to provide a Setup program for the Adventure Set programs. Setup programs tend to behave like black boxes, creating directories, copying files, and modifying your INI files behind your back. To get the most from this code, you need to understand not only how it works, but how to make it work on your system. Fortunately, it's simple. Just copy the \VBMAGIC subdirectory and its subdirectories to your hard drive. It is important to keep in mind that all of the source files and programs are saved on the CD-ROM with "read-only" attributes. To use these files, you'll need to change the attributes to "read-write" after copying the files to your hard disk. We've included a BAT file, PROGINST.BAT, to help you copy all the files to your hard disk. For most of the programs, that's all there is to it. A few programs, however, require custom controls (OCX or VBX files) or dynamic link libraries (DLL files), which are located in their own subdirectories on the CD-ROM. Be sure to read the following items carefully:

- The project WAVEMIX.VBP, explained in Chapter 15, requires the WAVEMIX.DLL, located on the CD-ROM in the subdirectory \SHARWARE\WAVEMIX\16-BIT. Copy that file to your \WINDOWS\SYSTEM subdirectory. WaveMix is provided as a courtesy by Microsoft Corporation. It is not a supported product. There is no registration fee.

- The MIDIIN1.VBP program, explained in Chapter 16, requires the VB Messenger custom control. This control is located on the CD-ROM in the \SHARWARE\VBMSG subdirectory in the file VBMSG.VBX. Copy that file to your \WINDOWS\SYSTEM subdirectory. The distribution version of VB Messenger is provided as a courtesy by its author, James Tyminski. VB Messenger is not free software. For information on how to obtain a registered copy of this handy custom control, see the README.TXT file in the \SHARWARE\VBMSG subdirectory.

- The projects FTPSAMPL.VBP and BROWSER4.VBP, explained in Chapter 18, require the files FTP.OCX and GETHOST.OCX, which are located in the \SHARWARE\FTPOCX subdirectory on the CD-ROM.

- The WEBSTER1.VBP project from Chapter 18 requires the WEBSTER.OCX custom control, which can be found in the \SHARWARE\WEBSTER\32-BIT subdirectory on the CD-ROM.

- The projects VIDCAP1.VBP and AVIPLAY2.VBP, explained in Chapter 19, require the CAPWNDX.VBX and MCIWNDX.VBX custom controls, which are installed on your hard drive by the VfW Development Kit Setup program. To install the VfW Development Kit, follow the instructions in Chapter 19, in the section *Installing the Video for Windows Development Kit*. After running the Setup program, you'll find the VBX files on your hard drive in the subdirectory \VFWDK\BIN. Copy them both to your \WINDOWS\SYSTEM subdirectory.

> **Note:** *In the source code directories, you'll also find executable versions of all the Adventure Set programs. Most of the programs will run directly from the CD-ROM. However, several projects have data files that need to be updated periodically. You should copy all the programs to your hard drive to test them properly.*

Images and Audio and Video Clips

In the \CLIPS directory, you will find many megabytes of multimedia files that are available for use in your applications. Most of the files are in the public domain, so you don't have to worry about paying any royalties. The only copyrighted files are the ones in the \CLIPS\VIDEOS\AVI\MEDPED subdirectory. These files, from the Media-Pedia demonstration product, are there purely for your personal viewing pleasure, and for an idea of the clips that are available, look in the same directory for the README files that contain information on how to contact Media-Pedia about obtaining video clips.

The images we have included in the \CLIPS\IMAGES subdirectory can be very helpful in creating interesting User Interfaces, as well as for creating cool Web pages. Experiment with these to create your own Web page, or use one of the image manipulation programs that we'll discuss soon.

Useful Visual Basic Shareware Tools

Here is a list of the shareware Visual Basic tools that are provided on the companion CD-ROM. You'll find more detailed information about each product by reading the description file that is included with each product. (See the subdirectories in the directory \SHARWARE on the CD-ROM.)

ADESK	A custom DLL for displaying Autodesk animations (FLI, FLC).
3DFXPLUS	A custom DLL for creating special 3D effects in your VB programs.
CANIMATE	A unique custom control for performing animation.
CDR_13	A program used for digitizing directly from CDs.
COOL	A full-featured WAV editor for Windows written by David Johnston.
CSRPLUS	A DLL that provides a collection of icons and backdrop patterns for VB (or any Windows programming environment), complete with easy-to-use functions for utilizing the new, appealing graphics in your own applications. You get nearly 100 new cursors and 18 eye-appealing backdrop patterns.

MUSICF A useful music TrueType font.

FTP_OCX A powerful group of OCX custom controls that can be used for interacting with many different Internet protocols. We used the FTP and GetHost controls in the book, but the others are also quite powerful.

SPECTRUM A small utility program that provides a real-time display of the power spectrum of the signal present on the Wave Input device of a Windows multimedia PC, which is typically the signal coming in through the microphone socket on the sound card.

VBMSG A custom control that allows you to tap into the power of Windows by intercepting Windows messages, while retaining Visual Basic's ease of use. With VB Messenger, you can subclass a Visual Basic form or control (or any Windows control or window) to intercept messages that are intended for the form or control.

VBPIANO A custom VB application that illustrates the use of MIDI to create a multi-functional digital piano.

WAVEMIX A DLL utility that allows multiple WAV files to be played simultaneously. It is designed to be as simple to use as possible but have the power to do what is required by games. The DLL supports eight channels of simultaneous wave play, the ability to queue up waves along the same channel, and wave completion notification.

WEBSTER A well-thought-out Web browser that is completely contained in a single OCX. Webster can be used for browsing documents locally, or on the World Wide Web. There is a 32-bit OCX, as well as a 16-bit DLL that can be used with VB 3.

WINJAMMR A full-featured MIDI sequencer for Windows. It uses standard MIDI files, giving you access to a vast number of songs. WinJammer also contains a companion program called WinJammer Player, which is used to play MIDI song files in the background.

Shareware Tools

We have included many help utilities and applications that will help you in your quest to create awesome multimedia applications. The utilities have been split into six categories, represented by the six subdirectories in the \TOOLS directory on the companion CD-ROM.

CONNECT	Software to aid in connecting to the Internet
IMAGE	Image manipulation software
SOUND	Sound playback and editing applications
UTILITY	Miscellaneous utility programs, plus Microsoft Win32 and WinG for Windows 3.1 users
VIDEO	Video and animation playback software
WEB	Web browsing programs and HTML editing utilities

Let's look at these categories individually, and talk about some of the software in each category. Many of these applications and utilities have their own installation programs, README files, and help systems, so do a little research on each program before you install it.

Connect

What: Instant Internet
Where: \CONNECT\INSTINET\DISK1
Description: Easy-to-use connectivity software that will aid in getting you up and running with a PPP or SLIP account in no time.
Setup File: SETUP.EXE

What: NETCOM NetCruiser
Where: \CONNECT\NETCOM
Description: NETCOM's proprietary Internet connectivity software. If you are starting from scratch on the Internet and need an easy way to get connected, NETCOM's software is tough to beat. All the popular Internet applications like email, Web browsers, and FTP programs are there. The only drawback is that you are forced to use NETCOM's connection service—which isn't necessarily bad, especially if you are new to the Internet and need an easy way to get online.
Setup File: SETUP.EXE

What: Miscellaneous TCP/IP connection software
Where: \CONNECT\TCPIP
Description: A couple of helpful applications for more experienced Internauts.

Image

What: LView Pro
Where: \IMAGE\LVIEW

Description: A simple, but powerful, image manipulation and editing program. Lview pro is best used for creating special effects on your present images. Lview supports many image formats, and can be used to create the transparent or interlaced GIFs that are very popular on the Web.
Setup File: None; copy files onto your hard drive, and run LVIEWP1B.EXE.

What: Paint Shop Pro 3.0
Where: \IMAGE\PSP3
Description: A powerful image-creation and manipulation program. Paint Shop Pro 3.0 is one of the best shareware applicatons we have ever used, and it's features rival those found in expensive applications like Photoshop. You can use many different methods for creating images, or use the editing function to add many diverse effects to images. Paint Shop Pro 3.0 can import and export an incredible number of different formats; it also contains an image browser that allows you to quickly look through images on your hard drive to find the one you want. This is one shareware package that is definitely worth the money to upgrade to the full version. Look at the VENDOR.DOC file for more information about registering Paint Shop Pro 3.0.
Setup File: SETUP.EXE

What: ViewSpace 3D environment viewer
Where: \IMAGE\VIEWSPAC
Description: This is a hot new technology from the guys at Caligari. They have taken the rendering engine from their product trueSpace and made it run extremely well with a minimum of requirements. ViewSpace uses the 3DR rendering technology to display 3D environments in real-time. The environments can be as complicated and detailed as your imagination—and, of course, your processor—will allow. ViewSpace is also starting to be used as an effective online Virtual Reality interface, because the file sizes for the 3D worlds are small. If you want to create the worlds that can be accessed by ViewSpace, we recommend purchasing trueSpace 2 from Caligari—for the money, it is one of the best modeling packages available for the PC.
Setup File: SETUP.EXE

Sound

What: WHAM
Where: \TOOLS\SOUND\WHAM
Description: A simple audio player that is frequently used as a helper program for Web browsers.

What: Wplay Any
Where: \TOOLS\SOUND\WPLAYANY
Description: Another audio helper program that has a few different features and supports a few additional audio formats.

Utility

What: Acroread
Where: \TOOLS\UTILITY\ACROREAD
Description: Runtime version of Adobe's Acrobat. Acroread, a remarkably intuitive postscript document viewer, is quickly becoming a favorite means of viewing documents on the Web for people with fast connections. Postscript documents also offer more control over what a document will look like on any user's system. Supposedly, the documents look identical on a PC, Mac, and a Unix system. HTML files, on the other hand, provide only a basic framework, and while the individual browsers can display the same document, they look very different.
Setup File: ACROREAD.EXE

What: Drag N' Zip
Where: \TOOLS\UTILITY\DRAGZIP
Description: A nice little utility for doing drag and drop file compression and decompression.

What: Mega Edit
Where: \TOOLS\UTILITY\MEGAEDIT
Description: A small and fast editing program that reads and writes many types of files.

What: Win32s
Where: \TOOLS\UTILITY\WIN32S
Description: Microsoft's 32-bit add-on for the Windows 3.x OS. Many new applications need these new 32-bit APIs. Increases the speed and performance of Windows 3.x.
Setup File: SETUP.EXE

What: WinG
Where: \TOOLS\UTILITY\WING
Description: Microsoft's attempt to bring the games market to Windows. Although many good ideas were implemented, they now have been made obsolete by Windows 95 and the Games SDK.
Setup File: SETUP.EXE

Video

What: MPEG for Windows
Where: \TOOLS\VIDEO\MPEGWIN
Description: Feature-filled MPEG animation player. Can be used with WinG for faster performance. Great as a helper for your Web browsers.
Setup File: SETUP.EXE

What: Quick Time Player (Runtime version)
Where: \TOOLS\VIDEO\QUIKTIME
Description: Apple's QuickTime video player for Windows. An alternative to AVI files. Very close in performance. Many people, especially multimedia developers, prefer QuickTime because it makes cross-platform development much easier.
Setup File: SETUP.EXE

Web

What: Home Page Creator
Where: \TOOLS\WEB\HPC
Description: A very simple Web document creation system. Great for creating the initial pages of your Web site.
Setup File: SETUP.EXE

What: HTMLed
Where: \TOOLS\WEB\HTMLED
Description: This intuitive HTML document editor easily adds HTML tags to text. With many features to make Web document creation a breeze, this editor is easy to use if you know a little about HTML already.

What: Microsoft Internet Assistant
Where: \TOOLS\WEB\IA
Description: Web browser and graphical HTML editor that runs on top of Word 6.0. No HTML experience needed, due to the graphical nature of the application. Just drag and drop elements where they need to be and Internet Assistant figures out the rest. The Assistant offers some very nice features, such as its ability to import RTF documents and translate them to HTML.
Setup File: WORDIA.EXE

What: Web Spinner
Where: \TOOLS\WEB\WEBSPIN

Description: Another good HTML editor. Try them all out and see which one suits you best.
Setup File: SETUP.EXE

Installing Video for Windows

If you are using Windows 95, then you can skip this section, since full multimedia capabilties are already built in. If you are using a previous version of Windows, read on. To play AVI video clips on your system, you must install the VfW runtime library, version 1.1e. Follow the instructions in Chapter 19, found in the section *Installing the Video for Windows Runtime Library*. The VfW runtime setup will copy numerous files to your \WINDOWS\SYSTEM subdirectory, will modify your WIN.INI and SYSTEM.INI files, and will install an updated version of the Windows Media Player.

The Explore the Grand Canyon *Demo*

If you want to see the ultimate use of VB as a multimedia development platform, you need to check out the demo version of the commercial product *Explore the Grand Canyon*. This package is a leap forward for interactive entertainment. Some of the features include: hours of video, thousands of images, several hours of narration and sound effects, and most impressive, a fully interactive 3D model of the Grand Canyon. The 3D model is the only part of the product that was not created completely in Visual Basic.

The fully functional version differs from the complete version in that the demo is limited to accessing only a single quadrant of the canyon. Even with only one quadrant available, you will be amazed at how much information is at your fingertips—and it comes in so many different formats! Just think, if the program is this good now, just imagine if you could see the other 48 quadrants.

For more information on obtaining the full release version of the product, you can contact the Coriolis Group at 1-800-410-0192, or send them email at: grandcanyon@coriolis.com.

Index

Adventure Set License Agreement

Please read this Coriolis Adventure Set software license agreement carefully before you buy this product and use the software contained on the enclosed CD-ROM.

1. By opening the accompanying software package, you indicate that you have read and agree with the terms of this licensing agreement. If you disagree and do not want to be bound by the terms of this licensing agreement, return this product in whole for refund to the source from which you purchased it.

2. The entire contents of this CD-ROM and the compilation of the software contained therein are copyrighted and protected by both U.S. copyright law and international copyright treaty provisions. Each of the programs, including the copyrights in each program, is owned by the respective author, and the copyright in the entire work is owned by The Coriolis Group, Inc. You may copy any or all of this software to your computer system.

3. The CD-ROM contains source code presented in the book, utilities, tools, multimedia demonstration software, and multimedia files including sound, video, music, and pictures. You may use the source code, utilities, tools, and multimedia files presented in the book and included on the CD-ROM to develop your own applications for both private and commercial use unless other restrictions are noted on the CD-ROM by the author of the file.

4. You may not decompile, reverse engineer, disassemble, create a derivative work, or otherwise use the programs except as stated in this agreement.

5. The Coriolis Group, Inc. and the author specifically disclaim all other warranties, express or implied, including but not limited to implied warranties of merchantability and fitness for a particular purpose with respect to defects in the disk, the program, source code, and sample files contained therein, and/or the techniques described in the book, and in no event shall The Coriolis Group and/or the author be liable for any loss of profit or any other commercial damage, including but not limited to special, incidental, consequential, or other damages.

6. The Coriolis Group, Inc. will replace any defective CD-ROM without charge if the defective CD-ROM is returned to The Coriolis Group, Inc. within 90 days from the date of purchase.

7. The source code and sample program files presented in this book are available on a 3 1/2" 1.44MB disk. You can obtain this disk by sending your request to: The Coriolis Group, Attn: VB Multimedia Adventures Disk, 7339 E. Acoma Dr., Suite 7, Scottsdale, AZ 85260, or call 602-483-0192. A $5 shipping and handling fee is required.